ENCYCLOPEDIA OF BRITISH FOOTBALL

ENCYCLOPEDIA
of
BRITISH FOOTBALL

Editors
RICHARD COX, DAVE RUSSELL
and WRAY VAMPLEW

Foreword by
GORDON TAYLOR
Chief Executive of the Professional Footballers' Association

Sponsored by

FRANK CASS
LONDON • PORTLAND, OR

First published in 2002 in Great Britain by
FRANK CASS PUBLISHERS
Crown House, 47 Chase Side, Southgate,
London, N14 5BP

and in the United States of America by
FRANK CASS PUBLISHERS
c/o ISBS, 5824 N.E. Hassalo Street
Portland, Oregon 97213-3644

Copyright © 2002 Frank Cass & Co. Ltd.

Website: www.frankcass.com

British Library Cataloguing in Publication Data

Encyclopedia of British football. – (Sports reference
library series)
1. Soccer – Great Britain – Encyclopedias
I. Cox, R. W. II. Russell, Dave III. Vamplew, Wray
796.3'34'0941'03

ISBN 0-7146-5249-0 (cloth)
ISBN 0-7146-8230-6 (paper)

Library of Congress Cataloging-in-Publication Data

Encyclopedia of British football / editors, Richard Cox, Dave Russell,
and Wray Vamplew; sponsored by the National Football Museum.
    p.   cm. – (Sports reference library)
Includes bibliographical references and index.
    ISBN 0-7146-5249-0 (cloth) – ISBN 0-7146-8230-6 (pbk.)
    1. Soccer – Great Britain – Encyclopedias. I. Cox, Richard William,
1953 – II. Russell, Dave, 1953– III. Vamplew, Wray. IV. National Football
Museum (Preston, Lancashire, England) V. Series.
    GV944.G7 E53 2002
    796.334'0941 – dc21
                                                          2002000332

Contents

Foreword

Most readers will already be familiar with quotations to the effect that football is 'more than a game'. Whilst it is never a case of life or death as some would have us believe, it is an important part of our cultural heritage.

Football has been an important part of the working man's life for more than a century. Today, it has infiltrated all sectors of society. It often features on the front as well as back pages of newspapers (national as well as local), TV companies compete against each other to secure coverage of matches, sponsors line up to have clubs promote their brands, and footballers are enlisted to open new buildings, shops and extol the virtues of just about every consumer product on the market from deodorants to washing machines. Most of football's superstars are now household names and adorn the walls of offices and teenagers' bedrooms throughout the land. I doubt that anyone yet has attempted to assess the most common topic conversation in pubs and bars across the land, but my bet would be with football being near to, if not at the top of the list.

Football features so highly in people's lives because it represents much more than what takes place on the field of play. It can provide a unifying force within the community, region or country. At whatever level it is played it is capable of stimulating great excitement through the artistic and athletic skills of its exponents, the suspense and drama of the match as it unfolds.

Unlike its predecessors, this *Encyclopedia of British Football* is not a listing of tables and results, biographical descriptions of its stars but an in-depth examination of the many different facets of the game from the anthropology of football to youth training schemes. Nowhere to my knowledge has anyone before tackled such a variety of diverse topics that include comic characters and crowd control, drama and drugs, law and literature, mascots and medals, etc. all within the same covers.

I congratulate the editors in progressing the study of our game and feel sure that you the reader will enjoy many hours perusing the pages which follow with interest and in so doing learn something new about the game you possibly thought you already knew everything about.

GORDON TAYLOR
Chief Executive
Professional Footballers' Association
June 2002

Introduction

Until the 1990s, the phrase 'compared with cricket' was one of the trustiest clichés available to any aspiring football writer. Almost as if unguided by human fingers, our typewriters and pens automatically produced these words in letters to prospective publishers as we stressed the relative paucity of good football literature and pressed our claims. Fortunately, this situation has now changed quite dramatically. As association football has recovered from its 1980s nadir to become one of the most fashionable and central areas of popular culture, so the bookshelves have begun to groan under the weight of works chronicling, debating and celebrating the game. This book is partly a response to the explosion of writing about the game and partly an attempt to enhance our understanding still further, seeking both to synthesise the best of existing knowledge and to add to it by addressing topics and issues that have not generally been considered so far. We hope that it will find a wide audience, offering information and stimulus both to those pursuing essentially academic studies of the game and to a broader body of fans with an intelligent general interest in the history and culture of the game. In the 1980s, it was not normal to bracket the words 'football', 'fan' and 'intelligence', but the vast majority of the football community has always had an intense and knowledgeable interest in the game. Hopefully, this work will add to and enrich that knowledge still further.

We have termed it an encyclopedia of 'football' rather than 'association football' or 'soccer' because ultimately that is the term most commonly used by the game's devotees. We hope that fans of rugby and other codes will accept this act of appropriation. It is obviously not the first football encyclopedia; Frank Johnston's *The Football Encyclopaedia: a Historical and Statistical Review of the Game*, published in 1934, is a candidate for that award. Similarly, many readers will be aware of *The Encyclopedia of Association Football* compiled by the aptly named Maurice Golesworthy and which ran to eleven editions between 1956 and 1973, Martin Tyler and Phil Soar's *Encyclopaedia of British Football* (first published in 1974), Phil Soar's *Hamlyn A-Z of Football Records* (first published in 1981), Keir Radnedge's *The Ultimate Encyclopaedia of Soccer* (first published, 1994) and other titles. Nevertheless, this work is, we believe, the first of its type. It comprises some 200 entries, which provide short, informative essays of between 500 and 2,500 words on key themes and issues in football and football history. In this sense it differs from the works above, which tend to offer either chapter length treatment of specific topics combined with collections of statistical data, or a number of relatively short entries. Such an approach also distinguishes it from the dictionaries and reference works such as David Pickering, *Cassell Soccer Companion* (first published 1994) and Jon Ballard and Paul Suff, *The Dictionary of Football* (1999) that have become popular in the last decade and which in some cases run to several thousand headings. A second element of novelty relates to our approach. In essence, we have tried to identify (under headings quickly recognisable to a wide range of readers) major elements of the British football world and place them in their social, political, economic and cultural contexts. This attention to the relationship between football and the wider society receives far more attention here than is normally the case. Finally, the book considers a wider range of subject matter than most of the previous literature. All this in no way denigrates these other titles, many of which have been invaluable both to the editors and to our contributors; it merely defines our distinct purpose.

Size restrictions constrained what could be included and much consultation, head scratching and heart searching was indulged in before final decisions were taken. This has resulted in a conscious decision to exclude entries relating to specific individuals and clubs. A biographical/club-based approach leads naturally to a proliferation of entries and to almost insurmountable problems of inclusion and exclusion. With the exception of a handful of collective biographies dealing with notable individuals in areas such as management and coaching and similarly collective pieces dealing with certain tournaments and suchlike, we have chosen to subsume specific cases into general entries and let interested readers pursue them through the index. Limitation of space has also prevented the inclusion of any substantial body of statistical data relating to such issues as appearance, scoring and attendance records, although relevant material of this type appears in some entries. Searchers after statistical truth are recommended to use the irreplaceable *Rothmans Football Yearbook*, the various publications produced by the Association of Football Statisticians, Barry Hugmann's *The P.F.A. Premier and Football League Players Records, 1946–1998*, and Gordon Smailes, *The Breedon Book of Football Records, 1871–2000*.

Having eventually agreed a list of headwords, we assigned each entry a rating: C (500 words); B (750); A (1,250) and A+ (2,500), reflecting the overall significance of the topic. In general, our contributors acquiesced in our judgements, but we have been flexible when it has been demonstrated that a particular topic is worthy of greater attention than we had at first thought. One or two entries have indeed been allowed to extend beyond 2,500 words where it was felt that they provided genuinely new or neglected information. Inevitably, overlaps have arisen between entries and although we have eradicated some of these, there are occasions when particular events or issues are referred to in more than one entry. Hopefully, any minor irritation that might result when perusing the whole is more than compensated for by the comprehensiveness of the entries when used individually. All entries cite the major sources used by the writer as well as suggestions for further reading. These two listings are intended to be informative and enabling rather than definitive and those seeking more exhaustive bibliographic tools are recommended to seek out R. W. Cox's three-volume bibliography of British Sport to be published by Frank Cass in 2002 and Peter Seddon's *A Football Compendium: An Expert Guide to the Books, Films and Music of Association Football* (second edition) (Boston Spa: British Library Publishing, 1999). Detailed updates of football literature also appear in *The Sports Historian* which is published twice a year by the British Society of Sports History.

One of the most interesting challenges has been to make the encyclopedia genuinely and not just nominally 'British'; as in the wider culture, sporting literature has too often equated 'Britain' with 'England'. One way of achieving this has been to include specific entries on aspects of the game in Ireland (defined as the 32-county state pre-1920, and as Northern Ireland from then onward), Scotland and Wales. However, this in itself is an inadequate way of ensuring appropriate coverage and all authors have been asked to include relevant material on the three countries whenever and wherever possible. We hope to have gone some way to achieving our aims in this direction. A similarly diffused approach has been taken in relationship to women and football; while the women's game receives an extended entry, relevant issues are raised at suitable points throughout the book.

Contributors were selected partly by invitation and partly by response to a call for authors raised through the British Society of Sports History. Wherever possible, we have tried to encourage younger writers or contributors who have recently begun to work in the field. This strategy was designed both to provide opportunities for new scholars and to ensure that some of the most up-to-date and innovative research was made available to a wider public in an accessible form. Writers were not asked to operate under any particular set of 'house rules', beyond the request that all entries should be up to date, informative and accessible. The personalities and predilections of different writers do show through, therefore. The major unifying feature, however, is the knowledge and enthusiasm that they bring to their task: all our writers are fans, and it shows.

The chronology has been included to help juxtapose developments in different aspects of the game and to allow the reader to set these against wider changes in other sports and society as a whole. Its value became apparent when identifying topics for the encyclopedia and, as it has grown, readers will undoubtedly identify other relationships for more detailed consideration. A more comprehensive version covering all sports is to be published by Frank Cass in 2002.

The entries here will not merely provide information and knowledge but will stimulate readers to undertake football research of their own. The project has been a valuable learning experience for the compilers and, as one might have predicted, it has highlighted gaps in the existing knowledge. There are still many areas of the game, particularly its amateur and semi-professional aspects, which badly need further study. It would be highly satisfying if a future version of this encyclopedia featured work that it had helped inspire.

RICHARD WILLIAM COX
DAVE RUSSELL
WRAY VAMPLEW
June 2002

A Note about Illustrations

Football has provided the inspiration and subject for many art forms from drama, through music and painting to sculpture and verse. Contributors recommended numerous interesting and exciting pictures illustrative of the subject on which they had written for inclusion. Unfortunately, the fees charged by commercial agencies placed most of these beyond our budget. Once this factor had been taken into account, our objective was to achieve a compromise which balanced the subject matter (i.e. the event, issue, topic, venue), geographical location (England, Ireland, Scotland and Wales), period in history (early, modern) and also the nature of the source material (i.e. artefacts, cartoons, photographs, prints and stamps, etc.). We also endeavoured not to reproduce the same illustrations (good as they might be) that have frequently appeared in other publications, although a few like Lowry's *Going to the Match* we desperately wanted to include but permission was not forthcoming from the artist's estate. We are very grateful to The National Football Museum for providing many of the illustrations which appear in the book. Every effort has been made to trace the primary source of illustrations; in one or two cases where it has not been possible, we wish to apologise if the acknowledgement proves to be inadequate; in no case is such inadequacy intentional and if any owner of copyright who has remained untraced will communicate with us a reasonable fee will be paid and the required acknowledgement made in future editions of the book.

The National Football Museum

England was the birthplace of the modern professional game of association football, the world's most popular sport. Football is an important part of England's heritage, its people's way of life and their sense of identity. Despite this country's unique contribution to 'the people's game', until recently there had been no national museum to celebrate this history.

This has now changed with the opening in June 2001 of The National Football Museum, a charity governed by a board of independent trustees, which aims to collect, preserve and interpret football's rich heritage for the public's benefit. And there could be no more appropriate home for The National Football Museum than Deepdale Stadium, the home of Preston North End FC, the first winners of the world's oldest professional football league in 1888–89. Preston has been playing continuously, at the same ground, for longer than any other English league club. The Museum houses collections of national and international significance and contains exhibitions which provide an interactive account of the history and the future of the game.

The Museum charity secured Heritage Lottery Funding in 1997 which was conditional on the Museum acquiring a rich and varied collection owned by FIFA, the world governing body of football. The FIFA collection, now owned by The National Football Museum, is one of several major collections housed at the Museum. These include the Football League, the Football Association and the Wembley collections.

The Museum has split its exhibitions into two distinct sections The 'First Half' explores the origins of the game, the experience of fans, and brings together great football moments with significant events in a broader social history. The 'Second Half' is a themed 'interactive' exhibition, containing activities that encourage participation. Objects, moving images, audio commentary and original sound archive *exclusive* to The National Football Museum bring to life the personalities and events that have helped to shape the game we know today. The Museum's curators have ensured that the interpretation is suitable for all the family. Football and non-football supporters alike are catered for in the multi-sensory exhibitions.

The Museum is delighted to sponsor this volume and to have many items from its collection reproduced in the text.

List of Entries

List of Contributors

Roy Abbott
Sherwood, Nottinghamshire
European Championship
History Highlights 1980–1989
History Highlights 1990–1999
World Cup, The
FA Premiership
Yo-Yo Clubs

Martin Atherton
University of Central Lancashire
Association of Football Statisticians
Football and the Deaf Community

John Bale
University of Keele
Geography

Peter Beck
Kingston University
Politics

Ian Beesley
Rossendale
Photography

Alistair Bennett
Football Trust and Foundation

Gherardo Bonini
Historical Archives of European
Communities, Florence
Trainers

Lee Bradley
High Peak College
Youth Training

Mark Bushell
The National Football Museum
Collectors and Memorabilia
Exhibitions
Footballs
Medals

Neil Carter
University of Warwick
Management
Managers

Tony Collins
De Montfort University
Alcohol
Codes of Football
Folk Football

Richard William Cox
UMIST
Club World Championship
Exhibitions
Partnerships
Record Defeats/Wins
Scorers of Note

John Coyle
Solihull
All-Rounders
Big Spenders
Careers Cut Short
Coaches
Directors
Discipline and Punishment
Ex-Church Teams
Exports
Fixture Lists
Footballing Families
History Highlights 1800–1849
International Football
Replays
Scottish Football Association
Talented Ball Players

Tim Crabbe
Sheffield Hallam University
Racism and Ethnicity

Mike Cronin
De Montfort University
Irish Football

Steve Cunningham
Banbury
Football for the Blind

Paul Darby
University of Ulster
FIFA
UEFA

Frank Galligan
Droitwich
Schools Football

Richard Giulianotti
University of Aberdeen
Great Goals
Tactics and Playing Formations

Steve Greenfield and Guy Osborn
University of Westminster
Agents
Crowd Control and Management
Law
Taylor Report

Roy Hay
Deakin University
Refereeing
Scottish Football
Scottish Football Association

Jeff Hill
De Montfort University
Anthropology of Football
Gambling
Historiography of Football
Nurseries of Talent

Richard Holt
De Montfort University
Amateurism and Amateur Football

Dave Hudson
De Montfort University
Marketing

Trevor James
Lichfield
Lilleshall

Martin Johnes
St Martin's College, Lancaster
Disasters
Welsh Football
Welsh Football Association

Sam Johnstone
University of Liverpool
FA Cup

Marc Keech
University of Brighton
British Teams in Europe
Coaching
Coaching Schemes
Fantasy Football
Youth Groups

Robert Lewis
Rawtenstall
Anti-Football Lobbies
Fan Culture
First World War
Former League Clubs
History Highlights 1850–1899
History Highlights 1900–1909
History Highlights 1910–1919
Hooliganism and Riots
Music
Names and Logos
Original 12, The
Public Schools

Jeremy Mailes
Brighton
All-Rounders

Tony Mason
De Montfort University
Press

Ali Melling
University of Central Lancashire
Women and Football

Gavin Mellor
Liverpool Hope University
Football and the Community
History Highlights 1940–1949
History Highlights 1950–1959
History Highlights 1970–1979
Radio
Social Class
Sociology of Football

Ian Moir
University of Birmingham
BUSA
Rules

Rex Nash
Liverpool
Fanzines
Football Supporters' Association
Independent Football Supporters'
Associations
National Federation of Supporters' Clubs
Television

Paul O'Higgins
University of Liverpool
Football League Cup
Record Crowds

Jeff Perris
Bingley Sports Turf Research Institute
Turf Management

Kyle Philpotts
PGA National Training Academy
Mascots

Ray Physick
De Montfort University
Caps
Dominant Clubs
Football Boots
Grounds
History Highlights 1920–1929
History Highlights 1930–1939
Inter-Cities Fairs Cup

Brian Pluckrose
Bisham Abbey
Bisham Abbey

Tom Preston
Prescot
Architecture and Design
Art
Costume (Strip)
Facilities
Floodlighting

Michael Price
Kings Norton
Football and the Gay Community

Ronald Price
Milton Keynes
Amateur Football – Administration
Amateur Football – Cup Competitions
Amateur Football – International

Competitions
Amateur Football – National and Local
Leagues

Tom Reilly
Liverpool John Moores University
Applied Sports Science
Drugs
Scientific Perspectives on Football
Injuries

Tony Rennick
Boston Lincolnshire
Advertising and Publicity
Amateur Football – Notable Clubs
Artificial Pitches
Captains
Comic Characters
Derbies
Giant Killers
Goalkeepers
Hard Times
History Highlights 1960–1969
Humour, Incidents of
Knighthoods
National Stadia
Successes off the Pitch
Record Transfers
Rituals and Superstitions
Veterans

Dave Russell
University of Central Lancashire
Amateurism and Amateur Football
Charity
Discipline and Punishment
Drama
FA Cup
Football Trust and Foundation
Football Games
Football Season
Literature
Programmes
Radio and Television Pundits
Recreational Football
Religion
Research Centres
Royal Patronage
Scouting
Services Football
Yearbooks

Robert Shiels
Edinburgh
Deaths on the Pitch

Matt Taylor
Portsmouth University
Administrators
Agents
British Players Abroad
Football Association
Football League
Imports
Professional Footballers' Association
Promotion/Relegation System
Re-elections to the Football League
Wages

John Tolson
De Montfort University
Transport

Peter Vamplew
University of Tasmania
Websites

Wray Vamplew
University of Stirling
Economics
Relocation of Clubs
Sponsorship
Technology
Violence

Jean Williams
De Montfort University
Drama

John Williams
University of Leicester
Policing

Joyce Woolridge
Bristol
Celebrity Supporters
Corruption
Discipline and Punishment
Drugs
Film and Newsreel
Footballers' Wives
Heritage
Fashion Icons
Press
Radio and Television Pundits
Scandals
Second World War
Tobacco

List of Abbreviations and Acronyms

AFA	Amateur Football Association	GM	General Motors
AFPU	Association Football Players' Union	GNVQ	General National Vocational Qualification
AFS	Association of Football Statisticians	HMSO	Her Majesty's Stationery Office
ASL	American Soccer League	IFA	Irish Football Association
BASES	British Association for Sport and Exercise Science	IMUSA	Independent Manchester United Supporters' Association
BBC	British Broadcasting Corporation	IOC	International Olympic Committee
BCSA	British Colleges Sports Association	ISA	Independent Supporters Association
BPSA	British Polytechnics Sports Association	ITV	Independent Television
BOA	British Olympic Association	ISHPES	International Society for the History of Physical Education and Sport
B.Sc.	Bachelor of Science		
BSSH	British Society of Sports History	IVAB	Inter Varsity Athletic Board
		LEA	Local Education Authority
BTEC	British Training and Education Council	LMA	Leisure Managers' Association
		MA	Master of Arts
BUSA	British Universities Sports Association	MBA	Master of Business Administration
CCTV	Close Circuit Television	MBE	Member of the British Empire
DfEE	Department for Education and Employment	NASL	North American Soccer League
DIY	Do-it-yourself	NFFSC	National Federation of Football Supporters' Clubs
D.Sc.	Doctor of Science		
EPO	Erythropoietin	NVQ	National Vocational Qualification
ESFA	English Schools Football Association	OBE	Order of the British Empire
FA	Football Association	PFA	Professional Footballers Association
FACA	The Football Association Coaches Association	PPA	Pools Promoters Association
		POW	Prisoner of War
FAW	Football Association of Wales	PSU	Police Surveillance Unit
FAIFS	Football Association of the Irish Free State	RAFFA	Royal Air Force Football Association
FFE	Footballers' Further Education	RAOC	Royal Army Ordnance Corps
FIFA	Fédération Internationale de Football Association	RNFA	Royal Navy Football Association
FISU	Fédération Internationale du Sport Universitaire	RFU	Rugby Football Union
		SAFA	Scottish Amateur Football Association
FMA	Football Managers' Association		
FSA	Football Supporters' Assocation	SFA	Scottish Football Association
		TV	Television
GAA	Gaelic Athletic Association	UAU	Universities Athletic Association
GFTU	General Federation of Trade Unions		

UEFA	Union des Associations	WUGS	World University Games
	Européennes de Football	WWW	World Wide Web
UNESCO	United Nations	YOP	Youth Opportunities
UK	United Kingdom		Programme
USA	United States of America	YT	Youth Training
VTS	Vocational Training Society	YTS	Youth Training Scheme
WRU	Welsh Rugby Union		

Acknowledgements

Many individuals have kindly contributed to this volume. For developing the original proposal for such a publication we would like to thank Dr Bob Neville. For editorial assistance in the early stages of the project we are indebted to Daniel Nunn who showed great enthusiasm for the project and would have undoubtedly contributed more had he had the opportunity to stay to the end. When the commissioning publishers withdrew from the project Stewart Cass kindly stepped in to rescue the encyclopedia and ensured its final publication. For his encouragement, constructive advice and prompt response to numerous enquiries we are most grateful to Jonathan Manley of Frank Cass Publishers.

Several individuals have been invaluable sources of information, none more so than David Barber, Press Officer at the Football Association headquarters in London.

For supplying illustrations we thank the various authorities who generously waived copyright fees.

We are grateful to Gordon Taylor, a widely respected figure in the world of British football, who kindly agreed to write the Foreword.

Finally, the responsibility for all errors and omissions lies solely with the contributors.

History Highlights 1800–1849

The first half of the nineteenth century witnessed a gradual transformation from the old forms of folk and street football to the beginnings of the game we know today. The late eighteenth century had seen an increase in the enclosure of agricultural land that had reduced the space available for popular recreation. The growth of industry, too, with its demand for long and regular hours of work reduced the time that town-dwellers had to indulge in forms of leisure.

In addition, football and other popular pastimes were under pressure as a result of changing social attitudes. The church, local authorities and subsequently central government took a stricter view of idleness, drunkenness and sexual indulgence among working-class people. The playing of games and sports was often linked with such excesses, at least in the minds of middle-class reformers. As an example the Society for the Suppression of Vice was formed in 1801 with the aim of bringing prosecutions against people for breaches of the Sabbath, including the playing of organised games. The Lord's Day Observance Society, formed in 1831 succeeded this organisation. In 1835, Parliament passed the Highways Act, which provided for fines of up to £2 for 'playing at football or any other game on any part of the said highways to the annoyance of any passenger'. The law was not always enforced with rigour, but it did provide those local authorities that were so minded with a means by which they could suppress street football.

If football was declining as a sport for the masses, it was gaining ground in another important sphere of society. Pupils at many public schools had played rough forms of football since the early eighteenth century, although traditional sports such as hunting with hounds were often more popular. These rough games and bloodsports reflected the rumbustious, not to say lawless, character of many such institutions. As part of the reform of public schools, associated with men like Thomas Arnold at Rugby, many headmasters promoted team games as a means of social control within the schools. Team games provided some sense of order and provided an outlet for the boys' energies as well as being seen as more civilised than hunting and other country sports.

The games played at each school as 'football' were vastly different in form and often took their distinctive shape and style from the space available. At Charterhouse the game was played in a long, narrow cloister, thus favouring a dribbling game with players running with the ball at their feet. At Harrow the football field was large but muddy, so catching and kicking was encouraged. Rugby School's large field encouraged a running game although the innovation which allowed players to run while carrying the ball in their hands was not introduced until the 1820s.

The variety of local rules posed difficulties when the boys left their schools, as it was virtually impossible to organise games involving former pupils of different establishments. In 1846 some old boys of Eton and Shrewsbury tried without success to form a football club while studying at Cambridge University. Two years later, another group of Cambridge undergraduates had more success. One evening fourteen students, representing schools which included Eton, Winchester, Harrow, Shrewsbury and Rugby spent over seven hours formulating a set of rules that could be used for matches played at the university. The Cambridge Rules awarded a goal for a ball kicked between the posts and under the connecting string (forerunner to the crossbar). Catching the ball was permitted, but running holding the ball was not: the catcher had to kick the ball at once. Goal kicks and throw-ins were also included, as was an offside rule that stipulated that a player could receive a forward pass so long as there were three or more opponents between him and the goal.

The Cambridge Rules were perhaps the most significant development in football in the early nineteenth century as they paved the way for future codes of rules. The socio-economic pressures of the agrarian and industrial revolutions were transforming the old, unstructured folk game into an early form of the game we recognise today. In this sense, the first half of the nineteenth century was a significant era in the development of football.

Sources:

Holt, R., *Sport and the British: A Modern History* (Oxford: Clarendon, 1989).

Walvin, J., *The People's Game: A Social History of British Football* (London: Allen Lane, 1975).

Vamplew, W., *Pay Up and Play the Game: Professional Sport in Britain 1875–1914* (Cambridge: Cambridge University Press, 1988).

Further Reading:

Malcolmson, R. W., *Popular Recreations and English Society 1700–1850* (Cambridge: Cambridge University Press, 1973).

Dunning, E. and Sheard, K., *Barbarians, Gentlemen and Players: A Sociological Study of the Development of Rugby Football* (Oxford: Martin Robertson, 1979).

Russell, D., *Football and the English: A Social History of Association Football in England 1863–1995* (Preston: Carnegie Publishing, 1997).

John Coyle

Academies

– see Lilleshall

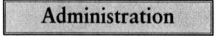

Administration

– see Football Association, Notable Administrators

Administrators

Charles Alcock was perhaps the leading figure in the early development of association football. As a player, journalist and administrator, he was instrumental in pop-ularising the game. Moreover, it was Alcock who came up with the idea for a knockout cup competition based on a house tournament at Harrow School which led to the creation of the FA Challenge Cup in 1871. Having played football at Harrow, Alcock was involved with his brother (J. P. Alcock) and other old Harrovians in the foundation of the Forest Club in 1859. In 1864, Forest was reformed as Wanderers FC with head-quarters at The Oval. Within two years, Alcock had been elected to the committee of the FA and by 1870 he was both its Secretary and Treasurer.

Cricket vied with football for Alcock's affections and his enthusiasm for both sports was combined in his journalism. It was here too that he made his living. He was Secretary of Surrey County Cricket Club from 1872 until his death in 1907 and wrote for the *Sportsman* and *The Field* before becoming owner and editor of *Cricket* in 1882.

A talented forward, Alcock played for England on a number of occasions, scor-ing in one international in 1875. He also was involved in, and wrote about, the transformation of football from a drib-bling to a passing game. By the time Alcock hung up his boots (but not his pen), Scottish and northern teams with new approaches to the game were beginning to upset the ascendancy of the southern teams of ex-public school and University men.

Like Alcock, whom he replaced as FA secretary in 1894, Frederick Wall was steeped in the amateur football world of London and the South of England. The emphasis he placed in his autobiography on the primacy of the Royal Engineers side of the early 1870s, rather than the Scottish and Lancastrian teams, in developing the passing game was a clear indication of where his loyalties lay. Wall was certainly no advocate of the professional game. He could be patronising towards the profes-sionals of the Football League – officials and players alike – and tended to idealise the 'golden age' of the game when results were less unimportant. But like many of his contemporaries at the FA he attemp-ted to manage professionalism and curb its excesses. And he had no time for the dogmatic amateurism of those who broke ranks with the governing body in 1907 to form the AFA.

Of all football's early administrators Wall has had perhaps the worst press. A snob and a sexist he may have been – he had apparently decided that football was not a suitable game for women after watching a match in 1895 – but Wall was essentially a product of his time and his social background and was not in fact as reactionary as he is often portrayed. Indeed rather than simply remembering him as the secretary who rejected invitations to the World Cups of 1930 and 1934, it is as well to note that Wall slowly came to recognise the significance of football's development abroad for the well-being of the English game. And while he was loathe to challenge the primacy of club over country, he was beginning to advocate changes in the selection of the national team, including the idea of consulting with leading managers in the north and south, when he retired from his post in 1934. Wall was knighted in 1931 and was rewarded with a golden handshake of £10,000 when he left the FA.

A contemporary of Wall at the FA and an even more prominent figure was the Sheffield solicitor Charles Clegg. Joining the governing body in 1866, Clegg served on the FA Council for 51 years, becoming chairman in 1890 and president in 1923. In 1927 he was knighted for his services to the Board of Trade, although it was widely considered to be recognition of his contribution to football. His power was such that he became known as 'the Napoleon of Football', while critics accused him of being an autocrat and a dictator.

Clegg was a keen and talented footballer. He played for a number of clubs in the Sheffield area, including Sheffield Wednesday, and was good enough to be selected to represent England in the first international fixture against Scotland in 1872. The experience was not an enjoyable one for Clegg as none of his teammates from the south passed or spoke to him and he vowed never to play for England again. He also took part in the first-ever floodlit match at Bramall Lane in 1878. He later turned to refereeing,

officiating a number of internationals and two FA Cup finals.

Like Wall, Clegg was an amateur at heart. He had fought against the legalisation of professionalism and regretted the increasing commercialisation of elite football but maintained that it was the responsibility of the amateurs to ensure that the honesty and integrity of the game were maintained. Driven by his religious convictions, Clegg had some success in opposing football's connections with drink and gambling. But his failure to outlaw the 'objectionable system' of transfers and exasperation at the continual infringements of FA regulations convinced him in 1910 to wash the FA's hands of the financial side of the professional game.

A Scottish migrant to Birmingham, William McGregor was the key figure in the foundation of the Football League. Although he was involved in the administration of all levels of football for most of his life, it is as the 'Father of the League' that he is best known. McGregor moved south from Perthshire in 1870 and opened a draper's with his brother near Birmingham city centre. Although not a player himself, he soon became involved in local football, particularly the Aston Villa club, whose committee he joined towards the end of the decade. It was in this position that McGregor sent his famous circular advocating a regular pro-gramme of fixtures among the leading sides in the country. The idea of 'fixity of fixtures' may not have originated with McGregor – indeed he admitted to have been influenced by the county cricket championship – but it was he who had the energy and the connections to put the idea into operation.

Once it had been launched in 1888, McGregor continued to play a central role in the development of the League. He was chairman of the Management Committee between 1888 and 1892, president from 1892 until 1894 and was the League's first Life Member from 1895 until his death in 1911. As a staunch Liberal, methodist and teetotaller, McGregor's background was similar to that of a number of his fellow Committee men, although his loyalty to the FA as football's governing body was probably more genuine than most.

John James Bentley was another pioneer of the professional side of the game popularised through the Football League. As secretary of Bolton Wanderers he had received McGregor's original letter in 1888 and served on the Management Committee for the next thirty years. He was president from 1894 until 1910 and in 1902 became the first League official to become vice-president of the FA. He played football as a youngster for his home village of Turton and represented Lancashire but made his mark as a journalist and administrator. In 1884, Bentley began work for the *Bolton Cricket and Football Field* and in 1886 became assistant editor of the *Athletic News*. He was editor between 1895 and 1900, a period which saw the circulation rise to almost 200,000 and helped to establish it as the unofficial mouthpiece of the Football League. Bentley was hardly a great writer but he was said to have introduced a topical and chatty style of sports journalism in which it was perfectly acceptable to call a football 'the ball'. Bentley was not a great orator but stood up to the gentlemen of the FA in the Council chamber and the pages of the sports press. He held a variety of positions with local and national football associations and clubs, including chairman of Manchester United from 1902 until 1910 and secretary between 1912 and 1914.

Charles Sutcliffe, a lawyer from Rawtenstall in Lancashire, was possibly the most influential football administrator of all in the period before the Second World War. Although a member of the FA Council for many years, he was unquestionably a 'League man'. He was the main architect of the Football League's rapid growth from a parochial clique to a truly national body and worked tirelessly devising new schemes in every area of its activities. Sutcliffe began his life in football as a player and then a committee member and director of his home town club Burnley. He was also an accomplished if a rather controversial referee. His election to the Management Committee in 1898 was the start of a forty-year association with the League, although he did not rise to the presidency until 1936. As a stout defender of League interests, Sutcliffe was the main advocate of the philosophy of mutual support, whereby the richer clubs within the League 'family' supported the poorer ones. For this reason he stood firm against FA threats to remove the retain-and-transfer system in the 1890s and was instrumental in establishing the legality of the system during the Kingaby case of 1912.

A small, frail man, Sutcliffe's physical appearance belied his strong character and ceaseless energy. Most of his schemes – from the system of constructing the fixture list to the Jubilee Fund for former players – were success stories but he did make mistakes, as his failed attempt to ruin the pool companies in 1936 showed. Aside from his League activities, Sutcliffe was president of the Lancashire FA, sat on the Appeals Committees of twenty different leagues, became a Liberal councillor and temperance worker and wrote regular newspaper columns.

It was a secretary, Alan Hardaker, rather than a president who dominated the postwar years of the Football League. In this role from 1957 to 1979, Hardaker attempted to modernise the League, and bring it kicking and screaming into the twentieth century. Although criticised by some as a dictator, he was not always able to get his way and so was left to defend the League and advance its cause with an increasingly hostile media and public which regarded it as a decaying institution.

Hardaker was the first secretary to have joined a League club, playing for a short time as an amateur with Hull City. His administrative experience came as Lord Mayor's secretary in Hull and Portsmouth and it was from the latter post that he applied to join the League as assistant secretary in 1947. On assuming the senior position, Hardaker soon expanded the League's operations by orchestrating the move from Preston to Lytham St Annes and increasing the staff from six to nearly thirty. He was committed beyond the call of duty, living in a house next door to the League's offices in Lytham and showing, according to one journalist, 'a degree of efficiency at times bordering on the ruthless'.

His plans to reform the structure of League competition were never wholly successful. His 'Pattern for Football' was an innovative attempt to adapt the League to a new environment in which football was one of many leisure choices. It was given a warm reception in the press but failed to get the required majority among the clubs although the idea of a League Cup – Hardaker's 'baby' but to some his 'folly' – was accepted. His outspoken nature got him into trouble at times and he clashed with Stanley Rous at the FA, whose interest in European and international football he did not share. For Hardaker, as for most of his predecessors and the majority of supporters, club always came before country.

In 1977, Hardaker's title was changed to Chief Executive and General Secretary and two years later he was replaced by Graham Kelly, although he refused a move upstairs as Director-General of the League. When he died suddenly of a heart attack in March 1980, Hardaker was still working for the League, drafting new ideas for 'Football in the Eighties'.

Never a radical but hardly a conservative, Stanley Rous played a pivotal role in converting the FA from an insular body to one aware of its place in the rapidly expanding international game. He became FA secretary in 1934 and stayed in the post until 1961, when he was elected president of FIFA, the world governing body.

Born into a lower middle-class family, Rous was employed as a schoolteacher at Watford Grammar School and made his initial mark on football as a respected referee. He officiated in domestic football and took charge of thirty-four international fixtures between 1927 and 1934. He was particularly interested in educational and technical aspects of football, and pioneered a range of schemes for coaches, players and referees.

Rous was extremely active during the Second World War, helping football to survive but also involving himself in broader plans for the future of sport and recreation, particularly as a founder member of the Central Council for Physical Recreation. His wartime fund-raising earned him a CBE in 1943 and, like Clegg and Wall, he received a knighthood in 1949. By this time, Rous had helped steer Britain back into world football politics by rejoining FIFA He was also involved in the creation of UEFA, the European confederation in 1954, helped set up the Inter-Cities Fairs Cup (the present UEFA Cup) and envisaged the development of a European League.

A traditionalist at heart, at FIFA Rous struggled to accommodate the emerging presence of Third World nations in search of increased representation on the world body and the increasingly lucrative World Cups. When he stood for re-election in 1974, he clearly expected to win but was skilfully outmanoeuvred by the Brazilian João Havelange, who was able to present Rous as 'old-worldly'.

Graham Kelly was the first paid administrator to move south, when he joined the FA as Chief Executive in 1988, having undertaken the same role at the Football League from 1979. His change of job was symptomatic of the changing power relations between the two bodies, with the governing body increasingly gaining the upper hand. Kelly played schoolboy football and was on the books at Accrington Stanley for a short time but he was really a supporter rather than a player. He was working as a bank cashier in his home town of Blackpool when he applied for a post as junior clerk at the Football League. He soon climbed the ranks at Lytham and was chosen to replace Hardaker as secretary in 1979 at the age of only thirty-three. Kelly's stewardship of the Football League came at a difficult period for the game. Faced with declining attendances, hooliganism and widespread unemployment, many clubs found themselves in severe financial difficulties. The policy of mutual support which had sustained the 92 League clubs for so long was under pressure from the wealthier clubs who wanted to secure better representation and larger shares of the income from television and sponsorship deals. Kelly played a key role in the attempted modernisation of the League and the television and reconstruction negotiations of the 1980s. Much of his energy, however, was spent trying to keep the influence on the game of the multi-millionaire publisher Robert Maxwell at arm's length. Kelly's move to the FA placed him firmly in the media spotlight. He was immediately involved in dealing with the ramifications of the Hillsborough disaster and the negotiations for the creation of the Premier League under FA control. He also dealt with a range of controversial cases from Cantona's famous kung-fu kick of 1995 to the Spurs loans scandal. Although a witty and articulate man off-screen, Kelly was never media friendly, as his stultifying performances during televised FA Cup draws proved. Kelly was forced to resign from the FA in December 1998, following allegations that he had been involved in a 'Cash for Votes' incident stemming from England's bid to host the 2006 World Cup, specifically sanctioning a £3.2 million loan to the Football Association of Wales.

Kelly's replacement, Adam Crozier, who took up his post in January 2000, represented a significant break with tradition. A 36-year-old Scot, Crozier had been in the advertising industry rather than football, suggesting that the FA were looking for a new set of skills as they engaged with football's rapidly changing environment.

Sources:

Inglis, S., *League Football and the Men Who Made It* (London: Collins Willow, 1988).

Gibson, A. and Pickford, W., *Association Football and the Men Who Made It* 4 vols. (eds) (London: 1906).

Green, G. *The History of the Football Association* (London: Naldrett Press, 1953).

Further Reading:

Mason, T., *Association Football and English Society, 1863–1915* (Brighton: Harvester Press).

Matt Taylor

Advertising and Publicity

The two big football stories that broke in the newspapers of 8 February 2001 could not have better emphasised the inequality in the game as a result of the breakaway of the top clubs into the Premier League in 1992. While Manchester United were announcing their alliance with the USA's richest baseball team, the New York Yankees, Third Division Hull City were calling in the administrators following a winding-up order brought by Customs and Excise and the Inland Revenue for outstanding VAT and PAYE debts of £500,000. Reports estimated that City's total debts amounted to between £2 million and £3 million, less than David Beckham was currently earning in a year. Among the stricken club's financial tangles awaiting the administrators' attention was a dispute over an unpaid bill of £6,000 at a Mr Chu's Chinese restaurant, with City counter-suing the restaurant over outstanding bills for advertising hoardings. With United, grown rich from the colossal advertising and endorsement revenue pouring into their swollen coffers since the Premiership's TV deal with BSkyB, and having signed a £30 million, four-year shirt sponsorship deal with Vodafone the previous year, the cause of the Tigers' £6,000 squabble was irony personified. Two quotes from the Guardian that day summed up how the attitudes within the game have changed in the television age. United director Bobby Charlton: 'We're not in it to make money. But obviously we will make money, because that's what we're good at.' A bemused Tommy Docherty, United manager of the 1970s: 'I keep scratching my head wondering what this is all about and whether the supporters care. People who support United are happy to go to the game, have a pint and something to eat. Everything else is incidental.' The Old Trafford club's transatlantic deal was, of course, designed to continue the globalisation of the team, the Manchester United 'brand' and bring the 'product' to the attention of the vast, hitherto untapped market of the United States. The idea was that United and Yankees would sell each other's merchandise. The Americans may not know much about football, or 'soccer' as they insist on calling it, but they certainly lead the way in marketing.

In the game's early days, before Madison Avenue, just down the road from Yankee Stadium, had become the world's advertising capital following the establishment of the first advertising agencies in the late nineteenth century, the most reliable method of advertising available was word of mouth. Long before television, sponsorship, even organised football itself had emerged, a momentous event took place in Scotland when, on 5 December 1815, the men of Selkirk took on the men of Yarrow. Selkirk's most prestigious supporter that day was the poetic Mr Scott, the Keeper of the Forest, who penned a commemorative ballad to celebrate the occasion. His stirring words were printed on broadsheets and distr-ibuted to the crowd of 2,000, providing them not only with a musical memento of the day, but the world's first football pro-gramme. Even today, in the electronic multi-media age, the humble match pro-gramme serves as a useful outlet for a club to promote its public image to its fans. What better captive audience is there? Modern pro-grammes are more like maga-zines, usually containing regular contri-butions from the manager, chairman or club captain. The opposition of the day are profiled, player by player, and the home team's recent results analysed, providing pre-match, half-time and post-match entertainment. Current offerings have come a long way from Mr Scott's effort and the later pro-grammes of the Victorian era. In those days the publications on offer were simple match cards with the players listed on one side and the reverse containing advertisements. The card publicising the FA Cup final between Aston Villa and West Bromwich Albion on 20 April 1895, for example, carried advertisements for tea, Scotch whisky, cigarettes, and, in view of the imminent return of the summer game, cricket bats. Aston Villa, after winning the trophy that year, received a deal of unexpected publicity a few months later when the 'little tin idol' was stolen from the shop window of a Birmingham boot and shoe maker, Mr William Shilcock. It was never found, but the newspaper stories the incident generated would have done Villa no harm, given the adage that there is no such thing as bad publicity. As match pro-grammes gradually evolved and became more sophisticated, by the early twentieth century some of the more progressive clubs were producing publications with newspaper-style titles. Aston Villa had *The Villa News*, Fulham *The Cottagers' Journal* and Chelsea *The Chelsea F.C. Chronicle*. Visitors to White Hart Lane could enjoy the delights of Tottenham Hotspur's grandly-titled *The Official Programme and Record of the Club*. Even in the 1990s the fans were provided with matchday reading material, but the 'messages from our sponsor' were ever-present. A 1994 copy of Manchester United's glossy, full-colour *United Review*, for instance, carried, among the footballing information their faithful followers wanted, full-page advertisements for their kit manufacturers Umbro, the Premiership sponsors Carling and (two pages this time) their shirt sponsors Sharp. A study of a Boston United programme from 1996 shows that even non-league outfits were aware of the power of advertising, on a scale matching their position in the footballing hierarchy. For the visit of Sudbury Wanderers in the third qualifying round of the FA Cup in October that year, United, then in the Unibond League, produced a programme promoting local firm Johnsons Seeds, official seed suppliers to Wembley Stadium. Henkel, the producers of Unibond, reminded fans that they manufactured not only fillers, sealers and adhesives, but also haircare products, toothpaste and hand cream. The club's sponsors of the time, local brewery Batemans, had the back page to themselves, but Sudbury fans would have been puzzled by a strange panel on the page listing reserve team patrons. The message read simply: 'Mick Baxter, 3 Hardwick Estate, Kirton.' There was no mention of who Mr Baxter was or what he did. Boston United fans already knew that he was a local roofer. All that was necessary for him to generate business was to advertise the fact that he was actively supporting the club.

This phenomenon of showing only the name of an advertiser, without making any claims as to the merits of the product on offer, can be seen during the post-match

Advertisements for RIZLA and OXO, Sunday Chronicle Football Annual 1954–55

OXO ad, Association Football by J.L. Jones
(1904)

COSSOR radio ad, News Chronicle Football
Annual 1948–49

interviews after every televised match which inevitably take place against a backdrop of corporate logos. Even the broadcasters ensure the viewers remember which channel they're watching, with 'BBC' or 'ITV Sport' prominent among the names of the sponsors of the teams, their kit or the competition they're curently engaged in. Every modern Premiership player has become a walking billboard, with his own name emblazoned across the back of his shirt, while the front carries the name of the club sponsor for all to see. Close-ups during the televised action also reveal that shorts and socks carry the maker's name. The club crest is also part of his uniform, as are his team colours. What all this means is that his message to the fans is: 'This is who I am, who I play for and where the money comes from.' Young fans, and others not so young, can vicariously relive the exploits of such heroes by wearing replica shirts, usually of a different design each season, giving the clubs and their sponsors even more publicity. Not only is this exposure free, the supporters pay inflated prices for the privilege.

Sources:

Conn, D., *The Football Business* (Edinburgh: Mainstream, 1997).

Hamil, S., Michie, J. and Oughton, C. (eds), *A Game Of Two Halves?* (Edinburgh: Mainstream, 1999).

Further Reading:

Barrett, N., *The Daily Telegraph Football Chronicle* (London: Carlton, 1999).

Hart, G. (ed.), *The Guinness Football Encyclopedia* (Enfield: Guinness, 1995).

Mason, N., *Football!* (London: Mason Temple Smith, 1974).

See also Business

Tony Rennick

Agents

Agents emerged as a feature of British football in the decades immediately following the legalisation of professionalism in 1885. Initially, they were full-time entrepreneurs exploiting the lack of organisation in early professional clubs, who had yet to establish recruiting and scouting networks. They were involved in the basic service of providing clubs with players. The governing bodies, however, were morally opposed to this activity and set about banning individuals and agencies attempting to make money by acting as the go-between for clubs and players.

Despite their bad reputation, agents were important figures in the development of the game. They performed an invaluable role in the growth of the international transfer market. Many of the British players who moved to the American professional league in the 1920s, the French league in the 1930s and the Colombian rebel league in the early 1950s dealt with intermediaries rather than the clubs themselves. The Italian agent Gigi Peronace was instrumental in the transfer of a number of Britons to Serie A in the 1950s and 1960s. He had acted as an interpreter for Juventus' Scottish manager William Chambers after the Second World War, and worked initially as an independent scout and agent in Britain before taking a more formal post as business manager at Torino, where he engineered the transfer of John Charles, among others. However, few of these were agents as we would recognise them today. The crucial difference is that they tended to represent clubs rather than players.

These days an agent is more generally a representative who acts on behalf of a player in negotiations both with football clubs who wish to employ the player, and with third parties to maximise the various commercial opportunities open to him. The visibility of agents has increased since the *Bosman* ruling, which allowed greater freedom of movement at the end of a contract, and their function has developed in line with the greater ease with which players may change clubs. The most obvious role of an agent is to maximise the financial rewards when a player moves to a new club or renegotiates an existing contract. If the agent is paid on a commission basis then the better the terms obtained for the player, the greater the resulting reward for the agent. The growth in the use of agents is linked to greater contractual freedom, after both the Eastham and Bosman cases, and the financial opportunities for players on and off the field. There has also been an increasing globalisation of the game, which has led to more overseas players appearing in British football and has also brought an international dimension to agents. It is important to recognise that a player's career has the potential to be cut short at any moment by injury or loss of form. A switch to a different club may affect a player's performance if he does not settle in a new area or is unhappy with an altered training and managerial regime. There are many examples of players moving clubs and seeing a promising career nosedive. An agent will need to advise a player carefully on the advantages and disadvantages of a transfer so that an informed decision can be made. An agent is in a fiduciary relationship with a player and must always act in the player's best interests. An agent must only act for one party within a negotiation and would be in breach of his contractual duty to the player if he received a payment from the club to entice the player to move. There have been a number of highly publicised allegations of improper payments being made in connection with transfers that have led to inquiries and some disciplinary action. In order to ensure propriety the football authorities have attempted to exert some system of control over the activities of agents.

There exists a system of licensing for agents at both international and domestic level. The Premier League provides guidance, including definitions of their role and functions, and methods of application. Barristers, solicitors and FIFA licensed agents do not require domestic approval, but licence applications are otherwise considered by a Board in conjunction with the Football Association and the Football League, and a successful applicant is required to lodge a £30,000 guarantee with the Football Association. A number of restrictions are placed on the agreements that can be made between players and agents, including: specifying that these shall be in writing, that the agreement can only last for a maximum of two years, that the agreement cannot be assigned, or transferred, to another party, and that the method of remuneration must be clearly stated in the contract. The Football Association keeps a register of agreements that may be inspected by the clubs or other relevant parties.

Agents are in an invidious position in that they may be disliked by many of the parties in football – managers, club owners and fans, who may see agent influence as malevolent. Agents clearly have a legitimate function, as there are enormous commercial opportunities both inside and outside the game. The avenues for sponsorship, product endorsement and advertising are increasing for the highest profile players, and agents can be used to exploit these opportunities and maximise income. It is in this role of trying to get the best deal for the client that the agent can come into conflict with the buying club. Furthermore, agents may be perceived by clubs and supporters as attempting to initiate transfers whilst players are in contract. Football has a long and distinguished history of contractual breaches by all sides, and agents are part of the contemporary bargaining process within the established culture of the industry. The football authorities have acted to regulate agent conduct and this process is likely to continue, as is the increasing role of player agents.

Sources:
FA Premier League Handbook (London: Premier League, 1999).

Further Reading:
Graham, G., *The Glory and the Grief* (London: Andre Deutsch, 1995).
Greenfield, S. and Osborn, G., *Regulating Football* (London: Pluto Press, 2001).

*Steve Greenfield, Guy Osborn
and Matthew Taylor*

Alcohol

Football is a fascination of the devil and a twin sister of the drink system.

So declared an Anglican vicar in Leeds in

1893. Satan's affiliations are beyond the scope of this article, but football's close association with drink, and especially beer-drinking, has been strong from pre-industrial times, when folk football games were played at fairs and festivals. Today, playing, administering, and watching football remain deeply interconnected with the pub, drinking and the alcohol trade in general.

The 1870s and 1880s saw innumerable early football clubs formed in pubs, using pubs as their headquarters, or playing on pitches connected with pubs. By the turn of the century football became an integral part of pub culture. In addition to the facilities offered to teams, regular updates of games in progress and match results were sent by telegraph to pubs on Saturday afternoons. Pubs also displayed trophies won by local teams, and savings clubs were set up in pubs so that their patrons could save money to travel to important away matches.

Despite this close association, many clubs had uneasy relationships with pub landlords, especially as publicans sought to cash in on football's popularity. It became common for clubs to move grounds to secure better facilities or more advantageous terms. Sunderland, for example, played their first matches on a field next to the Blue House Inn, but moved to a site at Ashbrooke when they found the £10 annual rent too much. Everton fell out with brewer John Houlding over the rent he charged them to play in the field adjoining his Sandon Hotel; in revenge, and to exploit the commercial opportunities available from football, he set up his own side, Liverpool FC. But not all relationships were acrimonious: when the landlord of the pub which Kilmarnock used for changing rooms decided to move in 1883, the club moved with him.

The extent of the drinks trade's involvement in the formative period of football can be seen in Vamplew's analysis of shareholdings in football clubs before 1915. He demonstrates that publicans played an important role in the financing and administration of football clubs. Of all shareholders in football clubs, 14.9 per cent were involved the drink trade, as were 14.7 per cent of directors of English First Division clubs and 10.1 per cent of Second Division clubs. In Scottish soccer, the involvement of the drinks trade was similarly high: 11.3 per cent of shareholders were involved in the trade, as were 21.8 per cent of First Division directors and 15.8 per cent of Second Division directors.

Football clubs would often appeal to local publicans and brewers for financial help. For example, Middlesbrough's promotion to the First Division of the Football League in 1902 led them to seek new capital to invest in the Ayresome Park ground, and an appeal was issued to members of the licensed trade to invest in the club. When Newton Heath went into liquidation in 1902, they were rescued by John Davies, a local brewer, renamed Manchester United, and the shares in the new club distributed among himself and other directors of his brewery. Other clubs were reliant on the good will and financial assistance of brewers for the purchase of grounds: both Watford and Oldham Athletic, to name just two clubs, were beholden to their local breweries for loans to purchase their grounds. During the depression of the inter-war years, it became commonplace for breweries to come to the financial aid of their local team.

It is important to note, however, that the development of modern football was not simply the work of brewers and publicans. The role played by teetotallers and temperance advocates was in many respects crucial, especially in the formation and early administration of the Football League. Of the League's founding fathers, Birmingham's William McGregor was a committed teetotaller; Charles Sutcliffe, the Football League's founding secretary, was a Sunday school preacher; Charles Clegg of Sheffield and Walter Hart of Small Heath in Birmingham were both active temperance reformers; and John Lewis, the League's leading referee, was inclined to impromptu lectures on the demon liquid. North of the border, the Scottish Football Association was actually founded at Dewar's

Temperance Hotel in Glasgow in 1873. In many towns, local church and Sunday school leagues were formed as alternatives to clubs and leagues which had their headquarters in pubs, in some places actually outnumbering their non-teetotal rivals.

But in general the cultural bond between drinking and football was too deep for the temperance movement ever to challenge seriously. Nowhere was this more obvious than in advertising, where breweries sought to exploit opportunities at football grounds, in newspapers and in match-day programmes. Few covered stands were complete in the inter-war years without the name of the local brewer painted on the roof, while sporting newspapers and club programmes derived not inconsiderable revenue from the advertisements placed with them by breweries. In the 1960s the advent of TV commercials saw players – among them Bobby Moore, Denis Law and the entire Liverpool team – being used to advertise beer and pubs in general.

The modern age of football sponsorship can be said to have arrived in the 1970–71 season with the inauguration of the Watney Cup knock-out competition for Football League teams, for which the brewer paid £82,000 (the tournament was also the first to use penalty shoot-outs to decide matches). Relaxations in the rules governing shirt advertising meant that by the 1980s clubs were signing sponsorship deals which saw the names of brewers and their products adorning team shirts. The 1990s saw the wholesale re-branding of competitions to attract sponsors in both England and Scotland. This was dominated by Bass, the Burton-on-Trent based brewery giant, who used the game to promote the names of its brands in major competitions, such as the Worthington (formerly League) Cup, the Carling Premier League and the Tennent's Scottish Cup. By 1998 Bass were spending over £1 million per month sponsoring the Premier League alone, but the return on its investment was also considerable – sales of its Carling lager rose by 31 per cent to become the UK's top-selling alcoholic brand.

During the first half of the twentieth century, beer advertising using football was often attacked by temperance advocates, who pointed to the contradiction between the healthy lifestyle seemingly promoted by the sport and the threat to health posed by alcohol. Today, although the temperance movement is an insignificant fringe, public health analysts echo some of their criticisms, especially when famous players are seen to be endorsing drinking. The idea that sportsmen and women should act as role models for the young is deeply ingrained into British sporting culture, yet history suggests that – at least as far as drink is concerned – professional footballers are not an ideal choice for such a role. The very nature of the professional footballer's trade means that opportunities to drink are legion. Clubs have long sought to regulate the alcoholic intake of players: for example, Arnold Hills, founder and owner of West Ham United, introduced a series of fines for players caught drinking or found to be drunk, even holding wages in trust in 1907 for players alleged to have drinking problems. Aston Villa went so far as to employ a private detective to investigate allegations of heavy drinking among players during the 1900s. Nevertheless, many players still acquired reputations as heavy drinkers. England and Derby County forward Steve Bloomer was well-known for his liking for a pint, making a number of appearances before the board of directors to explain his lack of sobriety. In this, he perhaps established the prototype of the hugely talented player with an over-fondness for drink, whose footsteps were to be followed over the decades by Jimmy Greaves, George Best and Paul Gascoigne, to list just three household names. Indeed, to some extent, it is their drinking feats which have endeared such players to fans, especially when accompanied by a sense of humour. Best in particular developed a self-deprecatory style in commenting on his own drinking habits: for example, when asked in the 1970s why he went to play in the North American Soccer League he replied 'Because I saw a sign saying Drink Canada Dry.'

Football's attitude to drinking by players has always been ambiguous. Although frowned upon by directors, managers often saw its worth as a medicinal aid – raising the spirits of injured players or as a pick-me-up at half-time, or, in the case of beer, for its supposed stamina-providing qualities – and as a means to inspire a sense of camaraderie and *esprit de corps* in a team. Heavy drinking as part of a 'bonding session' between team-mates is today an important part of many managers' motivational and man-management techniques, although its success or otherwise has never been analysed. However, it does appear that such sessions can achieve the opposite of their purpose when a player is either teetotal or a light drinker, and is consequently felt to be an outsider by his team mates or himself. In both men's and women's amateur football, drinking before, after, and often even during a match is a major part of its culture and appeal, perhaps best exemplified in the names of amateur clubs such as Real Ale Madrid and PSV Hangover in London.

The alcohol link does not end with retirement from the game. As Greaves and Best demonstrate, the alcoholic ex-player is sadly not a rarity. The relationship between football clubs and local breweries has also meant that there is a long tradition of players becoming pub landlords at the end of their playing careers. In the early days of the game it was also a regular occurrence for players to become publicans during their careers, and the offer of a pub tenancy became an especially attractive inducement to a player to change clubs. Scots players were often enticed to English clubs by the opportunity to run or work in a pub. At least six Blackburn Rovers players of the early 1880s were publicans during their playing careers, and in the 1890s it was rumoured that up to half the Sunderland side were publicans. Celtic were also well known for the number of footballing publicans in their side in the 1890s. Despite the abolition of the maximum wage in 1961, the life of a publican was still very much sought after by players at the end of their careers. A 1996 study of over 2,000 ex-players found that the most common post-playing occupation outside football was that of pub landlord, with 8.5 per cent of the surveyed ex-players taking a job in the drinks trade.

But it is not only playing football that is closely associated with drinking – it is just as much a part of watching the game. Observers of crowds attending early FA Cup finals in London noted the propensity for alcohol consumption by spectators, especially those travelling down from the North of England, for whom the extended train journey south was an opportunity for considerable indulgence. Nevertheless, in England at least, drinking was not initially felt to be a direct cause of spectator violence and disorder: the Report of the 1898 Royal Commission on the Liquor Licensing Laws went so far as to argue that 'the passion for games and athletics – such as football and bicycling – which has been so remarkably stimulated during the past quarter of a century, has served as a powerful rival to "boozing", which at one time was the only excitement open to working men'. That drink at football was not associated with crowd disturbances was highlighted by a leaflet distributed by Millwall to their supporters in the 1940s, entitled 'Don't Do It Chums', which warned them about their behaviour at matches but made no mention of alcohol. In Scotland, however, drinking to excess at matches became a recognised problem and one of the major causes of the 1909 Cup Final riot at Hampden Park was thought to be the widespread imbibing of spirits before and during the match. 'Old Firm' derbies between Celtic and Rangers became notorious for drunken disorder and 'bottle parties', whereby fans would shower the opposing team with beer bottles, empty or otherwise.

By the late 1960s violent crowd behaviour had become increasingly prevalent at football grounds and on journeys to and from matches in England and Scotland. With little hard evidence to support the contention, much of the blame was laid at the door of alcohol. After numerous reports into the causes of football hooliganism, and calls for the banning of alcohol from football grounds, the 1980 Criminal Justice (Scotland) Act made illegal the possession of alcohol at, or on the way to, a football match in Scotland. This was followed in 1985, at the height of the Thatcher government's concern over the law and order problems generated by the game, with the introduction of an even more draconian anti-alcohol regime into football in England and Wales. This legislation made it illegal to drink, possess alcohol or be drunk on the way to or at a match, although, unlike the Scottish Act, it did allow drinking at a football ground, provided that it took place in an area from which the pitch could not be seen.

However, this association between alcohol consumption and violence has been challenged by a number of observers, all of whom point to football supporters, such as the Danes, who combine prodigious drinking with peaceful reputations. The example of Italian 'Ultras', who, conversely, are extremely violent yet rarely drunk, is also used. In Britain, a 1977 study by the Strathclyde Police found that there was no significant difference in the number of crimes committed, including those due to drunkenness, between times when football matches were played and other times of the week. Peter Marsh and Kate Fox Kibby, in their 1992 book *Drinking and Public Disorder*, use this evidence to argue that claims of drink-inspired football hooliganism are a form of 'moral panic' with little basis in fact.

The change in the image of supporters of the Scottish national team – perceived in the 1960s and 1970s as among the most drunken and violent in world football, yet transformed into peaceful though heavy-drinking goodwill ambassadors for their country at successive World Cups and European Championships in the 1980s and '90s – provides compelling evidence that alcohol is neither the cause nor the symptom of spectator violence. Although there is as yet no commonly accepted explanation for the metamorphosis of Scottish fans, it would suggest that the social uses of alcohol are deeply related to prevailing ideas of national or local identity and their expression.

The bond between alcohol and football appears almost indissoluble. If, in the future, attitudes to drinking change along similar lines to the change in attitudes to tobacco, direct financial and sponsorship links may be broken, but it appears that drinking alcohol will always be an essential element of the lifeblood of football culture.

Sources:

May, P., *Sunday Muddy Sunday* (London: Virgin, 1998).

Vamplew, W., *Pay Up and Play the Game* (Cambridge: Cambridge University Press, 1988).

Weir, J., *Drink, Religion and Scottish Football 1873–1900* (Renfrew: Stewart Davidson, 1992).

Further Reading:

Mason, T., *Association Football and English Society 1863–1915* (Brighton: Harvester Press, 1980).

Ripley, M. and Wood, F., *'Beer is Best': The Collective Advertising of Beer 1933–1970* (London: The Brewers' Society, 1994).

See also Drugs

Tony Collins

All-Rounders

There are essentially two kinds of footballing all-rounder: the sportsman good enough to represent his country at two sports, and the versatile footballer able to operate in several different positions.

Max Woosnam can make a strong claim to being the most versatile British athlete of all time. In 1911, during his final year at Winchester College, Woosnam played cricket for the Public Schools against the MCC at Lord's and scored 144 and 33 not out. He proceeded to Trinity College, Cambridge, where he won blues at football, lawn tennis, golf and real tennis. He would gain still more major sporting honours, despite being severely debilitated by service with the Royal Welch Fusiliers during the First World War. At the Amsterdam Olympics of 1920 Woosnam won a gold medal in the lawn tennis men's doubles with Noel Turnbull, and a silver in the mixed doubles with Kitty McKane. In 1921, partnering the Anglo-Australian Randolph Lycett, he took the men's doubles title at Wimbledon. In this year he and Lycett also won a crucial Davis Cup match against Spain when they defeated Manuel Alonso and Count de Gomar. On the football field Woosnam was undoubtedly one of the finest centre-halfs of his day. As a Cambridge undergraduate he turned out for the Corinthians and Chelsea, while in the early 1920s he played regularly for Manchester City. Woosnam won two amateur international caps, but his highest honour was to captain the full England team against Wales in 1922.

Similar claims to the title of sporting polymath could have been made by Howard Baker. He won the first of six Amateur Athletics Association high jump titles while a schoolboy in 1910. His jump of 6' 5", made at the Huddersfield Cricket Ground in 1921, lasted as a British record for 26 years. Baker played 176 football matches for the Corinthians and kept goal 120 times for Chelsea. Originally a centre-half, he had an England amateur international trial in this position while with Blackburn Rovers. Baker only turned to keeping after one of his ankles was damaged during mine-sweeping operations on a Q boat in the First World War. He won 10 amateur caps for England and two full caps against Belgium (1921), and Northern Ireland (1926). Baker was adept in the swimming pool and represented Lancashire at water polo as a goalkeeper. He was also celebrated for his demonstrations of trick diving in swimming pools throughout Lancashire. He had an exceptionally long goal-kick and appears to have been an antecedent of Peter Schmeichel; he was known to make rash sorties into mid-field and fancied himself from the penalty spot, scoring one league goal. At tennis Baker won the Welsh covered-court doubles title in 1932 as a 40-year-old, and also played doubles at Wimbledon. He was a competent cricketer and played for the Lancashire Second XI.

Charles Wreford Brown was an international at football and chess. He is also credited with having given us the word 'soccer'. David Pickering has revealed that it was the habit among Victorian undergraduates to abbreviate words and add '-er' to the end; in this way, for example, breakfast became 'brekkers'. Wreford Brown is said to have abbreviated 'association' to 'asoccer', and later 'soccer'. He was a brilliant all-round athlete at Charterhouse and Oxford University, for whom he played first-class cricket. Wreford Brown played football for England against Wales and Northern Ireland in the 1890s and captained his country against Scotland. The combination of chess and football may seem bizarre, but anyone who can remember Simen Agdestein, an international footballer for Norway in the 1980s, might like to note that he has achieved considerable success as a chess grandmaster. Agdestein once said he would rather take on Anatoly Karpov than Franco Baresi. Wreford Brown appears to have been an obsessive chess player: during the British Championship at Hastings in 1933 it was only with great reluctance that he retired after having a heart attack at the board. In 1924 he played chess for Great Britain at the Paris Olympics. Wreford Brown was a centre-half with superb pace and judgement and at 5' 8" he was unusually strong in the air; more surprisingly, given his physique, he began playing as a goalkeeper. He was a vice-president of the FA and captained a tour of South Africa by the Corinthians in 1903.

There have also been a small number of players winning international honours at soccer and rugby. Reginald Birkett appeared in goal for England against Scotland in 1879, having previously been capped four times at rugby, a feat emulated by Charles Wilson. H. W. Renny-Tailyour played for Scotland against England in both 1872 and 1873 – the former at rugby, the latter at soccer. John Sutcliffe abandoned rugby soon after being capped by England in 1889 and joined Bolton Wanderers as a goalkeeper, performing with such success that he played for England six times between 1893 and 1903. In 1948 the Irish amateur Kevin O'Flanagan made his debut for Ireland at rugby, having already represented Northern Ireland and Eire on the soccer field.

The most common combination for the multi-talented sportsman was football and cricket. Before 1914 six players were capped by England at both sports. Four were amateurs, namely Alfred Lyttelton, Leslie Gay, Reginald Foster and C. B. Fry, an inescapable figure in this period. As an Oxford undergraduate, Fry equalled Charles Reber's world long jump record with a leap of 23' 6.5". The legend – which Fry frequently reinforced – is that the jump was made between puffs of a cigar. In 1895, as a stalwart member of the Oxford University Drama Society, Fry turned down the chance to play football for the Corinthians in order to appear as one of Portia's suitors in *The Merchant of Venice*. His one appearance as an international footballer came in March 1901, during a lacklustre fixture between England and Wales at The Dell. His performance was no more than competent and he did not retain his place. Fry spent much of his life on the *Mercury*, a naval training academy where his ogre of a wife held sway over a regime of terror that caused several deaths. Between 1892 and 1921 he achieved the small matter of 30,866 runs in first-class cricket, while in 1912 he captained England to victory in the Triangular Test Series against Australia and South Africa. As one of India's representatives at the League of Nations in the 1920s he was offered the throne of Albania.

Of the others, Alfred Lyttelton deserves special mention as the only cabinet minister to play football for England, having served as Colonial Secretary in 1903 after the resignation of Joseph Chamberlain. Lyttelton played in four Ashes tests against Australia in the 1880s as a wicket-keeper, and – bowling under-arm lobs – once took four Australian wickets for 19 runs at the Oval while still wearing his keeper's pads. His sole international football appearance was for England against Scotland. England lost 3–1, but Lyttelton scored with what *The Field* described as 'a hard shot from a scrimmage'. Lyttelton's death at the age of 56 came after he received a blow in the stomach from a cricket ball.

Two professionals won international honours in both games prior to the First World War: William Gunn of Notts County and Nottinghamshire and Jack Sharp of Everton and Lancashire. Sharp's team-mate in both sports, Harry Makepeace, was capped four times for

football between 1906 and 1912, but did not win international recognition at cricket until 1920, when he was nearly 40. Harold Hardinge of Sheffield United and Kent played for England against Scotland in 1910, but had to wait 11 years to make his Test cricket debut. Between the wars Andy Ducat of Aston Villa and Surrey won six caps for football and one for cricket, while Johnny Arnold of Southampton and Hampshire played in a Test match against New Zealand in 1931 and two years later won a football cap against Scotland. Andrew Ducat's football clubs were Southend Athletic, Woolwich Arsenal and Aston Villa. Ducat was captain of Villa in 1920 when they defeated Huddersfield Town 1–0 in the FA Cup Final. His record as manager of Fulham in 1923 and '24 was abysmal, but his international career as a footballer saw him win six caps against Scotland, Wales and Northern Ireland. In first-class cricket he scored 23,373 runs at an average of 38.63. His one Test match for England was in 1921 against Australia at Headingley, where he scored 3 and 2. Ducat died with his boots on at Lord's, where he had a heart attack while playing for the Home Guard against Sussex and Surrey. After playing a ball gently into the covers he keeled over on the wicket and died. There was much dispute as to how his dismissal should be described, the scorers finally settling for the rather poetic '29 not out'.

Since 1945 there have been two English double internationals. Arsenal's Arthur Milton played against Austria in 1951 and went on to play six Tests for England from 1958, by which time he had abandoned professional football to concentrate on his cricket career with Gloucestershire. Willie Watson was a regular member of the England cricket team in the 1950s, winning 23 caps, and also appeared four times for England at football between 1950 and 1951, as well as being a member of the 1950 World Cup squad. Although Scotland do not possess Test status in cricket, the Hibernian, Rangers and Scot-land goalkeeper Andy Goram appeared for the national cricket side in the 1990s before being ordered to concentrate on football by Rangers' manager Walter Smith.

Tom Finney (left) *plays his last game. Preston North End v Luton Town, 30 April 1960*
(National Football Museum)

Although an international only at cricket, Chris Balderstone holds the unique record of appearing in a County cricket match and a Football League game on the same day. On 15 September 1975 he left the crease at Chesterfield, where he was playing for Leicestershire against Derbyshire, and travelled to Doncaster where he played for Rovers in a Division Four game against Brentford. Balderstone, who was capped by England at cricket, returned to Chesterfield and resumed his innings the following day.

Other players have been famed for their versatility in football. Jack Rowley, who played for England six times between 1949 and 1952, won his caps in four different forward positions. Jack Froggatt, a regular selection between 1950 and 1953, appeared in the diverse positions of centre-half and outside-left, while Tom Finney appeared on the right wing for his club, Preston North End, but usually played on the left flank for England. Leeds United's Paul Madeley appeared in every outfield position for the club, but for versatility it was hard to beat the Charles brothers, John and Mel. John, a powerfully built but skilful player, was equally

adept at centre-forward and centre-half. For Wales he turned out 17 times in defence and 15 at centre-forward, as well as appearing on occasion at inside-forward. Mel spent most of his career as centre-half or wing-half, but also played centre-forward for Wales on five occasions, once scoring all four goals in a victory over Northern Ireland.

In recent years the requirement for players to be skilled in several facets of the game have tended to make the true utility player less noticeable. At the same time the demands on players arising from the length of the season mean it is unlikely that we shall see another dual international; or, at least, not one playing both games at a high level at the same time.

Sources:
Charles, W. J., *The Gentle Giant* (London: Stanley Paul, 1962).
Ellis, C., *C. B.: The Life of Charles Burgess Fry* (London: Dent, 1984).
Frindall, B., *England Test Cricketers: The Complete Record from 1877* (London: Willow, 1989).
Lamming, D., *An England Football Internationalists' Who's Who 1872–1988* (Beverley: Hutton, 1990). Malies, J., *Sporting Doubles* (London: Robson Books, 1999).

Further Reading:
Goram, A. and Gallacher, K., *Andy Goram: My Life* (London: Virgin, 1998).
Haynes, B. and Lucas, J., *The Trent Bridge Battery: The Story of the Sporting Gunns* (London: Collins Willow, 1985).
Watson, W., *Double International* (London: Stanley Paul, 1956).

John Coyle and Jeremy Mailes

Amateurism and Amateur Football

Amateurism was a Victorian invention. The term meant a love of sport and was used to distinguish those who played for pleasure from those who played for pay.

Historically, spectator sports like pugilism and horse racing had been dominated by gambling interests, and betting led to corruption as performers sometimes found it more profitable to lose than to win. Those who encouraged sports in the elite schools of early Victorian Britain saw team games, especially football and cricket, as a means to impart moral and social virtues. They wished to create a new sporting elite where an upper-class code of honour could be combined with the middle-class virtues of exertion and competitiveness. Amateurs advocated participation over spectating and adopted an ethical code of 'sportsmanship', stressing respect for opponents and referees. Though not deliberately divisive, the amateur prohibition of payment of all kinds ran counter to the traditional culture of manual workers. Amateurism in its purest form was never accepted by many working-class sportsmen, who argued that it stopped the poor from competing on equal terms with the better off.

There is some evidence that games of street football had been played for wagers between teams of equal numbers in the first half of the nineteenth century. This, however, had no influence on the founders of the Football Association in 1863. Men like the solicitor Ebenezer Cobb Morley, the first FA secretary, who rowed and kept a pack of hounds, did not even envisage the possibility of professionalism. Charles Alcock, the son of a Sunderland ship owner and a Harrovian, who took over as FA secretary in 1870, inaugurated the FA Cup and the first international match. The players of the 1870s were mostly gentlemen 'amateurs', though there was no distinction at the time as professional football had not yet come into being.

It was the rapid success of the FA Cup which first raised 'amateurism' as an issue in the game. The new clubs in the textile towns of Lancashire like Darwen, Blackburn and Preston were attracting quite large crowds in the later 1870s and were clearly in a position to pay players and to lure the best Scottish talent into their teams. Teams like Blackburn Olympic and Preston North End chal-lenged the dominance of the southern public school teams like the Old Etonians, Royal Engineers, Old Carthusians and the Wanderers, who were mostly Old Harrovians. This culminated, in 1883, with Blackburn Olympic becoming the first northern side to win the FA Cup.

No amateur team ever won it again, and in 1884 the conflict between amateur and professional came into the open when William Sudell, the chairman of Preston North End, openly admitted to paying players. The FA was split over the issue. Many simply wanted to break with the professionals – as rugby was to do eleven years later – but senior figures like Alcock, who had experience of mixing amateurs and professionals in cricket as secretary of Surrey, did not want a split. In July 1885, after a long, and at times bitter argument, Alcock and his supporters finally got their way. Professionals were to be allowed to play in the FA Cup providing they had a two-year residence qualification with their club. When even this restriction was abolished in 1889, some of the leading amateur figures in the FA, including the president, Sir Francis Marindin, stood down. However, Lord Kinnaird, who had first sat on the FA committee at the age of 22 in 1869, took over as president and stayed for a further 33 years, keeping the gentlemen amateurs in control of the FA.

In response to the rise of the northern professional teams N. Lane 'Pa' Jackson formed the Corinthians in 1882 to bring together the best of the public school players, including the celebrated centre-forward, G. O. Smith, who played regularly for England in the 1890s. C. B. Fry, the great cricketer and all-round athlete was another Corinthian. In fact, the Corinthians provided all the England players for the games against Wales in 1894 and 1895, and a third of all those chosen to play against Scotland between 1882 and 1907, leading to accusations of southern amateur bias in team selection. The FA set up its Amateur Cup in 1893, but this was also dominated by northern teams, many of whom the southerners suspected of embracing shamateurism. The Amateur Cup attracted great interest in the small towns of the north-east of England, which were represented in 20 of the 22 Amateur Cup finals before 1914. An outstanding example was Bishop Auckland, founded in the traditions of muscular Christianity by Oxbridge theological students but soon taken over by local working men. Bishops appeared in seven finals before 1914, winning three. In 1902 the public schools set up their own cup, named after Arthur Dunn, an Old Etonian who had been injured in the famous 1883 FA Cup final with Blackburn Olympic. In 1907 the Amateur Football Association was founded as a breakaway group from the FA and assembled around 500 clubs from the south of England, mostly public school and old-boy sides. This social and geographic split was reminiscent of rugby in 1895. However, the FA kept control of the international side and of British football at the Olympic Games of 1908 and 1912. The Amateur Football Association's ambitions were seriously damaged by FIFA's refusal to recognise the organisation in 1908, and it returned to the fold of the FA in 1914.

The issue of amateurism remained potentially contentious, however. There was periodic concern over illegal payments and inducements to players and, in 1927/28, the FA suspended 341 players and over a thousand officials in the Northern League. On the field, as in the professional game, there was great rivalry both between the amateur north-nastern sides, such as Bishop Auckland and the highly talented Crook Town, and the best London teams. Economic recession severely weakened the northern sides between the wars, when talented players turned professional rather than staying in jobs in the locality and playing as amateurs. The south London side, Dulwich Hamlet, took over as the leading amateur club in the 1930s, winning the Cup in 1932, 1936 and 1937; Kingstonian, twice winners of the Isthmian League in the 1930s and Amateur Cup winners in 1933, were also a major force.

After the Second World War, there was a remarkable revival of gentlemanly amateurism in the form of a combined Oxford and Cambridge team, Pegasus, which won the Amateur Cup in 1951 and in 1953 in front of crowds of 100,000 at Wembley.

Pegasus, which had been founded in 1948 by Harold Thompson – later an Oxford don and chairman of the FA – were strict amateurs in style and values. With big crowds for top amateur games there were clearly payments available for the best amateur players in the north-east, London and the Home Counties. With professionals on a 'maximum wage', those who held a day job and received top-up payments could do quite well. This was a regular source of complaint from the 'true blue' amateurs, for whom Pegasus represented the moral and social ideal. At the same time, clubs in the Southern League and other major semi-professional competitions were constantly irritated by the loss of key players to nominally 'amateur' sides. Eventually, the FA realised that the situation was untenable and, in 1974, the distinction was finally abolished.

Sources:

Appleton, A., *Hotbed of Soccer: The Story of Football in the North-East* (London: Rupert Hart-Davis, 1960).

Butler, B., *The Official History of the Football Association* (London: Macdonald Queen Anne, 1991).

Grayson, E., *Corinthian Casuals and Cricketers* (Havant: 1983).

Mason, T., *Association Football and English Society* (Brighton: Harvester, 1981).

Porter, D. and Smith, A. (eds), *Amateurs and Professionals in Post-War British Sport* (London: Frank Cass, 2000).

Russell, D., *Football and the English* (Preston: Carnegie, 1997).

Richard Holt and Dave Russell

Amateur Football – Administration

The administration of football is an evolving story. The FA was formed in 1863 with the purpose of providing a standard codification of football. Nineteen years later, in 1882, this object was achieved when the national associations of Ireland, Scotland (SFA) and Wales formed an International

Board to agree future changes to the laws of the game.

Although problems since then have been many, the control of the game in each country has been maintained within one Association, although different administrative approaches have been adopted in relation to the organisation of amateur and professional clubs. The SFA, which is a federation of associations, includes the Scottish Amateur Football Association (SAFA). The SAFA was formed in 1909, mainly from Glasgow-based clubs, and affiliated to the national Association in 1922. The remaining three associations are a mix of clubs with control devolving through to county associations, and what used to be district associations. The Welsh association was initially based in the north of the principality, whilst, in Ireland, soccer was secondary to the other football codes of Gaelic football and Rugby Union. In practice, the impression given is that the national bodies devote their resources to the upper echelons of the game.

County football associations first emerged in the late 1870s. In the early days, their organisation was typically characterised by the appointment/election of two officers and the convening of an annual meeting to organise a cup competition. Representative matches against other associations formed their other main activity. When the range of competition was extended a role emerged for county associations in dispute arbitration between member clubs, and in the disciplining of errant players. In England, a South East Counties Amateur Championship was organised in 1902, supplanted in 1906 by a wider southern competition. (The northern counties organised a similar inter-county competition from 1925.) From 1906, county associations were given full responsibility for all soccer, amateur or professional, in their area. It was the refusal of the Surrey and Middlesex Football Association to accept responsibility for the professional game that led to the formation of the breakaway Amateur Football Association in 1907, a separation which was not resolved until February 1914. Renamed the Amateur Football Alliance in 1934, the organisation is now affiliated to

the FA but continues to oversee a network of leagues and cup tournaments on behalf of both southern and midlands-based public and grammar school old boys sides, as well as teams connected to London financial and legal companies.

In 1908, city-based associations, of which there were five, were restricted to affiliating clubs within a twelve-mile radius of a designated landmark, and between the wars there were occasional disputes relating to boundaries. Each association organises as it sees fit, with funds being derived from the proceeds of its cup competitions, membership fees, and fines. Today, these district FAs are divisions of the county football associations. In the 1930s, encouraged by the Government to improve the health of the nation – firstly through the National Fitness Council and subsequently through the Central Council for Physical Recreation – the Football Association offered grant aid to enable the formation of minor (under–19s) associations, within each county.

Direct and indirect club membership of the FA doubled between 1906 and 1948, and the legalisation of Sunday football in 1961 saw a further increase of about 70 per cent by 1967. Long-running controversies continued, however. In 1963, the FA maintained that clubs with amateur players should sign a declaration that they uphold the amateur regulations with regard to the level of expenses paid. As a result, almost all Football League clubs briefly resigned from the FA, which was also heavily criticised by the Isthmian League. In 1968 came the report of the Chester Committee, appointed by the Government to inquire into all aspects of soccer. It proposed a new application form to register what in effect were sham amateurs. It also criticised the FA for not properly funding its county associations and advocated the adoption of regional associations. In 1974 the distinction between professional and amateur was finally abolished, aided in part by the Inland Revenue's guidelines on what constituted allowable expenses for tax purposes.

The amateur game is now branded as the recreational game and, due to changes in social habits, there has been a decline in full-sided matches at weekends. This is compensated for by an increase in mid-week indoor short-sided competitions in facilities provided commercially and by local authorities.

Sources:

Green, G., *The History of the Football Association* (London : Naldrett, 1953).

Green, G., 'The Football Association', in Fabian, A. H. and Green, G. (eds), *Association Football* (London: Caxton, 1960).

Williams, G., *The Code War* (Harefield: Yore Publications, 1994).

Further Reading:

Greenland, W. E., *The History of the Amateur Football Alliance* (Harwich: Standard Printing and Publishing, 1966).

Ronald Price

Amateur Football – Cup Competitions

Until the abolition of amateur status in 1974, the FA Amateur Cup was recognised as the blue riband for leading English amateur clubs. Similar competitions were organised on a national basis elsewhere in the British Isles, occasionally at regional level, and widely at county and local level. Soccer competitions remain a popular method of raising funds for charity.

In the 1890s there was a strong undercurrent of opinion that the decisions of the FA were being made to suit the professional. After initially rejecting a proposal from Sheffield FC for an amateur tournament in 1892, the FA then launched such a competition in the following year. No fewer than 12 old boys' clubs were among the 81 entries for the first FA Amateur Cup in 1893/94. One of their number was successful when Old Carthusians defeated The Casuals 2–1 in the final. They became the first club to win both the FA Cup and FA Amateur Cup; only Wimbledon have ever matched this achievement. However, in 1902 the southern old boys' clubs

formed their own competition, concerned about the adoption by the FA of referees' guidelines, the frequency with which they encountered reinstated professionals (whose exclusion was recommended in 1903, but not effected until after the Great War) and the difficulty of fielding their best sides due to Saturday work commitments. The new competition was named in memory of Arthur Dunn, an Old Etonian and English international, who died tragically young in that year. The Scottish Amateur Football Association was formed in 1909 and it immediately introduced a cup competition, first won by Queen's Park. In 1911, the Welsh Junior Cup was designated for amateur clubs. In contrast, an amateur club, Dundela, won the senior Irish Trophy, the Irish FA Cup, in 1955.

The FA Amateur Cup was staged for 71 seasons, during which sides from the Northern League, the Isthmian League, and Athenian League – the top amateur leagues – secured more than 65 per cent of quarter-final places. From 1911, only four clubs outside of these leagues won the Cup. Bishop Auckland, a Northern League club from a small Durham town, won the competition on ten occasions, twice as many as their nearest rival, managing the trophy's only hat-trick of successes (1955–57). The club made a further eight appearances in the final in their history, and were defeated in the semi-final on nine other occasions. After the Second World War, entries to the FA Amateur Cup increased dramatically and the final became a major footballing event. In 1948, it attracted almost 60,000 spectators, and was transferred the following year to Wembley Stadium, where capacity 100,000 crowds followed for some particularly attractive games. The 1954 final between Bishop Auckland and neighbours Crook Town was an epic affair. Around 20,000 spectators travelled down from this corner of south-west Durham to see a thrilling 2–2 draw. Sixty thousand went to St James's Park, Newcastle for another 2–2 draw in the replay, with Crook finally winning a second replay 1–0 at Middlesbrough's Ayresome Park. From 1969, the winners of the Cup met their Italian counterparts for the Barassi Cup, named after the president of the Italian FA.

From the 1950s onwards, there was increasing concern that the senior amateur clubs and the better amateur players were exploiting the amateur regulations. Proposals were made to amend the competition, including restricting entry to clubs who did not charge for admission to their ground, and changes to the exemption system. However, the senior amateur clubs retained a strong influence at the FA and no changes were made. With the abolition of the amateur/professional distinction, the Amateur Cup was discontinued in 1974. Many former entrants competed for the FA Trophy, a competition that had been started in 1969 for professional clubs outside the Football League. After much consideration, a new competition, the FA Vase, was introduced in 1974/75, with Hoddesdon Town defeating Epsom & Ewell in the first final. By the late 1990s, entry to these competitions was aligned to a club's place in the national league pyramid. In 1999 a regional pilot was introduced for a national competition for clubs not entering the FA Vase.

Sources:

Ackland, N., 'The F.A. Amateur Cup', in A. H. Fabian and G. Green (eds), *Association Football* (London: Caxton, 1960).

Barton, B., *Servowarm History of the F.A. Amateur Cup* (Author publisher, 1984).

Ronald Price

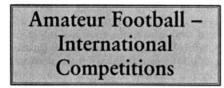

Amateur Football – International Competitions

The idea of sporting contests between nations was quickly seized upon by the founders of the association code as a method of increasing interest. Hence, football internationals were organised, with the first such official engagement being between England and Scotland in 1872; this historic engagement ended goalless. Until the Football Association

(FA) sanctioned a restricted professionalism in 1885, all football internationals in Britain were officially played by amateurs.

These restrictions were whittled away and, in their accepted sense, amateur football internationals began in 1906, after objections to their introduction within the FA Council were overcome. There were similar objections in Scotland, where an amateur international team was not fielded between 1891 and 1926. By the early twentieth century it had become clear that different organisations held different interpretations of what constituted an amateur footballer. The Fédération Internationale de Football Association (FIFA) had been formed in 1904 by seven continental European countries, and it adopted the convention that players receiving broken-time payments (the reimbursement of wages for time lost in playing) were amateurs. The English FA, which joined FIFA in 1906, and the other home associations which followed in 1910, did not accept that position and continued to try to resolve this and related problems, in what was clearly becoming an acrimonious debate. An agreed world-wide definition of amateur status was never fully arrived at, with the sham amateur thus being prevalent from the beginning. In Britain, there was also concern over the participation of the reinstated professional in amateur football, as well as over the issue of importation, whereby the better amateur player was offered employment outside football on the understanding that he played for the club of his employer.

The first officially recognised England amateur international was played against France in 1906. Between 1907 and 1914 the breakaway Amateur Football Association also staged 'amateur internationals'. In 1908, the FA Selection Committee began an amateur trial match for previously uncapped players between the north and the south. (Until the 1930s all English international teams were selected by one committee.) In 1935, despite the decline in the number of amateur internationals being played between the wars, a further series of trial matches was introduced, involving the FA Amateur XI against universities and representative sides from the armed forces.

The modern Olympics were first staged in Athens in 1896. Soccer has been included in each Olympiad except this first and the 1932 Los Angeles Olympiad. Some are of the view that the 1908 London Olympiad was the first serious Olympic football competition, when England represented Great Britain. It was not until 1928 that FIFA agreed a player qualification rule with the International Olympic Committee. This agreement led to the withdrawal of the four home associations from FIFA. They were of the view that, since every other sport at the Games was amateur (without broken-time compensation), football should follow suit. The withdrawal lasted until 1946.

Prior to the Melbourne Olympiad of 1956, a qualifying competition was necessary to ensure that the football could be fitted into the time-span of the games. At the 1960 Olympiad in Rome the knock-out principle was replaced by the mini pool system, with knock-out stages to conclude. The second Los Angeles Olympiad, in 1984, saw the inclusion of full-international players aged under 23 and who had not participated in the World Cup. This was modified at the 1996 Atlanta Olympiad to allow for the inclusion of three full-internationals over that age. Failure to reach agreement on the definition of a Great Britain side has prevented British Olympic participation since 1972.

The major amateur football international competition for the United Kingdom was the Home International Championship, which was put on a proper footing from 1953, with Northern Ireland winning the first championship. Between 1966 and 1974, UEFA staged three European Nations Amateur Cup Competitions, with Scotland the finalists in the first competition. In the 1960s several special events were staged, such as the FA Centenary Amateur Tournament (with all matches staged in the north-east of England), the Italian Amateur Tournament, and the Kenya Independence Celebration Amateur Tournament.

Amateur internationals ended in 1974 with the abolition of amateur status. They were replaced by games with teams selected from players outside the Football League.

Sources:

Ackland, N., 'The Amateur Internationals', in A. H. Fabian and G. Green (eds), *Association Football* (London: Caxton, 1960).

Green, G., *The History of the Football Association* (London: Naldrett, 1953).

F.A. Year Books (London: Heinemann, 1948–74).

Ronald Price

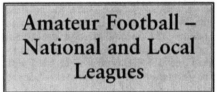

Amateur Football – National and Local Leagues

Following the establishment of the Football League in 1888, the league idea was adopted with enthusiasm by all sections of the football community, thus adding to the cup competitions provided by county associations and town charity cup committees. In these early competitions there was no formal separation of the amateur from the professional, and as a consequence they were often short-lived. From about 1897, there was a major attempt to set up leagues under the auspices of the county associations, with membership restricted to clubs within an agreed radius of a town, and player qualification based on residence within an agreed radius of a club's headquarters. Aspiring clubs in smaller towns, unhappy with this, often converted to professional status, only to fail quickly, and reform as amateur clubs within a short period. During the first decade of the twentieth century, leagues broke up as clubs sought to end the control exercised by county associations, with the emergence of new competitions managed by club representatives. The hierarchy of amateur leagues gradually developed, with successful clubs seeking other successful clubs to form stronger leagues over a wider area. The first county-based amateur league, for example, was formed in Lancashire in 1898. This pattern of the development of league football in England has close parallels in the other countries of the British Isles.

Problems occurred in some areas over the status of ex-professional players who were reinstated as amateurs. This issue led to the Northern League becoming a purely amateur organisation in 1906. The separation of amateur and professional continued apace, with amateur leagues being formed, such as I Zingari (Merseyside), in most districts. In Birmingham, Liverpool and Manchester, where semi-professional clubs had successfully developed as a stratum below Football League clubs, the amateur game was weaker than in the north-east and London. The second attempt to form a London amateur league (following a short-lived one in 1902) bore fruit in 1905 with the formation of the Isthmian League, whose founder members were elected on the basis of their recent records in the Home Counties' cup competitions. The Amateur Football Association created the Southern Amateur League in 1907, whilst the county associations of London and Essex formed the Spartan League to prevent other senior clubs from defecting to the rebel organisation. The Athenian League was formed in 1912 mainly by the amateur clubs from the London League (1896).

After the First World War, these leagues continued much as before, although some county leagues were weakened or closed by the formation of reserve team competitions by the Isthmian, Athenian and Spartan Leagues. The continuation of the London Combination for professional reserve teams led to the London League becoming a fully amateur competition. A few county associations established new county leagues by taking the better clubs from various area leagues. These were weakened by defection to the Spartan League, following the failure of a 1929 plan to amalgamate the four London area leagues. A further proposal to merge three of the four London area amateur leagues in 1944 failed, which – together with the increase in community spirit associated with local authority reorganisation in the 1930s – led to the establishment of new town clubs, and hence new leagues such as the Corinthian League (1945).

In 1973, Rothmans of Pall Mall agreed to sponsor a number of amateur leagues throughout the country, with the Hellenic, Isthmian, Northern and Western Leagues the first to be sponsored. Rothmans also built on an idea tried by Football League clubs involving financial rewards for good disciplinary records and goals scored. In addition, the concept of awarding three points for each league win was born in this package, which lasted until 1978. Since then, most leagues have arranged sponsorship deals, which when added to earnings from the football pools and broadcasting rights, provide a useful source of income for its member clubs.

In 1974 amateur status was abolished and amateur leagues simply became part of 'non-league football'. In the numerous re-organisations that followed, many famous names disappeared, including the Athenian League in 1984. With the creation of a formally recognised Pyramid of Football in 1991, it has become theoretically possible for a club to climb from park football to the Premiership, subject to the sometimes tricky tasks of achieving ground grading requirements and obtaining a bank guarantee. Colne Dynamoes, formed in 1963, followed this path until rejected by the Football Conference in 1990. Welling United, a junior club, moved onto the ground of the defunct Bexleyheath and Welling and eventually managed to maintain membership of the Football Conference from 1986 until their relegation in 2000.

The Football Association of Wales, after four years' work from 1988, established the League of Wales, and has created a regional structure to support it, whilst Northern Ireland and Scotland have begun similar strategies.

Sources:

Ackland, N., *Association Football* (London: Caxton, 1960) (Ch. 3–6 of Part 3, Volume 1).

Barton B., *Non League* (Second edition) (Author publisher, 1987).

Further Reading:

Wilson, M., *The Athenian Football League*, 3 vols (Author publisher, 1994, 1995, 1996).

Ronald Price

Amateur Football – Notable Clubs

In the game's early days all clubs were amateur, and the leading players of the time emerged almost exclusively from public school backgrounds. With time and money to spare, they played the game for fun, never for a moment considering seeking financial reward. A gentleman was expected to 'love the game beyond the prize' – although generous travelling expenses were accepted. The history books show that the early winners of the FA Cup, after that famous competition's inception in 1871, included such pillars of the establishment as Oxford University, Old Etonians and Old Carthusians (Charterhouse old boys). The Wanderers side – winners of the coveted 'little tin idol' five times in the first seven years – was formed by Old Harrovians, while the Royal Engineers, the 'Sappers from Chatham', overcame Old Etonians in the 1875 final fielding a side drawn exclusively from the officer class. Goalkeeper and captain Major W. Merriman led his team to victory aided by ten trusty lieutenants, including the splendidly hyphenated H. W. Renny-Tailyour and C. V. Wingfield-Stratford, together with the aristocratic P. G. von Donop. 'Major' Francis Marindin, renowned goalkeeper, full-back, referee and president of the Football Association, found himself eligible to play for both sides in that final, being both a Royal Engineer and an Old Etonian. The gallant major took the honourable course of playing for neither. Clapham Rovers, winners of the trophy in 1880, were a footballing offshoot of an established rugby side, their goalkeeper in their victory over Oxford University that year being Reginald Halsey Birkett, the first man to represent England at both football codes. The final the following year, however, when Old Carthusians beat Old Etonians in front of 4,500 spectators at The Oval, proved to be the last occasion on which two amateur sides contested the final. In 1882 Old Etonians prevailed against the professionals of Blackburn Rovers, but the following year lost to Blackburn Olympic, a collection of Lancashire artisans who prepared for the big game by way of a training session on Blackpool sands. Amateurism's final flourish was mounted by the Scottish amateurs Queen's Park, but they lost the 1884 final to Blackburn Rovers, a result that was repeated the following year. Queen's Park's appearance in the 1885 final was the last by an amateur side. An era was ended; football was now serious business.

The professional game, confined at first to the industrial areas of northern England and southern Scotland, gradually moved south (Royal Arsenal were the first southern club to turn professional, in 1891), but one club held out against the perceived threat and indeed continued to flourish. The Corinthians were formed in 1882 by N. Lane 'Pa' Jackson, assistant secretary of the Football Association and a fervent anti-professional. Corinthians drew their players from the ranks of the universities and public schools, as did the English national side of the day, and Jackson's idea was that if these players had 'plenty of practice together they would acquire a certain amount of combination'. He was dismayed that England had lost heavily in the 1881 and 1882 matches against Scotland, by 6–1 and 5–1 respectively. Although they had no ground of their own, and refused to enter the FA Cup, considering such competitions 'vulgar', the Corinthians became the dominant force in the game. In 1884 they demonstrated their supremacy by beating FA Cup winners Blackburn Rovers by an impressive 8–1.

In 1904 another upstart northern professional cup-winning side bit the dust. Bury had beaten Derby County by a record 6–0 in the 1903 final, but were swamped 10–3 by Corinthians. In 1886 Corinthians provided nine of the England side that beat Scotland 5–0, proving Jackson's point about practice making perfect: in both 1894 and 1895 all eleven England players against Wales were Corinthians. Jackson had instilled in his players the merits of dribbling and the short-passing game, which became known as 'Corinthian-style'. In 1897 the club began a series of foreign tours that took them to Europe, Africa and South America. They regularly overcame the national champions of the countries they visited, and in 1909 beat Bohemia. Following one such tour an Austrian opponent was so impressed by them after a match in Vienna as to recall: 'I remember how they walked onto the field, spotless in their white shirts and dark shorts. Their hands were in their pockets, sleeves hanging down. Yet there was about them an air of casual grandeur, a haughtiness that was yet not haughty, which seemed intangible. And how they played!'

It was not only their skill that marked the Corinthians out from the rest, however; they exhibited an inherent sense of sportsmanship and fairplay. When awarded a penalty, for instance, Corinthian players would deliberately shoot wide, while their goalkeeper would leave his goal untended, giving his opponent a clear shot, should his side concede a spot-kick. During one game it is even recorded that their captain, playing in and refereeing a match for which the official had not arrived, awarded a free kick against himself. In 1922 the Corinthians finally deigned to enter the FA Cup, but by then they were no longer the force they had once been, though they did provide the last England amateur captain in A. G. Bower in 1927. In 1939 they amalgamated with the Casuals, and still exist as Corinthian-Casuals, still strictly amateur but now with a home of their own at Tolworth, Surrey, and competing in Division Three of the Rymans League. Tradition dies hard, however. Questioning a referee's decision still results in a hefty fine, while receiving a red card makes a player an immediate ex-Corinthian. Their name, if not their attitude to the game, lives on in South America. The inaugural World Club Championship of 2000, in which Manchester United participated, was won by a Brazilian side, Corinthians, from São Paulo, playing in white shirts and black shorts and named in honour of the English sporting ambassadors following a good-will tour in the early years of the twentieth century.

If Corinthians were the amateur heroes of the south in their day, then their counterparts north of the border were undoubtedly Queen's Park. Scotland's oldest club, founded on 9 July 1867, they remained unbeaten for the first eight years of their existence, finally going down to The Wanderers in London on 5 February 1876. They won the Scottish Cup no less than ten times from 1874, and such was their influence on the game in the early days that in the Scotland v England match, played at the West of Scotland Cricket Ground, Partick, on 30 November 1872, no less than nine of the Scottish side were Queen's Park players. The other two, brothers James and Robert Smith, were former members of the Glasgow club but had moved south to join South Norwood in London. Selection of the Scottish side for this first unofficial international was the sole responsibility of Queen's Park captain, Robert Gardner. Although, as noted, they reached the FA Cup finals of 1884 and 1885, their adventures in the very first competition seem bizarre. Given a bye in the first round, Queen's Park were then drawn at home against Donington School, Lincolnshire in the second. The schoolboy side were unable to afford to make the trip to Glasgow, however, possibly because they had appointed a drill master at a salary of three shillings a week to improve their fitness, so were forced to pull out. Several of the competition's other 15 original entrants had also scratched, so only five clubs were left in the third round. Queen's Park again received a bye, so found themselves in the semi-finals without playing a match! A public subscription raised the funds to send them to The Oval, where their accurate passing style earned them a well-merited goalless draw against The Wanderers. Unable to afford to stay in London for the replay, however, the Scottish side headed home with their heads held high and their unbeaten record still intact. The Wanderers went on to win the first-ever FA Cup, beating Royal Engineers in the final, again at The Oval, on 16 March 1872. Queen's Park, now competing in the Second Division of the Scottish League, are still staunchly amateur and are based, as they have been since 1903, at

Hampden Park, the spiritual home of Scottish football, where their home games attract only a few hundred fans to the vast stadium. Their last moment of glory was the Second Division championship in 1981; of their ten Scottish Cup victories, the last was as long ago as 1893, fittingly the year in which professionalism was legalised in Scotland.

At the same time as the Scottish authorities were taking this momentous decision, plans were afoot south of the border to inaugurate a new national knock-out competition open to amateur sides only. The trophy was supplied by the FA and first competed for in the 1893/94 season. The first competition was won by Old Carthusians, but the old boys lost in the following season's final to Middlesbrough. The continued dominance of northern clubs sparked a defection of the majority of the public school and university sides to their own competition, the Arthur Dunn Cup, established in 1902/3, leaving the FA's own amateur competition largely in the hands of north-eastern sides such as Middlesbrough, Stockton, Crook Town and the greatest of them all, Bishop Auckland. Destined to become the most prominent amateur club of the twentieth century, the 'Bishops' were founded in 1886 as Auckland Town and, in their distinctive light and dark blue strips, won a record ten Amateur Cups and reached another eight finals. They qualified for the semi-finals no fewer than 27 times. In the 1950s, when they really dominated the amateur game, they played in four consecutive finals, losing to Crook Town in 1954 before notching up a hat-trick of successes against Hendon (1955), Corinthian-Casuals (1956) and Wycombe Wanderers (1957). After their record-breaking 1957 final they were presented with a specially made replica of the trophy. In those days their Northern League games against their fiercest rivals from Crook regularly attracted gates that were the envy of their Football League neighbours Darlington and Hartlepool United. They were inspirationally led by right-half Bob Hardisty, the captain of Great Britain's 1948 Olympic side who had regularly played alongside professionals during the Second

World War. In goal was the eccentric Harry Sharratt, who relieved the tedium in one-sided Northern League encounters by taking throw-ins and corners, and was not averse to playing the odd wall-pass off his own goalpost, much to the frustration of opposing forwards. Such was the quality of the Bishops players that, following the Munich disaster of 1958, right-winger Warren Bradley was transferred to Manchester United as part of Matt Busby's rebuilding plans. Within 15 months he was a full England international, and during his time at Old Trafford scored 21 goals in 66 appearances. Inside-left Seamus O'Connell was another to make an immediate impact on the professional game, scoring a hat-trick on his debut for Chelsea.

In the 1951 final Bishop Auckland were odds-on favourites to beat Pegasus, the Corinthians of their day, founded only in 1948 by future FA chairman Harold Thompson and made up of Oxford and Cambridge graduates. With no ground of their own, the combined university side had reached Wembley after playing seven away fixtures, coming from behind in five of them. A record 100,000 crowd, and millions of television viewers, watched as they beat the mighty Bishops 2–1 at Wembley. Pegasus enjoyed another Wembley victory in 1953 when they demolished Harwich and Parkeston 6–1. The scorer of two of their goals that day was Oxford University and Derbyshire cricketer Donald Carr, who went on to play two Tests for England (as an amateur, of course) before becoming secretary of the Test and County Cricket Board. Pegasus eventually disbanded in 1963. Legend has it that their genteel supporters, rather than indulge in the usual singing, would exhort their heroes to greater efforts by reciting poetry from the terraces, though it has never been confirmed that they originated the chant: 'Who ate all the canapés?'

Not long after the demise of Pegasus came the end of amateurism itself. In 1974, following years of controversy over 'shamateurism' – the payment of inflated expenses and other inducements to so-called amateurs – the FA decided that henceforth all footballers would be known simply as 'players'. The last Amateur Cup final of all was inevitably won by the 'Bishops', but this time not the famous County Durham side. Hertfordshire club Bishop's Stortford lifted the 1974 trophy, beating Ilford 4–1 at Wembley. After eight decades the FA Amateur Cup passed into history. Over the years it provided the stage for a fascinating struggle not only between north and south, but more especially between the Isthmian League and the Northern League. Wycombe Wanderers, Dulwich Hamlet, Kingstonian, Casuals, Leytonstone, Enfield, Wealdstone, Hendon and Bromley were among the Home Counties sides to lift the trophy, while if Bishops ever missed out then Crook Town, Willington and Stockton – their south Durham neighbours – were on hand to uphold the honour of the northeast. The last northern clubs to lift the Cup were North Shields in 1969 and Skelmersdale United two years later.

Bishop Auckland, who entered the twenty-first century as members of the Unibond League Premier Division, may have been the country's most consistent performers in the amateur spotlight over the years, but they were certainly upstaged in 1910 by the club next door, West Auckland Town. That year Sir Thomas Lipton, millionaire tea merchant and sailing companion of King Edward VII, decided to organise a tournament, dubbed the 'World Cup', in Turin in gratitude for being made a Knight of the Grand Order of Italy. After the FA had, in their insular way, refused permission for a professional side to take part as England's representatives, Sir Thomas, for reasons shrouded in mystery, selected West Auckland, third from bottom of what was then the Northern Amateur League. Why West Auckland? Was it because their shirts sported the same initials as Woolwich Arsenal? Perhaps their opponents were so fooled; in any event the English amateurs, most of whom were employed in the south Durham coalfield and had been forced to sell furniture and personal belongings to cover their travelling costs and lost wages, proceeded to win the tournament, disposing of Red Star Zurich and

Stuttgart before beating the host side Juventus 2–0 in the final. To prove the result was no fluke they undertook the trip again the following year and repeated their final victory, again beating Juventus, to win the trophy outright. To this day the West Auckland trophy cupboard houses the World Cup.

While the rest of the country cheered England's 1966 triumph over West Germany, celebrations in the pubs and clubs of a certain Durham mining village were understandably rather muted; they'd heard it all before. Twice.

Sources:
Barrett, N., *The Daily Telegraph Football Chronicle* (London: Carlton, 1999).

Butler, B., *The Official History of the Football Association* (London: Macdonald, 1991).

Butler, B., *The Official Illustrated History of the F.A. Cup* (London: Headline, 1996).

Soar, P., *The Hamlyn A-Z of Football Records* (London: Hamlyn, 1981).

Young, P. M., *A History of British Football* (London: Stanley Paul, 1969).

Further Reading:
Creek, F. S. N. C., *A History of the Corinthian Football Club* (London: Longmans, Green, 1933).

Drewett, J., and Leith, A., *The Virgin Book of Football Records* (London: Virgin, 1996).

Ponting, I., *Manchester United Player by Player* (London: Hamlyn, 1997).

Rollin, J. (ed.), *The Guinness Book of Soccer Facts and Feats* (Enfield: Guinness, 1983).

Tony Rennick

Anthropology of Football

Apart from autobiographies of football players, there has traditionally been little material on football from the inside. Even players' accounts, until recent years restricted to a coterie of famous players, were not usually very revealing about the experience of being a footballer, conforming as they did to a somewhat heroic view

When Saturday Comes, *one of the bestselling football magazines*

of both the game and the dressing room. Len Shackleton in *Clown Prince of Soccer* (1955) was one of the first to depart from this tradition, though in his case to level criticisms against the game's management rather than to offer a social realist view of sport. Not until Eamon Dunphy, a player with Manchester United and later Millwall, produced *Only a Game?* (1976), a book which received wider circulation the following year when published under the Penguin imprint, could an anthropology of football be said to have started. Dunphy charted in diary form an entire season as a player with Millwall, recording the boredom and fractiousness, as well as the pleasures and minor triumphs, of employment with an ordinary club. He established an approach that has since been adopted by others. Notable among such accounts of daily life in football are Gary Nelson's reminiscences on playing in the lower divisions of the Football League. Shelley Webb, herself a footballer's wife, has similarly produced an innovative gender perspective into the anthropology of the game, with her sketches of the life of the footballer's spouse. In rather more

dramatic form, and with the focus very definitely on the 'celebrity', there has been a series of confessional tales of attempts to cope with the stress that modern football brings. George Best, the first football 'superstar', veered rather too much towards sensational journalism in some of his forays into this field, but Tony Adams has judiciously dealt with his battle with alcoholism, and his erstwhile team-mate Paul Merson has equally candidly admitted to a drug habit. In these various forms the reality of football has been uncovered in a way that would not have been thought desirable even thirty years ago.

Alongside these innovations has been another form of anthropology directed at the behaviour – or more appropriately the misbehaviour – of football supporters. In both academic and popular styles there have been several attempts to describe and explain the culture of football 'hooliganism', a feature of the game which has attracted much attention in the media and politics since the 1970s. It gave rise to an important series of sociological studies, notably by Ian Taylor, Peter Marsh and the Leicester school headed by Eric Dunning, each of whom brought different emphases and interpretations to the phenomenon. In seeking to understand the attraction of hooliganism for the soccer spectator, rather than merely to condemn it, as so much of the media sought to do, this academic study fulfilled an important educational function, though not one to which politicians were inclined to pay much attention. It has, however, been the principal academic contribution so far to the anthropology of football.

Arguably, more has been achieved in the realm of popular writing. In the wake of the new-found appeal of football, stimulated by Italia 90 and the success of the Premier League, a new genre of football writing appeared, aimed mainly at younger males, which has added its own weight to the discussion of hooliganism. In particular, the writing of Bill Buford and Doug and Eddie Brimson brought a 'participant–observer' perspective to the hooligan phenomenon. But the new football writing did not confine itself to this theme. It achieved an enlargement of the anthropology of football by developing the perspective of the 'ordinary fan' in a number of interesting ways. Thus, for example, Colin Shindler explored personal obsession with a club (Manchester City), Harry Pearson humorously observed a whole region's passion for the game (the north-east), and Rick Gekosi was able to report from the privileged position of the fan in the boardroom (Coventry City). Some of the inspiration for this came from earlier work by the journalist Hunter Davies on Tottenham Hotspur, and some also flowed from the fanzine movement which, since the 1980s, has attempted to express the views of the ordinary fan. But the crucial influence, and the one which ensured that good writing on football would have a popular audience in the 1990s, was undoubtedly Nick Hornby. His *Fever Pitch*, an autobiographical account of the coming of age of an Arsenal fan, provided an astute and laconic observation on the part played by football spectating and supporting in the lives of young men. Its peculiar impact no doubt comes from its mirroring of the experiences of so many football fans, and it has ensured that readers of the better journals, like *FourFourTwo* and *When Saturday Comes*, will expect some attention to anthropological issues in their football literature.

Sources:

Buford, B., *Among the Thugs* (London: Arrow Books, 1997).

Dunphy, E., *Only A Game?* (London: Penguin Books, 1987).

Hornby, N., *Fever Pitch* (London: Gollancz, 1992).

Nelson, G., *Left Foot Forward: A Year in the Life of a Journeyman Footballer* (London: Headline Publishing, 1995).

Pearson, H., *The Far Corner: A Mazy Dribble Through North-East Football* (London: Warner Books, 1995).

Shindler, C., *Manchester United Ruined My Life* (London: Headline, 1998).

Webb, S., *Footballers' Wives* (London: Yellow Jersey Press, 1998).

Further Reading:

Adams, T. and Ridley, I., *Addicted* (London: Harper Collins, 1999).

Best, G., *The Good, the Bad and the Bubbly* (London: Pan Books, 1990).

Davies, H., *The Glory Game* (Edinburgh: Mainstream, 2000).

Gekosi, R., *Staying Up: A Fan Behind the Scenes in the Premiership* (London: Warner Books, 1997).

Shackleton, L., *Clown Prince of Soccer: His Autobiography* (London: Kay, 1955).

Jeff Hill

Anti-Football Lobbies

The forces that have lobbied against football over the years have invariably attacked the professional rather than the amateur game. In the 1880s, some representatives of organised religion denounced the fervour of football's supporters, and its tendency to divert the working man from his home, family and religion towards drinking, gambling and frivolous pursuits. Early criticism also came from socialists and radicals, who felt that professional football was another 'opiate of the people', distracting them from the seriousness of the class struggle.

The main opposition to the professional game in the early days, however, came from the alliance of some upper- and middle-class players and administrators, who asserted that football had become a pot-hunting glory game, whose participants were not averse to cheating, obsessed with money, and which was followed by hordes of working-class fanatics who ignored the finer points of the game. These critics saw football as the ultimate team game, ideally encompassing fair play, physical exercise and the sacrifice of the self to team effort, helping to build character and preparing young men for the struggles of life. This refrain carried on intermittently until the First World War, when professional footballers and their supporters were accused of being unpatriotic by continuing to play and not providing enough recruits for the war effort. Campaigns were fought over the legalisation of professionalism in 1884/85, the influence of the Football

League after 1888, and many other issues relevant to the professional game.

The anti-professional complaint was taken up by others who saw the game's influence as both evidence and cause of the physical decline of the English nation; Social Darwinist ideas of racial fitness were overlaid on the shift from active playing to passive watching. For those obsessed with British military capabilities and the burden of Empire, the ideology of athleticism was often linked with militarism and imperialism up until the 1930s. Criticism of football, often influenced by snobbery and class bias, was also connected to debates over the passive consumption of 'mass culture', such as cinemas, music halls, dance halls and popular literature.

The increase in football-related violence in the 1970s aroused new opposition, including residents' groups opposing football stadium moves or extensions, media campaigns against hooliganism, and some government intervention. The election in 1979 of a Conservative government advocating 'strong state' policies led to an increase in legislation which identified football as a major target – sometimes an easy one – for law and order legislation aimed at young men. Central here were the Sporting Events (Control of Alcohol) Act (1985), the Public Order Act (1986), and the Football Spectators Bill (1988). There were also increasing media attacks on football by the right-wing press.

The Popplewell Report sought to impose an identity card scheme that was only defeated by public campaigns and the influence of the Taylor Report. The accession of the more football-friendly Major government brought a welcome change of emphasis, but by then the Conservatives' modernising agenda of free-market philosophy married to strict legislation was well on the way to repositioning football as middle-class family entertainment.

Sources:

Mangan, J. A., *The Games Ethic and Imperialism* (Harmondsworth: Penguin, 1986).

Mangan, J. A., *Athleticism in the Victorian and Edwardian Public School* (Cambridge: Cambridge University Press, 1981).

Redhead, S., *Football with Attitude* (Manchester: Wordsmith, 1991).

Redhead, S., *Sing When You're Winning* (London: Pluto Press, 1987).

Russell, D., *Football and the English* (Preston: Carnegie, 1997).

Further Reading:

Green, G., *The History of the Football Association* (London: Naldrett, 1953).

King, A., *The End of the Terraces. The Transformation of English Football in the 1990s* (London: Leicester University Presss, 1998).

Robert Lewis

Applied Sports Science

Sports science in the context of football refers to the use of scientific principles or expertise within the game. The base of knowledge that this use implies embraces all of the component disciplines of sports science such as biomechanics, nutrition, physiology, psychology and so on. Scientific methodology can be applied to the systematisation of training, the preparation of players for impending matchplay, the formal analysis and feedback of behaviour and performance during competition, the adoption of contemporary management science approaches to running the club, and the utilisation of scientific practices in talent detection and its development.

The use of sports science consultants at English football clubs was sporadic in the 1970s and 1980s. Sports science support programmes tended to depend on the open-mindedness of a few managers who were alert to the limitations of traditional methods employed in coaching and training. In the early 1970s two top League clubs funded systematic research programmes, but neither manager survived at the club to implement the findings. In the 1980s an increasing number of consultants gained part-time employment, largely to help the clubs with physical conditioning and psychological counselling of players. This support was not always representative of best professional practice, since the clubs had no means of determining in advance the quality of their hired consultant. This situation was remedied with the development of an accreditation system for 'sports science support' by the British Association for Sports and Exercise Sciences in 1988, and later refined for purposes of working with elite athletes by the British Olympic Association's register of scientists. Separate registers are held for conditioning, nutrition, performance analysis, physiology and psychology, and individual expertise is related to specific sports, including football.

Sports science support programmes in Britain escalated after the inauguration of the English Premier League in 1992. By the end of the decade a majority of Premier League clubs had sports science personnel on their payroll. Some, such as Middlesbrough FC, had designated purpose-built laboratories at their training locations and formalised links with adjacent universities. In many cases the utilisation of sports science personnel has low investment costs, such as in nutritional or psychological support where work can be on a one-to-one basis with individual players. In other instances clubs have invested in state-of-the-art computer-aided video technology where specialists in 'notation analysis' of matches are taken on board. Notation analysis refers to the study of match events in a systematic way so that performance profiles can be displayed for the team's overall pattern of play and individuals' contributions to it.

The Football Association marked its adoption of sports science with the publication of *Insight: The F.A. Coaches Association Journal* in Autumn 1997. Its content is largely scientific, incorporating research reviews, feature articles, and updates on relevant research publications. The Association's strategy for sports science was implemented in 1998, with the permanent appointment of two physiologists and two psychologists to its staff. A year later it commissioned major research support for the national teams by appointing a research team for the purposes of notation analysis of all representative matches at under-age and senior levels.

Football practitioners now readily incorporate scientific information into their plans. These include, for example, strategies for coping best with heat stress when competing overseas, minimising the effects of jet-lag when travelling across multiple time zones, and scheduling training regimens according to the phases of the competitive season. A more long-term view is taken with instructive feedback on performance in matches, or with the use of reflective practices in training contexts. By these means players are gradually empowered to take responsibility for their own progress as professionals.

Source:
Reilly, T. (ed.), *Science and Soccer* (London: E. and F. N. Spon, 1996).

Tom Reilly

Architecture and Design

Until recently, good architecture was a rarity at British football stadia. Most grounds possessed a ramshackle configuration of piecemeal structures, often clad in drab corrugated sheeting, and punctuated by brutal floodlight pylons.

Football fans frequently seem to hold excessive affections for their own team's often architecturally undistinguished stadium. Geographer John Bale identified such sentiments as an example of topophilia, defined as an emotional attachment to place. Topophilia on the part of fans and the apathy of directors no doubt contributed to the complacency shown by football clubs towards the adequacy of their architecture, until the consequences of the Hillsborough disaster of 1989 compelled a greater concern.

The earliest British grounds date from the 1880s, when club committeemen began to realise the commercial possibilities of charging admission to an enclosed field of play. Successful clubs began to erect pavilions and small grandstands to provide shelter and better facilities for their wealthier patrons. In order that spectators could obtain a better view, clubs raised embankments or built timber terracing. The first substantial purpose-built English ground was Everton's Goodison Park, built in 1892. In Scotland, Celtic Park and Ibrox were at the same level of advancement.

Archibald Leitch (1866–1939) is generally considered to have been the most prolific football ground designer. His archetypal ground consisted of a grandstand and three sides of open terracing, though there were numerous variations on this plan. Ayresome Park, Stamford Bridge, Hampden Park, White Hart Lane, and Anfield were among many of his grounds that generally conformed to the basic shape. In Scotland an elliptical layout was preferred, whilst in England, rectilinear forms predominated. Leitch's work at Fulham's Craven Cottage has Grade II listed building status. Craven Cottage's corner pavilion (1906) was once a common feature, especially in Scotland. Its architecture is echoed in the richly detailed facade of the Stevenson Road stand, whilst on the ground-facing side, the roof's central gable, which bore the club name, was a typical Leitch motif. The final version of Aston Villa's Trinity Road stand (1922) was even more elaborate than Fulham's, possessing a grandeur unmatched at any other ground.

Another Leitch trademark was a pattern of criss-crossed ironwork on the balcony wall of an upper seating tier. Such a feature embellished Goodison, Roker, and Fratton Parks, and remains today in his native city in the South Stand at Ibrox. The sumptuous facilities of this structure originally included a bizarre castellated press-box on the roof. The magnificent street facade in red brick has a classical grandeur and remained the only part of Ibrox to survive the radical rebuilding of 1978–81, and has since been tactfully modernised by a new roof and seating tier.

Leitch was an engineer rather than an architect, and even the best of his stands' facades were mere pastiches of classical styles. However, Arsenal had the rare vision, for a British club, to commission structures in the modern international style. Claude Waterlow Ferrier's 1931 West Stand at Highbury is concrete, and distinguished by a curved marquise on the ground side of the roof. William Binnie's East Stand (1938) is similar to its counterpart, containing extensive facilities and the club's celebrated entrance hall. However, the most impressive external aspect of this listed structure is the typically British art deco frontage. Though a bold modern design, the Lobb Partnership's 1993 North stand retains a 1930s ambience.

During the post-war period, British football architecture was in the doldrums. Some innovative designs were submitted, including Wembley architect Maxwell Ayrton's extraordinary new stadium for Derby (1945), and Wolves' Futuristic European-style proposal of 1959, but these got no further than the model stage. Sheffield Wednesday's 10,000 seat aluminium-clad cantilever stand of 1961 (the first cantilever had been erected at Scunthorpe's Old Show Ground in 1958) was a watershed design, but the club has never again pursued such radical ideas.

Apart from a few modifications to existing stadia, the 1966 World Cup did not herald a new era of stand or stadium construction. Only Manchester United effected any exciting permanent improvements. The cantilevered United Road Stand, by architects Mather and Nutter, was the first with executive boxes. It was also envisaged as the first stage of a 'masterplan' redevelopment of the whole ground, the original oblate rectangular boundary of Old Trafford lending itself to such a long-term evolution. However, the entire plan was not complete until 1993, and even then United's resurgence prompted almost immediate rebuilding.

The Safety at Sports Grounds Act (1975) signalled the end for the massive multi-span stand roofs that had graced English football. Those at Wolves and Charlton were dismantled before the end of the decade. Such features were held in affection by many fans, together with the ordinarily undistinguished but unique minutiae commonplace at British football grounds. Such curiosities include West Bromwich's Throstle, Airdrie's pavilion,

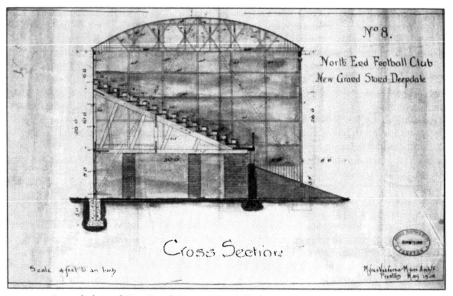

N° 8.

North End Football Club
New Grand Stand Deepdale

Cross Section

Scale 4 feet to an Inch

Ground plans of West Stand, Preston North End, 1906 (National Football Museum)

and Blackburn's famous Victorian turnstile block. Old style grounds survived another ten years until the Taylor Report (1990) into the Hillsborough tragedy insisted on the replacement of terracing by seated areas within four years. This stimulated new building programmes, and some clubs even decided to relocate. However, certain architects were concerned that, given British clubs' record of uninspired architecture, the opportunity for good design could be lost.

The Sports Council and Lobb Partnership collaborated on designs for a modular master-plan that could be progressively improved as funds became available. A 20,000-seat stadium could be built in five phases, utilising an innovative cantilever roof with extensive provision for modern facilities. Huddersfield Town showed an early interest in the 'Stadium for the Nineties' project, resulting in the Sir Alfred McAlpine Stadium in 1994. Modified from the original concept, the structure is truly startling, with each stand roof held in place by enormous banana-shaped trusses. The stadium is multi-functional, and is shared with Huddersfield Rugby League Club. Nearly twenty English and Scottish league clubs have

now built new stadia, including Millwall, Middlesbrough, Bolton, Derby, Stoke, St Johnstone, Sunderland, Reading, and Wigan.

Smaller clubs, such as Scunthorpe and Walsall, have also built new grounds, though, as the Lobb Partnership feared, these are in uninspired pattern-book styles, redolent of industrial units. Non-league Dorchester's Avenue Stadium has, however, been designed in a refreshing post-modern idiom.

Other clubs have opted to stay in their century-old locations, radically altering their traditional appearances as they have evolved into true stadia. Newcastle, Nottingham Forest, Liverpool, Celtic, and Birmingham City are virtually unrecognisable from only a decade ago. Chelsea have re-developed Stamford Bridge as part of the Chelsea Village complex. The famous bowl shape has been superseded by a more compact configuration, surrounded by hotels and apartment blocks.

The decision to rebuild Wembley stadium has stirred much controversy over what sports it should provide for, its size, structure and cost. A design by the famous architect Norman Foster, which comprised a sleek, high-tech structure with a

300-foot arch supporting a retractable roof, was at first approved but at the time of writing is on hold. The original stadium of 1923, designed by John Simpson and Maxwell Ayrton, exuded the monumental idiom of imperial architecture. After 77 years' service it is to be demolished, together with the emblematic twin towers, which were to have been retained in earlier proposals. The new Wembley was to have been capable of hosting World Cup and Olympic events, but after great controversy, it has now been ruled that the needs of athletics are not compatible with the original design, and the new national stadium will be predominantly a football venue. Nevertheless, Foster's extraordinary design demonstrates that the public and football authorities are now receptive to the construction of bold, innovative structures.

Sources:

Anon., *Football Grounds* (Seventh edition) (Surrey: Dial Press, 1999).

Bale, J., *Sport, Space and the City* (London: Routledge, 1993).

Inglis, S., *Football Grounds of Britain* (Third edition) (London: Collins Willow, 1996).

See also Grounds

Tom Preston

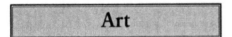

Art

Football has a relatively lacklustre artistic tradition in comparison with such sports as cricket, racing, or boxing. Nevertheless, a surprising diversity of British artists have found inspiration in soccer, and it has increasingly been regarded as a legitimate subject.

Caricaturists provided early comic depictions of folk football, and works survive by Thomas Rowlandson (1756–1827) and Isaac Robert Cruikshank (1789–1856). Oil paintings of the traditional game were less common. *The Football* (1839) by Thomas Webster (1800–86) shows village boys in their best clothes, indulging in a typically boisterous game, probably played during a feast day.

The public school ascendancy of the early soccer establishment is reflected by the rather vapid art characteristic of the decades before the First World War. Typical subjects include matches played at the universities and major schools. Prints of such paintings were popular gifts in magazines like the *Boy's Own Paper*. Only rarely did such paintings feature professional football. *Sunderland versus Aston Villa*, by Thomas Hemy (1852–1937), gives a vivid impression of a major league match of the late Victorian period. Designer John Hassall (1868–1948) contributed some remarkably evocative football imagery in this period. His simple depiction of a solitary standing player for the covers of Gibson and Pickford's four-volume *Association Football and the Men Who Made It* (1905) almost encapsulates the epoch.

For the masses, football art at the turn of the century consisted primarily of the pen-and-ink sketches common in newspapers prior to the emergence of action photography. Such free-flowing renditions typically depicted a montage of incidents during the course of a match, including personalities in the crowd and caricatures of players. The work of many unsung local artists, including some superb draughtsmen, reveals much of Victorian and Edwardian football.

Throughout the earlier period of soccer's history, British followers of progressive continental art movements showed little interest in football as a subject. By the 1920s and '30s, however, innovations in the visual arts began to filter through to the few works depicting British football. Paul Nash (1889–1946) was receptive to modernism but remained loyal to traditional English themes. Significantly, his work was brought to a wider audience through his long association as a poster artist with the Shell Oil company. *Footballers Prefer Shell* (1933), one of a famous series, was painted in an informal cubist style, depicting a deserted goalmouth and grandstand, with a football hovering over the goal line. The corporate re-design by London Transport also sponsored some innovative graphic design during this decade. Italian Futurist ideas were

Peter Howson's Just another Bloody Saturday *(1987)*(© Angela Flowers Gallery)

evident in the work of Sybil Andrews (1898–1992) and Cyril Power (1874–1951). Together they created a striking football motif (1933) for the London Underground.

The Festival of Britain revived public interest in the arts during the early 1950s, and the Football Association launched a competition for artists, in celebration of its ninetieth anniversary. *Football and the Fine Arts*, displayed by the Arts Council during 1953/54, marked a watershed in soccer's relationship with the visual arts. The exhibition gave the impression that, for the population at large, English football provided a release from the humdrum nature of their dispiriting industrial experience, often played against the backdrop of bleak urban environments. A typically evocative work was Arthur Hackney's (1925–) *Spectators returning home after Port Vale v. Accrington Stanley*, as appropriately grim as its title, in which an anonymous herd of fans march homeward under a threatening twilight sky.

The works exhibited were fairly typical mid-century British art, echoing the taste of Sir William Coldstream, chairman of the selection committee and a pivotal figure in the naturalistic Euston Road movement. Some contributors had strong associations with the Euston Road group – notably, Claude Rogers (1907–79). His *West Bromwich v. Chelsea 1952–1953*, was a depiction of Albion's celebrations in the aftermath of a Ronnie Allen goal, the paint laid on in abundant post-impressionist style. Despite the presence of some sculpture and abstract compositions, naive paintings were also prominently displayed, and indeed the abiding image of the exhibition remained L. S. Lowry's (1887–1976), *Going to the Match*, a vivid evocation of 'football's golden age', inspired by a scene outside Burnden Park, Bolton, the crowd represented by the artist's distinctive match-stick figures.

Regrettably, the soccer authorities and clubs failed to capitalise on the momentum generated by the exhibition, and for the next three decades football art lacked a focus for national patronage. However, prominent British artists such as William Roberts, Carel Weight, Ruskin Spear and Peter Blake, did find inspiration in the game. The latter produced a caricatured tribute to the Spurs double-winning side of 1961, and his *F is for Football* is a montage of nineteenth-century Baines' promotional cards and twentieth-century cigarette cards. Football photography has also demonstrated a bolder aesthetic tendency since the mid-1960s. In the past decade, the efflorescence of new British football writing, exemplified by *Fever Pitch*, has also been paralleled in the graphic arts. Design commentators Jeremy Leslie and Patrick Burgoyne have captured the extent to which soccer's iconography has permeated popular culture. 'From pitch markings to team strips and from match programmes to club badges, football has created its own coherent graphic language that transcends national and cultural boundaries.'

The scope of arts within the community has broadened, as some artists have abandoned traditional media and embraced notions of design and public art unacknowledged a generation ago. Even trends toward conceptual art are detectable in recent work. Mark Wallinger (1959–) has exhibited an oversized Manchester United scarf in the manner of a DNA spiral, as a biological interpretation of *United*. The artist has also produced other incisive works on football, and Wallinger perceives himself in the satirical tradition of eighteenth-century English artist William Hogarth. Contemporaries have been articulating similar themes. Matthew Ensor (1954–) has produced much work with football subjects, including some iconic parodies of Manchester United players. Peter Howson (1958–) and Jock McFayden (1950–) have contributed a Scottish perspective. Indeed, Howson had a critically acclaimed one-man show of football paintings in 1998. His energetic, muscular footballers are enunciated in bold strokes of raw colour.

Clubs' growing awareness of their heritage has resulted in a recent abundance of football statuary. Bronze likenesses of past heroes such as Shankly, Busby, Wright, and Bremner have been unveiled, though Jacob Epstein's bust of Herbert Chapman has adorned the Highbury foyer since the 1930s. Some sculptures represent heroes so identified with their communities that these have been erected in city squares far from the grounds. Examples include Stanley Matthews (Hanley Town Centre), Jackie Milburn (Newcastle), and Duncan Edwards (Dudley). Preston's Deepdale ground possesses perhaps Britain's largest portrait: a pointillistic seat mosaic of 1950s star Tom Finney.

By the 1990s, the validity of football as subject matter had been acknowledged. Exhibitions at London's 'Gallery 27' and Manchester's City Gallery were held as part of the Euro 96 celebrations, and the momentum has continued. In December 1999, the Professional Footballers' Association paid a record £2 million for a British painting when they purchased Lowry's *Going to the Match*. PFA Chief Executive Gordon Taylor recognised that in the past there had been a deficiency of literature and art surrounding the world's greatest game.

Sources:
Exhibition Catalogue, *Football and the Fine Arts* (London: Arts Council, 1953).
Leslie, J., and Burgoyne, P., *F.C. – Football Graphics* (London: Thames and Hudson, 1998).
Langton, H., *F.I.F.A. Museum Collection: 1,000 Years of Football* (London: Quintessence, 1996).
Exhibition Catalogue, *England's Glory: an Exhibition of Football* (London: Gallery 27, 1996).

Further Reading:
Exhibition Catalogue, *Muddied Oafs: an Exhibition of Football* (London: Gallery 27, 1998).
Exhibition Catalogue, *Offside: Contemporary Artists and Football* (Manchester: Manchester City Art Galleries, 1996).

See also Drama, Photography

Tom Preston

Artificial Pitches

As long ago as 1906 an idea had been put forward for a synthetic playing surface to be laid at Olympia in West London to enable indoor football to be staged. The £5,000 scheme, devised by a Mr E. Cleary, was to include the new, trendy electric lighting but it ended in failure, much to the relief of the FA, who saw a possible threat to the traditional outdoor version of the game. Three quarters of a century later, however, Queen's Park Rangers were the pioneers of a venture at their Loftus Road ground that was to see a handful of clubs take the bold step of trying to combat the notorious British weather.

It was fitting that Terry Venables was Rangers' manager at the time. Ten years earlier the former England international had co-written, with Scottish journalist Gordon Williams, the futuristic footballing novel *They Used To Play On Grass*. In the book the remarkably prescient Venables had fictionally described several aspects of the game that have since become fact. All-seater stadiums, players' freedom of contract, club sponsorship and a European Super League are all accepted as part and parcel of the modern game. Only artificial pitches have come and gone.

Venables would no doubt have been aware that Cleary's idea had belatedly caught on across the Atlantic. In 1965 the world's largest indoor sports stadium had opened – in Texas, inevitably. The Houston Astrodome was initially built with a natural grass playing surface but such was the solar glare from the roof's glass panels that these had to be painted, and under these conditions the grass withered and died. This problem was solved in March 1966 when the Chemstrand Corporation installed their newly-developed artificial grass, Astroturf. The Astrodome was back in business, and within ten years the idea had spread to venues across the United States. At the elite level baseball, grid-iron football and the newly-emerging soccer all embraced the new surface.

The material used at Loftus Road from the beginning of the 1981/82 season was not Astroturf, however. Venables and club chairman Jim Gregory visited Canada and brought back samples of a new, improved version. Omniturf comprised a sand-filled surface topped with polypropylene, and it was on Omniturf, after an outlay of some £350,000, that Queen's Park Rangers and Luton Town made history when their Second Division fixture went ahead on the new Loftus Road pitch on 1 September 1981. The innovation was well received initially, a typical tabloid headline declaring 'It's Fantastic on Plastic', but the novelty was soon to wear off. The extra pace of the ball and its unnaturally high bounce provoked complaints lodged by Blackburn Rovers and Leicester City in October 1981 and, despite Rangers' attempts to rectify these problems by adding extra sand, the FA, just as in 1906, were reluctant to embrace the new technology with any marked enthusiasm. The Football League initially sanctioned the use of Omniturf only for a three-year trial period. UEFA watched the British experiment with scepticism. Rangers, however, seemed to thrive on their 'fantastic plastic'; in 1982, still in Division Two, they qualified for their first ever FA Cup final, going down to Spurs only following a Wembley replay – though, of course, the later games in the competition were all on grass. In 1982/83 they won the Second Division championship, and the following season finished in fifth spot in the First Division. The welcome extended to Omniturf in the top flight was less than enthusiastic, however, even though it had been the stage for an international hockey festival, a rugby sevens tournament and had once staged three football matches in a single day. When Gregory sold the club to Marlar Estates in February 1987, new chairman David Bulstrode ordered a return to grass and the Loftus Road experiment was over.

In the meantime, however, three other Football League clubs had taken up the banner for all-weather pitches. No doubt recalling their part in the first ever League game on the new surface back in 1981, Luton Town themselves went ahead with a similar scheme, but this time utilising a much-improved product. As part of a £1 million refurbishment of their Kenilworth Road ground, Luton opted in the summer of 1985 for an artificial pitch made up of Sporturf International, developed by the Leicestershire firm of En-tout-cas. The new material consisted of a foundation of broken stone below a layer of bitumen macadam, with an open texture facilitating easy drainage. Above this was a sand infill supporting the synthetic grass itself, made up of polypropylene fibre blades resting on a synthetic rubber shock-absorbing base. The Hatters, like Queen's Park Rangers before them, seemed to adapt well to the plush surface: they reached three Wembley finals in their plastic days and finished the 1986/87 season an impressive seventh in Division One, their best ever placing. In bringing the club an estimated £3 million in extra revenue over the six seasons it was in place, the pitch staged the first ever representative game on plastic, when England took on Ireland in an Under-15 fixture. Luton also hired it out for international hockey and lacrosse. American football made an appearance, as did cricket. Local football also benefited, with an estimated 120,000 players earning a chance to show off their skills. Kenilworth Road had become a community sports centre as much as a football ground. Luton manager Ray Harford was greatly impressed with the new surface, while it lasted. Before an away game against Coventry City he inspected the Highfield Road grass and announced: 'It'll never replace plastic.'

The year after Luton's initiative, Oldham Athletic followed suit. Boundary Park, the Latics' home since 1899 is, at 509 feet above sea level, one of the highest in the League, and the pitch had always been prone to freezing. A £60,000 undersoil heating system had been installed in 1980 which enabled Oldham Rugby League Club to fulfil a threatened fixture, and on Boxing Day 1981, with Blackburn Rovers' Ewood Park ground out of commission because of the weather, the League allowed a switch in venue. But attendances continued to fall, so the 16 miles of undersoil piping were removed

and En-tout-cas had another customer. With £305,000 of the total cost of £385,000 being provided by Oldham Metropolitan Borough Council, Boundary Park became not only home to the Latics but also a community sports centre. Before the pitch could be relaid, however, the notorious six-foot incline had to be levelled; after all, it was meant to be a football pitch, not an artificial ski slope! Oldham retained their new pitch for five seasons, during which they won promotion to Division One and reached the League (Littlewoods) Cup final, after beating West Ham 6–0 in the home leg of the semi-final during an unbeaten run of 32 matches on their artificial surface. They also earned between £50,000 and £60,000 a year from hiring it out for community activities.

Oldham's Lancashire neighbours, Preston North End, found themselves in dire financial straits in the 1980s. Rooted in the Fourth Division, and with gates of below 5,000 not uncommon, the club was forced into a piecemeal sale of their Deepdale ground to the local council. The final transaction, involving the pavilion and car park, brought in £220,000 and enabled the new partnership of club and council to invest £300,000 in an artificial pitch. In May 1986 North End called in En-tout-cas. Deepdale, like Boundary Park, became a community sports centre and proved very popular in this guise. The synthetic pitch was equally well received by Preston's fans; a survey showed that 65 per cent of them were pleased with the new surface, with only 5 per cent preferring the traditional grass. Unfortunately for the club, however, success on the field did not follow. In 1991 the Football League finally decreed that artificial pitches were to be phased out, and on 18 May 1994 Preston North End, the 'Invincibles' of old, played the last game on plastic under League auspices. It was against Torquay United in a Third Division play-off.

While all this was going on in England, north of the border the only Scottish club to relinquish the traditional playing surface was Stirling Albion. Forced by financial problems to sell their Annfield ground to Stirling District Council in 1983 for £250,000, Albion leased it back for £3,000 per annum, but the following year the East Stand failed a council safety check. More council money was promised, but following the fashion of the times, only on condition that Annfield be opened up to wider community use. Once this was settled, a £1 million redevelopment package was agreed, involving not only the pitch, but a new floodlighting system, seats and safety barriers on the terracing. Of this total, £450,000 was earmarked for the new pitch, which was of the same type as those at Luton, Oldham and Preston. The pitch was laid in the summer of 1987 and on 5 September of that year Ayr United were the visitors for the first Scottish League match to be played on an artificial surface, the SFA having agreed to a three-year trial. This period was not extended, however, and Albion were forced to return to grass when the three years were up. Annfield was sold off for housing and Albion moved into Stirling's new community sports centre, part of a new business and retail park, at Forthbank.

Although the wholly synthetic surfaces have now passed into history, lessons were learned while they were in place. Oldham's new pitch, for instance, laid in 1991, was not completely natural. It comprised grass mixed with tiny plastic fibres to strengthen its roots. 'Fibreturf' has since been used at other venues, including Villa Park and Old Trafford: the game has not completely returned to its grass roots!

Sources:
Barrett, N., *The Daily Telegraph Football Chronicle* (London: Carlton, 1999).
Inglis, S., *The Football Grounds Of Great Britain* (London: CollinsWillow, 1993).

Further Reading:
Hart, G. (ed.), *The Guinness Football Encyclopedia* (Enfield: Guinness, 1995).
Nawrat, C. and Hutchings, S., *The Sunday Times Illustrated History of Football: The Post-War Years* (London: Chancellor Press, 1995).

Tony Rennick

Association of Football Statisticians

The Association of Football Statisticians (AFS) was founded by Ray Spiller in 1978 as 'The Football Experts', and came about as an extension of the large number of programme collectors, whose fairs took place around the country. Spiller felt that many of those attending these events must also keep statistics and historical data on their favourite clubs and on football generally, and that there was a need to make such information more widely available through a formalised association. Initial contact to determine whether such a group would be supported was made through the pages of the *Football Programme Directory*, and generated a great deal of interest. In order to provide a means of disseminating information, articles and requests submitted to the fledgling organisation, and to put the large number of respondents in touch with each other, the first newsletter (also entitled *The Football Experts*) was published in December 1978. Despite some early criticism of the quality and content of the newsletter, the organisation continued to attract new members, and the name of the organisation was changed to the Association of Football Statisticians in 1979.

The newsletter, renamed *The AFS Report*, is now a quarterly publication, and has contained a wealth of interesting and informative information over the years, covering all aspects of football at amateur, professional and international levels. Examples of the more esoteric details often published in the *Report* include the facts that the two league games between Wrexham and Lincoln in 1976/77 drew exactly the same attendance, and that Brian Clough was born on the same day that Persia became Iran. Other unusual issues covered during the lifetime of the *Report* include articles on professional footballers who have been awarded the Victoria Cross, and a season in Yugoslavia in which two end-of-season matches ended with score-lines of 88–0 and 134–1 – promotion was apparently to be decided by the number of goals scored by the winning teams!

The *AFS Report* passed 100 issues in 1998, and its regular features include obituaries of former players and officials, appeals for information, and book reviews. The AFS also publishes an *Annual*, as well as a number of subsidiary booklets on particular topics, such as FA Cup records, and the *Definitive History* series of books, which provide a complete statistical record of individual clubs. The AFS now boasts in excess of 1,500 members, who regularly meet on their travels around the country watching football. Many members are now employed by league clubs as official statisticians and historians, and AFS members are regularly consulted by the media on such matters. Ray Spiller relinquished control of the AFS in 1999 and the organisation now forms part of the Exxus publishing company.

Sources:
AFS Annual.
AFS Report 1979.
The Football Experts 1978–79.

Martin Atherton

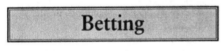

Betting

– *see* Gambling

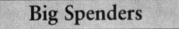

Big Spenders

British football's transfer market has grown dramatically since 1905, the year in which the first £1,000 transfer took Sunderland inside forward Alf Common to Middlesbrough in a move that helped the Teesside club avoid relegation from Division One of the Football League. Since then a number of clubs have acquired a reputation for big spending, although in the context of today's transfer deals, such reputations are merely relative.

If Middlesbrough were English football's first big spenders, Blackburn Rovers were certainly the second, breaking the transfer record in successive years. In 1911 they paid £1,800 to Falkirk to sign James Simpson, before signing Danny Shea from West Ham United a year later for £2,000. In 1920, Birmingham City paid a total of £6,800 for two players, and two years later Sunderland, whom we shall meet again, spent a combined £10,700 on two players, one of whom, Warney Cresswell of South Shields, joined for a record £5,500. In 1928 Arsenal paid the first five-figure transfer fee, £10,890, securing David Jack from Bolton Wanderers – the exact amount paid for Jack is unclear but this is the most frequently cited figure – and the Highbury club continued to spend heavily as they built up their dominating side of the 1930s.

After 1945 a boom in attendances helped to produce a rise in transfer spending on players whose pay demands were still constrained by the maximum wage. In 1947 Notts County purchased the Chelsea and England forward Tommy Lawton for £20,000, and Derby County snapped up Manchester United's John Morris for £25,000 in 1949. However, the real big spenders of the era were Sunderland, dubbed the 'Bank of England' club for their willingness to pay high transfer fees. The Welsh international forward Trevor Ford joined them from Aston Villa for a record £30,000 in 1950, and players such as Len Shackleton, Billy Bingham and Stan Anderson arrived at Roker Park for five-figure fees.

The brief exodus of British talent to Italy in the early 1960s influenced the domestic transfer market. When Denis Law, who had joined Torino for £100,000 in 1961, returned to England a year later, his new club, Manchester United, paid a record £115,000. Earlier, Tottenham Hotspur had paid £99,999 to secure Jimmy Greaves from AC Milan. Tottenham were active in the transfer market throughout the 1960s and early 1970s, signing Southampton's Martin Chivers for £125,000 in 1968, Martin Peters (West Ham) for £200,000 in 1970 and Ralph Coates (Burnley) for £190,000 in 1971. They set a trend which was followed by Leicester City (£300,000 for three players in 1971) and Manchester United (£325,000 for three players in 1972).

Manchester United, Arsenal and Everton led the way for big spending in the mid-1970s, the last named establishing a record for a cash fee (i.e. not involving a player exchange) in 1974 when signing Burnley's Martin Dobson for £300,000. In 1976 Everton also signed two players for £200,000 each, and they purchased two more for a combined £340,000 in 1977. However, the club enjoyed little on-field success. Despite a steady rise in transfer fees at a time of high inflation in the British economy, it still came as a shock when in February 1979 Nottingham Forest, not noted as big spenders, paid the first £1 million fee to secure Birmingham City forward Trevor Francis.

Over the following ten years transfer fees continued to rise and by 1988 five players moved for more than £2 million. Manchester United led the way, spending over £500,000 on individual players on thirteen occasions during the 1980s, although Liverpool paid the highest individual fee when re-signing Ian Rush from Juventus in 1988 for £2,800,000. Almost rivalling the Old Trafford club was Scotland's Rangers. Transfer fees for players moving to Scotland had always lagged behind those in England, but in 1987 Rangers paid Tottenham £1,500,000 to sign Richard Gough, one of eight transfer fees of over £500,000 paid by the Glasgow club during the 1980s.

Rangers' high spending continued into the 1990s and they established a Scottish record in July 1998 when purchasing Andrei Kanchelskis from Italy's Fiorentina for £5,500,000. Fuelled by income from the television deal with BSkyB, the leading English clubs continued to outstrip their own spending records during the 1990s. Liverpool spent £2,900,000 on Dean Saunders from Derby County in 1991, then in 1995 found £8,500,000 to sign Stan Collymore from Nottingham Forest. Blackburn Rovers acquired Alan Shearer from Southampton for £3,300,000 in 1992, then paid Norwich City £5 million for Chris Sutton two years later, forming a Championship-winning forward pairing.

Manchester United broke their own record four times, signing Roy Keane (£3,750,000 from Nottingham Forest in July 1993), Andy Cole (£6,250,000 from Newcastle United in January 1996), Jaap Stam (£10,750,000 from PSV Eindhoven in May 1998) and Dwight Yorke (£12,600,000 from Aston Villa in August 1998). Meanwhile Arsenal paid a total of £14 million for four players (including Marc Overmars and Emmanuel Petit) in the summer of 1997. Perhaps the real big spenders were Newcastle United. Having paid £6 million for Queen's Park Rangers' Les Ferdinand in July 1995, they found over £10 million to acquire Faustino Asprilla and David Batty before breaking the British transfer record, signing Alan Shearer for £15 million from Blackburn in July 1996. In November 2000 Rio Ferdinand moved from West Ham United to Leeds United for £18m, and in July 2001 Manchester United paid Lazio £28m for Juan Veron. By the time this encyclopedia has been published another big-spending club may well have beaten that record: such has been the history of the British transfer market.

Sources:

Inglis, S., *Soccer in the Dock: A History of British Football Scandals 1900 to 1965* (London: Willow, 1985).

Rothmans Football Yearbook, from 1970/71 onwards (London: Queen Anne Press, 1970–99).

Thompson, G., *South Shields F.C.: The Football League Years* (Harefield: Yore Publications, 2000).

See also Record Transfers

John Coyle

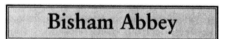

Bisham Abbey

For 800 years Bisham Abbey, set in beautiful grounds on the banks of the river Thames, had been both a home and place of refuge for the English nobility and aristocracy.

In 1780, Bisham was bought by the

Vansittart family and was their home until 1947, when Phyllis Vansittart-Neale first loaned and then sold the building to the Central Council of Physical Recreation in memory of her two nephews who were killed in the Second World War. It then became the first National Recreation Centre in Britain.

More recently, it has become one of five centres of excellence for the country's leading sportsmen and women and is part of the network of sites that comprise the UK Sports Institute. It has been the training centre for England's football during recent years. It is here that the press are often seen to be conducting interviews with the manager and filming players as they practise.

As a centre of sporting excellence, the Abbey is equipped with a modern gymnasium, with extensive free weight-training facilities. There are four indoor and ten outdoor tennis courts (including three clay courts); four outdoor football and rugby pitches; two floodlit Astroturf pitches marked out for hockey; two squash courts; and a dance studio where a variety of activities including aerobics take place. There is also a nine-hole par-three golf course within the Abbey grounds, which is a members-only course. In the early 1970s residential accommodation blocks were built within the grounds for sportsmen and women using the facilities.

Brian Pluckrose

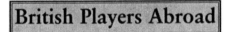

British Players Abroad

British footballers have not been good travellers. As well as the cultural and linguistic barriers to foreign settlement, few players have been inclined to leave the largest, most prestigious and, by their own accounts at least, best quality leagues in the world. Those Britons who have played abroad have tended to stay only for short spells and have generally been unable or unwilling to integrate into the host culture.

The first exodus of footballers abroad in the early twentieth century was as coaches rather than players. With little demand for their expertise at home, players reaching the end of their careers in Britain increasingly looked to the opportunities offered by clubs and associations in continental Europe. Some became key figures in the development of the European game. William Garbutt coached at Genoa between 1910 and 1915, and at Naples, Bilbao and Milan between the wars. He was also involved in the Italian national team's preparations for the 1924 Olympics. Jimmy Hogan left Bolton Wanderers in 1911 for a coaching position in Holland and spent most of the next 25 years coaching national and club sides in Austria, Hungary, Germany, France and Switzerland, including a spell with the famous Austrian *Wunderteam* of the 1930s. The highpoint for the British coach abroad may have been the inter-war years, but there was still a demand for Britons after 1945. In 1947 the FA reported 31 British footballers employed by clubs and associations in continental Europe, while the coaches of the national teams of Costa Rica, Egypt and Trinidad were all former Football League stars.

As European football developed, some footballers began to seize the opportunity to earn a living playing abroad. In 1912 Victor Gibson signed for FC Sète, in France, from the amateur club Plumstead. Officially employed by the club chairman in his shipworks, Gibson nevertheless became known as the first 'professional' in French football. On becoming manager in 1914 he signed some two dozen 'shamateur' players from across the channel before moving on to Barcelona, where he was trainer and groundsman as well as a player.

The introduction in 1932 of a professional league in France provided further opportunities, particularly for players who were unemployed or disaffected at home. The British were regarded as particularly attractive acquisitions in France, partly because of their footballing abilities but mainly because no transfer fees were necessary due to Britain's absence from FIFA. When the first round of fixtures kicked off, 43 British footballers, representing over 40 per cent of the foreign contingent, were contracted to the 20 clubs comprising the League, but by 1938 there were just five. Even the more talented players found themselves unable to adapt to the very different culture of French society and football. Most of the star recruits – such as internationals Andy Wilson and Alex Cheyne at Nîmes and Peter O'Dowd at Valenciennes – made little impact and returned home within a couple of years.

The periodic creation of professional leagues in North America provided another major overseas market for British football labour. The American Soccer League (ASL), established in 1921, was the first competition to take an active role in the recruitment of British footballers. Scots were conspicuous from the start, especially in teams like J & P Coats, a Scottish-owned firm based in Pawtucket, Rhode Island, and those of Holyoake and Fall River, Massachusetts, whose mills had long-established Scottish links. Many of the imports in the ASL's early seasons moved to the United States of their own accord, but increasingly clubs like Bethlehem Steel, backed by wealthy companies and free-spending owners, were prepared to raid the British leagues directly to entice players.

For a short time in the mid-1920s, Scottish clubs lost some of their best players with no compensation in the way of transfer fees. Tommy Muirhead, a Scottish international with Glasgow Rangers, joined the Boston Wonder Workers as player-manager in 1924, bringing with him leading players like Morton's Alex McNab and Partick Thistle's Johnny Ballantyne. For these players, the increase in wages – estimated at between double and three times what could be made at home – was worth the risk of migrating to a new continent. Yet by the time the ASL folded in 1931, the British presence had dwindled and the majority of imports had returned home.

British players were also heavily represented in the North American Soccer League (NASL), which lasted from 1968 to 1984. By 1971 over one quarter of the personnel were British citizens, a figure which reached just under 40 per cent by 1977 but declined thereafter. Many well-known internationals – such as George Best, Bobby Moore, Trevor Francis, Dennis Tueart and Peter Beardsley – played in the NASL, often at the beginning or the end of their careers. NASL clubs initially targeted players who had been unable to forge a career in Britain, or else could be taken on loan during the European close season. Yet by the late 1970s the migration of more talented players and an extended American playing season began to interfere with the game at home. Disputes between NASL and British clubs over the registration of players, and the complaints of British managers who had to start the domestic season with key players missing or injured, led to the outlawing of loan transfers in 1979.

The migration of certain players was contrary to international football regulations. In 1950 seven British footballers travelled to Bogotá in Colombia to play in the Di Mayor, a rebel professional league unaffiliated to FIFA. They were part of a much larger import of South American and European professionals brought in without the normal recognition of contracts and payment of transfer fees. Four of the British group, including the Stoke City and England centre-half Neil Franklin and Manchester United's Charlie Mitten, actually signed contracts, but their foreign adventures were short-lived. Franklin spent two months and played only six matches in Colombia, citing as reasons for his premature return the climate, the food and the lifestyle, as well as the poor standard of play and behaviour of players and spectators. Along with the other Colombian migrants, he was fined and suspended by the FA on his return, and transfer-listed by his club.

From the mid-1950s, Italy emerged as a new destination for the cream of British talent. The Welsh centre-forward John Charles joined Juventus from Leeds United in 1957, and in 1961 Joe Baker, Jimmy Greaves, Gerry Hitchens and Denis Law all moved to Italy for fees ranging from £73,000 to £100,000. The success of this group was mixed. Baker, Greaves and Law all failed to settle, returning to Britain within a season amidst complaints about the defensive style of play, stringent club discipline and press intrusion. By contrast, Hitchens enjoyed nine seasons in Italy – with Inter, Torino, Atalanta and Cagliari – while Charles won both respect and championship medals. He is still remembered affectionately in Turin as 'King John'.

Since the 1980s more British footballers have plied their trade abroad (and in a greater number of countries and continents) than in any other period. Some, such as Kevin Keegan at Hamburg, Glenn Hoddle at Monaco, Chris Waddle at Marseilles and David Platt in Italy, have done so successfully. Keegan, for instance, won the League, reached the European Cup final and was twice named European Player of the Year while in Germany. But many more have failed to adapt to work and life in a new environment. The increasing wealth of clubs in the English Premiership has led to a significant reversal in the transfer traffic, and few top British players are now prepared to make their living outside the country.

Sources:

Franklin, N., *Soccer at Home and Abroad* (London: Stanley Paul, 1956).

Jose, C., *NASL: A Complete Record of the North American Soccer League* (Derby: Breedon Books, 1989).

Jose, C., *American Soccer League, 1921–31* (Lanham, Maryland: Scarecrow Press, 1998).

Lanfranchi, P. and Taylor, M., *Moving With the Ball: The Migration of Professional Footballers* (Oxford: Berg, 2001).

Mason, T., 'The Bogota Affair', in J. Bale and J. Maguire (eds), *The Global Sports Arena* (London: Frank Cass, 1994), pp. 39–48.

See also Exports

Matt Taylor

British Teams in Europe

The European (Champions) Cup is the annual competition organised by the governing body of European football, UEFA, for the league champions of each country from the previous season. Originally a knockout competition for 16 teams, the European Champions Cup began its reincarnation into the UEFA Champions League in 1991, and by 1994/95 the competition (after qualifying rounds) incorporated four groups of four, with the top two in each group reaching two-legged quarter- and semi-finals, followed by the final. In 1998/99 the tournament was further expanded to eight groups of four, progressing to four groups of four and then the quarter-finals, semi-finals and final. Expanded to take advantage of exorbitant television revenues, the competition now requires its champions to play seventeen matches to win the trophy. British clubs have won the trophy on ten different occasions.

Following the boastful claims of some British newspapers about the status of Wolverhampton Wanderers after success in friendlies against Spartak Moscow and Honved of Budapest in 1954, the French paper *L'Equipe* proposed a competition involving European clubs to settle such arguments. UEFA accepted the proposal, and what has traditionally been known as the European Cup was born. Originally UEFA preferred the title of 'European Champion Clubs' Cup', but aided by the development of floodlights UEFA was able to develop a competition which permitted mid-week fixtures, became immediately known as the 'European Cup', and incorporated the champions of sixteen nations in its first season of 1955/56. In this first season the traditional insularity of British football reared its head when the Football League banned Chelsea's participation, although Hibernian from Scotland participated and made it to the semi-finals. In 1956/57, however, champions Manchester United entered against League advice (although the club was encouraged in this direction by FA secretary Stanley Rous). Despite an impressive victory over Anderlecht, United went out in the semi-finals to the all-conquering Real Madrid, winners of each of the first five competitions. The promise of the youthful United side was never fully realised. On 6 February 1958, after securing a second semi-final place within two years, the plane carrying the United team crashed on take-off at Munich airport en route from Belgrade. Eight players died – Duncan Edwards, Roger Byrne, David Pegg, Tommy Taylor (all England internationals), Geoffrey Bent, Eddie Colman, Mark Jones and Liam Whelan – whilst Johnny Berry and Jackie Blanchflower never played again. United lost the emotionally charged semi-final against AC Milan.

Manchester United's Bobby Charlton lifts the 1966 European Footballer of the Year trophy, 1967(Peter Robinson; © EMPICS Sports Photo Agency)

Although Tottenham (1962), Liverpool (1965) and Manchester United (1966) reached the semi-finals, Celtic became the first British club to win the European Cup, in 1967. Celtic were the complete opposite of their opponents, Inter Milan, already champions in 1964 and 1965 and famed for their defensive play. Having fallen behind after six minutes to a penalty from Mazzola, Celtic were frustrated by the majestic Facchetti and his side's often-cynical defence. But goals from Gemmell and Chalmers, just five minutes from time, meant that Celtic had won the Cup. The following year – ten years after the Munich air crash – witnessed emotional scenes at Wembley as Matt Busby's Manchester United defeated Benfica, with their elegant centre-forward Eusebio, 4–1 after extra time, with goals from Charlton (2), Best and Kidd.

From 1969 to 1976, British sides were unable to clinch another trophy as teams such as Inter Milan and Ajax dominated the period, albeit with contrasting styles. In 1969 a disappointing Celtic were beaten 1–0 by Feyenoord of Holland, whilst in

1972 Celtic and Derby County reached the semi-finals. 1972 also saw Northern Ireland fail to put forward their champions for entry into the cup. The troubles in the province were deemed too dangerous to allow foreign teams to travel to away matches. Irish sides have had little success in the European Cup, and Welsh sides only competed in the qualifying rounds after the expansion of the competition in the 1990s.

As Colin Cameron has noted, prior to 1976 British football had blasted its way to European success without ever threatening to adopt the tactical guile employed by Continental clubs. Tottenham's 1961/62 campaign was marred by what manager Bill Nicholson called 'tactical naivete', best exemplified by conceding four goals to Gornik Zabrze of Poland before overpowering their opponents 9–5 on aggregate. Celtic and Manchester United's success was based on 'momentary brilliance', but having won the 1976 UEFA Cup, Liverpool emerged to dominate European football as Real Madrid had between 1956 and 1960. Ironically, English football at national level was at one of its lowest ever ebbs when a spectacular run of success for British clubs in the European Cup began. After England's sorry displays against Finland and Luxembourg, and Don Revie's resignation, Liverpool embarked on a triumphant campaign, which had as its signature game a remarkable three-goal semi-final comeback against St Etienne of France. The 1977 final was held in Rome where Liverpool beat Borussia Monchengladbach of (then) West Germany 3–1, with goals from Terry McDermott, Phil Neal and Tommy Smith.

Not satisfied with that achievement, Kenny Dalglish (a replacement for Kevin Keegan) and Alan Hansen were added to the squad for the 1977/78 season. Following a glorious semi-final against Monchengladbach, Dalglish clinched a second successive triumph in a 1–0 victory over Brugge of Belgium, in the final held at Wembley. In the 1978/79 season England's two entrants, Liverpool (as holders) and league champions Nottingham Forest (in their first appearance in the competition) were drawn against one another in the first round. The charismatic Forest manager, Brian Clough, engineered a remarkable 2–0 aggregate triumph and Forest went on to a third successive triumph for British football, beating Malmö, of Sweden, 1–0 in the final. The only goal was scored by Britain's first million-pound player, Trevor Francis. Forest, severely hampered by injury, repeated the triumph the following year with a 1–0 victory over Kevin Keegan's SV Hamburg, John Robertson scoring the winning goal.

In the 1980/81 season, whilst Forest surprisingly lost to CSKA Sofia of Bulgaria, Liverpool completed their third triumph in five years. After a hard-fought victory over Bayern Munich in the semifinal, the final against Real Madrid failed to live up to expectations, but left-back Alan Kennedy turned up unexpectedly in the Real penalty area to fire in the only goal from a very narrow angle. The success of Aston Villa in the 1981/82 season was astounding. With no real star players, manager Tony Barton in his first ever post, and only two previous European campaigns, Villa completed England's fifth successive triumph in the European Cup when Peter Withe converted Tony Morley's cross to secure a 1–0 victory over Bayern Munich. In 1983/84, Liverpool secured their fourth win in seven years with a dramatic penalty shoot-out victory over Italian champions, Roma, playing in their home stadium. But the following year, having again reached the final, the European Cup final was to be the setting for the first of Liverpool's two darkest moments in their history. On 29 May 1985, at the Heysel stadium in Brussels, 39 Juventus fans died as a result of crowd violence. Before the match, Liverpool fans 'charged' the Juventus supporters in a desegregated section of the terraces. As they fled, the Juventus fans were crushed against an old wall, which collapsed and left a global television audience dumbstruck. For the record, Juventus won the match, played in a surreal atmosphere, 1–0.

As a result of events at Heysel English clubs were banned from all European club competitions indefinitely, with Liverpool receiving an additional three-year ban from the time when English clubs were readmitted. Other British sides were allowed to continue. English clubs returned in 1990/91, but with Liverpool having won the League the previous season there was no English club in the competition. The moratorium had created a distinct 'gap' between British and continental clubs, best exemplified by Blackburn Rovers' lack of success in the 1995/96 season. Slowly, Manchester United began to improve their European performances, amplifying their development in the domestic game. Like Liverpool in the 1970s, they learned from a series of 'near-misses' in the latter half of the 1990s. In May 1999, having won the domestic double of League and FA Cup, and completed a remarkable triumph against their nemesis of previous years, Juventus, in the semi-finals, United took on Bayern Munich in the final. 1–0 down for much of the game, goals by Teddy Sheringham (in the last minute) and Ole-Gunnar Solskjaer (in injury time) completed one of the most memorable comebacks in European history and brought manager Sir Alex Ferguson an unprecedented treble.

Sources:

Cameron. C., *Football, Fussball, Voetbal: The European Game 1956–Euro'96* (London: BBC Books, 1995).

Nawrat, C. and Hutchings, S., *Sunday Times Illustrated History of Football* (London: Hamlyn, 1997).

Tyler, M., *The History of Football* (London: Marshall Cavendish, 1978).

Further Reading:

Ferguson, A., *Managing My Life: My Autobiography* (London: Hodder and Stoughton, 1999).

McWilliam, R., *The European Cup: An Illustrated History 1956–2000* (London: London Bridge, 2000).

Taylor, R. and Ward, A., *Kicking and Screaming: An Oral History of Football in England* (London: Robson, 1996).

Marc Keech

BUSA

The British Universities Sport Association (BUSA) provides competitive sport for students in higher education through the organisation of domestic championships, representative fixtures and international tournaments, principally the World University Games.

BUSA was established in 1994 following the amalgamation of the Universities Athletic Union (UAU), which previously controlled domestic university sport, and the British Universities Sports Federation, which dealt with international competition. UAU was itself formed in 1930 from the more loosely structured Inter Varsity Athletic Board (IVAB), which was first convened in February 1918. In 1922, association football was added to the IVAB programme of events. Prior to 1994 the sporting needs of students in colleges and polytechnics were satisfied by the British Colleges Sports Association and the British Polytechnics Sports Association. In the 1991/92 academic year it became apparent that the government was committed to the removal of the binary divide within higher education, and as a consequence the paramount requirement for a *single* student sports body was realised with the establishment of BUSA in offices in Union Street, London.

Today, in total, BUSA organises competitions in 44 different sports with approximately 50,000 regular participants. In association football BUSA's domestic programme offers different levels of involvement for male and female students. In the men's competition approximately 140 university first teams, 120 second teams, 95 third teams and 65 fourth teams participate on a weekly basis, normally on Wednesday afternoons, in Championship, Shield and Plate tournaments.

In the women's competition over 100 teams take part in the BUSA championship, making soccer the third most popular student women's sport behind hockey and netball. In total, therefore, there are over 8,000 male and female student players competing regularly in BUSA competitions.

The best student players undergo a trial process through which the English, Northern Irish, Scottish and Welsh Universities' national squads are selected. The highlight of the representative programme for all these sides, male and female, is the British University Games, held annually in the Easter vacation. At international level, the Fédération Internationale du Sport Universitarie (FISU), the world governing body for student sport, mandates BUSA to enter a *British* team in the World University Games (WUGS). The Games are held biennially and the 16-team men's football tournament, sanctioned by FIFA, attracts many teams of Olympic standard from every continent. Great Britain's best performance came in 1991 when, on home soil in Sheffield, the side were bronze medallists. The British team's record in WUGS since 1985 is as follows:

1985 Kobe, Japan
    8th out of 12
1987 Zagreb, Yugoslavia
    10th out of 16
1989 No team entered
1991 Sheffield, England
    3rd out of 16
1993 Buffalo, USA
    4th out of 16
1995 Fukuoka, Japan
    14th out of 16
1997 Sicily, Italy
    12th out of 16
1999 Palma, Spain
    9th out of 16

The impressive growth of the women's game in British Universities suggests that they will make their first appearance at WUGS in the near future. WUGS therefore represents the pinnacle of the student soccer pyramid, and several players have progressed from the British team to a professional career. For example, Jon McCarthy (Birmingham City), a player in the 1991 WUGS side, is a regular member of the Northern Ireland senior squad. His team-mate in 1991, David Wetherall, is currently playing for Bradford City FC, having made his name at Leeds United, while David Weir (Everton), a Buffalo squad member in 1993, competed for Scotland in the 1998 World Cup finals in France. The majority of the Great Britain WUGS teams are currently playing in the English, Irish and Scottish Leagues, the Football Conference or for senior non-league semi-professional sides. Thus, whilst satisfying the demands of grass-roots student players for regular competition, BUSA also serves through its involvement in the World University Games to progress the soccer education of elite student players, many of them talented late-developers, who ultimately enjoy professional careers in the game.

Sources:

BUSA, *Annual Reports* and *Handbooks* (1995–).

Ian Moir

History Highlights 1850–1899

Folk varieties of football were played in Britain from at least the Middle Ages; some existing in the English public schools employed their own distinct unwritten rules. As games became more ideologically important to 'character development' in these schools from the 1850s, rules were formulated, and clubs established by ex-public schoolboys, including Sheffield FC in 1855 and Notts County in 1864. The Football Association was founded by clubs in London and the south-east in 1863, and the FA Cup introduced in 1871 as a knockout competition for these clubs. In the 1870s the Cup was dominated by public school-related sides, such as Wanderers and the Old Etonians.

In Scotland, Queen's Park (1867) and Hamilton Academicals (1868) heralded the origins of organised football, and the first official international between England and Scotland was played in 1872. The pre-eminent clubs in the early days were Queen's Park, Vale of Leven, Dumbarton and Renton. The Glasgow clubs Celtic and Rangers began their rise from the late 1880s. The record Scottish FA Cup score occurred in 1885, when Arbroath beat Bon Accord 36-0. In Wales, the Welsh Cup commenced in 1877, the year after the formation of the Welsh FA. The principal Welsh clubs around this time were Druids (Ruabon), Wrexham, Newtown and Chirk.

Early technical developments in the game included the introduction of shinguards (1874); the crossbar (1875 – although tapes were used at times); the referee's whistle (1878); goal nets (1891); and the penalty kick (1891). The Scots (or alternatively, the Royal Engineers) initiated the passing game in the mid-1870s, using a square midfield with players passing between the 'wing triangle' and crossing the ball to beat opponents. Similar techniques were introduced to England by Partick Thistle, who influenced Darwen and Blackburn Olympic, some of the first English exponents of the passing manoeuvre.

Increasingly, competition between Lancashire clubs from 1878 onwards led to the surreptitious payment of players, and the importation of Scots 'professors'. The great improvement in the Lancashire challenge for the FA Cup brought good performances by Darwen in 1879, and Blackburn Rovers, beaten finalists in 1882. In 1883, Blackburn Olympic became the first club from outside the south-east to win the Cup, their victory of the Old Etonians ending the monopoly of the public school-derived clubs. Blackburn Rovers won the Cup three times between 1884 and 1886. All other winners until 1900 came from the north and Midlands, including Aston Villa, Sheffield Wednesday, Sheffield United and West Bromwich Albion. Preston North End established the record FA Cup score by beating Hyde 26-0 in 1887.

One of the most significant innovations in this period was the legalisation of professionalism in England in July 1885. Opposition to it came mainly from the amateur lobby in London, the south-east, Sheffield and Birmingham, although the latter city's premier club, Aston Villa, supported it. The Football League was founded in 1888 at the suggestion of William McGregor (Aston Villa), with the twelve clubs chosen being arguably the best and most attractive to spectators at the time. The founders were Aston Villa, Bolton Wanderers, Preston North End, Accrington, Wolverhampton Wanderers, Blackburn Rovers, West Bromwich Albion, Everton, Burnley, Derby County, Notts County and Stoke. Preston were the first Champions, and the first club to perform the 'double', in 1889. Accrington FC was the first club to succumb to the pressure of the League, resigning in 1893, and finally folding in 1896. The dominant clubs initially were Preston, Aston Villa, Sunderland and Everton. A second division was introduced in 1892, bringing in clubs such as Liverpool, Royal Arsenal, Grimsby Town, Newcastle United and Ardwick (Manchester City).

The Southern League was formed in 1894, encompassing clubs such as Southampton, Portsmouth and Millwall, and was important for the growth of professionalism in southern England. Many of these clubs later joined the Football League. The Scottish League commenced in 1891, with professionalism finally legalised in 1893. Here the significant clubs up to 1899 were Dumbarton, Celtic, Hearts, Hibernian and Rangers.

Promotion and relegation were introduced to the Football League in 1898 to avoid the system of 'test matches' that had operated previously between the top clubs in Division Two and the bottom clubs in Division One. One important feature in this earlier period (certainly in comparison with the post–1960 period) was the relative openness of the competition, with a number of different clubs enjoying success. Blackburn Rovers and the 'invincible' Preston North End were the dominant forces in the 1880s, Aston Villa and Sunderland in the 1890s. In Scotland, competition was also more equal before the near monopoly of Celtic and Rangers became consolidated in the next decade.

Sources:
Fabian, A. H. and Green, G., *Association Football* (London: Caxton, 1960).
Mason, T., *Association Football and English Society, 1863–1915* (Brighton: Harvester, 1980).
Rothmans Football Yearbook (London: Headline, various editions).
Russell, D., *Football and the English* (Preston: Carnegie, 1997).
Young, P. M., A *History of British Football* (London: Stanley Paul, 1968).

Further Reading:
Gibson, A. and Pickford, W. *Association Football and the Men Who Made It*, 4 vols (London: Caxton, 1905–6).
Green, G., The *History of the Football Association* (London: Naldrett, 1953).
Inglis, S., League *Football and the Men Who Made It* (London: Willow, 1988).

Robert Lewis

Caps

International caps were initially awarded to players following an appearance for their country against an opposing national team. This probably grew out of the public school system. Many of football's early administrators came from a public school background and the idea of the 'cap' as a symbol of national identity was most appealing. The number of appearances players make for their country is actually counted in caps, although today one cap is awarded for each friendly international a player plays in, and one for each international tournament played in.

It would seem that the Scottish Football Association (SFA) first introduced international caps. The SFA has a cap in its museum relating to the second international against England in 1873, although when the decision was made to award caps for this match is uncertain. In England international caps were not introduced until 1886. This followed a resolution moved by N. L. Jackson – assistant FA secretary and founder of Corinthians – at an FA Committee meeting on 30 January 1886, stating that 'all players taking part for England in future International matches be presented with a white silk cap with red rose embroidered on the front. These to be termed "International Caps".' The proposal went to a sub-committee where it was decided to accept Jackson's idea. The committee amended the design, opting for a royal blue velvet cap, with the date of the international to be imprinted onto the peak. The committee also decided that all players who had played an international during the 1885/86 season would be presented with an international cap retrospectively. So the first international caps were presented to players who played for England against Ireland in Belfast on 13 May 1886. It would seem that the other home international countries adopted caps around the same time as England. However, owing to political difficulties Northern Ireland only introduced caps in the 1937/38 season.

Since 1886 English international caps have undergone several design changes. They came to be embellished with gold braid, as well as a silver tassel; on modern-day caps the insignia has changed to include the initial of the opposing country on the peak. Caps are still blue velvet but the red rose has been replaced by three lions, the symbol which was given to England by Henry II, and one which has overt associations with English nationalism. The first English player to receive 100 caps was Billy Wright, captain of England during the 1950s, while the most capped English player is Peter Shilton, with 125 caps. Two other English players, Bobby Charlton and Bobby Moore, have also reached the milestone of 100 caps. Kenny Dalglish, with 102 caps, is the only Scottish player to pass the century mark, while Pat Jennings, of Northern Ireland, is the only Irishman to have achieved a century of international caps. Billy Meredith, formerly of Manchester City and United, holds the record for the highest number of caps in home internationals: 48 caps for Wales, including a run of 22 consecutive appearances between 1908 and 1920.

Sources:

Green, G. and Witty, J. R., *History of the Football Association* (London: Naldrett, 1953).

Ray Physick

Captains

Every game begins with the toss of a coin, but there is more to the art of captaincy than the ability to call correctly. A successful captain may not necessarily be the most talented player in the side, but he needs leadership qualities and the gifts of motivation and communication. When all these attributes come together – and the captain can also play a bit – then a team has something special. The British game has bred many notable club captains over the years; the best have gone on to do the same job at international level.

England's most memorable must surely be Bobby Moore, the West Ham United central defender whose potential as a natural leader was spotted at an early age. Born in Barking, East London, in 1941, he captained the England Youth side, for which he made a record 18 appearances, before becoming a West Ham professional in 1958. His polished, stylish play epitomised the philosophy of manager Ron Greenwood and was soon to be rewarded. In 1964 he led the Hammers to the club's first major honour when they beat Preston North End 3–2 in the FA Cup final. A year later Moore was climbing the steps to the Royal Box again as West Ham became the second English side to win the European Cup Winners' Cup after beating Munich 1860 2–0. In 1966, however, came, the greatest moment of all when, as England captain, Bobby Moore lifted the World Cup aloft following England's historic 4–2 triumph over West Germany. Three years, three wins, three different trophies – and he was still only 25.

Between 1962 and 1973 Moore's gifts of uncanny anticipation, composure under pressure and immaculate distribution more than made up for his comparative lack of pace, winning him a total of 108 England caps, a record at the time. He also captained the side on no less than 90 occasions. He made 642 League and Cup appearances for West Ham before moving to Fulham and adding another 150 to his total. Towards the end of a distinguished career he made another FA Cup final

Bobby Moore holds aloft the World Cup as his teammates celebrate around him
(Empics/Alpha; © EMPICS Sports Photo Agency)

appearance for Fulham in 1975, when the unfashionable Second Division club lost – to West Ham. He was voted Footballer of the Year in 1964 and awarded the OBE three years later, rewards merited by his overriding sense of fair play as well as his extraordinary technical gifts. Towards the end of his Football League career he joined the emerging North American Soccer League, turning out for San Antonio Thunder in 1976 and Seattle Sounders in 1978. He had brief managerial experience with Herning FC of Denmark, Oxford City and Southend United before spending three years as sports editor of *Sunday Sport*. An entire footballing nation mourned when Bobby Moore, whose sportsmanship recalled the Corinthian ideals of an earlier age, died of cancer in February 1993.

Later the same year the football world was saddened by the death of another inspirational captain, Danny Blanchflower. Robert Dennis Blanchflower, still revered by Spurs fans who recall the double-winning 'Glory, Glory' days of the 1960s, first saw the light of day in Belfast in 1926. He spent three years with Glentoran before leaving the Irish league side in 1948 for his first English club, Barnsley, who paid £6,500 for his services. In 1951 he joined Aston Villa for £15,000, then in 1954 Tottenham manager Arthur Rowe doubled that price to bring the cultured Blanchflower to White Hart Lane, in the process making him the most expensive half-back to date. It turned out to be money well spent.

Rowe's famous 'push and run' side that had won the Second Division in 1949/50 and the First Division the following season, was breaking up and languishing in the bottom half of the table. Danny made his debut on 11 December 1954, helping Spurs to a much-needed point in a goalless draw against Manchester City at Maine Road, and Rowe's relief was evident: 'The first match I'd been able to enjoy for some weeks.' Ill-health soon forced Rowe to leave the club, but when new manager Jimmy Anderson made Blanchflower captain at the expense of Alf Ramsey the club's fortunes began to change. The new skipper was at the helm when Spurs, by now managed by Bill Nicholson, won the coveted but elusive FA Cup and League double in the 1960/61 season, making them the first club to do so since Aston Villa way back in 1897. FA Cup success was repeated in 1962, and the following season Danny captained the first British side to win a European trophy when Tottenham overcame Atletico Madrid 5–1 in Rotterdam to lift the Cup Winners' Cup. On the international front, Blanchflower won a then record 56 caps for Northern Ireland and steered the unfancied Ulstermen, against all sensible odds, to the 1958 World Cup finals in Sweden, where they surprised themselves as much as anyone else by reaching the quarter-finals before going out to France.

Danny Blanchfower was the creative heart of the 'Super Spurs' side built by Nicholson. His vision, his ball control, his natural instinct for changing the pace of a game and ability to hit accurate passes over long distances were crucial to Tottenham's attacking style, which helped them to an impressive 115 League goals in their celebrated 'double' year, though he graciously admitted that the talents of his team-mates allowed him the time and space to flourish: 'I had the ball much more often than anybody else, so I should have done something with it! Shouldn't I?' This comment was typical of the man's puckish sense of humour: when Bill Nicholson's managerial debut ended with a 10–4 home win over Everton, Danny congratulated his new boss with: 'Well done, it can only get worse.'

A leg injury forced him to retire at the end of the 1963/64 season after a Spurs career encompassing 383 games. He was voted Footballer of the Year in 1958, and again in 1961. He had a brief stab at management with Northern Ireland (1976–79) and Chelsea (1978/79), though he enjoyed a long, successful career as a journalist, first with the *Observer* and then the *Sunday Express*, where he stayed for 25 years. Unlike most ex-players who followed this path, however, he wrote his own copy and the words that followed his by-line were not always to the liking of the authorities. He also ruffled a few media feathers when he became the first prospective subject of the TV show *This is Your Life* to tell Eamonn Andrews what to do with his big red book. Danny Blanchflower was always his own man.

While the Spurs captain was leading Northern Ireland in their Swedish adventure of 1958, Tottenham's near neighbours and traditional rivals, Arsenal, also provided an international captain at that tournament. Wales, also surprise quarter-finalists that year, were led by Dave Bowen, born in the rugby stronghold of Maesteg, but who had made the association code his game. He began his Football League career with Northampton Town in 1947 and quickly established himself as a forceful outside-left. Such was his impact that he was brought to the notice of Highbury boss, Tom Whittaker. When Arsenal signed him in 1950, Bowen was converted to left-half, and within eight months had made his first-team debut in his new position. The presence in the Gunners' side of Joe Mercer, himself an accomplished wing-half and the established club captain, restricted Bowen's first-team opportunities, as did a series of injuries. However, when Mercer himself was forced out of the game following a broken leg in 1954, the Welshman became a regular first-team choice. He was made captain during the 1957/58 campaign and at the end of that season led Wales in Sweden, where the accuracy of his passing, especially when feeding speedy winger Cliff Jones, proved as vital to the team's unexpected progress as his stalwart defensive qualities and leadership skills.

Wales, who had only qualified for the tournament on a technicality after the withdrawal of all Israel's opponents in the qualifying stages, drew all their three group matches, against Hungary, Mexico and Sweden, the hosts, to earn a play-off which again matched them with Hungary. A 2–1 win against the Mighty Magyars, who only five years earlier had humbled England 6–3 at Wembley, put Wales into the quarter-finals where they met hot favourites Brazil. In front of an enthralled Gothenburg crowd and without the injured John Charles, Bowen inspired Wales to a heroically defiant rearguard action against the awesome Brazilian attack. The deadlock was finally broken in the 66th minute, when the legendary Pele hit a shot that Bowen's Arsenal team-mate, goalkeeper Jack Kelsey, seemed to have well covered. The ball struck Stuart Williams, however, and was deflected into the net for the only goal of the game. Wales were out of the World Cup. To put Wales's performance into perspective, it should be pointed out that Brazil scored five against France in the semi-final, and did the same against Sweden in the final.

The inspirational Bowen was not destined to remain at the top of the game much longer. In 1959 Arsenal released him and he moved back to lowly Northampton. There was more to come, however. The Cobblers were in Division Four when Bowen, who had remained a resident of the town throughout his Arsenal days, arrived for his second spell at the club, this time as manager. Things did not look promising: not only was the team decidedly lacklustre, the ground was even worse. The County Ground, shared with Northamptonshire Cricket Club, was the Football League's last surviving three-sided ground, the fourth side being open to the cricket pitch. Not only that, half the turf on the cricket field side was used as a car park and picnic area when the summer game was in operation. New boss Bowen, whenever trying to sign a new player, would invariably arrange to meet him at the nearby motorway services, rather than have him put off by seeing the ground. In typical style, however, Dave Bowen responded to the challenge. Arsenal were the visitors in October 1960 when the County Ground finally got round to having floodlights installed. The following May, Northampton, who had joined the Football League in 1921, savoured their first taste of success by finishing third and earning promotion to Division Three. After only two seasons they were Third Division champions and then, incredibly, in 1964/65 they finished runners-up to Newcastle United in Division Two, and so completed an unprecedented rise from the League basement to the top flight in only five years. Taking their inspiration from Dave Bowen, that supreme motivator, the Cobblers had experienced the most dramatic change in a club's fortunes that the

game had ever witnessed. They only managed to stay in the First Division for one season, but what a season it was. Average gates reached a club record, at over 18,000, and for the visit of fellow-strugglers Fulham, on 23 April 1966, they attracted their highest-ever attendance of 24,523. Even the cricket side of the ground was brought into use, with a series of wooden bleachers being installed.

Who else but Dave Bowen could have led Wales to the last night of the World Cup and unfashionable Northampton Town to the heady reaches of the First Division? The man from Maesteg, famed for his typical Welsh fire and impassioned vocalising on the field, may not have been the most skilful player of his time but he was never matched for commitment. Arsenal may have discovered a new hero in Tony Adams, Wales can be proud of Ryan Giggs, and Northampton now have a new stadium at Sixfields: but there will never be another Dave Bowen.

Of all Scottish international captains over the years, none made a greater impact on the game than George Young. A true giant of a man in every sense, 'Granite George' spent his entire Scottish League career with Rangers, joining as a teenager in 1941 via the Blues' junior club Kirkintilloch Rob Roy. Initially a right-back, he was converted to centre-half by Rangers, although normally reverting to his original position for Scotland, and went on to become the predominant defender in the Scottish game at club and international level until his retirement in 1957.

While with Rangers he helped them to win six Scottish League Championships, and the Scottish Cup four times. They also won the Scottish League Cup twice, the first occasion being in 1946/47, the first year of the new competition. Their best season was 1948/49, when they lifted all three trophies, the first time in the club's history they had achieved the 'treble'. Young began his Scotland career by representing his country in two wartime internationals, before going on to win a record 53 official caps, the last of them coming in 1957. He captained the side 48 times (another record) and achieved a further milestone by appearing in 34 consecutive matches. His greatest disappointment was to be omitted from the Scotland team that qualified for the 1958 World Cup; he had envisaged the Swedish tournament as a fitting finale to an illustrious career. He also felt he had something to prove, in light of Scotland's World Cup record up to that point. In 1950 they had refused to go as they had not won the home international championship, and in 1954 they finished pointless in their group. He had been a member of the Scottish team that had gained impressive 1957 victories over Spain and Switzerland in the qualifiers, but then found himself dropped from the squad. The 2–1 win over Switzerland was to prove his 53rd and last cap. So distraught was the big man that he retired from the game at the end of the 1956/57 season.

That had been quite a year. Rangers made their first foray into the new European Cup but went out 3–1 to Nice after a first-round play-off. Arch-rivals Celtic eliminated them from both domestic cup competitions, but a 16-match unbeaten run, including a 6–4 win after coming from 4–1 behind, saw them retain the League championship. It was to be George Young's final honour. He managed the late lamented Third Lanark from 1959 to 1962, but then concentrated on his other interests, hotel management and sports journalism, although his deep knowledge of the game earned him a place on the very first pools panel when it sat on 26 January 1963.

George's newspaper column offered him a platform for reminiscing about a career that had coincided with the postwar boom in Scottish football and had so many highlights. His nickname of 'Corky' was earned by his habit of carrying around with him a lucky champagne cork from a bottle opened in celebration of Rangers' 1948 Scottish Cup final victory over Morton after a replay, the two ties attracting a total of 261,151 spectators. The following season, the year of Rangers' historic 'treble', George helped himself to two goals from the penalty spot as Rangers swamped Clyde in the final. In the 1953 final it was big George, all 6 feet

3 inches and 15 stones of him, who went into the Rangers goal after an injury to George Niven. Rangers drew 1–1 and then went on to beat Aberdeen in the replay. Together with Sammy Cox and Willie Woodburn, George was part of Rangers' 'Iron Curtain' defence of the time. Although genuinely two-footed and a skilful ball player, he is best remembered for his strength in the air and his prodigious clearances that could switch play in an instant from one penalty area to the other. Scotland lost a true giant when George Young passed away in January 1997.

Other captains have led club and country with distinction but there can be little doubt that Billy Wright, Terry Neill, Terry Yorath, Billy Bremner and the rest would feel proud and honoured to be part of a side led by any of the four remembered above.

Sources:
Bremner, B. and Rale, B., *Billy Bremner's Scottish Football Heroes* (Derby: Breedon Books, 1997).
Inglis, S., *Football Grounds of Britain* (London: CollinsWillow, 1996).
Matthews, P. and Buchanan, I., *The All-Time Greats of British and Irish Sport* (Enfield: Guinness, 1995).
Nawrat, C. and Hutchings, S., *The Sunday Times Illustrated History of Football: The Post-War Years* (London: Chancellor Press, 1995).

Tony Rennick

Careers Cut Short

This section looks at examples of players whose football careers were cut short, mostly by injury but in a small number of cases by their own decisions. Perhaps the most shocking cases involve those players who died as a direct result of injuries sustained while playing football. In 1892 James Dunlop of St Mirren died of tetanus as a result of a cut received in a match, while James Milne of Hibernian died from internal injuries sustained in a game in

Unfulfilled promise: Manchester United's
Duncan Edwards, March 1954
(Barratts; © EMPICS/Alpha)

1909. The most famous Scottish casualty was Celtic's goalkeeper John Thomson, who died as a result of fracturing his skull during a match with Rangers in 1931.

In England players who have died during games or as a direct result of injuries include Bob Benson (Arsenal, 1916), Tom Butler (Port Vale, 1923), Sam Wynne (Bury, 1928), Sim Raleigh (Gillingham, 1934), James Thorpe (Sunderland, 1936) and David Longhurst (York City, 1990). In the cases of Benson, Thorpe and Longhurst, a long-standing medical condition was found to have contributed to their deaths. Raleigh, Gillingham's centre-forward, died from a brain haemorrhage following a clash with a Brighton defender, Paul Mooney. Mooney was so distraught by events that he gave up playing football soon after the incident.

A number of active players have perished as a result of illness or non-footballing accidents. Nick Ross was still a Preston player when he died of consumption in 1894, while Chelsea's Tommy Meehan died as a result of sleeping sickness in August 1924, shortly after winning his only England cap. Birmingham City's international defender Jeff Hall died from polio aged 30 in 1959. A year earlier eight Manchester United players, including Duncan Edwards, Roger Byrne and Tommy Taylor perished in the Munich air crash. Car accidents have claimed the lives of several players, the most notable perhaps being England's Laurie Cunningham, killed in Spain in 1989. More unusual was the demise of Harold Hampson (Blackpool and England), killed in 1938 when a yacht in which he was sailing collided with a trawler.

Less tragic, but nonetheless poignant are those cases of players whose careers were cut short by injury. Newcastle's Peter McWilliam (1911) and Sheffield Wednesday's Bill Marsden (1930) had to retire due to injuries received playing for Scotland and England respectively. Manchester City's Jimmy Meadows did not play again after damaging his knee in the 1955 FA Cup final, while Burnley and England goalkeeper Colin McDonald had his career ended by a broken leg sustained when representing the Football League in 1961. Other international players forced to retire early due to injury have included Gary Bailey (Manchester United, aged 29), Kevin Beattie (Ipswich Town, 30), George Cohen (Fulham, 30), Mick Jones (Leeds United, 30), Harold Hassall (Bolton Wanderers, 26) and Rob Jones (Liverpool, 27).

Some players forced to retire have gone on to forge successful careers within football. Derek Dooley's playing career ended in 1953 when a leg he broke playing for Sheffield Wednesday had to be amputated. He went on to manage Wednesday and later became Managing Director of Sheffield United. Brian Clough, a prolific scorer for Middlesbrough and Sunderland had to retire aged 29, but went on to manage Derby County and Nottingham Forest to Football League titles. Steve Coppell, winner of 42 England caps before retiring at 28 with a knee problem, has enjoyed managerial success with Crystal Palace. Wilf McGuinness won two England caps but his career was effectively over at 22. He went on to manage his former club,

Manchester United, and later worked as a physiotherapist. Arthur Cox, who later managed Newcastle United and Derby County, had his career ended almost before it began, a broken leg as a 19-year-old trainee at Coventry forcing him to take up a coaching career.

Perhaps because of the attractions of football as a career there are few examples of players giving up of their own volition. Arthur Milton, capped for England at both football and cricket, shocked Bristol City in 1955 when retiring aged 27 to concentrate on his cricket career. Equally stunned were Wolverhampton Wanderers in 1969 when 24-year-old Peter Knowles, an Under-23 international, announced that he was giving up football to become a Jehovah's Witness. Attempts to persuade Knowles to reconsider proved fruitless. In 1985 Exeter City's Symon Burgher left the club, his religion preventing him from working on Saturdays. For the vast majority of players, however, quitting is not an option and those who leave the game do so only with a heavy heart.

Sources:

Lamming, D., *An England Football Internationalists Who's Who 1872–1988* (Beverley: Hutton, 1990).

Williams, R., *Football Babylon* (London: Virgin, 1996).

Further Reading:

Comfort, A. and Peacock, G., *Never Walk Alone* (London: Hodder, 1994).

Lawton, T., *When the Cheering Stopped* (London: Golden Eagle, 1973).

See also Deaths on the Pitch

John Coyle

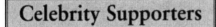

Celebrity Supporters

Many celebrities, especially from the worlds of entertainment and politics, have declared their allegiance to a particular football club, and some have become actively involved in their club's affairs. The celebrity supporter gains publicity and authenticity from their association with football. Clubs may also use their prominent fans as fund-raisers, promoters and benefactors.

There have always been close links between the entertainment industry and football. The music hall comedian George Robey, once a Millwall player, frequently appeared in charity matches alongside top professionals. He provided the Manchester United strip for the 1905 FA Cup final and held fund-raising concerts for the Players' Union. Comedians have been some of football's most high profile supporters, finding it a rich source of material. Tommy Trinder, one of the biggest variety stars of the 1940s and '50s, became Chairman of Fulham Football Club in 1955 until he was made Life President in 1976. Trinder kept the club he had supported from his childhood in the news, making Johnny Haynes the first £100 a week footballer and having to apologise frequently to his players for making jokes at their expense in his act. Eric Morecambe (a director at Luton Town) and Tommy Cannon (chairman of Rochdale) were other comics who became more deeply involved. Jimmy Tarbuck, Stan Boardman, Jasper Carrott and Bernard Manning are all examples of comedians whose regional identities were reinforced by their football allegiances. David Baddiel and Frank Skinner took this identification between football and comedy to its apogee in the 1990s as presenters of the BBC2 *Fantasy Football* programme, and as performers of the England pop anthem *Three Lions*. The alternative poet Attila the Stockbroker, in a more radical role, played a prominent part in the successful campaign to save Brighton and Hove Albion at the end of the 1990s.

Pop, rock and other stars have also been some of football's most prominent supporters. Tom Jones was made President of Newport County in 1969. Elton John has twice served as Watford's chairman, first from 1976–90, after acting as vice-president from 1973, then from 1997. He was also made honorary life-president in 1993, in recognition of his financial and personal contribution to the club. Mick Hucknall, singer with the appropriately named Simply Red, is one of Manchester

United's many celebrity fans, and helped to raise money for manager Alex Ferguson's testimonial year in 1999. Disc jockey John Peel's support for Liverpool is an important part of his public persona. Other pop stars and groups have recorded club songs. In the late 1980s and '90s, as football enjoyed an upswing in popularity, it became *de rigueur* for rock bands to parade their club loyalties as a point of identification with their audience and a badge of authenticity: Damon Albarn of Blur made much of his support for Chelsea; the Gallagher brothers from Oasis were frequently pictured at Maine Road watching Manchester City. In the 1930s film scriptwriter Emeric Pressburger was a dedicated Arsenal fan. The actor Tom Watt wrote a book about the Arsenal North Bank and also hosted a radio football phone-in show.

Harold Wilson was probably the first Prime Minister to cultivate a direct association between his government and sporting success, encapsulated by his comment that England only won the World Cup under a Labour government. Wilson was a passionate Huddersfield Town supporter and carried a photograph of the 1926 League Championship-winning side in his wallet, often showing it to visiting dignitaries. Unfortunately, a Russian general who mistakenly thought Wilson wanted his autograph defaced it. Roy Hattersley's devotion to Sheffield Wednesday was a frequent subject for his *Guardian* and *Punch* columns. *Football and the Commons People*, a book of MPs' essays about their favourite football clubs, demonstrated football's growing respectability in the 1990s. John Major, Tony Banks and David Mellor all appeared at Chelsea matches. Mellor began a post-political career as a pundit and radio broadcaster and was a member of the Football Task Force. However, Tony Blair's adoption of Newcastle United was suspected to be a matter of expediency for his image as a people's Prime Minister, rather than reflecting a genuine connection with the club.

Celebrity fans are predominantly male, though the best-selling cookery writer Delia Smith became a director of Norwich City Football Club in 1996, and in 1997 she and her husband became the majority shareholders.

The listing of celebrity fans is a popular feature of fanzines and internet football sites and has become a part of alternative fan culture. Pride is taken equally in the prominence or obscurity of the celebrities named.

Sources:

Bull, D., and Campbell, A. (eds), *Football and the Common People* (London: Juma, 1994).

Eyre, F., *Stargames: A Jog Down Memory Lane with the Stars* (Glossop: Senior Publications, 1984).

Houlihan, B., *The Government and Politics of Sport* (London: Routledge, 1991).

Redhead, S., *Post-Fandom and the Millennial Blues: The Transformation of Soccer Culture* (London: Routledge, 1997).

Joyce Woolridge

Charity

British football has a long history of charitable involvement at both elite and grass roots levels. As early as 1889 a South of England XI played the Old Carthusians in a 'charity festival' at The Oval to raise money for London causes, and this is unlikely to have been the first such event. The annual FA Charity Shield, inaugurated in 1908, is undoubtedly British football's longest surviving fund-raising function. The first game, between Football League champions Manchester United and Southern League counterparts Queen's Park Rangers, raised some £239 for hospital charities, while dependants of the *Titanic*'s victims were amongst the beneficiaries four years later. Initially, there was no set format as to the teams involved, although Amateurs versus Professionals was a fairly popular combination. League champions first played FA Cup winners in 1920 (Cup winners Spurs beating Burnley 2–0); with only occasional exceptions, this became a standard fixture from 1930. Often played in October, it became a pre-season showpiece in 1960, moving to Wembley Stadium in 1974. By the late 1990s, the fixture typically raised around

£500,000 pounds, distributed to around one hundred separate and wide-ranging charities.

Some clubs have been especially active in encouraging the charitable impulse. Brian Clough, for example, deducted money from his players' wages for Oxfam while manager at Nottingham Forest in the late 1970s and early 1980s. Many individual professional players have always quietly supported charities in a personal capacity. When Stanley Mortensen, the Blackpool forward of the 1940s and 1950s, was awarded the freedom of the borough in 1990, his long record with local charities was celebrated only a little less prominently than his footballing skills. As players have taken an increasingly high profile in the national culture in the late twentieth century, they have found themselves asked to take an equally high profile in the charitable sphere. In 1998, French international David Ginola, then playing for Tottenham Hotspur, took over as the patron of the Red Cross's campaign for landmine victims following the death of its previous champion, Princess Diana; while in the following year, Manchester United's Andy Cole established the Venture Kodak Andy Cole Children's Fund to raise money for homeless children in Zimbabwe. United's powerful name has similarly led to the establishment of a United for UNICEF campaign. In 2000, a number of leading figures, including England national coach Kevin Keegan, campaigned for the housing charity Shelter. In moments of national crisis, most obviously in wartime, football as a profession has also contributed to charitable appeals. In September 1914, most Football League players agreed to donate up to 5 per cent of their wages to the National War Relief Fund, and a number of games were organised over the ensuing months between League and army teams with the dual intent of raising money and stimulating recruitment.

The emphasis here has been on the professional player, but it is important to remember that much football-related charitable effort has been supported by or emanated from the fans: collecting buckets and sheets for innumerable organisa-tions have often appeared inside grounds over the years. Moreover, the amateur game has also been a constant source of funds. Before the establishment of the National Health Service in 1948 many towns held a 'Hospital Cup' tournament, raising small but useful amounts through entry fees or collections. The charitable impulse was certainly strong in the early phase of the women's game between 1918 and the early 1920s. In 1921 alone, the Preston-based Dick, Kerr Ladies played 67 charity matches, raising between £150 and £2,000 per match. It is likely that the association of the women's game with charity at this time helped temper some of the criticism that it faced and boosted attendances and interest – although, ironi-cally, the FA were able to use claims that money was being misappropriated as part of their case for banning the women's game in 1921. Perhaps the most striking example of charitable activity stimulating football, however, is provided by Glasgow Celtic, founded initially in 1887 by a Marist brother to raise money for soup kitchens amongst the city's Catholic poor.

Sources:

Green, G., *The History of the Football Association* (London: Naldrett, 1953).

Newsham, G., *In a League of their Own* (Chorley: Pride of Place, 1994).

Rothmans Football Yearbook, 1999 (London: Rothmans).

Dave Russell

Club World Championship

In 1982, Tyne Tees television screened a 90-minute drama 'The World Cup: A Captain's Tale', based on the story of the amateur team from the Durham pit village of West Auckland who beat Red-Star Zurich, Stuggart, Juventus and Turin to win the coveted trophy.

The competition was established by Glasgow millionaire Thomas Lipton in gratitude for his being made a Knight of the Grand Order of Italy. Renowned as having a flair for publicity, the grocery chain magnate presented the trophy and laid down the rules. When snubbed by the England football authorities, he invited West Auckland of the Northern Amateur League to represent England.

A new version of a world club championship was established in 1960, when the winners of the European Cup were invited to take on the winners of the South American Copa de los Libertadores, regarded as the strongest teams in the two strongest football playing continents. The competition was first won by Real Madrid, but was not contested every year. In 1971, European Champions Ajax of Amsterdam refused to go to play in South America following repeated incidences of violence in previous years. Celtic were the first British nation to contest it in 1967, the first year FIFA gave it official recognition. They lost two matches to one against Racing Club. Manchester United contested the Cup the following year, losing to Estudiantes 1–0 after a draw in the home leg at Old Trafford. Aston Villa, Liverpool and Nottingham Forest are the only other British teams to have taken part in the Cup, all losing to their South American counterparts.

From 1980, the competition was reduced to a single match on neutral territory, Tokyo. On 30 November 1999, Manchester United became the first British club to win the championship, beating Palmeiras of Argentina 1–0. In 2000 the competition was extended to include the champions from other football playing continents.

In 1999/2000, Manchester United caused quite a stir by deciding to withdraw from the FA Cup in pursuit of the more lucrative World Club Cup, this time played in Brazil. Many opponents of the club felt they got their just deserts when they failed to reach the final stages.

Sources:
Rothmans Football Yearbook 2000–2001 (London: Rothmans, 2000).
Soar, P., *The Hamlyn A-Z of Football Records* (Second edition) (London: Hamlyn, 1985).

Richard William Cox

Coaches

Despite the rapid growth of professional football in Britain from the late 1880s onwards, little attention was given to coaching. Manuals were produced at regular intervals offering insights on how to play the game, but few clubs thought it necessary to employ a person who would work with players to improve their skills and techniques. The clubs' views were summed up by the former England international Billy Bassett, then a director of West Bromwich Albion. Writing in the *Book of Football* (1905/6), Bassett lamented the fact that not enough was done in training to improve the quality of play. At the same time, though, he expressed the view that it was up to individual players to improve their own game. Furthermore, Bassett asserted that the arts of dribbling and tackling could not be taught, and that players could improve only by constant practice. This view, effectively ruling out the intervention of coaching, dominated British football up to the Second World War.

That said, Britain was often the main source of coaching expertise for other European countries. Steve Bloomer, the Derby County and England forward, was working as a coach in Germany at the outbreak of the First World War: he ended up being interned for the duration. Other Britons such as Curtis Booth, Ted Magner, Jackie Robertson and Howard Slade worked as coaches in Europe between the wars. Perhaps the most notable was Jimmy Hogan, a former Fulham, Burnley and Bolton Wanderers player who was appointed national coach in Austria after the First World War. Hogan formed a partnership with Hugo Meisl which helped Austria become one of Europe's leading football nations in the 1920s and 1930s. When Hogan returned to England in 1934 to become manager of Fulham, he soon found his methods were distrusted and he returned to Austria a year later. At this time many club managers were still employed for their administrative skills, and were not expected to have much contact with the playing side of the club. An exception was Arsenal, where Herbert Chapman took a leading role in team matters and encouraged coaches like Tom Whittaker (later Arsenal's manager) and 'Punch' McEwan.

Official attitudes began to change after 1934, when Stanley Rous was appointed secretary of the FA. Rous, a former schoolteacher and international referee, had noted that countries like Italy, Austria and France were beginning to overtake England in terms of skills, tactics and organisation. He enlisted another schoolteacher, Walter Winterbottom, to be the FA's director of coaching, a job he combined with that of England team manager from 1946. England did not enjoy great success under Winterbottom, but he identified and promoted a number of young coaches who were to be influential from the 1950s onwards. Bill Nicholson, who later managed the Tottenham Hotspur side which won the League and FA Cup 'Double' in 1960/61, assisted Winterbottom at the World Cup finals in 1958. Jimmy Adamson, later to be coach and manager at Burnley, was England's coach at the 1962 World Cup in Chile, the first time anyone had held this title. Two other coaches who were disciples of Winterbottom, Ron Greenwood and Bobby Robson, went on to manage England after success at club level. While Scotland took a little longer to adopt a similar approach it is noticeable that the two most recent Scotland team managers, Andy Roxburgh and Craig Brown, have come from a coaching background. Wales' manager between 1974 and 1979, Mike Smith, had been a schoolteacher and national director of coaching for Wales before taking on the national team.

The advances promoted by Rous and Winterbottom took some time to bear fruit, and talented coaches were often forced abroad to find work. George Raynor, a former professional player who took up coaching during the Second World War, was recommended by Rous to the Swedish FA. In two spells as national coach he took Sweden to an Olympic Gold medal (1948) and the World Cup final (1958). He also managed Juventus and Lazio, but his only involvement with the English game was in brief spells at Coventry City and Doncaster Rovers. George Ainsley, a former Leeds United player, coached in India, Pakistan, South Africa and Israel between 1950 and 1964, while George Curtis was Norway's national coach up to 1970. Danny McLennan, a Scotsman, held national coaching posts in Iraq, Jordan and the Philippines in the 1970s. Apart from Raynor, perhaps the most successful was Vic Buckingham, who managed Ajax of Amsterdam (1960/61) and Barcelona (1971) to domestic honours, in between spells in charge at West Bromwich Albion, Fulham and Sheffield Wednesday.

During the 1960s the role of the coach began to achieve greater recognition at club level. An important figure was Alf Ramsey, who succeeded Winterbottom as England manager in 1963. Ramsey, a former defender with Tottenham Hotspur and England, had taken Ipswich Town to the Football League championship in 1962. He was an innovative tactician who liked to work with players on the training ground and he employed two coaches, Harold Shepherdson and Les Cocker, to assist him with preparations for the 1966 World Cup, won by England. Ramsey set the tone for managers who worked with their players. Such managers were often dubbed 'tracksuit managers' and were epitomised by Brian Clough, who won the League championship with both Derby County and Nottingham Forest, and the Leeds United manager, Don Revie.

Not all good coaches were adept at management, however. Malcolm Allison, a former West Ham United player, proved to be an outstanding coach at Manchester City. He formed an effective partnership with the manager, Joe Mercer, as City won the League Championship, FA Cup and European Cup Winners' Cup between 1967 and 1970. As a manager, Allison did not achieve similar success. Don Howe, later coach of the England team, was Arsenal coach in 1970/71 when the club achieved the League and FA Cup 'Double'. Howe assisted the manager, Bertie Mee, who was not from a coaching background. Howe's spells in sole charge at West Bromwich Albion and Arsenal were less distinguished. More recently Brian Kidd, who had been first team coach at Manchester United during several of their Premiership-winning seasons, experienced relegation when manager of Blackburn Rovers.

Other notable coaches have enjoyed more success as managers. Dave Sexton, who was coach of England from 1983, led Chelsea to the FA Cup in 1970 and the European Cup Winners' Cup a year later. Howard Wilkinson, now the FA's director of coaching, won the Football League championship as manager of Leeds United. Arthur Cox, who took up coaching when injury ended his playing career, has enjoyed success both as a manager (at Newcastle United and Derby County) and as a coach with Sunderland, Fulham and England. It is apparent that club management and coaching often involve different skills, and the size and complexity of modern football clubs make it likely that these roles will be separated in the future. This is the case at many clubs in mainland Europe, where a business manager looks after administration and finances while the chief coach handles football matters. This potential change, along with a requirement for coaches to hold formal qualifications, may help to further raise the status of the coach within British football.

Sources:
Leatherdale, C. (ed.), *The Book of Football: A Complete History and Record of the Association and Rugby Games* (Westcliff-on-Sea: Desert Island Books, 1997, facsimile edition).
Rous, S., *Football Worlds: A Lifetime in Sport* (London: Faber, 1978).
Turner, D. and White, A., *The Breedon Book of Football Managers* (Derby: Breedon Books, 1993).

Further Reading:
Bowler, D., *Winning Isn't Everything: A Biography of Sir Alf Ramsey* (London: Gollancz, 1998).
Raynor, G., *Football Ambassador at Large* (London: Stanley Paul, 1960).
Wilkinson, H. and Walker, D., *Managing to Succeed: My Life in Football Management*

(Edinburgh: Mainstream, 1992).
Winterbottom, W., Wright, B. and Ferrier, B., *Soccer Partnership* (London: Heinemann, 1960).

John Coyle

Coaching

Coaching is the term given to the teaching of football. It has many elements, such as training, developing strategies, systems and styles of play (commonly known as tactics), performance analysis and managing a team. In the nineteenth century, the science of coaching did not exist. Instead the trainer, whose responsibility was to ensure that players were fit for the start of the season, was an experienced volunteer who provided guidance to players by concentrating on fundamental skills rather than the finer points of the game. One early example was George Ramsay, who helped young players at Aston Villa in 1875. Training began its evolution into what we know today as coaching when the Old Carthusians, playing the more skilful Old Etonians in the 1881 FA Cup final, departed from the traditional practice of individual skills by successfully adopting a strategy of 'combined play', which required planning and co-ordination. One of the first successful trainers/coaches was Jack Hunter, who played half-back for Blackburn Olympic. Olympic's unlikely progress to the 1883 FA Cup final saw them up against the firm favourites Old Etonians. Hunter took the team to Blackpool prior to the final. This was the first recorded occasion of sustained systematic training, with players leaving home for a period of time to live communally. The planned tactics of sideline runs and cross-field passes resulted in Olympic winning the Cup.

For many years British football virtually ignored the art and practice of coaching. In the late nineteenth century officials and players believed that young players would develop their 'natural' young talent from the example of senior players. This narrow view caused many retired professionals to look abroad, and before the First World War some former players were taking up appointments on the continent, although they had no experience of coaching and often did not speak any foreign languages. One of the first to leave was John Madden, capped by Scotland in 1893 and 1895, who managed Slavia Prague between 1905 and 1938. Between the First and Second World Wars, many other former players coached in Austria, Denmark, Germany, Holland, Italy, Portugal and Spain, but the most travelled and praised 'coach' was Jimmy Hogan, the former Burnley and Bolton centre-forward, who led the development of the game in several countries. Most notably, the Hungarians praised him after their victory over England in 1953. Chelsea's former Danish half-back, Nils Middleboe, said that British 'coaches' were sought after because of their background and reputation. Ivan Sharpe, the former player and journalist, bemoaned the insularity of the British game in 1959:

We neglected coaching, allowed excessive competitive spirit and rivalry to undermine the quality of play, and have been overhauled in artistic methods.

This early insight has been an often-repeated criticism in the last 40 years, and continues to be cited as the primary reason for the lack of international success by British nations.

Coaching manuals began to emerge in the early 1900s. Former Everton and Spurs player John Cameron wrote *Association Football and How to Play It*, followed by Bertram Saxellye Evers and Cyril Edward Hughes Davies publishing *The Complete Association Footballer* in 1912. The book was the most comprehensive guide to how to play the game prior to the First World War. By 1935 the FA had begun to publish coaching manuals, with techniques and tactics illustrated by photographs and diagrams. Previous publications were collated into the 1937 volume *Association Football*, edited by F. N. S. Creek. The editor was a former England international and acted as the official lecturer for the accredited coaches of the FA.

When Sir Stanley Rous took office as Secretary of the FA in 1934 he began to establish a system of courses where coaches could 'qualify' and make the most of their ability and experience. Walter Winterbottom became the first 'Director of Coaching' for the FA as part of his responsibilities as England manager. His 1952 publication *Soccer Coaching* was presented as an official FA manual and translated into many languages. Possibly the most influential British coach in recent years worked not for a club, but for the FA. Charles Hughes joined the FA in 1964 as assistant director of Coaching, manager of the England Amateur team and the Great Britain Olympic team. Hughes later progressed to Director of Coaching and Education. He criticised managers and coaches for their 'opinions' and 'theories' about what constituted successful coaching and tactical strategies, noting that football had become 'less entertaining' and 'more defensive', and citing the declining number of goals in matches. In 1980 he published the FA's coaching book of soccer, tactics and skills, which advocated a 'forward-thinking, forward-running, forward-passing' system of play. Hughes believed that misguided attacking strategies based around 'possession football' were to blame for the declining level of excitement in the game. He advocated the use of 'hard facts' to develop what he termed *The Winning Formula*, published as a book in 1990. By analysing many hundreds of matches Hughes concluded 'that when the number of consecutive passes in a move exceeds five, the chances of a shot at goal decrease'.

The 'Winning Formula' was based around a strategy of 'direct play', which involved moving the ball forward quickly but in a 'controlled manner'. Thus, high levels of technical ability needed to be retained, although they had to be harnessed as the most striking consequence of 'direct play' was the need for substantially increased levels of physical fitness – otherwise players would be unable to sustain the system. Skill development was often relegated in training sessions to develop fitness, and British football continued to embody the traditions identified by Ivan

Sharpe in 1959.

Hughes was roundly criticised in many quarters. He was accused of dehumanising football, nullifying imagination and neglecting skill. 'Direct play' forced players to pass the ball forward at almost every opportunity. Accuracy was sacrificed, and possession was often given away too easily, while players were often unable to distinguish between the need to retain possession by passing sideways or backwards, or play to the strategy and simply 'pump the ball forward'. Hughes's system was not a substitute for being able to play the game, and the obvious conclusion to many was that skilful players would be better at the system than unskilful players. As Bill Shankly once remarked, 'the game's about long balls and short balls', and the defining feature of coaching team play is to develop a player's ability to make the correct decision at the right time. Hughes denounced criticisms that 'direct play' sacrificed skills and the beauty of the game as 'factually inaccurate', but he was widely credited with much of the blame for the so-called decline of British football. In the 1980s 'direct play' manifested itself within the professional ranks as the 'long-ball game', a simplistic but rather accurate term that summarised the approach of clubs such as Cambridge United, Crystal Palace, Watford and Wimbledon, all of whom achieved a fair degree of success. Former Palace manager, Steve Coppell, said the system adopted was a pragmatic one given his playing staff: 'The Chairman wanted results, he was paying my wages and "direct play" was the best way to win.'

One of the more progressive coaches in British football during this time was Dave Sexton, formerly manager of Manchester United and coach to the England national team during Bobby Robson's reign as England manager. Robson and Sexton got on well with Hughes, but were known to disagree profoundly with him. Sexton took particular interest in new ideas in coaching and was to play a leading role in creating the 'school of excellence' at Lilleshall, as well as developing the concept within individual clubs. This concept is now a prerequisite for Premiership

clubs, and many other clubs have highly developed systems of coaching at their 'schools'. At Crewe Alexandra, Dario Gradi is widely credited with developing the technical ability of many young players who have moved to bigger clubs and obtained international honours.

In the 1980s, a European influence on coaching in British football began to emerge. Coaches dissatisfied with Hughes began to look elsewhere for a formula that would teach young players technique to match their foreign counterparts. Wiel Coerver is the Dutch coach credited with partly developing the fluid style of play endorsed by the national team since the 1970s. His manual *Soccer Excellence: The Revolutionary New Training Plan* (1985) encouraged the development of skills as the primary objective of coaching young players. Coerver's profile in the coaching of young people has grown steadily. Andy Roxburgh, former Scotland coach, is now technical director of UEFA, and is a firm supporter of Coerver's methods. In England, Howard Wilkinson has since been appointed as technical director of the FA, and has responsibility for the structure and function of coaching in English football. However, the continued failure of the English national football team in 2000 has resulted in the announcement of a new 'academy of excellence', based on the French FA model and the controversial appointment of the first foreign coach of the national side, Sven-Göran Eriksson. Ivan Sharpe would be happy that our narrow-mindedness is finally wearing off.

Sources:

Hughes, C., *Soccer Tactics, Skills and Coaching* (London: BBC, 1980).

Hughes, C., *The Winning Formula* (London: William Collins and Co., 1990).

Taylor, R. and Ward, A., *Kicking and Screaming: An Oral History of Football in England* (London: Robson, 1995).

Sharpe, I., 'Coaches' in Fabian, A. H. and Green, G. (eds), *Association Football*, Vol. 3 (London: Caxton, 1959) pp. 235–40.

Witty, J. R., 'Club Trainers' in Fabian, A. H. and Green, G. (eds), *Association Football*, Vol. 3 (London: Caxton, 1959), pp. 261–6.

Further Reading:
Coerver, W., *Soccer Excellence: The Revolutionary Training Plan* (London: Sidgwick & Jackson, 1985).
Sexton, D., *Tackle Soccer* (London: Stanley Paul, 1977).

Marc Keech

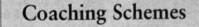

Coaching Schemes

Coaching schemes have been established to develop and educate coaches in their ability to tutor players, and to permit them to obtain a series of coaching 'qualifications'. Coaching schemes have, in part, reflected the increasing professionalisation of the sport. However, for far too long the British game has suffered from the majority of managers – particularly those who coach young players – having little or no coaching qualifications or experience. The importance of the coach had been largely ignored in British football, while abroad, significantly advanced scientific and technical approaches to developing coaches and coaching schemes markedly improved the technical ability of players.

It was not until 1934/35 that the FA created its initial programme, and it took many years for formal coaching schemes to develop. In 1954, six coaching courses were held, attended by 567 participants. With the addition of a further nine schemes organised by county federations, the net result was over 5,000 visits to youth and school football teams. By the late 1950s British football had slowly developed the initial structures of coach development programmes, and had begun to initiate coaching schemes. Supported by an annual investment of £12,000 the FA claimed that the country had become 'coaching minded', a view that was misguided at best. The problem was how to develop coaching schemes that could improve not only elite football, but also 'grass-roots' coaching. This issue was not addressed for many years as the FA primarily concentrated on providing schemes for coaches involved with more advanced levels of participation.

By the 1980s the FA had developed a structured programme of coach development with four main components. Having obtained their introductory Teachers Certificate, many young coaches progressed to their Preliminary award, which was recognised as a baseline for coaching basic skills to young people. Far fewer progressed to the Intermediate level than the FA would have liked. The Advanced Coaching Licence was the highest award, and colloquially called the 'full badge'. In 1996, the FA revamped its coaching system and introduced a series of vocational courses after 'widespread consultation through the game'. The changes in the coaching structure marked the beginning of more rigorous and robust assessment procedures, and also incorporated domestic awards within UEFA qualifications. There are now five levels of coaching. The Teachers certificate remains, while the Preliminary award has been replaced by the FA Coaches Certificate. The former Intermediate award has become the FA Coaching Licence, and is equivalent to the UEFA 'B' award. The Advanced Coaching Licence can be achieved in either 'senior' or 'youth' categories. Candidates may be assessed in both categories, although not in the same year, and the award is equivalent to the UEFA 'A' award. The fifth and newest coaching qualification is the FA coaching diploma and is equivalent to the UEFA 'Pro' award.

According to the FA, coaching is at the forefront of its long-term strategic plan, as techniques become more sophisticated. In October 1997, The Football Association Coaches Association (FACA) was launched in order to 'affect positively the attitudes, ethics, knowledge and performance of football coaches'. Howard Wilkinson, the FA Technical Director, has been at the centre of these developments, although it is too early to comment on how successful the FACA initiative has been.

There have also been developments in women's and girls' football, albeit at a much slower pace. In 1995 there were 251 female FA Preliminary students nationwide, which compared favourably with 119 in 1990. In the same period the number of female FA Teaching Certificate students rose from 327 to 426, while the number of FA Leaders students rose from 285 to 1,061. There are only five women in the country to hold a UEFA full coaching badge. Hope Powell was appointed as the first female head coach of the England women's football team in 1998.

Overall, the FA is working towards a programme of continuing professional development for all its registered coaches in order to keep them informed of new developments and initiatives. It has been one of the first National Governing Bodies to effectively initiate and fund a child protection programme, which began in 2000. Since 1995 the quality of coaching and coaching schemes in Britain has improved immeasurably, but there is still an immense amount of hard work to do. Despite the efforts of many committed and dedicated people in local areas, 'coaches' of youth teams around the country – many of whom are volunteers – offer to take training because their son or daughter wants to play in a team and, in some cases, continue to instil poor habits into many of our young people.

Sources:
Football Association, Information Pack (London: FA, 2000).
Sharpe, I., 'Coaches' in A. H. Fabian and G. Green (eds), *Association Football* (London: Caxton, 1959).

Further Reading:
See the FA's website:
www.footballassociation.org

Marc Keech

Codes of Football

Although the word 'football' is used throughout Britain as a synonym for association football, it is just one of seven modern forms of football which can all trace their roots back to the folk football of pre-industrial times. The other six codes can be divided into those deriving directly from the football rules of Rugby school – rugby union, rugby league, American and Canadian football – and Australian Rules and Gaelic football, which drew up their laws independently yet have aspects in common with each other.

Uniquely, soccer is the only code that forbids outfield players handling the ball. The myth that Rugby schoolboy William Webb Ellis 'created' rugby football by picking up and running with the ball – invented by the Old Rugbeian Society in 1895 – portrayed the handling code as an aberration, whereas it was soccer's insistence on using only feet which marked it out as the deviation from the norm.

The formation of the FA in 1863 was an attempt to unify the playing rules of football. The first draft of the FA's rules allowed running with the ball and hacking – kicking the shins – of the player in possession, but these were voted down and the modern game of soccer was born. In 1871 the Rugby Football Union (RFU) was formed by those who supported running with the ball.

In contrast to soccer, whose playing rules have maintained a remarkable stability since 1863, the rugby game began to fracture from 1880. In America, where after an early dalliance with soccer the major universities had taken up rugby, the number of players per side was reduced from 15 to 11 and the scrum replaced by a 'snap' at the line of scrimmage when a player had been tackled. In 1882 the concept of 'downs' was introduced, initially restricted to three attempts to carry the ball five yards but later extended to today's four downs in which to carry the ball ten yards. A new sport was born, reaching maturity in 1906 when the forward pass was legalised.

In England, rugby itself split in 1895 when 22 of the leading clubs in the north were forced to resign from the RFU. The immediate cause was the RFU's refusal to sanction 'broken-time' allowances to players who lost money by taking time off work to play. Underlying this was the RFU's fear that the working class players and spectators in the north would swamp 'their' game. The Northern Union, as the new organisation was called until 1922 when it became the Rugby Football

League, abolished the line-out in 1897, allowed open professionalism in 1898, and fundamentally changed the nature of the game in 1906 when it reduced the number of players to 13 per side, and replaced rucking and mauling for the ball after a tackle with an orderly play of the ball. In 1966, again in an attempt to make the sport more entertaining, the number of tackles allowed before a side had to relinquish the ball was set at four, increased in 1972 to six.

A similar process of adaptation and refinement of rugby rules took place in Canada. The scrum was replaced by a 'heel back' in 1882, in 1921 the number of players per side was reduced to 12, and in 1931 the forward pass was introduced. Unsurprisingly, given its geographical and technical proximity to American football, the 1940s and '50s saw an increasing Americanisation of the sport as scoring values, terminology and even the title of the governing body, the Canadian Rugby Football Union, were changed to bring it closer to its American cousin.

Rugby union itself was established as the major winter sport of the white dominions of the British Empire by 1900. Priding itself on its amateurism, it sought to resist pressures to become more entertaining and spectacular. But from the late 1960s this stance began to crumble: in 1971 the value of a try was increased from three to four points to encourage open play (and to five in 1992); in 1972 the RFU's first ever national club cup competition began; and in 1976 merit tables, the forerunner of the national league system, were introduced.

By the mid-1980s, the RFU's international influence had waned as the balance of rugby union's power shifted to the southern hemisphere, especially South Africa and New Zealand, leading to the inauguration of the world cup in 1987 and the momentous embrace of professionalism in 1995.

In contrast to the rugby codes' changes, Australian and Gaelic football have remained relatively static, though styles of play have altered. Gaelic football's first rules were published in December 1884 at the second convention of the Gaelic Athletic Association. The codification of its rules was a response by Irish nationalists to the growth of 'English' football, and the game became identified with the assertion of Irish national culture and opposition to British rule. Today it is played by teams of 15 players each. The goals resemble rugby goal-posts, with three points scored by kicking the ball between the posts and under the bar, and one point if it is kicked above the bar. Throwing the ball is forbidden, but it can be carried provided that it is bounced every four steps.

Australian Rules football traces its origins back to Thomas Wentworth Wills, who in July 1858 suggested that a football club be started in Melbourne. The Melbourne Cricket Club set up a football section and the playing rules were agreed the following year. Today the game's heartland remains in Victoria, but it has a strong following throughout Australia, especially in Western and South Australia. The game is played by 18 players per side and, uniquely, on an oval pitch. Four posts at either end of the pitch serve as goals: kicking the ball through the two centre posts brings six points, one point if it goes between the outer goalposts. Carrying is allowed if the ball is bounced every five or six yards and the ball can be kicked or hand-passed. As in rugby union, a player catching a kicked ball before it bounces can claim a 'mark', allowing an unimpeded kick.

The similarities between Australian and Gaelic football, fuelled by a need for international competition, led in the 1960s to matches between the two countries under a hybrid set of 'International Rules'. The artificiality of the matches has served to demonstrate only that the playing rules of each football code are crucial to its culture. In a similar way, the cross-code matches between Bath and Wigan in 1996, respective champions of English rugby union and rugby league, showed that it is the uniqueness of each code of football which gives each sport its individual appeal.

None of the other football codes can even attempt to rival the world-wide popularity of soccer. Although rugby union is played in many countries, it is the national sport only of New Zealand and, to an extent, white South Africa and South Wales. Rugby league is played seriously only in northern England, Eastern Australia, New Zealand and Southern France, while the four other codes are, as their names suggest, effectively mono-national sports. It is also noticeable that the handling codes are strongest in English-speaking countries.

Today soccer has become a truly global sport. In contrast, the other codes continue to reflect national, regional or social particularities – the source both of their strengths and of their weaknesses.

Sources:

Atkinson, G., *Everything You Ever Wanted To Know About Australian Rules Football But Couldn't Be Bothered Asking* (Melbourne: Five Mile Press, 1982).

Consentino, F., *A Passing Game: A History of the Canadian Football League* (Winnipeg: Bain and Cox, 1995).

Lennon, J., *The Playing Rules of Football and Hurling 1884–1995* (Dublin: NRC, 1997).

Moorhouse, G., *A People's Game: The Official History of Rugby League 1895–1995* (London: Hodder & Stoughton, 1995).

Peterson, R. W., *Pigskin: The Early Years of Pro-Football* (New York: Oxford University Press, 1997).

Williams, G., 'Rugby Union' in T. Mason (ed.), *Sport in Britain. A Social History* (Cambridge: Cambridge University Press, 1989).

See also Folk Football

Tony Collins

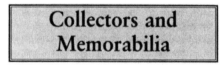

Collectors and Memorabilia

Until recent years, the collection of football memorabilia, although undoubtedly indulged in by fans, was neither particularly fashionable nor lucrative. Up until the mid-1980s it was a much less popular activity than collecting objects associated with other sports such as golf and cricket. The huge growth in football collectables from around that time mirrors the massive

Stamp celebrating the 1966 World Cup

boom in the game during the 1990s. This period is noted for a shift from the more traditional working-class supporter to a more affluent, middle-class spectator. This, combined with the commodification and commercialisation of the game, led to auction houses presenting sporting sales that either offered some football artefacts or were totally devoted to the game. Today dealers in sporting memorabilia specifically buy and sell football objects.

While the growth of auction houses and dealers specific to football has been reasonably slow, there now exists an organised collectors' network that makes it very difficult for people to find the bargains that could be had in the 1960s and '70s. Today's collectors are catered for by a wide variety of collecting clubs, associations, magazines, directories, specialist auction houses and dealers. Individual collectors may have a preference for items within a specific area of interest. They may also choose to collect contemporary collectables alongside memorabilia from earlier periods. Collectors are often aware that today's souvenir may become tomorrow's collectable. Many objects are quite affordable, as much memorabilia is essentially ephemera. It is relatively easy to amass a collection of programmes, autographs, postcards, cigarette cards, tickets, stamps, books and associated publications. This type of item can be bought for only a few pounds. Some collectors may want more than simple ephemeral objects and invest larger sums of money in collecting 'Living Memorabilia', such as football shirts, medals, equipment, and an assortment of objects awarded to, and owned by, footballers throughout the history of the game.

The more adventurous collector may choose to obtain works of fine art produced to celebrate the game, although in comparison to other sports there is little to collect, perhaps as a result of the adoption of the sport by the working classes in the late nineteenth century. Football also received much bad publicity during the First World War due to the fact that the Football League allowed the 1914/15 fixtures to be completed when many thought that they should be cancelled. As a result of these factors many sculptors, jewellers, potters and artists may have doubted the value of producing works of art associated with the game. Paradoxically, supporters of cricket and rugby, the recognised games of the public schools and gentlemen amateurs, could afford to direct their wealth into the commissioning of works of art. Even taking these circumstances into account, it has still been possible for the early collectors of football memorabilia, such as the late Harry Langton, to build up significant collections. Langton, who started buying in the 1950s, assembled a vast collection of paintings, prints, balls, boots, toys, games, ceramics and sculptures that eventually formed the basis of The National Football Museum's collections in Preston.

Prices for football related memorabilia continue to rise. Autographs can be bought for between £5 and £10. Shirts belonging to recognised players can be bought for £200 upwards, while a high-profile player's shirt may fetch several thousand pounds. The oldest international football shirt in the world, worn by England's Arnold Kirke Smith in 1872, sold for a record £25,000 while, at the time of writing in 2000, Geoff Hurst's 1966 World Cup shirt is expected to fetch £20,000. Similarly, former Liverpool and England star, Phil Neal – the most decorated player in English football history –

hopes to sell his personal collection of medals and trophies for a figure in excess of £100,000.

Sources:
Chilcott, D., *The Hamlyn Guide To Football Collectables* (London: Reed Consumer Books, 1995).

Further Reading:
FIFA, *F.I.F.A. Museum Collection* (Berlin: Verlags-GmbH, 1996).
Pickering, D., *The Cassell Soccer Companion* (London: Cassell, 1994).

See also Heritage

Mark Bushell

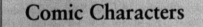

Comic Characters

'Real "Roy of the Rovers" stuff' is a phrase that has found its way into sporting language. Whenever a team snatches victory from the jaws of defeat, an unfancied lower-division side beats a Premiership giant, or a youngster scores the winning goal on his debut, commentators and headline writers even today invoke the name of the legendary Roy Race, who first appeared in the inaugural edition of *Tiger* comic as long ago as 11 September 1954. Young Roy appeared on the front cover of that issue as the blond, tousle-haired centre-forward of Milston Youth Club, but by the time his adventures were continued on the back page he had been signed by Melchester Rovers of the First Division. Thus began an amazing career with the fictional side in their distinctive red and yellow strip, which not only avoided clashing with that of any established team (with all due respect to Watford) but was also the easiest to reproduce using the colour printing technology available at the time. Roy graced the front cover of *Tiger* – not only winning matches for the Rovers but also solving the odd international mystery at half-time – until 1976, when his long service was rewarded with his own weekly paper, *Roy of the Rovers*. The veteran striker, by now Rovers' manager, was also editor of the new publication. Aided and abetted, on the field and off, by his trusty team-mates, including inside-right Blackie Gray and French right-winger Pierre Dupont, Roy helped his club to FA Cup victory in 1961 and the Division One title in 1980. No doubt his fans, who also followed Spurs and Liverpool, would have forgiven his creator Frank S. Pepper these moments of artistic licence. Throughout a career that lasted until 1993, when a decline in readership led to his spectacular demise in a helicopter crash, Roy had maintained an unblemished disciplinary record and scored over 5,000 goals, despite deliberately missing the odd penalty or blasting an easy chance high and wide to bring down an escaping jewel thief or would-be assassin in the stands.

The world of Melchester Rovers was surreally satirised from 1983 in the adult comic *Viz*, in the form of the strip *Billy the Fish*. Young Billy Thompson played in goal for Fulchester United, despite being born half man, half fish. No explanation was offered as to Billy's bizarre ancestry, nor his ability to hover in mid-air in his goalmouth. The rest of the team were no less fanciful: they included Red Fox, a scantily-clad (sometimes nude) Red Indian squaw; blind pensioner Rex Findlay, who never took the field without his guide dog, Shep; and Professor Wolfgang Schnell, who calculated every shot and header with mathematical precision. Billy and his chums continued their adventures in an animated TV series in 1990.

Between the extremes of the wholesome role model Roy Race and the outlandish Billy Thompson, a whole galaxy of football characters has graced British comics over the years. The traditional, heroic types included Limp-along Leslie (*New Hotspur* 1962–74, *Buddy* 1981–83, *Victor* 1983), the 14-year-old orphan crippled in a car accident that killed his parents, but determined to emulate his father by becoming a professional with Darbury Rangers. Leslie also appeared in the strip devoted to Iron Barr (*Spike* 1983/84, *Champ* 1984), who earned his nickname, and astonished young Leslie, by playing barefoot after taking over in the Rangers goal. In a strip subtitled 'It's Goals That Count' (*Hornet* 1965–76, *Hotspur* 1976–80) Nick Smith, another orphan, working in the circus for £3 a week with the sea-lions Horace and Hector, signed as a professional with Fourth Division Hamcastle United and went on to become England's inside-left. One of the country's greatest real-life stars also appeared in a cartoon strip. The prestigious *Eagle* ran a series from December 1950 entitled 'Football Hints By Billy Wright', in which the Wolves and England captain passed on his skills to young readers. Strangely enough, 'The Art Of Kicking' did not appear until No. 7 in the series.

If the comics' young readers couldn't aspire to the deeds of these heroes, there were many more light-hearted strips that gave a footballing twist to the eternal battle between schoolboys and conformity. Legge's Eleven (*Valiant* 1964–70), for instance, was the nickname of Rockley Rangers, also known as 'Britain's Strangest Soccer Team'. Led by the lanky Ted Legge, this team of eccentrics included Sir Darcy Lozenge, complete with monocle, another upper-class twit in the bespectacled Algernon Sims, hairy Scotsman Angus MacFee, Griffith Jones from wild and woolly Wales, debonair Frenchman Pierre Gaspard, the aptly-named Chubby Mann, hard man Badger Smith, the elusive Nipper Norton and the Tearaway Twins, Les and Ron. This merry band could play a bit; their assorted skills lifted them into the Second Division and in 1966 they valiantly overcame Brazilian side Grazia, who, in the comic world where anything is possible, were the current World Cup holders.

If this team contained a hero most readers could identify with, however tenuously, the same could in no way be said for another strip that appeared in the 1970s. Antchester United (*Plug* 1977–79, *Beezer* 1979), managed by Matt Bugsy and based at the Antfield Stadium, not only had all the talents but all the legs, and no doubt the country's biggest boot room. Many players in the real world enjoyed the dubious honour of being renamed via some of the worst puns in comic history. United's stars included George Beastie, Gnat Lofthouse, Kevin Beetle, Anty Gray, Brian Greenfly, Crawlin' Todd, David Larvae,

Francis Flea and Mantis Buchan. They even had Stirling Moth motoring up the wing. Mike Summerbee stood alone as the only player whose name survived intact. The regular referee for their matches was Samuel Peeps (who else?) and the official club programme, *The FlyPaper*, related the tale of the team of flies, beaten 36–0 and whose manager committed insecticide!

Yes, it's a funny old game, best summed up by Billy the Fish's boss, the deadpan Tommy Brown, manager of Fulchester United: 'As team manager my job has not been an easy one. I've been sacked, slandered in the gutter press, suffered a fatal heart attack, been kidnapped, taken to Mars, undergone a sex-change operation, and travelled back through time to caveman days. But that's football.'

Though the golden age of comics may have passed, the game is alive and well in cartoon form in the new millennium. Both the *Sun* and the *Mirror*, with Striker and Scorer respectively, cater for adult fans, featuring the modern footballer and his world of trophy girlfriends, lucrative endorsement deals and jet-set lifestyle, while *Dandy* and *Beano*, those children's favourites that have both survived since the 1930s, carry on the great comic tradition, each with a football-orientated character alongside old stalwarts such as Desperate Dan and Dennis the Menace. In *Dandy*, Owen Goal (geddit?) is a football-crazy young Dandy Town player yearning for the big time but never quite making it, while his *Beano* counterpart Ball Boy plays for his school team and is so obsessed with the game that, if Dad confiscates his ball and makes him work in the garden, he's not averse to booting a cabbage around. Heroes all, but there'll never be another Roy Race.

Sources:

Gifford, D., *Encyclopedia of Comic Characters* (Harlow: Longman, 1987).

Pickering, D., *The Cassell Soccer Companion* (London: Cassell, 1997).

Sabin, R., *Adult Comics: An Introduction* (London: Routledge, 1993).

Further Reading:

Gifford, D., *Happy Days: A Century of Comics* (London: Jupiter, 1975).

Morris, M. (ed.), *The Best of Eagle* (London: Michael Joseph, 1977).

See also Humour (Incidents of)

Tony Rennick

Corruption

Corruption in various guises has been present in the professional game from its earliest days. Proven cases of match-fixing or bribery of officials have been rare, and British football has generally enjoyed a reputation for probity in terms of its conduct and organisation on the pitch. Financial peculation off the pitch, usually involving transgressions of the game's own internal regulations, has been exposed more frequently.

Allegations of attempts to influence the result of matches by bribery, to ensure promotion or to avoid relegation, have proved virtually impossible to substantiate. Manchester City's Billy Meredith was suspended for a year in 1905 after being found guilty of offering Aston Villa's captain, Alec Leake, £10 to throw a match that would have secured the First Division title for City. Meredith tried to claim he was joking, but later said he had been instructed to approach Leake by the City manager, who was anxious to secure an equally illegal £100 win bonus. Usually such cases founder through lack of hard evidence; football's code of silence was broken in this instance because a third party overheard the conversation. Accusations of fixing games for gambling purposes are easier to prove. Enoch 'Knocker' West received a life ban for engineering the result of Manchester United's Easter 1915 game against Liverpool by bribing some of the Merseyside team's players. Suspicions were aroused when numerous bets were placed across the country predicting the 2–0 United victory, and the crowd booed the obviously lackadaisical play. West vigorously contested the sentence several times in court, but this ban was only lifted in 1945 as part of a general amnesty, when he was 59. In 1924, John Browning, a former Scottish international, was jailed along with another ex-player, Archie Kyle, for attempting to fix the result of a Scottish League fixture involving Bo'Ness and Lochgelly.

Perhaps the most notorious case of match-fixing occurred during the early 1960s, resulting in prison sentences and life suspensions for several footballers including two England internationals, Peter Swan of Sheffield Wednesday and Everton's Tony Kay. Both were found guilty of conspiring to fix the result of the Ipswich v. Sheffield Wednesday match in December 1962, when Kay was a Wednesday player. Other players were more deeply involved, but Swan and Kay gained most notoriety because of their standing in football. They were found guilty of ensuring Wednesday's defeat by Ipswich Town in 1962 and pocketing £100 each from betting on their own team to lose. Further cases were uncovered by a police investigation and eventually 33 players were prosecuted, ten receiving jail sentences of up to four years. The Wednesday players, along with colleague David 'Bronco' Layne, though minor figures in the scandal, bore the brunt of the notoriety.

The international implications of betting on football became apparent when the goalkeepers Bruce Grobbelaar and Hans Seegers, and Wimbledon's John Fashanu, were acquitted in 1997 for a second time of charges of match-fixing in 25 Liverpool, Southampton and Wimbledon games for a shadowy Malaysian betting syndicate. Grobbelaar later sued the *Sun* newspaper for libel over its published allegations, but although initially successful, an appeal court overturned the judgement in January 2001.

Under Far Eastern betting rules wagers on matches abandoned after half-time are not declared void and stand on the score when the match was called off. Four men were successfully prosecuted for taking advantage of this rule and sabotaging floodlights at two English Premier League games at Upton Park and Selhurst Park, both televised live internationally. The men were arrested before they could simi-larly disrupt a third game in 1999 between Charlton and Liverpool on behalf of a Hong Kong syndicate.

British clubs have also been on the receiving end of match-fixing in European competitions. Leeds United's 1–0 defeat by AC Milan in the 1973 European Cup Winners' Cup final was secured partly by the highly suspect performance of the Greek referee, who was suspended by UEFA and later struck off the refereeing list, though the result stood. British officials have largely escaped such censure.

The restrictions on players' wages and transfer fees in force until 1963 led to a widespread flouting of the regulations regarding extra payments to players to supplement their wages. Once the maximum wage for professionals was fixed at £4 in England in 1900, clubs routinely broke the rule, offering extra financial incentives to attract and retain the best players. At least seven clubs were punished for irregularities between 1901 and 1911. Steve Bloomer, one of the greatest stars of the time, was suspended for 14 days in 1906 for accepting an illegal signing-on bonus from Middlesbrough. Though these inducements were an open secret in the game, most were undetected, as it was to neither players' nor club officials' advantage to report them. Billy Meredith only revealed Manchester City's liberality with such payments in 1905 when he fell out with the club during his suspension for bribery. His accusations led to the first team being torn apart in June 1906. Its directors were suspended, its players barred from ever appearing for City again, and the club was fined £250.

When evidence of illegal payments was uncovered, punishments were draconian. In 1919, Leeds City was expelled from the Second Division for allegedly making illegal payments to players, and was forced to re-form as Leeds United. Sunderland was fined the enormous sum of £5,000 by the F.A for irregular payments in 1957. Some directors were given life bans and players adjudged to have received extra money were punished. The ending of the maximum wage did not spell the demise of illegal payments, though since then most cases of corruption have centred on 'bungs' – bribes offered to schoolboy players and their families or older professionals to join particular clubs, or to managers and agents as part of transfer dealings.

In 1970 Derby County was fined £10,000 for 'administrative irregularities'. Swindon Town's promotion to the Second Division in 1990 was overturned and the club relegated to the Third Division after an FA investigation uncovered widespread financial irregularities (and illegal betting – usually that Swindon would lose – by the previous manager Lou Macari and club chairman Brian Hillier). On appeal the club was reinstated to the Second Division but not to the First. A *World In Action* television exposé in 1980 accused Manchester United of luring schoolboy stars to sign for the club by offering their parents a range of incentives, including washing machines, refrigerators, cookers and even three freezers of ice cream. Heavy fines by the FA have not deterred clubs from making illegal approaches to promising youngsters.

In the 1990s both Chelsea and Tottenham Hotspur received huge punishments for financial corruption. Chelsea was fined £105,000 in 1991 for illegal payments on transfers. An Inland Revenue investigation discovered Spurs had made substantial payments to players signing for the club, sums that were then not declared for tax purposes. The FA enquiry in 1994 found Spurs guilty on 40 charges. Spurs were fined £600,000, 12 points were deducted from their next season's League total, and they were banned from the FA Cup for a year. Unlike Swindon Town, Tottenham successfully challenged the FA ruling in the courts, halving the 12-point deduction and avoiding relegation as a result. The team was also reinstated in the FA Cup.

Players, managers and clubs found guilty of corruption often resent being made scapegoats for practices they claim are widespread in the professional game. In 1993 the FA responded to the number of press allegations about 'bungs' to managers and players' agents that had been made in the press and set up an enquiry team to investigate transfer irregularities. Only one manager has actually been found

guilty, despite frequent tabloid stories involving high-profile figures. George Graham was banned for a year from football, and subsequently sacked as Arsenal manager, because he accepted a 'gift' of £140,000 in £50 notes from the Norwegian agent, Rune Hauge, followed by a further payment of £285,000 Graham was bitter that he was singled out for prosecution. The belief remains that most 'sleaze' and corruption in British football continues to go unpunished, and that it has reached new levels of financial complexity which make much of it impossible to unravel.

Sources:

Chaudery, V. and Gregoriadis, L., 'Floodlights Scam to Beat Bookies', *Guardian* (21 August 1999), p. 7.

Harding, J., *Football Wizard: The Billy Meredith Story* (London: Robson Books, 1998).

Inglis, S., *Soccer In the Dock: A History of British Football Scandals 1900 to 1965* (London: Willow Books, 1985).

Sharpe, G, *Gambling on Goals: A Century of Football Betting* (Edinburgh: Mainstream, 1997).

Williams, R., *Football Babylon* (London: Virgin, 1996).

Further Reading:

Campbell, D., Shields, A. and May, P., *The Lad Done Bad: Sex, Sleaze and Scandal in English Football* (London: Penguin, 1996).

Cosgrove, S., *Hampden Babylon: Sex and Scandal in Scottish Football* (Edinburgh: Canongate, 1991).

See also Careers Cut Short, Gambling

Joyce Woolridge

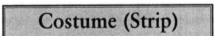

Costume (Strip)

Following the codification of public school football in the mid-nineteenth century, suitable items of apparel began to be recommended for the sport. Early playing kit was not dissimilar to that of cricket, and generally consisted of shirt, flannel trousers, sturdy boots, and a tasselled cap.

Figure of Blackburn Rovers player in early kit
(National Football Museum)

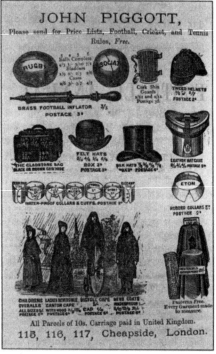

John Piggott equipment ad, Football Annual,
1886 (National Football Museum)

Routledge's *Football Handbook* for 1867 recommended to have one side with striped jerseys of one colour, say red, and the other with another, say blue. Not only were teams distinguished by contrasting colours, but individual players could be identified by specific cap or stocking designs, as for instance Queen's Park's English Cup tie against the Wanderers in 1875. Wanderers' Kenrick wore a cerise and French grey cap while fellow winger Heron sported an orange, violet, and black cap.

University and public school teams adopted specific colours or patterns for their shirts, though when working-class northern men began to play the game they generally did so in their workaday clothes. Direct survivals of early shirt designs include Queen's Park (narrow black and white hoops) and Blackburn Rovers (blue and white halves). Some early kits utilised bizarre colours, such as chocolate and mauve, or curious designs such as the spotted shirts of the early Bolton Wanderers. Other famous clubs took years or decades to establish what are now regarded as their traditional colours. Everton, for instance, sported an all-black strip in the early 1880s.

Around the turn of the century, football shirt designs had settled into a few standardised alternatives. For example: plain, stripes, hoops, halves, 'V's, bands, or sashes. In 1891, the Football League decreed that all clubs were to register their colours during the close season. In the event of a clash, the home team was instructed to change (this was altered to the away team in 1921). Some bizarre ideas were proposed, in view of the significance that club colours have since assumed. A century ago, Liverpool and Manchester United proposed that every home team always play in red, with away teams in white, in all League matches.

Early shirts were normally flannelette, with buttoned-down or laced collars, such styles surviving until the 1950s. Aston Villa preferred woollen jerseys with a broad light-blue band woven around the neck. Some clubs received permission to use their local borough's coat of arms and embroidered versions were sewn onto the breasts of shirts. Others devised their own heraldic-style badges.

Knickerbockers were preferred to cricket trousers from about the 1870s. They were made from serge, swansdown, or lambskin, and generally needed a belt. In 1904, in response to the then outrageous habit of hitching up shorts, as practised, for instance, by Manchester United's Charlie Roberts, the FA insisted that knickers cover the knee! Though losing some length, long baggy shorts remained fashionable throughout the inter-war period, one of the most distinctive, almost comical pairs belonging to Alex James of Arsenal and Scotland.

Initially, hosiery was not considered important in a footballer's uniform; players often sported individually coloured socks even in professional teams. Remarkably, it was only in 1937 that the Football League required clubs to register their colour and design. Very thick, often hooped socks were popular from about 1920 to 1960. Leeds United led a brief fashion for decorative garters in the early 1970s. Shin guards were reputedly invented in 1874 by the Nottingham Forest player Sam Widdowson. These were originally worn outside the socks, and held in place with leather straps, rather like cricket pads. Later versions could be inserted into socks but even these were bulky by comparison with the lightweight protection available today.

Confusingly, goalkeepers originally wore the same colours as their teammates. From 1909 they were distinguished by scarlet, blue, or white jerseys. Three years later, the favoured green jersey was also permitted. These were woollen, with a thick, rolled-down collar; only from the mid-1950s were lighter padded jerseys available. Only yellow jerseys were permitted in international games from 1921, although the same colour was also obligatory for Scottish FA Cup ties. Laws relating to the keeper's colours were slackened during the 1980s as kit manufacturers lobbied to produce a wider range of designs.

Goalkeepers can also wear caps and gloves, although many outfield players now also wear the latter as protection from the cold. Flat caps were once *de rigueur*, though woolly hats or baseball-type headgear are now preferred options. During the winter, keepers frequently don tracksuit bottoms, a practice popular since the 1970s.

In the early 1950s British football kit began to look very outdated in comparison to the sleek attire of the Europeans and South Americans. Modern 'V' neck shirts were introduced by mid-decade and lighter synthetic materials became acceptable. The 1960s look included round collars, continental-style shorts, and plain socks. Some clubs modernised traditional designs; simpler one-colour kits were adopted by Liverpool, Leeds, and Chelsea.

By the 1970s, collared shirts had returned with basic designs remaining fairly traditional, though sleeve-stripes had become virtually obligatory. The next decade brought radical alterations to the appearance of kits. From the late 1970s, sponsors' names could be displayed on shirts, though the restrictions were strict. Initially allowed only at non-league level, corporate names soon appeared on sewn patches, but major clubs began to order shirts with the sponsor's identity integrated into the fabric. In attempting to incorporate sponsorship logos, designers demanded more freedom in styling kits. Some shirts became outlandish, curious patterns and squiggly flourishes bearing a closer resemblance to casual summer wear. Team shirts were also becoming a badge of allegiance on the terraces and clubs began to realise the commercial potential of 'replica' shirts, maximising revenue by altering strip design virtually every season. Manchester United are among several clubs criticised for a proliferation of regularly updated designer kits. One of these proved embarrassingly non-practical. During a match at Southampton in 1996, United used a grey away strip which proved difficult to see in peripheral vision. More conventional shirts were adopted in the second half of the match. Shorts have become somewhat baggier during the 1990s, and some players also occasionally wear close-fitting thermal shorts under their kit.

Shirts were numbered experimentally in some English league matches in 1928 and for the 1933 Cup Final, but the practice was not made obligatory until the 1938/39 season. For many years, Celtic were the only major British club to resist shirt numbering. Numerals originally corresponded to specific positions, but in the Premier League and internationals this practice has been superseded by squad numbering. The English and Scottish Premier Leagues also oblige clubs to display players' surnames on shirts.

Officials originally wore ordinary clothes, but as physical demands increased referees and linesmen began to wear short trousers. Black was adopted as a neutral colour but referees continued to wear blazers and sometimes even ties into the 1930s. Following the Second World War, referees' attire was modernised, though long shorts remained until the 1970s. Black with white trimmings remain the preferred outfit, but the Premier League initially supplied green pin-striped tops, and other colour/design combinations have been used depending on context.

Sources:
Bickerton, B., *Club Colours – An Illustrated History of Football Clubs and their Kits* (London: Hamlyn, 1998).

Further Reading:
Fabian, A. H., 'Equipment' in A. H. Fabian and G. Green, G. (eds), *Association Football*, Vol. 2 (London: Caxton, 1960), pp. 75–8.
Morris, D., 'The Costumes', 'The Colours' and 'The Emblems' in Morris, D., *The Soccer Tribe* (London: Jonathan Cape, 1981), pp. 193–210.

Tom Preston

Crowd Control and Management

For all forms of professional sport the safety of the spectators is now of paramount importance. For football this has particular significance given the disasters that have occurred leading to the deaths of supporters. It was the tragic events at Ibrox, Bradford and Hillsborough that eventually prompted legislative action to govern safety. Prior to this, government policy, largely based on concerns around cost, had been to leave safety issues to the clubs and governing bodies. The post-Hillsborough era is now more heavily regulated than previously, with safety a fundamental issue. With football crowds there is the additional element of supporter behaviour, and this has also strongly influenced legislative action. Thus while safety is the prime aspect of crowd control and management, the related issue of public order is also of great concern.

The safety of football spectators may be provided for in a number of ways. First, the owner of the football ground itself will have obligations to spectators whether they are paying customers or not, extending to potential civil liability if a spectator is injured on the premises. In addition, after the Hillsborough disaster, the government created the Football Licensing Authority, under the Football Spectators Act (1989). The role of the authority is to operate a licensing scheme for grounds where a designated football match is played, advise the government on the introduction of all-seater stadia, and, most importantly, 'to keep under review the discharge by local authorities of their functions under the Safety of Sports Grounds Act (1975)'. To this end, the Football Licensing Authority has published a series of guidance documents and instigated a review of the 'Green Guide', a document which provides assistance on the requirements for safety at sports grounds. Hillsborough certainly put the issue of safety high up football's agenda, and the certification scheme under which grounds have to be licensed was designed to prevent such disasters recurring.

One of the prime manifestations of Hillsborough, and the consequent Taylor Report, was the move towards all-seater stadia. At the same time, the 'policing' of the ground was increasingly passed over to club stewards rather than managed by police officers. A major reason for this

Crowd control during the 1923 FA Cup Final (National Football Museum)

switch was the high cost of using police officers, which had to be borne by the club. Paradoxically, the move towards using stewards has lessened the effectiveness of the legislation, since stewards are apparently less likely to intervene in certain areas. Seated spectators are also clearly easier to control and identify through controls over the supply of ticketing and the development of membership schemes. Other measures such as CCTV mean that individuals can be more readily identified, and this has affected the public order dimension of crowd management.

Football and public order have long been uneasy bedfellows. In the medieval and early modern periods football games were highly regulated by the state, as it was felt that football was not a suitable pastime. While football did attain some level of respectability as part of the Victorian push towards values of muscular Christianity, it has still, at times, been heavily policed. This area has become more pronounced since the 1980s, with a series of legal interventions designed to control football fans. The Conservative administrations reacted to a number of flashpoints, particularly embarrassing incidents abroad, involving both clubs and the national side. Widespread domestic hooliganism coupled with the disasters led to the enactment of a series of legislative provisions, often specific to football, that have led to this area becoming heavily rule bound. These measures have included the Football Spectators Act (1989), the Football (Offences) Act (1991) and the Criminal Justice and Public Order Act (1994). This legislative process was continued by New Labour, with both the Football (Offences and Disorder) Act (1999), and the Football Disorder Act (2000) enacted during the Labour Government's first parliament – each arguably even more rigorous than those of the previous administrations.

The changing shape and control of grounds has had a number of effects. Firstly, the move towards all-seater stadia has produced an environment that encourages more families and women to participate in football, and figures show that there has been a move away from the more traditional bedrock of support in lieu of this. Grounds have become safer and generally more pleasant places with much improved facilities, and have encouraged a new audience which is, rather ironically, less likely to need the controls that have been introduced.

Sources:
Football Licensing Authority, *Annual Report and Accounts* (London).

Further Reading:
Greenfield, S. and Osborn, G., 'When the Writ Hits the Fan: Panic Law and Football Fandom', in A. Brown (ed.), *Fanatics! Power Identity and Fandom in Football* (Routledge: London, 1998).

Steve Greenfield and Guy Osborn

Deaths on the Pitch

Deaths on the pitch in modern football are now so rare as to be virtually unheard of. The pages of *The Lancet*, the prominent and influential medical journal, however, suggest a different picture historically. Concern in the late nineteenth century about the dramatic number of serious injuries and deaths led to a record being kept. The medical journalists did not carry out a campaign in the modern sense but merely recorded events. For both soccer and rugby there were in the period 1891–99 about 96 deaths.

It has to be recalled that during that era many games were loosely regulated events involving enthusiastic young men. The condition of the pitches and the availability of medical attention was poor. Heavy football boots and the leather ball added to the risks. The number of deaths is a reflection of current medical knowledge of sports injuries as much as the inherent dangers of playing the game.

Three important articles in *The Lancet* provide a valuable insight into earlier modes of play. In the issue for 24 March 1894 it was noted that 'in older times a man stuck to the ball till he lost it. His tor-

tuous course across the ground was often comparatively slow from commencement, and necessarily slow if he was successful in retaining the ball any length of time.' By the 1890s the ball was being 'hurried along by combined effort, being bandied from man to man as each runs at the top of his speed'. As the pace of the game increased so did the dangers. In the same article particular concern was expressed about the practice of charging a man trying to head a football: '... to smash cruelly into him and knock him over unnecessarily and perhaps savagely is clearly a brutality which is permitted by the rules'. Foul play and insubordinate behaviour did not go unnoticed as relevant factors.

The Lancet continued to record details and concluded on 22 April 1899 that the dangers, while statistically small, were still universally present, although by that period not so great as they had been some years earlier. It was written that 'the reason for this is that local and central organisations alike have learned to take more care that clubs whose members do not exhibit the proper sporting spirit should be punished'. This improvement in attitude continued until it was suggested in *The Lancet* of 1 November 1905 that there seemed to be fewer accidents than previously. The cause of the increase in incidents had been the introduction of a scientific style of play, marked by greater pace and accurate and quick passing, and collisions while travelling at rapid speed became frequent. The powers of referees had since become very strong, and that seemed to have reduced accidents.

Three deaths associated with football in Britain are worth remembering because of the points they illustrate. In April 1889 James Tattershall, a Leyland footballer, disputed a goal allowed by a referee and seems to have attacked him. The referee died. Tattershall was indicted for manslaughter but acquitted when it was shown that the referee had a pre-existing medical condition. Uncontrolled tempers and insubordination may have been common factors in rowdy games.

In November 1896 Joseph Powell of Arsenal went to kick a high ball during a game at Kettering. His foot caught on the shoulder of an opponent and Powell fell and broke his arm. He was attended to by some people who were said to be first-aiders, but one apparently fainted at the sight of the protruding bone. Infection set in and, despite amputation above the elbow, Powell died. At the subsequent inquest specific reference was made to the sloping ground. Even skilled professionals did not necessarily have the best facilities available to them.

Finally, in September 1931 John Thomson, the goalkeeper of Glasgow Celtic, went to collect the ball from the feet of a Rangers player, but in doing so Thomson's head hit the knee of the other player. Thomson sustained a fractured skull and died in hospital not long afterwards.

In the twentieth century there were few, if any other deaths on the football pitch. Professionalism had speeded up the game, but with time and experience temperaments became restrained and violent confrontation receded. Amateurs doubtless sought to follow the style and approach of the professionals. Moreover, professional footballers would not wish to risk their lucrative positions by sustaining unnecessary injuries. In the fullness of time insurance companies might dictate terms, and medical knowledge improve dramatically, though, of course, accidents will still happen.

Sources:
The Lancet (various issues, 1889–1905).
Law Gazette, 65, 1 (March 1997).
Shiels, R., 'The Death Of John Thomson', *Scottish Law Gazette*, 65, 1 (March 1997).

See also Careers Cut Short

Robert Shiels

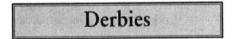

Derbies

The term 'derby match' or 'local derby' probably derives from the Shrove Tuesday folk football match played between the parishes of All Saints and St Peter's in the town of Derby. Deemed a threat to public

order in the politically charged 1840s, it was finally suppressed in 1846 after the intervention of a troop of cavalry. Nothing is guaranteed to inflame the passions of a football supporter more than a contest with 'the enemy', the team from down the road, especially when other factors mix with simple local rivalry. Religious division lies at the heart of the 'Old Firm' conflict in Glasgow, where the game, not just in the city but in Scotland, has long been dominated by Rangers, heroes of the Protestant establishment, and Celtic, formed in 1888 as representatives of the Irish immigrant community. In 1989 both camps were stunned when Rangers signed Maurice Johnston, from French club Nantes, from under the noses of Celtic, who had been trying to re-sign their ex-player. Crowds besieged Ibrox in an orgy of shirt-burning, incensed that Rangers had finally signed a Catholic. In the words of Jonathan Swift:

> We have just enough religion to make us hate but not enough to make us love each other.

The North London friction can be traced back to 1913, when Arsenal crossed the river from Woolwich and set up home near Tottenham. When league football resumed after the First World War, Tottenham, who had finished bottom of the First Division in 1915, expected to be safe from relegation as both First and Second Divisions were to be extended from 20 to 22 teams; but it was not to be. Following secret negotiations between Arsenal chairman Sir Henry Norris and League president John McKenna, the two top Second Division sides, Derby and Preston, were promoted, along with Arsenal, who had finished sixth. Spurs went down. Bitter rivalry was cemented by such shenanigans, to such an extent that many Spurs fans consider their team's greatest achievement to be not the historic Cup and League double of 1960/61 but the 3–1 defeat of Arsenal in the first Wembley FA Cup semi-final in 1991.

The Merseyside rivalry has just as strange an origin. When the Football League was founded in 1888 Everton were one of the original twelve clubs.

Martin Keown and Les Ferdinand compete for the ball in the North London derby between Tottenham and Arsenal

(© Stuart MacFarlane, Arsenal FC)

When chairman and landlord John Houlding tried to raise the rent of the ground where they played, the club moved across Stanley Park to Goodison, and Houlding responded by forming a new club. Both claimed the right to the name Everton; Houlding finally lost and Liverpool FC was born. Fans of both teams can be found to this day in the same family and were allowed to mix at Wembley for the League Cup final in 1984. A drawn match resulted in the famous old stadium ringing to cries of: 'Merseyside, Merseyside'.

In 1998, with Manchester United preparing for a crucial game against Bayern Munich that could put them into the quarter-finals of the Champion's League, their rivals Manchester City were scraping a draw with Third Division Darlington in the second round of the FA Cup. City fan Colin Shindler can be forgiven for describing in *Manchester United Ruined My Life* how it felt to be a little boy with his nose pressed up against the

sweet shop window watching United supporters take all the wine gums.

Other fairly intense rivalries can be found in Belfast, Birmingham, Bristol, Dundee (where Dundee's Dens Park and United's Tannadice Park are only 100 yards apart), Edinburgh, Sheffield and indeed any city or town where two clubs compete on a roughly equal footing. Over the years, the term 'derby match' has also come to embrace games between clubs in neighbouring towns. Particularly since the 1960s, these once 'friendly' rivalries have become anything but that. One of the most striking is that between Burnley and Blackburn Rovers, clubs lying just a few miles apart in East Lancashire. During a Fourth Division play-off game at Burnley in the early 1990s, Rovers' fans (some claim a Rovers player to have been responsible) paid for a plane to fly over Burnley's ground trailing a banner reading 'STAYING DOWN FOREVER'. When, in 1994, Rovers were beaten in a UEFA Cup game by Swedish part-timers Trelleborgs, graffiti appeared on a Burnley road sign declaiming 'Burnley. Twinned with Trelleborgs'. Who said it was only a game?

Sources:

Barwick, B., and Sinstadt, G., *The Great Derbies: Everton v Liverpool* (London: BBC, 1988).

Inglis, S., *The Football Grounds of Great Britain* (London: Collins Willow, 1996).

Shindler, C., *Manchester United Ruined My Life* (London: Headline, 1998).

Tony Rennick

Directors

While many football club directors have been low-key figures of whom little is known, others have maintained a much higher profile. Today many of the leading club chairmen and directors – for example Martin Edwards (Manchester United), Doug Ellis (Aston Villa), Ken Bates (Chelsea) and David Murray (Rangers) – are well known through their television appearances. Throughout the history of British football there have been other directors who have been notable for a variety of reasons.

A number of former players have moved from the football field to the boardroom, and this is not just a recent development. At least ten professional players who operated before 1914 went on to serve as club directors, including John Devey and Howard Spencer (Aston Villa), Jack Sharp (Everton), Billy Bassett (West Bromwich Albion) and Bob Crompton (Blackburn Rovers). In Scotland Rangers' international winger Alan Morton joined the Glasgow club's board in 1933 when his playing career ended. Billy Bassett, capped 16 times by England, became a director at West Bromwich in 1905 and remained on the board for 32 years, most of those as chairman. He was also a member of the Football League management committee, as was another ex-England player Phil Bach, a Middlesbrough director from 1911.

As well as the ex-professionals mentioned above it is worth mentioning two notable amateur players who served as directors. Vivian Woodward, capped 23 times by England, was appointed as a director while still playing for Tottenham Hotspur in 1908. When he left to join Chelsea a year later he resigned, but went on to serve on Chelsea's board. Harold Hardman, capped by England at amateur and full levels, became a director of Manchester United in 1912 and remained there almost continuously until his death in 1965. In 1951 he was appointed chairman and he worked closely with Matt Busby in building up the club during the 1950s and '60s.

In recent times many ex-players have held important positions on the boards of football clubs. These include Jimmy Hill (Fulham), Joe Mercer (Coventry), Stan Seymour (Newcastle United), Matt Busby (Manchester United), Francis Lee and Dennis Tueart (Manchester City), Derek Dougan (Wolverhampton Wanderers) and Dave Whelan (Wigan Athletic). There has also been a trend towards the inclusion of celebrities as directors, and while some have been appointed for publicity purposes others have played important roles. The comedian Tommy Trinder was prominent as chairman of Fulham, while Watford's Elton John played a significant part in his club's rise to Division One in the late 1970s and early 1980s. Charlie Williams, who played for Doncaster Rovers in the 1950s, and later found fame as a comedian, managed to combine the roles of ex-player and celebrity when he became a director of Barnsley in 1976. Williams was also one of the earliest examples of a black director at a football club, the first known black director of a Football League club being Ismail Gibrail, a Somalian businessman who joined Blackpool's board in 1967. Blackpool also recorded a notable first in 1996 when Vicki Oyston became the first female chairperson of a League club.

Other directors have been notable for their long service. Will Cuff was on Everton's board from 1895 to 1938, also serving on the Football League Management Committee and becoming League president in 1939. Perhaps those who are best remembered, though, are those directors whose careers involved controversy and scandal. Henry Norris, chairman of Arsenal, was responsible for moving the club to Highbury in 1913 and securing their place in Division One in 1919, as well as appointing the legendary Herbert Chapman as manager. However, Norris' involvement in football ended in 1929 when he was banned by the FA for financial irregularities. Sunderland chairman Bill Ditchburn was similarly suspended in 1957, although his ban was later overturned. More recently the publisher Robert Maxwell courted controversy by proposing to merge his club Oxford United with neighbours Reading. Maxwell later became chairman of Derby County and fell foul of the authorities when he tried to purchase a major shareholding in Watford.

Sources:

Inglis, S., *League Football and the Men Who Made It: The Official Centenary History of the Football League 1888–1988* (London: Willow, 1988).

Lamming, D., *An England Football Internationalists' Who's Who 1872–1988* (Beverley: Hutton, 1990).

Mason, T., *Association Football and English Society 1863–1915* (Brighton: Harvester, 1980).

Further Reading:

Ellis, D., *Deadly!* (Warley: Sports Projects, 1998).

Hill, J., *The Jimmy Hill Story: My Autobiography* (London: Hodder & Stoughton, 1998).

Tomas, J., *Soccer Czars: A Compelling Insight Into the Lives of the Tycoons Running the Big Clubs and British Football* (Edinburgh: Mainstream, 1996).

John Coyle

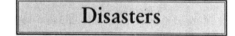

Disasters

What constitutes a 'disaster' is very much a subjective judgement, but it can be loosely defined as an event that causes death and/or destruction on a significant scale. Over the course of the twentieth century, football has suffered some horrific disasters, but it is in many ways surprising that such tragedies have not occurred more frequently. The rapid speed with which the game's popularity developed in the late nineteenth century meant that football grounds were built quickly and crudely. Any profits that clubs made were usually invested in players rather than spectators' facilities. Eager to see their teams successful, fans were usually happy with such priorities. Thus, as the century progressed and the game developed on and off the field, improvements in the condition of grounds were limited. Indeed, as financial problems became more common from the late 1970s onwards, the condition of many grounds actually deteriorated. Put simply, the assembly of large numbers of excited supporters on decrepit terraces was a recipe for disaster.

On 5 April 1902, at Ibrox Park, Glasgow, a wooden stand collapsed during a match between Scotland and England. People plunged forty feet through the broken boards; 26 were killed and over 500 injured. Play continued as the bodies were recovered from the wreckage. One observer noted that 'Not even the cries of dying sufferers nor the sight of broken limbs could attract this football maddened crowd from gazing upon their beloved sport.' At half-time the scale of the tragedy became apparent and the second half was played out in a token manner. The Ibrox incident was not the first accident at a football match. Occasional incidents of serious injuries caused by overcrowding were not unknown in the late nineteenth century, and bruises and crushes must have been fairly common occurrences for spectators at the more popular clubs. However, Ibrox in 1902 marked the beginning of a series of fatal football disasters that demonstrated unlearned lessons and frightening parallels.

Doubts over the quality of the wood used in the Ibrox stand led to an unsuccessful prosecution of the manufacturer for culpable homicide. The potential danger had not been unknown. A local newspaper noted that regular supporters 'in the know' avoided the collapsed end of the stand. The disaster spelt the end of wooden terraces. It thus produced a specific response that addressed the direct causes of the tragedy rather than an attempt to learn wider lessons. The disaster was seen as a technical failure in the building of stadia rather than a product of the industry's desire to pack in as many spectators as possible, with minimal expenditure on their safety and comfort.

A near-disaster occurred at the 1923 FA Cup Final, the first ever to be held at Wembley. Perhaps as many as 250,000 supporters packed the stadium amidst scenes of chaos in which 1,000 people were injured. The subsequent public recriminations ensured that future Cup finals were held on an all-ticket basis. However, the overriding legacy of the day was the belief that order had been restored by a single policeman on a white horse and the appearance of the King. Rather than creating an awareness of the potential danger of large crowds, the match was remembered for the essential orderliness and good behaviour of the English.

Nonetheless, concerns were widespread enough to lead to the holding of a public inquiry which recommended certain technical measures and the licensing of grounds by local authorities. The attitude of the FA to such intervention in what it regarded as an internal matter was demonstrated by its refusal to give evidence to the inquiry. The inquiry's report had almost no political impact and its recommendations had little effect on the management of football grounds.

Despite the huge popularity of football, and occasional isolated deaths in packed crowds, the remainder of the inter-war period saw no further disasters. The continued complacency of the football industry towards the safety of its customers was shattered by the Burnden Park disaster on 9 March 1946. An FA Cup match between Bolton Wanderers and Stoke City was witnessed by a crowd estimated at nearly 80,000. As paying supporters were joined by locked-out fans clambering in over walls, the overcrowding on the crude terrace was exacerbated by the opening of a gate by a spectator trying to escape. Helpless supporters were pushed down a barrier-less section of the embankment under the weight of the crowd; some were crushed to death, others trampled underfoot. Thirty-three people died and over 400 were injured.

The subsequent inquiry noted,

How easy it is for a dangerous situation to arise in a crowded enclosure. It happens again and again without fatal, or even injurious, consequences. But its danger is that it requires so little influence – an involuntary sway, an exciting moment, a comparatively small addition to the crowd, the failure of one part of one barrier – to translate the danger in terms of death and injuries.

The inquiry recommended the scientific calculation of ground capacities, mechanical counting of spectators entering and a system of central co-ordination of crowd control and management. Central to the proposals was, once more, the recommendation for a licensing scheme run by local authorities. Government plans for legislation based on the report failed to materialise amidst concerns that the safety of football fans was not a priority at a time when resources were already overstretched by the rebuilding of war-torn Britain. Instead, a system of voluntary regulation was implemented whereby clubs simply notified the FA that an unspecified authority had certified their ground as safe.

Falling attendances and limited investment in grounds meant that the safety of watching football did improve marginally over the next 20 years. However, the emerging problem of hooliganism meant that the issue of crowd management came to be viewed by clubs and authorities through a different lens. Crowd trouble did ensure that the British Football Associations now demanded annual safety certificates, but clubs were still very much entrusted with ensuring the safety of their supporters as they saw fit. It took another disaster to highlight the inadequacy of such a system of self-regulation.

On 2 January 1971, 66 people were killed at Ibrox Park, Glasgow. A myth persists that the cause is thought to have been leaving spectators turning around when a late goal was scored, but it was more likely a combination of bad design and a falling spectator. A fatal crush ensued on a stairway; two people had been killed in a crush on the same stairway in 1961. The subsequent inquiry again recommended a licensing system operated by local authorities. However, it noted that the cost to small clubs of implementing large-scale safety measures was potentially crippling, and argued that the risk to fans was not large enough to justify jeopardising the very existence of smaller clubs in the short term. Many supporters would have agreed that the future of such clubs was worth the risk they took in entering their grounds.

The obvious failure of football's self-regulation of safety meant that legislation followed. The 1975 Safety at Sports Grounds Act was based upon the Ibrox inquiry's recommendations. It established a system of inspection by local authorities and a series of technical safety requirements in football grounds. Because of the cost, the Act initially only applied to clubs in the English First Division and Scottish Premier Division (plus the three international rugby grounds in Britain). It was extended to clubs in the English Second Division in 1979. The system thus created an anomaly whereby small grounds such as Shrewsbury's (capacity 16,800) were designated under the Act but large stadia such as Sheffield United's (capacity 44,000) were not.

The impact and perceived importance of a disaster is not dependent upon the death toll. In football, nowhere is this clearer than with regard to the Munich crash of 6 February 1958. The aeroplane carrying Manchester United back from their European Cup quarter-final against Red Star Belgrade crashed, with the loss of 23 lives, while trying to take off after a refuelling stop in Munich. Eight of the Busby Babes, as the young team were known, were killed, including the supremely talented Duncan Edwards. The manager Matt Busby was also seriously injured. This tragedy continues to occupy a central place in football's folklore and was integral in creating the image of Manchester United as a unique club. Its memory has completely overshadowed the more deadly post-war disasters of Ibrox and Burnden Park. Football is a sport con-cerned with glory and heroes. In this light, the fate of its supporters is easily overlooked in the long-term perspective.

The 1980s were football's darkest decade. Hooliganism appeared to be escalating, culminating in events at the European Cup final at the Heysel Stadium on 29 May 1985. A wall collapsed, killing 39 Juventus fans who were trying to escape a charge by Liverpool supporters. The result was the banning of English clubs from European competitions. Two weeks earlier, on 11 May 1985, 56 fans had been killed in a fire at Bradford City's Valley Parade. With Bradford in the Third Division, their ground was not subject to the 1975 Sports Safety Act. Ironically, the match saw the club celebrate promotion and, as part of the preparations for bringing the ground under the Act, the fire risk presented by combustible rubbish under the fatal wooden stand had already been identified. The financial cost of ensuring safety meant that clubs tended to do only what legislation demanded. Had the Act covered all divisions then such a known risk would not have been allowed to remain unrectified.

The Bradford disaster highlighted the continuing dangers that ageing grounds across the country presented. The Safety at Sports Grounds Act was thus immediately extended to all clubs in the Football League, but the wider response to the disaster was entangled with the Heysel tragedy. Despite protests in Bradford and Parliament, a single inquiry under Lord Justice Popplewell was established to investigate Bradford, Heysel and a hooligan-related death at Birmingham. In the minds of ministers, like much of the public, the image of the football fan was integrally linked to the issue of hooliganism. Consequently, fans' interests as consumers, whose safety needed protecting, remained secondary.

The Popplewell report led to wooden stands across Britain being condemned and closed, but its recommendation that adequate exit gates be ensured in all perimeter fences was not fully noted. Large perimeter fences resembling cages had been erected at many grounds in order to keep hooligans off the pitch. Had they existed at Bradford, fans would not have been able to escape onto the pitch and the death toll would have been significantly higher. Their very existence was a classic example of how crowd management was viewed in the context of hooliganism rather than safety.

On 15 April 1989 such fences proved to be fatal for 96 Liverpool fans attending the FA Cup semi-final against Nottingham Forest at Hillsborough, Sheffield. Inadequate policing and signposting meant that fans were not distributed evenly across the three fenced pens that made up the Leppings Lane end. The overcrowding in the central pen became fatal when the police opened an external gate to relieve a crush outside the ground. Hundreds poured into the nearest pen, which was already full beyond capacity. Exit gates below were locked because of fears of trouble and the police were slow to realise that people were dying inside the crush against the fence. British football's most horrific disaster thus unfolded live before the eyes of a watching television audience. In the following days, newspapers published photographs of the dead and dying.

The impact of the disaster was immense, unlike all its footballing predecessors, and the subsequent recriminations bitter. Senior police officers spread misinformation that hooligans were to blame, and some tabloid newspapers followed this lead. The public inquiry under Lord Justice Taylor was to hear such allegations repeated, to the considerable anger of people in Liverpool. Taylor's report dismissed such theories unequivocally and laid blame for the disaster at the feet of the police.

Taylor's recommendations brought about a radically different philosophy of safety within football through the gradual introduction of all-seater stadia to the top two English divisions. Significantly, the disaster also awoke fans to the importance of safe grounds. Cost and a confidence in their own existing arrangements meant that many clubs were reluctant to embrace all-seater stadia, but the issue was forced by a government who increasingly saw football as an embarrassment and irritant.

Its insistence was due as much to the potential of all-seater stadia to reduce hooliganism as to the safety factor. Nonetheless, the disaster forced football to reassess how it treated its consumers, and indeed its whole future. Thus Hillsborough was a catalyst for not only the rebuilding of Britain's stadia but also the reinvention of the game itself. It helped focus ideas for a breakaway league and contributed to a chain of events that led to the emergence of the Premier League, a lucrative deal with Sky television and the current fashionability and wealth that pervades the upper echelons of football.

Hillsborough also stands out from other football disasters because of the legal actions that followed it. It was the last of a series of civil disasters that marred Britain in the late 1980s and changed the expectations of victims. Whereas Bradford fans had treated the disaster with a degree of fatalism, the aftermath of Hillsborough was marked by anger and demands for criminal prosecutions. A controversial inquest verdict of accidental death ensured that this was unlikely, forcing bereaved families to undertake private prosecutions against the senior police officers on duty that day. Token compensation payments were also no longer deemed sufficient amidst the widespread anger at the cluster of disasters caused by mismanagement and negligence. Hillsborough led to a number of important legal test cases that determined which classes of relatives were entitled to compensation.

The history of football disasters in postwar Britain illustrates how the safety of fans has not been treated seriously enough by clubs, football authorities or the State. Failure to introduce more comprehensive regulation sprang from concerns at the cost and a tradition of excluding sport from legislation. This tradition, which dated back to the nineteenth-century days of amateur idealism, was based upon a belief that sport's competitive but communal ethos had no need of intervention from the world of economics and politics. Yet football was a business with a moral duty to care for the safety of its consumers. Hooliganism may have increased external concern with football's affairs, but it ensured that the fans were viewed in terms of their potential to misbehave, rather than to die in dated grounds. It took the horror of the Hillsborough disaster before football and government fully reassessed their commitment to the safety of supporters.

Sources:

Baker, N., 'Have They Forgotten Bolton?', *The Sports Historian*, 18: 1 (May 1998), 120–51.

Inglis, S., *The Football Grounds of Great Britain* (London: Collins Willow, 1987).

McLean, I. and Johnes, M., *Aberfan: Government and Disasters* (Cardiff: Welsh Academic Press, 2000).

Scraton, P., *Hillsborough: The Truth* (Edinburgh: Mainstream, 1999).

Sheils, R. S., 'The Ibrox Disaster of 1902', *Judicial Review*, 4 (1997), 230–40.

Further Reading:

Elliot, D. and Smith, D., 'Football Stadia Disasters in the United Kingdom: Learning from Tragedy?', *Industrial and Environmental Crisis Quarterly*, 7: 3 (1993), 205–29.

Taylor, F., *The Day a Team Died* (London: Souvenir, 1983).

Martin Johnes

Discipline and Punishment

Discipline on the field of play is imposed by the referee and regulated chiefly by Rule XII of the Laws of Association Football, entitled 'Fouls and Misconduct'. Punishments which the referee may impose on players for offences committed during the match consist of indirect and direct free kicks, penalty kicks, cautions (also known as bookings) and sendings off. Additional penalties, fines and suspensions may also be incurred later. The FA's code of conduct regulates the behaviour of players and others involved in the game off the pitch. Clubs also have rules that players have to observe concerning, for example, failure to attend training or late

arrival for key events, and can impose their own disciplinary sanctions for breaches of those rules.

The FA Laws of 1881 stated that a caution might be given to players for ungentlemanly behaviour (a term which covered a wide range of offences) and that the referee could rule offending players out of play and order them off the ground. By 1890 a sending off usually resulted in professionals being suspended for a month without pay. An FA rule, which operated from 1884 until 1915, stipulated that unless players and clubs provided proof of their innocence of any breaches of discipline, their guilt would automatically be assumed. Penalties were often harsh and players had no right of redress or representation at disciplinary hearings. The Football League first introduced fines as punishments in 1935. A caution, indicated since 1976 by a yellow card, may be given at the referee's discretion for four broad categories of misdemeanours: entering or leaving the field of play without permission; persistent infringement of the Laws of the Game; dissent from any decision of the referee by word or action; and ungentlemanly conduct. Players can be sent off if, in the opinion of the referee, they are guilty of violent conduct (including spitting, since 1980), serious foul play, using foul or abusive language or if they have committed a second cautionable offence. A red card indicates a sending off. Red cards are punished by automatic suspensions for a number of matches determined by the gravity of the offence. Points are awarded for bookings and players will be suspended for accruing 16 points or more. Managers and other club officials can also be booked or sent off and be fined and banned from the dugout.

The imposition of disciplinary sanctions on the pitch is often contentious. Some bookings have been given for unusual reasons. Paul Gascoigne was booked when playing for Glasgow Rangers when he pretended to caution the referee while returning the yellow card which had fallen from his pocket.

Until the later twentieth century, the referee's power to send a player off was used relatively sparingly in senior football.

Leeds' Mark Viduka fouls Arsenal's Robert Pires (© Stuart MacFarlane, Arsenal FC)

when Tottenham's Frank Saul was sent off in December 1965, he became the club's first player to be thus dealt with since 1928. Punishment usually took the form of a one-month ban, but serious offenders could be dealt with extremely severely. In Scotland the longest suspension was handed out following a dismissal involving Rangers' Willie Woodburn. He had received two lengthy suspensions in 1953 and when, a year later, he was sent off for punching an opponent, the Scottish FA banned him for life. Woodburn appealed, but his ban was not lifted until 1957, by which time he was 38 and his playing career was effectively over. In England, Oldham Athletic full-back Billy Cook was banned for a year by the FA in April 1915 after his refusal to accept his dismissal led to the referee abandoning a League match at Middlesbrough – the first time such a course of action had been taken at senior level. The FA's concern with the game's reputation during the First World War may have been a factor here.

Another long suspension resulted from a game at Middlesbrough when South Shields defender Cyril Hunter received a six-month ban after being sent off in a match in April 1927. Watford's Frank Barson received a seven-month ban after being dismissed against Fulham in 1928. Barson, who had played for England, had been sent off many times during his career and received a total of 12 suspensions. Not even a petition delivered in person to the FA by the Mayor of Watford aided his cause in this instance. Other significant dismissals in this period included those of Glasgow Rangers' Jock Buchanan – who in 1929 became the first player to be sent off in a Scottish Cup final – and of Wrexham's Ambrose Brown. His departure on Christmas Day 1936 after just 20 seconds was to be the fastest sending off in British football until Crewe goalkeeper Mark Smith shaved a second off his record in 1994; his Sheffield Wednesday counterpart, Kevin Pressman, in turn cut this time down to just 13 seconds in August 2000.

Since the late 1960s and early 1970s, sendings off have become far more frequent as the game's authorities have tried both to clamp down on certain aspects of behaviour on the field and to maintain football's wider reputation and cultural position during a period of great public concern and debate over law and order. Whereas 37 players were dismissed in 1970/71 in the three major English competitions and the Welsh Cup combined, the 1999/2000 season saw 327 red cards in the FA Premiership and Nationwide League alone. This increase has led to various unwanted footballing firsts. In June 1968, Alan Mullery became the first ever player to be sent off while representing England, as a result of retaliation during a European Championship match against Yugoslavia. (Billy Steel in 1951, Billy Ferguson in 1966 and Trevor Hockey in 1973 took that particular record for Scotland, Northern Ireland and Wales respectively.) In August 1974, Liverpool's Kevin Keegan and Leeds' Billy Bremner became the first British players to be sent off at Wembley during the first ever Charity Shield match staged at the stadium. A goalmouth brawl, followed by a lengthy argument with the referee, earned them their marching orders, at which point they pulled off their shirts and threw them on the pitch. The fact that so many people witnessed this incident on television led to the FA taking punitive action, with both players receiving fines of £500 and seven-match bans. In 1985, Manchester United's Kevin Moran became the first player to be dismissed in an FA Cup final following a late tackle on Everton's Peter Reid (United went on to win). His winner's medal was initially withheld, but the supposed shame he endured (and the less than ringing endorsement of the referee's decision by many commentators) was held to be punishment enough, and the FA quickly relented.

As dismissals rose, the individual record for ill discipline fell to Willie Johnstone of Rangers, West Bromwich Albion and Hearts who was sent off on 17 occasions in British football, and a further four times during a spell in Canada; his tenth dismissal, for Albion against Brighton in 1976, was for kicking the referee. Among this generally depressing catalogue, a few sendings off have provided a certain humour for those not immediately affected. In the 1978/79 season, for example, Charlton Athletic's Mike Flanagan and Derek Hales were sent off for fighting *each other* during a cup match with Maidstone.

Arguably the most (in)famous dismissals in British football history are those of Argentina's captain Antonio Rattin in the World Cup quarter-final against England at Wembley in 1966, and of Eric Cantona when playing for Manchester United at Crystal Palace's Selhurst Park in January 1996. In a bad-tempered and foul-strewn game, West German referee Rudolf Kreitlein dismissed Rattin supposedly for verbal abuse (although Kreitlein later admitted that he could not speak Spanish) and it took seven minutes before the Argentinean finally agreed to go. The game in general and the incident in particular created extensive bad feeling between the two sides and their national associations. Cantona's dismissal, for kicking out at an opponent in retaliation, was not exceptional but its aftermath certainly was. Verbally abused by Palace fan Matthew Simmons as he left the field, Cantona lunged over the perimeter fence to deliver a kung fu kick and then aim a punch at his tormentor. As well as a nine-month ban from football and a £10,000 fine, Cantona received a two-week prison sentence, later commuted to 120 hours community service.

The first players to be tried in court for offences committed during play (a 1987 Glasgow derby) were Chris Woods, Graham Roberts, Terry Butcher and Frank McAvennie. They were charged with behaviour likely to cause a breach of the peace. In 1992 Brentford's Gary Blissett escaped prosecution for allegedly using his elbow to break Torquay's John Uzzell's cheek. In May 1995 Duncan Ferguson became 'the birdman of Barlinnie' when sentenced to three months for assaulting Raith Rovers' full-back John McStay in 1994: the prison sentence resulted from his already being on probation for an earlier off-the-field offence. In contrast, internationals Billy Wright and Gary Lineker were never sent off or booked. Wright's record was remarkable considering that he played as a centre-half for several years of his very long career.

There are periodic concerns about the levels of bad or violent behaviour on the pitch. In March 1999 the FA appointed a compliance officer, Graham Bean, to deal with serious breaches of discipline. Docking the wages of frequent offenders was discussed. But reactions to disciplinary clampdowns by referees can be hostile. In 1996 a House of Commons' motion called for a reduction in the 'excessive' use of yellow cards.

Sources:

Anon., *The Laws of Association Football, 1994–1995* (London: Pan, 1994).

FIFA website http://www.fifa.com

Golesworthy, M., *The Encyclopaedia of Association Football* (London: Robert Hale, 1956).

Ridley, I., 'Mr. Bean the wise old Owl', *The Observer* (Sunday 14 March 1999).

Williams, R., *Football Babylon* (London: Virgin, 1996).

Further Reading:

Campbell, D, Shields, A. and May, P., *The Lad Done Bad: Sex, Sleaze and Scandal in English Football* (London: Penguin, 1996).

Cosgrove, S., *Hampden Babylon: Sex and Scandal in Scottish Football* (Edinburgh: Canongate, 1991).

Murphy, P., Williams, J. and Dunning, E., *Football on Trial. Spectator Violence and Development in the Football World* (London: Routledge, 1990).

Nawrat, C. and Hutchings, S. (eds), *Sunday Times Illustrated History of Football* (London: Hamlyn, 1999).

Williams, R., *Football Babylon* (London: Virgin, 1996).

John Coyle, Dave Russell and Joyce Woolridge

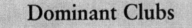

Dominant Clubs

The FA Cup was the world's first national knockout tournament when it was started in 1872. Initially, the competition was dominated by amateur sides; indeed, its first ten winners were all sides with an amateur background. The dominant team during this early phase was the Wanderers, who won the trophy on five occasions, including three years on the run from 1876 to '78. By the early 1880s, however, professional sides from the north of England began to dominate the competition. Although Blackburn Olym-pic were the first professional side to win the cup it was their neighbours, Blackburn Rovers, who became the dominant cup side during the 1880s. Like the Wanderers they achieved a hat-trick of wins, between 1884 and '86. Indeed, only the Wanderers and Blackburn Rovers have achieved a hat-trick of FA Cup wins. In the twentieth century the first team to retain the trophy was Newcastle United, winning the Cup in 1951 and 1952. Since then only Tottenham Hotspur have retained the trophy in successive years – 1961/62 and 1981/82. Manchester United hold the record for the most FA Cup successes, having won the competition on ten occasions.

In its early years the English Football League championship was dominated by Aston Villa and Sunderland. Prior to the First World War Villa won the title six times, while Sunderland ran out champions on five occasions. In the inter-war years the League championship came to be dominated initially by Huddersfield, and then by Arsenal. In fact, Huddersfield became the first team to win the title three years in succession (1924–26), a feat repeated by Arsenal between 1933 and '35. Arsenal dominated the 1930s, winning the title on five occasions.

In the post-1945 period, up to the foundation of the Premier League in 1992, Liverpool emerged as the dominant English championship side. They were the first post-war winners in 1947 and although they did not record their next championship until 1964, from this period onwards (prior to the foundation of the Premiership) they became champions of England on no less than 13 occasions. Their tally included a hat-trick of championships between 1982 and '84, making Liverpool only the third English team to win the League championship three years in succession. With the birth of the FA Premiership in 1992 Manchester United emerged as the dominant force, retaining the title on three occasions, with only Blackburn Rovers and Arsenal able to take the title away from Old Trafford.

The most coveted achievement in English Football is the League and FA Cup double. The first team to achieve this was Preston North End in 1889. During their double year Preston remained unbeaten in all competitions and did not concede a goal in their FA Cup run. Aston Villa, in 1897, became the next double winners, but it was 64 years before Tottenham Hotspur won the coveted prizes in the same season. Arsenal and Liverpool received the accolade in 1971 and 1986 respectively, but in the 1990s, as the wealthy clubs came to dominate football to an ever greater extent, the double has been won by Manchester United on three occasions, as well as by Arsenal. In 1993 Arsenal became the only English team to complete the League Cup and FA Cup double. The first English team to win a European trophy was Tottenham Hotspur, when they beat Atletico Madrid in the 1963 Cup Winners Cup Final. Manchester United were the first English club to win the European Cup, in 1968, but Liverpool have been the dominant English side in Europe. They have won the European Cup on four occasions, being the only English side to retain the trophy, and the UEFA Cup twice. The only English teams to win the European Cup more than once are Nottingham Forest and Manchester United, each having emerged as European champions on two occasions.

In 1973 Liverpool became the first English side to win the League championship as well as a European trophy, a feat they repeated in 1978 and 1984. They became the first side to win three trophies in a season when they won the European Cup, the League Championship and the League Cup in 1984. Manchester United emulated Liverpool in 1999 when they added the FA Cup to their European Cup and Premiership successes. Overall, Liverpool are the most successful English team. They have won 18 League champi-

onships, five FA Cups, five League Cups, four European Cups and two UEFA Cups. Manchester United's record in European and domestic competitions is second only to that of Liverpool. They have recorded 12 championships, 10 FA Cups, one League Cup and two European Cups, as well as winning the Cup Winners Cup in 1991.

Scottish football has been dominated by Celtic and Rangers both in the League and in the Scottish Cup. At its inception in 1891 the Scottish League was won by Dumbarton for two years in succession, although its first championship was shared with Rangers, but since then the dominance of the Glasgow sides has resulted in 48 outright championships for Rangers, while Celtic have been champions on 36 occasions. Celtic won a remarkable nine consecutive League championships between 1966 and '74, a feat matched by Rangers between 1989 and '98. Only three other teams have achieved more than three League titles – Hibs and Hearts four times each – while Aberdeen have been champions on three occasions. The Scottish Cup has also been dominated by the Old Firm, although in its early stages Queen's Park were consistent winners of the trophy, winning ten times between 1874 and 1893. However, as with the FA Cup, once the professional sides emerged amateur sides like Queen's Park were pushed to one side.

Only three Scottish clubs have won European trophies: Celtic became the first British team to win the European Cup in 1967, while Rangers and Aberdeen won the Cup Winners Cup in 1972 and 1983 respectively.

Source:

Radnedge, K., *The Complete Encyclopedia of Football* (London: Carlton, 1998).

Ray Physick

Drama

While football has never been a major source of inspiration for dramatists, a thin but noteworthy tradition of plays, sketches and revues dealing with the game at least to some degree can be traced back into the late nineteenth century, and becomes noticeably stronger in the later twentieth century. Perhaps the first such offering was George Gray's four-act musical drama *The Football King*, a hit in both London and the provinces in 1896. The work contained a re-enactment of part of an FA Cup final at Kennington Oval. Events surrounding the visit of a northern fan to the Cup final were also to provide a minor sub-plot in Lionel Monckton's hugely successful musical comedy *Our Miss Gibbs* (1909). For most of football's early life, however, it was the music hall rather than the 'legitimate' stage that showed the greatest interest in the game. Harry Weldon's *Stiffy the Goalkeeper* was one of the most popular comic sketches of the Edwardian period. The relationship between sport and the music hall was not just a one-way affair, however, with football fans taking songs and catchphrases into a developing terrace culture. During the club's FA Cup run in 1910/11, for example, Burnley fans celebrated the achievements of goalkeeper Jeremiah Dawson by wearing rosettes declaiming 'Stick it, Jerry', the catchphrase of comedian Lew Lake. The link between popular theatre and football as forms of entertainment at this time can also be seen in the shape of such journals as the *Illustrated Sporting and Dramatic News*, which reviewed music hall shows and contained football reports.

Probably the first 'serious' playwright to tackle the sport was Manchester's Harold Brighouse, whose *The Game* was first performed at the Liverpool Repertory Theatre in 1913. The play made much of the adulation given to star players (in this case, those of Lancashire's 'Blackton Rovers') but also acknowledged the basic honesty of the professional player, with Birchester's Jack Metherall refusing to throw a crucial relegation match against Blackton, his old club. However, although the published edition of the play actually included a footnote on the transfer system, Brighouse's ultimate interest was in the dramatisation not of football, but of inter-generational conflict, a subject that reached ultimate fruition in his classic *Hobson's Choice* (1915).

Although the inter-war period saw a handful of one-act plays based on the game, the use of the game as metaphor or symbol within drama was much more frequent than drama about football in this period, and indeed in much of the period to about 1970. These devices often reflected the era of the piece. R. C. Sheriff's play *Journey's End* (1928) was set in the trenches in March 1918. Raleigh, a young recruit, is talking here to the older Osbourne, a former schoolmaster and rugby international.

Osbourne: Rugger and cricket seem a long way from here.
Raleigh (laughing): They do, rather.
Osbourne: We play a bit of soccer when we're out of the line.
Raleigh: Good.

With both real and apocryphal 'frontline' games part of the popular memory of the 1914–18 conflict, the play uses the metaphor of football as both preparation for, and distraction from, war.

The 1940s and '50s saw occasional dramatic forays into the football world, most notably Glenn Melvyn's three-act comedy *The Love Match* (1953), starring Arthur Askey and Thora Hird, and which was made into a film the following year. Harold Pinter also included football related exchanges in some of his best-received pieces, including *The Dumb Waiter* (1960). However, it is from the late 1960s that the supply of plays becomes rather more constant. Important here was Peter Terson's *Zigger Zagger* (1967), which was first performed by the National Youth Theatre and dealt with issues relating to football hooliganism and youth culture ('zigger zagger, zigger zagger, oi, oi, oi' was a popular chant of the day). Terson, one of the leading young playwrights of his day, was then working at the Victoria Theatre in Stoke, and some of his fieldwork for the play was done at Stoke City's ground; City's strip was also used in the original performance.

From this point on, football dramas can be rather crudely categorised as either commercial works or community or 'fringe' plays, designed either to celebrate the achievements of a local club or to highlight a problem within the game. In the commercial sector, by some way the smaller of the categories, by far the best known is Arthur Smith and Chris England's *An Evening with Gary Lineker* (1992), an extremely successful comedy dealing with responses to England's departure from the 1990 World Cup. That a play dealing with football could be performed in the West End and receive such critical acclaim is clear evidence of football's rising position within the national culture at this time, after the problems of the 1980s. Paul Hodson's adaptation of Nick Hornby's *Fever Pitch* into a one-man show also proved popular on its launch in 1995, and helped maintain the Hornby phenomenon. The Andrew Lloyd Webber and Ben Elton musical, *The Beautiful Game* (2000), uses a football team as a convenient device for exploring relationships across Northern Ireland's religious divide. Celebratory community plays include Bill Grundy's *Up the Rams* (1970), dedicated to Derby County and one of the first of the genre; Willie Maley and Ian Auld's *The Lions Of Lisbon* (1992), written as a silver anniversary commemoration of Celtic's 1967 European Cup triumph; and *Theatre of Dreams* (1998) by Chesterfield fans Howard Borrell, Mike Firth, Fiona Firth and Phil Tooley. A number of Chesterfield players appeared in the early productions of this play by Spotlight Theatre, celebrating the Third Division club's remarkable run to the FA Cup semifinal in 1997. 'Issue-related' community plays include three that deal with racism: Paul Hurt's *Big Time* (1990); Clifford Oliver's *Kicking Out* (1995); and *Oooh Ah Showab Khan* (1997).

Football may appear to share with theatre several features of what could be called dramatic action. In both there are rules which are what Allen Guttmann has called 'designedly inefficient' in order to make the action possible. It would be more efficient for Othello to ask Desdemona if she had had an affair, but we the audience suspend our disbelief that he does not because we are familiar with the conventions of dramatic irony and suspense. Similarly, the laws of the game prevent goals being scored by hand, and the crowd accepts this artificiality of the rules in order that the spectacle has more intense highlights prior to conclusion. Iago's actions may, then, be foul, but they are within the orthodoxy of tragedy: to breach the laws of football would be to break the spell of the agreement of the constructed nature of the experience for both audience and performer. The key difference is that, unless improvised, the dramatic action is plotted and the football game, though linear, is unscripted – however much sports commentators may try to persuade us of their *déjà vu* regarding the outcome of the match!

Given the limited opportunities available to playwrights in comparison with those working in other sectors of the literary media, and the finite demand from audiences for drama of this type, football-related plays will always be relatively scarce. Nevertheless, the topic will certainly continue to provide rich opportunities for those working at local level or with younger people, while the level of output on the commercial stage will provide a useful index of football's national standing.

Sources:

Bale, J. and Moen, O. (eds), *The Stadium and the City* (Keele: Keele University Press, 1995).

Brighouse, H., 'The Game' in his *Three Lancashire Plays* (London: French, 1920).

Guttmann, A., *From Ritual to Record: The Nature of Modern Sports* (New York: Columbia University Press, 1978).

Seddon, P. J., *A Football Compendium* (London: British Library, 1999).

Sherriff, R. C., *Journey's End* (London: Everyman, 1937).

See also Art

Dave Russell and Jean Williams

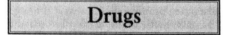

Drugs

A drug is a chemical substance which, by interacting with biological targets, can

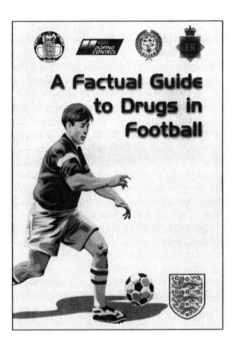

A Factual Guide to Drugs in Football

alter the body's biochemical systems. Drugs are designed to correct imbalances in biological systems induced by illness, injury or disease, rather than for any physiological effects on healthy individuals. Nevertheless, drugs whose actions are mediated by target tissues – such as amphetamines, whose effects on the central nervous system include altering mood and behaviour, or anabolic steroids, which can be used for optimising strength training stimuli on muscle ultrastructure – have been utilised in leisure and professional football contexts, respectively. Drugs that are used with the intention of causing a physiological response that enhances performance in sport are said to be ergogenic.

The use of exogenous supplements to maximise athletic performance in sport dates back to the ancient Olympic Games. In the third century BC, the physician Galen reported that athletes at the Olympics used stimulants to improve their physical capabilities. They also employed special diets. In the modern Olympic Games there is evidence of drug use from the early Olympiads, including for example the use to strychnine and brandy by the winner of the men's marathon race in St Louis in 1904. Only in the 1960s was the more systematic use of pharmacological ergogenic agents recognised as a problem. This had become evident with the death of a Danish cyclist at the 1960 Olympics in Rome as a consequence of amphetamine abuse. The British cyclist Tommy Simpson died while competing in the Tour de France in 1967, and two other deaths in cycling and one in football occurred the following year. In all cases there was evidence of the use of amphetamines. While use of amphetamines for offsetting fatigue followed from its administration to troops in the Second World War, the drugs that triggered the formulation of doping control measures were the anabolic steroids. These drugs had come into vogue in the late 1960s for sustaining strenuous training regimens, accelerating recovery from hard training and promoting muscle growth.

The International Olympic Committee took a lead in publishing its list of doping classes in 1967. The first list included stimulants and narcotic analgesics. Anabolic steroids were banned in 1974 when the laboratory methods for detecting these substances in urine samples were developed. Testosterone was the first endogenous steroid to be placed on the banned list, in 1963, a positive finding being declared when the testosterone to epitestosterone ratio exceeded a value of six. In 1985 beta-blockers and diuretics were added to the IOC's banned list, although these drugs tended to be used in target-sports and those with weight categories – for example, shooting and wrestling, respectively. Doping methods were added as a discrete category in 1985, incorporating blood doping, pharmacological, chemical and physical manipulations. Masking agents were added to the list in 1987, along with human chorionic gonadotrophin, a hormone naturally produced during pregnancy but which has performance enhancing effects on muscle function. Peptide hormones were added to the list in 1989 and included growth hormone and erythropoetin, used for enhancing strength and endurance respectively. With the recombinant technological developments of the 1990s, the availability of synthetic versions of these hormones to athletes (including footballers) presented a problem to scientists detecting these substances in accredited laboratories, a problem that remained unsolved at the end of the second millennium.

The governing bodies for football have in the main followed the lead of the IOC. FIFA in fact carried out the first official dope-testing in Britain during the 1966 World Cup finals, although there were no positive test results. UEFA set up its own committee in 1979, with the aim of handling the so-called doping problem. This action followed the ban imposed on a Scottish player, Willie Johnstone, following a positive test for the stimulant phencophamine at the World Cup finals in Argentina, when he had swallowed two tablets to treat his hay-fever before Scotland's game against Peru. This incident highlighted the problem associated with taking over-the-counter medicines which contain substances that are on the official banned list. The one other positive drug test at this elite level of football incriminated the Argentinian star Diego Maradona at the 1994 finals in the United States, following an urgent weight-reduction regimen in his physical preparation for the tournament.

When official testing for drug abuse in British football first began in 1978, it was primarily concerned with the detection of performance-enhancing substances. Since then, fears about increasing social drug use among the young, and the need to protect players from the long-term damage cause by misuse of medication, have widened the scope of testing. This has so far uncovered little evidence of the use of drugs to gain an unfair advantage, though a few cases of 'recreational' drug use by footballers off the field of play have been exposed. In the 1994/95 season the English FA adopted what it described as a 'pro-active' approach, in response to reports by a number of clubs that drug pushers had been observed approaching youth and professional players at training grounds, as well as wider societal concerns about the growth of recreational drug use.

Detection of social or recreational drug use, not intended to enhance performance, and controlled under the provisions of the 1971 Misuse of Drugs Act, became a second aim of a more comprehensive Doping Control Programme. Young players at Centres of Excellence, youth players aged between 16 and 18, and women in the FA Women's National League, were all to be included. Out-of-competition testing at training grounds supplemented the existing post-match tests. Alcohol testing is also permitted, although results are only brought to the attention of the medical officer of the player's club. An educational programme and specialist pamphlets were designed to accompany all testing, aimed specifically at younger players.

In 1994 Paul Merson, then an Arsenal player, confessed publicly to social cocaine use, although this was subordinate to his alcohol and gambling addictions. His honesty was widely applauded and he returned to professional football after a brief period of counselling and treatment. In 1999 a youth trainee at Newcastle United admitted to heroin addiction. The authorities' response to these and other cases has been to offer rehabilitation alongside punishment. Players guilty of taking performance-enhancing drugs would be charged with misconduct for bringing the game into disrepute. For social drug use, an eight-point programme of counselling and treatment, and a probationary period of between 12 and 18 months, are offered for a first offence, depending on the scale and level of the problem. The FA decides when the footballer is 'fit' to be allowed to resume playing.

Evidence of drug use among footballers is extremely difficult to obtain. Undoubtedly, there was some early experimentation with the amphetamine-like stimulants that became available in the 1920s. Leslie Knighton, the Arsenal manager, in his book *Behind the Scenes In Big Football*, revealed that Arsenal players were given a 'courage pill' by a supporter who was also a doctor to boost their performance in their FA Cup in 1925. The match's postponement rendered their first experiment useless, and the players refused to take them again after a second attempt had unpleasant side-effects. Stanley Matthews was prescribed 'pep pills', as used by the Luftwaffe on long-range bombing missions, to counteract a bad attack of influenza. He survived Blackpool's 1946 FA Cup game against Sheffield United without any ill effects, but paced his room frenetically all night. Major Frank Buckley, manager of Wolverhampton Wanderers, attracted huge publicity in 1939 when he ordered a course of 'monkey gland' injections and tablets to improve his team's fitness. Billy Wright later claimed he fed his supply to his landlady's tom cat, which became the envy of the neighbourhood. The exact nature of the substance injected is unclear but it is unlikely that it was anything other than a vitamin supplement or anti-influenza treatment.

Sensational allegations about 'doping' were a staple of 1950s Sunday newspaper exposés. According to the Welsh international Trevor Ford's 1957 autobiography, *I Lead The Attack*, oxygen, pheno-barbitone and dexedrine had all been used to revive players at half-time. A scandal erupted when drug-taking allegations were levelled against the 1963 First Division Championship-winning Everton side, but these were never proven.

Although random, out-of-competition testing in other sports has uncovered the illegal use of steroids, hormones, blood-doping with erythropoietin (EPO) – a technique suspected of wide misuse in professional cycling – and other substances to improve performance unfairly, the increasing number of drug tests in football has revealed only a relatively small amount of social drug use. In the domestic game, voluntary post-match testing of professional players for performance-enhancing substances was introduced in 1978, and made compulsory in 1989. From the 240 tests carried out between 1989 and '93 under the auspices of the UK Sports Council, in which two players from each team were randomly selected from 20 games per season, there were no positive results. This suggests either that anecdotal evidence about widespread drug use was unfounded, or that the number and type of tests were inadequate. Between 1994 and 1999 there were only 29 positive tests from the 2,090 carried out – only one for a performance-enhancing drug,

the others mainly for cannabis use. Overall, the number of positive tests continued to fall.

Allegations of drug use are often based on hearsay rather than fact, and systematic random sampling in a training context is highly expensive. Besides, performance in match-play is a complex phenomenon and it is difficult to demonstrate ergogenic effects experimentally. Scientific studies have shown with more confidence the positive effects of manipulating fuels for muscle activity (such as creatine or carbohydrate) on particular components of work-rate during play. Such substrates are stored within muscle and are available in common foodstuffs, and so dedicated regimens to optimise the ergogenic effects of their ingestion are not deemed illegal. The misuse of medications has probably been a bigger problem in professional football than of any performance-enhancing or recreational drugs. Cortisone and other anti-inflammatory injections have been widely used to allow players to carry on despite injuries, and in some cases have resulted in longer-term health problems, particularly arthritis. Team doctors must give written notification of corticosteroid use to the medical officer of the FA Doping Control Unit. The IOC permits the use of local anaesthetics only where there is medical justification. Another grey area is the increasing number of nutritional supplements available. Glenn Hoddle's endorsement of the legal supplement creatine, given to members of the 1998 England World Cup squad he managed, caused some controversy, particularly as there were claims that it had adverse side effects of weight gain and kidney damage.

Allegations about drug use still continue. Emmanuel Petit, the French Arsenal midfielder, claimed in 1999 that the increasing number of matches created by the expansion of the European Champions League had forced some top professionals to take drugs to cope with the impossibly heavy physical demands. He refused to name any players. The Scottish FA was also forced to defend its drug testing procedure after Berwick Rangers captain Martin Neil declared he had used amphetamines, LSD and cocaine throughout his decade-long career and had never been tested. However, internationally, football in 1999 continued to have a more liberal and enlightened attitude to drug testing than some other sports. FIFA refused to back an IOC proposal for a minimum ban of two years for those giving a positive sample, preferring to retain the options of rehabilitation and education.

Sources:

Dent, A. R., 'Doping Control in Professional Football', *British Journal of Sports Medicine*, 32 (1998), 96–7.

Donohue, T. and Johnson, N., *Foul Play: Drug Abuse in Sports* (Oxford: Basil Blackwell, 1988).

FA Memorandum, 'The Football Association Drug Testing Programme: Memorandum and Procedural Guidelines For the Conduct of Drug Testing, Season 1999/2000' (1999).

Hodson, A., 'The Football Association Doping Control and Health Education Programme', in *Insight: the F. A. Coaches Association Journal*, 3: 4 (Summer 1999), 52–5.

Mottram, D. R. (ed.), *Drugs in Sport* (Second edition) (London: E. and F. N. Spon, 1996).

O'Leary, J., *Drugs and Doping in Sport: Socio-Legal Perspectives* (London: Cavendish, 2001).

Williams, R., *Football Babylon* (London: Virgin, 1996).

Tom Reilly and Joyce Woolridge

History Highlights 1900–1909

Football continued in much the same vein as it had in the 1890s, albeit with increasing spectator interest. Football League divisional average attendances rose steadily from between 1900 and 1909: Division One from 9,000 to 16,000 and Division Two from 4,000 to 9,000. The best-attended clubs throughout the period were Aston Villa, Manchester City, Newcastle United, Everton, Liverpool, Manchester United, and Chelsea (from 1907 to 1908). The poorest attendances were at Glossop and Gainsborough Trinity, both in towns too small to sustain professional football for very long.

In 1904/05, both divisions of the Football League were increased to 20 clubs, and the newly-formed Chelsea were elected in 1905 without playing a game, because of their substantial new ground at Stamford Bridge. Southern professional clubs began to make an impact, although limited at first. Southampton reached the FA Cup final in 1900 and 1902, and Bristol City were beaten by Manchester United in the 1909 final. The 1901 final at Crystal Palace between Tottenham Hotspur and Sheffield United attracted a crowd of 111,815, then a record attendance. Spurs were the first southern professional club to win the Cup.

In the Football League, the decade was dominated by Liverpool, Aston Villa, Manchester United, Sheffield Wednesday, Everton, Manchester City, Sunderland and Newcastle United, the latter winning the title in 1905, 1907 and 1909. In the FA Cup, however, honours were spread a little more evenly. Bury, a competent First Division club at the time, actually won the Cup twice, in 1900 and 1903. Newcastle United appeared in the Cup final three times, in 1905, 1906 and 1908.

Scottish football at this time became dominated by Rangers and Celtic, with an intense rivalry engendered between the two, fuelled by sectarianism. The only other clubs to win the Championship were Third Lanark and Hibernian. As in England, winners of the Scottish Cup were more varied, as Hearts, Hibernian and Third Lanark triumphed alongside Glasgow's big two. In 1907, Celtic became the first Scottish club to perform the League and Cup double.

Two other significant events also occurred in Scotland. The first major football disaster happened at Ibrox in 1902, when wooden terracing collapsed under the weight of a large crowd of swaying spectators at a Scotland v. England international, causing the death of 26 people and injuring over 500. In 1909, there was a serious riot at Hampden Park following a Celtic v. Rangers match when extra time was not played, causing frustration that escalated into violence, arson and vandalism.

In England, the Players' Union was reformed in 1907, having amongst its main aims the abolition of the retain-and-transfer system and the maximum wage. The former had existed since the early days of professionalism to prevent clubs from 'poaching' players, but the wage limit of £4 per week was instituted by the FA in 1900 and implemented at the beginning of the 1901/02 season. Glossop, Middlesbrough, Sunderland and Manchester City were all punished by the Football League for exceeding maximum wage restrictions between 1904 and 1907.

The first threat of a players' strike occurred in September 1908, being averted by a last-minute compromise before the start of the new season. Members of the FA were also opposed to the transfer system, and tried to abolish it following the first £1,000 transfer fee paid by Middlesbrough for Alf Common in 1905. The scale of the fee illustrated the amount of money circulating in the game, and its importance to successful clubs. The FA move did not succeed, as it was opposed by the professional clubs who wanted some reward for losing valuable players. The FA also tried to place a limit on fees of £350 in 1905, but this lasted for only three months, again because of pressures from the market. In 1908, England played its first ever full international against foreign opposition, beating Austria 6–1. In the same year, the Olympic Games were held at White City, London, where England, representing Great Britain, won the inaugural football tournament, beating Denmark in the final. 1908 also saw the inauguration of the Charity Shield, with funds being donated by the FA to suitable charities. Manchester United, champions of the Football League, beat Queen's Park Rangers, champions of the Southern League, 4–0.

In 1907, the breakaway Amateur Football Association was created after a dispute in which the Surrey and Middlesex Football Associations refused to admit professional clubs in defiance of an FA directive. The split lasted until 1914, and indicated the still-prevalent opposition to professionalism amongst middle-class ex-public school amateur players and administrators, particularly in south-east England. This organisation initiated separate amateur-only competitions, and was supported by many famous amateurs, including N. L. Jackson and G. O. Smith.

Sources:
Rothmans Football Yearbook (London: Headline, various editions).
Mason, T., *Association Football and English Society, 1863–1915* (Brighton: Harvester, 1980).
Fabian, A. H. and Green, G., *Association Football* (London: Caxton, 1960).
Russell, D., *Football and the English* (Preston: Carnegie, 1997).
Tabner, B., *Through the Turnstiles* (Harefield: Yore Publications, 1992).

Further Reading:
Gibson, A. and Pickford, W., *Association Football and the Men Who Made It* (London: Caxton, 1905-06).
Inglis, S., *League Football and the Men Who Made It* (London: Willow, 1988).
The Book of Football (London: Amalgamated Press, 1906).

Robert Lewis

Economics

It is often alleged that sport has 'peculiar economics', and to an extent this is true. In conventional business an objective might well be to dominate the market and become a monopolist who can set higher prices and make larger profits than a company operating in a more competitive environment. This cannot occur in football. There is no game without a competitor. Manchester United v. Manchester United Reserves would eventually pall even for diehard fans of the Reds. Moreover, during the long history of commercialised football, the vast majority of clubs have not made profits, nor have they seen this as a prime objective. Most of them have preferred to be utility maximisers whose aim is to win cups and championships, rather than profit maximisers looking to earn revenue for their shareholders.

Nevertheless, economists can apply conventional analysis and concepts to much of what goes on in football. In looking at the demand for football the economist would examine how the variables of price, income, taste, and time operate in the market for the game. The lower the price of most goods, including those for leisure and sport, the greater will be the consumer demand. The reverse, of course, is also true – hence the protests about 'real fans' being excluded from Premiership football by the steep rise in the cost of season tickets. Price discrimination operates at most events, with higher prices being charged for better seats, and within football there is a quality aspect with higher prices for what is perceived as a better product, such as Premier League as opposed to non-League games. Disposable income is what determines how much fans have to spend on their consumption activities, and their tastes will influence the nature of this spending and whether they prefer to be spectators at a game or to watch it on a television screen at home or in a sports bar. The times at which matches are played can also affect the size of the crowd, especially the attendance of those travelling long distances to an away game.

On the supply side attention should be paid to the relative role of the various factors of production that are combined to create the football match – land, labour and capital. Land includes the fabric of the soccer ground as well as the area on which it is situated. Since the Taylor Report several clubs have sought to offset the costs of stadium redevelopment by selling their valuable inner-city sites and moving to a cheaper 'out-of-town' location. Labour obviously includes the players themselves, but also the backroom staff and those workers who manufacture the match equipment, tailor the team outfits and print the programmes and tickets. Capital in British football is predominately private, with only a few clubs, such as Huddersfield at McAlpine Stadium, sharing investment with the public sector. The motivation of investors can encompass those seeking a speculative gain, others looking for a safe rentier return, and the fans who are simply backing their team.

Even today, after the massive inflow of television and other non-gate revenues, few clubs are significantly profitable and huge dividends are a rarity. Nevertheless, it is clear that in many respects football clubs operate as conventional businesses. They are involved in purchasing equipment; renting or buying premises; recruiting, training and paying staff; promoting their product; and, of course, generating revenue. Those in football do seek additional sources of revenue. At the club level commercial widening takes place when more receipts are sought from traditional sources such as gate receipts by playing more games or by expanding stadium capacity where there is excess demand for seats. Within this revenue source clubs hope to sell more season tickets rather than rely on payment at the gate, as such sales guarantee an income prior to the start of the season. In contrast, market deepening occurs when new arrangements are made to secure revenue from sponsorship deals, merchandising, signage, media rights and other sources. A club at the cutting edge here would be Chelsea, with its concept of the Chelsea Village which currently encompasses two hotels, five restaurants, a night club, two shops, and, oh yes, a football pitch. The relationship is a symbiotic one. The football club brand enables these activities to have an image different from that of the conventional hotel or restaurant and, in turn, these activities help sustain the core business of playing football. Product innovation in football lies more in the province of the leagues and associations than the individual clubs. Product development involves creating a different type of contest. Here, apart from some five-a-side tournaments, football has lagged behind cricket with its one-day matches and athletics with its Grand Prix concept. In product improvement, however, football has been to the fore in changing the traditional product to encompass play-offs for promotion and relegation, and introducing a host of cup competitions to supplement the long-standing FA and SFA trophies.

Some economists view the various football leagues as business cartels, created in order to reduce economic competition. They see an arrangement of firms (football clubs) that agree to pursue joint policies with respect to key aspects of the environment in which they operate (Premier League, Football League, etc.). Such policies might cover pricing (minimum admission charges), distribution of revenue (pooling of gate receipts), output (fixture schedules), supply of inputs (restrictions on player mobility), cost of inputs (maximum wages) – all of which have featured in British league football. In many respects sports cartels resemble industrial ones, but with two major differences. First, most clubs have some degree of geographical monopoly with regard to their fan base, hence there is less danger than in a business cartel of a price-cutting war erupting to secure customers. Second, there is little chance of a club unilaterally opting to increase its output: indeed, it is hard to conceive of any club voluntarily quitting a league and remaining an effective competitor in the industry.

Nevertheless it is arguable that the degree of cartelisation has decreased in recent years. Only one plank of a strong cartel remains unscathed at the apogee of the English game: the existence of a central decision-making body with the power to discipline members for rule infractions. Cost-minimising regulations, such as maximum wages, salary caps, maximum team rosters, territorial restrictions on recruitment and impediments on player mobility are practically non-existent. Whether UEFA regulations will overcome the reluctance of the Premier League to reduce its size, and hence the demand for players, remains to be seen. On the other hand, group revenue raising policies are stronger, particularly regarding the selling of media rights – though some clubs would prefer to strike their own deals. But there are no regulations on admission prices or mechanisms to promote equality of playing strengths, a central feature of any crowd maximisation policy when home and away gates for matches between particular opponents are aggregated.

Football cartels emerge from the mutual interdependence of clubs: the gate revenue of any club depends on the performance of all clubs. Clubs may be sports competitors, but they can be economic partners. Only one team can win the championship but, in an effective cartel, all clubs can make profits. Yet historically most seem not to have focused on this economic side, preferring to spend any surplus funds on strengthening the team or developing the club's facilities rather than paying dividends to shareholders. This scenario is beginning to change and the 'bottom line' is becoming more important. A few clubs are now publicly quoted companies on the stock exchange whose owners seek a return on their capital commensurate to that achievable in other sectors of the economy. Technically this is in breach of a not yet rescinded FA rule, which limits football club dividends to 5 per cent of the notional face value of their shares. In 1983 Tottenham Hotspur circumvented this restriction by forming a holding company – free from such dividend limitations – to which the football club became a subsidiary enterprise. More than 20 other clubs have followed this route, though this still leaves the majority of clubs following traditional practice. Some observers suggest that, as happened in American sport, leisure and media groups may well take over football clubs to exploit the non-gate money activities in which they have more experience than the clubs themselves.

It should be stressed that what happens in the Premier Leagues in Scotland and England is not the norm for football as a whole. Publicly quoted companies are not yet the typical form of football club organisation. Moreover, despite the reactions of traditionalists to what they perceive as the rampant over-commercialisation of football, it is also worth emphasising that football is not big business by any conventional standards. The average Premier League club employs less that 200 people and at most the whole football sector may offer work to 10,000 employees, many of them part-timers. In a British labour force of some 28 million this is hardly significant. Very few clubs are capitalised at over £100 million and the annual turnover of most Premier League clubs is less than £50 million.

Sources:

Shackleton, J., 'Football as a Business', *Football Studies*, 3: 1 (April 2000), pp. 80–9.

Szymanski, S. and Kuypers, T., *Winners and Losers: The Business Strategy of Football* (London: Viking, 1999).

Further Reading:

Dobson, S. and Goddard, J., *The Economics of Football* (Cambridge: Cambridge University Press, 2001).

Hamil, S., Michie, J. and Oughton, C. (eds), *The Business of Football: A Game of Two Halves?* (Edinburgh: Mainstream, 1999).

See also Business

Wray Vamplew

Equipment

– *see* **Artificial Pitches, Football Boots, Footballs**

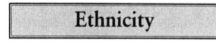

Ethnicity

– *see* **Racism and Ethnicity**

European Championship (formerly European Nations Cup)

The European Championship is a tournament organised by the European governing body, UEFA, for the national teams of all its members. It is held every four years and is played between the four-year cycles of the World Cup. It was begun in 1958 with the final taking place in 1960. It was originally called the European Nations Cup because, unlike today, there was no final championship; it was very much a cup competition, with games played on a home and away knock-out basis. The semi-finals and final were, however, played in one country so as to give it a tournament feel, the first such tournament being held in France. The trophy itself was named after Henri Delauney, the former general secretary of UEFA.

The inaugural tournament was beset by problems, mainly concerning those nations that did not consider the tournament worthy of entry. In fact only 17 nations deemed it important enough to enter; those who did not included all the British nations. However, on this occasion it was not only the British who saw an international competition as being beneath them. In fact it seemed that the only nations who took the tournament seriously were those who made up the majority of the Soviet Bloc. At the height of the Cold War this was probably a factor in the withdrawal of so many Western democracies.

The British nations were still very suspicious of competitive contact in tournaments that were not of their making. While they agreed to compete in World Cup tournaments after the Second World War, it cannot be said that they ever took them as seriously as they might have done. The national Football Associations also put pressure on clubs not to compete in the new UEFA competitions, reflecting their suspicion of contacts from abroad. This reluctance to compete may also be explained by the boom period that domestic football was experiencing at this time, with clubs attracting record crowds and a consequent increase in revenue. Despite several political conflicts involving those who did compete, particularly the spat between the USSR and Spain, the initial 1958/60 tournament was completed to popular approval – so much so that when the next phase came around there were only three dissenters.

West Germany was still embroiled in Cold War politics; England and Scotland simply maintained their aloof posture; but Northern Ireland and Wales did compete. However, they both went out in the first round to teams from the Eastern Bloc. Thankfully, during the tournament politics gave way to football as controversies were few and far between. After the 1964 edition, the European Championships began

Arsenal's Dennis Bergkamp beats Lyon's Brazilian defender Edmilson to score
(© Stuart MacFarlane, Arsenal FC)

to resemble something like what it is today.

By now all UEFA members, apart from Iceland, had agreed to participate. Due to the increase in numbers, qualification groups were set up, with the top team in each going on to the quarter-finals. The semi-finals and final were still played in one host nation, this time Italy. For the only time in the tournament's history the British nations were given the Home International Championships as their designated qualification group. That the English and Scottish deigned to compete in the 1966/68 edition, was no doubt due to the strides the tournament had made since its inception. That England had just won the World Cup on home turf would merely have shown what benefits could be gained from ultimate success in a major international competition.

As it was, England were the successful British qualifiers from their group and they achieved some success from their first entry into the competition. They finished third after defeating Spain in the quarter-finals, only to lose to Yugoslavia 1–0 in the semi-finals in Italy. A 2–0 win against the USSR in a third place play-off match meant a decent return from their first appearance. England were the only qualifiers for the 1970/72 edition, but this proved a blessing in disguise as they were totally outplayed in a defeat by their seemingly constant nemesis – West Germany. Wales were the only British qualifiers for the quarter-finals of the 1974/76 edition. How unfortunate it then was that the tournament finals still only covered the semi-finals onwards; it still remains a sad fact that the 1958 World Cup was the only finals of a major tournament that Wales have ever reached. However, they acquitted themselves well in defeat during the quarter-finals against a very strong Yugoslav team.

From 1980 onwards the format was again changed, with recognisable finals taking place in one host nation. For the first such tournament, held in Italy, eight teams would qualify and then play in two groups of four, with the top two going on to the semi-finals. This format gave the tournament a great deal more focus and exposure as it presented a recognisable event for the increasingly influential TV. England's appearance at the finals provoked outrage as it coincided with the first major incidents at international tournaments of what came to be known as the English disease – hooliganism. During their first encounter, with Belgium in Turin, the game was halted after tear gas used by the police to quell violent England fans affected the players as it wafted on to the field of play. While the game was able to restart, ending in a 1–1 draw, the tournament had been tarnished. Nor did the football offer much to enthuse about, as England went out in the first round, finishing third in their group.

The next appearance by a British nation occurred at the 1988 tournament, when England qualified for the finals held in West Germany. This proved to be just as much of a disaster as had their showing eight years earlier. While the team went home bottom of their group, without gaining a point, the fans repeated their notorious acts of destruction, with city streets now taking the place of stadia.

For the finals in 1992, England again qualified and again performed badly, going out in the first round bottom of their group. Scotland on the other hand performed admirably both on and off the pitch. While the team went out, in a difficult first round group, they at least performed with a semblance of grit and skill. Scotland's fans, meanwhile, behaved themselves immaculately, so much so that for many observers they were deemed the highlight of a rather sterile tournament.

A noteworthy year for both the tournament and English football followed in 1996. The popularity of the Championship had meant that the finals had been extended to incorporate sixteen teams, and as a reward for its construction of impressive new stadia England was given the honour of hosting this new, expanded tournament. While there were a few gripes about ticketing, the tournament was to be hailed as a great success. The much-feared threat of hooliganism never materialised; the feelings provoked were associated rather with fraternal bonding between fans from around Europe. There

was even the added excitement of a match between the 'old enemy' as Britain's only qualifiers, England and Scotland, were drawn to face each other in their first round group. England won the over-hyped match 2–0, which helped their progression to the next round, while Scotland unluckily missed out on qualification by one goal. As the English progressed to the semi-finals against West Germany the nation was gripped by a 'feel-good factor', which politicians tried to use for their own ends. While eventual defeat on penalties may have led to feelings of deflation, these only lasted for a short while as the nation could pride itself on a well organised and enjoyable tournament, whilst even having a team to match.

Sources:

Hammond, M., 'Euro 92 Finals', in *The European Football Yearbook 1992/93* (London: Sports Projects Ltd., 1992).

Henshaw, R., 'European Football Championship', in *The Encyclopaedia of World Soccer* (London: New Republic Books, 1979).

Ward, C., 'Euro 96', in *All Quiet on the Hooligan Front: Eight Years that Shook Football* (Edinburgh: Mainstream Publishing, 1996).

See also UEFA

Roy Abbott

Ex-Church Teams

Churches, along with public houses and places of work, can be said to be the chief institutions that gave birth to football clubs in Britain. Perhaps the most notable British club whose origins lay in the church is Scotland's Glasgow Celtic FC. Their inspiration in turn came from another team in whose formation the Catholic church was important, Hibernian FC of Edinburgh, formed by Canon Hannam in 1875. In 1887 Hibernian played Dumbarton in the Scottish FA Cup Final in Glasgow, and the well-attended match provided food for thought for a local Roman Catholic priest, Brother

Walfrid. Walfrid was a member of a teaching order whose ministry, in the east end of Glasgow, included many poor Irish Catholic families. Walfrid thought a football team could help to raise money for a church charity, the Poor Children's Dinner Table, as well as giving the locals a sense of pride and self-esteem. His parishioners took up his idea with enthusiasm and after their debut season, 1888/89, Celtic presented the sum of £421 to Catholic charities. In 1889 the Archbishop of Glasgow agreed to become a patron of the club, as did other members of the local clergy.

However, as Celtic became more successful (they were a founder member of the Scottish Football League in 1890) their links with the church declined. Walfrid took up a post in England in 1892, and by 1897 most of the charitable donations had dried up altogether. Profits were used to invest in new players – an increasing item of expenditure after 1893 when professionalism was legalised in Scotland – and a growing stadium. In 1897 the club became a limited company, although a sizeable minority of members wished to retain the charitable ethos. Nevertheless, Celtic fulfilled one of Walfrid's aims by remaining a source of pride for Glasgow's Catholics.

In England, the church was influential in the formation of several famous clubs. Aston Villa were formed in 1874 by members of Villa Cross Wesleyan Chapel in Birmingham, Fulham started out in 1879 as a church Sunday school team from Kensington, and Southampton's players were initially drawn from parishioners at St Mary's Church. They kept the name Southampton St Mary's until turning professional in 1892, seven years after their formation. To this day, Southampton are known as 'the Saints', although their connections with the church ended over a century ago. Stockport County was formed in 1883 as Heaton Norris Rovers by members of a local congregational chapel.

Like Celtic, many English church teams broke away from their origins within a few years of formation. The church may have viewed football as a way to keep young men from the temptations of money and the public house, but as the teams grew more successful, so those temptations grew stronger. In 1874 in Bolton a club was formed at Christ Church's Sunday school. The members chose the vicar to be president, but when the reverend gentleman insisted on attending meetings of the club the players declared their independence. In 1877 they held a meeting at a public house, the Gladstone Hotel, and called themselves Bolton Wanderers Football Club, severing their links with the church in the process.

One of the more enduring links between the church and football came in Barnsley. In 1887 the newly appointed curate of St Peter's church, Rev. Tiverton Preedy, formed a football team in an area hitherto dominated by rugby. Apparently Preedy turned to football because he was upset by the local rugby club's decision to play a game on Good Friday. A true muscular Christian, Preedy played in Barnsley St Peter's first game and acted as their chief fund-raiser. He recruited many local businessmen, including a family of brewers, to the club, remaining actively involved until 1893 when he took up a post in London. Four years later the club, who still retained the vicar of Barnsley as their president, dropped St Peter's from their name. A year later they joined the Football League and were happy to accept matches on Good Friday!

The church gave birth to a number of clubs, but once successful the clubs soon drifted away from their religious parentage.

Sources:

Dennis, B., Daykin, J. and Hyde, D., *Barnsley Football Club: The Official History 1887–1998* (Harefield: Marland, Simon, *Bolton Wanderers: A Complete Record 1877–1989* (Derby: Breedon, 1989).

Mason, T., *Association Football and English Society 1863–1915* (Brighton: Harvester, 1980).

McColl, G., *Celtic: The Official Illustrated History 1888–1996* (London: Hamlyn, 1998).

Further Reading:

Weir, J. (ed.), *Drink, Religion and Scottish Football* (Renfrew: Stewart Davidson, 1992).

John Coyle

Exhibitions

In England there is no tradition of exhibiting fine art objects and memorabilia connected with association football. One reason for this could simply be a distinct lack of artwork detailing the game. In order to remedy this the FA decided to launch the Football and the Fine Arts Competition in 1953. Open to painters, sculptors and other kinds of artists, the competition, and the exhibition that would arise from it, was considered by the FA to be an excellent way of celebrating its ninetieth anniversary. They believed that the exhibition would have lasting value. The exhibition was the first of its kind and was welcomed by press and public alike.

This was, as far as we know, the first major exhibition relating to the game, but it was not until the later 1980s that anything resembling a tradition of such activity began to be established. Key figures in this regard were a younger generation of curators and keepers anxious to give popular culture its rightful and (they hoped) appealing place within the museum world. In 1988, for example, the Harris Museum in Preston created an exhibition to celebrate the centenary of the Football League. '100 nil', which later toured several other cities, traced the game from its humble beginnings through to its development into the world's most popular sport. This was the first time that an exhibition had attempted to interpret the rich heritage of the association game to the public, covering a variety of topics including the crowd, hooligans, and women and football. This period also saw the development of football's first significant permanent exhibition in the form of the club museum, the first of which opened at Manchester United Football Club in 1985. With the commercial success of this museum, other clubs, notably Arsenal and Liverpool, have followed suit, creating similar purpose-built exhibitions dedicated to their past.

Major football events have increasingly been accompanied by exhibitions of various types. England hosted the European Championship in 1996 and many of the participating cities produced temporary football exhibitions. Leeds Leisure Services organised a particularly notable exhibition entitled 'More Than A Game'. This imaginative visitor attraction was a large-scale interactive exhibition, exploring and celebrating the game from the fans' perspective. High-tech displays brought the story of the world's most popular game to life. Visitors were also asked to take part in a 'smellorama', in which they could guess a selection of aromas associated with football. Housed in a set of mobile buildings next to Elland Road, home of Leeds United, the hands-on experience was a great success. One of the most important collectors of football memorabilia, the late Harry Langton, exhibited his private collections at the 1990 and 1994 World Cups. A number of regional museums also based temporary exhibitions around his collections during the European championships of 1996. His vast collection was purchased, in 1998, by FIFA. They, in turn, sold the collection to The National Football Museum in England at the Deepdale Stadium, Preston.

Sources:

The FA, *Football And The Fine Arts* (London: The Naldrett Press, 1953).

Further Reading:

FIFA, *F.I.F.A. Museum Collection* (Berlin: Verlags-GmbH, 1996).

Pickering, D., *The Cassell Soccer Companion* (London: Cassell, 1994).

Mark Bushell and Richard William Cox

Exports

Footballers have long been noted for their geographic mobility and this entry looks at British players who have spent a proportion of their careers overseas. The first exiles were the Scottish players who began to appear in English teams from the early 1880s, a flow which increased after professionalism was legalised in England in

1885 (it was not legalised in Scotland until 1893), and has continued to the present day. Here, however, we are concerned with excursions abroad.

The first foreign exodus came after 1923, when a number of British players were lured to North America by the prospect of high wages and the opportunity to avoid the effects of a trade depression at home. Tom Muirhead, a Scottish international, was among them, but many found playing standards low and soon returned to Britain. An exception was Sam Chedgzoy of Everton, who had won five England caps and emigrated to the United States aged 37 in 1926. He settled in Montreal, Canada, and continued to play for the local team until 1940. Robert Faulkner, a Scot who had played for Blackburn Rovers, also settled in Canada, winning three caps for his adopted country.

Another short-lived exodus came in 1950, when Stoke City centre-half Neil Franklin, capped 27 times by England, shocked the English football world by signing for a club in Bogotá, Columbia. That country was not recognised by the world governing body, FIFA, and Franklin found himself suspended from all football for a time. Eventually he was allowed to return to play League football in England, but he never again represented his country.

A more substantial movement of labour came in the late 1950s and early 1960s, when wealthy Italian clubs began to attract British talent. First to go was Leeds United's Welsh international centre forward John Charles, who joined Juventus of Turin for a British record fee of £65,000 in 1957. Charles, an immensely gifted player who could also operate in central defence, won three Italian championships while at Juventus. Others who moved to Italy at a time when the maximum wage was still operating in England were less successful. English forward Jimmy Greaves endured a brief, unhappy spell at AC Milan in 1961, and Scotland's Denis Law had a short stint at Torino, both soon returning to the Football League. England international forward Gerry Hitchens did better, playing for six years in Serie A for three different clubs.

The lifting of the maximum wage in England helped reduce the lure of the lira, but during the 1970s and '80s it again became common for top British players to venture abroad. Kevin Keegan left European Champions Liverpool in 1977 and spent three years at Hamburg. Another England international forward, Nottingham Forest's Tony Woodcock, joined Cologne in 1979, but thereafter Spain, Italy and France became the favoured destinations. Wales's Mark Hughes, England's Gary Lineker and Scotland's Steve Archibald had spells at Barcelona, while England winger Laurie Cunningham left West Bromwich Albion for Real Madrid. Italy's Serie A featured Englishmen Trevor Francis (Sampdoria and Atalanta), Luther Blissett, Ray Wilkins and Mark Hateley (all AC Milan) and Paul Gascoigne (Lazio), plus Scotland's Graeme Souness (Sampdoria) and Wales's Ian Rush (Internazionale). England stars Glenn Hoddle (Monaco) and Chris Waddle (Marseilles) took advantage of the 1980s football boom in France, as did Wilkins, who joined Paris St Germain. The exodus was given added momentum after 1985, when English clubs were banned from European club competitions following the Heysel Stadium disaster. Joining a foreign club was the only way for the top players to get involved in Europe at club level. In 1991 Gary Lineker was persuaded to end his playing days as a professional footballer in the newly established Japanese League.

Since the restoration of England's clubs in European competitions and the formation of the Premier League in 1992, England has become a net importer of footballing talent, while the Scottish leagues have also witnessed an increase in the number of imported players. Rangers began this trend in the mid-1980s, attracting top English stars followed by players from Europe, and other Scottish sides soon followed suit. The changes to the transfer system within Europe following the Bosman case in 1995/96 may lead to British players going abroad in numbers again. This allowed players to move to any club within the European Union at the completion of their contract without any transfer fee being involved. Scotland's late twentieth-century exports John Collins (Monaco) and Paul Lambert (Borussia Dortmund), plus England's Steve McManaman (Real Madrid) may, like Charles and Keegan before them, represent the start of a trend towards movement abroad by British players.

There has also been a clutch of British managers and coaches who have known more success abroad that at home. Jimmy Hogan, a player with Fulham and Bolton Wanderers before the First World War, became Austrian national coach in 1914, doing much to develop football skills and techniques in that country. George Raynor, a Yorkshireman with a modest playing record, was appointed Swedish national coach in 1946 and led the team to an Olympic gold medal two years later. After spells with Juventus and Lazio in Italy, and with Coventry City, Raynor returned to Sweden and coached the national side to the final of the 1958 World Cup, where they lost to Brazil. Another Briton who coached in Italy was Leslie Lievesley, formerly a player with Doncaster Rovers and Manchester United. He was coach of the outstanding Torino side of the late 1940s, and perished along with his players in the Superga air disaster in 1949. Bobby Houghton, a former Fulham reserve, was manager of Swedish club Malmö when they reached the European Cup final in 1979, losing 0–1 to Nottingham Forest. His assistant, Roy Hodgson, went on to manage the Swiss national team and Inter Milan before an unsuccessful stint in charge of Blackburn Rovers. Finally, despite his many successes in England, it is worth remembering that Terry Venables' only national championship title was won in Spain in 1985 when he was in charge of Barcelona.

Sources:

Charles, W. J., *The Gentle Giant* (London: Stanley Paul, 1962).

Harding, J., *For the Good of the Game: the Official History of the Professional Footballers' Association* (London: Robson, 1991).

Lamming, D., *An England Football Internationalists' Who's Who 1872–1988* (Beverley: Hutton, 1990).

Rush, I., *My Italian Diary* (London: Arthur Barker, 1989).

Turner, D. and White, A., *The Breedon Book of Football Managers* (Derby: Breedon Books, 1993).

Further Reading:

Adamson, R., *Bogota Bandit. The Outlaw Life of Charlie Mitten* (Edinburgh: Mainstream, 1998).

Franklin, N., *Soccer at Home and Abroad* (London: Stanley Paul, 1956).

Greaves, J. and Taylor, C., *A Funny Thing Happened on my Way to Spurs* (London: Kaye, 1962).

Hughes, M., *Sparky: Barcelona, Bayern and Back* (London: Cockerel, 1989).

John Coyle

FA Cup

The Football Association Challenge Cup (commonly known as the FA Cup) was the first knockout competition of its type in the world. Introduced in 1871 by then FA Secretary C. W. Alcock, and entered by just 15 clubs, its first winner was the Wanderers club, who beat the Royal Engineers at the Oval by a single goal. For the next decade a succession of southern amateur sides won the trophy, until 1883 when Blackburn Olympic became the first non-amateur and northern club to succeed. Tottenham Hotspur, then of the Southern League, became the last non-league side to take the Cup in 1901; they also stopped an unbeaten run of 18 victories by northern teams. The early finals had a decidedly gentlemanly flavour – the kick off of one 1870s final was delayed to allow players to watch the University boat race – and crowds were only several thousand strong. However, with the advent of professionalism and the spread of the game, the Cup final became one of the great centrepieces of the season, with the 1913 game attracting a crowd of 120,081 to the Crystal Palace. The Cup final moved to the newly built Empire Stadium, Wembley in 1923, a location that has become synonymous with the 'magic' of the FA Cup. The first Wembley final saw an estimated crowd of 200,000 watch Bolton beat West Ham 2–0, and became known as the 'White Horse' final, in recognition of a police horse named 'Billy' that helped herd many thousands of supporters off the pitch.

For many the road to Wembley is an opportunity to see less fancied teams compete against the giants of the English game. Perhaps the most remarkable giant-killing record in FA Cup history is that of non-League Yeovil Town (of the Nationwide Conference in 2000/01) whose victory over Blackpool in December 2000 gave the club its twentieth victory against League opposition. A 1948/49 run, which included a 2–1 victory over First Division Sunderland, saw them progress as far as the fifth round. Arguably the most successful individual 'giant-killer' has been manager Geoff Chapple, who, with Woking and then Kingstonian, oversaw seven victories against League opposition in the 1990s. Notable Cup final giant killings have included Sunderland's 1–0 victory over the strong Leeds United side of 1973, Second Division Southampton's defeat of Manchester United in 1976, and the Wimbledon victory over Liverpool in 1988.

Although finals can often be tense and less than satisfying as spectacles, they have often been enhanced by a particularly dramatic turn of events or by the importance that a game has taken on for a particular player. The game that best combined both of these features was undoubtedly the so-called 'Matthews Final' of 1953. With most football fans (mistakenly) believing that 38-year-old Stanley Matthews would soon be retiring, there was widespread hope for a Blackpool victory and the FA Cup winner's medal that had so far eluded him. Although technically not a great game, a thrilling climax saw Blackpool pull back a 3–1 deficit to beat Bolton Wanderers 4–3, the winner coming with only a minute remaining. But for Matthews' presence, it might well have been termed the 'Mortensen' final, with the Blackpool forward scoring the first ever FA Cup final hat trick (although the TV commentary referred to his first goal, which took a crucial deflection, as an own goal for much of the game).

Other players have been associated with specific finals for less happy reasons. In the late 1950s and early 1960s, for example, a number of games were marred by serious injuries; the 'Wembley hoodoo' became a stock journalistic phrase. Manchester City's Bert Trautmann (1956), Manchester United's Ray Wood (1957), Nottingham Forest's Roy Dwight (1959), Blackburn's Dave Whelan (1960) and Leicester's Len Chalmers (1961) all fell victim to it. Trautmann and Dwight at least had the pleasure of finishing on the winning side, with Trautmann, City's goalkeeper, actually completing the game despite what transpired to be a broken neck. The problems caused by these injuries helped fuel the call for substitutes that was eventually met in 1965, although, in 1959, the *Daily Sketch* could still proclaim that Forest's effort after losing Dwight was 'a soccer Dunkirk ... soccer as we know it, as we invented it – and as I hope we continue to play it'.

Forty-two different clubs won the FA Cup between 1872 and 2000, with Manchester United's ten successes in 15 finals representing the best record.

Through the telling and retelling of the sort of tales relayed above, the FA Cup has gained rich layers of what is usually termed 'tradition'. Significantly in this regard, it was the last major English competition to receive sponsorship, this only coming in 1994. Moreover, attempts to

Bill Shankly (left) and Stanley Matthews
(National Football Museum)

win the deal by brewers Fosters were rejected because association with alcohol was believed to tarnish its image. Given this strong sense of history and heritage that has been attached to the tournament, it is hardly surprising that the decision by its most successful club not to enter in the 1999/2000 season caused much outrage. Encouraged by the FA to go instead to Brazil, where, it was believed, participation in the FIFA Club World Championship would improve England's chances of hosting the 2006 World Cup Finals, Manchester United was accused of devaluing the traditions of the English game. However, while United's absence may have been a factor in producing the lowest average attendance (10,765) across the tournament since the Second World War, there were already signs that the Cup might be losing something of its hold on the popular imagination. Certainly, average attendances have remained more or less static throughout the period from 1987 at a time when attendances for league matches have been rising, with crowd size in the earlier rounds being particularly disappointing. The habit of many clubs of charging season ticket holders extra for FA Cup ties may also have been a factor here. For all this, however, the FA Cup still remains the most high-profile and uniquely prestigious domestic cup tournament in the world.

Sources:
Butler, B., *The Official History of the Football Association* (London: Queen Anne Press, 1993).

Further Reading:
Butler, B., *The Giant Killers* (London: London, 1982).
Walvin, J., *The People's Game* (Edinburgh: Mainstream, 1994).

See also Football Association

Dave Russell and Sam Johnstone

FA Premiership

While the Premier League is simply a different name for the old First Division of the Football League, the implications of its formation go much further. Although it was formed, officially, on 23 September 1991 the League was a culmination of negotiations that had begun during the 1980s. For it was then that regular live football had first hit the nation's television screens. Throughout the decade the broadcasting companies had combined to keep the cost of football down by negotiating contracts together. The monies being gained from these television rights were shared equally among all 92 members of the Football League.

The major clubs were not happy about the sharing of these, even then, major spoils. As it was they were frustrated by the two-thirds majority needed when it came to voting for change in the Football League's constitution; the smaller clubs were not going to vote to deprive themselves of much needed funds. Consequently during the 1980s threats were made by some of the leading clubs to resign from the Football League and set up a separate organisation that would negotiate its own television and merchandising contracts. Throughout the decade, however, the major clubs were able to negotiate certain changes to their benefit. For example, in 1985 the First Division were able to negotiate a deal whereby they would receive a 50 per cent share of all TV and sponsorship monies coming in. This was to appease them only for a short while, however.

Due to the commercial benefits of advertisers gaining national exposure for their wares, ITV were soon able to outbid the BBC for rights without breaking their own bank balance. As ITV were looking only to attract large national audiences rather than regional ones for its advertisers, they were only interested in clubs and matches that could supply this need. ITV therefore approached what has since become known as the 'big five' clubs about going their own separate ways. These 'big five' were Manchester United, Liverpool, Everton, Tottenham Hotspur and Arsenal. They all had several important aspects in common: they had a long traditional history; all were successful in the modern era; and they all could be called 'national clubs' – that is, they could count on relatively loyal support throughout the country, therefore supplying consistently large television audiences.

These clubs threatened to break away in 1988, but instead negotiated a new, improved contract for the next four years. However, the problem still arose that they had to share it with the other First Division clubs. Up until then the threats had been just that – no doubt due to the fact that, had these clubs followed up on their threats, they would have been isolated, outside the auspices of the European governing body UEFA, meaning that they would not have been allowed to compete in any future European competitions. However, on 15 April 1989 a tragic event was to occur that would change British football forever. On that day 96 football fans were killed at Hillsborough, due in part to inadequate facilities at the ground.

In response to the tragedy Lord Justice Peter Taylor was appointed to set up an inquiry. In his findings, released in January 1990, there came a damning condemnation of the country's football grounds, with recommendations that grounds in the top two divisions should be made all-seater. To achieve this the Football Trust was set up, with the remit of financing these alterations. Despite all the financial help from the Trust, clubs still complained that they could not meet all the costs. This inspired ITV, in the shape of Greg Dyke, Managing Director of London Weekend Television, to push the 'big five' once again to break away. This time all 22 clubs in the top division were included, so as to provide strength in numbers. He knew that ITV's current contract ran out in 1992, so he began negotiations fully two years before its end. The clubs were encouraged to go further than they had done previously by the confirmation that they would still receive the Football Trust money even if they resigned from the League. However, they still needed official support so as to appease UEFA.

They found this in the shape of the Football Association, who acceded to the fledgling Premier League's request, due to fears that their own existence was under threat. Again, this was in a sense due to the Taylor Report, which had criticised both themselves and the Football League over their lack of leadership and control. In response to this the Football League, in a report entitled *One Game One Team One Voice*, had recommended that the two bodies amalgamate to provide one unifying force within English football. The Football Association, however, saw this as a threat to its very existence and immediately set out its own plans for the future with the 'Blueprint for the Future of Football'. Central to this plan was the formation of a new league, which they would oversee. Despite internal rules put in place to prevent mass resignations from the League, a legal ruling by the courts stated that the clubs could indeed join the FA in forming the Premier League. The TV deal on which the whole League was based had yet to be settled, however. ITV's previously comfortable bargaining position had now been threatened by a new player in town – the Rupert Murdoch-owned satellite station BSkyB. This fledgling, and at the time ailing, station was putting all its financial muscle behind acquiring rights to the Premiership. At a meeting in May 1992 ITV upped their bid for the rights: immediately BSkyB put in a far higher bid. The issue went to a vote of the 22 clubs at the meeting, with a two-thirds majority needed for whichever bid was to be successful. While four of the 'big five' stuck with the ITV deal, as the independent station was still promising to concentrate on them, the majority of the other clubs voted for the BSkyB deal, as their money would be shared throughout the whole league. The voting went 14 to 6 (with two abstentions) in favour of the BSkyB deal. While BSkyB would pay £305 million for a five-year contract, the BBC also agreed to pay £44 million over the same period for recorded highlights. Added to this were all the sponsorship and merchandising rights that could be pooled. This was improved on further in 1997, when a new four-year deal was struck for £670 million. The relationship between the Premier League and BSkyB seemed a marriage made in heaven.

In June 2000, BSkyB agreed to pay £1.11billion for live braodcasting of Premiership matches, while NTL agreed £328 million (later withdrawn) and ITV £183 million to broadcast edited highlights.

For the Football Association, however, it would seem that their original intentions for the Premier League have been somewhat overshadowed. They receive virtually no financial benefit from the League and are not given any say when it comes to negotiating any commercial rights. Their hope that the League would be reduced to 18 clubs, so as to help in national team preparation, has only partially been acceded to, with the League now reduced to 20 clubs.

In its early years, the competition has been very much dominated by Manchester United, winners six times between 1993 and 2000 and runners-up when Blackburn Rovers (1995) and Arsenal (1998) proved victorious. There has been great concern about the dominance of a small elite (only ten sides managed a top-three finish from 1993) and the difficulty that promoted sides have experienced in establishing themselves in the Premiership. This was especially an issue in 1998, when all three sides promoted the previous season were relegated. However, these patterns represent a slight hardening of pre-existing trends from the 1980s (only 11 sides finished in the top three of the old First Division between 1985 and 1992, and six promoted clubs experienced immediate relegation in that period), rather than a specific product of the Premiership itself. While contemporary football economics will ensure that very few clubs ever win the Premiership, changing economic fortunes amongst the elite clubs, and the skill or otherwise of individual managers and coaches, will provide at least some competitive interest.

Sources:

Conn, D., *The Football Business: Fair Game in the 90s* (Edinburgh: Mainstream Publishing, 1998).

Kelly, G., *Sweet F.A.* (London: Collins Willow, 1999).

Further Reading:

Dempsey, P. and Reily, K., *Big Money Beautiful Game: Winners and Losers in Financial Football* (London: Nicholas Brearley Publishing, 1998).

Roy Abbott

FIFA

The Fédération Internationale de Football Association (FIFA), the governing body of world football, was founded in Paris on 21 May 1904 by seven European football associations (France, Belgium, Denmark, Netherlands, Spain, Sweden and Switzerland). The two key figures behind the inception of FIFA were the Dutch banker, Carl Hirschman and the Frenchman Robert Guérin, who was also the organisation's first President (1904–06). Both men viewed England as the natural head of the new federation, given its status as the birthplace of the modern game. Thus, the Football Association was approached on a number of occasions during the last decade of the nineteenth century and the early years of the twentieth century with a view to taking up a leadership role in the international governance of the game. However, the FA refused to involve itself, believing that while it existed there was no need for another governing body, and instead adopted an insular and somewhat arrogant attitude towards FIFA.

Although the FA eventually joined the world body in 1905, and assumed a leadership role with the Englishman Daniel Woolfall holding the presidency between 1906 and 1918, Britain's early relationship with FIFA continued to be fractious. In the wake of the First World War, the British associations, supported by Belgium, Luxembourg and France, called for the exclusion of the former 'enemy' nations of Germany, Austria and Hungary from the FIFA fold. When FIFA's neutral associations refused to countenance these demands, Britain withdrew. Despite being persuaded to rejoin in 1924, the British associations remained at odds with FIFA, particularly over the issue of amateurism. In a dispute over the International Olympic Committee's decision to formally ratify 'broken-time' payments for participants in the Olympic football tournament, the FA decided in 1928 to resign from the world body and, although the British still participated in international competition, it was not until 1946 that its football associations rejoined FIFA. In spite of the problems which Britain's abstentionist policy engendered, FIFA's list of constituents took on an increasingly diverse character as the early twentieth century progressed. During the presidency of the Frenchman Jules Rimet, the development of world soccer was particularly pronounced, with FIFA membership increasing from 20 countries in 1921 to 85 by 1954. As a consequence of this expansion, key figures in FIFA decided that it was necessary to decentralise its administrative functions and responsibilities, and this led to the eventual formation of six continental confederations which took over the governance of football in their regions.

Jules Rimet's other significant achievement was, of course, the creation of the World Cup, the first edition of which was played in Uruguay in 1930. Since then, the final stage of the competition has developed into a multi-million dollar global media and marketing spectacle involving 32 teams. The driving force behind the dramatically expanded and commercialised World Cup was the Brazilian businessman, João Havelange, who ousted the conservative Englishman, Sir Stanley Rous, in 1974 to become the first non-European FIFA President. Until the emergence of Havelange, the international federations' leading administrative figures had all been northern European (FIFA's list of presidents reads as follows: Robert Guérin, France, 1904–06; Daniel Woolfall, England, 1906–18; Jules Rimet, France, 1921–54; Rudolfe Seeldrayers, Belgium, 1954/55; Arthur Drewry, England, 1956–61; Stanley Rous, England, 1961–74). Although the numbers of affiliated members hailing from the developing world had expanded dramatically following the collapse of colonialism during the 1950s and '60s, FIFA remained somewhat Eurocentric, and its newer members from Africa and Asia found their needs and aspirations within world football routinely frustrated by a European-controlled administration. Recognising the possibilities which FIFA's one-nation-one-vote franchise provision offered, Havelange shrewdly manipulated these tensions and, in the run-up to the 1974 FIFA Congress, began making a series of election promises to FIFA's developing constituencies. Once elected, Havelange set out to fulfil his mandate and, having secured support from Adidas and Coca-Cola, was able to implement his ambitious development plans and expansion programmes aimed at satisfying the third world's calls for global equity within the context of world football. Thus, the World Cup was enlarged to 24 teams for the 1982 World Cup in Spain, and then to 32 teams for the 1998 edition in France, to facilitate greater representation from the third world. Development initiatives were set up throughout Asia and Africa, and new international under-age competitions were established to encourage FIFA's less developed members to play a fuller part in international football.

By the early twenty-first century FIFA was charged with the governance of a global football industry estimated to have an annual turnover of $250 billion. Although his motives and the manner in which he dispatched his presidential duties have been questioned, Havelange's stewardship of FIFA undoubtedly heralded an era of unprecedented democratisation both within world football's corridors of power and in terms of opportunities on the field of play. When he was replaced at the helm of FIFA by Sepp Blatter in 1998, the world body constituted 203 members and was organising eight international competitions, including the recently inaugurated World Club Championship.

Source:

Yallop, D., *How They Stole the Game* (London: Potic Products, 1999).

See also World Cup

Paul Darby

Facilities

The primary function of a football ground is to provide spectators with reasonable comfort for the viewing of games, and modern stadia also include a diversity of additional facilities. Early grounds could be very primitive: players frequently had to change at remote locations such as pubs, even after some grounds had been enclosed. Wealthier clubs built pavilions to provide improved facilities. Generally, however, grounds could be cold, muddy places with most spectators standing in the open in all weathers. Conditions for such fans did not improve much over the next century. Even clubs of the stature of Newcastle, Chelsea, and Sunderland still had vast tracts of uncovered terracing until the 1990s. Affluent supporters enjoyed a better state of affairs. Substantial main stands were built from the 1890s, with particularly luxurious facilities for directors. Private executive boxes are commonplace in modern stadia, but were a glamorous novelty at Old Trafford in 1965. Food and drink facilities have improved vastly since the days of traditional Bovril and meat pies. Nowadays, stadia possess a wide range of catering services, from fast-food outlets to luxury dining rooms.

Today's supporters enjoy much better toilet facilities than in the past. The standard of football ground toilets was highlighted by the BBC TV fanzine *Standing Room Only* in 1991. Increased numbers of female spectators require that 20 per cent of a ground's toilet provision be for women. The Football Stadia Development Committee suggest that clubs provide a minimum of one urinal per 70 men and one WC per 35 females attending games. For disabled spectators proportionally more adapted toilets are provided.

Journalists have generally been accorded excellent facilities at grounds. Radio and television brought in their own outside broadcast units as coverage increased from the 1960s. Specially constructed gantries were erected by major clubs, but today broadcasting facilities are generally integrated within the fabric of stadia. Although half-time scoreboards existed from at least the Edwardian period and possibly earlier, the trend towards a coordinated system of spectator information began with public address systems and electronic display boards in the 1960s. Jimmy Hill's Coventry City were a pioneer in this field, as Radio Sky Blue kept fans entertained and informed from 1964, complemented by a state-of-the-art electric scoreboard. Large-screen video displays are now commonplace at major stadia such as Highbury and Ibrox. The Sony JumboTron combines high definition with immaculate colour, and can act as the focal point of an entertainment package that includes advertising and replays of key action.

Manchester United opened a club museum in 1986, and other big clubs such as Celtic, Rangers and Liverpool have followed suit. Museums are one of the modern marketing strategies clubs use to target a family audience, resulting in stadia with special enclosures, crèches, and retail outlets. Clubs have realised that their revamped stadia are multi-purpose facilities which can be utilised to their optimum as office space, function rooms or conference venues.

Football pitches in Britain are usually reserved for the playing of that game alone. Unlike in the antipodes, the recuperative powers of the grass are not seen as warranting summer use for other sports. In any event, as the close season gets shorter, there is less free time available for non-football use. Historically the area surrounding the pitch has been used for athletics and cycling, which proved a major fundraiser for clubs in the late nineteenth century: at times both Rangers and Celtic obtained over 10 per cent of their income from such sources. These days rarely is the pitch used for income generation, save for those clubs with superior facilities who lease the ground for representative or neutral-ground football fixtures. Occasionally, most notably in the case of Crystal Palace and Wimbledon, clubs actually share grounds.

That the playing area remains sacrosanct makes sense in the light of the need to keep it playable despite the vagaries of the British climate. Less explicably, many clubs also under-utilised their stands and other capital assets, although this has changed with the firm entrenchment of profit-maximising commercialism in the modern game. Weddings and conferences are catered for, pop concerts fill the grandstands, and many clubs offer the aficionados museums and the ubiquitous shop. No British club has yet fully adopted the club concept epitomised by Barcelona at its Nou Camp estate, with its indoor sports halls, many restaurants and community facilities, though Chelsea are taking a more capitalist approach along similar lines with their Chelsea Village concept. For most clubs, however, it is the use of dining areas and entertainment space that brings in the money, with some non-commercial use of their facilities via their involvement in football in the community projects.

Source:

Inglis, S., *Football Grounds of Britain* (Third edition) (London: Collins Willow, 1996).

Further Reading:

John, G. and Sheard, R., *Stadia: a Design and Development Guide* (Second edition) (London: Architectural Press, 1997).

Tom Preston

Fan Clubs

– *see* **Fan Culture, Football Supporters' Association, Fanzines**

Fan Culture

Football fan culture may be defined as anything that surrounds and enhances the experience of being a supporter, including attaching oneself to a particular club and remaining loyal. Historically, this would have been the club of the local town or city, although recently media coverage has extended fan bases of the larger clubs nationally and even internationally. Watching football brings excitement, spectacle, colour, noise and vicarious experience to sometimes dull lives. Local identification and rivalry can enhance the experience through 'derby' matches. Early football commentators noted spectators' 'partisanship'; they sometimes disputed with the referee, booed and 'hooted' the opposition, demonstrating a symbolic citizenship or focus of local pride. Another symbolic tradition was the 'invasion' of London by provincial fans on FA Cup final day.

In the early years of the game, the average fan was youngish, white, male and from the skilled working-class or lower middle-class. Other groups attended games: there was always a minority of middle-class support (around 10 per cent) in the grandstands, and some women (probably 5 to 10 per cent). In an essentially male subculture that mixed 'rough' elements with 'respectable', there was naturally some humour, swearing, drinking, gambling and occasional violence. Supporters illustrated their allegiance, sometimes through songs, ribbons, rosettes and cards displaying 'Play up, Rovers!'. Attendance may have involved a visit to the pub or music hall. Matchcards, programmes and cigarette cards were all well-established by the 1890s. Occasionally, enthusiasm would be overtaken by frustration, and disorder would follow, including assaults on players, referees, property and other spectators.

Between the wars, football fandom remained essentially the same, but perhaps became a little more sophisticated. Supporters' clubs became more active, and the National Federation had 150,000 affiliated individual members by 1934, consisting mainly of middle-class and lower middle-class supporters. Their principal function was to raise money for clubs and help out with various organisational and practical tasks. They stressed good behaviour, usually complied with clubs' wishes and had little say in running clubs.

The media, especially local and national

Two young Oldham fans holding inflatable bananas almost as big as themselves, Charlton Athletic v Oldham Athletic, 1989 (© Tim Reder)

newspapers, have always been very important in popularising the game, and creating local club identities. This was evident before 1914, but increased dramatically by the 1930s with extensive national press coverage. The growth in football 'pools' gambling, although not necessarily connected with spectatorship, helped to forge another link between supporters and football. Radio expanded rapidly in the 1930s, and match reports began to be broadcast. Novels, comics and magazines including football themes were produced, the latter containing articles on clubs and individuals. One important aspect of this period was that football culture ceased to appear as a 'threat' to the establishment, appearing instead to demonstrate more humour, restraint and balance than before 1914.

Football experienced a massive surge in popularity in the Britain of austerity just after the Second World War, but attendances declined from the mid-1950s as alternative leisure pursuits expanded. Many of the trends of the late 1930s continued, however, and media coverage increased, especially on television, from the mid-1960s. This had the effect of creating football 'fans' who never attended games. Hooliganism, although existing before, became a major problem from the late 1960s, increasingly building on rivalries and hostilities endemic to football, and probably increased its attraction to young, aggressive working-class males, whilst deterring some other supporters.

Terrace 'style' became associated with these fans, evolving from skinhead, through suedehead, and 1970s 'glam' to casuals, 'Perry Boys' and 'scallies'. The latter sported fashionable trainers and designer wear, influenced by contact with smarter European fans like the Italian 'ultras'. The nadir of football's reputation in 1985, after Heysel and Bradford, led to a resurgence in more constructive fandom, especially with the founding of the Football Supporters Association to promote co-operation and a positive image. The still-growing fanzine movement also illustrates another aspect of fans' do-it-yourself culture.

There appeared to be a decline in hooliganism during the 1990s, and a move

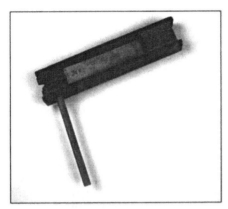

Supporter's rattle, c.1900
(National Football Museum)

Further Reading:
Giulianotti, R., Bonney, D. and Hepworth, M.
(eds), *Football Violence and Social Identity*
(London: Routledge, 1994).
Haynes, R., *The Football Imagination: the Rise
of Football Fanzine Culture* (Aldershot:
Arena, 1995).
Redhead, S. (ed.), *The Passion and the Fashion*
(Aldershot: Avebury, 1993).

See also National Federation of Supporters' Clubs

Robert Lewis

Fantasy Football

towards a more celebratory carnival atmosphere, illustrated by Scottish and Irish international fans and the 'inflatable' craze. Following the Taylor Report, the introduction of all-seater stadia and the increase in admission prices, football at the top level seems to be moving towards a more affluent middle-class audience rather than its traditional working-class support. One illustration of this is the increase in literature and glossy magazines about football, including club histories and fans' confessional declarations, following Nick Hornby's influential *Fever Pitch* (1992). The more comfortable, less threatening, more publicised re-invention of football and its image has begun to attract more female support as well, as clubs – perhaps deliberately – seem to be re-positioning the game as 'family entertainment'.

Sources:
Mason, T., *Association Football and English
Society, 1863–1915* (Brighton: Harvester,
1980).
Redhead, S., *Post-fandom and the Millennial
Blues* (London: Routledge, 1997).
Redhead, S., *Football With Attitude*
(Manchester: Wordsmith, 1991).
Russell, D., *Football and the English* (Preston:
Carnegie, 1997).
Williams, J., and Wagg, S. (eds), *British Football
and Social Change* (Leicester: Leicester
University Press, 1991).

It's often said that football is a game of opinion, and nowhere else can a fan's opinions be so thoroughly put to the test as in the arena of fantasy football. 'Fantasy' Football is a game that is based on the 'real' performances of actual players, and therefore the 'real' situations encountered by managers of professional clubs.

'Fantasy' sports began in America and were introduced to Britain by the London-based commercial enterprise Fantasy League. Fantasy football was brought to the public's notice by the *Daily Telegraph* in the 1993/94 season. The success of the *Telegraph*'s league soon spawned many spin-offs in other national newspapers, but most notably in local and regional newspapers where players from the lower divisions and non-league clubs could play in 'teams' alongside Premiership and European Clubs. Fantasy leagues have been designed for World Cups, the European Champions League, a 'European League', the FA Cup and a number of other competitions. Evidence of the popularity of fantasy football was to be found in the culmination of the 1994/95 season. The *Daily Telegraph*'s 'Fantasy League' was won by 12-year-old Jonathan Roberts from Blackburn, who beat 341,866 other entrants to the prize of a two-week holiday anywhere in the world to watch a match of his choice. The success of fantasy football in the *Daily Telegraph* was quickly followed by the newspaper's fantasy cricket. Other leagues and competitions have developed in rugby and golf. The concept of fantasy football grew in popularity on the back of the television show of the same name, first presented by comedians David Baddiel and Frank Skinner in 1994. The amount of the show devoted to fantasy football gradually declined as the programme became known for a series of interviews and sketches loosely based on football themes. Although highly popular, the show was also criticised for its endorsement of 'laddish' culture and occasional racist overtones.

There are two types of game. 'Set price' games usually appear in newspapers and magazines, although the games all differ slightly. Prior to the beginning of the season the publication lists players, separated into sections (goalkeepers, defenders, full-backs, centre- backs, midfielders and strikers). Each 'manager' is provided with a set amount of money. Originally this figure was around £20 million but in an effort to reflect spiralling transfer fees this number has risen to approximately £75 million in the last five years. Each team must buy one goalkeeper, two full backs, two centre backs, four midfielders and two strikers. Points are scored when players score or create goals, keep clean sheets and are lost through bookings, sendings-off, own goals, missed penalties and conceding goals. If players are suspended or injured then the fantasy side cannot gain or lose any points through that player. During the season, 'managers' are responsible for making adjustments to their teams such as transfers, different team selections and (in some leagues) substitutions in order to keep their team in the hunt for the 'title'. In most leagues, the number of transfers that can be made in one season is usually limited to around ten or twelve. Usually the starting 11 will determine how many points the team scores in a given week. The team with the most points at the end of its season wins its 'manager'.

'Auction games' developed in the latter half of the 1990s, within which individuals take part in an auction for players, usually with a small group of fellow 'managers'. Each player can only be select-

ed once and none of the players are assigned a 'set' price. Each team will thus be entirely different from every other. These games are usually run by commercial companies by post or, more recently, on the Internet.

By the end of the 1990s, fantasy football had developed a significant number of Internet sites. As well as some poor sites, fantasy football had been employed as an educational tool utilising the statistical emphasis of the game to teach mathematics, as well as developing skills in prose-writing, geography and history. In 1999 Fantasy League launched Schools Fantasy League, in which 270 schools and approximately 24,000 students and staff took part. For the 2000/01 season a link between Fantasy League and schoolmaster.net meant that the number of participants reached three times that of the previous season. However, the development of fantasy football through the Internet is another reflection of the commercialisation of football during the 1990s. There is always a cost involved to play online, and for the 2000/01 season premierwin.com offered an incredible £1 million to the winner of its league. Nevertheless, fantasy football provides fans with their chance to prove that they should be the 'manager' of their club rather than whichever much-maligned figure currently occupies its dug-out.

Sources:
www.fantasyleague.com – original site
www.schoolmaster.net/en/press.index.html
www.telegraphpremierleague.com – Telegraph
   Premier League online

Further Reading:
Carrington, B. '"Football's Coming Home", but Whose Home? And Do We Want It?: Nation, Football and the Politics of Exclusion', in A. Brown (ed.), *Fanatics! Power Identity and Fandom in Football* (London: Routledge, 1998), pp. 101–23.
www.premierwin.com – the £1 million pound fantasy football web site

Marc Keech

Fanzines

One of the most interesting developments in British football in the 1980s, fanzines are magazines produced by fans for fans, usually totally independent of clubs. Fanzines have become a key arena for fans to express themselves in modern football, and one of the main ways in the 1980s in which supporters convinced a hostile British public they were not just violent hooligans. With origins in the 1970s (the much vaunted *Foul*), fanzines are essentially a 1980s phenomenon, a response to the treatment of supporters, violence, the decline of football, and the attacks on it by Margaret Thatcher's governments.

Fanzines have many common characteristics, using humour, sarcasm and abuse to get their points across. Most revolve around individual clubs (with nearly every club having a fanzine by 1991) and often offer alternative viewpoints on the game. Their politics vary: some (like Leeds) have been very active in anti-racism, while others (Celtic and Rangers) celebrate identities that may be less commendable or progressive. But most support anti-racism (though sexism is a problem) and anti-hooliganism, and all start from the premise that fans are more than simply consumers of football, and have the right to criticise the players and the clubs they love.

Often clubs have been hostile to fanzines, with some banned from stadia, but in an age of massive cultural change within football, fanzines remain important in offering fans one of the few ways to express themselves free from media or club censorship or control.

Sources:
Giulianotti, R., 'Enlightening the North: Aberdeen Fanzines and Local Football Identity', in R Guilianotti and Armstrong, G. (eds), *Entering the Field* (Oxford: Berg, 1997), pp. 211–37.
Haynes, R., *The Football Imagination* (Aldershot: Arena, 1995).
Jary, D., Horne, J., and Bucke T., 'Football "Fanzines" and Football Culture', *Sociological Review*, 38: 3 (1991).

Further Reading:
Haynes, R., 'Vanguard or Vagabond? A History of When Saturday Comes', in S. Redhead (ed.), *The Passion and the Fashion* (Aldershot: Avebury, 1993).
Moorhouse, H. F., '"From Zines like these": Fanzines, Tradition and Identity in Scottish Football', in G. Jarvie and G. Walker (eds), *Scottish Sport in the Making of the Nation* (London: Leicester University Press, 1994), pp. 173–94.

Rex Nash

Fashion Icons

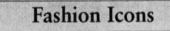

As young men with a higher than average disposable income, professional footballers have often served as style icons for working-class males. Their sartorial efforts have not always met with approval from fashion gurus; the pejorative phrase 'footballers' clothes' has become synonymous with bad taste.

Even Edwardian footballers were sometimes pictured on sporting postcards and cigarette cards in well-cut civilian suits, symbolising their social, as well as stylistic aspirations. Jim Iremonger of Nottingham Forest sported the starched, stand-up collar, dandyish Paisley necktie and tailored jacket of the smart turn-of-the-century male in an early cigarette card from the Clarke's Football Series of 1902. A *Topical Times* feature of 25 March 1939 entitled, 'The Best Dressed Players', spotlighted eight footballers in their hats and overcoats. The wardrobe of George Ainsley of Leeds United was deemed '[u]nconventional, comfortable and colourful', while Percy Grosvenor of Leicester City won praise for his 'sophisticated taste'. This at least suggests that footballers' style off the pitch was of increasing interest to supporters by the 1930s.

In the 1950s Arsenal's Denis Compton became a national icon of male stylishness through the high-profile advertising campaign in which he promoted the hairdressing product Brylcreem. The handsome

Compton, though of working-class origin, had a cross-class appeal, largely because he was also a debonair England international cricketer, adored for his cavalier batting. He encapsulated the image of raffish, middle-class sporting style, with his immaculately groomed, glossy dark hair, open neck shirt, cravat, flannels and blazer.

George Best's christening as 'El Beatle' by the Portuguese press, following his electrifying performance in Manchester United's resounding European Cup victory over Benfica in May 1968, is generally thought to be a defining moment. Increased media exposure of football on television, radio and in general interest magazines meant that some footballers were elevated to equal status with popstars as style icons. Best's dark, romantic, Celtic beauty was particularly suited to the flamboyant male attire of the 1960s. In 1968 the mail order catalogue company Great Universal Stores hired him as a model for a special line of trendy, youthful clothing in an attempt to exploit the increased spending power of the teenage male. Best also opened his own 'chain' of three George Best boutiques, beginning with *Edwardia* in Deansgate, Manchester in 1970, though his motivation for these investments was chiefly financial, rather than any desire to be a leader of fashion.

Kevin Keegan replaced Best as a late 1970s and early 1980s style icon; Keegan promoted the best-selling, pungent aftershave *Brut* and the bushy Keegan perm inspired hundreds of thousands of young men to curl their hair in homage. Not until Paul Gascoigne's 1990s 'Brutus' cut and his subsequent decision to bleach his hair platinum blond, was a footballing hairdo so widely copied. By the late 1980s there was an increasing focus on the display of the lean yet muscular young male body as the ideal in fashion and the media. The athletic, trained physiques of many footballers lent themselves perfectly to this development, and following the revival of football's popularity in the 1990s it was not uncommon to see players on the catwalk. Star professional footballers' high incomes made them enthusiastic, if not discerning, purchasers of exclusive designer labels like Armani,

David Beckham with wife Victoria and son Brooklyn, May 2000
(Steve Mitchell; © EMPICS Sports Photo Agency)

Thierry Mugler and Hugo Boss. In 1994 Liverpool's goalkeeper David James attracted much attention when he modelled for Armani.

Manchester United's David Beckham epitomised the importance of the professional footballer as a style icon in the late 1990s and early 2000s. Beckham's clothing, appearance and lifestyle were given huge prominence in the popular media. He often modelled designer clothing in men's magazines. A photograph of him on holiday wearing a man's sarong over a pair of loose fitting trousers sparked a long-running debate about proper masculine attire, and further suggestions that footballers had more money than taste. Beckham's streaked blond floppy-fringed hairstyle was enormously influential and led to him becoming the new 'Brylcreem Boy' in 1997. His appearance against Leicester City at Filbert Street on 18 March 2000 with a shaven head dominated the tabloid front pages and was featured in the main television news bulletins. His tattoos – his son Brooklyn's name in gothic script at the base of his spine and a 'guardian angel' between his shoulder blades – were revealed exclusively in *Esquire* magazine. Though the exploits of David Beckham and his popstar wife Victoria were frequently dubbed 'tacky' by commentators, their style was the object of intense interest and frequent imitation.

Sources:

Harding, J., *For the Good of the Game* (London: Robson Books, 1991).

Lovejoy, J., *Bestie: A Portrait of a Legend* (London: Macmillan, 1998).

McDowell, C., *The Man of Fashion: Peacock Males and Perfect Gentlemen* (London: Thames and Hudson, 1997).

Joyce Woolridge

Film and Newsreel

Feature films that have football as their main subject are rare in British cinema; it is even more uncommon for them to be both critical and box-office successes. A small number of football documentaries and considerable newsreel coverage of football since the end of the nineteenth century exists, providing a visual record of some of the most important games and personalities.

The first football feature films were silent shorts; the earliest known is *Harry the Footballer* (1911). In 1926 Billy Meredith, the ex-Manchester City and United player and Welsh international, became the first British footballer to star in a full-length film, *Ball of Fortune*, as a trainer who guides a young man cheated of his inheritance to soccer stardom. *The Great Game* (1930) was possibly the first British football film to incorporate actual match footage (the 1930 FA Cup Final between Arsenal and Huddersfield Town). This comedy about a club's machinations to avoid relegation was remade in 1952 with a cameo appearance from Tommy Lawton as himself and using Brentford

Town's players and ground. Denis Compton made a similar appearance in *Small Town Story* (1953).

The Arsenal Stadium Mystery (1939) demonstrates how football alone was often not considered sufficiently interesting to sustain a whole picture. Though the stars of the pre-war Arsenal team, their manager George Allison and trainer Tom Whittaker appear throughout, the plot centres on the murder at half-time of the caddish striker of Arsenal's FA Cup-tie amateur opponents, the Trojans. Footage of a genuine match between Arsenal and Brentford, and the Arsenal stadium, is used extensively.

Since then audience credulity has been stretched still further in films like *Escape to Victory* (1981), where football inspires the liberation of Nazi-occupied France. Michael Caine as Colby, an insubordinate, paunchy ex-West Ham player and England international, organises a POW team to take on the Germans at the Stade de Colombes in Paris. Bobby Moore, Mike Summerbee, John Wark and other British footballers play members of Caine's team, which refuses to escape at half-time so it can finish the match.

A recurrent theme is personal redemption through soccer. In *Yesterday's Hero* (1979) Ian McShane's playboy striker overcomes alcoholism to score the winning penalty in the FA Cup final. Footage of the 1979 League Cup final between Southampton and Nottingham Forest is used, with commentary by BBC broadcaster John Motson. In *When Saturday Comes* (1995) Jimmy (Sean Bean), a working-class brewery worker, fails a trial with Sheffield United because he gets drunk, but given a second chance scores three goals to defeat Manchester United in an FA Cup semi-final, inspired by the ghost of his dead brother. Ex-players Tony Currie and Mel Sterland make brief appearances.

Arthur Askey indulges in a novel display of hooliganism as an irascible, football-crazy train driver who accidentally flings his meat and potato pie at the referee (an optician) in *The Love Match* (1955). The spectacular end sees Askey driving his train around Burnden Park to watch a local derby from the cab. More serious treatment was given to organised 1980s football hooliganism in *The Firm* (1988) and *i.d.* (1995).

The engaging comedy *Gregory's Girl* (1980) revolves, unusually, around a female footballer, Dorothy, whose shapely yet muscular physique and superb ball control contrast starkly with the inferior skills of the scrawny, uncoordinated males of her Scottish school's football team. *Those Glory, Glory Days* (1983) explores how supporting the double-winning Spurs team of 1960 mitigated the pains of a girl's difficult childhood. Danny Blanchflower played himself. Its writer, Britain's first major female sports journalist Julie Welch, pioneered the autobiographical approach later used by Nick Hornby in the screenplay adaptation of his eponymous best-selling book *Fever Pitch* (1995).

The Saturday Men (1962) is a 29-minute behind-the-scenes documentary of a week with West Bromwich Albion, featuring supporters and directors as well as players. The first colour full-length documentary football film was *Goal* (1966), an impressive record of the 1966 World Cup, supposedly shot with 117 cameras.

The earliest known film in existence of an actual professional game is four minutes of an 1898 match between Blackburn Rovers and West Bromwich Albion. The FA Cup was filmed from 1899 onwards, but the first footage to survive is from the 1901 replay between Tottenham Hotspur and Sheffield United. Football became a popular subject in the newsreels produced to accompany main features. Competition between newsreel companies for exclusive rights was keen, and the 1923 Cup Final was pirated from a camera concealed inside a giant hammer.

Sources:
McKernan, L., *Topical Budget: The Great British News Film* (London: British Film Institute, 1992).
Richards, J., *Thorold Dickinson: The Man and His Films* (London: Croom Helm, 1986).
Seddon, P., *A Football Compendium* (Boston Spa: The British Library, 1999).
Films (London: Croom Helm, 1986).

Kinematograph Weekly
Sight and Sound

Further Reading:
Hornby, N., 'Hold on, Lads', *Sight and Sound*, vol. 3, no. 5 (199?), p, 40.
McKernan, L., 'Sport and the First Films', in *Cinema: The Beginnings and the Future* (London: University of Westminster Press, 1996), pp. 107–17.

Joyce Woolridge

First World War

Football continued to be played throughout the war, but in reduced circumstances. Critics of the professional game suggested as early as August 1914 that it should be abandoned as it was a distraction from the war effort. In campaigns in newspapers like *The Times*, critics including historian A F. Pollard, poet Robert Bridges and F. N. Charrington returned to the arguments of the public-school-educated upper and middle classes who had always stressed active participation, fair play, and amateurism as against 'spectatorism', gamesmanship, and the corruption of money. Some newspapers refused to publish match reports.

Critics suggested that thousands of fit young players should volunteer for the forces as an encouragement to paying spectators to do the same. A contrast was made with more socially exclusive cricket, rugby union and rowing clubs who had purportedly volunteered in numbers. Recruiting campaigns were set up at matches, with poor results – only one recruit at Arsenal and none at Chelsea or Nottingham Forest. It was also suggested that all spectators at professional matches should pay a tax toward the war effort.

The football authorities were defensive, but argued that continuing playing professional football boosted morale and that contractual obligations existed; the Football League and Southern League had agreed to pay players' wages until April 1915. Attendances naturally declined, so clubs were also in financial difficulties, and a reduction of wages by around 10 per cent went towards a relief fund. The Football Association also defended the game, saying that it had provided 100,000 recruits by November 1914, and there were only 600 unmarried professionals who had not volunteered. West Bromwich Albion formed a special Territorial company fromplayers and spectators, and in Lancashire there were 40 players from 11 Football League clubs in a total of 4,765 players volunteering.

By 1915 the Football League and Southern League ceased paying players, although the Scottish League paid £1 per match. Along with the FA Cup, the Football League's regular competition stopped after 1915, but there were regional competitions in Lancashire and the Midlands. Many other amateur competitions continued, players being recruited locally and from service personnel, although clubs sometimes had difficulties raising sides. In the South these included the Isthmian, Metropolitan, London and South Essex leagues. Most leagues in the North and Midlands survived, although there were withdrawals, and some lesser cup competitions persisted. In Scotland, Division One continued but Division Two was wound up, and leagues continued in South Wales. From 1917 to 1919 difficulties increased, but munitions workers' and army competitions started.

Women's football advanced during the war, factory and munitions teams forming for 'rational recreation', exercise and charity purposes – one aspect of women's emancipation in the period. Football remained the main leisure activity of working-class men, reflected in the Footballers' Battalion and the focus on community, local, and regimental teams, contrasting with the middle-class Sportsman's Battalion and its amateur ideals. One post-war consequence, however, may have been the change from association to rugby football in many public schools.

Sources:

Mason, T., *Association Football and English Society, 1863–1915* (Brighton: Harvester, 1980).

Veitch, C., '"Play up! Play up! and Win the War": Football, the Nation and the First World War', *Journal of Contemporary History*, 20 (1985), 363–8.

Bailey, J., *Not just on Christmas Day: An Overview of Association Football in the First World War* (Upminster: 3-2 Books, 1999).

Osborne, J. M., 'Sport, Soldiers and the Great War', *British Society of Sports History Bulletin*, 11 (1991), 17–34.

Fishwick, N., *English Football and Society, 1910–1950* (Manchester: Manchester University Press, 1989).

Further Reading:

Arnold, A. J., 'Not Playing the Game?: Leeds City in the Great War', *International Journal of the History of Sport*, 7 (May 1990), 111–19.

Mangan, J. A., *Athleticism in the Victorian and Edwardian Public School* (Cambridge: Cambridge University Press, 1981).

Robert Lewis

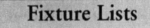

Fixture Lists

In many respects, fixture lists form the basis for all sporting competitions. Certainly they had influence upon the formation of the Football League in 1888. The League's founder, William McGregor, was motivated by a desire to secure regular, competitive fixtures for his club, Aston Villa, whose followers were finding a diet of cup-ties and irregular friendlies unpalatable. In Scotland, too, much of the impetus behind the formation of the Scottish Football League in 1890 was provided by the frustrations of a disjointed fixture programme.

The first Football League fixtures were agreed by the clubs themselves once the dates of the major cup competitions had been determined. In 1898 the clubs adopted a system for determining fixtures pioneered by Mr W. Fletcher, a system also used by other leagues. In 1915 Charles Sutcliffe, a member of the League's management committee, devised a system of his own which could handle the complexities of a two-division league. Sutcliffe's system was not universally popular as it involved the same teams meeting each other on consecutive Saturdays, but after complaints he modified his system to general satisfaction.

Sutcliffe was involved in perhaps the greatest controversy surrounding fixture lists. During the 1935/36 season the Football League's leadership embarked upon a campaign against the burgeoning football pools companies. The League felt the pools encouraged betting on football, something they fiercely opposed. Rather than take up the option to make their fixtures copyright, the League decided to scrap the fixture list for Saturday 29 February 1936, with each club not being notified of its opponents until 24 hours before kick-off. While this campaign, which became known as the 'Pools War', had some effect on the pools companies, clubs complained that it adversely affected attendances. After a second week of disruption, the original fixture list was restored. Shortly afterwards, in September 1939, the outbreak of the Second World War caused the fixture programme to be scrapped. When League football resumed in 1946 the same fixture list produced for the 1939/40 season was used.

Charles Sutcliffe retained responsibility for providing the League's fixtures until his death in 1939, whereupon the task passed to his long-term assistant, his son Harold. He carried on until his own death in 1967, although in 1957 the League secretary insisted that Harold should share his knowledge with a member of the League staff. At around the same time the League decided to seek to copyright the fixture lists. They brought a test case against Littlewoods and in May 1959 won a judgement that the fixtures were copyright. The League then reached agreement with the pools companies that guaranteed an income of £245,000 a year, thus helping to secure the League financially.

After 1967 the fixture list was determined by a computer program, inevitable given the complex factors that must be taken into account. Club location, local events, police requests and public holidays can all impact on fixture lists. The fixture list has also been disrupted by the increas-

ing demands of television, especially since the formation of the Premier League in 1992, with Sunday and Monday night football now a regular feature. Things have come a long way since 1888, but fixture lists remain the basis for competitive football.

Sources:

Inglis, S., *League Football and the Men Who Made It: The Official Centenary History of the Football League 1888–1988* (London: Willow, 1988).

Tischler, S., *Footballers and Businessmen: The Origins of Professional Soccer in England* (London: Holmes & Meier, 1981).

Further Reading:

Clapson, M., *A Bit of a Flutter: Popular Gambling and English Society c.1823–1961* (Manchester: Manchester University Press, 1992).

Clegg, B., *The Man who Made Littlewoods: The Story of John Moores* (London: Hodder & Stoughton, 1993).

John Coyle

Floodlighting

Floodlighting has been used to illuminate British football for the past 50 years, but remarkably the first experiments with artificial lighting began in the nineteenth century. In October 1878 a floodlit game was played at Bramall Lane between two representative Sheffield teams. The lamps were mounted on timber gantries and powered by dynamos. Floodlit games were also staged at other venues across the country, but electrical failure was common.

A decade later, further experimental games were played at some professional midland and Lancashire clubs, this time using non-electric Wells oil-fired lights. Celtic tried electric lighting with additional lamps mounted on wires suspended across the pitch. All such games were exhibition matches, but despite a favourable public reaction, the football authorities continued to disapprove of floodlighting even after advances in electrical technolo-

A floodlit Arsenal Stadium, Highbury
(© Stuart MacFarlane, Arsenal FC)

gy. During the 1930s, Herbert Chapman, the progressive manager of Arsenal, tried in vain to persuade the FA to sanction floodlighting. Floodlit football was officially banned from 1930 to 1950.

A series of spectacularly successful floodlit friendlies involving European club opposition in the early 1950s made a persuasive case for the viability of night-time football. Over twenty league clubs now had lights, though early installations were comparatively primitive. Slowly and reluctantly, the FA and League withdrew their objections and the first major floodlit game in England took place when Portsmouth played Newcastle United in a League game in 1956. Floodlighting made possible participation in mid-week competitions such as European tournaments and the League Cup.

In the early days, lights could be mounted on gantries along the side of the ground or on pylons at each corner. Some clubs could afford the extravagance of six pylons, though the precise configuration often depended on site restrictions. Early lamps were slow to activate, sometimes taking 15 minutes to achieve full illumination. To avoid casting shadows, some

floodlight pylons were very tall, becoming prominent local landmarks and providing a beacon for away fans to locate grounds. Scottish engineers preferred angled headframes on pylons so that lamps could be aimed more directly towards the pitch. Such 'drench-lighting' systems were also seen at some English grounds.

Colour television required more powerful lights and major clubs upgraded their systems with higher wattage lamps, and in some cases even taller pylons. More efficient lamps meant that fewer were needed, and some clubs were able to install neater systems on stand roofs. These days, floodlights are commonly incorporated within the fabric of roof structures. Corner-mounted installations are still common but the old lattice-like pylons have largely been replaced by slender, less obtrusive columns.

The FA Premier League stipulates that the floodlights of member clubs must give an average illumination of 800 lux, and proportionally lower levels are acceptable in lower divisions. Failure to comply can result in automatic relegation. Curious incidents of floodlight breakdown at some Premier League fixtures in the late 1990s led police to a Far-Eastern gambling syndicate involved in the attempted sabotage of certain British matches.

Sources:
Inglis, S., 'Floodlights', in *The Football Grounds of Great Britain* (Second edition) (London: Willow Books, 1987), pp. 40–5.
Anon., *IES Lighting Guide: Sports* (London: Illuminating Lighting Society, Publication No.7 (June 1974).

Further Reading:
Sports: Lighting Guide LG4 (London: Chartered Institute of British Services Engineers, 1990).

See also Technology

Tom Preston

Folk Football

It is probably safe to assume that some form of football has been played ever since humanity first discovered the endless fascination of playing with an inflated animal bladder. Whether played formally or informally, as recreation or as ritual, folk football, as the precursors of the modern codes of football have become known, encompassed the whole of the British Isles and can be traced at least as far back as the Roman Conquest.

The Romans brought a game with them called Harpastum which, along with Camp ball, Chulle, Cnapan and Jethart Ba', is one of the many names by which football has been known. The origins of these games are largely lost to historians, although some of the myths still survive. The games played at Kingston upon Thames and Chester were both reputed to have originally begun with the kicking around the town of the head of a captured Danish warrior, while the Derby Shrove Tuesday game was claimed to have been a celebration of a local victory over the Roman occupiers.

Other than in local legend, there is little evidence that organised football games survived from Roman times. But the depth of the game in the national consciousness can be seen in the regularity with which football is referred to in English literature. Probably the most famous reference is the Earl of Kent's disdainful reference to a 'base football player' in *King Lear*, but as well as Shakespeare, William Wordsworth, Isaak Walton, John Gay, Tobias Smollett, and Sir Walter Scott, among others, all made reference to the game.

Folk football was inextricably linked with the fairs, festivals and holidays of a predominantly rural nation. Shrove Tuesday, Christmas Day, New Year's Day and the Easter holidays were common match days. For these major matches football was a game for large numbers, ranging from the thousand men who contested the Derby game to the 100-a-side game at Alnwick. Common to all games was the propelling of a ball towards a goal, usually situated at prominent landmarks. For example, the goals were three miles apart for the Ashbourne game, while Whitehaven's goals were set at the docks and a wall outside the town. There is also some evidence of fields especially set aside for the game; for example, Hornsea, on Yorkshire's East coast, had a 'footeball grene' as far back as the 1680s.

The ball could be kicked, carried, thrown, hit or, more often than not, propelled using a mixture of techniques. In Ashbourne, the ball was carried rather than kicked, and in Derby itself the game was rather descriptively called hugball. Camp-ball, the football game popular in Norfolk and Suffolk, also involved carrying of the ball. The Scone game went so far as to expressly forbid kicking the ball. In contrast, the ball was rarely picked up during the Kirkwall Ba' game in the Orkneys before the 1840s. To those who believed that modern Association football was the sole heir to the older tradition, Montague Shearman's 1887 *Athletics and Football* commented that 'there is no trace in the original form of football to suggest that nothing but kicking is allowed'.

While the forms of football differed from area to area and time to time, there is little doubt that it was associated with the lower classes. As early as 1508 Alexander Barclay's poem *Eclogues* wrote that 'footeball' was the winter pastime of the 'sturdie plowman'. The long-term survival of this link is attested to by the comment of an anonymous Old Etonian, who in 1831 remarked that he could not 'consider the game of football as being at all gentlemanly. It is a game which the common people of Yorkshire are particularly partial to.' Further proof of the popularity of football can be seen in the number of recorded prosecutions for the illegal playing of informal matches down the centuries.

But the coming of urban industrial capitalism undermined the old customs and imposed a new rhythm of daily life, destroying both the opportunity and the inclination to play football. Although there were individual survivals of folk football, the time and work disciplines of the factory system, to say nothing of the suspicions aroused by large crowds of working people, meant that by late-Victorian times, folk football was largely a historical curiosity. Yet although the impetus for modern football was to come from the public schools, the rapidity with which it became popular with the working classes suggests that the residual memory of traditional football ran deep among those who had practised the sport over the centuries.

Sources:

Magoun, F. P., 'Football in Medieval England and in Middle-English Literature', *American Historical Review*, 35 (1929).

Malcolmson, R. W., *Popular Recreations in English Society 1770-1850* (Cambridge: Cambridge University Press, 1975).

Shearman, M., *Athletics And Football* (London: Badminton Library, 1887).

Tony Collins

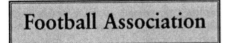

Football Association

The Football Association (FA) is the governing body of football in England. Formed in 1863, it is the father of all football associations and the only national body with no mention of its home country in its name. Variously described as 'the monarchy' and 'the highest parliament in English football', it is not only the supreme authority of the game in England but was instrumental in codifying and standardising the laws of football in the nineteenth century, and continues to play a central role in modifying the rules of what has become a world game.

From its early days the FA concerned itself with the development of the national FA Cup competition, established in 1871, and the organisation of the national team. But its responsibilities have always been much broader than this. It is responsible for the administration of the game as a whole: from the grass roots of junior, district and county associations through to professional football. Acting as an umbrella body, it authorises competitions and leagues throughout the country. Alongside the FA Cup, it runs seven national competitions, including the FA Trophy, the FA Vase and the FA Women's Cup. Although the Football League and the Premier League are run independently, they too come under the ultimate jurisdiction of the FA. It is also responsible for the recruitment and training of referees, disciplinary matters and appeals, player's registrations, coaching and development and international affairs.

The structure of the FA has not changed a great deal in its long history. It is governed by a Council of about ninety members, which meets six times a year, considering major issues and proposals put forward by a variety of committees dealing with every imaginable aspect of administration and development. The membership of the Council includes the elected representatives of 43 county associations, clubs in ten regional areas (or divisions), bodies such as the Football League and the Premier League and representatives of the universities and schools, the services and the Commonwealth associations. The FA has been a limited company since 1903 and all members of the Council hold directorships in the Football Association Ltd. The annual AGM is the main forum for drawing up and amending the rules of the FA.

The origins of the FA can be traced back to a meeting on 26 October 1863 at Freeman's Tavern in Lincoln Inn's Field involving captains and representatives of a number of London suburban clubs. The aim was to decide on a shared set of rules that would allow matches to take place without the problems that existed at the time. The clubs represented at the meeting were Barnes, Blackheath, Charterhouse, Perceval House (Blackheath), Kensington School, the War Office, Crystal Palace, Blackheath Proprietary School, The Crusaders, Forest (Epping Forest) and No Names of Kilburn. Ebenezer Cobb Morley proposed the formation of an association, and this was carried by eleven votes to one. The FA was born and Morley became its first honorary secretary.

However, there were still considerable differences of opinion over the precise laws to be adopted by the fledgling body. Morley presented a draft set of 14 rules to the new Football Association on 24 November 1863. These were based on an amalgamation of rules played by schools, universities and clubs. The biggest controversies surrounded the issues of catching and hacking. Seen by some as the essence of football's masculine toughness, hacking was criticised by others as an uncivilised habit. Those clubs who wanted minimal handling and the abolition of hacking were eventually victorious, and the first set of rules were enshrined at a meeting on 8 December 1963. The most vociferous supporters of hacking, Blackheath, immediately left the FA and became instrumental in the creation of the rival Rugby Football Union in 1871.

The publication of its rules aided the FA's expansion and it could claim 39 member clubs from as far afield as Lincoln, Oxford and York by 1870. It was the establishment of the FA Cup in 1871, however, which allowed the association to broaden its outlook and spread its influence. The inaugural competition comprised 15 clubs who, with the exception of Donington School and Queen's Park from Glasgow, were drawn from a narrow geographical and social background, but it soon attracted entrants from up and down the country. The FA's membership quickly rose and by 1881 it had 128 clubs and associations under its wing.

The emergence of professionalism in the game caused considerable problems for the FA. Dominated as it was by amateurs from 'old boys' teams from the south, the FA strongly opposed the payment of players. When the London club Upton Park complained that the Preston North End side they had played in an FA Cup tie was effectively professional, the FA expelled North End, along with Burnley and Great Lever, by the start of the next season. The accused clubs were open about paying their players and a group of clubs from Lancashire and the Midlands threatened to secede from the FA to create a rival British Football Association. The authority of the FA remained in the balance until the decision was made to legalise professionalism in 1885.

The amateur–professional tension at the heart of the game, and reflected in the structure of the FA, did not end there. Incensed by the rapid progress of the Football League and the apparent sacrifice of football to the forces of commercialism and professionalism, supporters of the 'true' amateur game attempted to make their voice heard in the Council chamber. A separate FA Amateur Cup was formed in 1893, but in 1907 the amateurs decided to break away to form their own Amateur Football Association (AFA). Over 500 clubs were recruited and recognition of the AFA as football's governing body was received from the Rugby Football Union and the Hockey Association. The experiment only lasted a short time, however, and the rebels returned to the FA as an affiliated association in 1914.

The FA's relations with international football have often been cool. With the other British associations, the FA joined FIFA, the world governing body, in 1905, but resigned in 1920 over its opposition to footballing contacts with its former wartime enemies. It rejoined in 1924 but resigned again in 1928 over the issue of 'broken time' payments and the definition of amateur status in the Olympic Games. Underpinning all this, however, was a perceived threat to the autonomy of the British associations, who had always done things their own way and felt that they should be allowed to continue to do so in the future. Thus the first three World

Cups in the 1930s passed the FA (and the other home nations) by, and 'international' football continued to be understood in terms of the annual fixtures against Scotland, Wales and Northern Ireland.

The arrival of Stanley Rous helped the FA to adopt a more international outlook. It rejoined FIFA in 1946 and sent its first team to a World Cup in 1950. It also became a founder member of the European governing body UEFA in 1954 and, unlike the Football League, supported the involvement of English club sides in European competition. It has long been an accepted senior federation in world football politics but there remains a feeling that the FA (and the British associations in general) enjoy a privileged position. Much of this stems from the existence of four separate associations within one state and the control of the British over the rules of the game. The British associations, for instance, retain a vote each on the International FA Board (which sanctions alterations in football's law), with FIFA having four votes in total.

Domestically, the FA was a conservative rather than a reforming body for much of the twentieth century. Dave Russell has described it during the inter-war years as 'Reithian' in spirit: determined to maintain its public service role while avoiding gimmickry and 'the vulgarities of the marketplace'. Much the same was true of the post-war years, although it was prepared to appoint officials from outside the football world, such as Denis Fellows and Ted Crocker, and by the 1970s was beginning to show a willingness to recognise the value of commercial activities.

Its involvement in the creation of the Premier League in 1992 was important in underlining the FA's position as the ruling body of the professional game as well as the grass roots. Yet, in the mind of the public at least, the FA is associated above all with the FA Cup and the England team. Its various other moves towards modernisation – from the appointment of a technical director in 1997 to the introduction of the first woman member of the Council in the mid-1990s – have generated far less interest than the appointment of Sven-Göran Eriksson as England's first foreign coach in 2000.

At the dawn of the twenty-first century, the FA is finally beginning to resemble a modern organisation. The move from its long-term home at Lancaster Gate to new headquarters in Soho Square is perhaps a sign of its willingness to shed its old, stuffy image. Public relations officers rather than football administrators now deal with the media. But the FA is still regularly criticised in the press for its incompetence, and if the crowds for FA Cup ties continue to drop and Eriksson's England lose matches, there is no reason to suppose that this will change in the future.

Sources:
Green, G., *The History of the Football Association* (London: Naldrett Press, 1953).
Green, G., 'The Football Association' in A. H. Fabian and G. Green (eds), *Association Football*, vol 1 (London, 1961).
Russell, D., *Football and the English: A Social History of Association Football in England, 1863–1915* (Preston: Carnegie Publishing, 1997).
Walvin, J. *The People's Game: The History of Football Revisited* (Second edition) (Edinburgh: Mainstream Press, 2000).

Further Reading:
Mason, T., *Association Football and English Society, 1863–1915* (Brighton: Harvester Press, 1980).

See also FA Cup

Matt Taylor

Football and the Community

The links between football clubs and the communities they represent are today some of the most studied topics in the history and sociology of sport. In recent years, eminent authors such as Tony Mason, Richard Holt, Jeff Hill, and John Bale have dedicated significant sections of their work to discussing the development of football clubs as sites for the expression of belonging to various community groups. In particular, they have concentrated on football clubs' abilities to engender pride in towns and cities, and have explained that, from the last quarter of the nineteenth century at least, football and other sports clubs have provided occasions for local solidarity when towns and cities can occasionally unite as wholes.

Historically, the FA Cup has been the most important football competition for producing occasions for the promotion of feelings of local belonging. A more 'democratic' competition than the League, the FA Cup has long provided small towns and cities with successes that have encouraged people to identify actively with their fellow townsfolk. The most obvious display of this type of local pride is, of course, the ritual of local people welcoming back FA Cup finalists to their town after a final, a tradition enacted throughout British football (but particularly in the north of England) from the 1880s onwards.

In addition to local pride, some academic research is now being conducted on the role of football clubs in developing other, geographically wider feelings of bonding and community. In addition to studies of football and local identity there is a rich history of research into links between football and national identity, but only now are those identities 'in between' the local and the national receiving the attention they deserve. Specifically, the role of football clubs in developing 'regional' community feeling and other sub-national senses of belonging such as 'northernness' are beginning to be explored.

Much of the work conducted on football and community has primarily been of a historical focus. It has studied how the relationships between football clubs and local communities were initially developed, and how they were maintained until the early 1960s. Much less work has been conducted on how the links between football clubs and local communities changed from the 1960s, leading to, for instance, football fans' increasing willingness to support national super-clubs at the expense of local teams. To explain why

this happened, it is important to consider the decline of local and regional identity in Britain since the 1960s, and how this was brought about by social and economic factors such as the rise of the national media, increases in geographical mobility, and the growth of suburban housing estates that undermined many traditional communities. However, it would be incorrect to overstate the contemporary decline of local identification through football and other sports. Most football clubs today still draw the majority of their supporters from their broadly-defined local regions, and as such continue to operate as principal sites for the production of community feeling.

This is to some extent due to the emergence of the community schemes run by clubs in recent decades. Since the beginning of professional football in Britain, football clubs have, as noted, enjoyed important and central roles in the communities they represent. However, in the 1970s, during a period of decreasing attendances and increasing hooliganism at British football, the taken-for-granted relationship between football clubs and communities started to decline. As early as 1968, a Department of Education and Science report into football (commonly known as the first Chester Report) advocated that, in the face of challenges such as hooliganism, football clubs should forge more formal links with their local communities. By 1978, the perceived decline in relations between football clubs and communities was such that the Labour government administered £1 million through the Sports Council to encourage football clubs to set up formal community schemes.

Using the money provided by the Sports Council, 39 Football and the Community schemes were launched in England in the late 1970s: 29 at professional football clubs and 10 at rugby league clubs. Most of the money was spent on building or improving resources such as sports halls, all-weather pitches, and changing facilities which, it was hoped, would be used as much by local people as by professional players. Community 'motivators' were also employed by some clubs to go out into the community and actively encourage people to associate with their local clubs. By making football clubs more readily accessible in this way, it was hoped that the Football and the Community schemes would play an important role in making clubs central to community life, while also providing local youths with an alternative to becoming involved with football only as hooligans.

The successes of the initial Football and the Community schemes were limited, not least because funding for the projects was short-term and many schemes simply ended when Sports Council support was no longer forthcoming. It was not until the deeply troubled mid-1980s that a fresh impetus emerged for football clubs to develop more formal relationships with their local communities. This time, funded by the government's Manpower Services Commission, the Professional Footballers' Association (PFA) set up six pilot Football in the Community schemes in 1986/87, all at professional clubs in the north-west of England. The aims of the schemes were to provide employment and training for unemployed people, to promote closer links between professional football clubs and communities, to involve minority and ethnic groups in social and recreational activities, to attempt to prevent acts of hooliganism and vandalism, and to maximise the use of facilities at football clubs. The success of the pilot initiatives was such that the scheme was soon able to expand. By 1990, over 50 football clubs operated Football in the Community projects, mainly in the north of England and Midlands, and by 2000 over 90 professional English clubs had active schemes.

The success of the Football in the Community project has demanded a great deal of financial backing. Since 1991, this burden has been readily accepted by the Football Trust and a number of sponsors such as *Pizza Hut*, *Wagon Wheels* and *Adidas*. Overall, support of this type has helped a number of football clubs regain something of the central place in local culture that they once held almost naturally.

Sources:

Bale, J., 'The Place of "Place" in Cultural Studies of Sport', *Progress in Human Geography*, 12 (1988), 507–24.

Hill, J., and Williams, J. (eds), *Sport and Identity in the North of England* (Keele: Keele University Press, 1996).

Holt., R., *Sport and the British: A Modern History* (Oxford: Oxford University Press, 1989).

Ingham, R., *Report on the Football and Community Monitoring Project* (London: Sports Council, 1983).

Russell, D., *Football and the English: A Social History of Association Football in England, 1863–1995* (Preston: Carnegie Publishing, 1997).

Further Reading:

Garland, J., Malcolm, D., and Rowe, M., *The Future of Football: Challenges for the Twenty-First Century* (London: Frank Cass, 2000).

Harding, J., *For the Good of the Game: The Official History of the Professional Footballers' Association* (London: Robson, 1991).

Mason, T., *Sport in Britain* (London: Faber & Faber, 1988).

Gavin Mellor

Football and the Deaf Community

Deaf football clubs date back to 1871, when Glasgow Deaf and Dumb Football Club – which still survives – was founded, making it one of the longest-established football clubs in the world. The initial growth of deaf football came in Scotland and northern England, and only spread to the south at the turn of the century, since when it has remained the major winter sport among deaf people. Football has always played an important social role for deaf people, serving as a means of bringing together members of what is a widely dispersed community. Pre- and post-match socialising is therefore a major element of deaf football.

Deaf players have not only played with and against each other, but have also featured in teams of hearing players. The standard of play is seen as better in the latter area, but due to problems of communication the socialising is less rewarding and this has often led to deaf players playing in both types of football in order to obtain different levels of personal satisfaction from playing the game. This integration has extended to the professional game, with several deaf players achieving success with league clubs. A number of players who have become deafened have continued their careers, including Cliff Bastin, the Arsenal and England winger of the 1930s, and more recently Rodney Marsh and Jimmy Case.

Deaf teams have had their own cup competitions since 1889 in Scotland, and 1926 in England, and international deaf football began in Falkirk in 1891, when Scotland drew 3–3 with England. A national deaf league emerged in the 1980s, but soon folded due to the problems posed by distance and expense. An international competition was established in 1924 as part of the Silent Games (often referred to as the 'Deaf Olympics'), with Great Britain winning the football section in 1928, 1935 and 1939. The first ever Deaf World Cup was contested in Madrid in 2000, and the Deaf European Championship attracts entries from all across the continent. International club tournaments have been a regular feature of the summer months since the 1970s.

Despite this history, British deaf football has undergone a period of decline in recent years, with many clubs closing down. This is partly due to the wider range of sporting activities open to deaf people, and partly due to changing social patterns within the deaf community. Young people no longer attend their local deaf clubs – the traditional focus of deaf sporting and leisure activities – and so the number of players clubs can draw on is shrinking. New technology allows deaf people to maintain contact more easily, and so the social attraction of deaf football has diminished. While it seems unlikely that deaf people will stop playing football, the prospects for the deaf competitions appear bleak, as the number of entries falls annually.

Sources:
Atherton, M., Russell, D. and Turner, G., 'Playing to the Flag: A History of Deaf Football and Deaf Footballers in Britain', *The Sports Historian*, 19: 1 (May 1999).

Further Reading:
Atherton, M., Russell, D. and Turner, G., *Deaf United: A History of Deaf Football in Great Britain* (Coleford: Douglas McClean, 2000).
Dimmock, A., 'Sport and Deaf People', in G. Taylor and J. Bishop, *Being Deaf: The Experience of Deafness* (London: Pinter Publishers, 1991), pp. 191–5.

Martin Atherton

Football and the Gay Community

While society is presumed to be increasingly liberal, homophobic perceptions are still identifiable within many societal structures and institutions, and indeed appear to predominate in the macho world of British football (both amateur and professional). As one definition of masculinity is celebrated as the dominant (hegemonic) ideal within football (athletic, macho, heterosexual, working class, white) others are subordinated and situated as contemptible in both status and form. In this sense the stereotypically gay man, viewed as effeminate, is abhorred within the football arena. Lesbian footballers who challenge the 'feminine' norm are also open to stigmatisation and discrimination on the grounds of their sexual orientation. The negative treatment of lesbian, gay and bisexual footballers due to their sexuality may take many forms: name calling, aggressive attacks and even what many assume to be harmless changing room banter framed around sexual innuendo and stereotypical beliefs. These may all be defined as cases of overt homophobic discrimination within the world of British football. Moreover, the possible existence of covert discrimination, perhaps taking an institutional form, might also affect the footballing career of an individual, whether amateur or professional. The prevalence of homophobia limits the extent to which lesbian, gay and bisexual footballers feel comfortable in a mainstream (non-gay) footballing environment, a situation that leads many individuals (especially in professional football, where the financial stakes are high) to attempt to pass as heterosexual in order to avoid stigmatisation. This 'culture of silence' carries with it a high price, as individuals are forced to deny public demonstrations of their true sexuality and live in constant fear of being 'found out'.

As certain people have taken the chance to be open about their sexuality in footballing circles their experiences have served as a warning to others who remain 'in the closet'. When the gay football referee Norman Redman refused to hide his sexuality or HIV-positive status from the footballing fraternity he was reportedly condemned for his actions and forced to move to a secret address after receiving abusive phone-calls and having excrement put through his letter box. Justin Fashanu's decision to 'come out' to the *Sun* newspaper in 1990 was made in order to identify with his fans. Fashanu had realised he was gay ten years earlier during his time at Nottingham Forest under the management of Brian Clough. Although he was not 'out' at this time, Clough knew of Fashanu's visits to gay clubs, a practice he was ordered to curtail. His manager was also responsible for subjecting the player to both public and private abuse. Fashanu hoped that if he was able to be truthful about his sexuality in the tabloid newspapers and remained positive about his role in British football he would be accepted as a gay footballer. However, this judgement was flawed and Fashanu suffered indignation from fans and family alike. While homophobic taunts such as 'You couldn't even score with your brother!' followed him out of the tunnel and onto the pitch, he was also vilified by his brother, John Fashanu, who initially felt threatened by Justin's public sexuality. This resentment later dissipated as John became a more supportive sibling.

A recent example of anti-gay reactions in professional football may be discerned from a high profile incident in which homophobic slurs were directed toward Graeme Le Saux (Chelsea) by Robbie Fowler (Liverpool) during an FA league match in March 1999. At the time, football pundits claimed that homophobic insults and jibes were a part of the game and to be expected. However, the then Sports Minister, Tony Banks, took the unusual step of intervening and initiating a public dialogue on the problems of homophobia in British football. His replacement, Kate Hoey, continued talks with the Football Association, but without specific outcomes. At the time of writing, it is generally believed that the issue will only be dealt with in a practical way at the moment when one or more high profile players come out.

These types of discrimination are not only to be found in the professional game. Amateur lesbian, gay and bisexual footballers are also open to homophobic responses, even from other players on their own team. It is in this context that a separate gay sports culture has emerged as a sub-cultural phenomenon within the structure of mainstream sport as a potential resistance to the heterosexist hegemony.

Although relatively little research has been forthcoming on gay football within this country, comparative studies from the Netherlands as well as Britain suggest that there are a number of reasons for the membership of individuals on gay sports teams. Explanations range from levels of homophobia feared to exist within a team that may lead to segregation from teammates, and a dislike of the 'macho' and competitive culture of mainstream sports, to a desire to play sport (football) in a socially accepting (and what some perceive to be erotic) atmosphere. In the gay sport environment lesbian, gay and bisexual players often experience increased freedom to express their sexuality and are able to enjoy the company of like-minded individuals in a social setting. There are now a growing number of amateur football teams that specifically cater for lesbian, gay and bisexual communities.

The first gay men's football club in Britain was Stonewall FC. Formed in 1991, the club has now run for nine seasons and currently boasts three squads.

The teams play in the mainstream Islington Midweek and West End leagues (London) and recently succeeded in winning the Gay World Cup. Other teams catering for gay and bisexual men are Village Manchester FC, the Left Foot Footballers Club and the Leicester Wilde Cats, a club for men and women. Teams for lesbians and bisexual women players include the Manchester Stingers, the South London Studs and the Manchester Spartans. Additionally, the Gay Football Supporters Network was formed in 1989 with the aim of enabling contacts between lesbian, gay and bisexual football supporters. This organisation also has five-a-side football teams in Birmingham, Leicester and Sheffield. Catering for a range of abilities and sexualities, these groups all share one aim: to offer marginalised individuals a chance to participate in 'the people's game' in a safe and accepting atmosphere.

Sources:

Connell, R. W., *Masculinities* (Cambridge: Polity Press, 1995).

Hekma, G., "As Long As They Don't Make An Issue Of It ..." Gay Men and Lesbians in Organized Sports in the Netherlands', *Journal of Homosexuality*, 35: 1 (1998), pp. 1–23.

Price, M. G. J., *Rugby as a Gay Men's Game: An Ethnographic Case Study*, MA Dissertation, University of Warwick, 1999.

Pronger, B., *The Arena of Masculinity* (London: GMP Publishers, 1990).

Simpson, M., *Male Impersonators* (London: Cassell, 1994).

Further Reading:

Messner, M. A. and Sabo, D. F., *Sex, Violence and Power in Sports: Rethinking Masculinity* (Freedom: The Crossing Press, 1994).

Messner, M. A. and Sabo, D. F. (eds), *Sport, Men, and the Gender Order* (Champaign, IL: Human Kinetics Books, 1990).

Young, P. D., *Lesbians and Gays and Sports* (New York: Chelsea House Publishers, 1995).

Michael Price

Football Boots

At its inception in 1863 the FA laid down guidelines as to what type of football boot should be worn. Rule 13 stated:

> No one wearing projecting nails, iron plates or gutta percha on the soles of his boots is allowed to play.

Initially players wore any pair of leather boots in their possession. But as the game progressed and leagues became widespread in the 1880s, specialised football boots emerged. Initially, most boots were manufactured locally, resulting in a great diversity of styles. They all shared common features, such as full toe and ankle protection: toes had to have added protection as it was usual for players to toe-kick the ball rather than use the instep. Boots were made of thick leather, which stretched above the ankle, and although some manufacturers claimed that their boots were light and pliable, by today's standards they would appear heavy and cumbersome. As the Football League established itself manufacturers began to supply teams directly. Perhaps the most famous boot was the 'hotspur' which was supplied to many league clubs. Many players used to buy their boots on the small side and stand in a hot bath allowing them to expand, the aim being to mould the boot to suit the size of their feet. As late as the 1940s, Jackie Milburn used to wear a new pair of boots down the pit where conditions were often wet.

Boots, c.1910 (National Football Museum)

Today's boots are lightweight and are cut low around the ankle and have a soft toe cap. This does expose the ankle to greater injury risk but it allows for greater speed and feel of the ball. There are several kinds of boots: most typically the studded, moulded rubber, pimpled stud and suction sole varieties. The studded boot can be fitted with studs at about a quarter of an inch, half an inch or three quarters of an inch in length. Studs can be made of leather, rubber, aluminium or plastic. There are usually six studs in a boot, though some manufacturers have added another under the big toe to improve balance. Moulded rubber boots are used in training or to play on hard or frozen pitches. These usually have fixed, shorter studs but must have ten per boot. On artificial pitches players can use pimpled stud boots or those with suction soles. Many players also wear an inner sole for extra comfort and foot protection. Most top professionals sign multi-million pound deals with the boot manufacturers. Players can sometimes be seen on television tying their laces, hoping that the camera will zoom in on them and give their sponsor a free advertisement plug.

Sources:

Howe, D. and Scovell B., *The Handbook of Soccer* (London: Pelham Books, 1988).

McArthur, I. and K., *Elegance Borne of Brutality: An Eclectic History of the Football Boot* (London: Two Heads Publishing, 1995).

See also Technology

Ray Physick

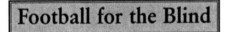

Football for the Blind

The general public is often surprised by the existence of football for the blind but it has proved increasingly popular from the second half of the twentieth century. The skill of blind football is rooted in orientation techniques and communication abilities – a case of ear-foot co-ordination.

Earliest records of blind football date back to the 1950s, when a very primitive version was played at the Royal National College for the Blind in Shrewsbury. The first recognised football was a leather case containing dry peas to give it some audibility and aid player mobility. In those early days there were few competitive games, but as blind players' ability developed, so did the desire to compete rather than simply play. Schools started to encourage blind football and inter-school games were arranged. The author recalls games between his team at Lickey Grange School for the Blind and Worcester College for the Blind being always full of passion and commitment – sometimes too much! At this time matches were five-a-side and mixed, with three totally blind and two partially sighted players.

By the mid-1970s, change was underway. Tarmac or concrete replaced grass as the best surface while the ball was made much lighter and easier to hear. It was now plastic with lead shot inside; the leather ball made quite a dull sound, especially when played on grass. The confidence and techniques of the players developed as a result, with matches even quicker and more competitive. Increasingly from this time, games came to be played on a tennis court-sized pitch, totally enclosed, to help players judge their position. The goals used are not of the conventional five-a-side type, as these would be easier to run into and thus more dangerous. They are instead made from hardboard or wire mesh netting with bells on, and are approximately six feet by four feet in area. When the ball hits the netting or boards players know immediately if they've scored.

Although it was deemed safer with two partially sighted players per team, blind players wanted their 'own' game. The first football league for the totally blind (technically referred to as 'B1' football) began in 1980 with seven teams of five totally blind players, with each team allowed two substitutes. Football for the partially sighted continued, graded according to the degree of sight as B2, B3 and B4. Although the initial season had teething problems, it was like a breath of fresh air and the League ran successfully for eight seasons. Many celebrities presented the end of season trophies and England international Steve Coppell was only one to be amazed and humbled at the ability he witnessed. The League had its controversial moments. For instance, questions were raised as to the sight classification of some players and, on one occasion, a team insisted on every player's sight being checked by the club ophthalmologist. Those who refused were asked to either withdraw or be blindfolded. This became a little contentious and those that refused left themselves open to criticism. After this unfortunate episode the League lost some of its appeal. One of the highlights of the 1980s occurred when Aston Villa allowed a demonstration of blind football before a First Division match between Villa and Luton.

In July 1985, BASRAB, the official organisation for disabled sport in Britain, organised the first European trip for blind players, to a tournament in Spain involving two Spanish teams and a Portugal side alongside the English side, which eventually finished second. A return tournament was held in Birmingham in 1987, but unfortunately, soon afterwards our domestic game went into a six-year decline and the league disbanded.

At the time of writing, there is a renewed drive towards totally blind football and attempts are being made to attract sponsors to allow participation in Europe and resurrect the domestic game. At one level, the future is now more encouraging than were those hard, early days, with blind football under the umbrella of the FA since 1998, while the International Blind Sports Association is keen for England to become an active voice in blind football in Europe and the World. However, the closure of specialist schools for the blind makes it increasingly difficult to attract blind footballers. Many blind children go directly into mainstream education – a frustrating situation, as they're probably unaware of the sporting opportunities they are missing.

Steve Cunningham

Football Games

Games replicating football matches in miniature, or in some way celebrating football culture, have existed from the very moment when football emerged as a mass spectator sport in the 1880s, yet another example of the vigorous service industry that grew up around the sport. Table-top games powered by finger, magnetic pull, lungpower and various mechanical devices have proved particularly popular. The oldest known table game was manufactured in Preston in 1884 and comprises a full set of players in the colours of Preston North End and Blackburn Rovers mounted on wooden blocks and designed to be moved around a squared board by hand. Suitably, it is now held in the National Football Museum at Preston. Blow football games, in which two manually manipulated goalkeepers are pitted against a ball propelled by small peashooters, were certainly in circulation by the early twentieth century at the latest, as were a variety of board and card games, football bagatelle and jigsaw puzzles depicting famous players.

Probably the most popular games were those that involved contestants flicking model players against a ball that they then tried to direct past a goalkeeper held on a stalk from behind the goal. Thus described, such games sound tedious in the extreme, but they have generated a distinctive and pleasurable set of skills and proved extremely profitable. *Newfooty*, invented by W. L. Keeling in 1929, was probably the first to attain a national market, but no game was to prove more pop-

PENALTY game, goalkeeper and two attackers with spring-loaded legs, c.1890
(National Football Museum)

ular than *Subbuteo*, devised by Peter Adolph in 1947. Adolph, a keen bird-watcher, named his creation after the Latin for the Hobby Hawk and he produced the initial sets from his Tunbridge Wells home. Soon taken over by the specialist games company Waddingtons, at its peak in the 1960s and 1970s 300,000 sets were being sold annually. It has been estimated that by 2000, 500 million sets had been sold in 50 countries (a *Subbuteo* World Cup was founded in 1987). The game was well marketed, with sets of players available in team or national colours, and black players were introduced into the United Kingdom version of the game in the 1990s to help counteract racism. Nevertheless, although over 50,000 sets were still sold every year in Britain alone in the late 1990s, Hasbro, the American company making the game since 1994, threatened to discontinue production in January 2000 citing the growing competition from computer games as its major reason. Although the decision was rescinded within days as a result of lively opposition, *Subbuteo* and the handful of other remaining tabletop games such as *Kick* and *Super Striker* had certainly lost ground dramatically to the games console and the personal computer.

Computer-based games began to appear in the late 1980s and within a decade had comfortably established themselves as the items of choice with particularly (although not exclusively) younger age groups. A football game topped the Christmas games software chart virtually every year from 1993 while, in 1997, three of the best selling 20, and 10 of the best selling 100, games packages were football related. Two hundred and sixty thousand copies of the most popular football game were sold in that year, with combined sales for the top three soccer titles alone reaching almost 600,000. The most popular games involve building a team, deciding tactical formations and then playing simulated matches at a chosen level of complexity. Featuring 3D graphics, action replays and live commentaries, rapid technological developments have made them ever more sophisticated and responsive.

Although the domestic market was always the dominant one in the football games industry, manufacturers were also quick to spot opportunities in the public domain. A goal shooting game involving model players mounted on stands certainly existed at Blackpool in the mid-1880s, although football arcade games began in earnest in 1896 when E. G. Matthewson invented a slot machine game encompassing two players. An eleven-a-side game had to wait until 1921. Computerised arcade games have become commonplace since the 1990s. Perhaps the most enduring of the non-domestic games (although it has been 'domesticated' in recent years) has been table football, involving the manipulation of rows of model players mounted on a metal bar. Table football was certainly emerging in arcades, pubs and clubs in the early twentieth century (the Football Museum owns a Welsh-made game from the 1900s), but it appears to have grown in popularity from the 1950s, establishing a strong following amongst students. The highest quality tables by manufacturers such as the French company René Pieree were selling for as much as £700 by the early twenty-first century.

Sources:

F.I.F.A. Museum Collection (Berlin: Verlags – Gmbh, 1996).
Leisure Intelligence, *Video and Computer Games* (London: Mintel, September 1998).
Payne, R., *Fifty Years of Flicking Football* (Harefield: Yore, 1996).
Pearson, L., *Amusement Machines* (Princes Risborough: Shire, 1992).

Dave Russell

Football League

Founded in 1888, the Football League was the premier league competition in English and Welsh football for over a century. Although often criticised for its insularity and conservatism, under its auspices professional football developed into a genuinely national game. What is more, the League has ranked alongside the FA as one of the foremost governing bodies of the game. Indeed, until recent years, the history of the Football League was virtually synonymous with that of English professional football. Since the creation of the FA Premier League in 1992, however, the League has seen its status and power reduced to the point where it has become peripheral in the organisation of football at the highest level.

The origins of the Football League can be traced back to the legalisation of professionalism in 1885. Faced with the burden of large wage bills to meet, in addition to other expenses, there was a recognition among the leading clubs that a regular schedule of matches was needed to replace the rather haphazard fixture lists which then existed. To that end William McGregor, a Scottish director of Aston Villa, circulated a letter in March 1888 suggesting that 'ten or twelve of the most prominent clubs in England combine to arrange home and away fixtures each season'. On 17 April the Football League was officially formed at a conference at the Royal Hotel in Manchester. It consisted of six clubs from Lancashire (Accrington, Blackburn Rovers, Bolton Wanderers, Burnley, Everton and Preston North End) and six from the Midlands (Aston Villa, Derby County, Notts County, Stoke, West Bromwich Albion and Wolverhampton Wanderers). The first round of fixtures took place the following September, and by April 1889 Preston North End had won the first championship without losing a single match.

The Football League's expansion was rapid. In 1892 the first division was enlarged to 16 clubs and a new 12-club Second Division was established, with many of the newcomers moving from the rival Football Alliance. By 1898 the League consisted of 36 clubs divided equally in two divisions, while the admittance of Chelsea, Clapton Orient, Hull City and Leeds City in 1905 took the total to 40.

Although it continued to be based around a core of clubs in the north-west and Midlands, the League also spread its geographical constituency by incorporating members from regions such as Yorkshire, the north-east and the south of England. In 1920, Cardiff City became the first Welsh member and a Third Division, was created by the election of the Southern League en bloc plus Grimsby Town. In 1921, this was renamed the Third Division (South) and a northern section was also added; by 1923, the membership of the Football League had reached 88 clubs. The League's final expansion to 92 clubs took place in 1950, and soon after, in 1958, the regional sections were abandoned in favour of separate Third and Fourth Divisions.

For much of its history, however, the Football League has been resistant to change. Its administrative structure reflected, and contributed to, this state of affairs. Before the 1980s, alterations in the constitution or rules of the League required a three-quarters majority, an arrangement which could frustrate even the most moderate of proposals. Moreover, the Management Committee (renamed the Football League Board of Directors in 1992), the body which was empowered to run the League and its competitions, had always been composed of representatives elected from the member clubs themselves. Disquiet regularly surrounded this potential conflict of interest between club and League. Changes in personnel have also been relatively rare: in its first hundred years, for instance, the League had only 12 presidents and six secretaries. It is hardly surprising then that the Football League has tended to be viewed as a deeply conservative body.

In this context, reforms have been difficult to push through. In the early 1960s, a plan for the reorganisation of the League into five divisions of 20 clubs each, with four promoted and relegated each season, was rejected by the membership. Drawn up by secretary Alan Hardaker and president Joe Richards, this 'Pattern for Football' was an attempt to streamline the League while at the same time increasing public interest. The reduced fixture list was to be buttressed by the addition of a new knock-out league. Ironically the latter was accepted, thus adding to an already congested fixture list and leading Hardaker to accuse the clubs of 'selfishness and shallow thinking'. In 1968 the equally progressive recommendations of the Chester Report were dismissed, as was a second report headed by Norman Chester in 1983, although ideas such as the reduction in the size of the First Division and changes in voting regulations were subsequently passed.

Even though it had expanded to embrace the whole of England and much of Wales, the Football League continued to be regarded as a parochial organisation. Its headquarters have always been in Lancashire, moving from Preston to Lytham St Anne's in 1959, and then back to Preston in 1998. In contrast with the metropolitan-based FA in particular, the League has always looked rather insular. Indeed, the relationship between these two bodies dominated English football for more than a century. In theory the functions and responsibilities of the two bodies were easy to differentiate: according to William McGregor, 'The League has its work to do; the Association has its work to do and there need be no clashing.' But the reality could be somewhat different. Initially the two bodies clashed over a range of issues, from the correct type of football boots to the release of players for international fixtures. The most significant conflicts centred on the financial dealings between clubs and players. The FA had after all opposed the transfer system from its introduction in the early 1890s, and was uncomfortable in administering the maximum wage rule. In 1910 the governing body finally formalised its 1904 decision by passing over the responsibility for club finances to the League.

There were signs of a more harmonious relationship. From the inter-war years, arrangements were made to deal with important issues jointly, and in 1930 the relationship became closer still when it was agreed that the League Management Committee should automatically be represented on the FA Council. But the underlying tensions between the two bodies often turned into open conflict. In 1965 all but one of 92 League clubs resigned *en masse* from the FA over a dispute regarding payments to amateurs. They soon rejoined but quarrels concerning the registration of players, disciplinary regulations and Cup Final tickets all strained the rela-

tionship during the late 1960s and early 1970s. The most serious disputes surfaced in 1972: first over the distribution of pools and other monies, and then over the negotiations for live transmission of an England fixture with West Germany. In March 1972, Hardaker declared 'a state of war between the League and the Football Association'. Agreement was finally reached in December but only after an arbitrator had been appointed to resolve the dispute.

Until the 1980s, economic arrangements within the Football League reflected its philosophy of mutuality. Income sharing and mutual support were considered crucial for maintaining the health of the rich and poor clubs alike, and maintaining the overall viability of the League. To this end, arrangements for sharing gate receipts were established during the First World War and from 1949 all clubs were expected to pay 4 per cent of gate receipts into a central pool for administrative purposes. The transfer system and maximum wage were also considered important devices to ensure equality of competition and thus prevent the wealthiest clubs winning all the trophies. These arrangements seemed to work fairly well. Despite short periods of supremacy (the three consecutive championships won by Huddersfield Town and Arsenal between the wars), the Football League was a relatively open competition for many years. Some clubs may have been richer than others but this did not preclude the possibility of one of the minnows rising up the divisions, or a member of the football aristocracy slipping down them.

These assumptions, and the economic arrangements which underpinned them, came under serious challenge during the 1980s. From 1983 clubs were allowed to retain their home gate receipts and further changes in the distribution of television and sponsorship money in favour of clubs in the higher divisions followed in 1985. The elite were also given more voting strength. This took place in the context of threats by the most powerful clubs to form a 'Super League' outside the Football League. By the early 1990s these threats had been transformed into something more concrete. Football League plans for power-sharing were rejected by the FA, which in 1991 produced its own 'Blueprint for the Future of Football'. The idea of a breakaway with FA support crystallised and in 1992 the entire First Division resigned from the Football League and formed a new FA Premiership.

The power struggle was finally over, and it was the League that had lost. Yet the Football League has survived. It now has 72 rather than 92 members, three rather than four divisions and a cup competition (the Worthington Cup) which increasingly seems to be regarded as an unnecessary diversion, at least for the Premiership clubs who still play in it. While it will probably never regain its former status, the retention of a UEFA Cup place for the winners of the Worthington Cup suggests that the Football League might still be able to exert some influence on football at the highest level.

Sources:

Churchill, R. C., *English League Football* (London: Sportsmans Book Club, 1962).

Hardaker, A., *Hardaker of the League* (London: Pelham, 1977).

Inglis, S., *League Football and the Men Who Made It* (London: Collins Willow, 1998).

Tomlinson, A., 'North and South: The Rivalry of the Football League and the Football Asssociation', in J. Williams and S. Wagg (eds), *British Football and Social Change* (Leicester: Leicester University Press, 1991), pp. 25–47.

Further Reading:

Butler, B., *The Football League: The First 100 Years* (London: Colour Library, 1998)

Taylor, M., *'Proud Preston': A History of the Football League, 1900–1939*, Ph.D. Thesis, De Montfort University, 1997.

Matt Taylor

[Football] League Cup

The Football League Cup is a knockout competition between all 92 members of the Football League in England. First competed for in the 1960/61 season, the Cup was the brainchild of former League Secretary Alan Hardaker, who has subsequently donated his name to the final's man-of-the-match award. The trophy itself, however, dates back to the late nineteenth century, when it was competed for by teams representing the Tyne shipyards.

The League Cup's early history was notable for the disdain shown by the bigger clubs, who often declined to enter, viewing the competition to be of little importance in an already crowded season, and this attitude has once again come to the fore in recent times. Attitudes first changed in 1965, when it was announced that the winners of the competition would gain automatic entry into European competition. Chelsea became the first to achieve this, ultimately reaching the semi-finals of the old Inter-City Fairs Cup. Tottenham Hotspur, however, remain the only club to achieve European success by virtue of qualification via the League Cup, winning the inaugural UEFA Cup in 1972. Unfortunately, despite the lure of European qualification, the increasing number of qualification places allocated to the domestic league has ensured that England's top clubs once again view the League Cup as a secondary competition, often using the games to blood younger talent and give squad players a run out.

The format of the competition has changed very little in its 40-year history. The one notable change has been the alteration in the final: originally a two-legged home and away affair, it was switched in 1967 to a one-off game played at Wembley. The two-legged nature of the early rounds remains in effect, however, helping to provide revenue for those smaller clubs lucky enough to draw a prestigious tie. Indeed the Football League views the competition as a vital component in the principle of wealth redistribution within football. This was a factor recognised in 1992 with the Tripartite Agreement, signed by the FA, the FA Premier League and the Football League, which ensured the future participation of top-flight clubs in the competition. The League Cup itself is estimated to generate more than £40 million annually, and the competition also runs a pooling system which assists clubs who suffer an early exit.

Queen's Park Rangers were the first Wembley winners, beating West Bromwich Albion 3–2, and it was not until 1977 that a replay was necessary, Aston Villa and Everton needing two before Villa secured a 3–2 victory at Hillsborough (replays being held away from Wembley). The Wembley game has since failed to secure a victor a further four times, in 1978 (Nottingham Forest–Liverpool), 1981 (Liverpool–West Ham), 1984 (Liverpool–Everton) and 1997 (Leicester City–Middlesbrough).

Part of the League Cup's revenue comes from sponsorship deals. Indeed the competition was the first major domestic competition to attract commercial sponsorship when the National Dairy Council became title sponsors in 1982, re-christening the trophy the Milk Cup. Since then the competition has been known variously as the Littlewoods Cup (1987–89), the Rumbelows Cup (1990–92), the Coca-Cola Cup (1993–98) and now, as part of a deal with Bass Brewers, the Worthington Cup (1999–). Bass have paid £23 million, including marketing support, for their current 5-year deal. TV coverage of the competition, which began in 1983/84, earns £25 million a season as part of the Football League's current deal with BSkyB and ITV, which covers all of the League's properties, including the League Championship. Gate receipts currently generate a further £17.3 million annually, and crowds totalling nearly 68 million have watched the League Cup over its 40-year history, providing an average attendance of 11,882 at the competition's near 6,000 games since its inception.

The League Cup's inaugural winners, Aston Villa, also share the record for most victories with Liverpool, the figure currently standing at five. The same two clubs also hold the record number of final appearances, at seven. Nottingham Forest became the first team to successfully defend the trophy, winning it in 1978 and 1979, although Liverpool also hold the distinction of winning the competition four times in a row (1981–84). The final

itself has also twice hosted local derbies, firstly in 1963 when Birmingham City met Aston Villa, and then again in 1984 when Liverpool and Everton clashed.

Whilst the future of the League Cup appears to be stable the competition will always be overshadowed by the more prestigious FA Cup. By the League's own admission the continued success of the competition is reliant on securing long-term European qualification for its victors as a means of providing an incentive for the nation's top teams, and helping to secure future TV and sponsorship money.

Sources:
Brown, T., *The Football League Cup Statistics Book* (Association of Football Statisticians, 1992).
The Football League, *The Football League Cup* (Lytham St Annes: The Football League, 2000).

Paul O'Higgins

Football Season

As association football emerged in the 1860s and 1870s, existing patterns of school and university football were maintained, with most club games confined to the period from September to April. However, it was the establishment of national leagues, with their distinct rhythms, that increasingly defined the 'football season' in the public mind. The inaugural Football League programme began on 8 September 1888, and most games had been completed by mid-March 1889. The steady expansion of the League over the period to 1921 necessitated the eventual use of late August as a starting date, with the season drawing to a close at the end of April, a pattern which changed little until the late century. Indeed, it was not until the 1950s that any significant change occurred, in the shape of the repositioning of the FA Cup final. Originally played in March, it soon moved to late April, coinciding with the last major Saturday of the League programme. In 1952, concern that the final's television audience was reducing gates led to Football League clubs successfully lobbying for the game to be moved back a week to the last official Saturday of the season, which usually saw a reduced fixture list. However, following the attraction of 10 million viewers to the 'Matthews final' of 1953, the game was finally moved back a further week as from 1954, thus providing a sense of dramatic climax to the season. The English season became neatly and effectively framed within two showpiece events when the FA Charity Shield was moved from October to mid-August in 1960. Other minor changes usually revolved around specific requirements, such as the need to extend the 1946/47 and 1962/63 seasons because of the amount of matches lost to bad weather. The 1962/63 season was probably the longest ever, with the FA Cup final played as late as 25 May and the Scottish First Division programme only completed two days later.

More lasting changes began with the introduction of the play-off system in England in 1987, which pushed the end of the season towards late May. At the same time, attempts to relieve fixture congestion and the partial cancellation of the League programme to allow time for the preparation of the national squad demanded an earlier start to the season. In 1999/2000, for example, the Nationwide League season began on 7 August and ended with the First Division play-off final on 31 May. In Scotland, similar pressures have also led to increasingly early starts. In the 2000/01 season, the Scottish Premier League programme began as early as 29 July. Calls for a mid-season break or a shift to a summer season have been routinely made, usually after periods of severe weather such as those experienced in 1947 and 1963. However, a small summer football lobby built up in the early 1960s argued that the switch would arrest the increasingly worrying fall in crowds. The directors of Crystal Palace were especially active here, and the fact that they successfully sued the *Daily Mail* after its football columnist, J. L. Manning, implied that they were suggesting this for personal gain is a significant comment on the economics of the game at this time. Interestingly, the Llandrynog and District Village Club's Summer League was founded as long ago as 1927 and, with around a dozen teams, still flourishes despite the opposition of the Welsh FA.

It is undeniable that for leading players the lengthening programme of matches, the possibility of playing in either the summer-based World Cup or European Championships every two years, and the need for extensive pre-season training, means that the football 'season' has become a memory, and the football 'year' a reality. Whether footballers, or indeed their fans, can sustain this remains to be seen.

Sources:

Inglis, S., *League Football and the Men Who Made It* (London: Collins, 1988).

Jones, E., *Llandrynog and District Village Club's Summer League: The Official History (1927–1995)* (Llandyrnog: The League Committee, 1995).

The Times, 16 and 18 May 1963.

Dave Russell

Football Supporters' Association

Formed in Liverpool in the aftermath of the 1985 Heysel disaster, the Football Supporters' Association (FSA) briefly galvanised fans into a radical democratising approach towards football, and for the first time gave supporters a genuine role within it, able at least to influence its decision-making processes.

The decision of Liverpool fans Peter Garrett and Rogan Taylor to found a new movement arose from the crumbling state of professional football: violence (and deaths) within stadia, decayed facilities, growing concern that the Conservative Government's proposed anti-hooligan measures would impact detrimentally on the majority of law-abiding fans, and a widespread sense that football was facing a potentially terminal crisis, are central to explaining the FSA's formation and rapid growth. With its individual, non-club, regionalised membership, well thought-out media strategies, and remit to campaign to empower fans, the FSA had an aggressive, vigorously expressed agenda that enabled it to quickly attract the support of thousands of (generally male) fans eager to realign football and fight for their rights within it, including creating genuine supporter representation. Closely connected to the burgeoning fanzine movement, a sense of politicised anger was essential to the FSA, and immediately after Heysel the organisation enabled fans to enter the corridors of power for the first time. This even extended to a strange alliance with football's governing bodies against the Conservative Government's plans for identity cards for supporters (the state's response to violence), which the FSA managed to defeat, primarily thanks to a well-organised and vocal political campaign, albeit with the help of Lord Justice Taylor in the aftermath of the Hillsborough disaster in 1989.

However, the FSA's undoubted successes masked the structural factors that were always likely to prevent it from becoming a long-term, broad-based organisation. Being formed from crisis meant that the FSA would struggle, with its non-club structure, to maintain membership, finance and ultimately influence once those crises appeared to have passed. Membership soared by 200 a week immediately after the Hillsborough disaster, only to drop away alarmingly over the next decade; it was believed to be no more than 1,000 or 1,500 by the mid-1990s. Its structure and ethos made it less attractive to fans of teams with staunchly oppositional fandoms that made them unwilling to co-operate with fans of other clubs: the Merseyside branch, for instance (always one of the largest in the country), comprised Liverpool, Everton and Tranmere fans. Additionally, the (not necessarily accurate) view amongst many supporters that the FSA was a politically motivated, middle-class organisation also damaged its appeal, and therefore its ability to speak for fans. As membership declined, so the leverage the FSA could exercise on clubs across the country fell, eliminating its

raison d'être. Moorhouse (1994) also argues that it was always an English organisation and that fans in Scotland never really took to it. By the mid-1990s, the FSA had fewer members than some single independent supporters' associations, and the structure of regional branches was clearly no longer functioning effectively, with some parts of the country (such as the north-east) entirely uncovered by the FSA.

Nonetheless, the FSA has retained a strong media presence, particularly over issues connected with the national team or government policy, and continues to do much unnoticed but vital work (running Fan Embassies for travelling British fans in Italy in 1990, in Sweden in 1992 and France in 1998, and for visitors to England for Euro 96), as well as having high-level access to local and national political authorities. The failure to maintain its mass membership of the late 1980s is, broadly speaking, attributable to its non-club structure, combined with deeply-rooted discourses of fandom that deny the possibility of acting politically or will only do so in moments of crisis. Equally, as King argues, traditional working-class male fans – what he calls the 'lads' – will not see the FSA as part of their interaction with football, or as representative of their views.

Maybe the crucial moment for the FSA was the formation of the FA Premier League in 1992: once control of football shifted from the Football League and Association to 20 Premier League club chairmen, the forces threatening to reshape the game fractured, making it more logical and effective to campaign at a local, club-focused level rather than on a national non-club basis: thus, since 1992, the FSA lacked the context to create and maintain a mass membership, in turn preventing it from generating the finance needed to sustain its activities. The absence of a single, all-pervading threat to the whole of football (such as the identity card scheme of the late 1980s) is probably highly significant in the declining fortunes of the FSA in the 1990s.

Sources:

Haynes, R., *The Football Imagination: The Rise of Football Fanzine Culture* (Aldershot: Arena, 1995).

Sir Norman Chester Centre for Football Research, *Football and Football Supporters after Hillsborough: A National Survey of Members of the FSA* (Leicester: Leicester University, 1989).

Further Reading:

Hargreaves, J., 'Sport and Socialism in Britain', *Sociology of Sport*, 9: 2 (1992), 131–54

King, A., 'The Lads: Masculinity and the New Consumption of Football', *Sociology*, 31: 2 (1997), 329–46.

Moorhouse, B., 'From Zines Like These? Fanzines, Traditions and Identity in Scottish Football', in G. Jarvie and G. Walker (eds), *Sport and the Making of the Scottish Nation* (London: Leicester University Press, 1994), pp. 173–95.

Rex Nash

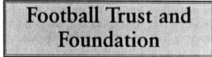

Football Trust and Foundation

The last quarter of the twentieth century witnessed the establishment of a series of organisations dedicated to the direction of money into projects that improved football's infrastructure and enhanced our understanding of its place in British society. The first such body was the Football Grounds Improvement Trust, established in December 1975. Faced with potentially expensive ground improvements by the requirements of the 1975 Safety at Sports Grounds Act, the Football League persuaded the Pools Promoters Association (PPA) to allow a levy on their 'Spot the Ball' profits to be passed on to clubs for crucial work. The PPA accepted this suggestion happy in the knowledge that their action would help head off pressure for taxation of these competitions. A board of six trustees including Sir Norman Chester and Tom Finney was established to vet applications to the Trust. In 1979, a parallel and similarly funded body named the Football Trust was established in order to

investigate a range of social issues surrounding the game, with hooliganism a central concern. The Sir Norman Chester Centre for Football Research, established at Leicester University in 1987, was funded exclusively by the Trust.

In 1990, the two bodies combined under the title Football Trust 90, although the simpler 'Football Trust' became the standard designation. Following the Taylor Report in 1990, the Conservative Government cut pools duty by 2.5 per cent in order to release £100 million for ground improvements over the next five years. Given this, an increase in funding available from *Spot the Ball* and the inter-related nature of so many of football's problems, it clearly made sense for such an amalgamation to take place. The Trust brought together representatives from within the game, the pools companies, the police and local authorities and played a major role in overseeing one of the most crucial periods of change in British football's history. In June 1997 the Trust came close to collapse. The establishment of the National Lottery in 1994 resulted in a large fall in revenues within both the pools and 'Spot the Ball', with the consequence that Trust funding fell from £37 million a year to just £9 million by 1996. The FA, FA Premier League and Sport England all pledged substantial sums of money to enable the Trust to continue.

Over the period from the 1970s, the Trust invested over £400 million in the game providing a major share of the costs for 15 new grounds, over 160 new and refurbished stands and 50 floodlight systems. Although most of the money was spent in England, the Trust also forged a partnership with the Scottish FA and the Scottish Sports Council leading to some joint activities. The English Football League had absorbed almost 90 per cent of funding up to 2000 and, with the Trust's 'Taylor' work largely finished and demands for greater attention to be paid to junior football mounting, a change of direction was inevitable. As a result, the Football Trust was dissolved and, in July 2000, the Football Foundation created in its place. The Foundation, a partnership between the Government, Sport England, the Football Association and the FA Premier League (which gives 5 per cent of its TV revenue to the organisation), is intended to revolutionise funding for grass roots football. It consists of a main board, chaired initially by Tom Pendry MP, and three advisory panels. 75 per cent of its annual budget (expected to be £60 million from 2001) will be used to put in place a new generation of modern football facilities in parks, local leagues and schools. The remaining 25 per cent will be split equally between various football and the community schemes emphasising social inclusion and the raising of educational standards, and outstanding ground improvement and safety work inherited from the Football Trust.

Sources:

Inglis, S., *League Football and the Men Who Made It* (London: Willow, 1988).
Rothmans Football Yearbook (1990/91; 2000/01).
The Times (4 March 1990).

Dave Russell and Alistair Bennett

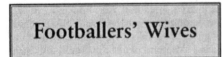

Footballers' Wives

As media attention on the private lives of footballers has grown, footballers' wives have become increasingly well-known. Their vital role in supporting and sustaining the professional through the vicissitudes of a football career has frequently been recognised by managers, who generally like their players to marry at a relatively young age. However, wives who seek to have a more active influence in their husbands' job are often branded as troublemakers.

In the early days of the professional game it was not unknown for footballers to pose with their wives and families for publicity photographs. *Topical Times* in 1919 printed a photo feature entitled 'Famous Footballers At Home', with the emphasis on cosy, stable domesticity. After the Second World War footballers' autobiographies discussed their wives, often portraying them as long-suffering women

who ran the family home and bore the brunt of their spouses' bad temper after defeat. Tom Finney appeared with his wife in a 1946 *Picture Post* feature as an example of a normal working-class family coping with life following wartime disruption.

However, probably the first footballer's wife to hit the headlines was already famous in her own right. In 1958, one of Britain's most eligible bachelors, Billy Wright, then captain of England and also the most successful club side of the Fifties, Wolverhampton Wanderers, married Joy Beverley of the singing trio the Beverley sisters. Details of their courtship were published in the Sunday papers and their 'secret' wedding was attended by thousands of fans. Despite the growing wealth and celebrity of footballers from the 1960s onwards it is rare for footballers' wives to be entertainment stars: Leslie Ash, the actress married to Lee Chapman, the singer Louise Nurding who became Jamie Redknapp's wife, and Spice Girl Victoria Adams, David Beckham's wife, were exceptions.

It was in the late 1960s that football wives really became the focus of sustained attention, but also began to attract derision as they became stereotyped as brainless bimbos with failed careers in modelling. *Shoot*'s 1969 regular feature, 'The Girl Behind the Man', consisted of full-page photographs of mini-skirted footballers' wives with a brief descriptive paragraph. This served chiefly to establish the wife's function as homemaker and mother, though some wives did have other employment. As Carol Moore, shown seated with her injured husband, Nottingham Forest's Ian Moore, said, 'There's more to being a footballer's wife than sitting in the stand glowing with pride at his achievements. When a star is hurt he needs comforting.' Though generally most wives had given up their jobs, usually hairdressing or working as receptionists, when they were married, some continued to run salons or dress shops. Hunter Davies, in his study of Tottenham Hotspur, *The Glory Game* (1972), concluded that the wives of the players had lower educational qualifications than their husbands, and also revealed that most of the footballers he interviewed saw no reason to give their wives any help with domestic tasks or childcare, with the notable exception of Alan Mullery. For most footballers' wives in the higher divisions, the demands of supporting their husbands, and the frequent moves which some players' careers demand, juggling a home and outside career is difficult.

From the 1980s onwards players' wives have also been collectively referred to in the football media as 'the wives', a group which will occasionally create problems for club and national managers alike by their refusal to accept a completely quiescent role and to be excluded from some activities. Bobby Robson, when England manager, invited players' wives and families for a week's holiday in Sardinia before the 1990 World Cup finals. Neil Webb's wife, Shelley, a journalist and television presenter, challenged Alex Ferguson's statement that there was no room for a crèche at Old Trafford and secured one adjacent to the players' lounge. However, the 'interfering' wife is usually the subject of club and fan condemnation. Victoria Adams was portrayed as a malign influence, particularly after comments that suggested she was unhappy in Manchester and would like David to move to a southern club nearer her family. Joy Beverley, decades before, had been similarly forced to rebut claims that Wolverhampton was not good enough for her.

Though fans are currently aware of the enormous amounts of work that footballers' wives often do behind the scenes to support and help their husbands, a 1990s Channel 4 documentary in the *Cutting Edge* series, which chose to portray a leading player's wife as a wannabe television presenter, model and shopaholic, demonstrated that the stereotype that players' wives are stupid or interfering still persists.

Sources:

Davies, H., *The Glory Game* (London: Weidenfeld and Nicolson, 1972).

Webb, S., *Footballers' Wives Tell Their Tales* (London: Yellow Jersey Press, 1998).

Wright, B., *One Hundred Caps and All That* (London: Robert Hale, 1961).

Joyce Woolridge

Footballing Families

Numerous interesting family connections can be traced within British football. There have been three instances of the most obvious family connection, father and son, representing England at full international level. George Eastham, capped once in 1935, was followed into the England side by his son, also George, who won 19 caps between 1963 and 1966. This feat was also accomplished by Brian Clough (two caps, 1960) and Nigel (14 caps, 1989–93) and by Frank Lampard (two caps, 1973 and 1980) and Frank junior (one cap, 1999).

More unusual were instances of father and son who appeared together in the same Football League team. Alec Herd and son David did so for Stockport County in 1951, and were followed in 1980 by Hereford United's Ian and Gary Bowyer. There have been numerous instances of brothers appearing in the same international team, the most notable being Jack and Bobby Charlton, who appeared together for England on 28 occasions between 1965 and 1970, including the 1966 World Cup Final. Arthur and Percy Walters were England's full-back pairing on several occasions between 1885 and 1890, a feat emulated by Gary and Phil Neville of Manchester United. Wales' team against Northern Ireland in April 1955 featured two sets of brothers: Ivor and Len Allchurch and John and Mel Charles. Jackie and Danny Blanchflower played together for Northern Ireland, while Scotland's Harold and Moses McNeil appeared against Wales in 1876. More unusual were the Goodall and Hollins brothers. John Goodall appeared for England 14 times between 1888 and 1898, while Archie made his ten international appearances for Ireland. John Hollins represented England once in 1967, by which time brother Dave had won 11 caps for Wales.

There have been even more substantial family connections at club level. Five Perry brothers appeared for West Bromwich Albion during the 1880s and 1890s.

Between 1923 and 1929 four Keetley brothers – Tom, Harold, Joe and Frank – turned out for Doncaster Rovers, although only three appeared together. The Clarke brothers – Allan, Derek, Frank and Wayne – appeared in the Football League for various clubs between 1965 and 1990, with Allan (Leeds United) and Wayne (Everton) winning League Championship medals. Since 1945 four sets of brothers have played together in FA Cup winning sides: Leslie and Denis Compton (Arsenal, 1950), George and Ted Robledo (Newcastle United, 1952), Jimmy and Brian Greenhoff (Manchester United, 1977) and the Nevilles (Manchester United, 1999). For long service it is hard to beat the Callender brothers, Tom and Jack, who amassed over 900 Football League appearances between them for Gateshead. Twin brothers in the same side are unusual but not unique, although the feat of twins Alfred and William Stephens, who both scored for Swindon Town against Exeter City in September 1946, has yet to be emulated.

Finally, England's, and indeed, Britain's best-known footballing family was perhaps the Milburns, who hailed from Ashington in Northumberland. Brothers James, Stan, John and George all played League football and cousin Jackie represented Newcastle United and England. Jackie himself had two famous cousins: the Charlton brothers!

Sources:

Gibson, John, *Wor Jackie: The Jackie Milburn Story* (Edinburgh: Sportsprint, 1990).

Harris, N., *The Charlton Brothers* (London: Stanley Paul, 1971).

Lamming, D., *An England Football Internationalists' Who's Who 1872–1988* (Beverley: Hutton, 1990).

Lamming, D., *A Scottish Soccer Internationalists' Who's Who 1872–1986* (Beverley: Hutton, 1987).

Neville, G., Neville, P., Pilger, S. and Barnes, J., *For Club and Country: the Hunt for European and World Cup Glory* (London: Manchester United Books, 1998).

John Coyle

Footballs

The origins of the spherical ball used within the game of soccer are unclear. What is clear is that the development of the football has, in contrast to other sports that use non-spherical balls, permitted the development of a very high level of kicking skill within the game. Games based around the use of a ball can be seen in relief carving, fine art, ceramic and metalwork from all over the world, notably Japan, and in Mexico, where the world's first rubber ball was used. During Columbus's second voyage to the Americas, Europeans witnessed local inhabitants playing a game with balls made from the gum of a tree. This game was a very important cultural activity, played between two seven-man teams. The game was known as tlatchi and took place in purpose-built stadia where huge sums of money were gambled on the outcome.

During the medieval period almost any roughly spherical object was acceptable for a game, including animal bladders and hogs' heads. However, the ferocity of most games meant that the more mobile, bouncy ball made from animal bladders was unsuitable to all but games based on throwing. This was as a result of the tendency of the inflated ball to burst during the more violent kicking and running sports. As a result many medieval ball games were played with a more solid ball – usually a leather covering filled with cork shavings or a similar material.

Technical deficiencies initially made rubber unsuitable for the manufacture of an artificial bladder. It was not until Mr Macintosh's nineteenth-century discovery of a suitable solvent for raw rubber that progress began to be made. This breakthrough enabled the production of thin rubber sheets, thus allowing inflatable rubber bladders of great strength to be manufactured. For the first time footballs were produced incorporating rubber bladders that could withstand heavy pressures. The quality of the ball was further enhanced with the formation of the FA in 1863. As the body responsible for the laws of the game they attempted to standardise the ball. It was agreed in 1872 that the ball must be spherical, with a circumference of 68–71 centimetres. It also had to be cased in leather or other approved materials and had to weigh between 453 and 396 grams at the start of a game. A rule change in 1905 made it mandatory that the outer casing be made of leather.

The ball remained largely unchanged for many decades but suffered from continuous problems caused by water absorption. On wet days the ball grew increasingly heavy as the leather soaked up large amounts of liquid. This, together with the lacing that protected the valve of the bladder, made heading the ball not only unpleasant but also painful and dangerous. Developments in recent years have seen the protection of the leather surface by a special polyurethane preparation, which has eliminated water absorption, thus maintaining a perfect ball weight even in heavy rain.

Today's balls combine a latex bladder with an outer casing made from synthetic leather. These polyester woven materials are sometimes impregnated with polyurethane for added strength and wear.

Sources:
Morris, D., *The Soccer Tribe* (London: Jonathan Cape, 1981).

Further Reading:
FIFA, *F.I.F.A. Museum Collection* (Berlin: Verlags-GmbH, 1996).
Pickering, D., *The Cassell Soccer Companion* (London: Cassell, 1994).

Mark Bushell

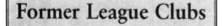

Former League Clubs

Throughout the history of the game, many football clubs have died in obscurity. However, some did achieve fame – albeit sometimes of a local or transitory nature – while some have been undeservedly forgotten. In England, a number of notable clubs of the 1870s and 1880s went into

decline from the late 1880s because of increased competition caused by professionalism. These included the Bolton clubs Great Lever and Halliwell, and Wednesbury Old Athletic in the Midlands. The first major casualty was Blackburn Olympic – the first provincial club to win the FA Cup – who succumbed to competition from the more powerful Rovers. Bootle, founded in 1878, were wound up in 1893 after one season in the Football League. Once Everton's main rivals for the title of Liverpool's premier club, they lost support to them throughout the 1880s.

Accrington FC and Accrington Stanley both suffered from lack of support in the town, and the proximity of better football at Blackburn and Burnley. The former folded in 1896 after five seasons in the League, while Stanley survived in the League from 1921 to 1962, when financial problems caused them to withdraw before the completion of their fixtures. Darwen FC were the probable originators of professionalism in 1878, and almost beat the Old Etonians in 1879. They were in the League from 1891 to 1899, but were affected by Blackburn Rovers's move to nearby Ewood. Wigan Borough were in Division Three from 1921 until 1932, but folded without completing their fixtures. New Brighton had two Football League clubs: New Brighton Tower and New Brighton FC. The former was an 'artificial' club founded to play on the Tower Athletic Ground, managing just three league seasons between 1898 and 1901, while the latter competed in Division Three from 1923 until 1951. Both clubs suffered from poor finances and eventually ceased activities.

Yorkshire's Bradford Park Avenue, founded in 1907, enjoyed three seasons in Division One from 1914 to 1921. (The club was re-formed in 1988 and, at the time of writing, plays in Division One of the Unibond League.) They declined after the Second World War, playing in the Third and Fourth Divisions, and collapsed soon after being voted out of the League in 1970. Another Yorkshire club, Leeds City, played at Elland Road before Leeds United. Founded in 1904, financial irregularities, including illegal payments to players, accelerated their decline, and they failed to complete their League fixtures in 1919.

In north-east England, Durham City were in the League from 1921 to 1928, without achieving any real success, being six times the worst-supported League club. Unsurprisingly, they collapsed in 1938. Middlesbrough Ironopolis were the top club in the town for a brief period, having one season in Division Two in 1893/94, but were defunct by 1894. Gateshead (originally as South Shields) were in the League from 1919 to 1960, facing severe competition from nearby Newcastle and Sunderland. To local anger, they failed to be re-elected in 1960, despite not having finished in the bottom spot.

Midlands clubs who reached the League but never achieved success include the Burton clubs and Loughborough. Burton is the smallest town in England to have had two clubs simultaneously in the Football League – Swifts and Wanderers, both playing in Division Two in the 1890s. They combined to form Burton United, who continued in the League until 1907, disbanding in 1910. Burton Wanderers' claim to fame is that they beat Newcastle United 9–0 and Manchester City 8–0 in 1894/95. Loughborough were one of the most unsuccessful League clubs. Very small attendances meant that they were poorly financed, but they did at least have the pleasure of beating Arsenal 8–0 in Division Two in 1896.

Scotland also had several clubs that achieved some measure of fame, but were affected by increasing financial pressures in the game. Edinburgh St Bernard's were founded in 1878, were members of the Scottish League from 1893 until the Second World War, and won the Scottish Cup in 1895. King's Park (Stirling) were in Division Two from 1921 to 1940, but never won anything substantial. Port Glasgow Athletic, founded in 1880, but defunct by 1912, were Champions of Division Two in 1901/02. The village club of Renton, which collapsed in 1922, were in the Scottish League from 1890 until 1898, won the Scottish Cup in 1885 and 1888, and were also finalists on three other occasions. Vale of Leven, another

early club, had three spells in the League, won the Cup three times, and were losing finalists four times. Abercorn (Paisley) were in the League from 1891 to 1915, and were Division Two Champions twice. Arthurlie (Barrhead) had 20 seasons in the League, but disbanded in 1929. Third Lanark is probably the most famous defunct Scottish club, with 79 seasons in the League, becoming Champions once and Cup winners twice. They folded due to financial irregularities in 1967.

Belfast Celtic joined the Irish League in 1896 and became one of the dominant forces in Northern Irish football, winning the championship fourteen times in the inter-war period. However, serious sectarian problems forced the club to close in 1948. Derry City were similarly affected in 1972, but re-formed to join the League of Ireland in the Irish Republic in 1984.

Sources:
Cronin, M., 'Soccer, Sectarianism and the Troubles: The Fall and Rise of Derry City Football Club', *Sporting Heritage*, 2 (1996), 7–23.
One Day in Leicester (Chislehurst: Association of Sports Historians, 1996), pp. 7–23.
Twydell, D., *Rejected FC: Histories of the ex-Football League Clubs*, 3 vols. (Harefield: Yore Publications, 1992–95).
Twydell, D., *Rejected FC of Scotland: Histories of the ex-Scottish League Clubs*, 3 vols. (Harefield: Yore Publications, 1992–95).

Robert Lewis

History Highlights 1910–1919

The popularity of professional football continued to grow until 1914, when the First World War intervened: the first serious interruption to the steady development of the game. Attendances rose from a Division One average in 1910 of around 16,000 to 22,000 by 1914, and in Division Two from 9,000 to 11,000 over the same period. There was an immediate fall in the only wartime League season of 1914/15, because of military commitments. The best-supported clubs were Newcastle United, Chelsea, Aston Villa, Tottenham Hotspur, Manchester City and Manchester United. Chelsea attained a huge average attendance of 37,105 in 1913/14.

For little Glossop, consistently one of the worst-supported clubs, 1914/15 was the last season in the Football League. After 17 seasons, they received only one vote for re-election, and were replaced by Stoke. In 1913, Woolwich Arsenal also found themselves in financial difficulties, and therefore decided to move their base to North London to attract larger crowds, despite objections from Tottenham, Chelsea and Clapton Orient. By 1914, six out of 40 League clubs were from the south: Arsenal, Bristol City, Chelsea, Clapton Orient, Fulham and Tottenham, reflecting the increasing geographical spread of a competition once confined to the north and Midlands.

In the Football League, Blackburn Rovers won the Championship in 1911/12 and 1913/14. Other successful clubs included Sunderland, Everton, Manchester United and Aston Villa; Manchester United's Championship victory of 1910/11 was their last major trophy for 37 years. The only real surprise to modern readers might be that Oldham Athletic only narrowly missed out on the title to Everton in 1914/15. The last proper season of the League during this period was that of 1914/15, football only returning to normal in 1919/20. Meanwhile, a wartime competition was set up with Midlands and Northern sections, and other leagues and competitions continued throughout the war, despite periodic difficulties in recruiting players and fulfilling fixtures. Service personnel and other guest players were often recruited. Women's football became a relatively popular periodic attraction, with matches being played by factory and munitions teams, often for charity or war funds.

The FA Cup, suspended during the war, was won in the earlier years by an assortment of clubs, including Newcastle United, Bradford City, Barnsley, Aston Villa, Burnley and Sheffield United, indicating yet again that the competition was not always dominated by the big-name clubs. Other regional cup competitions continued during the war, with new ones set up for sides from the armed forces.

The contrast between Scottish and English football became more distinct by this time, with the virtual monopoly of Celtic and Rangers in Scotland set against the relatively more open competition in England. In Scotland, the title was won by either Celtic or Rangers in all these years, the only serious challengers being Hearts, Morton, Motherwell, Raith Rovers and Kilmarnock. The Scottish League continued throughout the war, although Division Two ceased with effect from 1914/15. The Scottish Cup was suspended after 1914, and the only winners during the period were Celtic (three times), Dundee and Falkirk.

In England, the Players' Union continued in existence up to 1915, but was handicapped by its failure to abolish the retain-and-transfer system for players, or the maximum wage. Membership declined from about 1,300 in 1908 to around 400 in 1915, possibly as a result of the apathy of many players who saw it as representing only the 'star' players, and as a weak body. It failed in the Kingaby test case against Aston Villa, doing little to convince players that it could be effective, and it almost disappeared during the war. By 1914, it was calculated that only 12 to 15 per cent of players received the maximum wage, despite the union's efforts.

The first year of the war brought forth again the criticism of the professional game that had been simmering ever since professionalism had taken over the control of football, supplanting the gentlemen of the public schools, and diminishing the importance of the amateur game. Their snobbery and disdain was directed at this consumer-driven entertainment whenever a suitable opportunity arose. During the war, professional football was accused of being unpatriotic for continuing in 1914/15 and not providing enough recruits for the war effort, and for perverting a sport that had been seen as good, character-building exercise which engendered an *esprit de corps* and the teamwork necessary in wartime.

Sources:

Mason, T., *Association Football and English Society, 1863–1915* (Brighton: Harvester, 1980).

Fabian, A. H. and Green, G., *Association Football* (London: Caxton, 1960).

Russell, D., *Football and the English* (Preston: Carnegie, 1997).

Tabner, B., *Through the Turnstiles* (Harefield: Yore Publications, 1992).

Further Reading:

Gibson, A. and Pickford, W., *Association Football and the Men Who Made It* (London: Caxton, 1905–06).

Inglis, S., *English Football and the Men Who Made It* (London: CollinsWillow, 1988).

See also First World War

Robert Lewis

Gambling

Littlewood's pools ad, Athletic News Football Annual, 1934–35 (Littlewood's)

The extensive popularity of gambling, especially among the aristocracy and the working class, allied to football's own extensive appeal, has ensured that since the beginning of the modern game in the 1870s betting on the outcome of matches has been an ingrained feature of football. The early history of the game is riddled with instances of wagering. Many working men at the ground were said to have staked their whole week's wages on the outcome of the 1887 Cup Final between Aston Villa and West Bromwich Albion, though most football betting probably took place outside the ground in the form of coupon betting at fixed odds, either with bookmakers or through the local press. Considering the concerns felt by society's moral guardians over betting by working people – a habit thought responsible for hastening poverty – it is not surprising that the efforts of both bookmakers and the sporting press to organise sweepstakes based on the prediction of match results were generally frowned upon by the game's authorities. Indeed this stance was maintained well after the formation in the 1920s of the chief vehicle for football betting in Britain – the pools system.

The football pools originated in the 1920s with a system devised by John Moores and his brother Cecil, who founded the Littlewoods company and later became millionaires. Their system, followed by other leading companies such as Vernons and Zetters, as well as the smaller Shermans and Copes, allowed wagering on match outcomes for small stakes for a chance to win a share of the 'pool' of money placed by all betters. After the Second World War the 'treble chance' was introduced, a system of forecasting eight match results with the option of having several 'lines' on the coupon. So popular was this method, with its spectacular money prizes, that by the 1950s it is estimated that a half of the entire adult population were returning pools coupons, if not all on a regular basis, and investing some £60 million. 'Doing the pools' was often a family occasion, enjoyed as much by women as by men, and an important social pastime which gave pleasure and excitement to people because of the prospect of a win. Like the National Lottery, which began to overtake the pools as a form of popular gambling in the 1990s, the pools paid huge dividends to a lucky few.

Opposition from the football authorities had been grounded in the belief that pools betting would corrupt the game. Occasionally such fears have been justified. Instances have come to light of gambling syndicates conspiring with corrupt players to win money by 'fixing' results. For example, three well-known players (Peter Swan, Tony Kay and David Layne) were jailed alongside several lesser-known ones in 1965 for their part in perpetrating such a fraud. In the mid-1990s, following alleged attempts by Far-Eastern betting syndicates to fix matches in Britain, three Premier League players, including the former Liverpool goalkeeper Bruce Grobbelaar, were investigated by the police, though eventually cleared of the allegation of 'throwing' matches.

Sources:

Clapson, M., *A Bit of a Flutter: Popular Gambling and English Society c. 1823–1961* (Manchester: Manchester University Press, 1992).

Mason, T., *Association Football and English Society 1863–1915* (Brighton: Harvester Press, 1980).

Further Reading:

Chinn, C., *Better Betting with a Decent Feller: Bookmaking Betting and the British Working Class, 1750–1990* (London: Harvester, 1991).

Jeff Hill

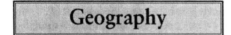

Geography

British football reflects a variety of geographical themes. These include: geographical changes found in the grounds in which the game is played; the environmental impacts of football grounds on the localities in which they are found; the spatial patterns of the professional clubs at the urban and national levels; the changing nature of national football 'success'; geographical variations in the 'production' of professional players; and the patterns of migration of such sports workers. Each of these geographies can be outlined in turn.

The micro-geography of the British football ground (traditionally not termed a 'stadium') has changed dramatically in the course of a century. It has become a less 'open' space. Its modern geography is one that displays the growth of segmented spaces. The enforced separation of players from spectators was an early division of football space, and other divisions followed. These included a separation of those spectators who had covered accommodation from those who braved the elements; of who were seated from those who stood and were able to mingle and select where they watched a game from; and of those who wined and dined in executive suites from those who were individualised in specified plastic seats. The hooligan syndrome of the 1960s and 1970s led to the growing enforcement of a prescribed positioning of spectators. Following the Hillsborough disaster, all-seater stadia became the norm. This confinement was accompanied by video surveillance and new commercial imperatives which changed the football ground into a multi-purpose leisure facility. The modern football stadium has facilities for banquets and conferences, a museum and a supermarket, a hotel and office space. It is an example of leisure laced with spending, attracting customers and consumers rather than fans.

Many British football stadia remain sited in residential areas of major cities. The effects of football on local residents can be both positive and negative. For example, local retailers – notably pubs – may benefit financially on match days; local fans find it beneficial to have their football club (almost literally, in some cases) on their doorsteps; accessibility to a stadium confers a saving in transport costs in comparison to those outside the immediate locality. For many urban residents, the presence of a professional football ground confers a sense of place and an icon of local pride.

At the same time, however, the events that occur inside a football stadium can create negative effects for those living in proximity to the stadium. The main negative effect of football matches, as perceived by local residents, are transport-related. Parked cars, traffic congestion, noise and air pollution all impose costs on local people. Hooliganism and vandalism are further, though less frequently reported, football nuisances. With the development of newer stadia following the Taylor Report into the Hillsborough disaster, the local complaint of football nuisances has declined. This is partly because the newer stadia have been sited within more compatible areas of land use – often on 'brownfield' sites as part of urban regeneration. Even so, some urban residents still complain that local transport infrastructure has failed to provide a milieu free from football's influence for those who do not wish to be part of a football culture.

The relocation of clubs in Britain has been overwhelmingly local, contrasting dramatically with the trans-continental moves familiar in North America. The move of Arsenal from Greenwich to Islington in 1913 remains quite untypical, and where clubs have moved the distances have rarely exceeded a few kilometres. Such tendencies reflect an intense sense of localness; the mooted move at the turn of this century of Wimbedon to Dublin or Cardiff was totally out of character with the strong sense of localism that is typical of the UK soccer scene. At a national level the distribution of professional football clubs in England and Wales has, over time, shown a general shift from north to south. Those clubs that have been demoted from the Football League have tended to be mainly in older industrial regions, reflecting the broader pattern of industrial change in the nation. Whereas in 1910, 70 per cent of clubs were found in the north and only 15 per cent in the south, the respective figures in 1990 were 25 per cent and 50 per cent. Likewise, there has also been a broad south-easterly shift in the 'centre of gravity' of Football League success.

It is popularly thought that the north of England is the 'seed bed' for the production of professional footballers. Several studies have mapped the birthplaces of professional footballers, and these tend to confirm the stereotype of the north as the hub of English football culture. In 1980, for example, the north produced over twice as many professional footballers as the national per-capita average. The south-east, on the other hand, produced less than three-quarters of the national norm. A particular hotbed of production was the north-east: the Charlton bothers, Jackie Milburn and Paul Gascoigne are all products of this region. However, there are signs that these differences are declining, since in 1950 the north provided nearly two and a half times the national average per capita, while the south-east supplied under half the number that would have been expected.

The broad pattern of migration in professional football has been from north to south, the over-producing regions supplying players to deficit areas. In recent years, however, there has been a substantial increase in the migration of overseas players to Britain. These have tended to be dominated by Scandinavians, notably from Norway (Ole Gunnar Solskjaer) and Denmark (Peter Schmeichel). Compared with several other nations in Western Europe, the number of migrant African players to Britain is small.

Sources:

Bale, J., *The Development of Soccer as a Participant and Spectator Sport – Geographical Aspects* (London: SSRC/Sports Council, 1979).

Bale, J. 'Geographical Diffusion and the Adoption of Professional Football in England and Wales', *Geography*, 63 (July 1978), 188–97.

John Bale

Giant Killers

On 9 February 2000 the tabloid headline writers had a field day. 'Supercaley Go

Ballistic. Celtic are Atrocious', screamed the back pages. The cause of their delight was not a footballing version of Mary Poppins but an event just as fanciful as the Disney film. The previous evening the mighty Celtic, former European Cup holders, had crashed out of the Scottish Cup, beaten 3–1 at home by Inverness Caledonian Thistle in a third-round tie. 'Caley', a club formed only six years previously by the amalgamation of two Highland League sides from Inverness, had quickly risen to the First Division of the Scottish League, but no one gave them a chance against the Premier League giants. When Paul Sheerin scored Caley's third goal from the penalty spot after 55 minutes the noise from the 4,000 blue-clad away supporters in Celtic Park's Lisbon Lions Stand went on for so long that their heroes might well have been distracted from the task in hand. They weren't, and went on to finish the game worthy winners, inflicting on Celtic their most humiliating defeat since their formation, 106 years before that of their upstart conquerors. This result was the beginning of the end for Celtic coach John Barnes.

The celebrations were not confined to the Highlands, of course. Fans of Celtic's traditional rivals, Rangers, would at last have a response to the taunts they had had to suffer from the green-and-whites since their own day of infamy on 28 January 1967 when they themselves had lost in the first round of the same competition, 1–0 away to Berwick Rangers, then in the Scottish Second Division. The Glasgow club, riding high at the top of the First Division with six wins and two draws out of eight games played, went out to a 32nd-minute Sammy Reid goal. Berwick's hero that day was goalkeeper Jock Wallace; the player-manager made a succession of great saves to ensure the Shielfield Park crowd saw history in the making. It was bad enough for Rangers to lose to a lowly club who had never finished better than eighth in Division Two, but to be beaten by the only Scottish League club from England was unforgivable! Heads rolled as a result: strikers Jim Forrest and George McLean never played for the Glasgow club again, and manager Scot Symon lasted only until

November of that year. In June 1970 their then manager, Willie Waddell, added a new coach to the Ibrox set-up – Jock Wallace.

Berwick's rustic stadium may have generated Scottish football's greatest shock for decades, but more was to come south of the border later the same year. The 1966/67 League Cup Final, held for the first time at Wembley, saw First Division West Bromwich Albion lose 3–2 to Queen's Park Rangers of Division Three after being two up at the break, both goals coming from ex-Rangers player Clive Clark. Second-half goals from Roger Morgan, Rodney Marsh and Mark Lazarus saw the West Londoners home in front of a crowd of over 97,000. Football League rules denied Rangers, as a non-First Division club, the reward of entry into Europe via the Fairs Cup, but they consoled themselves by going on to win the Third Division title that season by a massive 12 points. Wembley's latest show-piece fixture had got off to a cracking start and two years later saw another game that caused an even bigger upset. Once again the finalists were from the First and Third Divisions, this time Arsenal and Swindon Town. On a Wembley pitch that had been ruined by the International Horse of the Year Show, Swindon took a shock lead on 35 minutes when Roger Smart tapped home a sitter after Ian Ure had botched a back pass to keeper Bob Wilson. Arsenal besieged the Robins' goal after the interval, in one spell forcing nine corners in ten minutes, but it was not until four minutes from the end that Bobby Gould stabbed home the equaliser. In extra time the heavy rain seemed to sap the strength of the Arsenal players, many of them suffering the after-effects of flu, and just before the end of the first period Swindon left-winger Don Rogers drove home following a corner to put the underdogs back in front. In the last minute of extra time Rogers set off through the mud, starting from the half-way line, and slipped the ball past the hapless Wilson after a superb solo run. Swindon's 3–1 win did not earn them a place in Europe, but like Rangers before them they ended the season by gaining promotion to Division Two, finishing as runners-up to Watford.

All knockout competitions give small clubs the opportunity to take on their so-called betters, and none has provided more remarkable results than the greatest of them all – the FA Cup. Among the first giants to be killed were Nottingham Forest, back in December 1886, when they were drawn away in the third round to Lockwood Brothers, a Sheffield works team who did not even possess their own dressing rooms, having to resort to changing in a local pub. The biggest game in the factory workers' history was switched to Bramall Lane, and a crowd of 4,000 saw them humble the mighty Forest 2–1 with goals from Sellers and Betts. Lockwoods eventually went out of the competition to West Bromwich Albion, that season's beaten finalists, before disappearing back into obscurity.

It is not only the early rounds of the FA Cup that have thrown up unexpected results over the years: the final itself has produced its share. In 1901 Tottenham Hotspur became the first, and surely the last, non-league side to lift the coveted trophy. The Football League, formed in 1888, was at the time dominated by the professional teams from the north and the Midlands. The Southern League (won by Spurs in 1900) had been set up in opposition in 1894 but had not yet made any great impact. When Tottenham reached the 1901 final and were matched against Sheffield United – who could boast nine internationals and had the giant 'Fatty' Foulke in goal – the game was billed as 'Jack against his master', but it was Jack who came out on top. On 20 April a Crystal Palace crowd of 110,820, at the time the largest ever, saw Sheffield survive a 2–2 draw thanks to a controversial goal awarded after the referee had ruled that a shot from Bert Lipsham had been dropped over the line by Spurs keeper George Clawley. Both clubs suggested Villa Park for the replay the following Saturday, but for some reason the venue selected was Burnden Park, Bolton. With the railway companies of the day refusing to provide either set of supporters with the usual cheap excursion tickets, many found themselves priced out of attending, and the sec-

ond game attracted the competition's lowest crowd for a final before or since, a mere 20,470. Tottenham ran out comfortable 3–1 winners, with goals from Cameron, Smith and Brown. 'Sandy' Brown, one of the five Scots in the London side, had also scored twice in the first game, to give him a record 15 goals for the tournament and make him the first player to score in every round. Despite their historic achievement in becoming the first southern club to lift the Cup since the prestigious amateur Old Etonians eighteen years earlier, it was not until 1908 that Spurs joined the Football League, winning promotion from Division Two in their first season.

In more recent times two Wembley finals of the 1970s stand out as David-over-Goliath triumphs. In 1973, Leeds United, Wembley victors over Arsenal the previous season, were odds-on favourites. After all, they had not finished outside the League's top four in the last nine years and had already qualified for the final of the European Cup Winners' Cup. Their opponents, Sunderland, were a side from the Second Division who had spent the season battling against relegation to the Third. Amazingly it was the Wearsiders who won, with a goal after 32 minutes from midfielder Ian Porterfield. The Scotsman's strike was not only his first of the competition but had even greater scarcity value in that it was driven in with his right foot, a part of his anatomy he himself confessed was normally reserved for standing on. The game is also remembered for Sunderland goalkeeper Jimmy Montgomery's historic second-half double save from first Trevor Cherry and then Peter Lorimer. Sunderland's victory, their first Cup triumph since 1937, was celebrated by every neutral supporter in the land.

History was repeated in the 1976 final. This time the mighty Manchester United were matched with unfancied Southampton. In the semi-finals that season the two surviving First Division sides, United and Derby County, who finished third and fourth respectively in the League, were drawn against each other, while Second Division Southampton were matched with Crystal Palace of the Third. United's extrovert manager, Tommy Docherty, went on record as saying of his team's draw: 'This is the first time a Cup Final will be played at Hillsborough. The other semi-final is a bit of a joke, really.' The joke turned out to be on 'the Doc'. Southampton scored the only goal of the game courtesy of Bobby Stokes seven minutes from time, when the left-winger collected a through ball from ex-United Jim McCalliog and ran on to beat keeper Alex Stepney with what seemed a half-hit shot. Docherty, whose warning team talk had contained the one word 'Sunderland', could only look on in bemusement as the piratical-looking Saints skipper Peter Rodrigues paraded the trophy for the south-coast side. Southampton's last appearance in the final had been back in 1902, in their Southern League days. Even with the legendary C. B. Fry in their line-up they lost that day to Sheffield United.

The 1988 final, although contested by two First Division teams, was on paper as one-sided as any in history. Liverpool, chasing their second League and Cup double in three years, seemed to have completed the hard part after topping the table by nine points over nearest rivals Manchester United. Their opponents were unfancied Wimbledon, a League club for only 11 years, who had had a remarkable rise through the ranks. They had won the Fourth Division championship in the 1982/83 season, and gained promotion from Division Three a year later. At the end of 1985/86 they had scraped into the top flight, finishing third in Division Two behind Norwich City and Charlton Athletic. Now they found themselves in a Wembley final against the redoubtable Reds. Admittedly they did have a giant-killing pedigree. In 1975, when still in the Southern League, they had beaten Burnley – then lying seventh in the First Division – in the third round before losing by a single Leeds United-deflected goal in a fourth-round replay. But surely their Cup trail would have to end against the all-conquering Liverpool? Not a bit of it. Lawrie Sanchez, one of the smallest players on the field, headed in a Dennis Wise free-kick to give the underdogs a half-time lead. After the interval Wimbledon goalkeeper and captain Dave Beasant saved a John Aldridge penalty – the first one the Liverpool man had failed to convert in 12 attempts that season. It was the first penalty missed in a Wembley final and the nearest Liverpool came to the equaliser. Beasant, the hero of the day, became the first goalkeeper to captain a cup-winning side. 'Game, set and match to Wimbledon' was, not surprisingly, a typical headline next day.

Not all the small fry make it all the way to Wembley, of course, although it was not for want of trying in the 1977/78 season, when no less than six non-league sides reached the third round. Five of them went out at that stage, but Blyth Spartans of the Northern League carried the flag of the little 'uns into round four. They were drawn away to Second Division Stoke City and came away with a 3–2 victory that included one of the most bizarre goals in Cup history. Spartans had taken the lead after 11 minutes, when Terry Johnson scored from close range after keeper Roger Jones had dropped Robert Carney's corner. Stoke equalised in the second half through Viv Busby, and within six minutes a Garth Crooks header had given them the lead. Then came the north-easterners' amazing equaliser. Left-back Ron Guthrie, who had been a member of Sunderland's 1973 Cup-winning side, fired a free-kick against the Potters' defensive wall. The ball bounced off a defender and looped towards goal, with five Blyth players in pursuit. Between them they forced it against the left-hand post, from where it rebounded to Alan Shoulder, whose instinctive header came back off the opposite post before Steve Carney gleefully put it in the net. But there was more to come. In the last minute another free-kick, this time taken by right-back John Waterson, was headed back into the middle by Keith Houghton towards Robert Carney, who deflected it into the path of Terry Johnson, who in turn slammed home the winner. The Blyth players had proved themselves a force to be reckoned with, and none more so than Houghton. The inside-forward, a Wallsend policeman, had not been idle during the ten days for which the Stoke tie had been postponed due to heavy rain. The day before the match he had turned out for Northumbria Police against Strathclyde Police. In the fifth round Spartans were drawn away to Third Division Wrexham, themselves earlier victors over First Division Bristol City and Newcastle United, both at the second attempt. Blyth again took the Welshmen to a second tie: such was the Geordieland interest by this time that the game was switched to Newcastle's St James's Park ground. Thousands were locked out for the replay; the 42,000 who did gain admittance saw the Northern League outfit leading 1–0 until the 88th minute, only to lose 2–1. Wrexham finally went down 3–2 to Arsenal in the sixth round. In another quarter-final Second Division Orient beat First Division Middlesbrough before bowing out to Arsenal in the semi-final. Arsenal themselves lost at Wembley to lowly Ipswich Town, ending what the football correspondents called 'The Year of the Minnow'.

It was not the only year. FA Cup history is dotted with dates that are remembered by fans with either pride or embarrassment, depending on their loyalties. To take a random sample from each decade since the last war, the following spring to mind:

29 January 1949:
Yeovil Town 2 – Sunderland 1
Sunderland, sixth in the First Division and with the world's most expensive player – Len 'Clown Prince' Shackleton – in the side, crashed out to lowly Yeovil, lying sixth from bottom in the Southern League (there it is again) in the third round. The Somerset side's victory on their infamous sloping Huish ground was masterminded by their articulate player-manager Alec Stock, who scored the first himself and robbed Shackleton to set up the winner for centre-forward Bryant. Stock, who was destined to manage Queen's Park Rangers in their 1967 League Cup Final victory, summed up the dual role of playing and managing as a 'violent exercise on top of a pile of worries'. Sunderland certainly had the bigger pile that day.

10 December 1955:
Derby County 1 – Boston United 6
County, unbeaten at home all season and lying third in the Third Division (North) lost this second-round tie to the Midland Leaguers who put out a team including no fewer than six ex-Derby players, all of whom felt they had a particular point to prove – and prove it they did. The 6–1 score-line remains a record for a non-league side on a league ground. It was also completely unexpected. One diehard Boston fan is on record as saying: 'No, I shall not go to Derby because I can't stand the strain of seeing the United humiliated.' He certainly missed a treat. Boston's reward was a third-round trip to White Hart Lane where they lost 4–0 to Tottenham Hotspur but were in no way outclassed, Spurs skipper Danny Blanchflower describing them as a match for many First Division sides.

8 January 1964:
Aldershot 2 – Aston Villa 1
Seven-time Cup winners Villa were surprisingly held to a goalless draw at home by the Fourth Division Hampshire side in their third-round tie, but remained optimistic for the replay the following Wednesday. This game also failed to produce a goal until 20 minutes from the end, when a free-kick from near the right touchline was crossed by Aldershot inside-left Jim Towers. Villa keeper Sims dived to intercept the ball only to see it sail over his hands straight into the unguarded net. The second goal was even worse for the unfortunate Sims, a corner from the left taken by Chris Palethorpe curling in direct. Tony Hateley's last-minute goal for Villa was not enough, and they were out. An adage of the time said that whoever beat Aston Villa would go on to win the Cup (it had happened in each of the previous five seasons), but Aldershot couldn't keep the sequence going: they lost to Swindon Town in the next round.

5 February 1972:
Hereford United 2 – Newcastle United 1
For the first time since Yeovil's 1949 victory over Sunderland, in this third-round replay a non-league side beat a team from the First Division. Hereford were at the time second in the Southern League, so the Magpies should have been prepared

for the worst, especially after the 2–2 draw at St James's Park, which Hereford considered themselves unlucky not to win. Heavy rain meant the replay was postponed for 12 days, and when the teams finally took the field the Edgar Street pitch was little better than a mud-bath. The Newcastle players, confined to their Hereford hotel for ten days waiting for the weather to break, were forced to use Worcester racecourse as a training venue. When the tie finally got under way, on fourth-round day, Hereford held their First Division visitors at bay until Malcolm Macdonald scored with a typical header eight minutes from time. The England centre-forward had said in the press after the first game that Hereford had had their moment of glory and that he would score ten in the replay. He was out by nine. The article containing his boast had been pinned to the Hereford dressing-room wall and it was all the inspiration they needed. With four minutes left Ronnie Radford dispatched a mud-covered ball from all of 40 yards into the top corner of the Newcastle net to take the game into extra time. Enter substitute Ricky George. With eight minutes of extra time left he prodded home the winner from eight yards after being set up by Radford. Hereford met West Ham United at home in the fourth round four days later and held the Hammers to a goalless draw, only to lose the Upton Park replay 3–0. Their prowess had been duly noted, however: they gained admission to the Football League the following season, attaining promotion at the first attempt.

8 January 1980:
Harlow Town 1 – Leicester City 0
This third-round replay had been earned the previous Saturday at Filbert Street when Harlow's Neil Prosser had snatched an equaliser a minute from time. Leicester were chasing promotion from the Second Division at the time (they went on to finish the season as champions) while Harlow were a bunch of Isthmian League also-rans who in this, their centenary year, had reached the first round proper for the first time, after negotiating five qualifying rounds. They had already accounted for fel-

low non-leaguers Leytonstone-Ilford in the first round, and Third Division Southend United in the second after a replay. Surely Leicester City would prove a hurdle too far for the part-timers from Essex?

John Mackenzie thought otherwise. Four minutes before half-time the company accountant flicked at a Micky Mann free-kick only to see it rebound from Leicester defender Larry May. Mackenzie was first to the loose ball and sent a weak shot beyond Leicester keeper Mark Wallington. The ball came to rest a few inches over the line before a City defender could boot it clear but the referee was well enough positioned to give the decisive goal. The record crowd of 9,723 at the Sports Centre ground invaded the pitch in disbelief at the final whistle. The Cup dream was still alive. Among those who were suffering nightmares was the 19-year-old Leicester striker, a certain Gary Lineker. Harlow went on to meet Watford in the fourth round, losing narrowly at Vicarage Road by the odd goal in seven, Mackenzie scoring twice. With the end of the Cup run the glory days were over. Harlow Town folded in 1992.

4 January 1992:
Wrexham 2 – Arsenal 1
The two sides in this third-round tie could not have been further apart the previous season. Arsenal had ended it as champions, seven points clear of Liverpool; Wrexham had finished bottom of the entire League. They had also played at Scarborough in front of a crowd of only 625, the Fourth Division's lowest-ever attendance. Surely the unthinkable couldn't happen again? Oh yes it could. Although they'd spurned several early chances, Arsenal seemed to be coasting to victory by virtue of a single goal two minutes before the interval. Paul Merson had crossed from the left, leaving Alan Smith to score from close range. After 62 minutes the Gunners almost doubled their lead but Nigel Winterburn's shot came back off the woodwork. One goal proved not to be enough. With eight minutes left Wrexham were awarded a free-kick 20 yards out. Welsh international winger Mickey Thomas, 37 years old and not

renowned for his long-range shooting – i.e., from anywhere outside the six-yard box – let fly and the ball zipped into David Seaman's top right-hand corner. The crowd of 13,343 couldn't believe it. Nor could Thomas's team-mates. He'd never done anything like it all season, if ever. Arsenal's so-called cast-iron defence (they'd conceded only 18 goals in 38 League games the previous season) suddenly seemed prone to rust. With the crowd still cheering Thomas's strike, Tony Adams failed to clear a cross from the venerable Gordon Davies, Thomas's junior by only a year, and 20-year-old Steve Watkin poked the winner past Seaman. As the crowd, and the Wrexham team, went wild at the final whistle, Mickey Thomas would no doubt have reflected on the strange twist of fate the FA Cup had thrown up. In 1979 he had been a member of the Manchester United team that lost at Wembley to Arsenal. He'd waited 13 years for revenge and it had come at the Racecourse Ground, of all places. Unlucky Arsenal?

Just what is it about the FA Cup that causes all these so-called 'freak' results so often? Danny Blanchflower had a theory, based on bitter experience: his elegant Spurs team had been eliminated three times in the 1950s by Third Division sides. York City, Bournemouth and Boscombe Athletic, and Norwich City had all marched on at the expense of the Lilywhites. Danny's explanation was that 'the little guy with no fears and responsibility goes mad and turns the game into a riot where anything can happen'. But why do the top teams let them get away with it? Here's Danny again: 'The big fellow is often fighting against himself as well as the upstarts.' So there you have it. David always thinks he can win; Goliath is worried about losing. Long may it continue.

Sources:

Barrett, N., *The Daily Telegraph Football Chronicle* (London: Carlton, 1999).

Butler, B., *The Illustrated History of the FA Cup* (London: Headline, 1996).

Tibballs, G., *FA Cup Giant Killers* (London: CollinsWillow, 1994).

Further Reading:

Hart, G. (ed.), *The Guinness Football Encyclopedia* (Enfield: Guinness, 1995).

Nawrat, C. and Hutchings, S., *The Sunday Times Illustrated History of Football: The Post-War Years* (London: Chancellor, 1996).

Tony Rennick

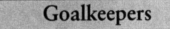

Goalkeepers

In his critique of the history of that most individual of positions, the ex-Scotland and Arsenal goalkeeper Bob Wilson claims that the job caters for every type of personality, every type of physique. A brief look at some of the characters that have graced the British game over the years bears this out.

Two of the most colourful of these, who shared the same irreverent outlook on the game, although from completely different backgrounds, were Bill 'Fatty' Foulke and Leigh Richmond Roose. Foulke, the son of an unmarried mother, was raised by his grandparents and emerged from a Derbyshire pit shaft in 1894 to sign for Sheffield United for the princely sum of £5, and went on to help the Yorkshire club to the League Championship in 1898 and FA Cup successes in 1899 and 1902. The giant Foulke weighed an impressive 15 stones when he signed for United, and had put on an extra seven stones by the time he left them 11 years later for Chelsea. London life suited the extrovert keeper, who was one of the first players to be provided with his own motor car and was often introduced to the crowd from the music hall stage. He is best remembered on the field for the way he used his phenomenal size, battering opposing forwards into submission and generally terrifying any opponent who came near his goal, but was always ready for a touch of light relief. He once turned out for Chelsea, much to the crowd's delight, wrapped in a bath towel because the only shirt the club possessed big enough to fit him clashed with the opposing team's colours. During the latter part of his career, the man-mountain moved to Bradford City, whose

*'I don't mind what they call me, as long as
they don't call me late for lunch'*
22-stone goalkeeper Bill 'Fatty' Foulke in 1905
(© EMPICS Sports Photo Agency)

Stoke City's goalkeeper Leigh Richmond Roose
*'His pants carried about them the marks of
many a thrilling encounter'*
(© EMPICS Sports Photo Agency)

manager took great delight in forcing the
still-expanding keeper to squeeze through
a narrow gateway to collect his wages
from the club's pay office. Despite his vast
size, however, 'Fatty' was an accomplished
keeper, good enough to win an England
cap against Wales in 1897, a match which
England won 4–0. William Foulke died in
1916, aged 42, after catching a chill saving
penalties for small change on Blackpool
Sands.

A contemporary of Foulke's was the
eccentric Roose, who, thanks to private
means, remained an amateur throughout a
peripatetic career which would eventually
take him via Aberystwyth to the Druids,
London Welsh, Stoke City, Everton,
Sunderland, Celtic, Huddersfield Town,
Aston Villa, Woolwich Arsenal, Llandudno
and the Royal Fusiliers, earning him 24
Welsh caps in the process. Roose was born
in 1877 in Holt, North Wales, the son of a
Presbyterian minister. He attended Holt
Academy, where the novelist H. G. Wells
was among his tutors, before moving to the
University of Wales in Aberystwyth to study
science. It was here that he is said to have
enjoyed an amorous encounter with the
music hall star Marie Lloyd. He had made

his debut for Aberystwyth in 1898 in an
impressive 6–0 win over Whitchurch.
Roose's display, which involved several
hair-raising sorties into enemy territory as
well as spectacular saves, brought him to
the attention of the young Tom Richards,
the future historian, who watched him in
action later the same season in an FA Cup
tie against Glossop North End. The professionals from the Midland League were hot
favourites, but lost 1–0 to the Welsh amateurs, thanks mainly to Roose. Richards
was to note proudly in his autobiography,
Atgofion Cardi:

Big, strong lads from the Pennines, with
hairy legs and in form to win the first-
round tie in the English Cup, for that
was the occasion. Their dreams were
ended by that wonderful goalkeeper
Roose, particularly by his diverting a
penalty into the middle of the gorse on
Buarth Hill ...

Roose helped Aberystwyth to victory in
the Welsh Cup in 1900, and the following
year moved to London to study medicine
at King's College Hospital, although,
characteristically, he was never to qualify.

Stoke City, at the time hard pressed financially, were grateful for the services of the amateur keeper and stepped in to sign him, though he did not always appear a sound financial investment: it is reported that he once cost the impoverished club over £30, a small fortune at the time, by chartering his own special train to take him from his London home to a match at Aston Villa. The unfortunate Potters were also presented with the goalkeeper's weekly expenses claim, which invariably began with the entry: 'Use of toilet ... twice ... two pence'! To be fair, however, he did keep his employer's laundry bill down: throughout his career he is said to have worn the same unwashed Aberystwyth Town shirt under his goalkeeper's jersey. Personal hygiene was also conspicuously absent from his nether regions, one match report inspiring the comment: 'His pants, we should say, carried about them the marks of many a thrilling encounter.' Sadly, the marvellously loopy Roose was killed during the First World War while serving with the Royal Fusiliers. He was posthumously awarded the Military Medal.

Foulke and Roose, of course, belonged to a different age, although the modern British game has also seen its share of characters. One of the most entertaining surely must be Bruce Grobbelaar, who treated Liverpool fans throughout the 1980s to displays varying from the sublime to the downright potty. Even before the game had started he would amuse the crowd with a display of cartwheels and ball-juggling, and these antics would continue once the game had got under way. One minute he would be charging through his own defenders, flattening more than one of them in the process, to take a high cross at the edge of his area; the next he would be tackling an opposing forward by the corner flag before dribbling the ball to the halfway line. Sometimes these tactics would work and the crowd would be delighted. At other times it would all go horribly wrong and he would have some of the most bizarre goals in history against his name. He was a gift from heaven to compilers of video 'howlers'. Grobbelaar was the living, breathing contradiction to the famous contention of Bill Shankly: 'They say that football is a matter of life and death. It isn't. It's far more important than that.' As a young man Grobbelaar had, like Roose, seen active service, fighting for Ian Smith's government forces in the then Rhodesia's bloody civil war, and seeing many of his friends die. After these experiences he always kept the game in perspective. He also took great delight in excusing his occasional gaffes by explaining that in Afrikaans his surname translates as 'clumsy'. Despite his unorthodox methods, however, Grobbelaar had a remarkable decade at Anfield, helping Liverpool to win the League Championship five times, the FA Cup twice, the Milk Cup/Littlewoods Cup three times, and the European Cup Winners' Cup. He must have been doing something right. The great Liverpool manager Bob Paisley is on record as saying that if Grobbelaar hadn't been committed to his adopted Zimbabwe (he was born in South Africa), then he would have been the natural successor to Peter Shilton in the England side.

Shilton would have been a hard act for even Grobbelaar to follow. Born in Leicester in 1949, Peter Leslie Shilton was keeping goal for his school team by the time he was nine years old. In 1965 he was a member of the Leicester Boys team that won the England Schools Trophy. But this wasn't enough: so determined was he to become a professional keeper that he devised a system of stretching exercises that involved him in hanging from the banister at the top of the stairs at home, sometimes with weights attached to his feet, sometimes with his parents pulling on his legs. The legacy of this self-inflicted torture was to give him arms two inches longer than normal for his height. Shilton was only 16 when he made his League debut for Leicester City, and 30 years later he made the headlines by playing his 1,000th League game for Leyton Orient. His League career had encompassed 286 matches for Leicester, 110 for Stoke City, 202 for Nottingham Forest – where he helped them to victory in the European Cup (1979 and 1980), League Championship (1978) and League Cup (1979) – 188 for Southampton, and 175 for Derby

County. He then moved to Plymouth Argyle as player-manager, notching up another 34 games. His travels then took him to Wimbledon, Bolton Wanderers, Coventry City and West Ham United. Only Bolton gave the veteran keeper a game – just one, and it was for Orient, his twelfth club, that he reached the historic landmark on 22 December 1996, helping the Londoners to a 2–0 home win against Brighton. The long-serving Shilton also gained a record 125 England caps, the first in 1970 and the last, at the age of 40, during the 1990 World Cup. This total, say the experts, would have been much greater had it not been for another great keeper with whom Shilton had to compete for international honours – Ray Clemence.

Raymond Neal Clemence was born in Skegness, Lincolnshire in 1948, and won a total of 61 caps between 1972 and 1983. He began his league career as an amateur with Notts County, then signed as a professional with Scunthorpe United before moving to Liverpool in 1967 as understudy to Tommy Lawrence. He made his League debut for the Merseysiders three years later and was an integral part of the great Liverpool side built by Bill Shankly and carried on by Bob Paisley. Shankly watched the young keeper eight times before signing him, but was finally convinced by Clemence's speed, his 'desperate courage' and the fact that he was well balanced in being left-footed but right-handed. Clemence's Anfield honours included three European Cup winners' medals and two UEFA Cup winners' medals. With Clemence in goal, Liverpool also won five League Championships, as well as the FA Cup and Football League Cup, once each. In the 1978/79 season his contribution to the championship-winning side was to play in all 42 League matches yet concede a miserly 16 goals, an amazing performance. In 1981 he moved to Tottenham Hotspur and in 1982 helped Spurs to another FA Cup triumph. He was forced by injury to retire during the 1987/88 campaign after over 1,000 senior matches, but continued at White Hart Lane in a coaching capacity.

Spurs' fans had welcomed Clemence

and seen him as the ideal solution to the side's goalkeeping problems, never satisfactorily solved since the controversial departure in 1977 of the hugely popular Pat Jennings to arch-rivals Arsenal. Born in Newry, Northern Ireland, in 1945, Patrick Anthony Jennings played Gaelic football as a youngster, an experience he says went a long way towards toughening him up for the goalmouth battles that were to be such a part of his professional life in the Association code. Pat moved on to play in goal for both Newry United and Newry Town before crossing the Irish Sea to sign for Watford, then in Division Four, in 1963, for a weekly wage of £15 – three times what he had been earning working as a tree feller. When new manager Bill McGarry arrived at Vicarage Road he was confident enough in the young Irish keeper's ability to make him a regular in the first team, and such were his performances that after one full season he was signed by Bill Nicholson, the Spurs manager. Jennings stayed at White Hart Lane for 13 seasons, making over 650 appearances in League, Cup and international matches, setting a club record of 449 League appearances in the process, and thus passing the total of 418 set by another goalkeeping legend, Ted Ditchburn. The softly-spoken Ulsterman of the huge hands and dark brown voice was voted the Football Writers' Footballer of the Year in 1973, the Professional Footballers' Player of the Year in 1975/76, and awarded the MBE the same year. He also beat Terry Neill's record of 59 Northern Ireland caps that season. He helped Tottenham to victory in the FA Cup (1967), the League Cup (1971 and 1973) and the UEFA Cup (1972). He is also remembered by millions of television viewers for the spectacular goal he scored for Spurs against Manchester United in the 1967 Charity Shield at Old Trafford, his huge kick upfield deceiving Alex Stepney in the United goal. At the end of the 1976/77 season, however, the unthinkable happened: Spurs finished bottom of the First Division and were relegated. New manager Keith Burkinshaw thought the club had capable deputies in Barry Daines and Mark Kendall, and also had to consider the expense of paying a world-class keeper on Second Division gates. Jennings made the short trip to Highbury and played for Tottenham's arch-enemies Arsenal for the next eight seasons, making another 350 senior appearances, including a winning appearance in the 1979 FA Cup Final. The last of his 119 international caps came on his 41st birthday, against Brazil in the 1986 World Cup. Ironically, Spurs had thought his best years were behind him when they released him at the age of 31. Clemence was 33 when he arrived at the club.

Shilton, Clemence and Jennings were all called the world's greatest during their distinguished careers; another who earned that accolade was Gordon Banks, Shilton's predecessor at Stoke City. Born in 1937, Banks played one season for his hometown club, Chesterfield, before moving to Leicester City in 1959 and Stoke in 1967. He won 73 England caps between 1963 and 1972, a record at the time. He was England keeper in the successful 1966 World Cup side, conceding only three goals in the tournament, and won League Cup medals with Leicester in 1964 and Stoke eight years later. He was also Footballer of the Year in 1972. He is probably best remembered for his save from the legendary Pele at Guadalajara in Mexico in the 1970 World Cup, ten minutes into England's group match against Brazil. Rising to meet a right-wing cross from Jairzinho, and only seven yards from goal, Pele powered his header downwards, aiming just inside the far post. Banks, who, expecting either a direct shot or a near-post cross, had taken up position at the near post and a couple of yards out, dived diagonally backwards. The ball bounced a yard in front of him before his right hand caught it and sent it spinning over the bar. Banks himself ended up wrapped around the post. Bobby Moore could only stand and applaud. Pele, who admitted it was the greatest save he had ever seen, looked stunned. 'Banksy', as the modest keeper was known throughout the game, tragically lost his right eye following a car crash in October 1972. He bravely tried to carry on, turning out in testimonial games, but at the age of 34

reluctantly had to give up the game at the highest level. He tried his luck in the United States, and after his first season with Fort Lauderdale was voted the Most Valuable Goalkeeper in the North American Soccer League. Banks himself summed up this less than dignified end to a magnificent career, which he considered little more than a circus act: 'Roll up, roll up to see the greatest one-eyed goalkeeper in the world.'

If these were some of the stars of the goalkeeping world there have been many others who have left their mark in various ways. Jimmy Montgomery of Sunderland never won an England cap due to the presence of Banks and Shilton while he was at his peak, but will always be remembered for the miraculous double save he pulled off in the 1973 FA Cup Final to enable the unfancied Second Division side to beat the odds-on favourites, the mighty Leeds United. Defender Trevor Cherry met a cross to the far corner of the Sunderland six-yard box with a diving header that seemed to have 'goal' written all over it until Montgomery threw himself to his left, only to deflect it straight into the path of the oncoming Peter Lorimer, possessed at the time with arguably the hardest shot in the game. He lashed the ball to the grounded keeper's right, only to see Montgomery somehow raise himself sufficiently to parry the shot and send it onto the bar and over the top for a corner. Sunderland went on to win the game 1–0 to give them their first Cup victory since 1937. One of the most memorable images in Wembley history remains the sight of the Wearsiders' trilby-donned manager, Bob Stokoe, capering onto the pitch at the final whistle, raincoat flapping behind him and heading not for Ian Porterfield, scorer of the all-important goal, but 'Monty', the target for a special bear hug.

Another keeper never to win an England cap was Sam Bartram, like Montgomery a north-easterner. Charlton Athletic's famous redhead played over 800 games for the south London club in a career that lasted from 1934 until 1956. The only honour he won in the game was an FA Cup winner's medal when Charlton beat Burnley in 1947, after having lost in the previous season to Derby County. If the Reds' fans would rather have seen a League Championship-winning side than a team of Wembley winners, the extrovert Sam was having none of it: 'Glamour over a hard grind' was his avowed preference.

One famous keeper who did gain international honours was Ronnie Simpson, who made his debut in the Scottish Southern League Cup for Queen's Park against Kilmarnock in 1945, at the incredibly young age of 14 years 304 days, thought to be a world record in senior football. He made his Scottish League debut against Hibernian a year later, aged 15 years 310 days. Despite such an early start, however, Simpson had to wait for his first cap until the England–Scotland match at Wembley in April 1967, when he became Scotland's oldest debutant at the ripe old age of 36 years 196 days. The selectors' faith was justified, Simpson helping the Blues to a 3–2 victory in England's first defeat as world champions. A month later Simpson, who had helped Newcastle United to victory in the 1952 and 1955 FA Cup Finals, won yet another medal as he played in the Celtic side that beat Inter Milan in Lisbon to become the first British club to win the European Cup.

Other record breakers include Chris Woods, who became the youngest keeper to play in a Wembley final when he represented Nottingham Forest against Liverpool in March 1978. He was 18 years 125 days old. Even younger was Derek Forster of Sunderland, who was only 15 years 185 days old when he played for Sunderland in the First Division against Leicester City in August 1964. A veteran who made Simpson look like a teenager was Neil McBain, who found his way into the record books when, as New Brighton player-manager, he turned out against Hartlepool in the Third Division (North) in March 1947. He was 52. Eric Nixon's unique place in history seems secure: in 1986/87 he became the first player to appear in all four divisions of the Football League in one season, turning out for Manchester City and Southampton in Division One, Bradford City in Division Two, Carlisle United in Division Three and Wolverhampton Wanderers in Divi-

sion Four. In 1988 Dave Beasant became the first goalkeeper to save a penalty in an FA Cup final when he kept out John Aldridge's spot-kick in the Dons' historic 1–0 victory over Liverpool. He was also the first keeper to captain his side to Wembley victory. Chris Woods deserves another mention for setting a new British record of 1,196 minutes without conceding a goal while playing for Glasgow Rangers in the 1986/87 season. His amazing run began on 2 November 1986 against Borussia Munchengladbach in a UEFA Cup tie, and ended when he was finally beaten from the penalty spot by unlikely opponent Adrian Sprott of Hamilton Academicals in the Scottish Cup on 31 January 1987. Vic Rouse of Crystal Palace kept goal for Wales against Northern Ireland in Belfast in April 1959, making him the first Fourth Division international. Alex Stepney, the Manchester United keeper who was on the receiving end of Pat Jennings' famous goal in the 1967 Charity Shield, found himself in the strange position of being his side's joint leading scorer, with two penalties, halfway through United's relegation season of 1973/74. Tony Coton made his debut for Birmingham City against Sunderland in December 1980 and within eight seconds touched the ball for the first time, saving John Hawley's penalty.

For all other members of the 'goalkeepers' union' who have not had a mention for reasons of space, it can only be said that they have all shared with the fans their moments of exhilaration and of despair. Rarely does a keeper have an 'average' game. He is destined forever to be portrayed as either hero or villain, famous or infamous. But isn't that why he takes on the job in the first place? He's not like the other players. He dresses differently. He is subject to different rules. He is confined (allegedly) to the penalty area. He wouldn't, of course, have it any other way. After all, goalkeepers are different.

Sources:

Hazlewood, N., *In The Way! Goalkeepers: A Breed Apart?* (Edinburgh: Mainstream, 1996).

Hodgson, F., *Only The Goalkeeper To Beat* (London: Macmillan, 1998).

Wilson, B., *You've Got to be Crazy* (London: Weidenfeld & Nicolson, 1989).

Further Reading:

Matthews, P. and Buchanan, I., *The All-Time Greats of British and Irish Sport* (Enfield: Guinness, 1995).

Tibballs, G., *Great Sporting Eccentrics* (London: Robson Books, 1997).

Tony Rennick

Great Goals

Great goals are central to football's global mythology. They are the most sublime moments in the game, and yet all too rare. The promise of their possible execution is what retains the routine involvement of many players and spectators. 'Great goals' display heightened levels of ingenuity, skill and physical fortitude, and stretch the human possibilities within football's fixed geometry. Appreciation of great goals tends to highlight popular antipathy towards the purely 'scientific' or instru-mental attitude towards goal-scoring: not all goals have the same value. Great goals showcase either an exceptional exercise in integrated team-work or an explosive individual intervention. In the former cat-egory, we tend to look for effective passing movements with a spectacular interven-tion (such as a clean shot or volley, or a diving header) as the *coup de grâce*. The Manchester United and Celtic teams of the 1960s and early 1970s, or the Liverpool and Everton sides of the 1980s, have been among the best known for sweeping moves and startling finishes.

In the latter category of individualist goals, we have three general kinds: mazy dribbles, long-range shots in open play, and free-kicks. The mazy, dribbled goal is perhaps the most difficult to execute and is thus the most celebrated. It requires stamina and speed to burst past several opponents, and exceptional technical skills to wrong-foot or evade challenges. The goal tends to be scored by football's great individualists, notably the wingers or the inside-forwards. Maradona's mazy goal against England in the 1986 World Cup final – beginning in his own half and ending with him rounding the keeper – is perhaps the finest illustration, although

Robert Pires scores for Arsenal
(© Stuart MacFarlane, Arsenal FC)

John Barnes's goal against Brazil in the Maracana in 1984 is similarly revered. Other goals in this category, constantly replayed on television, include Tony Currie's against West Ham in 1975, George Best's against Sheffield United in 1971, Davie Cooper's Dryburgh Cup final goal against Celtic in 1979, and Ricky Villa's Cup slalom for Tottenham in 1981.

Long-range shots require accuracy, power, timing and some personal adventure, to strike a moving ball into an almost unreachable part of a distant goal. Some skill may be exercised to bend the ball around a diving goalkeeper. Great goals in this category tend to be scored by attacking midfielders or strikers, such as Bobby Charlton, Peter Lorimer, Bruce Rioch, Graeme Souness, or latterly Alan Shearer. Free-kicks are a contest within a contest, a kind of gladiatorial duel between the 'dead-ball specialist' and the goalkeeper. In the UK, top exponents of the free-kick in recent years have included Liam Brady, Osvaldo Ardiles, Andy Ritchie (of Morton) and latterly David Beckham.

Goals that display inventive techniques in football are particularly celebrated, although the British contribution tends to be embarrassed by the quality of such goals scored by South Americans. For example, we have borrowed the banana kicks of Didi and later Brazilians, the bicycle kick made famous by Pele, the dead-ball strikes of Rivelino and later Roberto Carlos, and the double-swerve shooting of Zico. Great goals tend to draw strength from their context. The matches in which they are scored require some dramatic background such as being a major cup-tie or a clash between giants and purported giant-killers. The stadium should be as full as possible, the crowd boisterous and participatory, and the match itself might be at a tense stage, with the television commentator adding to the excitement. One goal that had all of these ingredients was Ronnie Radford's long-range strike for non-league Hereford over Newcastle United in an FA Cup-tie in 1972.

The advent of televised football placed a greater premium on spectacular goals in two ways. First, it enabled more fans to see a greater range of goals, specifically from matches they had not attended. Second, television's intrinsic interest in football's 'highlights' ensured that these spectacular goals would be constantly replayed, becoming the central part of viewing entertainment. An important aspect of the greatness of these goals is their relative rarity. To date, advances in player physique and equipment have not had a major impact in devaluing these spectacular goals. However, if FIFA's earlier plans to increase the size of goals are pursued further, in a bid to increase the number of goals scored during matches, then this may lead to a fundamental reassessment of the true quality of subsequent 'great goals'.

See also Scorers

Richard Giulianotti

Grounds

The design of British football grounds in the late nineteenth and early twentieth centuries owes much to the designs and influences of the Scottish engineer, Archibald Leitch. Much of his influence could still be seen as late as the 1970s and has only been finally swept away with the building of all-seater stadia in the 1990s.

Glasgow can lay claim to being Britain's major football city if measured in terms of football grounds. It is the only city which has three grounds with a capacity in excess of 50,000. Hampden Park, the home of Scotland's oldest football club, is also Scotland's national football stadium. It has recently been transformed into a 52,000 all-seater stadium, although in the past it has been the scene of record attendances for international and domestic matches. When Hampden Park moved to its present site in 1903 it had a capacity of 63,000. The ground's capacity was gradually extended, reaching its record attendance of 149,547 – then a world record – for the 1937 Scotland v England home international. A week later Hampden hosted the Aberdeen v Celtic Scottish Cup final before 144,307 fans (sometimes given as

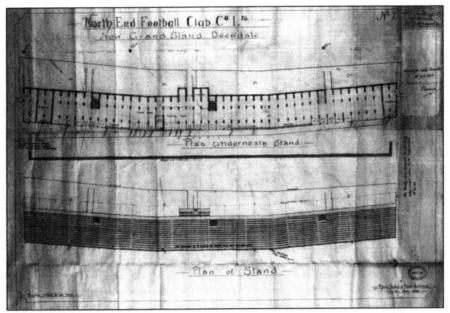

Ground plans of West Stand, Preston North End, 1906 (National Football Museum)

147,365), and is the highest attendance between two club sides in Britain. The ground was also the scene of the remarkable 1960 European Cup Final between Real Madrid and Eintracht Frankfurt in 1960.

Glasgow's other two grounds, Celtic Park and Ibrox, are, respectively, the homes of Celtic and Rangers. Celtic Park was opened in 1892 and, along with Goodison Park, was regarded as Britain's first major football ground. Initially the ground had a running track and a concrete cycle track around the pitch, thus making it a genuine sports stadium. Indeed Celtic Park played host to the World Cycling Championship in 1897. The stadium had an 80,000 capacity until 1971, and today it is a magnificent 60,000 all-seater football ground.

Ibrox was opened in 1897 with a 40,000 capacity. Alas, the ground is no stranger to tragedy. In 1900, a tall bank of open terracing was opened behind the goal with a capacity of 36,000. This was the scene of Britain's first big football disaster, in 1902. During a game between Scotland and England the terracing col-

lapsed, killing 25 fans and injuring over 500. On a more positive note the ground holds the record for the highest league attendance in Britain – 118,567, in 1939 for the New Year's Day Old Firm game. In September 1961 two fans died when a barrier collapsed on stairway 13. Two smaller incidents occurred in 1967 and 1969, with a total of 32 fans injured. Two years later, however, 66 fans died when barriers collapsed on the stairway as fans were leaving the Old Firm game. Today Ibrox is a much safer stadium with an all-seated capacity of almost 50,000.

The north-east of England has been home to three famous stadiums: St James's Park, Roker Park and Ayresome Park. The latter two being recently demolished only for their clubs, Sunderland and Middlesbrough, to transfer to two modern purpose-built football stadia. Roker Park's first and last visitor was Liverpool, the home side winning 1–0 on each occasion. In 1929 Leitch designed the main stand, based on the earlier stand built at Goodison Park. Its famous criss-cross iron facing was to become famous throughout the world of football. The ground's last

The pitch is prepared at Arsenal Stadium, Highbury
(© Stuart MacFarlane, Arsenal FC)

The players' changing room, Highbury
(© Stuart MacFarlane, Arsenal FC)

major improvements were in connection with the 1966 World Cup, allowing Sunderland to host three group-stage matches and the quarter-final match between the USSR and Hungary. Today, Sunderland's new stadium, the stadium of Light, has a 48,000 all-seated capacity and seems destined to become another of Britain's great grounds.

Ayresome Park was built by Leitch in 1903, with a capacity of 33,000. Like Roker Park it was a World Cup Stadium in 1966, hosting three group-stage matches. Middlesbrough left Ayresome Park in 1995 for their new home, the all-seated Riverside Stadium, which has a 34,000 capacity.

Football has been played at St James's Park since 1880. Initially Newcastle Rangers played there, but when they folded in 1892, East End moved in from Byker. Four years later East End became the now-famous Newcastle United. Newcastle joined the League in 1893. Following promotion in 1898 they extended their ground from a 15,000 capacity to 30,000. The Edwardian Newcastle United team was very successful, and from 1900 to 1914 they were regularly the best-supported team in the country. In 1905 the capacity was further increased to 65,000, while their average gate for the 1906/07 season was around 33,000. The club attempted to improve the ground during the 1950s, but their plans were met with resistance by the local council. In 1966 the FA wanted St James's Park to be a World Cup venue, but the local council refused to allow ground improvements and Newcastle lost out to Middlesbrough. It was a venue, however, for Euro 96. Following the Taylor Report the ground has undergone constant improvement, this time with council encouragement.

Liverpool is home to two of the most famous grounds in Britain, Anfield and Goodison Park. Anfield began life as the home of Everton, but since 1892 the red and white of Liverpool has prevailed. The ground is most famous for its Spion Kop, built in 1906 with a 32,000 capacity. The Kop obtained legendary status in the 1960s during the Shankly era, when the Kopites became famous for their wit, innovative chants and songs, and great roar. All in all the team, Shankly's charisma of and the intensity of the Anfield atmosphere made it an intimidating place for visiting teams. Today the ground has changed beyond recognition, the only feature remaining being the top-mast from the Great Eastern, which still flies the Liverpool flag at the Kop end. The ground pays a visible tribute to Paisley and Shankly via four gates decorated with symbols reflecting the success of their management. At the Anfield Road End stands the moving tribute to the 96 Hillsborough dead. It is a place where home and away supporters stand and reflect upon those who died so tragically; on match days the memorial is often decorated with the scarves of away supporters.

Upon leaving Anfield the Everton board acquired a piece of land across Stanley Park called Mere Green. They quickly built a new ground upon which they built two uncovered stands and a grandstand with 3,000 seats. Upon opening it was renamed Goodison Park. Goodison became England's first major football ground when it was opened, by Lord Kinnaird and Frederick Hall of the FA, on 24 August 1892. The first event, however, was an athletics meeting which drew 12,000 spectators. The following week the ground saw its first football match when Bolton were the visitors in a friendly. The Goodison Road main stand was regarded as one of Archibald Leitch's masterpieces when it was built in 1909, making it one of the most attractive grounds in the country. The ground was host to the 1894 FA Cup Final and the Cup Final replay in 1910. In 1913 it became the first league ground to be visited by a ruling monarch. It was also a World Cup ground in 1966, staging three group games as well as the semi-final between the USSR and West Germany. Today the ground, though all-seater, has not kept pace with the times and has a somewhat dilapidated appearance.

Manchester United's ground, Old Trafford, was opened in 1910. Its first visitors were Liverpool, who won 4–3. At the time it had the largest capacity in England, holding 80,000 spectators. It held the 'khaki' Cup final of 1915 and was chosen as a venue for the 1966 World Cup and for Euro 96. During the Second World War the ground was bombed, forcing the club to play its matches at Maine Road, the home of their arch rivals, Manchester City, until 1949. The ground has been extensively redeveloped since the Taylor Report, and since the 2000/01 season its capacity has been increased to 67,000, making it the largest football ground in Britain.

Alas, Hillsborough will always be remembered for the horrific disaster of 1989, which resulted in the deaths of 96 Liverpool fans. The ground was originally called Owlerton, but when it became a part of the new parliamentary constituency of Hillsborough the ground was also renamed. It has staged many FA Cup semi-finals and was chosen to host qualifying games for the 1966 World Cup and for Euro 96.

Architecturally, Highbury, home of Arsenal, is one of England's most significant grounds. Built in Art Deco style in the 1930s it too is having to give way to the forces of modernisation. Initially Arsenal wanted to extend their ground, but like other clubs they have been forced to give way to local residents and have had to find an alternative site for a new ground.

Aston Villa have been more fortunate than most top clubs and have recently been able to expand their ground without moving, although it has come with an architectural cost. Rinder and Leitch drew up plans in 1914 for Villa Park to hold 104,000. The club's shareholders, however, balked at the idea, pointing to their average attendance at the time of 30,000. Nevertheless, during the 1920s and '30s a form of the Rinder and Leitch plan did take shape at Villa Park, albeit on a more modest scale. Rinder and Leitch's design for the Holte End was largely retained, however, and when it was eventually built in 1939/40 it turned Villa Park into England's most modern stadium. In the post-war period this enabled Aston Villa to capitalise on the boom in attendances. Alas, the Holte End has also had to bend to the power of modernisation. For the 2000/01 season it has been rebuilt but,

surely, redevelopment could have allowed for some architectural retention?

After Hillsborough football grounds in Britain have undergone revolutionary change. Clubs in the English Premier League, the First Division of the Football League and clubs in the Scottish Premier League are required to have all-seater stadia. While these now offer greater safety and comfort for spectators, it has come with a heavy price tag for football's traditional fan base. Many such supporters can no longer afford to pay in excess of £20 for a seat: their places are now being taken by a more middle-class clientele. The change from stadia being a mixture of standing and seated sections to all-seater stadia has resulted in a significant reduction in capacity. Some clubs, most notably Manchester United, have had the wherewithal and the room to extend their grounds. This has resulted in a wealth gap opening up between England's top clubs and other clubs in the Premiership. As a result, clubs such as Liverpool, Everton and Arsenal, unable to expand their grounds sufficiently, are looking to build new grounds. This move away from their traditional home has met with local opposition, however. Liverpool, for example, want to move to nearby Stanley Park and build a 70,000-seat purpose-built stadium. The club has undergone an extensive public relations exercise in an attempt to convince the local community, but resistance has forced Liverpool City Council to organise a local referendum on the issue. The result is far from certain but it would seem likely that Liverpool will have to re-think their plans. The power of a local community in resisting football clubs over ground redevelopment was demonstrated in Newcastle, when residents successfully resisted Newcastle United's efforts to build a new stadium on the historic Town Moor. Newcastle were forced instead to expand St James's to the present capacity of 51,000.

In Scotland the reduction in ground capacities has produced an even greater wealth gap. Both Celtic and Rangers have ground capacities three or four times greater than their Edinburgh rivals. This has had a destabilising effect upon Scottish domestic football, with Rangers and Celtic threatening to quit Scottish football as they search for greater competition and greater gate receipts to help finance their European ambitions.

Following the Taylor Report clubs were given increased financial support for ground improvement, channelled through a revamped Football Trust. The grants, however, were distributed inequitably, with the richer clubs receiving significantly larger amounts than poorer teams in the lower divisions. Clubs outside the League faired even worse. This resulted in a situation whereby the champions of the Conference were barred from promotion because they had not completed the necessary ground improvements to conform with the League's Grade 'A' requirements. The league's criteria required Third Division clubs to have a minimum capacity of 6,000, with at least 1,000 seats. Clubs seeking promotion had to have their ground improvements completed by 31 December in the season of their intended application for promotion. This rule resulted in three Conference teams, in three successive seasons between 1994 and 1996, being denied promotion. The teams concerned – Kidderminster Harriers, Macclesfield and Stevenage Borough – could only meet the League requirements by the end of the season. This resulted in the anomaly of the 1994 champions, Kidderminster Harriers, being denied promotion even though their ground met the Grade 'A' requirements, while the team which finished bottom of the Third Division, Northampton Town, were unable to fulfil the required standard: Northampton only had 650 seats, instead of the required 1,000. They retained their League status because the League argued that 'our regulations regarding 1,000 seats apply to new clubs only'.

In the case of Kidderminster Harriers they failed to meet the 31 December deadline because their grant from the Football Trust arrived late. Moreover, both Kidderminster and Macclesfield considered ground sharing, but this was also rejected by the League. Once again the League upheld an inconsistent position, as

Chester had already played league football at Macclesfield's ground while their own ground was undergoing redevelopment. Also, Bristol Rovers play their league football at Bath City's ground, even though the ground does not meet the League's Grade 'A' requirements.

The Scottish League employs the same double standards as its English counterparts. Although achieving a promotion play-off place, Falkirk were denied the chance of competing for a place in the Scottish Premier League. Falkirk were refused the chance because their ground was deemed too small. They offered to play their home games at Murrayfield while their new stadium was being built, but this proved unacceptable.

Source:

Inglis, S., *Football Grounds of Britain* (London: CollinsWillow, 1996).

See also National Stadia

Ray Physick

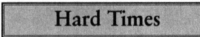

Hard Times

The top Premiership players of the television age are paid like rock stars and treated as such by the media, featured as often, it seems, in the show-business sections of the tabloids as on the sports pages. It seemed appropriate, therefore, that Arsenal and England centre-half Tony Adams should reveal in August 2000 that he was in negotiations to purchase a country house in Essex suitable for adaptation along similar lines to an establishment set up in the West Indies by guitar legend Eric Clapton. Adams was not, however, seeking to gentrify his image by setting himself up as lord of the local manor. What he envisaged was an addiction treatment centre for his fellow professionals hooked on drink, drugs or gambling: somewhere they could address their problems away from the glare of publicity. Clapton's retreat on Antigua, the rehabilitation centre appropriately named Crossroads, opened as a result of his own battle against cocaine and alcohol addiction, and Adams was well qualified to see the need for a similar facility to cater for troubled soccer stars.

Adams's autobiography *Addicted* had sold over 400,000 copies at the time of his announcement, and chronicled the story, both depressing and yet hopeful, of Britain's most high-profile recovered alcoholic. Living up to the fashionable 'play hard, drink hard' ethic, Adams had received a prison sentence just before Christmas 1990 after being charged with drink-driving. After serving a month inside he was inspired by the 8,000 Arsenal fans who turned out to see his first reserve game after his release. Picking up the threads of his career, Adams eschewed the regular nights out with the boys and took to reading Shakespeare and playing the piano. Ten years after his lowest point he was still on the wagon, ready and willing to help those he saw around him with similar problems. There were quite a few.

Arsenal team-mate and drinking partner Paul Merson had confessed to a triple addiction to drink, drugs and gambling. He moved to Middlesbrough, away from the temptations of London's bright lights; but his problems continued on Teesside, before a further transfer to Aston Villa resurrected his career. Paul Gascoigne, the superbly talented but prodigiously self-destructive midfielder, once an England colleague of Adams, was a self-confessed alcoholic and wife-beater. Stan Collymore, the gifted but wayward striker who had frustrated a string of managers, was regularly making the papers for all the wrong reasons, including a well-publicised assault on his glamorous showbiz girlfriend Ulrika Jonsson. Among the more sensational tabloid stories surrounding Collymore was the claim that he had been caught taking drugs while receiving treatment for depression at the Priory, an exclusive clinic in south-west London. Roy Keane, Manchester United's £52,000-a-week captain, was another to have confessed to a drink problem, and had been reported to have attended meetings of Alcoholics Anonymous. Alex Rae, Sunderland's Scottish midfielder, was a recovered alcoholic who had also had treatment for depression at the Priory.

What Adams envisaged was a refuge where these and others would be housed, not in the expensive private rooms provided by such trendy treatment centres as the Priory, but in four-bed dormitories, where the inevitable isolation brought on by addiction would be diminished. Mobile phones would be banned and football training would continue as normal. Adams envisaged that he would personally greet clients on arrival before handing them over to qualified experts. Noble sentiments indeed from a man ideally placed to recognise the pressures that new-found fame and excessive media attention can exert on the rising stars of today.

A number of players from an earlier generation would have had a closer interest than most in Adams' idea: those who had trodden the same path. Jimmy Greaves, the mercurial Spurs and England striker, saw his marriage wrecked through his addiction as the booze slowly but surely became more important than the game he loved. Greaves admits that he owes his recovery to Alcoholics Anonymous and their Twelve Steps to Recovery, and regularly uses his column in the *Sun* as a platform to urge today's young hopefuls to resist the lure of high living. Jim Baxter, the Rangers and Scotland midfielder, became, perhaps unwisely, a Glasgow publican after retiring from the game in 1969. His continued heavy drinking resulted in two liver transplants. The most famous of them all, the legendary George Best, walked out on Manchester United at the age of 26, much to the frustration of his manager, mentor and father figure Matt Busby. Best proceeded to embark on a jet-setting lifestyle that was to ruin his health and bring him to the very brink; he was hospitalised with severe liver and kidney damage in 2000, and was warned that one more drink could kill him.

Some have already died. In 1961 Albert Johanneson was plucked from the obscurity and poverty of the South African townships after being recommended to Leeds United by his schoolteacher. He became one of Don Revie's first signings as the future England manager built the Leeds side that was to win promotion from the old Second Division in 1963/64 and finish as runners-up in both the League and FA Cup the following year. The flying left-winger was top scorer in his first season for the club, and was the first black player the majority of fans had seen. He suffered the inevitable, moronic racist chanting from the terraces and was subjected to such harsh treatment on the pitch that team-mates Jack Charlton and Billy Bremner appointed themselves his on-field 'minders'. The pressure began to tell. Albert, undoubtedly gifted but never the most consistent of players, was replaced in the side by Eddie Gray. He moved to York City but had only one season there before injury caused his retirement in 1971. Forced out of the game that he loved and that had brought him fame, Albert turned increasingly for consolation to drink and to cannabis. By 1992 he was separated from his wife and two daughters and all that former team-mates knew of him was that he had hidden himself away in the seedy Chapeltown area of Leeds. Peter Lorimer, prominent in the club's old players' association, tried in vain to entice him back into the fold but all his efforts were rebuffed as the lost soul sank lower and lower. In 1995 Albert Johanneson's body was found by police in a flat in a Headingly tower block. He had been dead for days. He was 53.

An even more prominent player who had met a similarly tragic end was Hughie Gallacher, regarded by many in the game as the greatest centre-forward of them all, even though he stood only 5ft 5ins. Born in Bellshill, Lanarkshire on 2 February 1903, Hugh Kilpatrick Gallacher – 'Wee Hughie' – began his career with Queen of the South before turning professional with Airdrieonians in 1921. He helped the Lanarkshire club to Scottish Cup victory in 1924 before moving south of the border the following year to join Newcastle United, captaining the Magpies to the League Championship in 1927. Later moves took him to Chelsea, Derby County, Notts County and Grimsby Town before he returned to Tyneside, spending his last playing days with Gateshead before retiring from the game in 1939. In his League career he scored 387 goals in 543 games for his various clubs. His

Hughie Gallacher
(Reproduced with the kind permission of Imperial Tobacco Limited)

record at international level was even more impressive, his 20 appearances producing 22 goals, including five in the 1929 fixture against Northern Ireland. He was also a prominent member of the famous 'Wembley Wizards' who thrashed England 5–1 in 1928. Such a sparkling career had its darker side, however. While still with Queen of the South, and at age 17, he married, against his parents' wishes. The young couple, who could not afford a home of their own on Hughie's £6 a week, soon had a son, but baby Hughie died before his first birthday. A second child, this time a daughter, arrived too late to save the fragile marriage and in 1923, aged only 20, Hughie separated from his wife. During these troubled times he also suffered medical problems, spending some time on the danger list in a Dumfries hospital with double pneumonia. If Hughie's move to Newcastle helped his career, it did little to improve his private life. He sought an escape in alcohol and became involved with the 17-year-old daughter of a pub landlord, ending up in court following a fight with the girl's brother after the latter had objected to her seeing a married man. The romance continued in secret, however, and they were later to marry as soon as Hughie was free, although the divorce cost him £4,000 and left him penniless. A £10,000 transfer to Chelsea in 1930, together with generous personal terms, seemed to have solved his financial problems but alcohol continued to haunt him. On a tour of Hungary he was even accused of being drunk and disorderly on the pitch, though he ludicrously claimed that he had only used whisky and water as a mouthwash. After his final season as a League player, during which he scored 18 goals in 31 appearances for Gateshead, Hughie continued to live in the north-east and regularly turned out in charity matches for a number of years, though his private life continued its turbulent course. On 12 June 1957 he was due to appear in Gateshead magistrate's court on charges alleging assault and maltreatment of his 14-year-old daughter. He never kept the appointment. On 11 June, at the chillingly appropriate Dead Man's Crossing at Low Fell, just South of Gateshead, he stepped in front of the speeding York–Edinburgh express and was decapitated. A shocked witness claimed that, after accidentally brushing against him before his last fatal step, Wee Hughie's last word was 'Sorry!'.

Another player to take his own life, and another centre-forward, was the South African-born Stuart Leary, who became an England Under-23 international during a career that began with Charlton Athletic in 1951 and ended with Queen's Park Rangers in 1965. Leary, who also played first-class cricket for Kent, leaped to his death from a cable car near the summit of Table Mountain in 1988. Three years later Alan Davies, the Welsh international winger who had enjoyed his share of the glory days with Manchester United,

Newcastle United and Swansea City between 1981 and 1991, was found dead in his car near his Welsh home. He is thought to have been suffering from depression.

Over the years many other top stars, while not resorting to such drastic steps, have nevertheless discovered that fame and fortune do not continue after their playing days are over. Back in 1916 William 'Fatty' Foulke, the giant goalkeeper of the Victorian era, had frittered away a fortune and was reduced to charging a penny a time for holidaymakers to try to score penalties against him on the beach at Blackpool, with threepence the prize for successful punters. This undignified finale to his illustrious career resulted in his death after catching a chill. He was 42.

Arthur Rowley scored a remarkable 434 League goals, still a record, for West Bromwich Albion, Fulham, Leicester City and Shrewsbury Town in 619 matches between 1946 and 1964. He helped both Fulham and Leicester to promotion into the First Division but, after retiring to become a district manager for Vernons pools, he was almost forced to sell his medals to make ends meet, before Shrewsbury came to the rescue by playing a testimonial match in his honour. Several other players have, however, found it necessary to part with their treasured mementoes, including Ray Kennedy, the powerful striker turned midfielder, who was a member of the Arsenal side that had won the elusive League and Cup 'double' in 1970/71, himself scoring the dramatic winner two minutes from time against deadly rivals Spurs as the Gunners clinched the championship at White Hart Lane. Moving to Liverpool in 1974 as Bill Shankly's last signing before the great man gave way to Bob Paisley, he went on to win three European Cup, one UEFA Cup, five League Championship and one League Cup winner's medals with the Reds, as well as 17 England caps, but was tragically diagnosed, at the age of 35, as suffering from Parkinson's disease, a disorder of movement that also affects personality, emotions and speech. The Ray Kennedy collection was sold for £61,900. The League and Cup double-winning medals raised £17,000; the 1977 European Cup winner's medal £16,000. It all seemed scant reward, however; the debilitating disease had already cost Kennedy his marriage and his livelihood as a publican.

As the financial rewards available to top players spiralled ever upwards in the 1990s, two forgotten heroes, born too soon to enjoy the game's boom years, were drifting into poverty and obscurity. Bobby Tambling, the England winger who scored Chelsea's consolation goal when they lost the 'Cockney Cup Final' to Spurs in 1967, and who netted a total of 164 goals for the Blues during their days as the darlings of the West End, retired in 1973 and tried his hand at running a Hampshire sports shop, but was a hod carrier by the time Portsmouth County Court declared him bankrupt in 1994. Peter Marinello, who won a Scottish League Cup medal with Hibernian in 1969 before bringing his silky skills and film-star good looks to Arsenal as the 'Scottish George Best', returned to Edinburgh after his retirement in 1983 to run 'Marinello's', a trendy watering hole. The venture failed, however, and in 1995 Marinello, by then living in Bournemouth, was declared another footballing bankrupt. What price fame?

Sources:

Forsyth, R., *The Only Game: The Scots in World Football* (Edinburgh, Mainstream, 1990).

Pringle, A. and Fissler, N., *Where Are They Now?* (London: Two Heads Publishing, 1996).

Vasili, P., *Colouring Over the White Line: The History of Black Footballers in Britain* (Edinburgh: Mainstream, 2000).

Further Reading:

Chilcott, D., *The Hamlyn Guide to Football Collectables* (London: Hamlyn, 1995).

Greaves, J., *This One's On Me* (London: Arthur Barker, 1979).

Lees, A. and Kennedy, R., *Ray of Hope: The Ray Kennedy Story* (London: Pelham Books, 1993).

McElroy, R. and MacDougall, G., *Football Memorabilia* (London: Carlton, 1999).

Tony Rennick

Heritage

British football is characterised by a keen sense of its own history, and its supporters cherish a deep-seated nostalgia for the traditions of the past. Though individual collectors have amassed large amounts of memorabilia, until recently a collective sense that football's heritage should be preserved and celebrated more formally in museums or by other memorials has been lacking.

Cigarette and trade cards, programmes, medals, international caps, shirts, and trophies are just some of the memorabilia which have been collected by individuals since the nineteenth century. Magazines like *The Football Collector* and *Programme Monthly* share information about collectables. Even modern items can rapidly become desirable. The 1990s' Corinthian model figures of players and managers have a huge following and their own collectors' club. Some figures are deliberately made in small numbers to increase their rarity value. Football memorabilia have been relatively inexpensive to acquire, but the increasing popularity of the sport now means that rarer articles are keenly sought after. When in November 1989 Christie's held the first auction of football artefacts, the medal won by Arsenal's Alex James in the 1930 FA Cup Final raised £5,000. Since then a shirt worn by Arnold Kirke-Smith in the first Scotland and England International in 1872 has fetched £18,500, and a programme from the 1915 FA Cup final was sold for £9,800. Thirty of the England caps awarded to Billy Wright were sold for £42,050 in 1996. The record price for a single cap is £10,000, paid for one worn by George Cohen in the 1966 England World Cup finals.

Institutions are now among the biggest purchasers of football memorabilia. In 1999 the Professional Footballers' Association paid a then world-record price for a piece of modern British art, L. S. Lowry's *Going to the Match*, for £1,926,000. This 1953 painting shows a crowd entering Bolton's now demolished Burnden Park.

Soccer stars of the 1920s and 1930s as depicted on cigarette cards of the time
(Reproduced with the kind permission of Imperial Tobacco Limited)

Its purchase was considered to have saved for the nation an extremely evocative depiction of a traditional scene from football's golden age.

Football clubs have begun to recognise the profits that can be made from exploiting supporters' interest in and affections for their club's history and ground, even where the club has relocated to a new venue and its old stadium has been demolished. Ground tours are available at most of the top clubs in Britain and can attract thousands of visitors a year from all over the world. Though part of the appeal of these tours is to offer fans a glimpse behind the scenes, they trade upon the often sentimental attachment that many supporters develop for football stadia. A few clubs, notably Glasgow Celtic, Glasgow Rangers, Manchester United, Liverpool and Arsenal, have museums which celebrate past achievements, important events and stars, and emphasise the continuities between the modern game and its past. Recently, statues of famous footballing figures have been erected to mark their service to clubs or links with their home towns. Billy Wright (Molineux), Matt Busby (Old Trafford), Duncan Edwards (Dudley), and Jackie Milburn (Newcastle) have all been immortalised in this way. The faces of former Preston heroes Tom Finney and Bill Shankly are picked out in coloured seats at Deepdale.

Fans can also purchase replica shirts modelled on their team's past strips.

Manchester United's 1993 third kit was based upon the colours of their predecessors, Newton Heath. Blackburn Rovers was one of the first clubs to have its history published, in 1893. Other histories, like those of Everton, Queen's Park and Sheffield Wednesday, were written for their fiftieth anniversary celebrations in the 1920s. The majority were produced in the late 1940s, when there was a surge in interest in football's history.

In the 1950s Vic Wayling claimed to be the founder-curator of the first football museum at Hitchin, Hertfordshire. The sports journalist Harry Langton's collection of over 4,000 objects was later purchased by FIFA and will form the basis of the new Football Museum at Deepdale in Preston. The first national museum of football was established in Scotland as recently as 1994 and now has a permanent base in the South Stand at Hampden Park. Granada's 'International Football Hall of Fame' is planned to open in Manchester as a 'cathedral of football' in which names of great players, chosen by fans' votes, would be inscribed. The 'Hope and Glory Road' promised a blatantly sentimental reconstruction of a walk to the ground on match day, passing through a traditional turnstile, further evidence of the growing commercial power of cosy football nostalgia.

Sources:

The Football Association, *Football and the Fine Arts* (London: The Naldrett Press, 1953).

Further Reading:
FIFA, *F.I.F.A. Museum Collection* (Berlin: Verlags-GmbH, 1996).
Pickering, D., *The Cassell Soccer Companion* (London: Cassell, 1994).

See also Collectors and Memorabilia, Exhibitions, Facilities, Relocation of Clubs

Joyce Woolridge

Historiography of Football

Football has long been a popular historical subject. Since the late nineteenth century there has been a continuous stream of books, pamphlets and magazines concerned with the history of the game. For the most part these writings have adopted a conventional form of historical enquiry: personalities, institutions and matches have been the chief focus of interest. Such an emphasis results largely from the perspective adopted in the local and national press, from among whose reporters many football historians have come. Club histories are often the work of writers based at local newspapers, who use their contacts with clubs to gain information; biographies of well-known players also frequently issue from this source. The national press has produced historians who have directed their attention to the bigger picture: at this level, at different points in the twentieth century, J. A. H. Catton, Geoffrey Green, John Arlott and Hugh McIlvanney have all written with exceptional skill on the development of the game in Britain. In a rather more specialist vein the work of Simon Inglis on football grounds and John Harding's biographical studies have added significantly to this tradition. In the last decade of the twentieth century yet another variant appeared with the emergence in the wake of Nick Hornby's immensely successful *Fever Pitch* of a clutch of histories and testimonies written from a more personal perspective by the 'ordinary' fan. They served to stimulate, alongside the appeal of 'Italia 90' and the formation of the Premier League, a new interest in football, especially among young men in their twenties and thirties, at whom much of the new writing was aimed.

Only in the third quarter of the century, however, did academic histories of football begin to appear. Their appearance was the consequence of the growth during the 1960s and '70s of a new style of social history in British universities, concerned to examine the activities and interests of ordinary people 'from the bottom up'. Before this, social historians were not, in the main, inclined to regard football as a serious subject for historical enquiry. With due acknowledgement to James Walvin's *The People's Game*, the paradigm of the new approach, and a work which fully deserves the overused word 'seminal', was Tony Mason's *Association Football and English Society 1863–1915*. It deals in detail, using a variety of historical sources, with the fundamental question of how football developed as a game with particular affinities to the working class. In the twenty years since the appearance of Mason's work several historians have followed his lead, directing to football a series of questions about the nature of the game which spring from the broader field of social, economic and political history. These are less concerned with personalities and institutions than with structures, finances, and social relationships. Wray Vamplew, Richard Holt, Steve Wagg, Nick Fishwick and Dave Russell are all important members of this company of new historians.

Football history has been made difficult because of problems in acquiring good sources; clubs have not always been assiduous in maintaining archives, or helpful in permitting access to those that do exist. This has led to a possible over-reliance on the newspaper press as a source. Nonetheless, different sources would not necessarily have produced a different kind of history. Although there is some indication of alternative approaches developing based on linguistic analysis, it seems likely that football history will continue along the lines set out by Mason and Walvin for some time to come.

Sources:

Fishwick, N., *English Football and Society, 1910–1950* (Manchester: Manchester University Press, 1989).

Holt, R., *Sport and the British: A Modern History* (Oxford: Oxford University Press, 1989).

Mason, A., *Association Football and English Society 1863–1915* (Brighton: Harvester Press, 1980).

Russell, D., *Football and the English: A Social History of Association Football in England 1863–1995* (Preston: Carnegie Publishing, 1997).

Vamplew, W., *Pay Up and Play the Game: Professional Sport in Britain 1875–1914* (Cambridge: Cambridge University Press, 1988).

Wagg, S., *The Football World: A Contemporary Social History* (Brighton: Harvester, 1984).

Walvin, J., *The People's Game: A Social History of British Football* (London: Allen Lane, 1975).

Further Reading:

Hill, J., 'British Sports History: A Post-Modern Future?', *Journal of Sport History*, 23: 1 (Spring 1996), pp. 1–19.

Jeff Hill

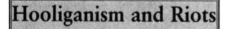

Hooliganism and Riots

Of all the subjects surrounding football discussed by academics and the media, hooliganism has been the most contentious. There have been many attempts to explain the phenomenon by historians, sociologists and others, but little agreement about its causes and frequency at different times. There is no consensus as to what exactly constitutes 'hooliganism'; relatively minor incidents have been counted as statistically equivalent to serious cases, and some analyses have included cases of 'verbal misconduct', thus increasing dramatically the number of 'incidents' occurring. Similarly, analyses in different countries suggest that explanations in one national context are less relevant in others. However, we may define it as including serious misconduct such as violence, vandalism and pitch invasions.

Football hooliganism is not new; it has been present since the beginning of spectator football, and no period has been entirely free of it. From the late 1870s to the late 1880s, football itself, and facilities for housing and handling crowds, were less well organised, and disturbances were caused by frustration at decisions by the referee, incidents on the field, overcrowding, poor organisation, and sometimes clashes with rival supporters. Most observers would agree that an earlier peak of incidents occurred during the 1890s and 1900s, but a decline began between the World Wars, continuing into the 1950s. A dramatic upsurge then commenced from the late 1960s.

The difference between the earlier and later incidents is that the former were generally smaller in scale (with some exceptions), and there was little evidence of an identifiable youth subculture becoming involved in violence before the 1960s. There is some evidence, however, of betting gangs creating disturbances, possibly to influence the result or cause the game to be abandoned. Crowd management was better organised in the 1920s and 1930s, and there seemed to be more self-policing of incidents in unsegregated grounds, as well as a better relationship with the police. This continued into the 1940s and 1950s, but isolated incidents still occurred. A growth in youth subcultures attracted to football in the 1960s led to increasingly oppositional behaviour and the growing segregation into 'ends' at grounds. The Saturday ritual of violence had taken hold, and continued through the 1970s and 1980s, becoming more sophisticated, and, seemingly, better organised. The obsessive attention of the media fuelled this phenomenon, thus generating a classic 'moral panic'.

Hooliganism is certainly connected to a feeling of identity with a football club or national team – especially England – and this can manifest itself in racism and xenophobia (in its widest sense), providing a convenient basis for the periodic involvement of right-wing political groups, including the National Front and the British Movement. For Scottish supporters, this has involved disorder at internationals against England (although since the later 1980s, fans of the Scottish national side have consciously adopted 'better' forms of behaviour in deliberate contradistinction to that of some English counterparts) and sectarian violence between Protestant Rangers and Catholic Celtic groups, both now and in the past. There is also evidence that sectarianism has erupted at other grounds, as in the Cappielow riot of 1899 between supporters of Greenock Morton and Port Glasgow Athletic. Major disruptions like this, or Hampden Park in 1909, are thankfully rare.

The evolution of the 'casuals' in the 1980s, with their stylish trainers, designer clothes and image, was probably influenced by contact with European hooligan fans, especially the Italian 'ultras'. The British equivalent may have started in north-west England or London, but became national by the mid 1980s. The media failed to recognise that this 'flash' style was connected more with stolen goods and the black economy, linked with the desired image of being 'hard' but smart, rather than with actual affluence. Indeed, the casual hooligans were just as deeply embedded in regional antagonisms and delinquent working-class behaviour as had been previous hooligan groups.

The issue became one of public order in the 1970s, accelerating after the election of Conservative governments from 1979, committed as they were to tougher law and order policies and a market economy. These governments originated specific anti-football legislation, including the Football Spectators Act, that sought to attack another identifiable 'enemy within' – the football hooligan. Football was described by a number of Conservative politicians and the right-wing press as an outmoded, violence-ridden institution requiring exposure to market forces and legal solutions that would exclude working-class hooligans. Possible reasons for the perceived decline in disturbances in the 1990s include subsequent changes in spectator demography, the introduction of all-seater stadia and the growth of rave/dance culture as an alternative youth attraction. Hooliganism has never entirely disappeared; rather, improved security measures have increasingly pushed it to new locations away from the ground. But, at the same time, it should in any case be stressed that it has never been the dominant form of spectator behaviour.

Sources:
Dunning, E., Murphy, P. and Williams, J., *The Roots of Football Hooliganism* (London: Routledge, 1988).
Giulianotti, R., Bonney, N. and Hepworth, M. (eds), *Football, Violence and Social Identity* (London: Avebury, 1993).
Murphy, P., Williams, J. and Dunning, E., *Football on Trial: Spectator Violence and Development in the Football World* (London: Routledge, 1990).
Redhead, S. (ed.), *The Passion and the Fashion: Football Fandom in the New Europe* (Aldershot: Avebury, 1994).
Williams, J. and Wagg, S. (eds), *British Football and Social Change* (Leicester: Leicester University Press, 1991).

Further Reading:
Armstrong, G., *Football Hooligans: Knowing the Score* (Oxford: Berg, 1998).
Giulianotti, R. and Williams, J. (eds), *Game Without Frontiers: Football, Identity and Modernity* (Aldershot: Ashgate, 1994).
Lewis, R., 'Football Hooliganism in England Before 1914: A Critique of the Dunning Thesis', *International Journal of the History of Sport*, 13 (1996), pp. 310–39.

Robert Lewis

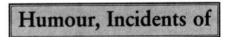

Humour, Incidents of

The late Bill Shankly once famously said that football was more serious than life and death but, luckily for those with a more realistic outlook, the game has always had its lighter side. There's an old saying that goalkeepers are crazy, and several of those custodians of the onion bag have provided moments of hilarity over the years.

One of the most memorable would have been witnessed by Shankly at his beloved Anfield. Gary Sprake, the Welsh international who was a key member of the Leeds United side of the late 1960s and early 1970s, confirmed his reputation as being gifted but erratic by throwing the ball into his own goal. Collecting a back-pass from centre-half Jack Charlton a minute before half-time, Sprake's intention was to throw the ball out to full-back Terry Cooper. Noticing that Cooper was closely marked, however, he changed his mind at the last moment but didn't check his throw in time; the ball bobbled ever so slowly over the line, much to the delight of the 40,000 crowd, who immediately burst into a joyous version of *Careless Hands*, a popular hit of the day. The Liverpool public address system added to the unfortunate keeper's misery and the increasing glee of the fans by playing the same song, by Des O'Connor, during the interval. Sprake had only confirmed, of course, that goalkeepers are a breed apart, and always have been, right from the early days.

One of the most colourful characters in the game was William 'Fatty' Foulke, for whom the expression 'larger than life' might have been invented,who stood 6 ft 2 ins and weighed 15 stone when he joined Sheffield United in 1894, reaching an amazing 22 stone towards the end of his career. Foulke, who also kept goal for Chelsea and Bradford City, as well as winning an England cap, used to say: 'I don't mind what they call me, as long as they don't call me late for lunch.' He meant what he said: he once arrived first at the breakfast table set for the entire Chelsea team and scoffed the lot. He was described in his day as: 'One of the curiosities of football; a wonder to every-one who visits the classic grounds of the game.' And with good reason: he once caused a game to be stopped after swing-ing on the crossbar and reducing it to matchwood. Neither were his opponents safe. He once grabbed a forward round the waist and dangled him upside-down in the muddy goalmouth. Another player foolhardy enough to penetrate Foulke's domain was bear-hugged and thrown into the back of the net. Referees were also known to incur his wrath: incensed by

what he considered an offside goal during the 1902 Sheffield United–Southampton FA Cup final, at the end of the game Foulke divested himself of his kit and went in search of the hapless referee, who locked himself in a boot cupboard to avoid the naked man-mountain.

Trying to earn a similarly fearsome rep-utation to Foulke's, Middlesbrough keep-er Tim Williamson, capped seven times for England between 1905 and 1913, padded himself out by wearing several jerseys in an attempt to emulate the legendary 'Fatty'. More outlandish sporting garb had earlier been donned by Welsh internation-al keeper Jimmy Trainer, playing for Preston North End against Reading during the 1893/94 season. As Preston proceeded to win the match 18–0, Trainer put on a mackintosh as the rain came down during the second half, taking it off only on the two occasions the ball reached him. No doubt he relished the easy time he was having; he had signed for Preston shortly after conceding 12 to them in a match while playing for Bolton Wanderers! Another mackintosh had been worn by Jim Milne, the Arbroath goalkeeper in the famous 1885 Scottish Cup tie in which Bon Accord lost 36–0. Milne, who report-edly never touched the ball throughout the whole game, also sheltered under an umbrella and kept himself occupied by smoking a pipe.

Yet another colourful keeper from the early days was Albert Iremonger, an England international who played over 500 games for Notts County between 1905 and 1926. Iremonger, who stood 6ft 6ins, hated being confined to his goal area and was not averse to venturing upfield to take the odd throw-in to relieve the bore-dom, much to the enjoyment of the crowd. His employers were not so amused, however: the County minute-book entry for 9 November 1908 reads: 'Iremonger appeared and was spoken to with regard to his gallery play at Trent Bridge and Bury.' Albert was also involved in one of the most ludicrous episodes in the history of the game. In a match against Blackburn he volunteered to take a penal-ty, which he slammed against the bar with such force that it rebounded over his head and landed at the feet of the Blackburn winger, who sped off in the direction of Albert's unguarded goal. Off scampered Iremonger in hot pursuit, his long legs eating up the lost ground until, with a last despairing effort, he whipped the ball away from his opponent – straight into his own net. At least Albert showed initiative, as did the Bolton Wanderers trainer when his side arrived by train to play Middlesbrough in the 1940s. As the kit hamper was unloaded, it was found that the team's shin-guards had been lost in transit. Unperturbed, that worthy strolled to the station bookstall and bought 22 paperback romantic novels to use as replacements. Bolton therefore achieved immortality by becoming the first team in the history of the game to take the field with all 11 players already booked.

Humour can originate quite effectively off the field as well as on it, as any owner of a television or radio is aware. During the transmission of a Sunderland–Spurs game in 1997, BBC commentator John Motson no doubt had the same end in mind while covering a Sunderland–Spurs game for the BBC in 1977. In a loss of colour during the transmission he offered helpfully: 'For those of you watching in black and white, Spurs are playing in yellow.' 'Motty' is also credited with arguably the most blindingly obvious statement ever made about the game: 'The World Cup – truly an international event.'

Motson is not the only commentator to come out with gibberish in the heat of the moment: they've all done it. Des Lynam proved that geography wasn't one of his strong points when he announced: 'Chesterfield 1, Chester 1. Another score-draw there in that local derby.' Brian Moore confused viewers intending to enter a postal competition with: 'Remember, postcards only, please. The winner will be the first one opened.'! Barry Davies took to extremes the notion of goalkeepers being a breed apart with his famous: 'Lukic saved with his foot, which is all part of the goalkeeper's arm.' John Helm was being nothing if not logical when he informed viewers: 'The USA are a goal down and if they don't get a goal they'll lose.' Stuart Hall waxed lyrically: 'If a

week is a long time in politics, it is an equinox in football.' The BBC's David Coleman is the commentator most associated with such gaffes, although many of the comments attributed to him are probably apocryphal or originate from other lips. Two of his supposed gems include: 'Nottingham Forest are having a bad run – they've lost six matches now without winning'; and 'Don't tell those who have just come in the final result of this fantastic match, but just let's have another look at Italy's winning goal.'

It's not only commentators; managers have also added their words of wisdom over the years, calling on their vast experience and intimate knowledge of the game. Laurie McMenemy rewrote the history books when he reminisced: 'The last player to score a hat-trick in an FA Cup final was Stan Mortensen. He even had a final named after him – the Matthews Final.' When managing the Irish side, Jack Charlton observed that: 'If in winning the game we only finish with a draw, we will be fine.' Terry Venables profoundly predicted: 'If history is going to repeat itself, I should think we can expect the same thing again.' And just to prove that all those stories of footballers' superstitions are exaggerated, Terry O'Neill made it perfectly clear: 'I'm not superstitious or anything like that, but I'll just hope that we'll play our best and put it in the lap of the gods.'

To give them credit, though, there have been some moments of conscious wit from the experts, as when Brian Clough compared an England player rather unfavourably to the renowned Muhammad Ali: 'Trevor Brooking floats like a butterfly, and stings like one, too.' Danny Blanchflower, during Northern Ireland's march to the 1958 World Cup quarter-finals, told a bemused press conference that his side's game plan was to equalise before the other team scored. Danny also explained one of the game's finer points to the Duchess of Kent at the Tottenham–Leicester City FA Cup final in 1961. During her introduction to the two teams before the game, the Duchess pointed out to Danny that the Leicester players wore their names on the back of their track-suit tops and asked why Spurs didn't do likewise. Back came the impish reply: 'Well, ma'am, you see, we know one another.'

Two players who appeared to know one another very well were Leicester's Alan Birchenall and Tony Currie of Sheffield United. During a match in 1974 they both chased a long ball, collided on the slippery pitch and slid over the goal line, where they ended up right in front of the pitch-level TV camera. They each gave the viewers a huge smile, then threw their arms round each other's shoulders and exchanged a sloppy kiss, to the disgust of the 'clean-up TV' brigade, but the delight of the country's fans. Birchenall's performance was so convincing he later mischievously claimed to have received an offer to contribute to a German gay magazine.

Another classic screen moment came on the final day of the 1982/83 season when Luton Town, away to Manchester City, needed a win to stay in the First Division, and eventually got it. When the whistle blew after substitute Raddy Antic's late winner, Luton manager David Pleat came capering on to the Maine Road pitch dressed in a beige suit and performing the sort of bizarre celebratory dance that will be remembered long after the match itself has been forgotten. As if to prove that football is now more show business than sport, with the actual game only part of the entertainment package on offer, spectators at the 1998/99 Bristol City–Wolverhampton Wanderers game were entertained at half-time by the club mascots, City Cat and Wolfie, belying the wholesome, cuddly image they were meant to promote by entering into a form of unarmed combat that used to reduce Stuart Hall to fits of giggling when he presented *It's a Knockout*.

At least all that padding meant they were not seriously hurt. Arsenal defender Steve Morrow would have been grateful for a mascot suit after the 1993 Coca-Cola Cup final. In celebrating the 2–1 win over Sheffield Wednesday, Gunners skipper Tony Adams hoisted Morrow, scorer of the winning goal, into the air, then immediately dropped him. A month later Arsenal went on to beat Wednesday again in the FA Cup final, but without Morrow, who was suffering from a dislocated shoulder. An injury to match Morrow's in irony was suffered not by a player but by an international manager. At the end of Scotland's ill-fated 1978 World Cup campaign, a dejected Ally MacLeod was conducting his final press conference when a stray dog trotted up and sat beside him. Desperate for a little sympathy from the hard-nosed hacks after his team's dismal showing, MacLeod lamented: 'Look at me now, not a friend in the world, only this mongrel dog.' He then went to stroke his only friend, which promptly bit him.

Sources:
Barrett, N., *The Daily Telegraph Football Chronicle* (London: Carlton, 1999).

Hazlewood, N., *In The Way! Goalkeepers: A Breed Apart?* (Edinburgh: Mainstream, 1998).

Nicklin, F., *Carling: The Ultimate Football Fact and Quiz Book* (London: Stopwatch, 1997).

Tibballs, G., *Great Sporting Eccentrics* (London: Robson, 1997).

Further Reading:
Glanville, B. (ed.), *The Footballer's Companion* (London: Eyre & Spottiswoode, 1967).

Kelly, S. F., *Back Page Football: A Century of Newspaper Coverage* (Harpenden: Queen Anne Press, 1995).

Pickering, D., *Cassell Soccer Companion* (London: Cassell, 1997).

Tony Rennick

Imports

The presence of large numbers of foreign imports in British football is a relatively recent phenomenon. Although a number of non-British players did perform in the top divisions of the UK leagues before the late twentieth century, few were imported specifically to play football. Indeed, between 1931 and 1976 the English FA imposed a residential qualification which required professional players to have lived in the UK for two years. In 1978, the Football League lifted its ban on overseas players which, despite continued restrictions, led first to a trickle and then, in the 1990s, a steady flow of imports.

The vast majority of foreigners in British football before the 1980s played as amateurs. The first notable example was Nils Middleboe, a Danish international half-back who had competed in the 1908 and 1912 Olympics. Middleboe signed for Chelsea in 1913, making an immediate impact and going on to play 46 matches for the club over five seasons.

The immediate post-war decades represented a highpoint of foreign recruitment, with amateur internationals such as Switzerland's Willi Steffen at Chelsea, the Pole Stanislaw Gerula at Orient and Iceland's Albert Gudmundsson at Arsenal. Few of these players, however, stayed more than a season. Though not strictly an import, the German goalkeeper Bert Trautmann was undoubtedly the best known foreign footballer of the 1950s. An ex-prisoner of war, Trautmann stayed in Lancashire after hostilities had ended and signed for Manchester City from non-League St Helens in 1949. He went on to play 508 matches for City over 14 years, appearing in consecutive FA Cup finals in 1955 and 1956. Trautmann gained a winner's medal in his second final appearance, a match which he completed despite breaking his neck! At the end of that season he became the first foreigner to be voted Footballer of the Year.

Scandinavians remained the most common and prominent European imports during the 1950s and '60s. Few were as loyal as Hull City's Danish international full-back Viggo Jensen, who joined the club after impressing scouts at the 1948 London Olympics and stayed for nine seasons. By contrast, many of the Scandinavians who migrated to Britain, particularly Scotland, were regarded as mercenaries with a lack of long-term commitment to their clubs. The Swedish centre-forward Hans Jeppson played just 11 matches for Charlton Athletic during a business trip to London in 1951, but is remembered nonetheless for his instrumental role in saving the club from relegation.

Tottenham Hotspur's purchase of Osvaldo Ardiles and Ricardo Villa in 1978 represented a watershed in the importation of foreigners. Both had played in that summer's Argentinian World Cup winning squad and moved to England at the peak of their careers. Ardiles, in particular, made a significant and lasting impact on the English game. He spent nine years with Tottenham, interrupted only by the Falklands War, before embarking on a managerial career which took him to four English clubs, including his former employers in 1993, for a 16-month spell. Ipswich Town's recruitment of the Dutch pair Arnold Muhren and Frans Thijssen in 1978 was equally significant. Muhren and Thijssen brought an elegant quality to the Ipswich play which helped the club to challenge for domestic and European honours, most notably victory in the 1981 UEFA Cup.

Until the 1990s, few of the foreign imports in British football acquired the status of adopted heroes. This changed with the arrival of the French striker Eric Cantona in 1992. Cantona won the League Championship with Leeds United in his first season, but it was with Manchester United, whom he joined in November 1992, that he achieved sporting success and public acclaim. He helped the club to win its first Championship since 1968 in 1992/93, adding three further Championships, including two League and Cup doubles, before his retirement in 1997. Cantona was voted PFA Footballer of the Year in 1994 and Footballer of the Year in 1996, but also acquired a reputation for volatility.

A series of prominent international stars followed Cantona to the English Premiership from the mid-1990s. Germany's Jürgen Klinsmann had a successful season with Tottenham in 1994/95 and returned for a short spell towards the end of 1997/98. Similarly, the Dutch forward Dennis Bergkamp was crucial to Arsenal's 1998 League and Cup double. European legislation to free up the labour market, within Europe and the higher wages that can be earned relative to many of their domestic leagues, now mean that the best players in the English and Scottish leagues today are invariably foreign imports.

At the beginning of the 2000/01 season there were just over 200 foreign players in the Premiership and Nationwide League, with the largest contingent coming from Nordic countries.

Sources:

Lanfranchi, P. and Taylor, M., *Moving with the Ball: The Migration of Professional Footballers* (Oxford: Berg, 2000).

Taylor, M., 'Through the Net', *When Saturday Comes*, 156 (February 2000), 27–8.

Further Reading:

Maguire, J. and Stead, D., 'Border Crossings: Soccer Labour Migration and the European Union', *International Review of the Sociology of Sport*, 33: 1 (1998), 59–73.

See also Record Transfers

Matt Taylor

Independent Football Supporters' Associations

First formed in the mid 1980s, Independent Supporters Associations (ISAs) are a new type of fans' group that seeks to penetrate the power structures of professional football. Sharing many of the attitudes and frustrations of the Football Supporters Association (FSA), and employing many of its campaign tactics, ISAs have specific characteristics that give them a greater long-term chance of maintaining a vibrant and active membership, and so influencing club policies.

The first were started at Chelsea and QPR in 1986 and 1987, and fitted neatly into the mid- to late 1980s project of 'reclaiming' the image of fans away from journalists and politicians. These early ISAs, always operating independently of their clubs, recognised an agenda beyond the individual issues behind their creation (particularly fan representation), and provided administrative and ideological models for subsequent waves. By the mid 1990s, ISAs had been formed at over 35

professional clubs, largely run by upper-working or lower-middle class male fans with certain traditions of ecstatic participatory fandom. Brown argues that, for ISAs,

> what has been and is at stake is the ability of 'young white males' (and others) to go to a stadium to watch live football. They represent a fundamental regeneration of football fandom – politicised, sometimes carnivalesque, highly organised, uniquely popular.

Some significant elements of resistance to the modern football project have equally been found at ISAs in Southampton, Leicester City, Sheffield United and Newcastle United, seeking to protect the rights of 'genuine' fans and developing genuine consultative processes, and contesting many of the more commercial and exclusionary norms of the modern game.

Active at local and national levels, it is ISAs' club-based, local focus that gives them a huge advantage over the regionally-based FSA. Exploiting the FSA's own tactics (especially using local media to publicise issues and put pressure on clubs), ISAs have proved adept at making themselves key players at a number of clubs, and at some in particular have become central to consultative processes. IMUSA at Manchester United was also a key part of the relentless lobbying campaign against Sky's bid for United that resulted in its blocking by the Labour Government in 1999. Like the FSA, ISAs have generally been formed out of crisis, primarily if the team is performing poorly: this partly explains the rise of ISAs at Sheffield United and Southampton, two of the most active in the country.

As with the FSA however, ISA membership and activism can fluctuate violently: Sheffield United's ISA (BIFA) saw membership collapse from over 1,700 in 1995 to 300 two years later, after forcing unpopular chairman Reg Brealey to step down seemed to leave them without a role to play. Most have less than 2,000 members. Nonetheless, ISAs have replaced the FSA as the dominant form of organised fandom, and represent a well-organised, vocal section of the modern crowd.

Sources:

Brown, A., 'United We Stand: Some Problems With Fan Democracy', in A. Brown (ed.), *Fanatics! Power, Identity and Fandom in Football* (London: Routledge, 1998), pp. 50–67.

Nash, R., *Fan Power in the 1990s*, Ph.D. thesis, Department of Sociology, University of Liverpool, 1999.

Ruben, C., *Political Football*, MA dissertation, Department of Physical Education, Warwick University, 1993.

Further Reading:

BIFA official website: http://pine.shu.ac.uk/~cmssa/bifa.html

Hargreaves, J., *Sport, Power and Culture* (Cambridge: Polity Press, 1986).

Jary, D., Horne, J., and Bucke, T., 'Football 'Fanzines' and Football Culture', *Sociological Review*, 38: 2 (1991), 581–97.

King, A., 'The Lads: Masculinity and the New Consumption of Football', *Sociology*, 31: 2 (1997), 329–46.

Lee, S., 'Grey Shirts to Grey Suits: The Political Economy of English Football in the 1990s', in A. Brown (ed.), *Fanatics! Power, Identity and Fandom in Football* (London: Routledge, 1998), pp. 32–49.

See also Fans

Rex Nash

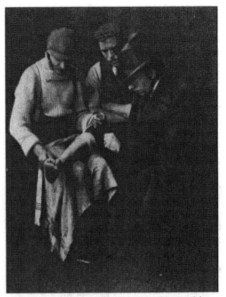

Doctor's morning – inspecting a damaged leg, 1906 (National Football Museum)

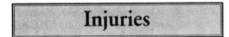

Injuries

An injury refers to a disability, acute or chronic, that interferes with the conduct of normal activity. There is no consensus as to what exactly constitutes an injury in football, but an operational definition would be one that precludes participating in the next game, or in training for two consecutive occasions. Injury statistics mostly include only those players who report for medical treatment. In Europe an estimated 50 to 60 per cent of all sports injuries, so defined – and 4 to 10 per cent of all injuries treated in hospitals – are due to football. Definition of the severity of an injury is also contentious, with main classifications of minor, moderate and major, depending on the length of time needed for recovery.

In calculating the risk of incurring a football injury, the real exposure of players must be considered. Exposure can be expressed as injuries likely per 1,000 hours of play. An alternative is to relate an injury to a corresponding player exposure rate, each match (90 minutes) representing 22 player exposures.

Most epidemiological studies indicate that injuries to footballers are about three times more likely in competition than in training. Furthermore, playing in the top professional League causes roughly twice the amount of injuries observed in corresponding reserve team matches, the incidence of injuries being intermediate between these two rates in top youth games.

The vast majority of football injuries – over two-thirds of the total – can be regarded as minor. About one-quarter are moderate in severity, necessitating absence from full activity for between one to four weeks. The remainder (about 10 per cent) cause absence for longer than one month and tend to be serious sprains or strains, or bone fractures.

Lower extremity injuries represent 65–88 per cent of the total injuries incurred by football players, both male and female, youth and adult. The most vulnerable joint is the knee (20 per cent) followed by the ankle (17 per cent). The remaining injuries are distributed among the regions of thigh (14 per cent), groin (13 per cent), leg (12 per cent), foot (12 per cent), back (5 per cent) and other (7 per cent). Some of the injuries can be caused by internal phenomena such as muscle weakness, imbalance between muscles that flex and extend the lower limb joints, asymmetry between left and right sides of the body, and poor flexibility – especially in the hamstrings and the adductor muscles on the inside of the thigh. Others can be due primarily to external influences, such as contact with another player, with the playing surface, and so on. These two factors interact: for example musculoskeletal deficiencies may render the player vulnerable when making tackles, or lack of fitness can be a limiting factor towards the end of a game.

Whilst many of the musculoskeletal injuries reported in football are common to sports participants in general, some are peculiar to the game. Among the relatively minor injuries are the contusions associated with bruising physical contact, and the occurrence of tears in hamstring muscles.

Professional players and youths in the clubs' 'football academies' benefit from modern physiotherapy methods available to them to hasten recovery. Groin strain is an umbrella term describing a range of specific soft-tissue injuries in this region, which can be more stubborn in responding to treatment. Injuries to the anterior cruciate ligament, a thin strand of tissue within the knee joint, compromises the joint's stability, and serious damage requires surgical treatment. The recovery is nowadays much faster than in previous decades, due to enhanced operative procedures and progressive rehabilitation regimes. The worst scenario is when anterior cruciate ligament damage is accompanied by trauma to the medial ligament (on the inside margin of the joint) and the medial cartilage (soft tissue on the end of the bones

that cushions impacts between adjacent bones of the lower and upper leg). Many players now resume their competitive activity after surgical repair of the affected tissues and appropriate systematic rehabilitation for an injury that used to terminate playing careers. Certain injuries, notably compound fractures of the lower leg bones, are not always adequately responsive to repair strategies and can prevent a return to top-level play.

The duration of professional footballers' active career in Britain now exceeds that of their counterparts in previous decades. The personal rewards for success in the game are powerful motivators to continue playing for as long as possible. Systematic injury prevention measures include proper pre-match warm-up, monitoring of fitness, post-match recovery strategies and rehabilitation when injured. Avoidance of over-training syndrome, due to training or competing excessively, is especially important in young players. A strategy for avoiding over-training injuries (including back injuries, Achilles tendonitis, psychological 'burn-out' and so on) is incorporated in the Football Association's *Charter for Quality* for the emergent academies developed in 1997 within approved professional soccer clubs.

Sources:
Ekblom, B. (ed.), *Handbook of Sports Medicine and Science Football (Soccer)* (Oxford: Blackwell Scientific Publications, 1994).

Further Reading:
Reilly, T. (ed.), *Science and Soccer* (London: E. & F. N. Spon, 1996).

Tom Reilly

Inter-Cities Fairs Cup

In 1950 Ernst Thommen, then vice-president of FIFA, proposed the establishment of an international competition between clubs, or city-wide teams, from cities which hosted industrial fairs. His idea was to give a competitive edge to friendly matches played between teams during trade fairs. Following a meeting in Basle in 1955 the first competition eventually got under way in June 1955, with a match between Basle and London. The regulations for the competition were drafted by Sir Stanley Rous. Essentially these were that only one team from a city could enter, that matches would coincide with the cities' trade fair, and that the competition would be called the International Industrial Inter-Cities Fairs Cup. The trophy was called the Noel Beard trophy. Two English teams entered – London, which was made up of the 11 professional teams playing in the capital, and Birmingham, which was represented by Birmingham City. The first competition was organised into four mini leagues with the four group winners qualifying for the semi-final. The first competition was scheduled to last two years, but because of fixture congestion it took three years to complete. The first final was a two-legged affair between London and Barcelona. Following a 2–2 draw in the first leg, Barcelona won the second leg 6–0 at the Nou Camp in front of 70,000 fans. The second Fairs Cup took two years to complete, 1958–60, but henceforth it would be an annual tournament running parallel with the European Cup and the newly established Cup Winners' Cup. This time, despite reluctance from the Fairs Cup committee, cities nominated their senior side to enter, rather than a city selecting its team. This created an anomaly of the Fairs Cup allowing teams to compete in two European club competitions simultaneously. They could represent their city in their Fairs Cup and qualify for the European Cup by winning their domestic championship. This situation lasted for one season, 1959/60, when teams such as Barcelona were still competing in the Fairs Cup and had qualified for the European Cup by becoming Spanish champions. By 1968 the competition had expanded to 48 clubs and had become a qualifying tournament based on league position. From the 1969/70 season the competition was renamed the Inter-Cities Fairs Cup, sometimes called the European Fairs Cup.

The last four years of the competition saw English winners – Leeds twice, in 1968 and 1971, Newcastle in 1969 and Arsenal in 1970. The competition was brought fully under UEFA control in 1971 and renamed the UEFA Cup. The first and last winners of the Fairs Cup, Barcelona and Leeds, competed for the original Noel Beard trophy with Barcelona beating Leeds 2–1 at Nou Camp in September 1971.

Until the 1996/97 season the UEFA Cup final was played over two legs. However, UEFA were keen to raise the prestige of the competition, while also alleviating fixture congestion. From 1998, the UEFA Cup final has therefore become a traditional showpiece final played on a neutral ground. If the two teams are level after extra time the final is decided on penalties.

Sources:

Radnedge, K. (ed.), *The Complete Encyclopedia of Football* (London: Carlton Books, 1998).

See also UEFA

Ray Physick

International Football

This entry will examine British international football, in particular the history of the British International Championship, a competition known as the Home Internationals. We shall also focus on the development of friendly matches against overseas opposition. The record of British sides in the World Cup and European Championships and the history of amateur internationals will be examined elsewhere.

The first official international match took place on 30 November 1872 at the West of Scotland cricket ground near Glasgow. An English 11, raised by Charles Alcock, secretary of the FA, took on a Scottish team with the aim of popularising football in Scotland. Although this game ended scoreless, it seemed to have the desired effect, as the Scottish FA was formed in March 1873, and the England–Scotland match became an annu-

England v Italy, Milan, May 1939

al fixture. It is worth noting that teams styled England and Scotland had met five times between 1870 and 1872 at London's Kennington Oval. The Scottish teams were drawn from London-based Scots, and these games are not regarded as full internationals.

Interest in football soon spread and the FA of Wales was founded in 1876, its first function being to select a team to play Scotland in Glasgow. Wales lost that debut game 0–4, and they also lost a return fixture at Wrexham 0–2. The Irish Football Association was formed in Belfast in November 1880, but Ireland's first international did not take place until 1882 when the team suffered a record 0–13 drubbing by England. Another significant development took place in 1882 when the four British associations met to discuss and agree the laws of the game. They then met annually, and in 1886 it was formalised as the International Football Association Board. The Board, upon which FIFA has been represented since 1913, is still responsible for determining the laws of football.

In the 1883/84 season, when Scotland met Ireland for the first time, the British International Championship was established, each country meeting the others over the course of the season. Scotland confirmed their status as Britain's leading team by winning the initial championship with a clean sweep of victories, and they, along with England, dominated the championship in its early years. The first breaches in this duopoly came in 1902/03 when Ireland was involved in a three-way tie, then in 1906/07 when Wales won the championship outright. Ireland won their first outright title in 1913/14, clinching matters with a 3–0 win over England at Middlesbrough. Between the wars the championship was dominated by Scotland, who won five outright titles between 1921 and 1926. Their chief rivals were Wales, winners of six outright championships between 1920 and 1937. Ireland played as Northern Ireland following partition and the formation of the FA of Ireland in 1921. Weakened by the loss of the Southern Irish players, they won only 12 matches between the wars. From 1946 England began to dominate the championship, and when the series ended in 1984 England had won 34 outright titles, Scotland 24, Wales seven and Northern Ireland three, including the final championship which they clinched on goal difference.

In both 1950 and 1954 the British Championship was designated a qualifying group for the World Cup. FIFA agreed to accept both the winners and runners-up, but in 1950, prior to the decisive match against England, the Scottish FA announced they would only go to the World Cup as group winners. England won 1–0, and despite appeals from both the Scottish and English captains the Scots did not go to Brazil. Four years later, although England again won the title, Scotland participated in Switzerland. The 1966/67 and 1967/68 competitions were combined to form a qualifying group for the 1968 European Championships, England again emerging triumphant even though Scotland had won the championship for 1966/67.

During the 1960s and 1970s the Home Internationals began to decline in significance and popularity as a result of the increasing importance of other international competitions at national and club level. From 1969 the championship was played in a short period at the end of the domestic season, but this innovation failed to increase its appeal. The only game to attract large crowds was the England v Scotland contest. In 1983 the FA and the Scottish FA agreed to continue this fixture, but to discontinue matches against the other home countries, bringing the championship to an end. England met Scotland annually until 1989, when the fixture was discontinued as a result of crowd disorder. Since then the countries have met only in European Championship matches.

For many years the only international matches played by British teams were the Home Internationals. England's first official international against foreign opposition came in June 1908 when they beat Austria 6–1 in Vienna, the first leg of a European tour that took in matches with Hungary and Bohemia. The first foreign team to visit England was Belgium, defeated 6–1 at Highbury in March 1923. Between 1910 and 1951, England also played a number of 'Commonwealth' internationals, mainly in South Africa and Australia, although these were accorded full international status. Scotland's first meeting with a European side came when they met Norway in May 1929, and Wales' first non-British opponent was France in May 1933. Northern Ireland also made their debut against foreign opposition against France, although not until 1951.

Although England played a considerable number of friendlies against foreign opponents, no British teams took part in the first three World Cups, despite invitations from FIFA, the result of a major dispute between the British associations and FIFA. In 1928 FIFA had agreed to allow broken-time payments for amateur players who participated in international matches. The British believed this would destroy the basis of amateur sport and they withdrew from FIFA, not returning until 1946. The absence of British teams weakened the standing of the early World Cups but probably did more damage to the home countries. It reinforced the insularity prevalent within British football and probably contributed to some disappointing performances on the world stage after 1950. While the Home Internationals were still important within Britain, the rest of the world was moving on. It was to be some time before that vital message was fully understood by those within British football.

As well as 'full' internationals, a range of other matches designed to provide crucial experience for younger players or those on the fringes of the international squad has developed since the Second World War. England played its first 'B' international against Finland in May 1949, and continued to play such fixtures into the early 1950s. These were discontinued until 1978 when a 'B' squad toured Asia and New Zealand, and have been played only sporadically from that point. More firmly rooted have been the games for younger players, with all home countries establishing under-23 sides from the early 1950s. From 1976, the designation changed to under-21, with the first game under the new order taking place between England and Wales at Wolverhampton in the December of that year. Following the abolition of the amateur/professional distinction in 1974, various discussions were held as to the best way of recognising leading non-league players. Eventually the FA introduced semi-professional internationals in 1979, with Scotland and Holland the first opponents. Wales joined the small group of nations that play international football at this level in 1984.

Sources:
Farror, M. and Lamming, D., *A Century of English International Football, 1872-1972* (London: Robert Hale, 1972).

Glanville, B., *The Story of the World Cup* (London: Faber & Faber, 1997).

Hayes, D., *England v. Scotland: The Auld Enemy* (Chorley: Sport in Word, 1996).

Lamming, D., *An England Football Internationalists' Who's Who 1872-1988* (Beverley: Hutton, 1990).

Lamming, D., *A Scottish Soccer Internationalists' Who's Who 1872-1986* (Beverley: Hutton, 1987).

Further Reading:
Davies, G. and Garland, I., *Who's Who of Welsh International Soccer Players* (Wrexham: Bridge Books, 1991).

Robinson, J., *The European Football Championships 1958-1992* (Cleethorpes: Soccer Book Publishing, 1992).

John Coyle

Irish Football

Football is presently Ireland's third most popular team game, having failed to wrest the nation's affections away from the Gaelic games of hurling and Gaelic football. Football has its Irish roots in the game of Cad, which was popular across the country from the time of its origins over a thousand years ago. While laws were implemented against the playing of such mob football games in England, such laws were never applied in Ireland. The Statutes of Kilkenny, which banned hurling in 1527, so that people might practise archery, did not mention Cad or any obvious variant of football in its list of undesirable pastimes. By the eighteenth century a ball game resembling mob football was widely played in the area around Dublin known as the Pale. In places such as Oxmantown, Kilmainham, Miltown and Drumcondra, men of various trades met together regularly to play their ball game.

The advent of modern codified football in Ireland is difficult to locate precisely. A general argument that has been made by several writers locates the arrival of football within the school and university system. Irish boys attending English Public Schools, where football was played, brought the game home with them: a game which then prospered within the Irish Universities, most notably Trinity College Dublin. Such arguments undoubtedly go some way in explaining the arrival of football in Ireland. However, football became a popular game in Ireland among all classes, but especially those lower down the social scale, and was not the preserve of a public school and university elite. The diffusion of football through the educational system in Ireland also fails to explain the advent, relatively quickly, of organised competitive football in Ireland.

The man who must take most credit for spreading football to Ireland is John M. McAlery. On his honeymoon in Scotland, McAlery watched a game of football and was captivated. In 1878 he arranged for Queen's Park and Caledonians to travel to Ireland to take part in an exhibition match to publicise the game. The match took place at the Ulster Cricket Club ground in Ballymafeigh. In the wake of the successful exhibition, McAlery formed Ireland's first football club, Cliftonville, in 1879. In 1880 he oversaw the foundation of the Irish Football Association (IFA). Founded nearly two decades after the FA, the IFA had the luxury of a model to follow. This explains, in part, the rapid development of an Irish Cup competition from 1881, an Irish League from 1890, and the playing of the first international match in 1882. That first international, against England, demonstrated that while off-field developments were moving ahead with pace, the footballing skills of the Irish left much to be desired. They lost the game 13-0.

While McAlery and his colleagues within the IFA quickly put competitive structures in place, Irish football was dominated by Ulster, and specifically Belfast interests. The Gaelic Athletic Association (GAA), which administered the various Gaelic games, banned its members from playing football as it was seen as a 'foreign' or 'garrison' game. In the early years of its existence, the IFA relied on the support of British troops in Ireland to make its competitions commercially viable. Thus while the Black Watch regiment and the Gordon Highlanders should be applauded for winning the Irish Cup in its early years, and the North Staffordshire Regiment, the Scottish Borders and Royal Scots recognised for their participation in the Irish League, their presence created problems for the national success of football. The IFA was spurned by the GAA, and many others who supported the Irish nationalist cause because of the role played by British military forces within the game. As a result, despite football's huge popularity across Ireland at the participatory level, the IFA-controlled game struggled to develop a genuinely national presence. It took until 1906 for a non-Belfast side to win the Irish Cup, and Shelbourne and Bohemians remain the only teams outside Ulster ever to have taken the Cup. The Irish League has never been won by a team outside of Ulster, and did not even leave the city of Belfast until 1952, when Glenavon were victorious.

The domination of football at the administrative and competitive level by Ulster was unhealthy, and, as a result of the political turmoil in Ireland between 1912 and 1922, could not last. In 1892, the Leinster Football Association had been formed, with the sanction of the IFA, to develop football in and around Dublin. Such a decision was a tacit admission that the IFA was viewed by many nationalists as an unpalatable body because of its perceived close links to the British administration and army presence in Ireland. In the years of the Irish revolution, teams from outside Ulster refused to play their fixtures because of the political situation. In 1919, all the Dublin clubs withdrew from the Irish league. With the official division between Northern Ireland and the Irish Free State (later the Irish Republic) in 1921, football split. The IFA administered football in the six Northern counties, while a new body, the Football Association of the Irish Free State (FAIFS), took control of the game in the 26 southern counties. The FAIFS copied the structures that had formerly existed under the IFA, and from the 1921 to 1922 season ran its own cup and league competitions. In 1923, football's world governing body, FIFA, admitted the FAIFS as a member. The first international played by an Irish team selected by the FAIFS was away to Italy in 1926, a game that was won by the home side 3–0.

Domestically, the competitions organised by the IFA and the successor to the FAIFS, the Football Association of Ireland (FAI), have developed with few problems since the 1920s. The IFA competitions have been dominated by Belfast teams, while those of the FAI have predominantly been the preserve of Dublin sides. Both the IFA and FAI competitions have struggled to attract large-scale support, and Irish football has always been overshadowed by the larger and more glamorous English and Scottish leagues. The interest in football outside Ireland has always been heightened by the long tradition of Irish players and managers travelling to Britain to pursue their football at the highest level.

Two issues have dominated Irish football in the twentieth century. The first was at the international level. In the wake of Irish independence, the home nations refused to recognise the FAIFS. It was not until the 1940s that the home nations agreed to begin playing matches against the Irish Republic. In 1949, at Goodison Park, the Irish Republic became the first foreign team to beat England on home ground, winning the game 2–0. The problems between the IFA and the FAI were compounded by their naming and selection processes. Despite a FIFA ruling in 1954, the IFA continued, until the 1960s, to describe its teams as Ireland, and not by their official title, Northern Ireland. Equally, it took until the 1950s for both Associations to recognise the border with respect to player selection. Until the 1950s, both the IFA and the FAI had selected their players from all 32 Irish counties. As a result, there is a small band of players within the record books, such as Manchester United's Johnny Carey, who played for both the Irish Republic and Northern Ireland. At the international level, both Northern Ireland and the Irish Republic have, considering the limited size of their respective populations and the relative weakness of their domestic leagues, performed respectably. Both international teams have qualified for the World Cup finals: Northern Ireland in 1958, 1982 and 1986, the Irish Republic in 1990 and 1994. The success of the Irish Republic's team in 1990, and their achievement of reaching a quarter-final match with hosts Italy, captivated the nation. While Italia '90, and four years later US '94, were joyous journeys for the Republic and their supporters, the second major theme in Irish football impacted on the Republic's participation in the World Cup finals.

The second important issue has been the sectarian tensions present within Ireland's football. The final qualifying game for the 1994 World Cup finals pitted Northern Ireland against the Republic of Ireland. At a time of heightened political tension, and against a backdrop of frequent paramilitary activity, the decision was made to exclude all away supporters from Northern Ireland's Windsor Park ground. The Republic qualified for the finals, and their first game was against Italy, a match they won 1–0. Amidst scenes of great celebration, members of the loyalist Ulster Volunteer Force entered a Catholic bar in Loughinisland and killed six men watching the game on television. The sectarian elements in Northern Irish society identified their targets by which of the two Irish football teams they chose to support. The problems of sectarianism, although impacting on international fixtures, have more normally affected the domestic game in Northern Ireland. Games between Catholic and Protestant teams have been a source of tension throughout the twentieth century. In 1948 the Catholic side Belfast Celtic played the Protestant team Linfield at the latter's Windsor Park ground. The game ended in a riot, during which the Belfast Celtic player, Jimmy Jones, had his leg broken. In response, the board of Belfast Celtic withdrew the team from the League, arguing that it was no longer possible for them to play football in such a climate of sectarian tension. The situation was heightened

from the late 1960s with the advent of the modern troubles in Northern Ireland. The centre for the early years of the troubles was Londonderry, and its football team, Derry City, inevitably became embroiled in what raged around them. Derry City played its football at the Brandywell, which was located in the predominantly Catholic Bogside area. From 1968 until 1972, Derry City's matches were regularly postponed or relocated because of security fears. From 1971, Derry City were ordered by the IFA to play all their home games at Coleraine's ground, as many Protestant teams within the League were refusing to travel to Londonderry because of the troubles. Derry City could not continue in such circumstances and they left the League in October 1972. The continuation of sectarian tensions, and the problems of Catholic teams in a predominantly Protestant league, have meant that Derry City has been relocated to the FAI league in the Irish Republic since 1984, and that other Catholic teams who have remained under the auspices of the IFA, such as Donegal Celtic and Cliftonville, have struggled to fulfil certain key fixtures because of sectarian tension.

Irish football has had a fascinating history. Its past has been influenced by the political landscape within which it is located, while the development of its football has been tempered by the larger leagues in England and Scotland.

Sources:
Brodie, M., *100 Years of Irish Football* (Belfast: Blackstaff, 1990).
Byrne, P., *Football Association of Ireland: 75 Years* (Dublin: 1996).

Further Reading:
Cronin, M., *Sport and Nationalism in Ireland: Gaelic Games, Soccer and Irish Identity Since 1884* (Dublin: Four Court Press, 1999).
Sugden, J. and Bairner, A., *Sport, Sectarianism and Society in a Divided Ireland* (London: Leicester University Press, 1993).

Mike Cronin

History Highlights 1920–1929

When football recommenced after the First World War the Football League First and Second Divisions were expanded to 22 clubs. Arsenal became the first ever team to win promotion other than by merit, to the newly expanded First Division; West Bromwich Albion were the first post-war champions in 1920; Liverpool became the first club to win consecutive championships in their expanded form in 1922 and 1923; but Huddersfield took the next three titles, thereby becoming the first team to win three consecutive championships.

Following the war the Cup final venue, Crystal Palace, was still under Army control. Between 1920 and 1922 the final was therefore held at Stamford Bridge. In 1923, the Cup final was moved to Wembley, then known as 'The Empire Stadium'. Bolton won the famous White Horse final, beating West Ham 2–0. For the first and only time the Cup left England, in 1927, when Cardiff beat Arsenal 1–0.

Perhaps the most significant development of the decade was the change to the offside rule. Up to 1925 a player was deemed offside when there were fewer than three players between the attacker and the opponent's goal line. This was changed to two players following a proposal by the Scottish FA in 1925. During the 1924/25 season 1,192 goals had been scored in the English First Division. The following season, under the new offside rule, this increased to 1,703 goals, an increase of 42 per cent, or an extra goal for every game played. This produced significant tactical changes as defences had to adapt. Prior to 1925 the centre-half played in the middle of the park, helping in defence and instigating attacks. Following the rule change the centre-half became a more defensive player, while the inside forwards fell back to play a midfield role. Herbert Chapman was responsible for introducing these tactical changes, which had a far-reaching influence

on the game. He also changed the role of the full-backs, who were pushed wider to mark the wingers, thereby allowing the two wing halves to perform midfield roles. The system became known as the W–M formation.

Two strikers took full advantage of the new offside rule, George Camsell of Second Division Middlesbrough and Bill 'Dixie' Dean of Everton. In the 1926/27 season, Camsell scored 59 goals, including nine hat-tricks. The following season Dean beat the record by scoring 60 goals in the First Division. Camsell's tally of nine hat-tricks is still a record, while Camsell and Dean remain the only two players to have scored more than 50 goals in a season, in either of the top two divisions.

In 1920 the Third Division was formed. All members forming the League, with the exception of Grimsby Town, had been members of the Southern League. Crystal Palace were its first champions. In the following year, it took on the title the Third Division (South) when the Third Division (North) was also formed. This was made up of clubs from the Lancashire Combination, the Midland League, the Cheshire League, the Central League and the North Eastern League. All teams had to be equipped for the professional game. Stockport were its first winners. Thus the Football League had grown from 44 clubs in 1919 to 86 clubs in 1921, a phenomenal growth since its foundation in 1888. Despite this growth the economic recession resulted in the maximum wage being reduced from £9 to £8 in 1922, while summer wages were set at a new maximum of £6.

The first live football radio broadcast, on 22 January 1927, was from Highbury, where Arsenal met Sheffield United. Easier identification of players was becoming essential in the new media age. Thus numbers on shirts were worn for the first time in 1928 by Arsenal and Chelsea, in separate matches against The Wednesday and Swansea respectively.

In 1928, *Athletic News* introduced a 'Spot the Ball' competition. Punters paid sixpence to enter, with a prize of £500 for the most accurate guess.

In Scotland the League title was won by Rangers eight times during the decade, with only Celtic breaking their dominance in 1922 and 1926. Rangers only did the double once, however – in 1928. In 1920/21 Rangers established a British points haul winning 76 points out of a possible 84.

A dispute between the First and Second Divisions threatened the dominant position of the Scottish League for a while. There was no automatic promotion to the First Division from the Second: promotion could only be won via election, a situation the traditional clubs abused. Consequently, the Second Division split away, forming a rebel Central League outside the jurisdiction of the Scottish League. The rebel clubs paid significantly higher wages than the League clubs. As a result clubs such as Dumbarton and Cowdenbeath began to attract players from Rangers and Celtic. The rebels won their point and from 1922 the Second Division was re-established with automatic promotion for the top two teams. In Northern Ireland, Belfast Celtic was very much the team of the decade, winning four consecutive League titles between 1926 and 1929.

Internationally, the British Football Associations' relationship with FIFA was severed in 1928, following a dispute over broken-time payments. This resulted in the home of football having no representatives competing for the first World Cup.

Scotland's Wembley wizards travelled south in 1928, thrashing England 5–1. The Scottish forward line of Jackson, Dunn, Gallacher, James and Morton became immortalised as Scotland's greatest ever attacking force. It was also the first season in which England lost all three home internationals. Moreover, in 1929 England suffered its first defeat to a non-British team, losing 4–3 to Spain in Madrid.

Sources:

Kelly, S. F., *Back Page Football: A Century of Newspaper Coverage* (London: Queen Anne Press, 1988).

Radnedge, K. (ed.), *The Complete Encyclopedia of Football* (London: Carlton Books, 1998).

Ray Physick

Knighthoods

When England played Argentina in a Wembley friendly in February 2000 the crowd of over 74,000 observed a minute's silence. Players wore black armbands as they stood in silent tribute to Sir Stanley Matthews, who had died a few days earlier in a Stoke hospital following a fall on holiday in Tenerife. Sir Stan, as he was affectionately known, was 85 when he died, and was the first professional footballer to be knighted when he received the accolade in 1965. He also remains the only footballer to have been knighted while still playing professionally. Born in Hanley on 1 February 1915, he made his League debut for Stoke City at the age of 17, his dedication to the game and to his personal fitness enabling the 'wizard of dribble', the world's best remembered outside-right, to enjoy an amazingly long career at the game's highest level. He was apparently in the veteran stage when he moved to Blackpool in 1947, but helped the Seasiders to three Wembley finals, although it was not until 1953, after the historic 'Matthews Final' against Bolton Wanderers, that he finally earned an FA Cup winner's medal. By now he was 38, but there was much more to come. He had earned his first England call-up at the tender age of 19, but he was 41 when he earned the last of his 54 international caps in 1957. He re-signed for Stoke in 1961, at the age of 46, and so popular was his return that his home debut attracted a crowd of over 35,000; a mere 8,000 had turned up for the previous game at the Victoria Ground. He helped Stoke to the Second Division championship in the 1962/63 season, repeating a similar success an incredible 30 years earlier. His last League game (his 71st) for the Potters, against Fulham in a 1965 First Division fixture, came five days after his 50th birthday and made him the oldest player ever to appear in the top flight. He was the first winner of the Football Writers' Player of the Year award in 1948, and won it again in 1963. He was also the first European Footballer of the Year in 1956. To go with

Sir Stanley Matthews attends the last game at the Victoria ground, May 1997
(National Football Museum)

his remarkable talent he had an innate sense of sportsmanship; he was never booked throughout his illustrious career. The first footballing knighthood could not have been awarded to a more worthy, or popular, recipient.

A contemporary of Stanley Matthews, and to some a more complete player, was Tom Finney, the 'Preston Plumber' who was born in the Lancashire town on 5 April 1922. He spent his whole professional career with unfashionable Preston North End and was knighted in 1998. While Matthews was a traditional right-winger who invariably beat his full-back on the outside before delivering a pin-point cross, Finney could play on either wing and also at centre-forward. Indeed, of his 76 England caps earned between 1946 and 1958, 40 were as outside-right, 33 as outside-left and three as leader of the attack. He had a powerful shot in either foot and was a prolific goal-scorer, his 30 goals for England standing as a record for many years. His final game for Preston came at Deepdale on 30 April 1960 and marked the end of an era: a crowd of over 27,000 sang Auld Lang

Syne, accompanied by a brass band. The players and officials joined in as they lined up with linked hands on the pitch. At the end of the game Tom Finney made a farewell speech before retiring from football to concentrate on his plumbing business. It was this local business that had kept him a home-town player for almost two decades, without a single domestic honour to show for it.

The only two other footballing knights to have earned the honour solely for their playing abilities are Bobby Charlton and Geoff Hurst, both members of England's World Cup-winning side of 1966. Charlton's knighthood came in 1994, Hurst's four years later.

Bobby Charlton was born in Ashington, Northumberland on 11 October 1937 into the famous Milburn family (the legendary Jackie Milburn, the Newcastle United and England centre-forward, was his mother's cousin). A bright lad, Bobby earned a scholarship to Morpeth Grammar School, but the football world will be eternally grateful that he did not take up the offer. In the words of his primary school headmaster, Mr James

Hamilton: 'It's one of those snooty schools where they play rugby. We got him transferred to the grammar school at Bedlington.' It was an inspired move. Bobby was selected as a trialist for the England schoolboys' side and it was at this game, at Maine Road, Manchester, that Matt Busby first saw him in action. In 1953 the young Bobby signed as an amateur for Manchester United and turned professional the following year. He scored twice on his first-team debut, appropriately against Charlton Athletic in 1956, and a glittering career was born. He survived the Munich air crash in February 1958 and in April of that year earned his first England cap, scoring against Scotland. His last cap came in 1970, and his total of 106 appearances for his country remained an England record until Bobby Moore eclipsed it in 1973. His total of 49 England goals still stands as a record, however. His 754 senior appearances for United brought him another 247 goals, and he helped the Old Trafford club to win the European Cup in 1968, the FA Cup in 1963 and the Football League Championship in 1957, 1965 and 1967. In 1966, as well as picking up a World Cup medal, he was voted Footballer of the Year not only in England, but also in Europe. After leaving Old Trafford in 1973 he had brief managerial spells with Preston North End – where he netted a further 8 times in 38 appearances as player-manager – and with Wigan Athletic, before returning to United in 1984 to take up a seat on the board and to run the club's coaching school. Bobby Charlton will be remembered not only for his powerful long-range shooting with either foot and his ability to pass defenders at speed, but for his sportsmanship and his inherent modesty. He remains one of the game's best-loved ambassadors.

Charlton's fellow knight from the 1966 World Cup triumph, Geoff Hurst, was born on 8 December 1941 in Ashton-under-Lyne, the son of an Oldham Athletic half-back. It was not with a Lancashire club that he made his name, however, but with West Ham United, for whom he signed as a professional in 1959, initially as a wing-half. In his first two seasons with the club he failed to make an impact, making only eight League appearances, but when manager Ron Greenwood moved him up to centre-forward his career blossomed. He helped West Ham to FA Cup victory in 1964, and the following season – during which he netted 40 times – he returned to Wembley with the Hammers when they won the European Cup Winners' Cup. He will always be remembered, however, for his third consecutive appearance in a Wembley final, when he scored a hat-trick in England's historic 1966 World Cup victory over West Germany. He remains the only player to achieve this feat in a World Cup final, yet he almost never made the team. Considered by many pundits of the day to be only a peripheral choice for Alf Ramsey's England squad, he only made the side after an injury to Jimmy Greaves in the group match against France. Hurst was selected for the ill-tempered quarter-final against Argentina and scored the only goal of the game with a header from a cross by West Ham team-mate Martin Peters. In the semi-final against Portugal Hurst laid on the pass that provided Bobby Charlton with England's second goal in a 2–0 victory, and then came his memorable three goals in the final itself, his third goal (and England's fourth) immortalised by Kenneth Wolstenholme's famous 'They think it's all over – it is now!' Geoff Hurst's England career lasted until 1972 and brought him a total of 24 goals from 49 appearances. He played 410 League games for West Ham, scoring 180 goals, before moving to Stoke City in 1972. He had spells as player-manager with Cork Celtic and Telford United before spending 18 months as manager of Chelsea. He then concentrated on his insurance business, but by 2000 he was chairman of the FA Premier League Hall of Fame at London's County Hall and, alongside his 1966 team-mate Bobby Charlton, a leading ambassador for England's 2006 World Cup bid.

Other footballing knights have received the honour not for their playing prowess but for their managerial flair. The first of these was Walter Winterbottom, who took charge of the England side in 1946 and stayed at the helm, first as chief coach and then, after an embarrassing 1–0 defeat by Switzerland in Zurich in 1947, as the national side's first full-time manager, a position he held until 1962. The title of manager was somewhat misleading, however, as the team was picked by a selection committee of club directors, and Winterbottom, who had no experience of club management, saw his chief role as a coaching one. Indeed, it was Winterbottom, ex-Manchester United half-back turned RAF PE instructor, who presided over the FA's coaching scheme, launched in the early 1950s. He was also instrumental in setting up the England Under-23 team. He led England in four World Cup tournaments, in 1950, 1954, 1958 and 1962, and remains the longest-serving England boss of all time. He was in charge for a total of 139 matches during his tenure and was knighted in 1978.

When Walter Winterbottom resigned as England manager after the 1962 World Cup in Chile he was replaced by Alf Ramsey who, unlike his predecessor, had an impressive record at club level. Beginning his professional career as a right-back with Southampton in 1946, the Dagenham-born Ramsey moved to Tottenham Hotspur in 1949 and was a member of the Spurs side that won the Second Division in 1950 and the First Division the following year. He won 32 England caps between 1948 and 1953, one of his three goals coming in the infamous 6–3 Wembley humiliation at the hands of Hungary in 1953, before retiring as a player in 1955. That year he became manager of Ipswich Town, then in the Third Division (South). He led the unfashionable Suffolk side to the divisional title in the 1956/57 season, and then shocked the football world by leading his 'Ramsey's Rustics' to championships of the Second Division in 1961 and the First Division in 1962. What he had achieved as a player with Tottenham he had repeated as Ipswich manager. The professionalism and dedication he brought to the job, and his opinion of 'amateurs', were epitomised while he was watching Ipswich's reserves in action. The club chairman, eager to congratulate Ramsey on the club's surprise championship success, was dismissed with

a terse: 'Do you mind, I'm working.' This was the dedication the national side needed. He was appointed England manager in 1963 and claimed his place in football history by leading his side to World Cup final success in 1966. His memorable team talk during the interval before extra time in that classic encounter against West Germany included the inspirational: 'You've beaten them once, now go and do it again. Look at them, they're knackered.' Prophetic words indeed. He remained in charge until 1974, when he was sacked after England's failure to qualify for the 1974 World Cup. His record remains impressive, however: of the 123 matches played under his leadership 78 were won, 32 drawn and only 13 lost. Alf Ramsey was knighted in 1967, becoming the game's first managerial 'Sir'.

Two other managers have received knighthoods, both Scotsmen and both for their achievements at Manchester United. Matt Busby, born in Lanarkshire in 1909, had a relatively undistinguished playing career, his only honours being a single international cap (against Wales in 1933) and an FA Cup winner's medal for Manchester City in 1934. His success as a manager at Old Trafford was remarkable, however. After his playing days with Manchester City and Liverpool were over he was appointed United manager in 1945, and led them to FA Cup success in 1948, when they beat Blackpool 4–2. First Division championships followed in 1952, 1956 and 1957, and United were only denied the elusive League and FA Cup 'double' in the latter year by Aston Villa, who triumphed 2–1 at Wembley. The following year saw the promising young United team, popularly known as 'Busby's Babes', all but destroyed in the Munich disaster, but Busby himself survived the catastrophic events of 6 February 1958 to rebuild the side. A scratch team of juniors, reserves and new signings hastily brought into the club played Sheffield Wednesday at Old Trafford in the fifth round of the FA Cup only nineteen days after Munich, and won 3–0. United went on to beat West Bromwich Albion and Fulham to reach Wembley for a second successive year, but the fairy-tale the whole footballing nation wanted to believe in ended with Bolton Wanderers scoring twice without reply. Busby, who had built one great team, began to build another that went on to dominate the game in the 1960s. With stars such as Bobby Charlton (like his manager, a Munich survivor), George Best and Denis Law, United won the FA Cup in 1963, and the League Championship in 1965 and 1967. In 1968 Busby finally achieved what he had been convinced his 'Babes' could accomplish: victory in the European Cup. United's resounding 4–1 defeat of Benfica at Wembley brought the coveted trophy to England for the first time since its inception and earned Busby his knighthood that year. It also proved his swan-song: the following January he announced his retirement from management. He was appointed to United's board in 1971 and became club president in 1982.

If the 1960s belonged to Matt Busby, then the 1990s were Alex Ferguson's. Born in Govan, Glasgow, in December 1941, Ferguson joined amateur side Queen's Park as an inside-forward in the summer of 1958 and spent two years at Hampden before moving on to St John-stone. His other clubs included Dunferm-line, Rangers, Falkirk and Ayr United. During his playing career he won Scotland caps at amateur, schoolboy, youth and senior levels, but it is as an inspirational manager that he will be remembered. After cutting his managerial teeth at East Stirlingshire and St Mirren, he became Aberdeen manager in 1978 and led the Pittodrie outfit to three Scottish League Championships (1979/80, 1983/84 and 1984/85), four Scottish Cup victories (1982, 1983, 1984 and 1986) and the Scottish League Cup in 1986. In 1983 Aberdeen won their first European trophy, beating the illustrious Real Madrid 2–1 in the Gothenburg final. Such a record brought Ferguson to the attention of Manchester United, and he crossed the border to Old Trafford in November 1986. Success was not immediate, and it was 1990 before he landed his first trophy, the 1990 FA Cup, after a replay against Crystal Palace, but the flow of silverware into the Old Trafford trophy cabinet continued apace throughout the next decade. In 1991

skipper Bryan Robson lifted aloft the European Cup Winners' Cup after a 2–1 victory over Barcelona in Rotterdam. In 1992 United won their first-ever Football League Cup, beating Nottingham Forest by a single Wembley goal. The following season, 1992/93, United won their first League (by now the FA Premier League) championship since 1967, finishing ten points clear of Arsenal. The following season they not only retained the Premiership title but also lifted the FA Cup after demolishing Chelsea 4–0 in the Final. United's dreams of a remarkable 'treble' were dashed by Aston Villa, who won the Coca-Cola Cup (formerly the League Cup) final by the surprising margin of 5–1, but United's efforts that season made them only the fourth side in the twentieth century to lift the League Championship and the FA Cup in the same season.

Sadly Sir Matt Busby was not to witness the Reds' latest triumph: he had passed away on 20 January 1994 at the age of 84. The 1994/95 season was something of an anticlimax, as United finished second in the Premiership and lost the FA Cup final to Everton, but in 1995/96 they bounced back with another 'double', ending the Premiership season four points clear of Newcastle United and beating Liverpool 1–0 in the FA Cup final. The Premiership crown was retained in 1996/97, but the following season United didn't win a trophy. The glory days were far from over, however. Ferguson ended the 1990s in an unprecedented blaze of glory with an amazing 'treble' in the 1998/99 season: the Premiership trophy, the FA Cup and the Champions' League trophy (formerly the European Cup) all found their way to Old Trafford. Not surprisingly, Alex Ferguson was knighted in 1999 and it was as Sir Alex that he led Manchester United to Premiership success yet again in the 1999/00 season, ready for yet another assault on Europe.

If these are the footballing knights familiar to today's fans, they are, however, not the only individuals to have been so honoured. In 1927 Charles Clegg, FA president, became the first football administrator to be knighted for his services to the game. Frederick Wall, who became FA secretary in 1894 and held the post for the next forty years, became Sir Frederick in 1930. In 1949 the visionary Stanley Rous, who had refereed the 1933/34 FA Cup final before becoming secretary of the FA, was knighted for his part in returning England back into the FIFA fold and thence to the World Cup for the first time. He also pioneered the Inter-Cities Fairs Cup, which became the UEFA Cup.

In more recent times Denis Follows, who succeeded Sir Stanley Rous in 1962, and FA chairman Bert Millichip have been dubbed, but such honours have merited little attention on the nation's back pages. To the dedicated followers of the beautiful game, the first footballing knight of the twentieth century was Sir Stan, and the last Sir Alex.

Sources:

Barrett, N., *The Daily Telegraph Football Chronicle* (London: Carlton, 1999).

Kelly, S. F., *Fergie: The Biography of Alex Ferguson* (London: Headline, 1997).

Matthews, P. and Buchanan, I., *The All-Time Greats of British and Irish Sport* (Enfield: Guinness, 1995).

Nawrat, C. and Hutchings, S., *The Sunday Times Illustrated History of Football: The Post-War Years* (London: Chancellor Press, 1996).

Further Reading:

Glanville, B., *Football Memories* (London: Virgin, 1999).

Glanville, B. (ed.), *The Footballer's Companion* (London: Eyre & Spottiswoode, 1967).

Russell, D., *Football and the English* (Preston, Carnegie Publishing, 1997).

Tony Rennick

Law

The law encroaches upon football in a number of different ways, from regulating behaviour on the playing field to controlling the buying and selling of clubs. Different areas of law can be applied to different aspects of football. For example, it is criminal and tort law that regulates on-field relationships between players and contract law that governs the position of clubs and the players they employ. Competition law can be used to control aspects of the commercial practices that increasingly dominate football, such as the buying and selling of television rights. Parliament has also intervened to pass numerous pieces of legislation that have sought to address issues of stadium safety and the control of football fans.

As football is a physical contact sport, there are numerous examples of players being injured on the field of play. Most of these injuries occur during the normal course of play and are accepted as one of the risks that players run. However, if injuries are deliberately or carelessly inflicted it is possible that some form of legal action can result. A criminal assault on the football field is the same as an assault carried out elsewhere, and the fact that it takes place during the course of sport does not provide any immunity. There are a number of examples of players being convicted for on-field assaults. The overwhelming majority of these relate to amateur football, particularly where off-the-ball retaliation has taken place. Ordinary physical contact that takes place during the normal course of the game is not actionable even if injury results. For a criminal prosecution to succeed there must be some evidence of intent or recklessness on behalf of the perpetrator. In theory, a police officer who witnesses an assault, such as a punch or deliberate elbow, on the pitch could arrest and charge the offender. Due to the potential public order problems with spectators that this might cause it generally does not happen. Perhaps the most infamous example of an assault inside the ground was that carried out by Manchester United's Eric Cantona, at Selhurst Park in 1995, on a supporter who abused him as he walked from the ground after being sent off. Cantona was originally sentenced to a term of two weeks' imprisonment, though on appeal this was reduced to 120 hours of community service. Cantona was also banned by both his club and the football authorities but returned, to resume his career.

Events on the field have led to instances of players suing each other for injuries that have occurred. However, this is a fairly recent phenomenon, with the first example of a negligence action taking place only in 1985. This case, *Condon v. Basi*, concerned an incident during an amateur match but there have been more recent examples of professional players resorting to the courts. In 1994 Paul Elliot brought an unsuccessful action against Dean Saunders and Liverpool FC, while Gordon Watson succeeded in his 1999 claim against Kevin Gray and Huddersfield Town for the career-threatening injury that Watson received in a carelessly executed tackle. The increased level of players' salaries now means that professional players have a great deal to lose if a career is cut short by injury. This type of litigation, over careless tackles that cause injury, is likely to increase unless some form of alternative compensation scheme is put in place.

As professional football has developed economically, areas of commercial law have become more applicable. The legal status of some of the leading clubs has altered as the model of the football club as a public limited company has emerged. Such clubs are open to takeovers, and this may involve the use of competition law: BSkyB's attempted purchase of Manchester United plc was disallowed as being contrary to the public interest. Similarly, the packaging and sale of the broadcasting rights to matches has been investigated for potential breaches of competition law. As clubs have sought to maximise areas of merchandising, the law has been used to prevent unlicensed traders selling copies of 'official' products.

The increasing incursion of law into football needs to be set against a context of increasing litigation throughout society more generally. The greater the level of commercialisation of football, and the more football develops as a multi-million pound business, the greater will be the use of the law to resolve disputes as, financially, more is at stake. At an amateur level, however, the use of the law will be much less frequent, and is more likely to revolve around what happens on the field than in the boardroom.

Source:
Dunning, E., *Sport Matters* (London: Routledge, 1999).

Steve Greenfield and Guy Osborn

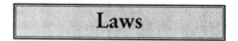

Laws

– *see* Rules

Lilleshall

Lilleshall Hall in Shropshire is now synonymous with the pursuit of sporting excellence, most notably through its association with football.

Located near Newport, Lilleshall Hall was originally built in 1829 as a hunting lodge for the Duke of Sutherland, and the architect was the highly regarded Sir Jeffry Wyatville. In 1951 it became a National Sports Centre. The funds for its acquisition and initial development as a sports centre had become available through a fund-raising effort in South Africa that had occurred in appreciation of the United Kingdom's assistance during the Second World War. During the 1950s and 1960s, with further government investment, the facilities were developed to enable Lilleshall Hall fully to fulfil the role of a National Sports Centre. With 30 acres of playing fields, a variety of artificial surfaces, tennis courts and extensive indoor facilities, it became a magnet for sports organisations and members of the sports community who wished to pursue sporting excellence in a highly professional and supportive context. With its residential capacity of 180, the National Sports Centre was an attractive venue for courses for coaches as much as the sportsmen and sportswomen under their supervision and guidance. In particular it became associated with the coaching programmes of the British Amateur Gymnastics Association and the Football Association.

By the 1970s it was the main coach education and coaching centre for the FA. Literally thousands of coaches and footballers have passed through programmes at Lilleshall Hall, and such programmes continue to this day.

It is the establishment in 1984 of the FA's National School for Football that warrants Lilleshall's special place in footballing history. The National School was a major attempt to promote excellence in football coaching and education by providing teenage boys with the opportunity to develop their footballing skills on a full-time residential basis, while still continuing their more conventional education at the Shropshire LEA's Idsall Comprehensive School in nearby Shifnal. This pioneering residential initiative was significant in two ways: boys were enabled to develop in this intensive regime in readiness for a professional playing career; but it also provided a model from which politicians evolved the concept of funding specialist sports colleges within the state education sector. The emergence of such colleges was not, however, the reason for the decision to close this unique and specialist School in 1999. Rather, it was its very success which led various senior football clubs to establish their own club-based academies, which have now come to fulfil a similar role at local level.

Among the 200 or so boys who passed through its programme the names of Michael Owen, Joe Cole and Nick Barmby can serve to illustrate that Lilleshall Hall drew together a number of players who were to prove very prominent in the first-class game at the turn of the millennium.

See also Coaching

Trevor James

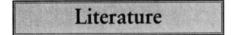

Literature

Amid the great mass of sporting literature thrown up in the last half century or so, decent creative writing about soccer scarcely exists.

Viewed from the perspectives of literary criticism, it is hard to disagree with D. J. Taylor's observation on the predicament

The Boys' Realm of Sport and Adventure
(National Football Museum)

of football writing. The general avoidance of the topic by 'serious' writers, and the often patronising or negative reception given to books that try to reverse this trend, illustrates the game's relatively low cultural status for most of its history. In earlier periods, only Arnold Bennett and J. B. Priestley, among 'leading' novelists (an extremely subjective term, of course), gave the game any sort of attention. Bennett's knowledgeable and witty coverage of the rivalry between Knype and Bursley (a thinly-disguised Stoke City and Port Vale) in *The Card* (1911) contains amusing comment both on the links between local political ambition and the football field, and on the lifestyles of professional footballers:

Both [clubs] employed professionals, who, by a strange chance, were nearly all born in Scotland; and both also employed trainers, who, before an important match, took the teams off to a hydropathic establishment, far, far, distant from any public-house. (This was called 'training'.)

Priestley's *The Good Companions* (1929) actually contains very little at all about football, but his ability to capture, in an early section, its attractions for a working-class community, and the novelty of his willingness even to do so in a work of some literary ambition, means that the following passage thoroughly deserves its frequent citation.

It turned you into a member of the community, all brothers together for an hour and a half, for not only had you escaped from the clanking machinery of the lesser life, from work, wages, rent, doles, sick pay, insurance cards, nagging wives, ailing children, bad bosses, idle workmen, but you had escaped with most of your mates, and your neighbours, with half the town, and there you were, cheering together, thumping one another on the shoulders, swapping judgments like lords of the earth, having punched your way through a turnstile into another and altogether more special kind of life.

Amongst more recent works, *The Thistle and the Grail* (1954) by Scottish novelist Robin Jenkins provides a closely observed portrait of junior football, and gained rather belated critical praise in the 1990s. Keith Alldritt celebrates Sir Edward Elgar's keen support of Wolverhampton Wanderers in his *Elgar on the Journey to Hanley* (1979), while, at a very different social level, Barry Hines' *A Kestrel for a Knave* (1968) contains an exquisite portrait of a school games lesson. Mr Sugden, the bullying games master forced by cold weather to pretend to be Bobby Charlton rather than Denis Law ('It's too cold to play as a striker today. I'm scheming this morning, all over the field like Charlton') was later immortalised in the film adaptation *Kes* (1969) by ex-games teacher and wrestler, Brian Glover. As football's cultural status began to rise from the late 1980s and early 1990s, a number of novelists including Martin Amis, Julian Barnes and Irvine Welsh included football references in their work. D. J. Taylor has also tried to remedy the literary deficiencies he has identified, in *The English Settlement* (1996), a novel concerning the employment of an American business consultant by a strug-

gling Fourth Division side.

Whether the majority of fans have been greatly concerned by the game's marginal position within literary culture is debatable. For many, the often hastily written and formulaic fiction that has long surrounded the game has proved a popular source of easy pleasure and an aid to fantasy and imagination. The largest market for such works has probably always been among children, teenagers and young males, and it is often hard to decide which of these groups specific titles have been aimed at.

Sports stories were to be found in late Victorian boys' magazines, but it was probably in the early 1920s that popular football fiction really took hold, possibly reflecting the surge of interest in the game that followed the resumption of 'normality' after the First World War. A key figure here was Sydney Horler who produced almost twenty titles between *Goal* (1920) and *Whilst the Crowd Roared* (1949). His two major creations were Angus McPhee, a Scottish trainer-coach, and Tiger Standish, who combined work for British intelligence with an outstanding career as a free-scoring centre-forward. Horler also contributed to the *Aldine Football Novels* series, which ran to 88 titles between 1925 and 1931. The Aldine books and the Amalgamated Press's *Football and Sports Library* were the best known of a number of series of short (64 pages was a common format), cheap (4d or 6d) novels aimed largely, although not exclusively, at a teenage market. These works married various popular fictional genres and featured an easily recognisable gallery of standard characters drawn from the traditions of melodrama, including loveable working-class backroom staff, crooked directors, scheming and evil foreigners and virtuous females. The romantic interest in these stories was a prominent feature: in *What's the Matter with Millport* (1922), the hero's beloved even manages to collapse into his arms on the pitch, her flight from kidnappers coinciding with his dispatch of a vital FA Cup goal. Interestingly, the heroes were often amateurs, or, if professional, only driven to that state by loss of memory or ill fortune. Ginger Gee, hero of the great Marigolds FC in Jock MacPherson's *Stick it Ginger!* (1922), for example, turns out not to be the 'gutter urchin' he appears, but the long-lost son of a wealthy army general. This emphasis on the amateur tradition in books aimed at working-class audiences, although partly a stylistic borrowing from the public school story, does suggest that there were still suppressed concerns about the professional game at this time, and a desire to celebrate the sporting leadership of the disinterested amateur. The appearance of a small cluster of titles in these series about the women's game in the early 1920s is suggestive of both its popularity at the time and the strength of the debates it engendered.

Although some of these traditions continued in boys' comics into the 1950s and beyond, popular football novels tended to take rather different directions from about the 1940s, although the levels of production never again reached those of the 1920s and early 1930s. The success of Leonard Gribble's *The Arsenal Stadium Mystery* (1939), which was made into a successful film in the same year, and *They Kidnapped Stanley Matthews* (1950), led to a steady trickle of football-related crime novels which has continued to the present day. Football certainly featured to varying degrees in P. B. Yuill's 'Hazell' stories, published in the mid 1970s, and detailing the life of a London-based private detective. 'Yuill' was in fact the pen name of a writing partnership between Gordon Williams and the then Queen's Park Rangers player, Terry Venables. (Their earlier futuristic novel, *They Used to Play on Grass*, had appeared in 1971.) A TV series followed.

In an age when tabloid journalism eagerly explored the personal lives of the emerging football superstar, the 1970s and 1980s saw the beginnings of the 'adult' football novel, with a new emphasis on sex and personal problems. Typical here were the four Jackie Groves novels produced by journalist Norman Giller and ex-England international Jimmy Greaves between 1979 and 1981, featuring a maverick American-born striker. The punning title of *The Ball Game* (1980), a story that charts Jackie's adventures with militant feminists during a spell back in America, suggests the subject of much of the action in these stories. Nevertheless, the accompanying focus on the use of alcohol as a way of coping with the pressures of the game does gain a certain interest and resonance from Greaves' own well-publicised battles against alcoholism. Novels of this type have, in keeping with popular literature in general, become ever more sexually explicit from the 1970s. Sex certainly plays a major role in a distinctive genre of the 1990s, the hooligan novel. Although novels and short stories focusing on this issue were not unknown before this period – Dick Morland's *Albion! Albion!* (1974) was probably the first – the decline of hooliganism within grounds, coupled with the enormous changes that took place in the structure and marketing of football in the 1990s, seems to have created an imaginative space within which hooligans can be viewed by readers as a safely distanced but still intriguing source of vicarious pleasure. Key titles in this context include Gavin Anderson's *Casual* (1996), Eddy Brimson's *Hooligan* (1998), Kevin Sampson's *Awaydays* and John King's *The Football Factory* (1996 – probably the most commercially successful of the genre), *Headhunters* (1997) and *England Away* (1998).

A body of creative writing also exists which to some extent stands outside the broad categories noted above. Sports journalist Brian Glanville has produced a steady flow of novels and short stories since the 1950s, many of which deal rather more seriously with lives and problems within the football world. Glanville's short story collections, such as *Goalkeepers are Crazy* (1964), have received a warm critical reception. Equally lauded in some quarters was J. L. Carr's *How Steeple Sinderby Wanderers won the FA Cup* (1975), a gentle fantasy charting the progress of a village side to Wembley in the 1930s. Its greatest attraction is perhaps provided by brilliant parodies of various journalistic styles.

So far in this discussion, 'football literature' has been equated with 'creative fiction', but the phrase should also cover the large body of factual, investigative writing that the game has always attracted. The 1950s was something of a watershed in this regard, and the work of Percy Young, an academic musicologist by profession, played an important role in setting the standard. Alongside a number of club and general football histories, his *Football: Facts and Fancies* (1950), *The Appreciation of Football* (1951) and *Football Year* (1956) represented romantic but intelligent attempts to define and describe the game's character and appeal. Much of the best work that followed in this vein came from sports journalists such as Brian Glanville, Geoffrey Green and Hugh McIlvanney, whose collected writings *McIlvanney on Football* (1994) have given him a new readership among younger audiences. Perhaps the most highly regarded work of this type was Arthur Hopcraft's *The Football Man* (1968). A freelance journalist who wrote about a lot more than just football, Hopcraft brought wit and perception to his attempt 'to reach the heart of what football is'. While Hunter Davies' *The Glory Game* (1972), an intimate portrait of a season in the life of Tottenham Hotspur, and one or two other titles, continued this tradition of intelligent writing, works of this type remained rare. Once again, it is tempting to lay the blame for this – especially in the late 1970s and 1980s – at the door of the game's limited cultural kudos.

The improved status of football from the end of the 1980s was both reflected and to some extent achieved by a flurry of writing about the game that continued throughout the decade and has finally given football something of the sustained quality of literature previously largely absent. An important early contribution was *Saturday's Boys* (1990), a set of essays edited by Harry Lansdown and Alex Spillius, which explored football fandom. The key text, however, was Nick Hornby's *Fever Pitch* (1992), one of the publishing phenomena of the decade and probably the most widely reviewed and discussed football book of all time. Hornby's skilfully crafted dissection of football as obsession, interwoven with a wider autobiography that spoke eloquently to the suburban middle classes, both

arrived at and helped define the moment when an interest in football became an essential part of the middle-class social agenda. Although it has become fashionable to decry Hornby and the so-called *soccerati* that followed him as middle-class males in search of a spurious proletarian identity (Hornby was honest about this aspect of his love for Arsenal), the best of the writing that followed into the space he helped create has much enriched football literature. The best received elements of football's 'new writing' include Harry Pearson's perceptive and occasionally surreal survey of the game in the north-east, *The Far Corner* (1994), the collections of fiction, memoir and journalism that Simon Kuper gathered in his *Perfect Pitch* volumes from 1997, and Colin Shindler's wry observations on the lot of a Manchester City supporter, *Manchester United Ruined my Life* (1998). There has been much else of value, although one of the unfortunate by-products of Hornby's success has been that rather too many of us who had followed a team through the wind and rain felt that others might be interested in reading about the experience!

Although players, managers and others from within the football world began to produce autobiographies in increasing numbers from the late 1940s and early 1950s, much that ensued was limited and unchallenging. Set against this standard blandness, Eamon Dunphy's *Only a Game?* (1976) was a revelation. Dunphy's story of daily life at Millwall Football Club was brutally honest both about himself and others, and it raised the potential for a new style of autobiography that few have attempted to emulate. Unsurprisingly, Dunphy made a successful career as a journalist after retiring from the game. The period from the late 1990s witnessed some signs that the footballer's autobiography might rise above a set formula. Then Charlton striker Gary Nelson's *Left Foot Forward* (1996) provided another well-observed 'journeyman's' view of the game, while both Tony Adams in *Addicted* (1998) and Tony Cascarino in *Full Time: The Secret Life of Tony Cascarino* (2000) have shown that a good collaborative relationship with sympathetic writers (Ian

Ridley and Paul Kimmage in these instances) and an 'interesting' personal life can produce sports literature of substance.

Sources:
Melling, A.,'"Ray of the Rovers": The Working-Class Heroine in Popular Football Fiction, 1915–1925', *International Journal of the History of Sport*, 15: 1 (1998).
Seddon, P. J., *A Football Compendium* (London: British Library Publishing, 1999).
Taylor, D. J., '"Rally Round You Havens"': Soccer and the Literary Imagination', in S. Kuper (ed.), *Perfect Pitch. 1: Home Ground* (London: Headline, 1997).

Further Reading:
Russell, D., *Football and the English: A Social History of Association Football in England, 1863–1995* (Preston: Carnegie Publishing, 1997).

Dave Russell

History Highlights 1930–1939

The decade opened with the team of the 1920s, Huddersfield, losing to Arsenal, the team of the 1930s, in the FA Cup final. During the Cup final Graf Zeppelin hovered over Wembley, a harbinger of burgeoning German military power. The following season, 1930/31, Arsenal won the first of their five championships in the 1930s: between 1933 and 1935 they equalled Huddersfield's treble of championships. Sadly, Chapman failed to take Arsenal to the third title, dying suddenly in January 1934.

While Arsenal were a dominant force, clubs in the north and north-west of England were reeling under the impact of economic depression, with several clubs from the lower leagues being forced out of League football. In September 1931 Wigan Borough resigned from the League after playing 12 games, becoming the first ever side to do so. With unemployment at its peak, in 1933, Sheffield United tried to amend rule 32 to allow clubs to admit

unemployed people at half price, but the motion fell. Further south, Thames, elected to the League in 1930, recorded the lowest ever league attendance of 469 against Luton.

Despite economic depression the main challenge to Arsenal still came from the north. Sunderland, Manchester City and Everton each won the Championship and the FA Cup at least once, while Newcastle, Sheffield Wednesday and Preston won one FA Cup each.

In 1930/31 West Bromwich Albion became the first team to win promotion to the First Division and the FA Cup in the same season. In the 1933 Cup Final, numbers were worn on the back of shirts for the first time in a Cup final. Everton wore 1 to 11, while Manchester City wore 12–22. The traditional third round shock facilitated Everton's path as Third Division (North) Walsall defeated Arsenal 2–0. The 1938 FA Cup final became the first live game to be shown on TV in its entirety. Only 10,000 viewed the game on TV, while 90,000 were in the stadium. With little interest shown, the experiment was abandoned for the following year. The final was the first Wembley final to be decided by a penalty, scored in the last minute.

There were several individual goal-scoring records of note. During 1935 Ted Drake scored seven goals, for Arsenal, in a league game against Aston Villa. This feat was bettered in 1935 by Harold Bell of Tranmere who scored nine goals in a game and, the following year, by Joe Payne of Luton Town, who found the net ten times playing against Bristol Rovers, a record that still stands.

A major controversy between the Football League and the Pools' Promoters Association led to the League scrapping all its fixtures on 29 February 1936. The League attempted to stop the pools' companies using league fixtures to promote gambling, and wanted to crush the pools companies. To circumvent the pools companies the League withheld the revised fixtures until the Friday, but ultimately their plans failed and the pools promoters continued to use the League's fixtures with impunity.

In 1931 John Thomson, possibly Scotland's greatest ever goalkeeper, died in a game against Rangers while diving at the feet of Sam English, who was blameless. Over 30,000 people, Catholic and Protestant, attended his funeral. Meanwhile the Old Firm still dominated, but Motherwell managed to win the title in 1932, the only time the Championship left Glasgow in the inter-war period. In 1938 East Fife became the first Second Division side to win the Scottish Cup, beating Kilmarnock 4–2 after a replay. The traditional Old Firm New Year fixture, in 1939, saw the largest ever attendance for a league game in Britain, when 118,567 came through the turnstiles. Meanwhile, Jimmy McGrory retired in 1938, having scored 550 goals in first class football, a British record. He made 378 appearances for Celtic, scoring a remarkable 397 goals. In Northern Ireland, Linfield managed four league titles across the decade, although Belfast Celtic remained the most successful club, winning five successive titles between 1936 and 1940.

In international football, Scotland lost their undefeated record against non-British opposition when they lost 5–0 to Austria in Vienna in 1931. Two years later, Wales played their first international against non-British opposition, drawing 1–1 with France in Paris. England managed to defend their unbeaten *home* record against foreign sides, although it was often a close-run thing. They played the great Austrian team at Stamford Bridge in 1932 and, although outclassed for periods of the game, managed to win 4–3. Other notable English performances were in 1934 when England beat world champions, Italy, 3–2 at Highbury, with a team containing seven Arsenal players; while in 1938 they beat the Rest of Europe 3–0. In 1937, Scotland played England at Hampden Park in front of Britain's record attendance of 149,547, the crowd witnessing a 3–1 win for the home side. The politics of the age entered the game when England played Germany in Berlin on 15 May 1938, and the English team gave the Nazi salute. *The Times* seemed proud: 'the English team made a good impression by raising their arms in the German salute'.

However, some other papers and many later commentators saw the gesture as a major mistake by England's football ambassadors. England won 6–3. The following day Aston Villa beat a German X1 3–2, but left the stadium to howls of derision because they did not follow the example of the national side.

Sources:

Kelly, S. F., *Back Page Football, A Century of Newspaper Coverage* (London: Queen Anne Press, 1988).
Radnedge, K. (ed.), *The Complete Encyclopedia of Football* (London: Carlton Books, 1998).

Ray Physick

Management

In business terms, management involves extracting the maximum potential benefit from available resources. In football's production process a manager's real impact is rather less than the media sometimes suggest. Players score goals and make tackles, and the quality of players a club is able to buy is dependent on its financial situation. Yet management can be the essential ingredient that makes the difference between success and failure. The functions of the football manager seem to be an ability to judge players and provide them with additional motivation, together with a sound knowledge of tactics.

Most clubs today are still small businesses, although some have become relatively sophisticated organisations. At the top there are the directors, with responsibility for the club's overall strategy. Below them the operations of a club are broadly divided into two: a football section and a commercial section. On the football side, managers are now supported by a host of specialist assistants such as coaches, fitness trainers, physiotherapists and dieticians. Most top clubs have also established their own academies to groom younger players. With clubs recognising the need to maximise their income, many employ a chief executive who directs the marketing and financial performance. This can entail the arrangement of sponsorship and corporate hospitality, as well as the marketing of a range of branded goods. A recent development has seen media companies investing in football, with some clubs possessing their own television channels.

In contrast, football's origins were humble. Early football clubs from the 1870s and 1880s were moulded by Britain's voluntary tradition. They were run by members who formed committees which amongst other things selected the team. Concerns over how clubs were run surfaced during the 1880s due to the increase in competition, and in particular the legalisation of professionalism in 1885. Football clubs were now businesses, albeit small ones. With players being paid, clubs had to increase their revenues. Grounds were developed to meet the game's rising popularity, and in the 1890s many clubs turned themselves into limited liability companies.

Directors were then in overall charge of team affairs, but daily supervision of the players was divided between the trainer and the secretary, who was usually the club's only paid official. Many secretaries, like George Ramsay of Aston Villa, had played for the club during its amateur days. He was a clerk by trade and had overall responsibility for the club's administration, and also occasionally recruited players. Ramsay was the club's secretary from 1886 to 1924 but was responsible to a directorate which was dominated by Fred Rinder for much of the time.

Managers were rarely called managers before 1920, and held various titles. Some were secretaries, others secretary-managers. However, there were early pioneers in the art such, as William Sudell at Preston North End and Tom Watson at Sunderland and Liverpool. By the early 1900s more football clubs began to employ secretary-managers as the demands of the job increased. Directors also had to run their businesses and gradually devolved more responsibilities to them. Some directors were also aware of the game's increased media coverage, and the growing trend to look for scapegoats when results were poor.

Football managers often employed the military model of management in dealing with players, and this continued throughout the twentieth century. They also reflected British management's tradition of the 'practical man', as no qualifications were required for the job. During the inter-war period managers were appointed in increasing numbers, most of whom were former players. Some were given responsibility for both administrative and football matters. The man who did most to change the perception of the football manager was Herbert Chapman. He established the manager as the fulcrum of the club, particularly at Arsenal between 1925 and 1934, when it was claimed he 'organised victory'. Chapman's career marked an early change from the amateur/voluntary tradition towards a more professional approach to football management.

Interference by directors, however, was an everyday fact for most managers. Only a handful, like Jimmy Seed at Charlton Athletic, enjoyed Chapman's autonomy. At Sheffield Wednesday in the 1930s, for example, Billy Walker's attempts to emulate Chapman were frustrated by the club's conservative directors. Some directors, such as James Taylor at Preston North End in the late 1930s, still felt team matters were best left in their hands. At Newcastle United this thinking persisted into the 1950s and, overall, directorial interference has never disappeared, as it is directors who carry ultimate responsibility.

After 1945 there was an increase in the scale of business of leading clubs. One consequence was the secretary-manager's post being gradually split into two. The secretary now dealt with the club's administration, while the manager had responsibility for the team, if not complete control over it. More managers, however, were beginning to follow Chapman's lead. At Tottenham Hotspur, for example, Arthur Rowe was credited with inventing the 'push and run' style when his team won the Championship in 1951.

Managerial expertise came to be recognised by directors and players alike as a vital ingredient of the football business. Players increasingly expected managers to demonstrate a knowledge of coaching and tactics, and directors began to realise an expert was required who could 'play' the transfer market and/or had renowned coaching or motivational skills. Managers came to be regarded as technical experts and were rewarded with a greater autonomy. But with these extra responsibilities came more stress. The job was very public and a football manager was consumed by his work, leaving him with little time for family or leisure.

With the abolition of the maximum wage in 1961 there was a gradual economic rationalisation as big city clubs such as Manchester United, Liverpool and Leeds United began to dominate. Liverpool's success may have been the result of a dynasty of managers, beginning with Bill Shankly, but it was the astute financial management of Peter Robinson which provided these managers with the necessary resources. The increase in autonomy coincided with the rise in football's coverage on television. By the 1970s managers were clearly identified (if arbitrarily) by the media as being responsible for a team's results. Some managers, such as Malcolm Allison and Ron Atkinson, attained celebrity status due to their charismatic personalities and 'quotability'.

The last 30 years have probably seen the manager at the peak of his powers. His role may now be coming to be more narrowly defined as clubs become larger enterprises. The Hillsborough tragedy; satellite television; the Premier League; the stock market flotation of many leading clubs: all have contributed to football's growing commercialisation in the 1990s, and this in turn has increased a player's power in the marketplace. The *Bosman* ruling of 1995 brought a deluge of foreign players who, like domestic players, demanded large salaries. Players were now seen as valuable assets who required careful handling. British managers were forced to adapt a more scientific approach to details such as fitness and diet. With so many foreign players, it is perhaps inevitable that some clubs, such as Chelsea, have engaged foreigners as managers.

Consequently, English clubs are now following, if not imitating, the European model where the manager is regarded as a tactician, with the wage negotiations of players taken out of his hands. The job of a football manager remains insecure, as illustrated by the job's very high turnover. A manager's importance will perhaps increase due to the need to give teams an edge in an increasingly competitive environment, but this may make managers more expendable as clubs search frantically for that vital quality which could make the difference between winning and losing.

Sources:

Fishwick, N., *English Football and Society, 1910–50* (Manchester: Manchester University Press, 1989).

Mason, T., *Association Football and English Society 1863–1915* (Brighton: Harvester Press, 1980).

Russell, D., *Football and the English: A Social History of Association Football in England, 1863–1995* (Preston: Carnegie Publishing, 1997).

Wagg, S., *The Football World: A Contemporary Social History* (Brighton: Harvester Press, 1984).

Further Reading:

Szymanski, S. and Kuypers, T., *Winners and Losers: The Business Strategy of Football* (London: Viking, 1999).

Turner, D. and White, A., *The Breedon Book of Football Managers* (Derby: Breedon Books, 1993).

Neil Carter

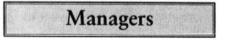

Managers

Early football managers were mainly administrators and subservient to directors. (For an historical overview see Management.) Some, however, such as William Sudell at Preston North End in the 1880s and Tom Watson at Sunderland (1889–96) and Liverpool (1896–1915), were successful. Watson was the first manager to win the Football League Championship with two different clubs; the others are Herbert Chapman, Brian Clough and Kenny Dalglish.

It was Herbert Chapman who modernised football management. Chapman's legacy was to transform the role of the manager, giving him responsibilities for team selection and tactics plus the buying and selling of players. He began with Northampton Town, who won the Southern League in 1909. As secretary-manager of Huddersfield Town (1921–25) he won the Cup in 1922, and then the Football League in 1924 and 1925. Chapman left for Arsenal in 1925. They won the FA Cup in 1930, plus two League titles in 1931 and 1933, before he died suddenly in January 1934.

After 1945 managers gained greater stature. At Manchester United, Matt Busby assembled three great teams between 1945 and 1969. The first won the Cup in 1948 and the League in 1952. The next, the 'Busby Babes', a product of United's successful scouting system, twice won the League before the Munich air disaster in 1958. He then built up another team based around the Law–Best–Charlton triumvirate, which finally won the European Cup in 1968. The following year Busby was knighted.

Alf Ramsey was England's first full-time, professional manager (1963–74), and will forever be associated with England's 1966 World Cup triumph. In recognition of this, he became the first manager to be knighted, in 1967. Ramsey had previously won the Football League with Ipswich Town in 1962. His 'wingless wonders' won the World Cup, placing an emphasis on work-rate over skill – an approach which came to be widely copied.

Scotland also produced notable managers. Under Willie Maley (1897–1940), Glasgow Celtic won 11 championships in 15 years from 1905. Managed by Willie Struth (1920–54), Glasgow Rangers dominated the 1920s and 1930s, winning 15 titles out of 20. Under Jock Stein (1965–78), a Protestant, Celtic became the first British team to win the European Cup, in 1967. Celtic also won a record nine consecutive championships between 1965 and 1974. Stein became Scotland manager in 1978, but died suddenly on 10 September 1985, after Scotland played Wales.

When Liverpool appointed Bill Shankly as manager (1959–74) it marked the start of a managerial dynasty, known as the 'Boot Room', which made Liverpool the

Bill Shankly captured in a rare jovial moment – he had just signed Kevin Keegan (May 1971)
(Peter Robinson; © EMPICS Sports Photo Agency)

most successful club in English football history. Shankly's powers of motivation and simple methods brought Liverpool three Championships plus two FA Cups. They also won the UEFA Cup in 1973. Shankly was succeeded and surpassed by his assistant, Bob Paisley (1974–83). Building on Shankly's foundations, Liverpool won six titles plus three European Cups in 1977, 1978 and 1981. Joe Fagan (1983–85) won three trophies in his first season, including Liverpool's fourth European Cup, but retired following the Heysel disaster. Kenny Dalglish (1985–91) inherited the Anfield chair, winning the 'double' in 1986 – uniquely as player-manager. Liverpool won the League again in 1988 and 1990, but their FA Cup triumph in 1989 was overshadowed by the Hillsborough disaster. Dalglish resigned in 1991 but returned to manage Blackburn Rovers (1991–95), who won the Premiership in 1995.

Brian Clough won Championships with two relatively small clubs, Derby County (1972) and Nottingham Forest (1978). His managerial career began in 1965 with Hartlepool United and finished at Forest in 1993. In hindsight, Forest's European Cup triumphs of 1979 and 1980 look like one of the greatest feats in football history. Outspoken and an authoritarian, Clough was usually assisted by Peter Taylor, especially at Forest and Derby.

Manchester United's domination of English football during the 1990s owes much to Alex Ferguson. A Scottish patriarch in the mould of Busby, Stein and Shankly, he arrived at United in 1986 following a successful period with Aberdeen (1978–86). Winning the FA Cup in 1990 marked the beginning of United's ascendancy. Between 1993 and 2000 they won six Premierships, including three 'doubles' – 1994, 1996 and 1999. United also completed an unprecedented 'treble' in 1999 by winning the European Cup. A few weeks later Ferguson was knighted.

The influx of foreigners into English football during the 1990s was complemented by foreign managers. Arsène Wenger has been the most successful. He took over at Arsenal in 1996, winning the 'double' in 1998 with a science-orientated approach, which is perhaps an indication of football management's future direction.

Sources:

Russell, D., *Football and the English: A Social History of Association Football in England, 1863–1995* (Preston: Carnegie Publishing, 1997).

Turner, D. and White, A., *The Breedon Book of Football Managers* (Derby: Breedon Books, 1993).

Wagg, S., *The Football World: A Contemporary Social History* (Brighton: Harvester Press, 1984).

Further Reading:

Rogan, J., *The Football Managers* (London: Queen Anne Press, 1989).

Studd, S., *Herbert Chapman: Football Emperor* (London: Souvenir Press, 1998).

See also Management

Neil Carter

Marketing

Any examination of the role of marketing in football needs to be preceded by a definition of marketing itself and a consideration of the key elements of sports marketing. Marketing can and should be considered both a function within and a philosophy of the organisation. The marketing philosophy is a belief that the whole organisation needs to be market-focused in order to satisfy customer needs better than competitors. The marketing function is basically responsible for the management of the marketing mix: elements which in their simplest form consist of market research and the four Ps of product, price, promotion and place. The principles of marketing can apply to all football organisations, whether they are professional or amateur, profit-making or non-profit-making. There are two distinct but complementary elements to any definition of sport marketing. Firstly, there is the marketing *of* sport, which involves football leagues, associations, clubs and individuals marketing their events, products and services directly to football consumers. Secondly there is marketing *through* sport, which involves the activities of consumer and industrial organisations that use football as a vehicle to market their products and services to football consumers. Football marketers therefore need to be concerned with the marketing of their sport to both the sport consumer and to those who use the sport as a marketing vehicle – i.e., sponsors and advertisers.

The professional football industry is just one part of the leisure sector, and as a result marketing a football event or club is in many ways similar to marketing other leisure utilities and services such as the theatre, cinema and concerts. However, the unique characteristics of the sport product, and the unusual market conditions, have required marketing personnel to adopt different marketing strategies from those used in other service sectors. Unlike other industries the sports market is characterised by joint interdependence, in that the clubs together provide the core product: the game. It is therefore not possible to consider the marketing of individual football clubs in isolation from the marketing of the sport as a whole, since marketing plays an important role at the league or association level of the sport. It is the league authorities who will decide on the nature of the core product offered, such as league structure, rules and regulations, match scheduling, television and sponsorship contracts and income distribution. At club level the sports marketer traditionally has no control over the core football product and its outcome, and therefore is often responsible for developing ancillary product and service extensions that complement the sporting spectacle and contribute more to a football consumer's overall satisfaction. Football consumers are often considered to be different from consumers in other industry sectors, because they have an emotional attachment to the sport or club and see themselves as 'fans' rather than customers. This unique characteristic can be a double-edged sword for football marketers. On the one hand, this fan loyalty provides commercial opportunities for product and service extensions in areas such as merchandising. However, it can also leave sports marketers open to accusations of exploitation if not handled with care and sensitivity. UK football clubs also hold an important position within their communities, which again has important implications for sports marketers in terms of their public relations activities.

The marketing of sport as a specific component within sport management has been particularly evident in the United States since the early 1980s, where sports franchises have taken the lead in adopting traditional marketing principles and practices commonplace in other leisure and service industries. In the UK, football organisations have been slow to adopt such practices and have suffered from 'marketing myopia' – that is, seeing themselves as being in the football industry rather than in the entertainment and leisure industry. The English Football League saw attendances decline from 30 million in 1966 to just 16 million in 1986. This long-term decline was, in part, the

result of the changing leisure demands of a more affluent society, with alternative attractions such as DIY, shopping, and in-home entertainment eroding football's customer base. But it was also the result of the industry's failure to adapt to these changes.

By the late 1980s the football industry was characterised by financial and business mismanagement, dilapidated stadia, hooliganism, poor quality leagues and international footballing failure. Since the early 1990s both the football clubs and the league authorities have adopted a more market-focused approach to their operations, implementing marketing strategies that have been commonplace in the United States professional sports industry for some time.

Sources:

Gavron, J. 'Association Football: A Battered Sport and a Troubled Business', *The Economist*, 31 May 1986, 45–53.
Mullin, B. J., Hardy, S. and Sutton, W. A., *Sport Marketing* (Champaign, IL: Human Kinetics, 1993).

Further Reading:

Fynn, A. and Davidson, H., *Dream On: A Year in the Life of a Premier League Club* (London: Simon & Schuster, 1996).
Shank, M., *Sports Marketing: A Strategic Perspective* (Englewood Cliffs, NJ: Prentice Hall, 1999).

Dave Hudson

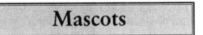

Mascots

A mascot is a person, animal, or object supposed to bring good luck. The use of mascots goes back to antiquity, though they did not always go by that name. A popular Italian operetta called *La Mascotte* ran for over 1,000 performances between 1880 and 1882 with a plot involving a farm girl who brings good luck to whoever possesses her. The slang word 'mascotte' is the derivative of the provincial word 'masco', meaning 'witch'. The operetta was translated into English and

The Gunnersaurus, Arsenal's mascot
(© Stuart MacFarlane, Arsenal FC)

staged in Britain and the United States. The translated title became *The Mascot*, and the concept of a mascot as person, animal or object providing good luck was thus established.

The World Cup in England in 1966 saw the start of a new trend of mascots, beginning with World Cup Willie. He was followed by Juanito (1970, Mexico), Tip und Tap (West Germany, 1974), Gauchito (Argentina, 1978), Naranjito (Spain, 1982), Pique (Mexico, 1986), Ciao (Italy, 1990), Striker (USA, 1994), Footix (France, 1998) and the Atmos (Japan/South Korea, 2002).

Such is the marketing value of the mascot that its very creation is now the province of specialists far removed from the football industry. The name Footix was chosen carefully, as it had to be easily pronounceable in many languages (and have no negative connotations), as well as being protected as a registered trademark. The computer-generated mascot Atmos is the product of Interbrand, the company responsible for brand names such as the Fiat Punto, Ford Mondeo and Prozac.

Mascots are today a feature of many sports, and in British soccer most clubs and teams have recognised the entertainment and marketing value of establishing their own mascot character. In the early days of soccer the mascot was often a dog or a small child that would lead the team on to the field. Although young children still often fulfil this function, official mascots are more often people dressed as giant furry animals. They are usually selected to be a character that represents

some aspect of the club's tradition, nickname, or an aspect of its locality. For example, Fred the Red at Manchester United and Ossie the Owl at Sheffield Wednesday.

The mascot's role is to act as a focus for the fans' enthusiasm, to entertain at half-time and to parade the touchline, meeting and greeting. The fact that its image can later be used to sell more merchandise adds to its value to the club. Unfortunately, at times they can get carried away in their enthusiasm and distract attention from the match. Hercules the Lion (Aston Villa) was sacked for hugging and kissing Miss Aston Villa. There was a mass pitch brawl at a match between Wolves and Bristol City featuring Woolfie, the Three Little Pigs, and the City Cat. The FA of Wales decided to draw up a code of conduct for mascots after fining the Swansea City mascot, Cyril the Swan, £1,000 for bringing the game into disrepute after he went on to the pitch and hugged the scorer of a goal.

Kyle Philpotts

Medals

Commemorative medals connected with football's prestigious events have been awarded since the earliest years of the organised game's history. No one can be sure when the first medals were awarded, although it is clear that for the major competitions medals were awarded from the outset. A medal is the physical expression of a player's victory, and could be kept and cherished throughout that player's life. Medals, therefore, came to represent the highlight of any footballer's career. In the most important cup competitions medals were, and still are, awarded to the runner-up team as well as the victors. Some medals have been presented unofficially. Players for Bury FC were given special medals by the club to commemorate their 6–0 victory over Derby in 1903, an FA Cup final record to this day.

Traditionally medals were of gold or silver-gilt, and prior to the First World

War players often had the choice of a medal, pocket watch, or even money! Surprisingly, players who chose medals sometimes had to have them engraved at their own expense. Many medals, therefore, were not ascribed to individual players and thus often remain unidentified. To the collector of football memorabilia the career of the medal winner is every bit as important as the medal itself, the fame and world standing of the recipient often affecting the value of their medal or collection of medals.

During the First World War the FA and Football League banned the awarding of medals and trophies, due to the limited availability of metals and the cost of production. However, in 1917 they allowed medals to be presented as long as the game was for charity and the production costs were not taken out of the gate receipts. Similar action was taken during the Second World War. When, after the Second World War, competitions were resumed, there was still a limited availability of precious metal. As a result of the scarcity of gold, Charlton Athletic, defeated 1–4 in the 1946 FA Cup Final, received two medals. Directly after the game their players were presented with bronze medals, whilst the victorious Derby team received gold medals. It was only some time later that the Charlton players were finally presented with their gold runners-up awards.

Medals come in all shapes and sizes, and usually depict images of footballers who are either static or in the process of kicking or heading a ball. Although the majority of medals are circular in shape, the introduction of European competition among British clubs in the late 1950s saw the development of more abstract, angular designs. Rather than incorporating the heraldic detailing of the traditional British designs the European medals are more graphic in their combination of images and lettering.

It is every player's ambition to build up large collections of medals, but few are as lucky as three nineteenth-century players, Charles Wollaston, Lord Kinnaird and James Forrest, each of whom won five FA Cup winner's medals.

Sources:
Chilcott, D., *The Hamlyn Guide To Football Collectables* (London: Reed Consumer Books, 1995).

Further Reading:
FIFA, *FIFA Museum Collection* (Berlin: Verlags-GmbH, 1996).
Pickering, D., *The Cassell Soccer Companion* (London: Cassell, 1994).

Mark Bushell

Museums

– see **Heritage**

Music

Music in one form or another has provided a background accompaniment to organised football since the 1870s, especially following the development of professional football and the corresponding growth of crowds. Sometimes this has involved musical instruments, but more often it has taken the form of relatively spontaneous singing among spectators. This has acted as one more means of unifying identity within groups of spectators when confronted with rival teams. Modern developments have seen recordings by players and fans associated with clubs or international teams, and a specific sub-genre of popular music has evolved.

Early evidence of the behaviour of football supporters is difficult to accumulate, but, as for Blackburn Olympic in 1883, there are many cases of brass bands playing to welcome home cup or championship-winning teams. There are also isolated examples of instruments like bugles and rattles being used. The singing of hymn tunes, possibly amended, and popular music hall songs such as *I Love a Lassie* (Harry Lauder) were noted at Bradford City and Nottingham Forest's grounds in 1911. Some songs became associated with certain clubs, such as *The Rowdy Dowdy Boys* (Sheffield United in the 1890s), *On* the Ball, City (Norwich City from at least 1902), and Southampton's *Yi Yi Yi* chant. Roughly 100 songs about football were published in the late Victorian and Edwardian eras, mainly concerning the public-school game and its virtues.

By the 1920s, there is more evidence of songs and chants on the terraces, although probably not at the levels reached from the 1960s onwards. Songs included *The Wearing of the Green, The Minstrel Boy, My Old Kentucky Home,* and modified songs, as in *Kick, Kick, Kick, Kick, Kick It* (to the tune of *Chick, Chick, Chick, Chick, Chicken*) and *Keep the Forwards Scoring* (to *Keep the Home Fires Burning*). The singing of *Abide With Me* at Wembley Cup finals from 1927 onwards had a poignancy for those who had lost comrades in the war.

Songs with a sectarian edge were certainly sung at games between Rangers and Celtic in the 1920s. These matches were always accompanied by lots of singing and the waving of banners, tricolours and Union Jacks. Celtic fans sang *Rebel* or Irish songs such as *The Fields of Athenry, The Wild Colonial Boy, The Faith of our Fathers* and many others, with variations. By the 1950s some specific songs sung on 'The Jungle' included *I'll Sing a Hymn to Charlie* (Tully), *Oh Hampden in the Sun* and *McGrory's Delight*. Rangers' *Billy Boys* replied with *No Surrender, The Sash my Father Wore,* and others, illustrating the possibility that oppositional chanting and singing in British football stemmed from sectarianism.

In England in the period immediately after 1945, football's musical style appears to have been rather similar to that of the pre-war decades, with *Blaydon Races* (Newcastle), Portsmouth's *Pompey Chimes* ('Play up, Pompey'), West Ham's *I'm Forever Blowing Bubbles* and Birmingham City's *Keep Right on to the End of the Road,* originating from the club's 1956 FA Cup run, particularly prominent pieces. However, the 1950s saw the beginning of changes, with a few multicultural influences creeping in, including American forms (two, four, six, eight, chants, for example); the Brazilian samba beat (*Brasil, cha, cha, cha*) from the World Cup, and West Indian calypso songs. The great explosion of singing on the terraces came from 1963, when the Beatles and *Merseybeat* transformed the British popular music scene. Crowds on Liverpool's Spion Kop started singing these songs (and amended versions), especially Gerry and the Pacemakers' *You'll Never Walk Alone,* and this spread very quickly to other clubs. By 1964/65 there were many parodies and variations of pop songs, television commercials and traditional songs.

By the late 1960s and early 1970s, the increasing violence, or threat of violence, associated with football meant that some songs and chants, such as *He's only a poor little Cockney,* became taunts and insults to the opposition. The 1970s brought musical influences into football again, as young fans copied various styles from skinhead to glam rock – David Bowie, Slade and Gary Glitter – and Punk. Some songs from this era seem to have become perennials, undergoing many amendments, like *Guantanamera* and *Go West.* New songs were composed and distributed on song-sheets (later fanzines), or rehearsed in local pubs. From the later 1980s, other songs became associated with particular clubs, as for example *Blue Moon* (Manchester City), *The Wonder of You* (Port Vale), *Glad All Over* (Crystal Palace), *Delilah* (Stoke City) and *Goodnight Irene* (Bristol Rovers).

The 1980s and '90s also saw the emergence of a genuine cross-over culture from popular music to football and vice versa. Oddly enough, the origins of professional football and the development of the popular music hall were both aspects of a new working-class consumerism that arose from the 1880s, with increasing leisure-time and higher incomes. Nevertheless, despite the singing of popular songs on the terraces, there was little evidence of a sustained cross-over until recently. The professional game was not often the subject of published popular songs, and there seem to be few sustained links between popular musicians and football. This changed in the late 1970s and early 1980s, when the punk and post-punk musical movements brought the attitude that 'anyone could do it'. This led to self-produced recordings, music fanzines and ideas that spilled over into football. Fanzines such as *The End* produced by The Farm, a band who supported Tranmere Rovers, illustrate this phenomenon. Similarly, other bands such as 808 State and Half Man Half Biscuit produced football-connected songs. In the 1980s, the *Madchester* music scene brought the styles of The Stone Roses, James, The Happy Mondays and others to the terraces, many of the musicians and fans being genuine supporters of various clubs. The 1990s continued this trend, with bands like Oasis supporting Manchester City.

Such a cross-over brought an increase in the recording of football songs. Some had been recorded in earlier periods, but these were few and far between. The 1950s brought a number of calypso-style recordings, probably the most famous being the *Manchester United Calypso* in 1956. By the 1960s, records concerning clubs were produced by them to celebrate reaching a cup final or the winning of a trophy, but most languish in an obscurity well-deserved by their mediocrity. Some have perhaps transcended that lack of quality, such as *The Anfield Rap* (Liverpool, 1988), *Blue Day* (Chelsea, 1997), or the England songs *World in Motion* (New Order, 1990) and *Three Lions* (Lightning Seeds/Skinner and Baddiel, 1996), with its now-famous, and much-imitated, *Football's Coming Home* chorus. Chelsea's *Blue is the Colour* (1972) seems to have survived despite its banality. There appears to be a growing market for CD collections of club songs, chants and obscure popular songs celebrating football – a sure sign that this largely self-created sub-genre of popular music has yet to reach its peak in terms of popularity.

The increasing globalisation of the game throughout the media has led to other musical influences permeating the British game, including bands in the stadium. These have appeared on television in several recent World Cup campaigns, and seem to have precipitated the formation of bands that follow two Yorkshire clubs, Barnsley and Sheffield Wednesday. There

has also been a link established between football and the growing popular use of classical music, especially since Italia '90 when Pavarotti's recording of *Nessun Dorma*, from Puccini's opera *Turandot*, which had been adopted as the tournament anthem, was taken up by the BBC as the theme to its own coverage. Similarly, high-profile *Three Tenors* concerts were held in connection with the 1990 World Cup, and its 1994 successor in the United States. The fact that a leading classical musician such as violinist Nigel Kennedy, an Aston Villa devotee, can identify so closely with the football world is possibly a further illustration of growing middle-class interest in the game (or, at least, willingness to acknowledge such an interest) in the 1990s. So too, perhaps, was the production of the opera *Playing Away* (1994) with libretto by playwright Howard Brenton and music by Benedict Mason, which focused on events surrounding a fictitious European Cup final.

Sources:

Burns, P. and Woods, P., *Oh, Hampden in the Sun* (Edinburgh: Mainstream, 1997).

Redhead, S., *Football with Attitude* (Manchester: Wordsmith, 1991).

Redhead, S. *Post-Fandom and the Millennial Blues* (London: Routledge, 1997).

Russell, D., *Football and the English* (Preston: Carnegie, 1997).

Thrills, A., *You're Not Singing Anymore* (London: Ebury Press, 1998).

Further Reading:

Bulmer, L., and Merrills, R., *'Dicks Out!': The Definitive Work on British Football Songs* (Tunbridge Wells: Chatsby Publishing, 1992).

Seddon, P. J., *A Football Compendium* (Boston Spa: British Library Publishing, 1995).

Robert Lewis

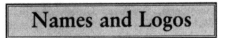

Names and Logos

Clubs have had nicknames and badges since the 1860s, when association football was first organised on a significant scale.

Both are means by which clubs and supporters express their own identities, and distinguished themselves from others.

Nicknames have generally been derived from attributes associated with the clubs, such as team colours, traditional regional occupations or perceived characteristics, although the derivation of some names is obscure or debatable. Some are more imaginative than others, with a number of clubs known simply as City, Rovers, United and the like. Blackburn and Doncaster seem only to be referred to as Rovers, and Cambridge and Colchester as the U's (United). Others have names derived from shirt colours, such as Birmingham City (Blues), Bournemouth (Cherries), Bristol City, Altrincham and Swindon (Robins), Cardiff (Bluebirds), Manchester United (Red Devils), Lincoln (Red Imps) and Burnley (Clarets). More complex colour choices have led to Norwich being known as the Canaries (yellow and green), Alloa as the Wasps (yellow and black hoops), Watford as the Hornets (formerly red, green and yellow stripes), Hull City as the Tigers (amber and black stripes), Queen's Park as the Spiders (because of the thin black hoops on their shirts) and both Newcastle and Notts County as the Magpies (black and white stripes).

Some nicknames obviously derive from the club name, as in Wolves (Wolverhampton), Spurs (Tottenham Hotspur), Citizens (Manchester City), Hammers (West Ham), Villans (Aston Villa), Gills (Gillingham), 'Gers (Glasgow Rangers), Killie (Kilmarnock), Accies (Hamilton Academicals), Hearts (Heart of Midlothian), Hibees (Hibernian), Latics (both Wigan and Oldham Athletic), and so on. Yet others have connections to the name of the ground, or location of the town. Examples here include Fulham (Cottagers, from Craven Cottage), Berwick (Borderers), Carlisle (Cumbrians), Brighton (Seagulls), Blackpool (Seasiders), Torquay (Gulls), Sheffield Wednesday (Owls, because they played at Owlerton), Chesterfield (Spireites, because of the town's famous crooked spire) and York (Minstermen).

Regional occupations offer another fruitful source for names. Clubs in this cat-

egory include Grimsby (Mariners), Luton (Hatters), Macclesfield (Silkmen), Northampton (Cobblers), Walsall (Saddlers), Sheffield United (Blades), Stoke (Potters), and Arsenal (Gunners). Both Crewe and Swindon have been called the Railwaymen. A most unusual example is Wycombe Wanderers, known as the Chairboys, from the traditional High Wycombe occupation of chair-making. Everton were also traditionally known as the Toffees or Toffeemen, although this name seems to have fallen out of favour.

Some clubs have had several nicknames over the years. Barnsley have been referred to as the Saints (originally Barnsley St Peter's), the Colliers (occupational), and the Tykes (generic). Crystal Palace used to be the Glaziers, but are now the Eagles. Leeds used to be the Peacocks, in honour of an earlier home, the Old Peacock Ground, but are more normally termed United. Leicester City have been the Filberts (after Filbert Street), but are now generally the Foxes. Preston have been the Old Invincibles, Lambs, Lillywhites and Proud Preston (from the town crest), as well as simply 'the North End' or 'PNE'. West Bromwich were traditionally the Throstles (a thrush is on their badge), but are generally known to their fans as the Baggies.

Some names are impossible to classify, and have obscure origins. Bury are known as the Shakers, because they were apparently about to 'shake' bigger opponents, and Newport County as Ironsiders, possibly because their ground was off Cromwell Road (and Oliver Cromwell's nickname was Ironsides). Peterborough are the Posh because they were supposedly the 'poshest' club in the area. Bolton Wanderers' nickname (Trotters) has nothing to do with pigs, but refers to a dialect word for practical jokers. Nicknames like the Addicks (Charlton), Grecians (Exeter), Buddies (St Mirren), the Honest Men (Ayr United), Terrors (Dundee United), Bairns (Falkirk) and Loons (Forfar) are humorous names whose derivation is somewhat obscure.

Club badges and logos have mainly been derived from town and city crests and coats of arms, modified in a football context. Clubs using modified coats of arms include Watford, Rochdale, Reading, Wrexham, Bristol City, Chesterfield, Luton and Millwall. Others follow the club nickname, as with Derby (Ram), Brighton (Seagull), Bristol Rovers (Pirate) and Arsenal (Fieldgun). Some also carry mottoes, such as Blackburn's 'Arte et Labore' and Aston Villa's 'Prepared'. Animals and birds feature frequently, as in Crystal Palace (Eagle), Bradford City (Bantam), Cardiff (Bluebird), Millwall (Lion) and Mansfield (Stag).

Some have evolved newer logos to convey a sense of 'modernisation', particularly since the 1970s. Examples include Bolton's BWFC logo, Nottingham Forest's stylised tree and Torquay's designer gulls. Despite some modish departures among club logos and badges, they tend towards the traditional in Britain, with an emphasis on the historical longevity of the game and its communal roots.

Sources:
Rothmans Football Yearbook (London: Headline, various editions).
Guinness Book of Football (London: Guinness Publishing, 1998).
Witty, J. R., 'The 92 League Clubs', in A. H. Fabian and G. Green (eds), *Association Football* (London: Caxton, 1960), vol. 2, VII, 6, pp. 323–434.

Further Reading:
Avis, Football Club, *Soccer Crests* (London: Author publisher, 1969).

Robert Lewis

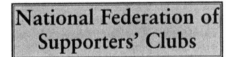

National Federation of Supporters' Clubs

The first national organisation for football fans, the National Federation of Football Supporters' Clubs (NFFSC) was the only representative grouping for supporters until 1985. Formed in 1927, the NFFSC was a peculiarly English group bringing together fans of amateur and professional clubs. Its historian, Rogan Taylor, suggests its entire history can be explained by reference to its lower-middle class make-up.

The NFFSC's federal structure combined supporters at both professional and amateur clubs to work for the common good of the game. Formed in the early years of the century (normally to raise funds for their clubs), until the 1960s supporters' clubs helped to pay for new stands and even players' wages. However, the federation's relationship with clubs and football's authorities was always distant and awkward, as its right to consultation was never recognised (the NFFSC did not officially meet the Football League or Association until the 1970s). Equally, it never sought to carve a role for itself within football, nor to represent fans to football's authorities. Taylor suggests that the NFFSC motto ('To help, not to hinder') sums up its lower-middle class, conservative agenda of helping the clubs and football *in toto*, and its avoidance of progressive issues such as those relating to the democratisation of the game.

However, while this was sufficient in the 1940s and '50s to lead to claims of a mass membership (accurate figures are difficult to calculate due to its loose federal structure), radical changes in the 1960s proved the undoing of the NFFSC. Football's increasing desire for greater revenue in that decade saw many clubs take over their social clubs, with many simply expelled from stadium facilities they had paid for (as at Coventry City). Ironically, this commercialisation was partly the consequence of the NFFSC's successful lobbying in the 1950s for a Lottery Act, which opened up a new source of funding for clubs. Equally, the declining crowds at professional football, new media approaches towards the game (particularly its star players), and increasing disorder rendered the NFFSC increasingly redundant. Unable, or unwilling, to develop distinctive responses to these issues, reluctant to use the media, and still seeking to benefit clubs rather than fans, the NFFSC quickly became irrelevant within the rapidly changing scene of professional football. This was reflected not just in the falling numbers of clubs affiliated to the NFFSC, but also in the increasing average age of members and delegates.

By the time the Football Supporters Association was formed in 1985, the NFFSC was thoroughly incapable of articulating the viewpoint of supporters or making any impact on the game. Often aligned with the Conservative Government in the mid to late 1980s – at least one of its leaders was a Conservative councillor – the NFFSC fundamentally set itself apart from most fans, particularly those involved in the fanzine revolution. Dominated by lower-middle class, conservative men, the NFFSC had no role to play: its attempts in the mid to late 1990s to work pro-actively with other types of fan group like the Football Supporters Association, to develop an effective media presence and to build a genuine presence within professional football, testify to its parlous state, and previous failures to construct a distinctive role, image or agenda.

Sources:

Taylor, R., *Football and its Fans* (Leicester: Leicester University Press, 1992).

Further Reading:

Haynes, R., *The Football Imagination: The Rise of Football Fanzine Culture* (Aldershot: Arena, 1995).

See also Football Supporters' Association, Independent Football Supporters' Associations.

Rex Nash

National Stadia

The most famous football ground in Britain, if not the world, is Wembley, England's national stadium and home to the FA Cup final since 1923. Generations of fans, when their side has qualified for a final appearance, have sung about 'Wem-ber-ley' over the years, and the ground, together with Argentinian international Osvaldo Ardiles, even made the pop music charts in 1981 when the Spurs squad, before their clash with Manchester City, released *Ossie's Dream*, opening with the immortal line: 'Ossie's going to Wembley; his legs have gone all trembly.' No matter how dire the players' musical efforts, this terrible rhyme affectionately summed up the state of reverence in which the north London ground is held in the national consciousness.

By 1923 the FA were looking for a new venue for their most prestigious annual fixture. The FA Cup final had, since its inception in 1872, become a national institution, and was deserving of a national stadium. The first final was held at The Oval, when 2,000 spectators paid a shilling each to see the Wanderers beat the Royal Engineers. The Lillie Bridge athletics ground, near the Thames, was selected the following year, when a morning kick-off enabled the victorious Wanderers and their opponents Oxford University to watch the Boat Race as part of the day's sporting entertainment. In 1874 the final returned to The Oval, which was to be its home until 1892, by which time the rising popularity of the game had resulted in 25,000 being attracted to see West Bromwich Albion beat their fellow professionals Aston Villa. This figure, generated by the increasing interest in a game that was by now largely professional, was more than the Surrey cricket ground could comfortably accommodate, so for the 1893 final the FA moved the game out of the capital for the first time, selecting another athletics stadium, at Fallowfield in Manchester. A record 45,000 were there as Wolverhampton Wanderers beat Everton, and the following year Notts County overcame Bolton Wanderers at Goodison Park in front of 37,000. Everton were the country's richest club at the time, and had attracted the Football League's highest attendances over each of the first ten years of its existence. Furthermore, Goodison was the first purpose-built football ground on which the Cup final had been staged. Could this be the game's first national stadium?

It was not to be. With The Oval out of contention, another London venue, with a far greater capacity than Goodison, was chosen – Crystal Palace, which was to host the final for the next two decades. In 1895 the Sydenham stadium housed 42,560 spectators, and attendances rose over the years until 1901, when the capital staged the first North v South clash, Tottenham Hotspur and Sheffield United sharing four goals. The game that day was watched by 110,820, a world record that stood until 1913, when Aston Villa beat Sunderland 1–0, with 120,081 inside the ground and many more watching from high in the trees surrounding the arena. Crystal Palace was to host only one more final, in 1914, when Burnley and Liverpool attracted 72,778. Despite the outbreak of the Great War the 1915 competition went ahead, the final between Sheffield United and Chelsea being contested at yet another ground, Old Trafford, after the FA had taken War Office advice that football would be good for morale on the home front. Hostilities then caused the tournament to be suspended until the 1919/20 season. Stamford Bridge was the venue for the final of 1920 and the two following years but, with a capacity of a mere 85,000, it was too small to become the game's permanent home. Crystal Palace, although big enough, had never been designed as a football ground; many of the 120,000-odd who watched the 1913 final complained that they never saw a thing, as they were accommodated not on banked terracing but on grassy banks more than 50 yards from the action. A showpiece national stadium was desperately needed, and what better excuse to build one than the 1924 British Empire Exhibition?

The sleepy suburb of Wembley, six miles north-west of London, was the site chosen for the spectacle to be staged as a celebration designed to bring Britain's colonies closer together. In 1921 FA President Sir Charles Clegg had agreed a 21-year deal to stage the annual showpiece at the new Empire Stadium designed to host the show. The Duke of York, the future King George VI, cut the first sod on 22 January 1922, and the gleaming white edifice – the greatest sports stadium in the world – began to rise majestically. At a cost of £750,000, Wembley was finally completed just four days before West Ham United faced Bolton Wanderers in another classic North v South clash in its opening match, the 1923 FA Cup Final. Into its construction had gone 25,000 tons of concrete, 2,000 tons of steel and 500,000 riv-

ets. It was 890 feet long, 650 feet wide and 76 feet high, with the famous twin domed towers 50 feet higher still. Here was surely, at last, a national stadium to be proud of. FA secretary Sir Frederick Wall was a happy man: 'At last we have found a ground for everybody who wants to see the Cup final.' The official Wembley press release was even more enthusiastic: 'The new Empire Stadium is as big as the Biblical city of Jericho. A hundred thousand people have been to the Final at Crystal Palace, but half of them couldn't see. Now there is room for everyone.' Unfortunately there wasn't. The stadium had 104 turnstiles and 72 corridor entrances, which it was thought would be more than enough to admit everyone who turned up. After all, the stadium's official capacity was 127,000 and the previous year's final, at Stamford Bridge, had attracted only 53,000. On 28 April 1923, however, an estimated 200,000 crowded into Wembley, many of them forced on to the pitch by pressure of those pouring in at the back. As disaster loomed, a number of mounted policemen rode to the rescue, most notably Constable George Scorey on his 13-year-old horse 'Billy', a distinctive grey whose colour marked him out in subsequent photographs. With the help of some of the players, the police patiently edged the crowd aside, walking slowly in ever-increasing circles until reinforcements arrived and order was restored. The game finally got under way, 45 minutes late, and Bolton eventually won what has become known as the 'White Horse Final'.

No stadium could have had a more dramatic baptism, but at least lessons were learned. The following season the Cup final was designated an all-ticket affair, and throughout the 1920s and 1930s crowds of over 90,000 watched the season's finale in relative comfort. The first 100,000 crowd, now the stadium's official capacity, was admitted for the 1950 final, and this figure remained constant until 1986, by which time ground improvements had reduced it slightly. The stadium's owners, Wembley plc, have complied with the all-seater rule since 1990, with a consequent further reduction to 79,045. This was how things stood until 2000, when it was decided that the ageing stadium was no longer able to compete in the modern world and plans were made to demolish it to make way for an ultra-modern replacement on the same site.

Of the FA Cup finals that have been held at Wembley since the dramatic events of 1923, probably the most famous is the 'Matthews Final' of 1953, when Blackpool came from 3–1 down to defeat Bolton 4–3. Either side of the first footballing knight's triumph, Newcastle United won the Cup three times in the 1950s. In 1958 the nation willed the Manchester United side, rebuilt after the devastating Munich disaster, to overcome Bolton, but it was not to be. In 1961 Tottenham Hotspur became the first team in the twentieth century to complete the coveted League and FA Cup double, beating an injury-hit Leicester City 2–0. Sunderland, Southampton and Wimbledon have all been unlikely winners of the famous trophy, but memorable games in other competitions have also taken place on the hallowed stage. In 1951 the whole country cheered when the student side Pegasus beat the mighty Bishop Auckland in the Amateur Cup final in front of a full house. Third Division sides Queen's Park Rangers and Swindon Town unexpectedly lifted the Football League Cup trophy in 1967 and 1969, respectively. In 1965 West Ham United beat Munich 1860 in the final of the European Cup Winners' Cup, and three years later Manchester United became the first English side to win the European Cup, with a 4–1 win after extra time over Benfica.

Not only club matches have been played at Wembley, of course. The home of the England team since its opening, Wembley saw the home side humbled in 1953, when Hungary became the first foreign side to win on English soil with a comprehensive 6–3 victory. The stadium hosted the most momentous match in its long and chequered history in 1966, the World Cup final, when England beat West Germany 4–2. Commentator Kenneth Wolstenholme's famous line 'They think it's all over – it is now!' has passed into football folklore. In 1974 disaster followed on triumph. Needing a Wembley victory against Poland to qualify for the finals of that year's World Cup, England could manage only a 1–1 draw, the Polish hero being Jan Tomaszewski, the goalkeeper dubbed a 'clown' by Brian Clough on TV before the game. Further Wembley heartbreak was to come in 1996 when a nerve-wracking penalty shoot-out saw England lose a European Championship semi-final to Germany, the eventual winners.

Germany were also England's opponents in the last international to be played at the old Wembley. The Premiership was suspended on Saturday 7 October 2000 when England strode onto the Wembley turf for their opening fixture in the qualifying competition for the 2002 World Cup. England lost 1–0 to a Dietmar Hamann goal, but home fans' disappointment was overshadowed by the announcement shortly after the game that England manager Kevin Keegan had resigned, throwing the England camp into turmoil one game into the world's greatest tournament. Wembley's last game, like its first, will be remembered long after the score has been forgotten.

Although Wembley's owners spent around £40 million on the venerable stadium from the late 1980s, by the end of the millennium it was beginning to show its age. Toilet facilities had always been inadequate and the catering facilities generated complaints after every big game. The front ten rows of seats behind the goals provided unacceptable sightlines, and at the very rear the Olympic Gallery – named to commemorate the 1948 Games held at Wembley, installed around the rim of the roof and seating 4,000 in relative comfort – was reached by stairways obstructing many of the cheaper seats. Even in the gallery itself many fans had only restricted views of the pitch, due to the scoreboards suspended from the roof. As its status as a listed building precluded expansion beyond the outer wall, the only solution, if the national stadium was to remain in the capital, was for demolition and the erection of a new stadium on the existing site. After the 2000 Germany game the bulldozers moved in and an era was over.

Northern Ireland
In Northern Ireland, West Belfast is the home of the province's richest club, Linfield, and their ground, Windsor Park, has hosted international matches since its opening on 2 September 1905, when Belfast neighbours Glentoran were the visitors. Built on land formerly known as Bog Meadow, 'the Shrine', as it became to hard core 'Blues' supporters, originally had a capacity of 60,000, but gradual improvements over the years have increased the fans' comfort whilst reducing the overall capacity to 28,000, including 9,160 seats. The most modern stand, on the north side of the ground, cost £2 million to build and contains 6,800 of these seats.

FIFA President João Havelange opened this gleaming cantilevered construction in October 1984. Local residents were less than impressed, claiming that their fireplaces had been rendered all but unusable due to the wind-tunnel effect of the new structure. On the other side of the ground the more traditional main, or South Stand, still survives as a monument to that famous Scottish engineer, Archibald Leitch, whose work across the Irish Sea up until the outbreak of the Second World War included the development of, among others, Parkhead, Ibrox, Hampden, Old Trafford, Highbury and White Hart Lane, though these modern grounds would now be unrecognisable to Leitch. Not so Windsor Park; the front of the South Stand still has an open paddock in front, a feature now only a memory in the modern Premiership. The stand, which was opened in 1930 with a match against Glasgow Rangers, Linfield's Scottish Protestant brothers-in-arms, is also restricted to only two-thirds of that side of the ground, the stand extension that formerly filled the remaining third having been dismantled on safety grounds after the disastrous Bradford fire of 1985. The stand situated at the east end of the ground, the appropriately-named Railway End, resembles a steam-age station more than a sporting venue, its roof boarded with a serrated wooden frontage. The west end of the ground still boasts an open expanse of terracing, the Spion Kop, once a feature of so many English grounds.

Behind the Kop is another pitch, used by The Swifts, Linfield's reserve side. Floodlit football finally came to the ground in October 1956, FA Cup specialists Newcastle United providing the opposition in the inaugural match.

Windsor Park, not surprisingly given its troubled location, has seen its share of unpleasantness over the years. In December 1949 a game between Linfield and Belfast Celtic, the city's leading Catholic club, ended in a sectarian riot, leaving a Celtic player with a broken leg; and in April 1972, in a spell during which Northern Ireland had been forced to play all their home games outside the province, a terrorist bomb blew up part of the Railway End stand. In 1979, following the murder of Lord Mountbatten in Ireland, Linfield's home leg of their European Cup tie against Dundalk of the Irish Republic was similarly switched to Holland. The 1980/81 Home International Championship was abandoned after both England and Wales refused to play in Belfast.

Outside this unhappy period Windsor Park has, however, been witness to several milestones in the national side's history. In 1951 France were the first non-British side to play there; then, in 1958, the year that all four home countries qualified for the World Cup finals, Northern Ireland shocked the football world by reaching the quarter-finals. They booked their tickets to Sweden after beating Portugal 3–0 in Belfast and then eliminating the strongly-fancied Italy at the group stage, with goals from Cush and Jimmy McIlroy. The draw for the 1982 tournament placed Northern Ireland in the same qualifying group as Scotland, and a packed Windsor Park saw the two home countries play out a goalless draw. Home victories against Sweden (3–0), Portugal (1–0) and Israel (1–0), however, saw Northern Ireland through to Spain. Four years later they were again drawn against home country opposition, this time England, who won the Windsor Park encounter 1–0. This was the Irishmen's only home reverse, however, as fans at 'the Shrine' watched Romania (3–2), Finland (2–1) and Turkey (2–0) all leave Windsor Park pointless. Northern Ireland qualified, along with England, and were off to Mexico.

To match their three successful World Cup qualifying campaigns, Northern Ireland have delighted Windsor Park fans by winning the Home International Championship outright on three occasions: 1913/14, 1979/80 and 1983/84 (the final year of the tournament). With Linfield's home Irish League attendances averaging only around 3,500, the club's main source of gate revenue is the 15 per cent they receive from international matches. With annual games against England, Scotland and Wales now ruled out, they must continue to rely on World Cup and European Championship qualifiers (Northern Ireland have never reached the final stages of the latter tournament). There are always friendlies, of course. On 29 April 1964 the Windsor Park faithful were treated to a 3–0 victory for Northern Ireland over Uruguay. Making his home international debut was a certain George Best.

Scotland

Hampden Park stadium is owned by Queen's Park, the nation's oldest club – founded in 1867 – and still an amateur one. The present ground is the third of the club's homes to bear the name, taken from a street of terraced houses named after John Hampden, an English Civil War Parliamentarian. The first Hampden Park, in the Queen's Drive area of the city, was home to the club from 1873 until 1884, when the building of the Mount Florida to Crosshill railway line forced them to move to the second Hampden, across Cathcart Road. This ground was vacated in 1903 and renamed Cathkin Park, home of Third Lanark until that club's sad demise in 1967.

On 31 October 1903 Hampden Mark Three – the ground that was to become famous for its intimidating 'Hampden Roar' – was officially opened by the Lord Provost of Glasgow, Sir John Ore Primrose, the amateurs beating Celtic 1–0 in the Scottish First Division. The following April the ground was the venue for the Rangers v Celtic Scottish Cup final, watched by a record 65,000 crowd. With Archibald Leitch's firm as main contractors, the ground was gradually improved

over the years. It began life in the classic Leitch mould: bowl-shaped, with enormous areas of banked terracing. Instead of the usual stand down one side with a pavilion alongside, however, this time he plumped for two 4,000-seater stands along the south side, with the pavilion between. When this rather self-conscious wooden edifice was destroyed by fire the stands were joined in 1914 by a much more impressive four-storey brick structure with a roof-mounted press box. In 1929, the club built Lesser Hampden behind the west end of the ground and this became the home of the club's reserve and junior sides. In 1927 the terraces were expanded to accommodate a further 25,000 fans, and in 1937 the North Stand, containing 4,500 seats, was added at the rear of the terracing on that side. By now the capacity of the ground had reached an amazing 150,000, making it – until the opening of the Maracana Stadium in Rio de Janeiro in preparation for the 1950 World Cup – the world's largest.

The extra space did not go to waste: the European Cup final was staged at Hampden on 18 May 1960 and an incredible 127,621 were packed in to see Real Madrid demolish Eintracht Frankfurt 7–3.

On 17 April 1937 a world record had been set when 149,547 fans passed through the Hampden turnstiles for the Scotland v England game. Reports at the time also estimated that another 10,000 forced their way in and saw the match for free. The game had no bearing on the International Championship that year, as Wales had already won the title and the Triple Crown, but the important thing from Scotland's point of view was that they had beaten the 'auld enemy' 3–1. Another piece of history was made that day: England wore numbered shirts for the first time. A week later another record went when 147,365 saw Celtic lift the Scottish Cup after beating Aberdeen 2–1. This remains a record for a club match in Europe. It could have been even higher – an estimated 20,000 tried to get in illegally but couldn't. Another milestone was reached on 15 April 1970 in the second leg of the European Cup semi-final between Celtic and Leeds United, Celtic winning 2–1 to win the tie 3–1 on aggregate. The crowd of 136,505 is still the highest ever for a European competition game. The Glasgow public don't just bother to turn out for the prestige matches either; Hampden's first floodlit fixture, a friendly between Rangers and Eintracht Frankfurt on 17 October 1961 saw the Blues go down 2–1 in front of no less than 104,493 spectators. The nearest Queen's Park came to a six-figure crowd was 95,772 for a match against Rangers in January 1930, during one of their brief spells in the First Division.

Such attendances are unlikely to be repeated, however. The official capacity of the now-outdated stadium was reduced to 135,000 following the disaster at Burnden Park, Bolton in 1946 and a further reduction, to 81,000, followed in the wake of the Safety of Sports Grounds Act (1977). Although Queen's Park had roofed over the West Terrace in 1967, the following year 1,400 South Stand seats were destroyed by fire and Hampden was in serious trouble. The North Stand was due for replacement, the vast cinder-covered terraces were unsafe and the stadium's future as the spiritual home of Scottish football seemed threatened. Queen's Park, on their modest gates of only a few hundred, could not fund the necessary rebuilding work themselves, so in 1971 the Scottish FA, backed by all Scottish League clubs, the local authority and the Sports Council, began talks with the Labour government of the day with a view to financing a major reconstruction. The estimated cost was £11 million, of which the government agreed to provide half. By 1980, however, the estimated cost had risen to £17 million. Even more unpromisingly, the sympathetic Labour government had been voted out. Margaret Thatcher's government revoked the grant of £5.5 million and Queen's Park came close to selling their historic home. Glasgow City Council had already withdrawn their support for the scheme and Rangers had also expressed their doubts. The SFA launched an appeal, however, and by 1981, with donations from the Football Grounds Improvement Trust and the Football Trust, enough money had been raised for work to begin. The first phase, lasting until 1986, involved demolition of the North Stand together with the concreting over of all the terracing. This reduced the capacity further, to 74,370, including 10,000 seats. Phase Two, which was intended to cover the open terraces and install more seats, had been scheduled to get under way in 1988, but the Taylor Report following the Hillsborough disaster meant that plans had to be modified to include seating throughout. A new South Stand was also proposed. Costs were escalating, and with the traditional Scotland v England fixture, Hampden's most lucrative, being removed from the football calendar after the 1989 game, the future looked bleak. The following year only 12,081 turned up to watch Scotland take on Romania. By now Hampden's very *raison d'être* was being called into question: with Wales's successful return to Cardiff Arms Park, why, it was asked, couldn't Scotland follow suit and play future internationals at Murrayfield? This notion was rejected, however, and the National Stadium Committee, consisting of Queen's Park, the SFA and the Scottish League, pressed ahead. In May 1992 the stadium was closed for its latest facelift, the next seven international fixtures being shared between Ibrox and Pittodrie, home of Aberdeen.

On 23 March 1994, the new Hampden admitted 36,809 for a friendly against Holland. This was almost a full house, but later that year the capacity was temporarily reduced again, this time to a mere 9,000, as yet another modernisation scheme got under way. The main stadium was again closed, with Queen's Park playing next door at Lesser Hampden, its 800 capacity being more than sufficient to house their few faithful fans. Future World Cup qualifiers, and hopefully further European finals, will return when the next version of Hampden opens its doors. The twenty-first-century stadium will have an all-seated capacity of 52,000 and be home to a Scottish museum of football exhibiting, among other memorabilia, the distinctive square Hampden goalposts. A media centre, a medical research centre and a residential fitness centre are also proposed. As an act of faith in the future of the latest version of Queen's Park's home, both the Scottish FA and the Scottish League plan to relocate their Glasgow offices to the new stadium. Murrayfield will have to be content with rugby internationals.

Wales

If Northern Ireland have had the same home, barring civil unrest, for almost a century, they still have a little way to go to beat Wales' record. Until 1997 the oldest surviving football stadium in the world still in regular use was in fact a rugby stadium – Cardiff Arms Park, home of Cardiff Rugby Club and the Welsh Rugby Union. The stadium, named after the Cardiff Arms coaching inn that once stood nearby, was built on land reclaimed after the eminent engineer Isambard Kingdom Brunel had been commissioned to divert the River Taff as part of a redevelopment of Cardiff city centre. It had already been staging rugby matches for 20 years when the Welsh soccer team first took to the field there on 3 March 1896, and perhaps wished they hadn't as they lost 9–1 to England. Five more internationals were staged at the Arms Park until 1910, when Cardiff City, after eleven years of wandering around the capital, finally found a permanent home at Ninian Park, named in honour of Lord Ninian Crichton Stuart, the club's foremost financial backer and later MP for Cardiff. The new ground, between Sloper Road and the Taff Vale railway, was opened on 1 September 1910 with a friendly against Aston Villa, watched by a crowd of 7,000. Before this prestigious match could get under way, however, the City players had had to rise at daybreak to clear broken glass and rubbish from the pitch; the ground had been built on the site of a former city dump. In March of the following year Ninian Park staged its first international, when Scotland were the visitors, and Welsh international football seemed to have found a home of its own.

The story is more complex, however. Cardiff City, who joined the Football League (Division Two) at the beginning of the 1920/21 season, made an immediate impact on the game. They won promotion in their first season, and lost the 1923/24 First Division title only on goal difference to Huddersfield Town. In 1925 they lost the FA Cup final by a single goal to Sheffield United, but two years later became the first – and so far only – club to take the coveted trophy out of England when they beat Arsenal by the same margin. In the midst of all this club success, Wales won the 1923/24 International Championship by completing the 'Triple Crown', beating all three home countries for the first time ever. Ninian Park hosted the first of these historic victories, when Wales played Scotland on 16 February 1924, and Cardiff City provided both captains that day: centre-half Fred Keenor of Wales and left-back Jimmy Blair of Scotland.

All this success brought great prosperity to the club, and enabled significant ground improvements to be made. In 1920 the Canton Stand went up at the north end of the ground and, unusually for the time, provided the luxury of bench seats for those watching the action from behind a goal. In 1928 the Grangetown End terrace was treated to a second large roof, City's Wembley triumph providing the necessary finance. Then the good times came to an end. The 'Bluebirds' were relegated twice within three seasons. In November 1931 a Third Division home fixture against Queen's Park Rangers attracted a crowd of barely 2,000, with not a single spectator braving the elements on the Popular Side, or Bob Bank (it cost a shilling to stand there). Worse was to come: on 18 January 1937, with City still in Division Three, the Main Stand was burned down after thieves had tried to blow open the club's safe. The old wooden structure was replaced with a new brick and steel stand and in 1947, during the game's post-war boom in attendances, the terraces on that side of the ground were extended. Just as well, for in 1952/53 City finally made it back to the First Division and attracted record average attendances of almost 38,000. The Bob Bank benefited from the latest boom by being doubled in both height and depth, and by having a roof fitted over its new rear section. On 5

October 1960 Swiss side Grasshoppers of Zurich were the visitors for the first game under the ground's new floodlights, and on 14 October 1961 the old stadium attracted its record crowd of 61,566 for the visit of England. Other prestigious games hosted during the Bluebirds' glory days were a friendly against the touring Moscow Dynamo in November 1945, the rampant Russians winning by an impressive 10–1, and a 3–2 winning result for Wales against the Rest of the UK in a match to celebrate the centenary of the Welsh FA. In 1971 Cardiff City surprised the rest of Europe, beating Real Madrid by the only goal of the game in a home European Cup Winners' Cup tie in front of a crowd of 47,500, but once again hard times beckoned. By early 1991 the Bluebirds, now languishing in Division Four, could only attract 1,629 diehard fans to brave one home fixture. The club's finances were so bad that three sides of the stadium, by now a crumbling wreck, were closed in order to save on policing costs. An air of desolation now pervades the place, reminiscent of its origins as a rubbish tip.

Not all Welsh internationals have been staged in the capital, however. Wrexham had argued for years that their own Racecourse ground in the north was the true home of Welsh football; Cardiff and the south were only interested in rugby. The authorities seemed to agree. Although playing football on a cricket pitch in the middle of a racecourse may seem bizarre in the modern age, that is exactly how Wales' oldest surviving club spent their early days. The first ever Welsh international, against Scotland in March 1877, took place there, overlooked by the Turf Hotel, where the players were still changing and reaching the pitch via boards placed over the racetrack when England were the visitors in 1902. The Wrexham Races were run for the last time in 1912, however, and football became the main sporting activity, apart from occasional boxing bills and athletics meetings in the 1920s. In 1921 Wrexham were admitted to the Third Division (North) of the Football League, and when the Supporters' Club was founded five years later the

ground began to be developed. The end behind the Plas Coch (Red Hall) goal was covered, then the cover extended over the whole of that end of the ground, the Popular Side later receiving similar treatment. In the 1930s the Mold Stand was extended by a wing stand, with seats in the upper tier; in 1947 dressing rooms were added underneath and the Town End improved by the addition of concrete terracing. In 1948, for the Wales v Northern Ireland match, a crowd of 33,160 enjoyed the new facilities, a record that stood until January 1957 when Manchester United were the visitors for an FA Cup tie in which the Welshmen lost 5–0. The Supporters' Club's fundraising activities enabled the club to add floodlights in 1959, and when Wrexham gained promotion from Division Four at the end of the 1961/62 season the balcony of the local Majestic Cinema was transplanted on to the Town End, and roofed over with the rear stalls replaced by a tea bar and club shop! This weird structure, known as the 'Pigeon Loft', looked increasingly incongruous when two more conventional, modern, stands were added during the 1970s. Despite these improvements, Wrexham's status as a national stadium was never secure. Between 1945 and 1971 they had staged only ten internationals, versus Cardiff's 42. On 27 May 1982 only 2,315 – the lowest figure for a match in the Home Internationals for 90 years – turned out to watch Wales v Northern Ireland. Four years later the Welsh FA ominously moved their offices from Wrexham to Cardiff, and then in 1989 FIFA decreed that after 1992 no standing was to be permitted at any World Cup venues. With only 5,250 seats available at the northern outpost it seemed that the old ground had run its course.

Wales' only other international venue has been Swansea. In February 1894 the first international in South Wales was played when Wales took on Ireland at St Helen's, half a mile from Swansea City's present home, the Vetch Field, which had been used by Swansea Villa since the 1880s. In 1912 a new club, Swansea Town (renamed Swansea City in 1970), was formed, and the newly improved Vetch, which had almost been turned into a gas-works by the Gas Light Company, saw the locals take on Cardiff City in a Southern League match before a crowd of 8,000, all of them standing on open banks. Not that the players were any more comfortable: the pitch had no turf throughout its first season and they had to wear kneepads to protect themselves from the clinker surface. The following season the ground boasted grass and a new stand (the present South Stand), with seating for 1,100. When the Swans became founder members of the Football League's new Third Division in 1920, a further stand was added in the corner of the ground overlooked by the nearby Territorial Army drill hall. The Vetch staged its first international, against Ireland, in April 1921, and went on to host a total of 18 until 1988, when, along with the Racecourse Ground, it fell victim to FIFA's all-seater policy.

With a total of only 14,000 seats available between them, Cardiff, Wrexham and Swansea were written out of the equation and the Welsh FA had no option but to return to the Arms Park, vastly improved since it had hosted its last soccer international in 1910, and large enough to hold any crowd the Welsh football team could attract. On 31 May 1989 West Germany were the visitors for a friendly, and a crowd of 31,000 watched in comfort. Not all Welsh fans seemed to appreciate their new home, however; two of their more lunatic element killed a spectator during a World Cup qualifier in November 1993 by firing a flare into the North Stand. Despite this act of mindlessness, the Arms Park went from strength to strength, hosting not only football and rugby matches but also rock concerts and even a visit from the Pope. In 1992, for example, it earned a staggering £35 million in visitor revenue, more than the entire city could boast in tourist income that year. Cardiff was not yet finished, however; even the modernised Arms Park was not considered a good enough home for the newly professional handling code. In 1995 the WRU made a submission to the Millennium Commission of the National Lottery for the construction of an entirely new stadium on the existing site, seating

75,000 and with a retractable roof and underground parking for 1,500 cars. The old ground was duly demolished and in 1999 the ultra-modern Millennium Stadium played host to the Rugby World Cup. On 29 March 2000 the new arena staged its first football match when an incredible 66,500 watched Ryan Giggs score Wales' consolation goal in a 2–1 win for Wales against Finland. This friendly was originally scheduled for the decaying Ninian Park, but Welsh manager Mark Hughes had argued the Welsh FA into the switch. With admission reduced to a standard £5, the choice proved inspired, giving Wales their highest attendance in history. Two months later even this was beaten – the revenue from the Finland game was sufficient to make a further 5,750 seats available, at a bargain £10 for adults and £5 for children, for the next fixture. An enthralled 72,250 were there to see Wales, this time without Giggs, hold Brazil until ten second-half minutes of South American magic conjured up goals from Elber, Cafu and Rivaldo. The result was not as important as the setting: next day the *Western Mail* carried a typical Welsh verdict on the game: 'I've never felt so good about a 3–0 beating.' Is this to be the pattern of the future for Welsh football, away from its grass roots?

Sources:

Butler, B., *The Official Illustrated History of the FA Cup* (London: Headline, 1996).

Inglis, S., *Football Grounds of Britain* (London: CollinsWillow, 1996).

Inglis, S., *The Football Grounds of Europe* (London, Willow, 1990).

Taylor, R. and Ward, A., *Kicking & Screaming: An Oral History of Football in England* (London: Robson Books, 1996).

See also Grounds

Tony Rennick

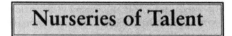

Nurseries of Talent

The transfer market, through which football clubs buy players from other clubs, is almost as old as professional football itself.

By employing superior financial resources some clubs have been able to corner the market for scarce playing talent and secure their own dominance. At the close of the twentieth century the labour market had been extendèd to overseas players, a process which helped a minority of clubs to import international talent to their teams. But while the transfer market has operated to a varying degree among all professional clubs, none have relied on it as the only source of new players. All clubs have sought to develop young players through their own youth teams, which are themselves supplied from often extensive scouting networks by which new talent is identified in local amateur football and integrated into the club. Thus a pyramidal hierarchy has developed, with clubs at the bottom feeding talent through to those at the top. The network operates on an informal basis with, as yet, no equivalents arising of the continental system in which some clubs actually own nursery clubs. The nearest equivalent was Portsmouth's use of Southern League Waterlooville as nursery-cum-reserve team in the early 1970s, following the abolition of their official reserve side for financial reasons. Informal links have developed between a small number of Premiership and Nation-wide League sides, such as that established between Liverpool and Crewe in the late 1990s, which allows the bigger clubs some very limited claim on promising players. Most elite clubs are also very happy to loan young players on the fringes of their first-team squads to smaller clubs for periods of up to a full season, in the expectation that the experience they gain will be far more valuable than that gained in academy or reserve team football.

In this structure some areas have been notable producers of talent. In the 1890s, for example, Bristol Rovers claimed to recruit most of their players from the local leagues in Eastville Park. One of England's most celebrated players of the inter-war years, Eddie Hapgood, was discovered in this way – though not by Bristol Rovers but by the London club Arsenal. He was apprenticed for a couple of years to Kettering Town of the Southern League, before making his appearance in the First Division. A number of Scottish players, including some famous managers, have come from the local leagues of the Bellshill area, in the mining district outside Motherwell. On a larger geographical scale the amateur clubs of the north-east of England have long been seen as a rich seam of football talent, supplying not only Newcastle United, Sunderland and Middlesbrough with players such as Jackie Milburn, Raich Carter, Wilf Mannion, Paul Gascoigne, and Peter Beardsley, but also feeding clubs farther afield. Burnley in the 1950s and '60s fielded a strong First Division team made up largely of north-easterners recruited through the club's scouting system there, subsequently selling many such players on to bigger clubs for large fees. Manchester United has similarly drawn many players from Ireland, including the renowned George Best.

Most League clubs are able to claim the discovery, or bringing on, of at least one player who has acquired fame after leaving the club: in recent years, for example, Scunthorpe United started Kevin Keegan on his career, Crewe Alexandra groomed David Platt, and Blackpool produced Alan Ball. Few clubs, however, can point to outstanding success achieved with teams not created by resort to the transfer market. Arsenal, the dominant club of the inter-war years, combined scouting for new talent, which produced players like Hapgood and Cliff Bastin, with the use of the transfer market to secure Charles Buchan, David Jack and the all-important Alex James. Their successors in the 1950s – Manchester United and Wolverhampton Wanderers – both enjoyed triumphs with teams built around players schooled in their own nursery. Many of Manchester United's 'Busby Babes', who won the Championship in 1956 and 1957, were also local men, although centre-forward Taylor was an expensive signing from Barnsley. Probably the British club to attain greatest success with local players was Celtic, whose European Cup-winning team of 1967 was an all-Scottish one, most of its members having been born in Glasgow, and none recruited for big transfer fees.

Sources:
Ferrier, B., *Soccer Partnership: Billy Wright and Walter Winterbottom* (London: Heinemann, 1960).
Green, G., *Soccer in the Fifties* (London: Ian Allen, 1974).
Walvin, J., *The People's Game: A Social History of British Football* (London: Allen Lane, 1975).

Further Reading:
Nawrat, C. and Hutchings, S., *The Sunday Times Illustrated History of Football* (London: Octopus Publishing, 1998).

Jeff Hill

[The] Original 12

The Football League, founded in 1888 following a suggestion from William McGregor (Aston Villa), comprised arguably the best professional clubs in England at the time. Six clubs were from Lancashire and six from the Midlands.

ACCRINGTON FC
Frequently confused with Accrington Stanley, this was an entirely different club founded in 1878. 'Th'Owd Reds' were one of the first clubs to use professionals. Situated between Burnley and Blackburn, the club always struggled, and resigned in 1893 rather than be relegated to the Second Division. Accrington then joined the Lancashire League but folded in 1896.

ASTON VILLA
Established in 1874 by members of Villa Cross Wesleyan Methodist Chapel, the club quickly became a key side in the Birmingham area. They were dominant in the 1890s, winning the Championship five times and the FA Cup twice. They declined in the 1950s and 1960s, but League Cup triumphs followed in the 1970s and '90s. Their best recent period was 1980–1982, when they won the Football League title and the European Cup.

BLACKBURN ROVERS
Founded in 1875, Rovers were one of the first clubs to break the southern amateur monopoly in the FA Cup, winning three times in the 1880s, and again in 1890 and 1891. Their best League spell was from 1911 to 1914, when they won the title twice. Transformed by Jack Walker's money, they triumphed again in 1994/95 after many years without a major trophy.

BOLTON WANDERERS
Founded in 1874, they used professionals from a very early date. Always better in cup competitions, they have won the FA Cup four times, but never the Championship. They spent many years in the top division until the 1960s. Their best periods were in the 1920s and 1950s, their worst in the 1980s. They had recent short-lived Premiership spells in 1995/96 and 1997/98.

BURNLEY
Founded in 1881, Burnley initially suffered from poor gates and indifferent results, spending long periods in Division Two. The club had a better time from 1913 to 1930, winning the Championship (1921) and the FA Cup (1914). The smallest English town to support regular top-level football, a further League Championship in 1960 was their last important trophy, and since the 1970s they have often struggled, coming periously close to losing League status in 1987.

DERBY COUNTY
Formed in 1884, they were largely unsuccessful until the 1970s, winning only one major trophy, the 1946 FA Cup, despite having many skilled players over the years, including Steve Bloomer, Hughie Gallacher and Raich Carter. Their best period was the 1970s, when, transformed by the management team of Brian Clough and Peter Taylor, they won the Championship in 1971/72, a feat repeated under Dave Mackay in 1974/75.

EVERTON
Established in 1878, their first League title came in 1890/91. Spending most of their time in the top division, they have won nine Championships and five FA Cups.

Less successful in the 1920s, 1950s and 1970s, their best performances recently came between 1984 and 1987, when they won the FA Cup, the Cup Winners' Cup, and the title twice.

NOTTS COUNTY
Formed in 1862, their only major trophy remains the FA Cup in 1894. In the early days, they had periods in the First Division from 1897 to 1913, but spent most of the time after that in the lower divisions. Their greatest achievement in recent years has been playing in the top division from 1981 to 1984 and in 1991/92.

PRESTON NORTH END
In 1888, North End were the best club in England, and proved it by being the first champions and the first double winners in 1888/89. Another title followed in 1889/90, but nothing after that. Their only other major trophy was the FA Cup in 1938. They moved between the First and Second Divisions until 1960, sinking lower in recent years.

STOKE
Established in 1863, they were unsuccessful in the League, failing to be re-elected in 1890, and resigning in 1909. They rejoined again in 1919, having a longer sojourn in the First Division from 1933 to 1953. Like the other smaller clubs discussed here, they have declined, spending several seasons in the lower divisions. Their only major trophy was the League Cup in 1972.

WEST BROMWICH ALBION
Founded in 1879, Albion is another club to have suffered in recent years, despite having won the FA Cup five times, the last occasion being in 1968. Although they have spent long periods in the top division, their only Championship was in 1919/20, and recently they have lacked the ability to return to the top flight.

WOLVERHAMPTON WANDERERS
Wolves were formed in 1877 as St Luke's, and they probably enjoyed their best years in the 1950s, winning three titles, when they were seen as England's representa-

tives against European clubs. They have also won the FA Cup four times and the League Cup twice. They spent a long time in the top division, but latterly have not looked capable of returning.

Sources:

Witty, J. R., 'The 92 League Clubs', in A. H. Fabian and G. Green (eds), *Association Football* (London: Caxton, 1960).

Guinness Book of Football (London: Guinness Publishing, 1998).

Rothmans Football Yearbook (London: Headline, various editions).

See also The Football League

Robert Lewis

History Highlights 1940–1949

For the first five years of the 1940s, it was simply impossible for British football to exist with any sense of normality. For a period after the outbreak of war in September 1939 the English FA had decided to halt all matches and suspend players' contracts in aid of the war effort. However, as the authorities realised that a long period of conflict lay ahead, football's ability to maintain public spirit and morale at home was recognised, and the FA launched a wartime programme of football based on various cup competitions and regionalised leagues. As many footballers were in the process of being called up to the forces, particularly to perform physical training roles, it was agreed that guest players would be allowed to appear for teams when they were short of men.

The standard of football during wartime was extremely variable. Some clubs struggled to raise a team and most had very little time to train. Not surprisingly, crowds were often very low as fear of bombing and poor expectations kept people away from matches. There were some exceptions. International matches continued throughout the war and, as in the case of Scotland v England at

Hampden Park in May 1940, drew attendances of up to 75,000. Winston Churchill indicated his strong approval for wartime football at just such an international between England and Scotland in 1941, when he was introduced to the teams prior to the match. Seven Cabinet ministers also attended the game.

Because of the fractured nature of competition, it is difficult to assess the relative strength of teams in the wartime period. Arsenal were undoubtedly strong in the south, winning the South A League in 1939/40, the London League in 1941/42 and the South League and the South League Cup in 1942/43. In the north, Preston North End won the Northern Regional League and the League Cup in 1940/41. However, it was Blackpool who dominated the war years in the north, winning the Northern League three years running between 1941/42 and 1943/44. This was no doubt because of the club's proximity to a major RAF base which accommodated such professionals as Stanley Matthews for much of the war.

As the war ended in 1945, football attempted to return to some level of normality. The FA Cup was reintroduced for the 1945/46 season, the eventual winners being Derby County, who beat Charlton Athletic 4–1 in the final. Far from being an occasion for celebration, though, the first FA Cup competition of the post-war period will be best remembered for the sixth-round match between Bolton Wanderers and Stoke City at Burnden Park on 9 March 1946. The official attendance at Burnden was put at 65,419, but it is estimated that a crowd of around 85,000 attempted to gain entry into the ground. As a result, part of the terracing became so overcrowded that crush barriers collapsed, killing 33 and injuring 500. This was, at the time, British football's worst disaster.

The crush at Burnden Park was a clear indicator, albeit a tragic one, of the popularity of football in Britain in the immediate post-war period. As the League competition got underway again on 31 August 1946, nearly one million people flocked to the 43 matches which took place. As the 1940s progressed, attendances remained exceptionally high, and

by 1948/49 an annual attendance of 41,271,424 was recorded at English football: a record for any single season. The large crowds caused problems of safety at many grounds (as evidenced by the Burnden Park tragedy) and other problems such as high levels of industrial absenteeism. Clearly, British people entered the post-war period with an almost insatiable appetite for football. However, football was not alone in this regard. Cricket crowds also boomed during this period, and other sections of the leisure industry, such as the seaside holiday trade, also enjoyed substantial growth.

When League football returned in 1946, playing success resided in the south and remained there for the rest of the decade. Arsenal won the League Championship in the 1947/48 season and the FA Cup in 1949/50, while Charlton Athletic lifted the Cup in 1946/47. But it was the performances of Portsmouth that will be most remembered from this period. With a team strengthened by ex-servicemen, professional players who had been stationed in the Portsmouth area during the war, the club won consecutive championships in 1948/49 and 1949/50, despite being totally disregarded by many experts. This achievement made them the undoubted team of the decade in England.

In Scotland, that honour fell to Rangers, who managed three titles between 1947 and 1950, and a League, Cup and League Cup treble in 1948/49. However, Hibernian began a resurgence that was briefly to threaten Glasgow's long-established domination. In 1948, they won the title for the first time since 1903, after finishing as runners-up in 1947. Belfast Celtic's Irish League title in 1947/48 gave the club a record sixth consecutive championship in a run that had begun in 1935/36. Unfortunately, sectarian tensions forced the club to leave the League in the next season. One of the most noteworthy events on the international scene was undoubtedly England's 2–0 defeat at the hands of the Republic of Ireland at Goodison Park. This was England's first ever defeat on home soil by a 'foreign' side, although political history and the fact that the Irish players were drawn from the Football League allowed many to ignore this fact.

Sources:
Nawrat, C. and Hutchings, S., *The Sunday Times Illustrated History of Football* (St Helens: The Book People Ltd, 1998).
Russell, D., *Football and the English: A Social History of Association Football in England, 1863–1995* (Preston: Carnegie Publishing, 1997).
Walvin, J., *The People's Game: The History of Football Revisited* (Edinburgh: Mainstream Publishing, 1994).

Further Reading:
Rollin, J., *Soccer at War, 1939–1945* (London: Collins, 1985).

See also Second World War

Gavin Mellor

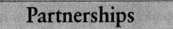

Partnerships

It has often been said that a certain player would never have had the success they experienced without the support of another player or mentor. This manifests itself when such a partnership is broken, for example by one of the two moving to another club or when one of the players is on international duty.

Successful partnerships on the field of play usually revolve around front-line or offensive players such as a winger and centre-forward, or in more recent times two strikers. Examples include Cliff Jones and Bobby Smith in the successful Tottenham side of the early 1960s, Kevin Keegan and John Toshack in the successful Liverpool team of the 1970s, Alan Shearer and Chris Sutton at Blackburn Rovers in the early 1990s, and Dwight Yorke and Andy Cole at Manchester United in the late 1990s.

It is as though one player has an extra-sensory perception of where the other player will be and how he would like the ball fed to him. Their joint success is often based on a tall player who reaches the crosses and feeds the ball to the feet of a good striker, two good ball-players good at playing each other off in a quick one-two, or a sweeper who is good at placing the ball for his partner to run onto. However, this is not always the case and there are examples of reliable full-backs who in partnership maintain a tight defence at the back (Ray Wilson and George Cohen in England's World Cup winning team) or penetrating midfielders with a partner constantly covering them when in attack. The greater movement of players between clubs and the rotation of players within a squad probably militates against such partnerships evolving or enduring in the way they once did. However, it is still common for managers to justify their purchases on the basis of providing a partner for another.

Occasionally it has been remarked how a player is capable of playing exceptionally well for one manager and not for anyone else. In the 1970s and '80s Nottingham Forest released a significant number of players for large sums who, playing under other managers, failed to replicate their form and justify their price-tag. Gary Birtles and Neil Webb both left Brian Clough's Nottingham Forest for Manchester United, but rapidly lost form. The tendency for successful partnerships has been said to be in decline as the rotation of players has become commonplace for clubs with large squads playing in several competitions.

Partnerships off the field of play are not so common, probably the best known being that of Brian Clough and Peter Taylor. A former goalkeeper and former striker with contrasting personalities appeared to complement each other in a partnership which brought success at club level, from taking unfortunate Hartlepool United to Fourth Division success in the late 1960s, to Nottingham Forest twice winning the European Cup in 1979 and 1980.

Within most successful teams there is at least one two- or three-way partnership, emphasising the team nature of the sport.

Sources:
Pawson, T., *The Goalscorers: From Bloomer to Keegan* (London: Cassell, 1978).
Rothmans Football Yearbook (London: Rothmans, 1981 onwards).

Richard William Cox

Photography

Photographers have been taking pictures at football matches since the nineteenth century, and football is now the most photographed sport in the world. Although television has become football's preferred medium, there is still an insatiable appetite for the 'frozen image'. Images of players' facial and physical acrobatics find an audience eager to study every gesture, grimace, and gyration.

The earliest examples of football photography date from the 1860s. The photographs are generally of formal groups of moustachioed gentlemen in long woollen shirts and hefty boots. The photographer, working from approximately 1840 to 1880, and perhaps realising the limitations of the medium, had the experience of recording only the static parts of the visible universe for his satisfaction. Photographs of formal groups at important social events such as christenings, weddings, military service, and membership of sporting or social clubs provided plenty of material for him, and the formal team photograph therefore soon became an important part of the tradition of sports photography. By the early 1900s, these photographs were reproduced as postcards along with individual player portraits. They were so popular that even reserve team players had postcards of themselves to give to adoring fans.

Moving objects, however, presented two problems. The cameras and film emulsions available at this time were slow and cumbersome, with exposure times in minutes as opposed to fractions of seconds. Even people moving at walking pace appeared as blurs. Only by reducing the exposure time could an acceptable image be produced. This technical advancement was hindered for four decades by the slow sensitivity of the photographic emulsions available. The second problem was that of relative speed – in other words, the relationship between the speed of the subject and the distance between it and the camera. As photographic emulsions became more sensitive exposure times became shorter. It was then possible to 'freeze' some action, but only if the subjects were relatively distant; objects close to the camera would still blur. The solution was the development of lenses that would bring the action closer.

Around 1880 the introduction of gelatine-silver bromide emulsions made instantaneous shots possible, as this film emulsion was much more sensitive to light than the previous wet collodian process. Action shots were now possible. The most important early examples of such 'frozen action' photographs are those taken by the photographer Eadweard Muybridge. Muybridge was the first person to conceive of a 'photo finish' in horse racing. His series of photographs of horses running, taken in 1878 and 1879 with a row of 12 to 24 cameras recorded for the first time movements too fast for the eye to perceive, and proved conclusively how a horse ran. The second problem was partly resolved with the production of the first telephoto lenses in 1891. At the turn of the century all the technological requirements were there for action photographs.

At this time there was only a limited market for football photographs. Artists' impressions were the vogue mainly because of the limitations of printing processes available to newspapers and magazines. However, by 1904 the advances made in print technology guaranteed reasonable photographic reproduction. There was great opposition from trade unions, illustrators, and engravers, but in 1907 the *Daily Mail* became the first paper fully illustrated with photographs. Editors soon realised that football photographs sold papers. Important games received extensive coverage, using a narrative style of reporting. The 'photo-story' came into being. Every aspect of the game was covered, from the pre-match preparations to the crowd leaving the ground, a format continued today by television. Crowd photographs showed the game in a wider social context: what sort of people went to games, in what numbers, and how they behaved. The most famous such photograph was that taken in 1923 of the crowd encroaching on the pitch at the first Wembley Cup final. It showed Constable George Scorey on his white horse 'Billy' trying to clear the pitch, and this photograph became so famous that the 1923 FA Cup final became known as the 'White Horse' final. In fact, the other police officers on darker horses simply did not show up so well against the dark background of the crowd. Football photography had expanded its boundaries and was beginning to develop a style of its own.

The development of the 35mm camera in the 1930s had a major impact on coverage of the sport. Not only was the camera light and portable, the film was more sensitive and the lenses longer and faster. Faster shutter speeds were available: 1/500th of a second will freeze action, 1/1000th will stop the action of runners' legs. One of the most famous photographs that utilised the new technology is that of the legendary Tom Finney playing against Chelsea at Stamford Bridge in 1956. The pitch was water-logged after heavy rain and, while attempting to turn whilst sprinting down the wing, Finney lost his balance and skidded along the pitch. A photographer using a long lens and a fast shutter speed captured the moment in the famous 'Splash photograph'. A horizontal player, partially obscured by a fountain of water, encapsulated all the athleticism, determination and drama of a football match.

The dramatic increase in the number of photographers at games in the later twentieth century led the FA to develop guidelines for the control and organisation of photographers. By 1999 rules requested that photographers must not use flash guns or their own artificial light sources, and that they must not pass over a restrictive line marked behind the goal line where they sat. While the FA have brought in these rules primarily for the safety of players and photographers, the increase in advertising boards around the pitch has reduced the areas available to photographers even further. No photographer can sit, stand or lie in front of an advertising hoarding if the match is being televised. Photographers are also usually asked to sign contracts at every individual football match they attend. A number of clubs have attempted to gain control of all images made on a match day – even of images taken within the vicinity of their ground.

In recent years there have been significant changes in the content of football photographs. The rise of footballers as stars has meant that a photograph with David Beckham with his shirt off has more value than a shot of another Premiership player scoring a fantastic goal. The playing of games at times other than the traditional Saturday afternoon has meant that photographers have tighter deadlines. At many games, photographs leave at half-time to transmit or process images for the next day's paper. As this, along with the bias towards big teams with big stars, becomes more evident, published photographs may not be a true reflection of the game or its result. The technological development of electronic images which has been so rapid in the last few years means that most newspapers can pull good quality pictures directly from the television coverage. As this practice increases we shall see a demise in true football photography. Soon spectators will not be allowed to take cameras to matches – TV stations and the larger, richer clubs are becoming increasingly protective of their media rights. This increased control over the production and use of images will result in a fundamental change in the content of football photographs. The images will come even more to function as advertising for a product rather than reportage of a sporting event.

Sources:

Campbell, B., *Exploring Photography* (London: BBC 1978).

Frizot, M. (ed.), *A New History of Photography* (Koln: Koneman, 1998).

Gernsheim, H and A., *A Concise History of Photography* (London: Thames and Hudson, 1965).

Spender, H., *'Lensman' Photographs 1932–52* (London: Chatto and Windus, 1987).

Szarkowski, J., *The Photographer's Eye* (London: Secker & Warburg, 1980).

Ian Beesley

Policing

The 1924 *Committee on Crowds* report following the crowd disruption at the first Wembley FA Cup final in 1923 held the view that football clubs should heed the advice of the chief of police about the numbers of police officers needed to manage English football crowds, and that those who disregarded his advice should incur heavy responsibility. Right up until 1968 this largely informal arrangement on football policing obtained, when the Harrington Report on *Soccer Hooliganism* noted that unless 'trouble' was really expected at matches, 'the number of police at many football matches is really only a token force usually distributed around the perimeter of the pitch'. Harrington also commented that 'at times the mere sight of police officers in strength seems to antagonise and inflame the crowd'. In 1969, the *Report of the Working Party on Crowd Behaviour at Football Matches* (the Lang Report) commented that one policeman for every 1,000 spectators was the generally accepted minimum for policing football matches in England, though for certain grounds and matches, and where large crowds were expected, 'it would be right, in close consultation with the club, to increase substantially the police force available for duty'.

The generally imprecise and usually small number of police officers used at football grounds in England up until the late 1960s – Scotland's 'Old Firm' meetings were rather a special case – is probably attributable to two things: firstly, the generally improving and orderly behaviour of English football crowds from the turn of the century, and secondly, the lack of any clear guidance on the precise distribution of responsibility for managing crowds inside these 'private' venues, and thus on the number of officers clubs should be liable to pay for. As a rule of thumb, clubs might be expected to pay for a proportion of the officers inside the stadium but for none outside. Even today, payment for football policing is a sensitive issue at the local level, and is generally

organised on an *ad hoc* basis, in negotiation between clubs and the local force.

By the time of Harrington, police were already expressing official concern about rising hooliganism and the lack of support for dealing with it from other members of the football audience. Football police duty was beginning to change from a welcome, and generally quiet overtime opportunity, to something altogether more challenging and action-orientated. Around this time, too, fan segregation began to be introduced inside major English stadia: firstly, by offering lines of police officers inside grounds to divide rival fan groups, and then later by the provision of unscaleable lateral and perimeter fencing manned by police officers. At this stage, club stewarding was minimal. Stewards, who were usually untrained club fans who were hired or given a 'free' match ticket for their work, had no formal responsibility for crowd safety or management. At best, they directed supporters to their seats; at worst they stayed out of harm's way and watched the match.

By the mid-1970s, serious problems of football policing had already extended *outside* stadia. The more notorious travelling fan groups now demanded a police escort to, and from, their organised transport, and English hooligans began to embark on assaults abroad, culminating in the Heysel tragedy of 1985, thus requiring more extensive police liaison between international forces, which was eventually formalised under the Trevi agreement. By this stage, too, a more aggressive and collective policing style emerged for football and other potential occasions of public disorder in Britain, with officers assigned to distinctive small 'riot' units – PSUs – which signalled a generally more 'militarised' approach to policing public disorder in Britain in the late 1970s and early 1980s.

By 1983, an FA memorandum to Football League clubs made it mandatory for clubs to engage in detailed prior planning with police, to arrange for the segregation of rival groups of fans, and to liaise with police on ensuring sufficient escorts for supporters. By this stage, police resourcing of football matches had become a considerable strain. The *Popplewell*

(Interim) Report of 1985 concluded that an average of one officer for every 75 spectators was now the norm in England, which meant up to 5,000 policemen each weekend policing matches, and record levels of hooligan arrests in the mid 1980s. A more intelligence-led and technology-driven surveillance approach to crowd management, which now meant a national police data bank on hooligan offenders and police-operated CCTV systems at top English stadia, had failed substantially to reduce the reliance on large numbers of police officers on the ground. But it did produce a number of high-profile 'undercover' police operations inside hooligan gangs, though in a number of these cases prosecutions against alleged hooligans collapsed because of 'inconsistencies' in police evidence presented in court.

The stadium disasters at Bradford City (a fire, in 1985) and at Hillsborough (fans crushed to death in 1989) prioritised the issue of supporter *safety*, rather than fan *hooliganism*, probably for the first time in Britain since the Ibrox stadium disaster of 1971. Hillsborough, especially, focused attention on the ways in which the management and policing of football crowds had been overdetermined by concerns about fan misbehaviour, at the expense of supporter safety. It also pointed up critical failings in arrangements for ensuring supporter well-being inside grounds, a responsibility which should properly have rested, according to the *Taylor Report* (1990) on Hillsborough, primarily with the clubs, not the police.

Since Hillsborough, a new stewarding regime has operated at all League grounds in England, and clubs and the police together have the job of ensuring good order inside the new generation of all-seater, largely fence-free football stadia, which have been developed at the highest levels. At many top English stadia today the police presence inside the ground is actually at a minimum, with clubs instead hiring their own trained private security staff to deal with issues of crowd management and low levels of fan disorder. Some clubs are also able to operate 'police-free' games today. New legislation – for example, to criminalise fan intrusions onto the

pitch and its surrounds – have helped to dampen stadium hooliganism, and concerns of the police National Football Intelligence Unit, a new clearing house for intelligence on hooliganism, tend to focus these days on football gang activity outside grounds and that involving English fans abroad. Hooligan arrests at club matches, though rising again at the turn of the century, have slumped in England since the mid 1980s high of over 7,000 to just over 3,100 in 2000, while police numbers at football matches have more than halved, even as football crowds have risen substantially since the post-war low point after Heysel in 1985/86 – from 16.5 million to around 25 million today. Policing football today is certainly not the 'soft option' it might have been in the 1950s, but nor is it quite the trial it undoubtedly was at the height of the English hooligan crisis in the late 1980s.

Sources:

Armstrong, G. and Giulianotti, R. 'From Another Angle: Police Surveillance and Football Supporters', in C. Norris et al. (eds), *Surveillance, C.C.T.V. and Social Control* (Aldershot: Ashgate, 1998).

Home Affairs Committee, *Policing Football Hooliganism* (Two volumes) (London: HMSO, 1991).

Lord Justice Taylor, *The Hillsborough Stadium Disaster, 15 April 1989, Final Report* (London: HMSO, 1990).

John Williams

Politics

Leading British footballers might see themselves as engaged in a purely sporting activity – today, this descriptor might be expanded to cover the game's increasingly lucrative character – but when playing foreign opposition they have often been viewed by governments, the media and public opinion as representatives embodying and projecting national values and qualities in some kind of gladiatorial contest. Politics merely compound the game's usual competitive element.

Notwithstanding this feature and political football's emergence as a commonplace metaphor for the 'state of the nation', British football is presented frequently as rightfully occupying a world separate from that of politics. For example, in February 1999 William Hague (Leader of the Opposition) used Prime Minister's Question Time to accuse Tony Blair of 'lecturing' British football on the Glenn Hoddle affair and 'poking his nose' into matters outside the government's responsibility. Just as Hoddle was attacked for bringing theology onto the pitch, so the prime minister's critique of the England manager was adjudged to infringe what has been presented as an autonomous feature of twentieth-century Britain.

At the same time, a succession of headline-making problems led many to argue that British football required a more active government approach. Admittedly, things had moved on from the low point in the 1980s when British football was dismissed as a 'slum sport' in a state of terminal decline, and the Thatcher government struggled with serious problems relating to ground safety and hooliganism. During the 1990s, positive images, at least at the higher levels, were qualified by the game's tendency to lurch from crisis to crisis, such as those occasioned by excessive profiteering, media links or the perceived shortcomings of the various footballing authorities. Nor, given the cult of personality, was the situation helped by a series of high-profile failings involving not only Hoddle but also Tony Adams, Paul Gascoigne, George Graham and Paul Merson, among others.

Football's revived popularity and high media visibility both accentuated the impact of such problems and enhanced the game's political potential. British football became steadily caught up in the political arena and the calculations of politicians. Certainly, Blair and Hague often seem to be reading from the same script. Both politicians, albeit reaffirming traditional separatist images, have acknowledged the game's political importance, most notably 'the pride we all get in identification with our club or our national side' (Blair) and the manner in which the game – to quote Hague – 'boosts national identity and pride'. Shifting patterns of allegiance, alongside socio-economic changes, have eroded traditional footballing ties, but the professed identification of Blair and Hague with Newcastle United and Rotherham United respectively, as well as with the national side, reaffirms the enduring force of football's ability to construct identities and beliefs possessing a resonance well beyond the ground. Opinion polls suggest consistently that for, say, the English and the Scots, football represents a significant – perhaps the most significant – source of national pride in the modern world. In this '90 minute patriot' vein, Eric Hobsbawm observed that 'the imagined community of millions seems more real as a team of eleven named people'. He recalled listening with several Austrians to a radio commentary of the Austria–England match played at Vienna in 1930: 'I was England, as they were Austria'.

Football's political dimension has been not only underrated but even denied by government, the media and the footballing authorities. For example, Frederick Wall, long-time FA secretary (1895–1934), described the national sport as 'merely a sporting entertainment'. But this seemingly apolitical line, though intended to distinguish Britain from the increasingly politicised game allegedly characteristic of continental Europe, reflected a political approach underpinned by Wall's distinctive version of British values. Moreover, it glossed over British realities. Indeed, during the 1928/29 season, Wall himself irritated British officials when conceding publicly the occasional imposition of pressure from government to field only 'first-class teams ... as it regards it as essential that British prowess should be well maintained'.

Nor would Wall, who was already fully versed in the politics underpinning the FA's relations with the other home football associations and FIFA, have forgotten the media and parliamentary campaign directed against the continuation of competitive football during the early part of the First World War. The British associations emerged anxious to salvage, even enhance, their reputations, as evidenced by their initial post-war refusal to play teams from the ex-enemy states, even at the cost of withdrawal from FIFA between 1920 and 1924). Subsequently, the politicisation of sport in, say, Mussolini's Italy or Hitler's Germany ensured that fixtures involving British sides inevitably assumed a political complexion, especially given Britain's great power status in both the footballing and political-economic spheres. Despite publicly professing an apolitical stance, British governments, viewing football as an instrument of cultural propaganda that refuted impressions of national decline, often apprised the footballing authorities of the importance for 'our prestige' of putting up a 'really first class performance' – that is, a victory achieved through fair play. The Germany–England match played at Berlin in May 1938 offered perhaps the most vivid example of official intervention; thus the England team was instructed to give the Nazi salute during the German national anthem. The worst thing was to lose in an unsporting manner, as evidenced by the strong official disapproval of Chelsea's misbehaviour on its 1936 Polish tour.

Following the Second World War, Cold War considerations imparted a political edge to fixtures against Soviet bloc states, as highlighted by Moscow Dynamo's 1945 British tour, the 1953/54 England–Hungary matches, or Arsenal's 1954 Moscow visit. Even today, the shadow of the Second World War continues to dog England–Germany fixtures, as happened during Euro 96 and the initial press coverage of Euro 2000 and the preliminary games of the 2002 World Cup tournament.

The post-1997 Blair government soon exhibited an awareness of the manner in which both the hosting of major international sporting events and Britain's maintenance of a leading role in the world game 'made in Britain' served the national interest in a globalised society. Tony Banks, Minister for Sport (1997–99), undertook an active global lobbying campaign to garner support for Britain's bid to host the 2006 World Cup – his efforts were seconded by Blair's contacts with the FIFA president – while citing 'the national interest' in not antagonising FIFA when pressurising Manchester United to participate in FIFA's 2000 Club World Championship rather than defend the FA Cup.

The notion that football should be above politics remains deeply ingrained in the national mindset, but it is increasingly common to acknowledge not only the politics of football itself but also the constant blurring of the separation between football and politics. Football is now deemed of sufficient political, economic, social and cultural importance to warrant government attention, even intervention, although 1999 controversies centred upon the new Wembley Stadium and the Football Task Force raised serious questions about the co-ordination of government policy. Likewise, British football, though welcoming a close working relationship with government on specific issues (such as the 2006 World Cup bid), displays an understandable, often stubborn, preference to retain a relatively autonomous role.

Clearly, British football cannot avoid future involvement in the political arena, even if, despite the political exploitation of England's 1966 World Cup victory, there remain strict limits to what government can achieve on the field of play itself. Nor can the game be expected to resolve national insecurities and uncertainties.

Sources:
Allison, L., 'The Changing Context of Sporting Life', in L. Allison (ed.), *The Changing Politics of Sport* (Manchester: Manchester University Press, 1993), pp. 1–14.
Beck, P., *Scoring for Britain: International Football and International Politics, 1900–1939* (London: Frank Cass, 1999).
Hobsbawm, E., *Nations and Nationalism Since 1780: Programme, Myth, Reality* (Cambridge: Cambridge University Press, 1990).
Russell, D., 'Associating with Football: Social Identity in England, 1863–1998', in G. Armstrong and R. Giulianotti (eds), *Football Cultures and Identities* (Basingstoke: Macmillan, 1999), pp. 15–28.

Peter Beck

Press

Modern sport and the modern newspaper grew up together. Newspapers contributed to the growth of sport in many ways. They provided free publicity listing what was on where and when. They described the events and published the results. In the second half of the nineteenth century, with the organisation of many sports in an embryonic state, it was newspaper editors who offered management and prizes and regularly provided judges and referees. In the twentieth century they would print increasingly sophisticated action photographs.

Britain had three sporting dailies in 1890. *The Sporting Life*, *The Sportsman* and the *Sporting Chronicle* all focused on horse-racing and betting intelligence as their core content, but many other sports were also included, most notably football. *The Sportsman* for example provided extensive coverage of the association game, especially in the south of England. But it was the weekly *Athletic News* which became the leading football paper in Britain from the 1880s until the 1920s. It had begun in Manchester as a 'weekly journal of amateur sport' in 1875, but, as football grew in popularity with a season lasting from September until early April, so the coverage of what has been called the *Times* of football came to be unrivalled, reporting every football match of any significance nationwide. Shortly after the beginning of League football in September 1888 this penny paper moved from Saturday to Monday. Sales of 25,000 a week in 1883 had doubled by 1891, doubled again by 1893 and were up to 170,000 in 1919. The number of readers was probably far greater. Many of the writers were influential officials of either the Football Association or the Football League, who were given 1,500 words for important games which they used not simply to describe the play but also to interpret it. By 1914, just as *The Times* was the house journal for the British upper class, so the *Athletic News* was the voice of football and the paper of the discerning football enthusiast.

Bradford City fans celebrate their club retaining Premiership status on the last day of the 1999/2000 season.

(© Ian Beesley)

Football magazines: Soccer Star *(17 August 1957) and* Shoot/Goal *(10 April 1976)*

At the beginning of the twentieth century there were 170 provincial daily papers and about 100 evening ones and most of them had sports pages, or pages which included sport. The main attraction of the local evening paper, apart from its cheapness, was that it could be first with the results. The first 'football special' was probably Birmingham's *Saturday Night* which lasted from 1882 to 1898. It was quickly followed by *The Football Field and Sports Telegram* in Bolton (1884), whose Saturday night football coverage was exceptional, and soon most towns where football was popular had one, usually produced on coloured paper and locally called the Pink, Buff or Green 'Un. Most of them flourished until the 1970s and in some cases beyond. Even in the year 2000 a handful still appeared, patriotically supporting the local professional team and reflecting the life of the local football sub-culture. The Sunday papers were probably the first national papers to take sports coverage seriously. The *Sunday Referee* published football results in 1877. Both the *Umpire* (1884) and the *Sunday Chronicle* (1886) devoted considerable space to sport.

In 1905 sport, with football prominent, took up almost a fifth of the space in both the *News of the World* and the *Umpire*. The popular national dailies soon followed suit. The *Daily Mail*, for example, had a sports page from its inception in 1896. By the 1920s and 1930s, these papers were filling column upon column with football news and results. In the 1930s the rising popularity of the Sunday papers, the *News of the World* and the *People*, and their circulation wars, elevated football coverage to even greater importance; both papers doubled their football coverage between 1920 and 1939. The *People* pioneered a new aggressive style in football reporting, placing sport on the back page and focusing more on human interest, controversy, mild scandal and action photography. Gone were the detached reports with their long sentences and scholarly paragraphs, to be replaced by more aggression in both language and style.

The *Athletic News* tried to compete with this but ended up merging with the *Sporting Chronicle* in 1931. *The Times* still featured as much amateur as professional sport, and concentrated on factual narrative rather than comment. The local press diversified its coverage, including more human interest stories about players, though one of its main functions was to provide results for the football pools.

After 1945, despite increasing radio and television broadcasting of the game, the press remained the chief means by which football was publicised and represented. The local papers continued to give daily coverage of local teams in a largely uncontentious manner. A more 'sensationalist' approach pervaded the popular national papers. The *Daily* and *Sunday Express* and the *News of the World* followed the *People*'s lead, and journalists like Alan Hoby, Trevor Wignall and Desmond Hackett were notable for their features exposing corruption and for an increasingly patriotic invective in reporting the national team's fortunes. In the quality press a new breed of intelligent, literary football journalist emerged. Geoffrey Green, Brian Glanville, J. L. Manning and Hugh McIlvanney established themselves as authoritative commentators in the 1950s and 1960s.

From the 1960s onwards, as most spectators' experience of the game came through television, football writing in the popular press became increasingly combative and concerned with scandal and criticism. In 1969 the tabloid *Sun* newspaper was taken over by Rupert Murdoch. Sport, particularly football, was hugely important to the *Sun*'s circulation, and it introduced a crude, terse and sometimes abusive style of reporting that influenced the rest of the popular press. In the 1980s and 1990s England managers became targets for nationalist tabloid campaigns, the private lives of players and others were exposed and denounced, as 'stories' eclipsed match reports. Football scandals were frequently promoted to the front pages. Julie Welch and Cynthia Bateman pioneered the entry of women into football journalism, and they were followed by a small number of female writers in the quality press. The broadsheets reacted to football's increased popularity and respectability in the 1990s by including separate sports sections with more lively personality and fan-based features, while maintaining their reputation for literate and responsible comment from writers like the *Guardian*'s David Lacey.

The number of sports pages in the broadsheets also grew. The *Guardian*, *Observer*, *Daily Telegraph* and *Times* included more serious discussion and features but there was more football gossip too. *The Times*, which had not sent a football reporter abroad until 1948, now sent whole teams to major footballing events such as the European championships and the World Cup. Six or eight pages on sport, of which half would concentrate on football, became the norm. Writing and reading about football had become as much part of a way of life as the game itself.

Sources:

Fishwick, N., *English Football and Society, 1910–1950* (Manchester: Manchester University Press, 1989).
Russell, D., *Football and the English* (Preston: Carnegie, 1997).

Further Reading:

Mason, T., 'All the Winners and Half Times', *Sports Historian*, 13 (May 1993), pp. 3–10.
Wagg, S., 'Playing the Past: the Media and the English Football Team', in J. Williams and S. Wagg (eds), *British Football and Social Change: Getting into Europe* (Leicester: Leicester University Press, 1991).

Tony Mason and Joyce Woolridge

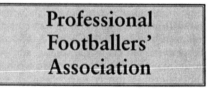

Professional Footballers' Association

The Professional Footballers' Association (PFA) acts as the trade union of football professionals in England and Wales. Its main duties are to protect and promote the interests of its members in negotiations with the football authorities, with a view to the abolition of all restrictions which adversely affect the livelihood of players. Yet it has always operated simultaneously in a benevolent capacity, providing legal aid and assistance to its players, helping members in financial need and assisting transfer-listed or disengaged players in finding employment.

The PFA was founded as the

Association Football Players' Union (AFPU) on 2 December 1907 at a meeting at the Imperial Hotel in Manchester. Previous attempts to establish a union in 1893 and 1898 had failed due to lack of support and recognition from the governing bodies, but the new union initially received both. The first meeting was chaired by the Welsh international winger Billy Meredith, and the union soon won the backing of FA and Football League officials and club chairmen.

However, in 1909 the union's intention to take disputes directly to the courts brought it into conflict with the FA. The governing body regarded this as a breach of its rules, withdrew recognition of the union, and, at its annual meeting in July, ordered both officials and rank and file members to resign. The union, which had meanwhile affiliated to the General Federation of Trade Unions (GFTU), prepared itself for strike action when the new season began in September. In the end, the authorities refused to back down and a compromise – which secured union recognition in return for resignation from the GFTU – was reached on the eve of the new season. The union suffered a further setback in 1912 when it failed to establish the illegality of the transfer system in a test case involving former Aston Villa player Charles Kingaby.

Despite strengthening its membership and expanding its benevolent activity, the union's primary objectives of abolishing the retain-and-transfer system and the maximum wage rule proved fruitless until after 1945. With Jimmy Guthrie as chairman between 1946 and 1957, the union established itself as a more militant body and enjoyed increased publicity, as well as forcing concessions from the football authorities on wages and other payments. It also came to depend on the support of external organisations, such as the Ministry of Labour and its arbitration machinery, and the Trades Union Congress which it joined in 1955, along with sympathetic individuals in Westminster and Fleet Street.

The election of Jimmy Hill to the chairmanship in 1957 signalled an advance in the success of the union and the condi-

tions of its members. Hill was an articulate and intelligent footballer, who was comfortable with the media and was able to manage the organisation's image to great effect. Fundamental to this was the 1958 change in title from the rather antiquated and cumbersome Association Football Players' and Trainers' Union (adopted after the First World War) to the Professional Footballers' Association.

In the early 1960s the PFA finally swept away the main pillars of the football industry's arcane employment laws. By the summer of 1960 the union was involved in an official dispute with the Football League and, backed by the threat of a nationwide strike, the League agreed to the abolition of the maximum wage in early 1961. Two years later the retain-and-transfer system was declared 'an unjustifiable restraint of trade' in a High Court case involving George Eastham and Newcastle United. In the aftermath of the Eastham case, the PFA negotiated a new contract system which allowed the player greater freedom to negotiate wages and conditions, and prevented clubs from retaining players on reduced terms. An Independent Tribunal with PFA representation was also established to resolve disputes. Football's contract system received further criticism in the Chester Report of 1968 and in the report of the Commission on Industrial Relations in 1973, but it was not until 1978 that freedom of contract was finally achieved.

By this time the PFA was beginning to assume a role which was rather different from a traditional trade union. It has long been instrumental in the establishment of insurance and pension schemes for its members, and in the widening of opportunities for footballers to receive further education and vocational training. More recently it has been closely involved in the creation of community development and anti-racism schemes. It is represented on the Professional Football Negotiating and Consultative Committee and is active in the international footballers' body, Fifpro. More than simply representing professional footballers, the PFA has become a leading voice in determining the present and future state of the game.

The AFPU had a Scottish section, but this seceded in 1913. Today the Scottish PFA is still independent from the PFA, and is a member of the GMB along with two other sports organisations – the Rugby Players Association and the British Swimming Coaches and Teachers Association – and a hundred or so other small unions.

Sources:

Dabscheck, B., '"Defensive Manchester": A History of the Professional Footballers' Association', in R. Cashman and M. McKernan (eds), *Sport in History* (St. Lucia: University of Queensland Press, 1979).

Guthrie, J., *Soccer Rebel* (London: Davis/Foster, 1976).

Harding, J., *For the Good of the Game: The Official History of the Professional Footballers' Association* (London: Robson Books, 1991).

Hill, J., *Striking for Soccer* (London: Sportsman's Book Club, 1961).

Further Reading:

Russell, D., *Football and the English: A Social History of Association Football in England, 1863–1995* (Preston: Carnegie Publishing, 1997).

See also Wages

Matt Taylor

Professionalism

– *see* **Amateurism and Amateur Football**

Programmes

Football programmes first appeared in the late nineteenth century and were usually single sheets that simply recorded the names of players and officials, along with a few other organisational details. They gradually became slightly more sophisticated, especially for cup finals and international games, but they remained often basic and quite crudely produced well into the 1950s and early 1960s. Especially outside the English and Scottish First Divisions, glossy covers and paper remained unknown and a spectator's 3d or 6d often bought him or her little more than team details, skeleton biographies of visiting players and terse managerial notes, set within a sea of box adverts for local shops and services. (At least the Hamilton Academicals programme was worth £5 in part-exchange value at a local furniture store in the 1960s.) A few clubs were more adventurous, notably Chelsea, who became the first club to produce a magazine type format featuring photographs and more substantial notes, comments and interviews (and free of adverts) in December 1948. Most programmes were of similar size and shape (c.20 x c.15 cms) and have remained so into the twenty-first century, although Crystal Palace pioneered a smaller, pocket-sized number from the mid-1950s and persisted with it for many years. Tottenham Hotspur, on the other hand, stayed loyal to a folded sheet of awkward size and flimsy material into the 1960s.

From the mid-1960s, production values improved at some grounds as clubs sought to provide a rather more modern and sophisticated image for a game that could no longer rely on the loyalty of its traditional fan base. Between 1966 and 1974, all English League clubs saw their programmes enhanced by the insertion of the *Football League Review*, an in-house magazine designed to show the League in particular and the game in general in a positive light. Chelsea's programme for the Inter-Cities Fairs Cup tie against AC Milan in February 1966 contained the first use of colour photography in a club programme, part of an 'ambitious plan to make our team, our ground, and our administration the envy of the football world'. The experiment was not a standard feature, however, and for most clubs, colour was not a prominent feature until the 1980s. From the late 1980s and early 1990s, programmes tended to take on a slightly more lively, varied and humorous tone, probably in the belief that they had to compete with the rival attraction of fanzines. Player profiles once restricted to

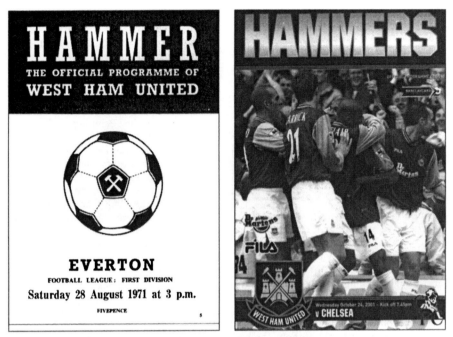

Programmes from different eras:
West Ham United v Everton, 1971; and West Ham United v Chelsea, 2001

'favourite' team, colour and food began to be concerned with other players' clothes sense, speed into the shower and so forth, while manager's notes became less formal and sometimes less bland. A few, such as Colin Murphy's grammar-free musings penned while at Lincoln City in the 1980s, developed almost cult status. By 2000, most Football League and Scottish League programmes ran to between 30 and 40 pages and cost usually about £2. Although not an insignificant cost, this usually represented better value for money than in decades before the 1970s.

Collecting programmes does not seem to have been a common hobby among fans until the mid 1960s – this might also have influenced the improvement in programme design from that time – but from then on a number of specialist dealers began to appear; Charlton Athletic's programme shop was an early and important source. The first guides for collectors appeared in the 1970s, several of them produced by Norman Lovett of the British Programme Collectors Club. The aim of collection varies but often focuses on achieving specific targets, such as gathering all programmes of a particular club over a set period or possessing at least one programme from every League club. Given the interest in collecting from about 1965, the monetary value of programmes from that point is limited and they remain one of the more affordable football collectables. Pre-1939 programmes have a much greater value, however, and a few items from the late nineteenth and early twentieth centuries have sold for four-figure sums.

Although most programmes are read and forgotten extremely quickly, they are an important part of the match-day experience. Some fans (including, it must be admitted, this author) feel uneasy if they cannot obtain one; the game seems somehow diminished, even unreal, without proof of its existence in hand or pocket. They are also a powerful stimulus to nostalgia in later years and provide a useful (although rarely considered) historical source.

Sources:

Chelsea v AC Milan, programme, 16 February 1966.

Chilcott, D., *The Hamlyn Guide to Football Collectables* (London: Hamlyn, 1999).

Shaw, P., *Collecting Football Programmes* (London: Granada, 1980).

Dave Russell

Promotion/Relegation System

Promotion and relegation are means of ensuring the mobility of teams between divisions in a particular league. Promotion is normally achieved by finishing in a designated position at the top of the division or through winning a play-off competition. In contrast with cricket and the rugby codes, and North American sports, variations of the promotion and relegation system have operated throughout the history of British football.

The promotion and relegation system was introduced between the two divisions of the Football League when the second was established in 1892/93. Initially movement was determined by the result of sudden-death 'test' matches played on neutral grounds between the lowest three First Division and the highest three Second Division clubs. From 1895/96 a play-off group involving the bottom two clubs in the top division and the champions and runners-up at the lower level replaced these one-off matches. The 1897/98 series, however, saw Stoke and Burnley play out an allegedly arranged goalless draw which assured both a First Division place. From 1898/99 the test match system was discarded in favour of an automatic two-up two-down system of promotion and relegation. From 1923, the champions of the new Third Division southern and northern sections replaced the bottom two clubs in the Second Division. The demoted members were allocated to geographically appropriate sections, with some clubs, notably Walsall, being required to switch sections in order to balance the numbers. A system of four-up four-down was introduced between the Third Division and the new Fourth Division from 1958/59, but two-up two-down remained in place at the higher levels.

Proposals to increase the number of promoted and relegated clubs throughout the League had been a feature of annual meetings from the beginning of the century, but the idea gained impetus in the 1960s. League secretary Alan Hardaker advocated a four-up four-down system so as to increase interest and attract higher attendances, a suggestion which was endorsed by the 1968 Chester Report. In 1973, a compromise was finally reached allowing for three clubs to be relegated and promoted each season.

A play-off system was re-introduced by the Football League in 1986/87. Initially it consisted of a knock-out competition involving the club finishing one position above the relegation places alongside the three clubs below the automatic promotion places with a two-legged final determining the finally promoted club. However, from 1988/89 play-offs involved only promotion contenders and a year later the finals were moved to Wembley Stadium. At the same time as the first play-offs, a system of automatic promotion and relegation was introduced between the bottom Football League club and the champions of the Football Conference, on the proviso that the promoted club met the League's ground criteria.

Although promotion and relegation between the Scottish divisions took place it was not made automatic until the 1921/22 season. In 1893/94, for instance, Clyde, third in the Second Division, had been elevated at the expense of champions Hibernian. In keeping with its periodically changing structure, the Scottish Football League has also adopted a variety of methods of promotion–relegation.

Sources:

Crampsey, B., *The First 100 Years: The Scottish Football League* (Glasgow: Scottish Football League, 1990).

Inglis, S., *League Football and the Men Who Made It* (London: CollinsWillow, 1988).

Matt Taylor

Public Schools

The English public schools played a very important role in the development of the modern game of football. Many different forms of unrefined football had been played in Britain since at least the Middle Ages. Different versions existed in the various schools, and rules began to be codified in schools such as Eton (1815) and Aldenham (1825). Westminster had the 'game in cloisters' in the eighteenth century, a dribbling form of football, and a similar type of cloister game is mentioned in the Charterhouse school song of 1794. Reform of the public schools followed those of Thomas Arnold at Rugby, and influenced other reforming headmasters, who placed more emphasis on the character-building aspect of games, including football.

The game was to be played for its own sake, with a stress on fair play and the subordination of self to the team. Headmasters such as Cotton and Bradley (Marlborough), Vaughan (Harrow), Woodard (Lancing), Almond (Loretto) and Thring (Uppingham) stressed this combination of 'muscular Christianity' and physiological Darwinism. Contact between ex-public schoolboys at university prompted them to institute some common rules so that they could form teams and play others, as each had their own form of the game. The earliest such code was the Cambridge Rules (1848), evolved at the university, and also adopted by others such as Forest FC and Barnes FC, clubs both founded by ex-public school men. J. C. Thring wrote a code called *The Simplest Game* in 1862, having previously attempted to unify the rules at Cambridge in 1846.

Football began to be diffused more widely as ex-public school men became teachers or returned to their native areas. Sheffield FC was founded in 1855, and the Sheffield Rules, a mixture of Harrow and Eton football, were written in 1856. In the 1860s and 1870s came other clubs, including Stoke (by ex-pupils of Charterhouse), Turton and Darwen (Harrow) and Blackburn Rovers (Malvern). Other public schoolboys spread the game through their involvement with the Church Lads' Brigade, boys' clubs and so forth. In 1863, old boys' clubs in the Metropolitan area founded the first Football Association, and determined the rules that were to unite the national game.

The schools themselves provided many of the better players in the early days. Westminster supplied ten England internationals between 1873 and 1894, including Moon, Veitch and Rawson. Charterhouse was one of the major powers, winning the FA Cup (1881), and later the FA Amateur Cup and the Arthur Dunn Cup many times, and providing internationals like

Footer at Harrow School *by Walter Cox (1887)* (National Football Museum)

G. O. Smith, W. N. Cobbold, A. M. and P. M. Walters and C. Wreford Brown. The Old Etonians reached the FA Cup final six times between 1875 and 1883, winning twice, and fielding such leading contemporary players as Lord Kinnaird, L. Bury, Arthur Dunn, R. C. Gosling and A. G. Bonsor. Old Etonians won a total of 39 full England caps between 1873 and 1903. Public school amateurs continued to play for England well into the 1900s, with some, like A. G. Bower (Corinthians), selected in the 1920s. The public schools also provided most of the early administrators of the FA, including Lord Kinnaird, C. W. Alcock, Major Marindin, C. Wreford Brown and N. L. Jackson.

The FA founded the FA Cup in 1871, and it was won by public-school derived teams – including Wanderers, Old Etonians and Old Carthusians – until 1883. The advent of professionalism destroyed the power of the 'old boys'' clubs, as first Darwen, Blackburn Rovers, and Blackburn Olympic challenged their dominance, the latter beating the Old Etonians to win the FA Cup in 1883, ending their monopoly forever. Resentment about the takeover of 'their' game by professionals rumbled on for years, as some ex-public school men vigorously denounced the influence of money. The FA Amateur Cup was founded in 1893 as partial compensation, but this too quickly became the preserve of working-class teams. The Arthur Dunn Cup, established in 1902/03 eventually became the premier tournament for the old boys' sides. Ex-public schoolboys including Charles Wreford Brown and the one-time England captain N. C. Bailey were instrumental in setting up the breakaway Amateur Football Association that existed from 1907 to 1914. Opposition to professionalism persisted, even during the First World War, when professional footballers and supporters were accused of being unpatriotic in continuing to play during 1914/15. Such continuous and persuasive opposition, combined with some snobbery, led to many schools changing from association to rugby football after the war, but schools such as Westminster, Charterhouse, Aldenham, Brentwood, Chigwell, Eton, Lancing, Malvern, Repton, Shrewsbury and Winchester continued to play. Clubs like Corinthians, founded by N. L. Jackson in 1882 to uphold amateurism, continued successfully, merging with the Casuals in 1939. Pegasus, a combined Oxford/Cambridge team containing a number of public school old boys, did well in the 1950s, winning the FA Amateur Cup in 1951 and 1953.

Sources:

Chandler, T. J. L., 'Games at Oxbridge and the Public Schools 1830–80: the Diffusion of an Innovation', *International Journal of the History of Sport*, 8: 2 (September 1991), 171–204.

Dunning, E. and Sheard, K., *Barbarians, Gentlemen and Players* (Oxford: Martin Robertson, 1979).

Fabian, A. H. and Green, G. (eds), *Association Football* (London: Caxton, 1960).

Mangan, J. A., *Athleticism in the Victorian and Edwardian Public School* (Cambridge: Cambridge University Press, 1981).

Young, P. M., *A History of British Football* (London: Stanley Paul, 1968).

Further Reading:

Green, G., *History of the Football Association* (London: Naldrett, 1953).

See also Schools Football

Robert Lewis

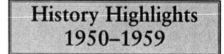

History Highlights 1950–1959

The 1950s began with England's entry into their first World Cup competition. The four British football associations had rejoined FIFA in 1946, and FIFA generously designated the home championship as a World Cup qualifying group, with two teams qualifying. Scotland, somewhat perversely, decided that they would only go to Brazil if they won the home championship. After a 1–0 defeat by England at Hampden, Scotland finished second in the group, and despite the protestation of their players, the Scottish FA maintained their position and did not travel to Brazil.

England's appearance in the 1950 World Cup will be remembered almost entirely for one match: their 1–0 defeat by the USA. England had started the championship well, with a win against Chile. But against the Americans, a totally unfancied team of part-time players, England inexplicably lost, despite having the majority of the play. The result was so unexpected that when it came over the wires in Britain, some newspapers thought it a typing error and changed it to 10–1.

England's record in international football, particularly in World Cups, was to remain undistinguished for the remainder of the 1950s. In Switzerland in 1954 England were defeated in the quarter-finals by Uruguay, while in Sweden in 1958 they did not even qualify from the group stages. Scotland's record was even worse. In 1954 they finished bottom of their group with two defeats, while in 1958 they only managed one draw from three games. The 1958 World Cup was, to date, the only one in which all four home countries reached the final stage. Both Wales and Northern Ireland performed exceptionally and qualified for the quarter-finals, where the Welsh were beaten by the eventual winners, Brazil, and the Irish by France.

Possibly the most significant international fixtures played during the 1950s were those between England and Hungary in 1953 and 1954. The first of these matches, a 6–3 win for Hungary at Wembley, was England's first defeat by continental opposition on home soil and, although warning signs had been evident in England's performances for a number of years, nobody was prepared for the scale of the defeat. This match, coupled with the return fixture in Budapest in 1954, which Hungary won 7–1, finally ended certain sections of the English press's arrogant assumption that England was the finest football nation in the world, regardless of who won the World Cup.

In domestic competitions, some of the most memorable incidents of the decade occurred in the FA Cup. In 1953, Stanley Matthews finally won a major domestic medal at the age of 38 as he inspired Blackpool to defeat Bolton 4–3 in one of the greatest comebacks in the competition's history. In 1956, Manchester City's German goalkeeper Bert Trautmann broke his neck in the final while making a series of match-winning saves, but remarkably played on until the final whistle. Newcas-tle United also achieved fame through the FA Cup in the 1950s, winning the final three times in four seasons between 1951 and 1955.

In Scotland, the decade enjoyed probably the most open League competition that the country has ever seen. Hibernian took the title in 1951 and 1952 and only the goal average prevented them completing a hat-trick in 1953. While Rangers to some extent reasserted their dominance by taking four titles across the decade, Aberdeen won their first ever title in 1955, Hearts their first for 61 years in 1958, and Celtic their first for 16 years in 1954. Linfield and, to a lesser extent, Glentoran, dominated the Irish League, although Glenavon and Ards both won their first titles in 1952 and 1958 respectively. In the Football League, two clubs battled throughout the 1950s for the status of the decade's most successful team. Wolverhampton Wanderers and Manchester United, under the respective managerships of Stan Cullis and Matt Busby, both won the First Division title three times each in the 1950s. In addition, both teams enjoyed success against continental opposition: Wolves against a Honved team that contained many of the Hungarian players who had humiliated England in 1953 and 1954; United as England's first entrants into the European Cup. Chelsea had been invited into the European Cup as League Champions in 1955, but had been refused permission to take part by the Football League. Interest-ingly, Hibernian (despite not being Scottish champions) had entered in the inaugural 1955/56 season and progressed to the semi-finals. However, one year later League Champions Manchester United refused to bow to the League's insular attitude and accepted the offer to take part. United performed admirably in the competition, reaching the semi-finals where they met the mighty Real Madrid. Almost inevitably, they lost the tie 5–3 and proceeded no further.

As champions of the 1956/57 season, Manchester United again entered the European Cup. This time, however, their attempt to reach the final is not remembered for playing success or failure, but rather for a disaster which proved to be the most tragic incident in British football in the 1950s. Returning from a quarter-final match in Belgrade, United's aeroplane stopped to refuel in Munich. Unfortunately, in poor weather conditions the plane crashed on take-off, killing 23 passengers including eight 'Busby Babe' players. As a team, a city, and a nation grieved the passing of so many talented players, United went about rebuilding their team and extraordinarily reached the FA Cup final only three months after the air crash. This remarkable feat won United many admirers and, it is claimed, laid the foundations for the club to develop its unusually high support in the 1960s and beyond.

Sources:

Nawrat, C. and Hutchings, S., *The Sunday Times Illustrated History of Football* (St Helens: The Book People Ltd, 1998).

Russell, D., *Football and the English: A Social History of Association Football in England, 1863–1995* (Preston: Carnegie Publishing, 1997).

Walvin, J., *The People's Game: The History of Football Revisited* (Edinburgh: Mainstream Publishing, 1994).

Further Reading:

Dunphy, E., *A Strange Kind of Glory: Sir Matt Busby and Manchester United* (London: Heinemann, 1991).

Kelly, S., *Back Page Football: A Centenary of Football Coverage* (London: Aurora, 1995).

Gavin Mellor

Racism and Ethnicity

From its roots within the Victorian social elites and the civilising project associated with 'muscular Christianity', through the era of expressive mass working-class audiences, to the increasingly commercialised game of today, football has provided one of the largest public arenas in which racism can be openly expressed and ethnic identities celebrated. The phenomenon of racism within the game first became a subject of widespread concern during the late 1970s and 1980s, a time when there was increasing evidence of racist behaviour related to football, and attempts by extreme right-wing movements to use football as a basis for recruitment. But interest in the issue is also partly related to the increasing representation of black players among the ranks of professional footballers since that time. With the emergence of black players at all levels of football, phenomena such as racist chanting and abuse became a common occurrence at many football grounds. In more recent times we have also seen the arrival of sizeable numbers of continental European players, and this has in turn led to new sets of cultural responses among football supporters.

Typically, issues relating to racism and ethnicity within the game have been related to the growing presence of black players in football, but this concentration on the phenomenon of 'black players' has meant that less attention has been paid to the cultural context of racism and the institutional barriers to further progression within the game's career hierarchies. Where questions of fan behaviour have been addressed it has largely been in the context of a wider concern with aspects of football fan culture and 'hooliganism'. Many references to the racist attitudes of 'hooligans' and the activities of the far right were made in early football literature, and during the 1980s the executive arm of the state responded to these fears by taking a heightened interest in the control of 'football hooliganism'.

Lord Justice Taylor's report into the Hillsborough stadium disaster stated that

> if there is a specific offence of chanting obscene or racial abuse, *hooligans* [authors' emphasis] will know precisely what is prohibited and that they do those things at their peril.

These comments were taken on board when the Football (Offences) Act (1991) made it 'an offence to take part at a designated football match in chanting of an indecent or *racialist* nature [author's emphasis]'. This recognition of racism in football by an executive power is significant in that it flows directly on from the more fundamental interest in dealing with 'football hooliganism'. It was not informed by a broader concern with how the cultural context of football provides a platform on which racism can be expressed and celebrated; neither was it concerned with the social processes that underpin that racism. Rather, there is an association between racism in football and the general 'unacceptable' and 'rowdy' behaviour of football fans involved in 'hooligan' activities.

The pervasiveness of the concern about racism as a cognate of hooliganism has meant that complex and often ambiguous expressions of racism and anti-racism in football have largely been ignored. In order for 'racism to count' within this logic, the exponent has to be a fully paid-up card-carrying neo-Nazi. In this sense the concern with hooliganism makes it possible for more banal racist practices to be made legitimate and rhetorically denied through such declarations as 'It's not racist – he's only winding him up.'

Such a syndrome is equally relevant to the institutions of football. Within the game the racist–hooligan can be vilified and condemned at all levels, from the FA, to individual clubs and players, and this is in many ways why there has been almost complete support for the 'Let's Kick Racism Out of Football' campaign. Yet, at the same time, there is a long-standing reluctance on the part of football's institutions even to discuss the issues as they apply to themselves. Recently, when interviewing the chief executive of a lower division League club, what was striking about the encounter was the ease with which the respondent used racial stereotypes to explain that the parental zeal for education and commerce was the reason why so few Asians are involved in football. This was confidently contrasted with the plight of young Afro-Caribbeans: 'At the moment for the black boys, there's three ways out of the ghetto: to be sportsmen,

to be pop stars or to be drug dealers – that's the three. I'm quite sure that it's better for them being sports stars.' At the same time as articulating such ideas this football administrator could voice his support for the 'Let's Kick Racism Out of Football' campaign and condemn the 'Nazi hooligans'.

It is thus perhaps more useful to conceptualise racism in football in terms of the processes by which 'whiteness' has been normalised within the game's spectator, player, and institutional cultures. John Williams has spoken of the 'naturalness' of racist assumptions, and how football simply 'has a way of saying things', an accommodative code or a form of (racist) 'banter' which incorporates rather than alienates the growing number of black players in League football. It is within this context that we might recognise that the issue has been viewed in the way it has, because racism in the stands is rather more overt, obvious and easier to identify than the semi-institutional forms which tend to characterise professional football culture more generally.

The key point is that football-related racism is not confined to football stadia, since supporters, players and directors do not live in those stadia but travel to them from other locations. Just as racism exists in football club dressing rooms, training pitches and boardrooms, its expression in the stands is related to complex processes rooted in homes, neighbourhoods, friendship networks and neighbourhoods. Indeed many football grounds are located in inner-city areas with large ethnic minority populations which are, to some extent, 'invaded' on match days by people with historic family ties but little extended contact with the area.

In this respect it is useful to turn the spotlight away from the 'racist–hooligan' and reflect upon the ways in which a variety of players, from different ethnic backgrounds, have been implicated in the game's racialised cultural processes during the post-war era. In the 1920s and 1930s the legendary Tranmere Rovers and Everton goal-scorer, William Ralph Dean, who scored 60 goals in the 1927/28 season alone, came to be known to the fans as

'Dixie'. Part of 'Dixie' Dean's story reveals the complex legacy of imperialism and race on Merseyside and how the understandings of race come to be played out in football vernaculars in quite ordinary, everyday fashion. Dean had a dark complexion and a mop of curly black hair, and while playing for Tranmere Rovers – his first club – the supporters marked out these distinctive features by giving him the nickname 'Dixie'. Dean resented the title and insisted on being called 'Bill' by acquaintances and friends. His biographer, Nick Walsh, wrote about his resistance to embracing the name. 'The reason perhaps was that at that time he felt "Dixie" had connections with colour problems connected with the Southern states of America, and therefore contained an inference that he was of that origin, or half-caste'.

Whatever its source 'Dixie' inferred some reference to race that was being projected onto his body, and his reticence to accommodate such a notion was dramatically illustrated in 1938, when after having played well enough in a game, he was one of the last to leave the field. As he reached the stands, in among the back-slappers lauding their heroes a man emerged from the crowd and grabbed Dean close, whispering in his ear: 'We will get you yet, you black bastard.' To an approaching policeman, Dean said: 'It's all right officer. I will look after this.' He thereupon punched the man, knocking him flying into the crowd. Cheers followed from some onlookers and the policeman rushed towards Dean, only to shake him by the hand and comment enthusiastically: 'That was a beauty, but I never saw it.'

'Dixie' Dean was also renowned for his fondness for humorous tales which would often be at his own or Everton's expense. One which he told repeatedly again referred to this awareness of issues of race and racism. An Everton director was one day strolling along Upper Parliament Street in Liverpool when he came across a coloured boy playing football. The boy was on his own kicking and heading the ball with remarkable skill against a large brick wall. The Everton director watched with utter amazement and fascination, and was so impressed with the boy's evident talent he approached him and said, 'How would you like to play for Everton, my boy? I am a director of the club and I could easily arrange for you to sign up to play for the first team.' 'Not bloody likely,' the boy replied. 'It's bad enough being black in this city.' The story is funny precisely because it plays with Everton's status as a poor footballing relation on Merseyside, but equally, it invokes the profound racism and racial segregation that exists in the City of Liverpool while maintaining 'whiteness' as the cultural norm within the world of football.

Yet while 'whiteness' is normalised within football environments through the silence that surrounds it, a willingness to tolerate and even engage in racial 'banter', wind-ups, and other cultural norms associated with white working-class masculinity, has on occasion become part of the 'character test' applied to players from ethnic minority backgrounds. As David Hill described it in his biography of John Barnes, 'On his first day at the training ground he sat at a bench with a couple of his new team-mates. Cups of tea were put before the two established players. Barnes looked up at the woman who brought them. He said: "What am I, black or something?" Everyone fell about.' Barnes pre-empted his own initiation. He gave permission, for better or worse, for his team-mates to relate to him in the traditional Liverpool way. I'm black. It's a joke. Everyone relax. 'Barnes has got a brain,' says a Liverpool insider:

But to use it there's got to be someone serious to use it with, and you're not allowed to be serious. If John was on television and he gave a serious interview, he would get some stick. And it's hard to take that sort of stick when you're trying to be part of the team. You've got to act like everyone else does.

It is significant that it was in the hyper-real televisual world which football embraced during the 1990s that a new chapter was opened in football's 'race relations' history. During an FA Carling

Premiership game between Crystal Palace and Manchester United in January 1995, the white Frenchman Eric Cantona, who had a reputation for being easily provoked, was receiving 'close attention' from Palace centre-back Richard Shaw. After becoming increasingly frustrated, in the 57th minute of the game Cantona kicked out at the player following a clumsy challenge.

Chants of 'off, off, off' quickly enveloped the stadium, interspersed with individual abuse directed at Cantona. Almost inevitably the referee produced a red card and the crowd erupted. As Cantona made his way from the field his manager Alex Ferguson avoided eye contact, showing no emotion. Cantona turned towards the tunnel, walking alongside the pitch within ear shot of mocking Palace fans in the main stand. All around the ground people were waving and chanting 'cheerio, cheerio, cheerio'.

Suddenly Cantona launched himself feet first at a spectator, Matthew Simmons, who had been shouting xenophobic and foul abuse at the player. However, in stark contrast to the reaction to Dixie Dean's behaviour 57 years earlier, in the midst of a media furore Cantona was arrested and convicted of assault and forced to undergo a ten-month playing ban alongside a community service order. Perhaps more significant though was the contribution that Cantona's response made to the debate about racism and anti-racism in football. As John Barnes commented at the time of the launch of the 'Let's Kick Racism – Respect All Fans' initiative later that year:

To be honest with you in the long run, some good may come out of [Cantona's assault] because that really brought it home that because mostly where [racial abuse] is actually done, black players have not responded to it, so people just make light of it because it can't be that bad because nothing has happened. Now he has actually responded to it they have actually seen how important the issue is because until something like that happens people don't realise how important it is because if someone was to call me a 'black bastard' I will laugh

it off and walk off and people would say well it is not that important because he hasn't said anything about it ... but you have also got to look at the person and the person's personality and his character, and Eric is a real volatile character and he responded to it. I have not ever done anything like that but I have felt like doing it, but I have not actually done it, so as I say there is an irony that it has actually taken a white Frenchman.

Nevertheless, this campaign against racism in football emerged at precisely the time when the orthodoxy of moral approaches to anti-racism was being questioned within other areas of British life. The crude labelling of 'racists' as 'moral degenerates' which initially lay at the heart of the campaign has done little to identify and tackle the more banal and ritualised forms of racism within football's institutions and among its devoted fans. However, while such narrow images of racism continue to dominate public perceptions and government interventions, a generation of more sophisticated peer-group activities at the local level and structured development plans at the institutional level are beginning to emerge.

Recently, a wave of media, activist and political interest in the game has led to the emergence of a broader agenda concerned with the under-representation of black and Asian supporters, the absence of Asian professional players and the identification of discrimination within the institutions of football. The sheer intensity of interest in the game, pressure brought to bear by Jaz Bains' study into Asian participation, and a variety of local interventions are making it harder for football to avoid this increasingly pervasive 'gaze'.

Accordingly, a new political agenda is beginning to point to the very ordinary, casual and everyday nature of racism in football and the need to connect responses to manifestations of racism, to focus on racist *actions*, on the time when people enact racism, rather than on the uniformity of the perpetrators' commitment to it as an ideology.

Sources:

Bains, J. with Patel, R., *Asian's Can't Play Football* (Birmingham: D-zine, 1996).

Hill, D., *Out of His Skin: The John Barnes Phenomenon* (London: Faber & Faber, 1989).

HMSO, *The Hillsborough Stadium Disaster – 15th April 1989: Final Report of Inquiry by Lord Justice Taylor* (London: HMSO, 1990).

Walsh, N., *Dixie Dean: The Story of A Goal Scoring Legend* (London and Sydney: Pan Books, 1977).

Williams, J., *Lick My Boots – Racism in English Football* (Leicester: Department of Sociology, University of Leicester, 1992).

Further Reading:

Back, L., Crabbe, T. and Solomos, J., *The Changing Face of Football: Racism, Multiculture and Identity in the English Game* (Oxford: Berg, forthcoming).

Carrington, B. and McDonald, I. (eds), *Racism and British Sport* (London: Routledge, 2000).

Tim Crabbe

Radio

The relationship between British football and radio began in January 1927 when the BBC broadcast its first commentary on a professional match: a League game between Arsenal and Sheffield United. By 1931, the BBC was broadcasting over 100 games per season, and radio had secured a central role in the rapid inter-war expansion of football. Through broadcasting League, FA Cup and International football matches to a national audience, the BBC ensured that most sections of British society had access to the game, and helped develop football into one of the shared experiences that contributed to the British people's sense of nationhood.

For radio to play an important role in the growth of football, it was, of course, vital that the majority of the nation owned radio sets. While only 30 per cent of households owned radio licences in 1930, that figure had risen to 71 per cent in 1939, when 8,900,000 licensed sets were in use. The BBC also had to regard foot-ball as a subject worthy of attention which, in the Corporation's early years, was not always the case. By the late 1920s, however, the technical challenge of broadcasting live football to the nation, coupled with the Corporation's limited willingness to engage with topics that did not necessarily accord with Sir John Reith's mission to raise public taste, ensured that football was seen as an important fixture in the BBC's regular schedule.

The BBC's leading commentator in the early years was journalist, Arsenal director, and later manager, George Allison. In his and other commentators' reports, the BBC was anxious that the audience should be able to visualise the verbal descriptions of matches being broadcast, so set about devising a system of informing listeners at all times of the position of the ball in relation to the pitch. The solution came in the shape of a chart in the *Radio Times* which showed a football pitch divided into numbered squares. With this as a reference, the audience were instructed to listen out for a background voice broadcast alongside the main match commentary which would inform them of the number of the square in which the ball resided.

By the early 1930s football, and particularly 'show-piece' matches such as the Cup final, had become important and popular additions to the BBC schedule. However, the popularity of football on the radio did not meet with universal approval, especially within the Football League. With football attendances declining at many smaller clubs in the 1930s because of rising unemployment, the Football League were nervous that radio broadcasts of games further encouraged people to stay at home rather than attend matches live. As a result, in June 1931 the League banned all broadcasts of its fixtures: a decision that stood until after the Second World War. The Football Association did not share the Football League's concerns and, although the FA Cup final was not broadcast in 1929 due to a dispute over fees, subsequent finals, many internationals and some Cup games continued to be broadcast during the 1930s.

Concerns within the Football League about the impact of radio broadcasts on football attendances continued in the immediate post-Second World War period. However, the League's ban on broadcasts did disappear as the regular fixture programme restarted in 1946, ensuring that the consumption of Saturday afternoon football on the radio became a national pastime for many people. In addition, Saturday magazine sports shows such as the BBC's *Sports Report* (1949) began in the late 1940s, filling most of their broadcast time with reports on football fixtures and interviews with the game's key personnel. This displayed and reinforced the importance of football to the BBC's schedules, and helped cement the place of football in the national consciousness.

Following the immediate post-war period, football maintained and further enhanced its position in the schedules of regional and national radio stations. With the increase in interest around football in the early 1990s, radio reacted by expanding its range of football-based programmes to include some interesting new additions. In August 1990, BBC Radio 5 first broadcast *Six-O-Six*, an irreverent football fans' phone-in show in which journalist Danny Baker invited fans to call in with their experiences of following the game. This 'democratisation' of football radio broadcasting has been much copied since Baker first aired his show, and, indeed, has come to form the main basis of some national radio stations' sports broadcasting. One of these stations is Talk Sport, an independent national British radio station which has emerged to provide the first serious challenge to the BBC's national monopoly on sports radio broadcasting.

Sources:

Russell, D., *Football and the English: A Social History of Association Football in England, 1863–1995* (Preston: Carnegie Publishing, 1997).

Walvin, J., *The People's Game: The History of Football Revisited* (Edinburgh: Mainstream Publishing, 1994).

Further Reading:

Allison, G., *Allison Calling* (London: Staples Press, 1948).

Haynes, R., "'There's many a slip 'twixt the eye and the lip": An Exploratory History of Football Broadcasts and Running Commentaries on BBC Radio, 1927–39', *International Review of the Sociology of Sport*, 34: 2 (1999), 143–56.

Gavin Mellor

Radio and Television Pundits

Radio and television commentators and pundits have become celebrities in their own right, though arguably they have never been afforded the same degree of national adulation as cricket experts. By bringing the game to millions of listeners and viewers who do not physically attend a football match, commentators have helped to stimulate interest in professional football since the radio broadcasting of football began in 1927. Pundits have also played a major role in the formation of opinion and controversy about football matters.

Among the first radio commentators to achieve fame for his personal style was George 'By Jove' Allison, later to become manager of Arsenal. He commentated on the 1928 FA Cup Final between Huddersfield and Blackburn Rovers, the first final to have live 'running commentary'. Allison went to the United States to observe American sports commentators and subsequently injected a measure of breathless immediacy and 'pep' into his delivery. He attempted to convey the excitement of the action to listeners by reacting to the play: 'He's got it ... no he hasn't!' Raymond Glendenning adopted the more gentlemanly, measured standard BBC mode, and future commentators have similarly either tended towards the classic style or a more populist delivery. Both men can be seen and heard in the film *The Arsenal Stadium Mystery* (1939). The Arsenal inside-forward Charles Buchan left football in the 1920s to become a radio broadcaster and journalist, but ex-players have generally not been used as commentators in terrestrial broadcasting, more usually providing 'expert' opinion and summaries, alongside a professional broadcaster as partner.

The pre-eminent BBC radio and TV commentator of the 1950s and 1960s was the authoritative Kenneth Wolstenholme. Wolstenholme won his place in football history with his oft-replayed concluding comments on the 1966 World Cup Final: 'Some people are on the pitch. They think it's all over. It is now!' He was replaced by the BBC in 1971 because his delivery was considered old-fashioned. John Motson eventually succeeded him, becoming a household name because of his appearances on the BBC's *Match of the Day* Saturday evening highlights programme since 1971. Motson's style is characterised by boyish enthusiasm, kept in check by his deliberate delivery and emphatic pronunciation and encapsulated by his trademark comments, 'Oh, I say' and 'Very much so'. His vocal idiosyncrasies and his ever-present sheepskin coat are much celebrated and parodied in fan culture. Motson appeared on *This Is Your Life* in 1996 and in the same year published his own best-selling *Motty's Diary*. In 2001 he also began commentating for BBC Radio. His commentaries are marked by his love of statistics and a fund of esoteric trivia. One of his most famous observations was about how fitting it was that Manchester United's captain in the 1977 Cup Final, Martin Buchan, was ascending the 39 steps to the Royal Box at Wembley. Motson's relatively demotic accent contrasted with the more sophisticated received pronunciation and calmer style of the BBC's other main television commentator, Barry Davies. Brian Moore provided urbane, mellifluous and controlled commentary for ITV from 1967 until his retirement in 1998.

Peter Jones and Bryon Butler were BBC Radio's chief commentators in the 1970s and 1980s. Alan Green, the man who arguably created a constituency of listeners for BBC Radio Five Live's football coverage, introduced a more opinionated style and stance during his tenure as senior commentator from 1984 onwards. His frequently provocative reflections on play are pithily expressed in his abrasive native Ulster tones: 'Roy Keane's a lout' being

one of his most infamous interjections. Green's trenchant observations have brought him into conflict with some of the leading figures of football, most notably his 'feud' with Sir Alex Ferguson, who considered that his judgemental attitude went beyond the commentator's remit. Green frequently shares commentary with Mike Ingham, a broadcaster in the standard BBC mode. 'Finishing' a live match commentary is the most prestigious part, and to do so is a sign of superiority.

If the commentator is the 'voice of football', providing the soundtrack to football's most memorable moments, punditry shapes opinion and creates controversy. From the 1960s the pundit has become an indispensable feature of football radio and TV broadcasting, and pundits have become objects of love and loathing in equal measure. Most pundits are current or former professionals or managers chosen for their expert knowledge. Panels of such experts were pioneered by ITV for their World Cup coverage in 1970 and soon became a permanent fixture. ITV's panel for the 1974 finals, chaired by Brian Moore, was a particularly bold choice of some of the more forthright voices in football, including Malcolm Allison, Jack Charlton, Brian Clough, Paddy Crerand, Derek Dougan. Jimmy Hill, ex-Fulham player and former chair of the PFA, crossed from ITV to the BBC to front *Match of the Day* in 1972, and served as one of the most recognisable and caustic pundits, fond of castigating foul play and ungentlemanly behaviour. Ex-Liverpool defender Mark Lawrenson, Alan Hansen and former West Ham midfielder Trevor Brooking formed the core of the regular *Match of the Day* expert panel in the 1990s, under the chairmanship of Des Lynam and later Gary Lineker. Hansen's frequent complaint, 'Where was the defending?', added a sharp edge to the more cautious comments of his colleagues. BSkyB's Saturday football results show has taken the expert panel further by seating Rodney Marsh, Clive Allen, Frank McLintock and George Best in front of monitors commenting on live action that the viewer cannot see. Ron Atkinson's quirky use of English, as in phrases like 'early doors', has made him a regular choice for providing expert summary during ITV televised coverage in the 1990s and 2000s.

Andy Gray, ex-Everton and Aston Villa forward, has been the 'voice' of BSkyB's satellite Premiership coverage since 1992. Gray's experience of the game and grasp of tactics make his punditry knowledgeable and respected. At one time he illustrated his analysis using counters and a model pitch on *The Boot Room* show, but more sophisticated computer graphics and videotape facilities allow for the almost instantaneous dissection and explication of on-pitch incidents. Gray's prolix, opinionated and passionate style, delivered in a broad Scots accent, marries gritty realism with a Latin American hyperbole and brio. His foil is the unflappable and coolly professional Martin Tyler.

Punditry has seen a boom since 1990, as more air and screen time have been allotted to football coverage. Ian St John and Jimmy Greaves were pioneers of the more alternative, humorous forum for punditry in their London Weekend Television show, *Saint and Greavesie*, which was shown across the ITV network from 1985 to 1996. However, the template was provided by broadcaster and writer Danny Baker's Radio Five football phone-in show, *6.06*, which, following Baker's dismissal, was subsequently taken over by the Conservative MP David Mellor and *Sun* columnist Richard Littlejohn. During Mellor's tenure the show achieved the highest listening figures, but his perceived pomposity drew much criticism and the appellation 'Mellorphant'.

Women have been conspicuously absent as commentators or pundits on radio or television; they tend to be used rather as presenters or reporters, as in Hazel Irvine's work for the BBC in Scotland. Gabby Yorath (now Logan) became co-presenter of ITV's football magazine programme *On The Ball* in 1999, though her opportunities for expressing opinions are limited. Helen Chamberlain has provided humorous, alternative comment on football as a presenter of Sky's *Soccer AM* programme since the 1990s.

Sources:

Green, A., *The Green Line: Views From Sport's Most Outspoken Commentator* (London: Headline, 2000).

Tudor, A., 'The Panels' in T. Bennett, S. Boyd-Bowman, C. Mercer and J. Woollacott, *Popular Television and Film* (London: BFI, 1981), pp. 150–8.

Wagg, S., *The Football World: A Contemporary Social History* (Hassocks: The Harvester Press, 1984).

Durant, S., 'Lamb in Sheep's Clothing', Interview with John Motson, *Guardian*, 14 December 1998. http://www.guardian.co.uk/Archive

Joyce Woolridge

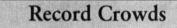

Record Crowds

The issue of record crowds is one that has been historically controversial, due to inadequate techniques for measuring crowd attendance, and a reliance on estimates, especially in the early period of the game. In 1925, the Football League insisted that all clubs return attendance data to the League headquarters and figures for this level of football, at least, do become considerably more solid from that point.

The vast majority of club crowd records date back to the time of terraces and unrestricted entry into the ground, during what has been dubbed football's 'Golden Era', generally acknowledged to run from the years immediately preceding the Second World War up to seven years after it.

Local derbies and cup games, especially finals, figure prominently in any list of record attendances. The FA Cup final of 1923, the first held at Wembley Stadium, holds the unofficial record for Britain's highest attendance at a football match, with an estimated 210,000 spectators present, although the official figure of paying customers stands at 126,047. This example highlights the difficulties in analysing attendance figures from this period, when, as in this match, it was common for gatecrashers to increase significantly the number in attendance without being recognised in official statistics. The 1923 Cup final though did raise concerns over crowd safety, and a subsequent inquiry found the procedures for the admission of spectators to be inadequate. Fear of overcrowding, coupled with an escalation in hooligan activity, led to a more thorough system of ground entry. In Scotland the 1937 Scottish Cup Final between Celtic and Aberdeen holds the record for attendance at a cup tie, with a crowd of some 146,433 inside Hampden Park. The same stadium also saw 135,826 watch Celtic battle Leeds United in the second leg of the European Cup semi-finals 33 years later.

The record British attendance for a league game stands at the 118,567 inside Ibrox Park for a 1939 Old Firm clash. The English record is somewhat lower, at 83,260 for a match between Manchester United and Arsenal, held at Maine Road while Old Trafford was being rebuilt following damage sustained during Second World War bombing raids. The record for one day's English League attendance was reached on 27 December 1949 when a total of 1,272,185 watched 44 league matches, producing an average attendance of 28,913. The day saw 70,000 watch Aston Villa lose at home to Wolverhampton Wanderers, and 56,000 witness Sheffield United drawing with Preston North End. Cardiff City hold the record attendance for a Welsh club, drawing 57,893 on 22 April 1953 against Arsenal.

The 1970s and 1980s saw a general decline in attendance levels precipitated by the perceived threat of increased levels of hooliganism and an economic recession, although figures began to rise again at the turn of the 1990s. The implementation of all-seater stadia following the Hillsborough disaster, in which 96 Liverpool fans lost their lives, ensured a drop in ground capacity for most clubs and a subsequent drop in attendance levels, although the majority of elite clubs within England and Scotland are once again beginning to reach their old terrace capacities in their redeveloped stadia.

The formation of the Premier League in 1992 brought with it a new list of attendance statistics thanks to the League's adoption of a 'year zero' policy as part of its marketing strategy. As a result the Premier League's attendance record has changed several times since its inception, now standing at 67,744 for Manchester United's game at the redeveloped Old Trafford against Newcastle on 20 August 2000. How long this will remain as the benchmark is uncertain, with several clubs aiming to redevelop their stadiums with similar capacities in mind, and the possibility of Manchester United further enlarging Old Trafford.

However, it remains unlikely that the record crowds achieved in the 1940s and 1950s will be exceeded. As the official literature for the new 90,000 capacity Wembley stadium notes, 'capacities of 100,000 and over are products of the days when fans were closely crowded together, usually standing on terraces', and concerns surrounding safety and comfort make a return to such figures unlikely.

Sources:
Rothmans   Football   Yearbook   (London: Rothmans, 1981 onwards).

Further Reading:
Tabner, B., *Throught the Turnstiles* (Harefield: Yore Publications, 1992).

Paul O'Higgins

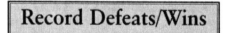

Record Defeats/Wins

No British club has managed to get through a whole season undefeated, or without a win, although several have come close. Leeds United hold the record for the fewest defeats in a season (two out of 42 League games in 1968/69) and Stoke City the record number of defeats (31 in 1984/85).

The highest losing/winning margins are to be found in cup competitions, the record in the FA Cup being 26–0 when Preston North End defeated non-league Hyde in the first round of the FA Cup in 1887. This was surpassed by Arbroath, who knocked Bon Accord out of the Scottish Cup in the first round in 1885 by

36 goals to nil, the very same day that Dundee Harp defeated Aberdeen 35–0, easily the highest victories in any British first-class match. The biggest margin in the First Division of the Football League is West Bromwich Albion's defeat of Darwen 12–0 in 1892. Celtic hold the equivalent record in the Scottish League with an 11–0 defeat of Dundee in 1895. Several league clubs have suffered 10–0 defeats, but only Darwen and Brechin City have had a hat-trick of such defeats in one season.

In international matches, England beat Australia 17–0 in Sydney in 1951, although this was not recognised by the FA as an official international. Northern Ireland suffer the stigma of being the victims of England's (13), Scotland's (11) and Wales' (11) record wins.

Sources:

Soar, P., *The Hamlyn A-Z of Football Records*, second edition (London: Hamlyn, 1985).
Rothmans Football Yearbook (London: Rothmans, 1981 onwards).

Richard William Cox

Record Transfers

When Rio Ferdinand joined Leeds United from West Ham United in November 2000 the £18 million price tag made him the world's costliest defender. It was also the largest ever fee involving British clubs, beating the £15 million Newcastle United had paid Blackburn Rovers for the services of Alan Shearer four years earlier. Shearer's move had made him the most expensive player in history, the previous record being the £13 million paid by AC Milan to Torino for Gianluigi Lentini in 1992. On the same day as Ferdinand was watching his new team-mates beat Arsenal 1–0 at home, another record signing was making an emphatic debut north of the border: Tore Andre Flo, Rangers' new Norwegian striker, had left Chelsea just days earlier and marked his first game for the 'Gers with a goal in their 5–1 defeat of deadly rivals Celtic. The fee of £12 million

was a record for a transfer involving a Scottish club. The previous Scottish record had been held by Celtic, who had paid just half that amount to bring another unsettled Chelsea striker, Chris Sutton, to Glasgow.

Astronomical though these sums appeared at the time, they were relatively modest compared to what was happening in the rest of Europe. Leeds' previous home fixture had been a Champions' League game against Real Madrid. In the Spanish side that won 2–0 had been Luis Figo, the Portuguese striker signed the previous season from Barcelona for £37 million. The record fee involving a British club stood at the time at £23 million, again paid by Real Madrid, to lure French forward Nicolas Anelka from Arsenal.

While the British press made much of Ferdinand's move, speculating on the wisdom of spending so much on such a relatively inexperienced defender (he was only 22 at the time and not a regular international), they were at least not as hysterical as their predecessors. When struggling Middlesbrough paid the first four-figure transfer fee in history, parting with £1,000 to lure England inside-forward Alf Common from Sunderland in February 1905, one sports journalist called it 'Flesh and blood for sale'! Another pondered: 'We are tempted to wonder whether Association football players will eventually rival thoroughbred yearling racehorses in the market.' Common soon justified the outlay. On 25 February 1905 he scored the only goal of the game at Bramall Lane to give Boro their first away win for two years, appropriately against another of his former clubs. Sheffield United had sold him to Sunderland in 1902, in the game's first £500 transfer. By January 1908 the Football League were so concerned at the spiralling cost of transfers generated by Common's moves that they imposed a £350 limit, but the idea lasted less than a year, the purchasing clubs getting round the restriction simply by putting artificial price-tags of that amount on unwanted reserves and including them in the deal as financial ballast.

After Alf Common the floodgates were opened and financial milestones were regularly reached over the years as fees moved steadily upward. Blackburn Rovers doubled Common's price when they paid West Ham £2,000 for Danny O'Shea in 1912. The first £2,500 fee was paid by Manchester City when Horace Barnes moved from Derby County in 1914. In 1922 Syd Puddefoot became the first £5,000 player when West Ham sold him to Falkirk. The same year Mick Gilhooley was involved in the first £5,000 transfer between English clubs when he left Sunderland for Hull City. James Gibson attracted the first £7,500 fee when he moved to Aston Villa from Partick Thistle in 1927, but it was David Jack's move the following year from Bolton Wanderers to Arsenal that got the football world really excited. The fee of £10,000 (or £10,670 or £10,890 – clubs have always been reticent about actual figures) prompted Sir Charles Clegg, president of the FA, to issue the warning that no player in the world was worth that amount. The clubs obviously thought differently, however. In 1947 Billy Steel became the first £15,000 player when he moved from Morton to Derby County, and the same year Notts County paid £20,000 to Chelsea for the services of Tommy Lawton. The £25,000 mark was reached in 1949 when Johnny Morris left Manchester United for Derby.

Within 11 years the record had doubled again, Denis Law moving from Huddersfield Town to Manchester City for more than £50,000 in March 1960. The Scottish international also became the first British player to attract a fee of £100,000 when City sold him to Torino in July 1961. Law was also the first British player for whom a British club paid a six-figure sum, when the Italian club sold him a year later to Manchester United for £115,000. Jimmy Greaves had almost earned this distinction in November 1961 when Tottenham Hotspur brought the ex-Chelsea striker back to England from Italy, but Bill Nicholson, Spurs' manager, wishing to protect the young Greaves from the inevitable pressure and publicity, insisted that the price paid to AC Milan was a mere £99,999! It was to be October 1968 before £100,000 was paid by a club north of the border, when Rangers parted with

that amount for Hibs' striker Colin Stein.

Onward and upward: the first six-figure deal between British clubs took Alan Ball from Blackpool to Everton for a reputed £110,000 in August 1966, the price no doubt inflated by his part in England's World Cup triumph. In 1970 another World Cup winner, Martin Peters, left West Ham for Tottenham for an estimated £200,000 (although Jimmy Greaves went the other way as part of the deal), and in 1977 Kevin Keegan left Liverpool to further his career in Hamburg, Germany paying £500,000 for his services. This was the first half-million fee involving a British club. David Mills became the first player to be transferred between British clubs for such a fee, when in January 1979 he joined West Bromwich Albion from Middlesbrough for a quoted £512,000. The million-pound transfer had to come. On St Valentine's Day, 14 February 1979, Nottingham Forest entered the record books when they lured Trevor Francis from Birmingham City for the magical figure, although the romance of the affair was slightly diminished when it was revealed that City received only £975,000. By the time VAT, Francis's 5 per cent cut and the fee due to the Football League Provident Fund were added, the total came to an estimated £1,150,000, however, and Francis became Britain's first million-pound footballer. He was by no means the last. In September 1979 Wolverhampton Wanderers sold Steve Daley to Manchester City for £1,437,500, then, within days, bought Andy Gray from Aston Villa for £1,469,000. In July 1980 Manchester United broke the £1,500,000 barrier when they signed Bryan Robson from West Brom, and on 7 July 1988 Paul Gascoigne became the first player to attract a £2 million fee when Tottenham paid Newcastle United that sum to bring the colourful Geordie to White Hart Lane. Ian Rush cost Liverpool over £3 million to tempt him back from Juventus in June 1987, and Chris Waddle moved from Tottenham to Marseille two years later for £4.5 million. In July 1992 Spurs sold another star abroad, receiving £5.5 million for Paul Gascoigne from Rome club

Lazio. The fee matched those paid in two deals the previous August when another Italian club, Bari, had bought David Platt from Aston Villa, and Trevor Steven had left Rangers to join Waddle at Marseille. Andy Cole left Newcastle for Manchester United in 1995 for £7 million, and Stan Collymore signed for Liverpool the same year in a deal that netted £8.5 million for Forest, making him Britain's costliest player until Shearer's £15 million move in July 1996. Leeds manager David O'Leary and chairman Peter Ridsdale were quick to justify their seemingly extravagant move for Ferdinand, and the player's estimated £30,000 a week wages, at a time when, following the *Bosman* ruling, the then current transfer system was vulnerable to possible abolition under EC labour rules. It was a price well worth paying for an emerging player with possibly ten top-level years ahead of him, they told the press. Their overriding priority was to keep Leeds in Europe. The vast rewards from a successful run in the Champions' League, with all the resultant television revenue, made it a sound financial decision to lay out such a sum. And who could argue with that? After all, hadn't Middlesbrough paid £1,000 all those years ago just so that Alf Common could keep them in the First Division?

Sources:
Barrett, N., *The Daily Telegraph Football Chronicle* (London: Carlton, 1999).
Hart, G. (ed.), *The Guinness Football Encyclopedia* (Enfield: Guinness, 1995).

Further Reading:
Kelly, S. F., *Back Page Football: A Century Of Newspaper Coverage* (London: Aurora, 1995).

See also Big Spenders

Tony Rennick

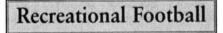

Recreational Football

Recreational football is a useful if loose phrase, describing the great range of British football that is played outside the major professional and semi-professional leagues. Although almost completely ignored in the academic literature, it has always comprised far and away the biggest element of footballing activity. At the beginning of the twenty-first century, at least a million players perform at this level each week.

Although they would not necessarily have recognised the term, recreational sides existed from the earliest history of the organised game. Workplace, church and local friendship groups provided the most common starting points for such clubs. Given the lack of formal sporting facilities in the nineteenth century, many of them presumably played on the most unsuitable of grounds, with fields begged and borrowed from various sources and public house changing rooms the norm. With the growth of provision of public playing fields, especially after the foundation of the National Playing Fields Association in 1925, more clubs were able to play and prepare in slightly better conditions. (Even today, however, any park footballer will have favourite tales of Himalayan pitches and malfunctioning showers.) Football at this level was boosted greatly in 1961 when the FA shed one of its last Victorian values and recognised Sunday football: until that point, although the game was played on Sundays, clubs could not affiliate to the FA. The FA Sunday Cup was inaugurated in 1964, with Umbro taking over sponsorship in the late 1990s, a clear sign of the popularity of the game at this level. A significant number of Sunday sides have been based on and named after public houses. With the growth of all-weather and indoor pitches at local authority leisure centres from the 1970s, so-called 'small side' football, usually five-a-side, has become another extremely buoyant sector of the recreational game, league and cup tournaments proliferating alongside the informal weekly kick-abouts that many continue to indulge in years after their bodies first told them to stop.

Recreational clubs are often quite brittle structures, with players leaving en masse for better opportunities or after arguments over sometimes quite trivial issues. Although many clubs, especially in smaller communities, have long and continuous traditions, many are therefore short-lived. Cooperville White Star were a leading side in Bradford, West Yorkshire in the 1950s and 1960s, moving up through four different leagues before folding in 1966 when reduced to just seven players. Many readers will recognise such a history.

Much of the reward gained is ultimately social and emotional rather than sporting. Football clubs are often just extensions of, or the basis for, male friendship groups, and humour and a 'good laugh' are essential ingredients. The naming of sides often reflects this with Real Ale Madrid, JCB Eindhoven and Perfidious Albion just three of the wittily named Sunday sides at large in the 1990s. Unsurprisingly, the Sunday game in particular is a rich source of anecdotes about excuses for missing matches (a player's claim that his dog died of a heart attack after falling off a skateboard won a best excuses competition in the 1990s), overweight goalkeepers and hung-over strikers. Less appetisingly, there have been periodic concerns about the levels of ill discipline in recreational football. Refereeing can be a particular trial and, in 1996, Halifax referees went on strike in protest at the attitude and behaviour of some players. The actual level of violence against both players and officials, however, tends to be quite small, and is often exaggerated as the result of a few high-profile cases.

For all the 7–7 draws between sides that could only field nine players each, it must be stressed that the best recreational football is of a very high standard indeed and plays a vital role in building a basis for the game at higher level. Although Sunday football has an especially jokey image, some of its best sides contain extremely talented players and the recreational game in general has always been the training ground for many professionals. Similarly, many who have been rejected by professional clubs have revived their careers in park football, while a small number of sides have progressed from the public park to a high level of the football pyramid. Welling United, for example, worked

through from the Eltham and District League to the Vauxhall Conference between 1971 and 1986. Even the weakest teams and players have their moments of glory, when a surprise win, a good goal, or even just a good tackle suddenly makes the world seem a better place. Of critical importance is the fact that all referees begin their training at this level. The establishment by the FA and partner organisations in 2000 of the Football Foundation, a body designed to increase funding at this level of the game, was a long overdue recognition of its value and importance.

Sources:

May, P., *Sunday Muddy Sunday: The Heart and Soul of Sunday League Football* (London: Virgin Publishing, 1998).

Wharton, R., *A Pick of the Best of Bradford Amateur Football* (Bradford: Author publisher, 1989).

Dave Russell

Re-elections to the Football League

Lasting from its first season in 1888 until 1986, the Football League's election system acted as a quality control mechanism, allowing it to review and modify its membership on an annual basis. The system required those clubs with the weakest playing records in the lowest division at the end of each season to retire and re-apply for membership of the League. All member clubs would then vote to either re-admit or replace them with an applicant from outside the competition.

Originally the bottom four clubs were required to re-apply, although this was reduced to three in 1896, then to two in 1908. With the creation of the Third Division North and South in 1921, the lowest two clubs in each section were forced to apply for re-election in separate ballots. The creation of the Fourth Division in 1959 brought the number of retiring clubs in the lowest division back to four.

Before the First World War, re-election proved a useful means of strengthening the composition of the League and aiding its expansionist policy by bringing in clubs from hitherto untapped areas. Between 1888 and 1915, 17 clubs failed to be re-elected. Some, like Stoke, Blackpool and Lincoln City, subsequently returned, but others, such as Loughborough, Burton United and Gainsborough Trinity, had to make do with a future outside the leading football competition in England and Wales.

The consolidation that followed the creation of the Third Division sections in the early 1920s led to accusations that the League was operating a 'closed shop' by protecting its existing members. As associate rather than full members, the Third Division clubs were denied a vote in the election ballot, but from 1922 each section was allowed to recommend the clubs it wished to be elected. Invariably, self-protection and group loyalty led to support for retiring members at the expense of outside applicants. Barrow, for example, finished bottom of the Northern Section on four occasions between 1924 and 1930, but were re-elected each time. Between 1921 and 1939 only seven clubs in the two sections lost their League places.

The so-called 'Old Pals' Act' was more evident still after the Second World War. In 1947, a record 27 non-League clubs applied to join the competition, but all four retiring members were re-elected. Even clubs applying for re-election in consecutive seasons were in little danger, as votes were often split between a number of non-League applicants. Before the 1970s only New Brighton (in 1951) and Gateshead (in 1960) failed to be re-elected.

The early 1970s saw Cambridge United replace Bradford Park Avenue, and Hereford United step in for Barrow, but the system was clearly in need of reform. From 1977 the Football League Management Committee selected just two clubs to challenge the four retiring members. In the following two seasons, Wimbledon and Wigan Athletic benefited at the expense of Workington and Southport. Over the next eight years, however, no new clubs were elected, and in 1986/87 re-election was replaced by an automatic promotion and relegation arrangement with the Football Conference.

Sources:
Inglis, S., *League Football and the Men Who Made It* (London: CollinsWillow, 1988).
Taylor, M. and Coyle, J., 'The Election of Clubs to the Football League, 1888–1939', *The Sports Historian*, 19: 2 (November 1999), 1–21.

Matt Taylor

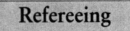

Refereeing

Early football games were played without officials, relying on a democratic decision among the players to determine infringements. In the 1860s and 1870s, with disputes about rules and infringements becoming more common on and off the field, umpires emerged – one nominated by each side – who, as in cricket, made decisions only when appealed to by the players. The growth of the game and the appearance of professionalism inevitably meant that disputes over interpretation of the rules in the heat of a match would become more common. A third, more objective official, the referee, appeared some time in the 1870s, and gradually thereafter assumed greater influence. Umpires were first mentioned in laws of the game in 1874, referees in 1881. The FA had a code of guidance for referees and umpires by the start of the 1885 season and, in 1891, the referee was made the sole judge of fair play, while umpires became linesmen and were clearly demarcated as the referee's assistants. Neutral linesmen for important games followed from around 1898/99.

At the start of the 1889/90 season the necessity for an appeal was removed, and the referee could award free-kicks at discretion. Penalty kicks were introduced for serious breaches of the rules in the attacking zone in the 1890s. The increasing powers of the officials indicated that intentional foul play had become part of the game. The officials' tasks were made easier by the introduction of a crossbar rather than a tape strung between posts, and of goal nets, mentioned in 1877 when the FA and the Sheffield Association

Sol Campbell scores a disputed goal for Arsenal
(© Stuart MacFarlane, Arsenal FC)

agreed to a common set of rules. Umpires had carried flags to indicate decisions, which they retained when they were banished once again to the touchlines. Referees used whistles to control play from the 1870s.

As today, discontent with the decisions of the officials was a regular if not frequent occurrence in the early days. More serious were attacks on referees at or after games, which resulted in ground closures, the setting up of a Referees' Union to protect its members in 1908/9, and attempts by the FA to raise standards among officials, as reflected in the establishment of a Referees' Association of 1893/94 and the Referees' Committee in 1899.

That early referees and umpires were members – usually, but not always, non-playing members – of clubs or associations, caused some friction as justice was not always perceived to be done. Gradually, they became a separate corps of independent officials, usually drawn from the middle classes. Players called for the introduction of professional referees as

their own livelihoods came to depend more and more on the game. The middle-class origins of the early referees were still noticeable in 1978, when a survey estimated that 88 per cent would be so described. An examination of the current list of Premier League referees indicates that this is still the case.

Sir Stanley Rous had a long career as a football referee in the 1920s and 1930s before becoming secretary of the FA, and later president of FIFA. He claimed credit for introducing the diagonal system of control, where the referee's movements are co-ordinated with those of the linesmen or assistant referees to provide the maximum coverage of the playing areas. Other innovations which he supported included coloured cards for cautions or sendings off, first tried internationally at the Olympic Games in 1968, the arc outside the penalty area borrowed from Italy, and the board with the numbers of players being exchanged, which he first saw in Malaysia. Nevertheless not all his decisions were favourably received. Rous admits to an unfortunate choice of officials for the latter stages of the World Cup in England in 1966, which led to accusations of bias from South America, and from his successor as President of FIFA, João Havelange.

That said, British referees have usually been highly regarded overseas for their professionalism and resistance to pressures of various sorts. Referees have always had to cope with changes in the laws of the game, and with directives from governing bodies, now particularly FIFA. Interpretations had varied between countries, for example, over charging the goalkeeper, a particular source of controversy between Britain and continental Europe in the first half of the twentieth century. FIFA's directives have been aimed at promoting a uniform approach by referees, though they have not always succeeded.

Debates over professional referees, having two on-field officials and the use of technology to help reduce error remain inconclusive, and experiments such as advancing a free-kick in case of dissent by the offending team continue. FIFA is actively promoting referee training and the quick advancement of good young officials, male and female. Women are officiating at male games in growing, if still small, numbers. It remains true however, as Pat Partridge, one leading British referee said, that 'No amount of training could improve a referee's two greatest assets – his eyesight and his courage'.

Sources:
Mason, T., *Association Football and English Society, 1863–1915* (Hassocks: Harvester, 1980).
Rous, S., *Football Worlds: A Lifetime in Sport* (London: Faber & Faber, 1978).
Thomson, G., *The Man in Black: A History of the Football Referee* (London: Prion, 1998).

Further Reading:
Elleray, D., *Referee!* (London: Bloomsbury, 1998).

Roy Hay

Religion

Organised religion played a major role in the initial development and sustenance of Association Football. Late Victorian clerics from across the religious spectrum saw football as an important source of moral, spiritual and physical education, and it has been suggested that as a result of such 'muscular Christianity' perhaps 25 per cent of early clubs were in some way connected to church or chapel. A significant number of professional clubs, including Aston Villa, Bolton Wanderers, Glasgow Celtic and Wolverhampton Wanderers, owe their origins to religious organisations. Although the conflicting demands placed on players by religious obligations (such as attendance at a specific place of worship) and the search for sporting success, led to many sides breaking away from the host institution, religious bodies and their offshoots remained major sponsors of the amateur game well into the twentieth century. As late as the 1950s, the (mainly Presbyterian) Glasgow Battalion of the Boys' Brigade ran what was probably the world's largest league, fielding over 200 sides. Only with the growth of often pub-centred Sunday football since the 1960s was religious based amateur football finally pushed to the margins, at least in England.

Although generally supportive of football as a recreational sport the churches have not always been sympathetic to the professional game, with a vocal minority seeing it as a rival to, and distraction from, organised religion and other aspects of public culture, and as a site of personal greed and generator of false passions. In 1938, the Bishop of Liverpool even found the pre-FA Cup final singing of *Abide With Me* a source of spurious emotion. In the light of this, it is interesting that a number of recent academic observers have argued that the game, while not a religion as such, can certainly work very much like one for some individuals in contemporary society. Certainly, given the sense of pilgrimage that can accompany attendance at games, the rituals involved and the sense of expectancy, even ecstasy, that football can engender, this seems a fertile argument. (The complex relationship between football and religion on a world scale was underlined in May 2000 when a sculpture of Manchester United's David Beckham was integrated into the base of Buddha's effigy in Bangkok's Pariwas Temple.)

Religion has undoubtedly been a cause of conflict within British football, and most particularly in Northern Ireland and Glasgow, where sectarian tensions have often found expression through the game. Conflict between supporters of Belfast Celtic – very much the side of Catholic West Belfast from its foundation in 1891 – and rival Protestant sides such as Glentoran and Linfield, pepper the history of the Irish game. This culminated in the club's withdrawal from the Irish League in 1948 after a Boxing Day pitch invasion at Linfield's ground resulted in its (Protestant) centre-forward having his leg broken. Similar politico-religious problems saw Derry City leave the Irish League in 1972 and eventually join the League of Ireland in 1985. In Glasgow, tensions between fans of Celtic, founded by a Marist Brother in 1887, and Rangers, established in 1872 and ever more overtly 'Protestant' in counter-distinction to the new rival, have been deep, and expressed through a variety of outlets from the symbolic to the physical. When, in July 1989, Rangers broke with a 70-year-old tradition of denominational discrimination by signing Catholic and ex-Celtic player, Maurice Johnston, he received death threats from both communities and an arson investigation was started following a fire at his home. However, it is worth noting that at least one authority on Scottish football, H. F. Moorhouse, believes that the sectarian element has been overplayed in the traditional account of Scottish football, and that many from both sides of the divide defined themselves as 'religious moderates' and welcomed Johnston's signing in 1989, and similar ones since. Both clubs tried hard to minimise sectarian impulses from the 1990s, and although the resignation of a Rangers vice-president after singing sectarian songs at a post-season celebration in June 1999 led to some

questioning as to whether they had been successful, the very fact of his leaving was perhaps indicative of changing mentalities.

In terms of personal beliefs, individual religious persuasion or group values have led to individuals either abandoning the game (as in the case of Peter Knowles, below) or being discouraged from playing it: it has sometimes been argued that the belated development of football culture among British Muslims owed at least something to religious factors. In general, though, tensions between the two areas are few. From the outset, many professional footballers have been practising Christians, and although some have been involved in organisations such as Christians in Sport, founded in 1976, for many players religion is often largely a private matter. Strong personal statements or patterns of behaviour have, however, occasionally made personal belief a matter of public concern. In a celebrated case, Wolves and England Under-23 international Peter Knowles retired from the game in 1969 because it prevented him from behaving in Christian fashion seven days a week. He was baptised as a Jehovah's Witness at the end of the year, although the club held on to his contract until 1982. In 1974, Bobby Tambling, a full England international then playing with Crystal Palace, became another to leave the professional game in order to work as a Jehovah's Witness. The most striking example of religious views impinging on a football career, however, was undoubtedly that concerning England coach Glenn Hoddle in February 1999. At the heart was Hoddle's importation of an acceptance of reincarnation into his long-professed Christian beliefs, leading him to argue in an interview with *The Times* that disability was essentially a punishment for sins committed in a previous life. After a furious public backlash, the FA removed Hoddle from his post.

Generally, however, religion plays a non-controversial role. *Rothmans Yearbook*, for example, listed over 50 chaplains serving at English clubs in 2000, with many teams using ministers in a pastoral role with trainees; indeed, the Football Scholarship scheme lays down a specific role for them in this context. Despite the increasingly secular tone of British society, religion continues to exert a certain quiet and productive influence in the modern game.

Sources:

Cronin, M., *Sport and Nationalism in Ireland since 1884* (Dublin: Four Courts Press, 1999).

Murray, B., *Glasgow Giants: One Hundred Years of the Old Firm* (Edinburgh: Mainstream, 1988).

Russell, D., *Football and the English* (Preston: Carnegie Publishing, 1997).

The Times (2 September 1969; 11 July 1989; 30 January to 3 February 1999; 1 June 1999).

Further Reading:

Percy, M. and Taylor, R., 'Something for the Weekend Sir?' Leisure, Ecstasy and Identity in Football and Contemporary Religion', *Leisure Studies*, 16 (1997), 37–49.

Shirley, P. and Hoddle, G., *The Faith to Win* (London: Harper Collins, 1998).

See also Rituals and Superstitions

Dave Russell

Relocation of Clubs

Following the 1985 Bradford fire disaster and the 1989 Hillsborough tragedy, both associated with stadium design and maintenance, the report of Lord Justice Taylor demonstrated clearly the decaying fabric of many stadia, initially a source of civic pride, now – as virtual slums – a source of shame. His recommendations regarding all-seater stadia forced many clubs to consider relocation as the most cost-effective way to implement his proposals. Some clubs, such as Walsall, had already recognised the dilapidated state of their ground and were committed to move to improved premises. Others shifted because of financial pressures, positive and negative. Football grounds on urban sites are prime targets for housing or business use, and some received offers they could not refuse. Others, such as Bristol Rovers in 1986, were forced by mounting debts to sell their ground and move in with Bath City at Twerton Park. Charlton's decision to leave The Valley was prompted by the projected costs of renovating the ground to meet safety standards, and an offer from Crystal Palace to share their ground. When they returned to The Valley it was to be replaced at Selhurst Park by Wimbledon, who were hoping to sell their Plough Lane site for lucrative redevelopment. Finally there are a few clubs such as the north-east duo of Middlesbrough and Sunderland, who have seen a move as a way of coping with larger crowds, actual or potential. Even lower down the leagues, Scunthorpe United was faced with spending a six-figure sum to raise the capacity of the Old Show Ground, and chose instead to relocate.

Yet relocation is nothing new. Indeed, of the 179 moves by the 92 clubs which comprised the Football League in 1988/89, 88 per cent of them took place before 1921. In the following 60 years most clubs stayed where they were but the last two decades of the twentieth century saw a burst of relocation activity. Since the late 1980s, 50 Premier and Football League clubs have actively considered relocating. Indeed, more clubs relocated their ground in the last decade of the century than at any time since the first ten years.

Inevitably, these relocations caused angst among supporters of the teams concerned. Since membership of a team is transient and rarely local in origin, fan loyalty extends, for some, to the more enduring ground where the team plays: the concrete link between the club and its supporter base. Here we are moving into the area of what John Bale has labelled 'topophilia' – or love of place – with any attempt to relocate their stadium generally being met initially by strong resistance from local patriots who have devoted their leisure time to attending matches at a particular site. Generally, fans have been at best badly informed and at worst ignored by the clubs, who seem to have learned little from the example of Sheffield Wednesday who, in 1898, canvassed their fans as to where they should move to.

Although at the time Owlerton (now Hillsborough) was miles beyond the city boundary and poorly served by public transport, attendances in the first season at the new ground averaged some 3,000 more than at the previous one. This was a lesson in democracy which went almost unheeded in ensuing years. Only one club has followed the democratic line pursued by Sheffield Wednesday a hundred years ago. When it decided to sell its Old Show Ground to developers, Scunthorpe consulted its fans on three possible sites, and actually went to the most favoured one at Glanford Park. The result was a trebling of season ticket sales and a rise in gates of 32 per cent in the first four seasons at the new ground. A few others, such as Northampton, have kept fans informed as to what was likely to happen. Generally, however, communication and consultation have been minimal.

Local councils can play a crucial role, as either enabler or as obstacle. One has only to contrast the 14 refusals of the planning applications of Wycombe Wanderers with the initiative taken by Huddersfield Town, who invited Kirklees Metropolitan Council to nominate the facilities it would like in a new stadium and then worked in partnership to develop the award-winning Alfred McAlpine Stadium. Certainly the fans of Charlton, fighting to bring their team back to the Valley, appreciated the position. They fielded candidates in the council elections of May 1990, securing nearly 11 per cent of the vote and helping to unseat the Chairman of the Planning Committee. The collective political protest no doubt helped persuade Greenwich Council to approve revised plans, and in December 1992 Charlton returned 'home'. Although some councils appreciate the economic loss of a team departing their area, others still remember the hooligan days and would prefer to see football clubs banished to the outskirts of town, or even to some other authority's backyard.

Sources:

Bale, J. and Moen, O., *The Stadium and the City* (Keele: Keele University Press, 1996).
Inglis, S., *Football Grounds of Britain* (London: CollinsWillow, 1996).

Further Reading:

Duke, V., 'The Drive to Modernisation and the Supermarket Imperative: Who Needs a New Football Stadium?' in R. Giulianotti and J. Williams (eds), *Game Without Frontiers: Football, Identity and Modernity* (Aldershot: Arena, 1994).
Taylor, R., *Football and its Fans: Supporters and their Relations with the Game* (Leicester: University of Leicester Press, 1992).

Wray Vamplew

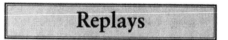

Replays

The notion that a drawn cup match should be replayed at the ground of the visiting team in the original match was enshrined in the rules of the FA Cup from its inception in 1872. The first replayed FA Cup game was probably the 1873/74 tie between Sheffield Club and Shropshire Wanderers. Both the original game and the replay were drawn, and Sheffield progressed via the toss of a coin. The same season witnessed the first replay in the Scottish FA Cup, Clydesdale overcoming Third Lanark 2–0 after two draws. The first replayed FA Cup final came in 1875, when Royal Engineers beat Old Etonians 2–0 following a 1–1 draw. The Scottish FA Cup final was replayed for the first time in 1876, Queen's Park beating Third Lanark at the second attempt.

Replays in FA Cup finals have actually been quite rare: after Barnsley's replay victory in 1912 there was no replay until 1970, when Chelsea beat Leeds United 2–1 at Old Trafford after a 2–2 draw at Wembley. However, between 1981 and 1983 the final went to replays in three successive seasons. Replays have been more common in finals of the Football League Cup, and the 1976/77 final, between Aston Villa and Everton, required two replays before Villa emerged victorious. Chelsea are the only British team to have won a major European final after a replay, defeating Real Madrid 2–1 in Athens in 1971 to clinch the Cup Winners' Cup after a 1–1 draw.

The record for the greatest number of

replays in the FA Cup goes to the 1971/72 fourth qualifying round tie between Alvechurch and Oxford City. Alvechurch won 1–0 in the fifth replay, the teams therefore meeting a total of six times. In the competition proper seven ties have gone to a fourth replay, the most recent being Arsenal's third round game with Sheffield Wednesday in 1978/79. Arsenal won the fifth meeting 2–0 and went on to lift the FA Cup that season. In the Scottish FA Cup, the Beith v Broxburn tie in 1908/9 took four replays to resolve. The final three games were played on consecutive days, 3–5 February 1909, and winners Beith then had to face St Mirren on 6 February. Perhaps unsurprisingly, St Mirren won the game 3–0.

In 1991, the FA decided that all ties in the FA Cup competition proper would be decided by penalty kicks after the first replay. In November 1991 Rotherham United became the first team to progress in the FA Cup via a 'shoot-out', overcoming Scunthorpe United after two drawn first round games. A similar system had been introduced in the Scottish FA Cup from 1989/90 and the final of that season was decided on penalties, Aberdeen beating Celtic 9–8 after a 0–0 draw. The Football League Cup had seen the introduction of 'shoot-outs' in the early rounds from 1976/77: Doncaster Rovers were the first team to benefit from this, overcoming Lincoln City in August 1976 after a drawn first round replay. The later stages of the League Cup featured multiple replays for some time, and in 1989/90 Swindon Town beat Bolton Wanderers 2–1 in the fourth round following three drawn games.

Not all replays are a result of drawn games. In the early years of the FA and Scottish Cups disputes were common, and games were often replayed when protests from beaten teams were upheld. In 1889/90 the third round FA Cup tie between Sheffield Wednesday and Notts County was replayed twice after protests from both teams. In March 1974, the FA ordered a replay after crowd trouble had disrupted the sixth round tie between Newcastle United and Nottingham Forest. In 1985 Leicester City's 6–1 victory over Burton Albion was annulled because an object thrown from the crowd had injured the Burton goalkeeper. The replay was held behind closed doors at Coventry, Leicester winning 1–0. A similar incident led to Peterborough United's 9–1 win over Kingstonian in November 1993 being expunged from the records. That game was replayed behind closed doors at Peterborough, the home team winning 1–0. Finally, in February 1999 the Arsenal v Sheffield United tie was replayed at the request of the Arsenal manager and directors, after their team had breached the etiquette of the game. They took advantage of a 'free throw' following an injury to score what proved to be the winning goal. The game was replayed at Highbury, and Arsenal won 2–1, the same score as in the original game. Multiple replays may be a thing of the past, but unusual ones are clearly not.

Sources:

Brown, T., *The Ultimate FA Cup Statistics Book* (Basildon: Association of Football Statisticians, 1994).

Pawson, T., *100 Years of the FA Cup: The Official Centenary History* (London: Heinemann, 1972).

Smailes, G., *The Breedon Book of Scottish Football Records* (Derby: Breedon Books, 1995).

John Coyle

Research Centres

Although the academic study of football had begun in earnest in the 1970s, it was not until the opening of the Sir Norman Chester Centre for Football Research at Leicester University in April 1987 that the game possessed a dedicated research centre. It was rooted in the University's Sociology Department, which had already established a strong reputation for its work on football hooliganism through the work of Eric Dunning, Patrick Murphy, John Williams, and others. Funded in its entirety by the Football Trust, it has engaged in a wide range of research projects for various football bodies and interested organisations, including studies of black footballers and women and football, while maintaining special expertise in the area of fan behaviour.

Although the Chester Centre had to endure a little gentle satirical comment at the hands of journalists finding the marriage of sport and academia a target impossible to resist, its success coupled with the football boom of the 1990s legitimised the notion of the football research centre. In 1995, the Football Research Unit was established within the Department of Economic and Social History at Liverpool University under the directorship of Rogan Taylor, a leading figure in the independent fan movement of the 1980s and a former researcher at the Chester Centre. The Unit's major contribution has probably been the establishment of an MBA (Football Industries) in 1997, the first full-time course of its type in the country, although other work in a number of areas has been pursued. The establishment of the Institute of Football Studies at the University of Central Lancashire followed, in 1996. This is a joint venture between the University and The National Football Museum at Deepdale, Preston, initially directed by Dave Russell. The Institute will eventually provide major support for the Museum and concern itself with all aspects of the game, but under current head Rob Hulme, work is focused on a DfEE-funded project developing a range of teaching and learning materials for use with school students.

A number of other centres, although not exclusively concerned with football, have made major contributions to the game. In 1992, a number of academics originally working at the Sir Norman Chester Centre set up the Centre for Research into Sport and Society, currently led by Patrick Murphy, and also at Leicester University. This has produced a number of studies and surveys of the game. Leicester's association with the academic study of sport was further enhanced in 1996, with the establishment of the International Centre for Sports History and Culture at the city's De Montfort University. Originally headed by Wray Vamplew, the Centre has employed several of the most notable historians of the game, including Tony Mason and Pierre Lanfranchi, and since 1999 has run an MA in the Management, Law and Humanities of Sport on behalf of FIFA. Staff at Manchester Metropolitan University's Institute for Popular Culture have been at the forefront of studies of football fandom, while important work on football and the law has been carried out at the Centre for the Study of Law, Society and Popular Culture at the University of Westminster and the Anglia Sports Law Research Centre at Anglia Polytechnic University.

While still prone to occasional critical or humorous comment of the type noted earlier, the football research centre, either as freestanding entity or part of a wider grouping, established itself in the academic and footballing landscape in the late twentieth century. Born out of the game's troubles in that period, it is unlikely to disappear in the more favourable but increasingly complex days of the twenty-first century.

Sources:

Newsletter of the International Centre for Sports History and Culture, 1996– (Leicester: International Centre for Sports History and Culture).

Williams, J., et al., *FA Premier League Fan Survey, 1994–* (Leicester: Sir Norman Chester Centre for Football Research).

See also Scientific Perspectives

Dave Russell

Rituals and Superstitions

When the opposing captains lead their teams out of the players' tunnel and take to the field of play, to the accompaniment of the roar of the crowd, the scene resembles nothing more than the entry of the gladiators into the Roman amphitheatres of old. Indeed, some historians would have us believe that it was the ancient Romans who first introduced football to Britain, in the form of the game of Harpastum, one of their less bloodthirsty pastimes. When a team returns to home territory after a Wembley victory in the FA Cup final, the coveted trophy, draped in the club colours, is displayed to the cheering crowds from the top of the obligatory open-topped double-decker bus. The scene is reminiscent of a Roman general's 'triumph', the ceremony bestowed on him by a grateful Senate following a successful campaign spent subduing some troublesome band of Gauls or Brigantes. For the soldiers' reward of gold pieces, read win bonuses. What we watch today is merely a sanitised form of what George Orwell called 'war without the shooting'. If this is the case then we can be grateful that the Emperor's dreaded 'thumbs-down', sanctioning the despatch of some unfortunate fallen combatant in the arena, lives on in a less drastic version in the form of the red card brandished by the referee. This gesture, no less dramatic though thankfully less final, is still greeted with roars of approval – at least from half of the assembled multitude.

Continuing the analogy of football as ritualised combat, the exchange of shirts after an important game can be seen as the equivalent either of carrying a vanquished enemy's standard from the battlefield or of being subjugated into accepting the superiority of the victor by wearing his colours, just as conquered tribes were conscripted as Roman auxiliaries. The small boys (or girls), dressed in similar style to their favourites and accompanying them into the arena, may be known as mascots these days, but bring to mind the squires who led their medieval knights into the field. One such squire even became a knight himself and appeared in all the top tournaments: David Beckham's first appearance in Manchester United colours was at the age of 12, when he appeared as the United mascot at an away game against West Ham.

Football clubs do not rely entirely on mascots to bring good luck, however. The Newcastle United team of the early twentieth century, for instance, who won three League Championships in five years and reached five FA Cup finals out of seven, were convinced that it was all down to luck: they would win if they passed a wedding on the way to a game and lose if they

saw a funeral. Gillingham were long convinced that their Priestfield stadium had a gypsy curse hanging over it from the time in the 1940s when the then manager of the club had been involved in a motoring accident near the ground in which a young gypsy girl had been killed. So paranoid about this curse were the Kent club, even in 1992, that they appointed a supporter, a Catholic priest, to lift it. They promptly won their next three home games. They must have been inspired by Derby County, who had caused the eviction of a gypsy encampment when they moved to the Baseball Ground in 1895. Convinced that the departing Romanies had left a curse behind them, the club captain, Jack Nicholas, sought out an obliging gypsy just before the 1946 FA Cup final. After the traditional passing over of silver the hoodoo was lifted, and Derby went on to beat Charlton Athletic 4–1, though they must have thought they had been double-crossed when a seemingly goal-bound shot from two-goal hero Jack Stamps was easily saved by Charlton keeper Sam Bartram after the ball burst!

In 1994 Beazer Home League side Dorchester Town, struggling at the bottom of the League, called in a vicar to bless their pitch and lift a curse left by a dissatisfied supporter, a part-time druid. The cleric's words were followed by a druidic chant from the remorseful fan and the next day Town won their first game for months. Ipswich Town put their winning run in the 1953/54 season down to a seven-leaf clover, a present from a US fan. Oldham Athletic must have had some such talisman among their kit when they toured Rhodesia in 1967. They lost only one match out of 11, scoring 45 goals in the process, despite a local witch doctor protecting their opponents' goals with 'magic' lines.

Another curse, the so-called 'Wembley Jinx', was said to have been behind a number of injuries to players affecting FA Cup finals for more than a decade, although the first incident occurred during an England–Scotland match. In the 1950/51 fixture, won 3–2 by Scotland, England's Wilf Mannion challenged Billy Liddell for a high ball and came off worse, fracturing his cheekbone. He left the field on a stretcher. His injury was sustained in the thirteenth minute – was this an omen? It was certainly the start of something. In the 1952 final between Arsenal and Newcastle United, the Gunners' Wally Barnes suffered a knee injury in the first half. He twice came back on with the knee heavily strapped, but eventually had to leave for good after 27 minutes. Some of the gloss was taken off the famous 'Matthews Final' of 1953 by the injury to Bolton left-half Eric Bell that left him a right-wing passenger for much of the game. In 1955 Manchester City's Jimmy Meadows was forced off after 20 minutes with knee ligament problems in the final against Newcastle United. The following year Manchester City were again involved. Their German goalkeeper Bert Trautmann, newly elected Footballer of the Year, played the last 15 minutes with a broken neck after diving at the feet of Birmingham City's Peter Murphy. In 1957 it was the turn of Manchester United; goalkeeper Ray Wood was concussed following a collision with Aston Villa's Peter McParland, and Jackie Blanchflower had to go in goal. In 1959 Nottingham Forest won the Cup but only after Luton Town's Roy Dwight had been carried off in the first half with a broken leg.

In 1960 Wolves beat Blackburn after Rovers' Dave Whelan had been forced to bow out with a similar injury. Spurs clinched their historic 'double' at Wembley in 1961 with an uncharacteristically lacklustre performance, after Leicester City had lost right-back Len Chalmers after only 18 minutes. When Tottenham won the Cup again in 1962 by beating Burnley, the *Daily Telegraph*, bearing the so-called jinx in mind, ran the headline: 'Spurs retain Cup at Wembley: not a stretcher in sight.' Two injury-free finals followed, but then in 1965 Liverpool's Gerry Byrne spent all but the first five minutes of the Reds' extra-time victory over Leeds with a broken collarbone. The end was in sight, however: the hoodoo was finally lifted not through sorcery or exorcism but courtesy of the FA. On 3 July 1965 they finally sanctioned the use of substitutes.

One player who appeared well out of reach of any jinxes going around was Ted Farmer, the Wolves player of the early 1960s. He scored his 21st league goal in his 21st League game on 21 January. And it was his 21st birthday! At the other end of the superstition spectrum was Len Shackleton, soccer's 'Clown Prince'. The colourful 'Shack', with a name containing 13 letters, had first played for England schoolboys aged 13, and made his first full international appearance for England in 1946 – on 13 April. Later that year he was transferred from Bradford Park Avenue to Newcastle United for a then Second Division record fee – £13,000. He didn't let this omen affect his game in his debut, however: he scored six as Newcastle hammered Newport County 13–0. It could have been 14–0, but Charlie Wayman obligingly kept the sequence going by missing a penalty.

Albert Nightingale could have used a bit of Shack's luck a few years later. The unfortunate inside-forward was a Sheffield United player when Bramall Lane was hit by ten German bombs in December 1940, destroying half the John Street Stand and leaving the playing area a smoking ruin, pitted with craters. By 1950 he was on the books of Huddersfield Town when the Leeds Road ground had its West Stand burn down in mysterious circumstances. In 1956 he was with Leeds United when an electrical fault in Elland Road's West Stand caused that structure to go up in smoke.

In order to avoid such terrible luck as that suffered by the hapless Albert, footballers down the years have resorted to some bizarre practices to ward off the 'evil eye'. Derby County's goalkeeper of the 1890s, Jack Robinson, insisted that the team's results depended on his having his traditional rice pudding before games. 'No pudding, no points' was Jack's motto. When Arsenal goalkeeper Dan Lewis, himself a Welsh international, let in a soft shot that gave Cardiff City the only goal of the game in the 1927 FA Cup final, he blamed his new jersey, claiming it was too slippery. This rather lame excuse led to a tradition, which still persists, of all Arsenal keepers washing new jerseys before use.

Dick Pym, the England goalkeeper who turned out for Exeter City and Bolton Wanderers in the 1920s, would always examine his train ticket before away trips. If the digits of his ticket number totalled 13 then he wouldn't travel. He also insisted on always having a lump of coal in his pocket, even when playing.

Even in the present hi-tech era some activities of players seem rooted in the dark ages. A goal-scorer was once content with his team-mates' congratulations consisting of a quick handshake or perhaps a friendly ruffling of his hair. These days every goal seems to be followed either by the scorer being engulfed in a heap of bodies or by some obscure ritual involving the whole team. These esoteric ceremonies can involve running backwards together, crawling on all fours around a corner flag, hopping around the centre circle, or even more bizarre celebrations. In an attempt to enlighten the rest of the nation as to what these mysterious caperings actually meant, the BBC in the 1990s introduced a special 'What's that all about, then?' round into their quiz show *A Question of Sport*, but the resultant publicity merely incited the players to even more arcane tomfoolery. Some goal-scorers, wishing to distance themselves from such communal indignities, confine their celebratory antics to individual gymnastics in the form of a handspring or two. One who did, and wished he had not, was Chelsea's Nigerian striker Celestine Babayaro. After a goal for his new club in a pre-season friendly he attempted what looked like an ambitious triple back-flip with toe-loop and pike, which failed to impress his new bosses as it all went wrong and he ended up with a broken ankle.

Less dangerous rituals and superstitions are still commonplace, however. Many players insist on always having the same peg in the dressing room; some always want to be last on to the field; goalkeepers often kick each post for luck. One of the most common is the compulsive donning of kit in a certain order, such as one boot before the other. This is probably best epitomised by ex-player Barry Venison, a regular presenter on ITV's *On The Ball*. Using the communication skills that no doubt earned him his media job, but displaying a worrying lack of dress sense, he explained: 'When I was a player I always put my right boot on first, and then obviously my right sock.' Bad luck, Barry.

Sources:
Nicklin, F., Carling: *The Ultimate Football Fact and Quiz Book* (London: Stopwatch, 1997).
Pickering, D., *Cassell Soccer Companion* (London: Cassell, 1997).
Young, P. M., *A History Of British Football* (London: Stanley Paul, 1969).

Tony Rennick

Royal Patronage

Although British royalty has never been associated with football in the way that it has with sports such as horseracing, polo and show-jumping, royal patronage has been extended to the game from the late nineteenth century as the monarchy has sought to establish tentative links with popular culture. Football, for its part, has actively sought the cachet that royal connection brings. With these respective ends in mind, no doubt, the Prince of Wales accepted an invitation to become the first royal patron of the FA in 1892. After respectfully postponing all FA Cup replays for one month following the death of Queen Victoria in January 1901, the FA then persuaded him to continue as patron after his coronation as Edward VII, and from then on the reigning monarch has always served in this role.

George V's visit to an England v Scotland international in 1909 probably marks the first attendance at a major game by royalty, and he broke new ground again in 1914 when becoming the first monarch to attend the FA Cup final. To an extent, this may have reflected the King's genuine interest in sport: the King George V Cup, for example, was introduced in show-jumping in 1911. More probably, it lies alongside the King's attendance of the first Royal Variety Performance in 1912 as a gentle embracing of popular entertainment in an increasingly democratic age.

Royalty, if not always in the form of the monarch, has been in attendance at the majority of FA Cup finals ever since this moment. George V was to become even more closely associated with the match in 1923, when his appearance just before the kick-off of Wembley's famously over-crowded first final was held to be one of the key factors preventing a major catastrophe. Others in the game noted the benefits of royal acknowledgement and, in 1932, the commercially astute Arsenal FC persuaded the Prince of Wales to open Highbury's new West Stand. His reign as Edward VIII was far too brief to allow him to add more royal lustre to the game, and the FA joined in the general sigh of relief following his abdication by commissioning the Spode Pottery to produce a so-called 'loving cup' to celebrate the coronation of George VI in 1937. One of these was presented to each First Division club, with the expectation that a loyal toast would be raised in it every New Year.

The 'Coronation Cup Final' of 1953 took the form of the error-strewn but dramatic game between Blackpool and Bolton. After Blackpool's last-minute 4–3 victory, captain Harry Johnson called for three cheers for the new Queen from the centre of the pitch. From the late 1950s, the Queen became the first monarch to bestow honours upon professional footballers and managers, and she played a central role in the opening ceremony of the 1966 World Cup. Three years later, she celebrated the achievements of Bobby and Jackie Charlton in that tournament by naming two of her racehorses after them. Prince Charles has never been a particular devotee of the game, but he gave practical help to the FA in its bid to host the 2006 World Cup by attending and arranging a number of functions and receptions and, in 1998, actively supported the 'Kick Racism out of Football' initiative by visiting a scheme involving Charlton Athletic and a Sikh youth side. In the late 1990s, the royal princes Harry and William exhibited a rather more engaged attitude to the game than most of their forebears. Harry's enthusiastic support of the England team during his attendance at the 1998 World Cup group match against

Columbia was well captured by the media, and added a little to both his appeal with some audiences and to the aura of glamour increasingly surrounding the game at elite level.

Sources:
Green, G., *The History of the Football Association* (London: Naldrett, 1953).
Russell, D., *Football and the English: A Social History of Association Football in England* (Preston: Carnegie Publishing, 1997).
Pickering, D., *Cassell Soccer Companion* (London: Cassell, 1994).

Dave Russell

Rules

The laws of association football serve to maintain the necessary balance between the players' freedom to improvise and express themselves on the pitch, and the need to introduce controls to enable the game to be played fairly between different classes, cultures and countries, and by both sexes. While the contemporary game has become increasingly law-bound, and that inevitably some of the pure play quality in soccer has been lost in this process, it is nonetheless true that football is unquestionably the world's leading sport for players and spectators alike. Football laws therefore successfully perform the vital function of permitting certain prescribed conditions which enable factors other than ability to be equalised for all participants. If the relationships between players on the field are too rigidly or too loosely bound, the game will suffer.

Rudimentary football laws have existed for centuries. Medieval football laws were passed from generation to generation by word of mouth, since the vast majority of players were illiterate. The absence of written laws and central organisation meant different varieties of these mob games were played in different localities in Britain. The emotional spontaneity of the struggles was considerable, and standard limitations were rarely imposed on the size of pitches, the number of players or the duration of matches. Moreover, few restrictions were placed on the tactics the player might employ, and practically none were imposed to keep their passions in check. Nor were there officials to enforce such rules as did exist. Mob football reflected the violent, relatively unregulated tenor of life in society at large. The game shaded into other folk-games, and elements of what would now be seen as soccer, rugby, hockey, boxing and wrestling were often embodied in a single game such as 'knappan', 'hurling', or 'camp-ball'.

The present laws of the game can be traced as far back as the public school codes of the mid-nineteenth century. The wild, ill-disciplined football of the past was incompatible with the educational aims of the masters' and the pupils' ethical, if novel, desire for fair play. Starting with the Rugby School rules of 1845, more civilised laws were committed to print which constrained the degree of acceptable violence on the field of play. Such controls reflected societal changes, yet the public school laws retained their individuality and preserved sufficiently high levels of conflict, tension and excitement without, which the interest of players would have flagged.

The quest for a uniform national code of laws in the latter part of the nineteenth century focused on the maintenance of this delicate balance. The process was not, however, undertaken by experts constructing a national game according to logical principles. Rather, the laws evolved in a haphazard fashion, resolving issues as they arose. Thus, up until 1886 the laws developed along a number of clearly defined but disparate lines. The Cambridge Rules of 1848 and 1863, Thring's Rules of 1862, the Sheffield Rules of 1867 and the Scottish Rules of 1873 exhibited a heterogeneity that defied the FA's early attempts at unification following its formation in 1863. Gradually the different codes came together, disagreements were argued out, laws were arrived at by compromise, tested in practice and modified as tactical and technical progress revealed their weaknesses. The most potent catalyst for unification towards the end of the century was the desire for competition at local, regional and national level. Improvements in road transport, the advent of the railways, the acceptance of the Saturday half-holiday and the spread of the newspaper stimulated the clamour for a uniform code. The FA's tenuous hold on the association game strengthened with the establishment of the FA Challenge Cup in 1871, the first international match between England and Scotland in 1872, the legalisation of professionalism in 1885, and the formation of the Football League in 1888. Such innovations simultaneously led to a tremendous improvement in playing standards, and precipitated change in football law. In 1886 the FA gracefully surrendered their right as chief lawmaker to the International Football Association Board, composed of two representatives from each of the four home nations. In 1913 two delegates from FIFA were admitted to the International Board. Since then the International Board has been extremely conservative. Its policy is only to make changes when there is positive evidence that change is necessary. For example, before 1925 skilful exploitation of the offside rule gave far too much advantage to defenders. The laws gave too much advantage to defenders. Eventually, in 1925 the law was changed to insist on only two (instead of three) defenders between the attackers and the goal line. The effect was instant. In the 1925/26 season there was a 42 per cent increase in goals scored in the Football League. Between 1925 and 1937 there were several more minor changes, and the laws were completely re-drafted in 1937/38. Each clause was made as short as possible, and the punishment for each offence was stated immediately after each law. In 1959 the International Board issued a *Memorandum on the Application of the Laws* that stated that future problems were to be resolved by 'Official Decisions' relating to the laws rather than by tinkering with the laws themselves. Today, there are 17 laws of association football applying equally to all players amateur and professional, male and female, throughout the world. They may be subdivided into four main groups.

1. Matters relating to the game before the match begins
   1.1 Field of play, the ball, the number of players (Laws 1, 2 and 3)
   1.2 Equipment and protection of players (Law 4)
   1.3 The officials in charge of the game (Laws 5 and 6)
2. Matter relating to the playing of the game (Laws 7 to 11)
3. Special features of the game – throw-ins and free-kicks – the penalty kick, goal kick and corner kick being particular kinds of free-kicks (Laws 13 to 17)
4. The Penal Law (Law 12)

Recently, the International Board has acted through the laws to combat undesirable trends such as time-wasting, violent tackles and deliberate foul play. Interpretations and clarifications are published by national associations in the form of questions and answers, together with reasons and intended effects. Thus, as guardians of soccer law, International Board members serve to promote improvements to the technicalities of play, and also to preserve the moral, character-forming qualities intended by the founders of the game in the nineteenth century.

Source:
Dunning, E., *Sport Matters* (London: Routledge, 1999).

Further Reading:
Lover, S., *Soccer Rules Explained* (London: Eric Dobby Publishing, 1998).

Ian Moir

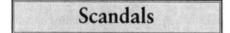

Scandals

Scandals in the personal lives of those involved in football have frequently been given as much attention and publicity as other matters more closely related to the game. Until the 1960s football scandals dealt with financial corruption or accusations of cheating and match-fixing. However, since then, as professional sportsmen have increasingly been held up as role models for the young and afforded ever-greater celebrity status, footballers' off-the-pitch behaviour (often conveniently ignored in the past) has become the subject of intense media scrutiny.

Excessive intake of alcohol and its consequences have led to several notable football scandals. George Best is generally acknowledged to have been the first British soccer star to experience voracious media interest about his private life, and his drunken exploits continued to make headlines long after his career had finished. He was sentenced to three months imprisonment in 1984 for assaulting a police officer. Both Jan Molby, the Danish international and Liverpool midfielder, and Tony Adams, the Arsenal captain, served custodial sentences for drink-driving offences. Molby was jailed for three months in 1988 following a two-mile high-speed car chase by police. In 1990 Adams smashed his car into a brick wall and was given four months in Chelmsford Prison, and disqualified from driving for two years.

Incidents relating to social drug use began to gain publicity from the late 1990s, while a number of players have also attracted attention because of gambling problems. England internationals Stan Bowles and Peter Shilton ended their careers with large gambling debts, with Bowles thought to have lost around £750,000 over the course of his career.

The 'incident in a night club' has become a cliché of football scandals. In 1965 the suspension of members of the Chelsea team who had broken the club curfew to go drinking in Blackpool was an early example of what was subsequently to become standard newspaper fare. Terry Venables, George Graham, Eddie McCreadie and John Hollins were among the eight men sent back to London by their manager Tommy Docherty in a blaze of publicity, made greater because Chelsea were First Division Championship contenders. Brawling, other violence, and damage to property appear to be frequent consequences of footballers' nights out. England's preparations for the European Championships in 1996 were accompanied by loud controversy which erupted when lurid photographs of Teddy Sheringham and Paul Gascoigne in the Jump Club in Hong Kong were displayed on the tabloid front pages. Images of players strapped in a dentist's chair and having alcohol poured down their throats hardly seemed suitable training for the tournament.

Paul Gascoigne's career has been punctuated by a number of such high-profile incidents which have received extensive press coverage, ranging from the relatively minor offences of belching in an interview and insulting Norway, to the serious charge of wife-beating. His notoriety earned condemnation from many quarters, but also won him admiration from those fans who considered some of his behaviour subversive, and the excessive media attention he received tantamount to persecution. In the 1990s compilations celebrating the exploits of 'football's bad boys' became popular subjects for magazine articles and books. In 2001 Leeds United player Jonathan Woodgate was found guilty of affray following a racist attack on an Asian student outside a Leeds nightclub. He was given 100 hours of community service.

Sexual scandals featuring managers, players and other football figures regularly dominated the Sunday papers from the 1970s onwards. When, in 1993, Welsh international Mickey Thomas, then at Wrexham, was sentenced to 18 months' imprisonment for passing forged bank notes to the club's YTS players, the judge commented that he had failed in his duty as a distinguished international sportsman looked up to by many youngsters throughout Wales. However, Thomas became something of a cult figure when it became known that he had been subjected to a horrific assault with a sharpened screwdriver while engaged in sexual activity in a parked car with another man's wife just eight days before. So great is the appetite for such stories that even the peccadilloes of chairmen make headlines. The confessions of Manchester United's multimillionaire chairman Martin Edwards' mistresses appeared in the *Sunday People* and the *News of the World* in 1990 and 1994. A far bigger furore greeted revela-

tions in 1998 of a taped conversation in a Spanish brothel. Newcastle United chairman Freddy Shepherd and vice-chairman Douglas Hall supposedly described Newcastle women as 'dogs', their supporters as gullible for buying overpriced replica shirts, and striker Alan Shearer as 'Mary Poppins'. The subsequent outcry caused their temporary resignations.

An international scandal ensued when England captain Bobby Moore was accused of stealing a bracelet from a jeweller in Bogotá during the 1970 World Cup. Though he was arrested, he was later given a conditional release from what is generally acknowledged to have been a false charge. Criminal activities by football's personnel have continued to fascinate tabloid readers. The ex-Arsenal player Peter Storey was convicted of running a brothel in 1979, and jailed at various times since then for involvement in a counterfeiting scheme, car theft and importing obscene tapes inside his car's spare tyre.

Sources:

Adams, T. with Ridley, I., *Addicted* (London: CollinsWillow, 1998).

Campbell, D., May, P. and Shields, A., *The Lad Done Bad: Sex, Sleaze and Scandal in English Football* (Harmondsworth: Penguin, 1996).

Cosgrove, S., *Hampden Babylon: Sex and Scandal in Scottish Football* (Edinburgh: Canongate, 1991).

Williams, R., *Football Babylon* (London: Virgin Books, 1996).

See also Careers Cut Short, Gambling

Joyce Woolridge

Schools Football

Although the English Schools Football Association (ESFA) was founded in 1904 the game had been established in schools throughout the country for some time beforehand. Significant influence had been brought to bear by the country's leading public schools on a game that had previously been considered violent, raucous and certainly not suitable for young gentlemen. Although this rationalising influence was founded in the exclusivity of the Oxbridge 'melting-pot' in the second half of the nineteenth century, and was adopted by those public schools that favoured the round ball game, it was in the country's elementary schools that the game we now refer to as soccer took root and flourished.

The South London Schools FA was the first known school football body and was founded in 1885. It was the forerunner of many other associations centred largely upon the heavily populated industrial areas where the professional game had already taken root. In May 1890, the Sheffield Schools FA invited South London Schools to play at Hillsborough, and this marked the beginning of inter-district rivalries which continue to this day. The first schoolboy game prior to an FA Cup final came in 1894, between boys from Manchester and Sheffield in front of some 40,000 spectators. South London Schools played West Ham Schools at the Crystal Palace in 1897 for the Corinthian Trophy.

There was development elsewhere and in 1889 Kidderminster Harriers presented a trophy for competition between local schools, signifying that the game was sufficiently established in the area. Brighton Schools FA was formed in 1892 with a membership of 22 schools, and games were played on Preston Park on Saturday mornings; while in Leicester, there were organisations for both rugby and association codes set up in 1892 and 1893 respectively. The Leicester 'Fosse' Club (now Leicester City) was particularly generous to the schools, granting the use of their ground for inter-city schools matches, and presenting a silver cup, a banner, 22 silver medals and a set of jerseys to help schools football in the city. Football in Oldham, Lancashire was organised by the Oldham Schools Athletic Organisation, and Oldham shared with Leicester the distinction of being the only area that supported both codes of football at that time (1896). The organisation in Sheffield was particularly strong and was one of the earliest, having been formed in 1887. It was

apparently not unknown for crowds of up to 15,000 spectators to attend local schools finals, and in addition to competition with South London Schools, regular fixtures also took place with teams from Manchester, Liverpool, Sunderland, Nottingham and North Staffordshire from about 1890, with other occasional fixtures. It should be noted also that in many of the districts, these developments also included associations for other sports – either as independent associations or as sections of a school's 'Athletic' or 'Sports' association.

The first schools international fixture was played between England and Wales at Walsall in 1907, with England winning 3–1, and the first game against Scotland was in 1911 at Newcastle. Games were not played against Northern Ireland until 1934 (Belfast). Perhaps significantly, the first European opposition was West Germany in 1956 at Portsmouth, with the English side winning 5–1.

Association football continued to be played in some of the country's leading public schools and in the growing number of local authority grammar schools created as a result of the Act of 1926. As a general rule, there was little or no competition between schools in the independent and state sectors. Many of the new grammar schools, however, opted to play rugby (and some of them hockey) although in some, the two codes of football co-existed happily. Some of the older grammar schools have left a rather more indelible mark on English football history, the present club at Blackburn, for example, being originally formed by old boys of Blackburn Grammar School, and Tottenham Hotspur being the product of former pupils at both St John's Presbyterian School and Tottenham Grammar School. Other clubs with a schools pedigree include Leicester City (Wyggeston School Old Boys), Sunderland (Sunderland & District Teachers Association) and Northampton Town (Northampton Schoolmasters).

The growth of grammar schools football saw the creation of the Grammar Schools Festival at Bognor, and later at Skegness, in the 1960s, in which teams from each county played in friendly competition. Initially, the grammar schools had their own organisation, the Council of Senior Secondary School Football Associations (CESSFA), but this eventually joined ESFA, as the closure of many grammar schools following the introduction of comprehensive education denuded it of members. Festival ties are still proudly worn by those who took part in those early festivals, although the event was renamed the English Schools Festival with the demise of the grammar schools that resulted from the development of comprehensive education in the 1970s. The venue has now moved, first to Morecambe and more recently to Pakenham in Norfolk, and continues to cater for county teams at under-19 level. Out of this have grown festivals for other age-groups, notably those at under-11 (at Jersey and North Tyneside respectively), under-13 (Durham) and under-14 (Isle of Wight).

The organisation of schools football in England still centres on the local district associations, many of which are now over 100 years old, and oversee the running of football in local schools from primary age right through to sixth-form level. Each association runs league and cup competitions and selects representative sides, which play in competition against teams from other district associations. At a second level, the county associations, to which local associations also affiliate, look after county representative teams and county knockout cup competitions. This structure is thought by many to be rather cumbersome, requiring as it does the dual affiliation of local associations.

ESFA now runs a whole range of competitions from five-a-side at under-11s through to full international games at under-18 level, and competition for girls has been included since 1991. All district and county associations are now directed to make provision for girls' football. Ironically, the world's most successful schools sports organisation was forced in 1999 to give up the jewel in its crown – the under-15s national side – to the FA, who felt that such talent would be more effectively groomed under its own wing, rather than that of teachers. This move has

not been well received by many who have given their lives to promoting the game among the nation's young people. Funding, for many schools' associations, has also become a major issue. Many school sports organisations had local authority funding withdrawn during the constraints of the 1980s, and now rely either on their own fund-raising initiatives or upon the generosity of senior county football associations and/or local businesses. This situation, in the age of countless football millionaires, is one that senior football authorities choose either to ignore or regard as unimportant. It is likely, for example, that a small fraction of the weekly wages of one Premiership player could fund all county schools football for a whole year, yet apparently football authorities are resisting the audacious suggestion that just a little funding might be usefully directed towards the game in schools.

Sources:

ESFA, *ESFA Handbook* (English Schools Football Association, 1907–).

ESFA, *England Schoolboys – international players' records 1907–1999* (English Schools Football Association, 1999).

Marples, M., *A History of Football* (London: Secker & Warburg, 1954).

Mason, T. *Association Football and English Society, 1863–1915* (Brighton: Harvester Press, 1980).

Walvin, J., *The People's Game: The History of Football Revisited* (Edinburgh: Mainstream Publishing, 1994).

See also Public Schools

Frank Galligan

Scientific Perspectives on Football

Scientific perspectives are evident in the formal curricula of University programmes related to football, conferences in which information about football is shared among experts, and academic courses designed to assist individuals in furthering their careers within the football industries.

The First World Congress of Science and Football was held in Liverpool in April 1987. The event represented a milestone in bringing together those scientists whose research work was directly related to football and practitioners of football keen to obtain current information about its scientific aspects. It represented an attempt to bridge the gap between theory and practice so that scientific knowledge about football could be communicated and applied. Practitioners included players, trainers, coaches, managers, paramedical and medical staff: among the delegates who attended from overseas, Gerard Houllier and Egil Olsen became managers of English Premier League clubs a dozen years later.

The World Congress of Science and Football is held every four years under the auspices of the International Steering Group for Science and Football, which is itself affiliated to UNESCO. After the success of the inaugural event in Liverpool, later Congresses were held in Eindhoven (Netherlands) in 1991, Cardiff (Wales) in 1995 and Sydney (Australia) in 1999. The fifth meeting is fixed for Lisbon (Portugal) in 2003. The list of Congress themes is comprehensive, including, for example: football surfaces, group dynamics in match-play, pre-match stress and performance, soccer violence, and strain in adolescent footballers. The themes embrace all of the football codes (including Australian Rules and Gaelic football) so that common research and practical threads among these games can be debated. The published *Proceedings of the Congress Communications* provide invaluable resource material for updating students and researchers about scientific investigations concerned with football.

There have been other milestones in the advancement of scientific applications to football. A consensus statement concerned with food and nutrition as they applied to soccer was approved at FIFA headquarters in 1994. Proceedings were published later that summer in a special issue of the *Journal of Sports Sciences*. The consensus publication was in part instrumental in altering the rule about administering fluids to players during match-play, which was first implemented in the World Cup finals in the same year.

Post-graduate research projects focusing on football were largely limited to a few at Liverpool Polytechnic (which became Liverpool John Moores University in 1992) and Salford University in the 1970s. The University of Leicester set up its research unit in the 1980s to focus on sociological aspects of soccer. It was funded by the Football Trust and made a major contribution to the analysis of the football hooligan phenomenon. The credibility of academic research was further enhanced by the theses of Jan Ekstrand at Linkoping University (Sweden) in 1982, entitled 'Soccer injuries and their prevention', and Dirk van Gool at the Catholic University of Leuven in the late 1980s, a study of physiological aspects of the game. In 1994 Jens Bangsbo at the August Krogh Institute, Copenhagen (Denmark) was awarded a D.Sc. for his thesis entitled 'Physiology of soccer – with special reference to intermittent exercise'. The doctoral thesis of Barry Drust awarded at Liverpool John Moores University for work conducted in part during the Copa America tournament in Uruguay in 1995 represented the start of a rush of post-graduate research projects at a number of academic institutions within the United Kingdom.

The first formal academic programme in Science and Football was offered at Diploma level at Liverpool John Moores University in 1991. The course was developed to a full-blown B.Sc. (Hons) degree programme in 1998. The fundamental sports science disciplines are studied first, prior to their application to football, so that graduates on the course have a solid biological basis to their intellectual training. In contrast, the University of Liverpool offers an MBA (Football Industries) course geared towards prospective administrators and managers, as a collaboration between its Football Research Unit (established by Rogan Taylor in 1994) and its Business School.

The study of football is now accepted unquestionably as a viable area of academic work. Practically all institutions within the United Kingdom offering undergraduate programmes in sports science or sports studies allow options to study football in project work. Furthermore, some institutions offer short part-time courses for footballers to gain academic accreditation for their learning while continuing to work on developing their professional careers. These trends towards a greater acceptance of football as a fruitful field of academic study, and of the continued education of footballers in parallel with advancing their playing careers, are likely to continue for the foreseeable future.

Source:

Reilly, T., *Science and Soccer* (London: E. & F. N. Spon, 1996).

See also Anthropology of Football, Geography, Research Centres, Sociology of Football

Tom Reilly

Scorers of Note

Identifying the greatest goal-scorer of all time has always invited controversy, and will continue to do so. Measures range from the total number of goals scored in a career, through the most influential goals, to strike rate (goals scored per match) and the ability to create goals from 'nothing'. Then there are the spectacular goals remembered for generations for their brilliance, even though they might have come from the feet of defenders or other traditionally non-attacking players or positions. For the average fan it sometimes has nothing to do with the above, but is related to the team the scorer played for; a strong sense of national or club loyalty causes their impassioned heart to overrule any sense of rationality. Perhaps the player most often nominated for such a title would be Pele of Santos and Brazil. It is the fluency and relative ease with which he scored some spectacular goals on the World Stage during the 1962, 1966 and 1970 World Cup Finals that stick in many peoples' minds.

In British terms, a front-runner must be 'Dixie' Dean who, during his career for Tranmere Rovers and Everton, had a phenomenal strike rate. In his best season (1927/28) he scored 60 goals in 39 appearances. Such a strike rate has never been surpassed. Close behind are Jimmy Greaves and Denis Law. Both players were in league football at the same time, Jimmy Greaves playing a formidable role in the highly successful Tottenham Hotspur team of the early 1960s and Denis Law a key part of Manchester United's revived fortunes in the mid to late 1960s. Each player was known as something of a 'poacher', and both struck fear into defenders of the time because of their remarkable speed in bringing the ball under control and firing or volleying it into the net, despite close marking. They were succeeded in subsequent years by the likes of Charlie George (a key figure in Arsenal's double-winning side of 1970), Joe Jordan (for Leeds and then Manchester United), Kevin Keegan (Liverpool's multi-title winning side of the late 1970s), Malcolm MacDonald (Newcastle United), Kenny Dalglish and Ian Rush (both Liverpool) in the 1980s. Eric Cantona, Andy Cole and Ruud Van Nistelroy (all key figures in Manchester United's all-conquering team), Alan Shearer (Black-burn Rovers and Newcastle United) and Ian Wright (Arsenal) followed in the 1990s. Clubs in lower divisions of the Football League have also had their heroes. Ted MacDougall (Bournemouth) and Steve Bull (Wolves) were among the top scorers in recent decades.

The introduction of television and, especially video replays from different camera angles, helped illustrate the genius of great scorers to those who never saw them play live, and also to fans at grounds whose vision of events was restricted in one way or another. The introduction of the BBC's *Match of the Day* 'Goal of the Month' and subsequent 'Goal of the Season' competitions in the late 1960s added publicity to the debate.

Football League records show that Arthur Rowley was the highest goal-scorer of all time, with 434 goals in 619 mainly lower-division matches between 1946 and 1965. Jimmy McGrory holds the same record for the Scottish League, with 410 goals in 408 matches between 1922 and 1938. Ian Rush has the record for scoring the highest number of FA Cup goals (43), and also holds the same record for the League Cup (49).

Sources:

Soar, P., *The Hamlyn A-Z of Football Records*, second edition (London: Hamlyn, 1985).
Rothmans Football Yearbook (London: Rothmans, 1981 onwards).

Richard William Cox

Scottish Football

As with the rest of the United Kingdom, football was being played in Scotland long before it became formally organised and codified in the nineteenth century. Varieties of the game differed regionally and locally, but there was sufficient popular involvement to ensure that the modern game had a secure basis as it evolved. The dominant force in the early Scottish game was the Queen's Park club formed in 1867. Queen's Park entered the FA Cup in its first season in 1872, and again in the 1880s, progressing to the final in 1884 and 1885, where it lost to Blackburn Rovers on each occasion. Retaining its amateur ethos in the face of insurgent professionalism, Queen's Park gradually lost influence, though its stadium, Hampden Park, was to remain the main international venue in Scotland. Queen's Park was not the only Scottish club to challenge the English, and the Leven Valley club Renton beat the 1888 FA Cup holders, West Bromwich Albion, and proclaimed themselves champions of the world.

The first international matches (within the United Kingdom) were played in 1871/72, with the rugby code taking precedence and the Association game following at the West of Scotland cricket ground on 30 November 1872, resulting in a scoreless draw against England. This led to a persistent rivalry that produced some stirring victories for the Scots. The Wembley Wizards of 1928, Jimmy Cowan's match in 1949 and the 1967 defeat of the World Cup

holders, have to be balanced by some more spectacular losses, including those of 1955, 1961 and 1975.

The Scottish Football Association was founded in 1873 by eight clubs who subscribed for a challenge cup that Queen's Park won for the first three years of competition. The Scottish League followed in 1890, initially without the great amateur club, and with a simmering debate about professionalism already evident. Within a year of its legalisation in 1893 around 800 professional players were registered. The heartland of senior professional football in Scotland has been the Central Lowlands, particularly its major urban centres, with all but a few clubs drawn from these areas. In the 1990s two clubs from the Highland League were admitted. The Scottish Borders is one of the few areas where another code of football, rugby union, remains dominant. The central belt areas like the Leven Valley and North Lanarkshire, which were represented by numerous teams in early competitions, now find themselves with few or no senior clubs. Several Scottish senior clubs only just survive on the strength of local sponsorship and the access to patronage that the game still provides, rather than on attendances, which are often numbered in the low hundreds. In general, weekly aggregate attendances in Scotland have been around 100,000 or 110,000 since the post-war peak, with two-thirds of these attending the top three games involving the 'Old Firm' (Rangers and Celtic), and one of Aberdeen, Hearts or Dundee.

From the 1870s at the latest the Scots began to emphasise a passing rather than a dribbling game, exported by the 'Scots professors' to England and the wider world. Yet the Scots have always retained affection for the 'tanner ba' player whose close control and mesmeric individual talent often outweigh the player's strategic contribution to the game. Names that spring to mind include Jimmy Johnstone, Patsy Gallagher and Charlie Tully of Celtic, and Willie Henderson and Torry Gillick of Rangers.

For most of the last century Scottish football has been overshadowed by the rivalry of the 'Old Firm'. Between them Rangers and Celtic have won the Scottish league championship 85 times in the 103 occasions it has been contested since 1890/91. Periodic challenges from Edinburgh, Dundee and Aberdeen clubs have been only briefly sustained. Views as to the causes and effects of the 'Old Firm' dominance remain matters of controversy. The pattern where two or three clubs dominate the domestic competitions in a country is not unique to Scotland, even though the underlying sectarian divisions have given this rivalry a particular edge.

Over the years Scotland has produced some of the game's greatest players, managers, referees and administrators. In the modern era John White and Dave Mackay of Tottenham Hotspur, Jim Baxter of Rangers, Denis Law of Manchester United and Kenny Dalglish of Celtic and Liverpool, would stand comparison with any of their generation. But in terms of influence on the game, a small group of managers would probably be the most significant Scottish figures. Willie Maley of Celtic and Bill Struth of Rangers bestrode the 1900s and 1930s to 1950s respectively, while Jock Stein at Celtic did likewise from the 1960s to 1980s, adding European success to his laurels. South of Scotland, Sir Matt Busby of Manchester United, Bill Shankly of Liverpool, and Sir Alex Ferguson at Manchester United moulded successive teams that achieved European as well as domestic pre-eminence. Among administrators Lord Arthur Kinnaird played for Scotland by virtue of parentage and went on to win the FA Cup with Wanderers and Old Etonians, before becoming treasurer and later president of the FA from 1890 to 1923. William McGregor, a Perthshire draper, was a major figure in the foundation of the Football League. Sir Robert Kelly of Celtic and John Lawrence of Rangers exercised strong domestic influence in the upper echelons of the game, and David Will has represented the four home unions in FIFA for several years. Peter Craigmyle, Jack Mowat, and Tom 'Tiny' Wharton had international reputations as referees.

Apart from home internationals and domestic league and cup competitions, Scotland has hosted major European games, including the unforgettable

European Cup final between Real Madrid and Eintracht in 1960 in front of 135,000; another less evocative one involving Bayern Munich and St Etienne in 1976; the European CupWinners' Cup finals in 1961, 1962 and 1966; and one leg of the UEFA Cup finals in Dundee in 1987.

Scottish influence on the world game has been much more through the export of players and organisers than through triumph in competitions, with only Celtic's European Cup victory in 1967, and European Cup Winners' Cup wins by Rangers and Aberdeen, to show at club level, and nothing apart from home international championships for the national side. Qualification for the FIFA World Cup – first achieved in 1954, and then in sequence from 1974 to 1998, with a hiatus in 1994 – has uniformly been followed by departure after the preliminary round of competition, usually by the narrowest of margins. Performances in the European championships have followed a similar pattern. Scottish supporters, who had a fairly well-founded reputation for unsavoury behaviour, reinvented themselves in the 1980s as the Tartan Army, whose obsessive bonhomie won the approval of host countries and tournament organisers. This acted as a protection and distinction from English fans over the same period.

Two major disasters punctuate the history of the game in Scotland, both at Ibrox Park. The first, in 1902, occurred when a stand collapsed during an international, resulting in 25 deaths and many injuries. The second, in 1971, came during an Old Firm game when both sides scored in the last minutes. The crowd leaving down a very steep set of exit stairs tumbled over each other, resulting in 66 deaths. The inquiries which followed led to improvements in public safety at football grounds, but there was a much more thoroughgoing overhaul of the conditions under which people were expected to attend games. These included, a decade later, measures to control the alcohol consumption of spectators, following an Old Firm riot at Hampden Park.

Violence was also a regular occurrence around the Scottish game from its earliest days. The first Hampden Riot, after a replayed Cup final in 1909, stands alone as the one occasion when the fans of the Old Firm rioted in unison against the authorities as a consequence of a decision not to play extra time. In the 1930s, gang warfare in Glasgow had its football equivalents and, after what seems to have been a relatively peaceful period in the immediate post-war years when crowds were at their peak, incidents involving Scottish club sides at home and abroad multiplied, leading to a number of inquiries and policy changes. Though the sectarian rivalry between Celtic and Rangers is the best known, these fans have never had a monopoly on violent behaviour in Scotland, and at least in relative terms some of the worst behaviour occurs elsewhere.

Below the elite level Scottish football has had a successful semi-professional organisation of so-called junior leagues, not to be confused with youth and development competitions, though many good young players used to be farmed out to juniors to learn their trade. There are also amateur competitions throughout the country, but the schools, Boys' Brigade, and similar organisations are no longer as influential as they once were in the development of junior players. A wide-ranging inquiry was conducted into the state of youth development by a former secretary of the SFA, Ernie Walker, but its recommendations remain to be fully implemented. At the elite level the Scottish team managers in the last two decades have been qualified coaches who have come through UEFA and FIFA training. It is fair to say that Andy Roxburgh, now Technical Director at FIFA, and Craig Brown have been more highly regarded abroad than at home. Women's football has existed from the earliest days, but has struggled for recognition in what has been a male-dominated sport. The Scottish women's team is now taking part in European competitions.

Scotland suffers from its marginal position in the European football scene and from its history as one of the four home unions. Its leading clubs – which are among the strongest financially, but just below the elite level in playing performance – are therefore driven to consider playing in other competitions, even though in 1998 a new ten-team Premier League was instituted to improve domestic competition.

Sources:

Crampsey, R. A., *The Game for the Game's Sake: The History of Queen's Park Football Club, 1867–1967* (Glasgow: Queen's Park Football Club, 1967).

Crampsey, R. A., *The Scottish Footballer* (Edinburgh: Blackwood, 1978).

Crampsey, R. A., *The Scottish Football League: The First Hundred Years* (Glasgow: The Scottish Football League, 1990).

Forsyth, R., *The Only Game: The Scots and World Football* (Edinburgh: Mainstream, 1990).

Hutchinson, J., *The Football Industry: The Early Years of the Professional Game* (Glasgow: Richard Drew, 1982).

Murray, B., *The Old Firm: Sectarianism, Sport and Society in Scotland* (Edinburgh: John Donald, 2000).

Rafferty, J., *One Hundred Years of Scottish Football* (London: Pan, 1973).

Roy Hay

Scottish Football Association

The Scottish Football Association (SFA) was founded at a meeting held at Dewar's Hotel, Glasgow, on 13 March 1873. The meeting took place a few months after the first official international match between Scotland and England had taken place. The international fixture was the result of a joint initiative of the Queen's Park club and Charles Alcock, Secretary of the (English) Football Association. Queen's Park were the driving force behind the formation of the SFA, and it was they who called that meeting in March 1873, ostensibly with the aim of establishing a Scottish equivalent of the FA Cup. There were six other clubs present at the meeting: Clydesdale, Dumbreck, Eastern, Granville, Third Lanark and Vale of Leven. The clubs agreed to a cup competition and decided that an Association should be formed to administer it. Archibald Campbell of Clydesdale was elected the first president of the SFA, and Archibald Rae of Queen's Park was chosen as secretary.

The SFA is the second oldest football governing body in the world after the FA. Initially the SFA organised the international matches, which provided its main source of income, and the Scottish FA Cup. The SFA's proselytising role in Wales and Ireland led to the setting up of similar associations in these countries. Disputes over rules led to a series of meetings with the FA and the other British associations. In 1882 an agreement was reached that the home associations should each have an input into the determination of the laws, and from this came the International Board in 1887 which was responsible for the Laws of the Game until the emergence of FIFA.

By 1883 there were 11 provincial associations and 133 member clubs, including one from Newfoundland. Scottish clubs were initially members of the FA as well and took part in the FA Cup, seven teams playing in 1887. However, that year the SFA passed a rule that prevented its members from holding membership of another association, effectively barring Scottish clubs from the FA Cup. The FA had allowed professionalism in England from 1885, and although professional Scots players were keenly sought in England, the SFA was implacably opposed to professionalism at home. At the Annual International Conference held in Glasgow in 1884, T. Lawrie of Queen's Park, president of the SFA, moved 'that all Associations should unite to stamp out professionalism and that all National Associations should recognise penalties inflicted on them'. However, by this time moves to legalise professionalism were under way in England. The formation of the Scottish Football League in 1890 increased the pressure for professionalism within the Scottish game, but the SFA did not yield until May 1893. At the decisive meeting J. H. McLaughlin of Celtic, proposing the motion to accept professionalism, argued that 'you might as well attempt to stop the flow of Niagara with a kitchen chair as to endeavour to stem the tide of professionalism'. McLaughlin's argument was accepted, though with some reluctance, and he went on to become SFA president in 1899.

Perhaps as a result of its amateur background, the SFA has maintained a reputation for conservatism. For many years international selections were announced from the steps of the SFA's offices at Carlton Place, overlooking the Clyde. In 1928 the team to play England at Wembley was announced in this fashion, and the announcement was greeted with jeers. The team went on to win 5–1 and become immortalised as the 'Wembley Wizards'.

Scotland did not play internationals against non-British opponents until 1929, and, along with the other home countries, opted out of FIFA between 1928 and 1946 over payments to amateur players. In 1950 the British Championship was designated a qualifying group for the World Cup. FIFA agreed to accept both the winners and runners-up, but in 1950, prior to the decisive match against England, the SFA announced that they would only go to the World Cup as group winners. England won 1–0, and despite appeals from both the Scottish and English captains the Scots did not go to Brazil. In 1954 Scotland did participate, and the SFA appointed its first national team manager, Andy Beattie. However, Beattie was not allowed a free hand in selection, and he resigned in disgust after the tournament. Not until Jock Stein was appointed manager, on a part-time basis only, was the manager allowed to pick the team. Perhaps because of this, World Cup results were very disappointing until 1974. Thereafter, the national team has regularly qualified for the final stages, though it has not yet managed to get through the first round of the finals.

The SFA presided over the largest stadium in the world, Hampden Park (though it was owned by Queen's Park), with record attendances until they were overtaken by those at Maracàna Stadium in Rio de Janeiro. In 1937, 149,547 spectators watched Scotland play England, and one week later 146,433 turned up for the Cup final between Celtic and Aberdeen.

By 2000, the SFA had 6,148 affiliated clubs and 135,474 registered players, more than 2 per cent of the population of the country. The SFA, now based at Hampden Park in Glasgow, presides over six minor associations for amateur, junior, schools, welfare, women's and youth football. It also has almost 2,300 registered referees, of whom nearly 200 are on the Senior List. The Scottish Football Association Museum Trust, set up in 1990, was a joint enterprise with City of Glasgow Council aiming to establish what was believed to be the first national museum devoted to football, located in new Hampden Park. The museum opened in 2001.

Sources:

Crampsey, R. A., *The Game for the Game's Sake: The History of Queen's Park Football Club, 1867–1967* (Glasgow: Queen's Park Football Club, 1967).

Crampsey, B., *The Scottish Footballer* (Edinburgh: Blackwood, 1978).

Leatherdale, C. (ed.), *The Book of Football: A Complete History and Record of the Association and Rugby Games* (Westcliff-on-Sea: Desert Island Books, 1997; facsimile edition, originally published 1905/06).

Further Reading:

Forsyth, R., *The Only Game: The Scots and World Football* (Edinburgh: Mainstream, 1990).

Scottish Football Association, official website.

Roy Hay and John Coyle

Scouting

A scouting system has existed since the late nineteenth century, although it probably became rather more sophisticated in the inter-war period as the larger clubs began to pay more attention to recruitment and training. The number of scouts employed varies according to the resources of individual clubs, the smaller clubs making do with perhaps 12 or 15, while larger ones can employ up to 40 or 50. They are usually based in a particular region and can build up remarkably detailed knowledge of the game in their area. Some are ex-professionals but the majority have traditionally played only at amateur or semi-professional level. The essence of their job is either to identify good prospects or to watch players that have been 'spotted' by other sources. In both cases, lengthy reports are compiled for managers, examining all aspects of the player's physique, technical ability, attitude and sometimes even character and lifestyle. Many of the crucial initial negotiations between a club, a player and his family are also initiated by scouts. However, especially at smaller clubs, scouts who live in close proximity are likely to be hooked into all manner of other activities. Fred O'Donohue, whose colourful autobiography *Scouting for Glory* (1996), gives one of the few inside pictures of the scout's life, undertook coaching work, acted as occasional reserve team trainer and kept an eye on apprentice players living in club houses during his time at Blackburn Rovers in the 1970s.

The most striking point is that virtually all of this activity is carried out on a part-time basis. Only the larger clubs have ever appointed full-time scouts (although, from the later 1990s, full-time staff at schools of excellence and academies have take on some of the responsibilities once devolved to part-timers), and usually only one such individual has been in place. Those that took on this role often preferred the term 'chief representative' to 'chief scout', as their work often involved acting as an intermediary between their employer and other clubs on transfer and other matters. Most, however, have always operated on an expenses-only basis, with fairly modest bonuses paid to them for each player signed and acknowledgements of what turn out to be particularly good signings. When Fourth Division Rochdale sold Alan Taylor to West Ham United in the 1970s for £80,000, Fred O'Donohue's reward for initially bringing the player from non-league Morecambe was a letter of thanks and a set of wine glasses and decanter. Given the enormous amount of time involved in the scouting process – the time at matches can be quite small in comparison to that spent travelling and writing reports – this represents a remarkable level of subsidy for the clubs. They in turn defend the situation by pointing out that, given the tiny number of players watched who actually progress to the professional ranks, any other system would be financially inefficient. Although some scouts can feel bitter and exploited, most seem to accept the system and extract rich and compensatory emotional rewards. O'Donohue, whose autobiography lists in graphic detail the tiny level of his financial rewards, also noted that there are things 'a scout can earn which are beyond monetary value'. The sheer satisfaction of having launched the successful career of a young player has always been the greatest of these. It is probably also the case that the job is so demanding – Leslie Bedford claimed to have watched 161 games in one season while full-time chief scout at Sheffield Wednesday in the 1950s – and has such an uncertain career structure, that scouts prefer to maintain a full-time job and see scouting as a kind of vocation. The remarkable level of commitment that scouting demands is in any case powerful testimony to the passion and enthusiasm that the game can draw upon.

Successful scouts are rarely household names, and are surprisingly little considered by supporters. One of the best known was undoubtedly Manchester United's Bob Bishop, the club's chief scout in Northern Ireland for 37 years until 1987. Bishop's list of discoveries included Jimmy Nicholson, David McCreery, Sammy McIlroy, Norman Whiteside and, most famously, George Best. His career even inspired a TV play starring Ray McInally in the 1980s.

Sources:

Interview with Leslie Bedford, Chelsea v West Bromwich Albion match programme, 21 March 1964.

O'Donohue, F., *Scouting for Glory* (Penwortham: Author publisher, 1996).

Dave Russell

Second World War

Throughout the Second World War, the government considered the continuation of football at both professional and amateur levels vital for maintaining both morale and fund-raising. The professional game survived radical short-term experiments and depleted resources to enjoy a brief but spectacular post-war boom.

When war was declared on 3 September 1939, an Air Raid Precautions ban on the assembly of crowds brought the game to an abrupt halt. But organised football quickly resumed. In October a new English League Championship was launched with eight regional groups, decided on goal average, and a League Cup competition. Further major reorganisation took place in subsequent seasons, intended to ease travel and manpower problems. In 1940/41 clubs were divided between North and South Leagues, although dissident London clubs played in a breakaway London League from 1941 to 1942. The North League had two consecutive Championship competitions in 1942/43, and a Western League was established. Various regional league cups were also contested each season. In Scotland two regional leagues were formed for the first season, but after that local leagues were organised. Cup competitions flourished throughout Britain.

Initially, attendances were low. Fear of air raids and fluctuating line-ups discouraged spectators. But numbers gradually rose as the war went on, and prestige matches attracted huge gates. The biggest draws were the 30 wartime home international matches (these were not given full international status and no caps were awarded) and the special charity representative matches between national and forces' teams. The FA ban on radio broadcasts of live football was lifted in time for commentary on a match between Blackpool and Manchester United to be relayed to the front on 14 October 1939.

All professional footballers' contracts were suspended when hostilities began. Many players enlisted in the Territorials and the War Reserve Police, became physical training instructors for the forces, or found civilian work. But by 22 September 1939 the War Emergency Committee of the English FA agreed to a 30-shillings match fee (increased to £2 in 1942) and allowed registered players to appear as guests for other clubs. Despite a few occasions when spectators were drafted, most clubs were able to field adequate teams, often including famous stars as guests. Touring sides composed of top stars entertained the troops abroad, and 75 players died on war service.

The fortunes of professional clubs fluctuated. As receipts slumped, some, like Port Vale and Charlton Athletic, were forced to shut down for part or the whole of the period. Others, like Preston North End and Aston Villa, were in profit by 1945. Non-League Bath City, Lovell's Athletic (a Newport toffee factory team) and Aberamon Association FC joined the depleted Western League in the 1942/43 season. Some grounds were damaged by bombing, or were requisitioned by the military or civil defence authorities – Molineux became a delousing centre for a time. Many amateur clubs closed down for the duration, but others survived and new amateur competitions were formed.

After the transitional season of 1945/46, with a Victory League and the revival of the FA Cup, football's pre-war organisation was restored.

Sources:

Inglis, S., *League Football and the Men Who Made It* (London: Willow Books, 1988).

Lanfranchi, P. and Taylor, M., 'Professional Football in World War Two Britain', in P. Kirkham and D. Thoms (eds), *War Culture: Social Change and Changing Experience in World War Two Britain* (London: Lawrence & Wishart, 1995), pp. 187–97.

McCarthy, T., *War Games: The Story of Sport in World War Two* (London: Queen Anne Press, 1989).

Rollin, J., *Soccer at War 1939–45* (London: Willow Books, 1985).

Further Reading:

Miller, D., *Stanley Matthews: The Authorized Biography* (London: Pavilion Books, 1989).

See also History Highlights 1940–1949

Joyce Woolridge

Sendings Off

– *see* Discipline and Punishment

Services Football

In terms of football at least, the Army has been very much the senior service. The Royal Engineers, based at Chatham, were one of the most dominant teams in early English football history, pioneering a version of the passing game, winning the FA Cup in 1875 and appearing in three other finals in the 1870s. Team captain Major Francis Marindin became a key figure within the FA, serving as president from 1874 to 1890, and eventually emerging as a key critic of the professional game. Soldiers, and indeed sailors, also played an important role in the spread of the game around the world, helping to establish its roots in India, China, Chile and other locations. The Army Football Association (AFA) was founded in 1888 to co-ordinate the game within the service, and the Army Challenge Cup inaugurated in the same year – the Second Battalion of the Argyll and Sutherland Highlanders were the first winners. The AFA affiliated to the FA in 1894 and was given a seat on its governing committee that it still holds. Affiliation to the Scottish, Irish and various county associations followed by 1907. The game was being taken seriously enough to necessitate the introduction of a rule in 1890 banning teams from cup matches if the players had been off duty for more than seven days before a game. Military leagues were sanctioned in 1902, and in the same year an Army team played its first game against civilian opposition in the form of Tottenham Hotspur. The Army athletics ground at Aldershot became the headquarters of Army football in 1913, and could attract crowds of 15,000 to Army Cup finals.

The Royal Navy Football Association (RNFA) was founded in 1904, with the Navy Cup established in the same year, and the RNFA affiliated to the FA on the same basis as the AFA in 1907. The foundation of the Royal Air Force Football Association in 1919 completed the initial establishment of footballing provision in the services. An inter-services tournament between the Army and Navy was inaugurated in 1905, and this was opened to the RAF in 1921. Matches were also arranged between British forces and their European counterparts, with the Kentish Cup, first contested between the armies of Britain, Belgium, and France, begun in 1921. By the late 1930s, members of the three services enjoyed a rich network of tournaments encompassing every level of the game from the overtly recreational to the highly competitive. The women's game emerged in the 1990s, with an inter-services tournament established in 1998. The service game was also the focus for early experiments with the commercial sponsorship of football, brewers Watney Mann backing an inter-service Silver Jubilee event in 1971, and cigarette company Rothmans sponsoring a six-a-side tournament for the Army of the Rhine in 1972.

Playing and watching football has undoubtedly proved crucial in the maintenance of morale in the forces, especially in wartime. Although formal matches were rare in the First World War, endless scratch games at training camps and behind the lines at the front helped maintain a sense of normality. The Second World War saw a far more formal structure maintained, with many games played for charity. Professional footballers were recruited in both wars. Their supposed reluctance to join up was a source of controversy in 1914, although many did enlist through the Seventeenth Service Battalion of the Middlesex Regiment, the so-called 'Footballer's Battalion'. Conscription prevented any repetition of such problems in 1939. For some players the Second World War was a professional disaster, ending careers prematurely, but for others it provided increased self-confidence, improved fitness and the opportunity to play regularly with top players. Seventy-five players lost their lives during the conflict.

The influx of professionals meant that the quality of services football was undoubtedly high during the war, but it probably reached its zenith in the period of National Service from 1945 until its abolition in 1962. With innumerable professional players serving in the forces, teams of the highest quality could be raised. The Army side that played the Portuguese Army in 1957 included three full internationals (including Lance Corporal D. Edwards of the Royal Army Ordnance Corps), four under-23 and two youth internationals (one of whom was Private R. Charlton, another RAOC representative). AFA Secretary Lieutenant-Colonel Gerry Mitchell was effectively the link between professionals in the Army and their clubs and the football authorities (his counterparts fulfilled similar roles in the other forces), and this close involvement led to his serving for a period as a full England selector. Although previous standards could not possibly be maintained after 1962, the best football has remained at a high level: in 1999, at least eight players in the English and Scottish Leagues, including Northern Irish international Maik Taylor, had begun their football career in the Army.

Sources:

Anon., *One Hundred Years of Army Football* (Aldershot: Army Football Association, 1988).

Murray, B., *Football: A History of The World Game* (Aldershot: Scolar, 1994).

Rollin, J., *Soccer at War, 1939–45* (London: Collins, 1985).

Further Reading:

Lanfranchi, P. and Taylor, M., 'Professional Football in World War Two Britain', in Kirkham, P. and Thoms, D., *War Culture: Social Change and Changing Experience in World War Two Britain* (London: Lawrence and Wishart, 1995).

Dave Russell

Social Class

Association Football has, of course, long been regarded as the 'people's game'. For almost the entire history of the sport, it has been commonly assumed that football's natural constituents were members of the broadly defined working class: 'decent workaday folk' as the historian Nicholas Fishwick termed them, enjoying 'the winter pastime of millions'. Indeed, in the 1990s when academic and popular commentators sought to interpret the contemporary rise of middle-class spectatorship at British football, it was almost always assumed that middle-class fans were largely absent from the game in the period before 1990, and that middle-class fans were now invading a form of popular culture that did not properly belong to them.

In its earliest period as an organised sport, football was anything but a working-class pastime. The game was codified in the public schools of England, and until the early 1870s at least, to be a footballer was to be a 'gentleman' and a member of the local or even national elite. From then on, however, the game was quickly disseminated to other social groups and, although the upper and middle classes continued to play and watch the game in large numbers until the 1880s, by the time of the formation of the Football League in 1888 the social composition of successful northern football teams and their fans ensured that the game was increasingly identified as a working-class concern. Despite this, it is important to note that formal control of football clubs never moved from the middle-classes in this or any period of the game's history, causing problems for social historians and sociologists who have sought to interpret football as a traditional site of working-class self-expression and self-identification. Indeed, some, principally European Marxist, authors have claimed that football's historical control by a complicit and manipulative middle-class has long ensured that the game has functioned as a form of social control over an unknowing and ultimately duped working class.

Drawing on similar notions of social domination, the working-class profile of football in the first two decades of the twentieth century drew much criticism from the labour movement in Britain. They too saw the game as an 'opiate of the people' and as distraction from what they perceived to be more important political concerns. Ironically, elite, right-wing groups also abhorred the working-class nature of football in the same period, expressing concern about the effects that its large, boisterous and occasionally violent crowds would have on public morals. Prior to the inter-war period, football's associations with working-class culture guaranteed it enemies in almost all sections of society.

From the inter-war period until the 1950s, the number of opponents that football had in society began to diminish. The real or perceived decline in disorder at football matches from the 1920s, and the subsequent presentation of football crowds as exemplars of working-class restraint and good humour, secured the game a centrality in British culture which it had previously lacked. In accordance with this, football became much more a truly national game in the inter-war period, drawing increased support from the middle classes. While the virtual absence of reliable empirical data on the social structure of football crowds for any period of the game's history makes it impossible to assert the percentage rise in middle-class support for football in this period, Gavin Mellor's study on the subject does conclude that a significant number of middle-class people were following the game in the 1930s, 1940s and 1950s.

Whatever the level of middle-class support for football in the period up to the 1950s, the game retained the public image of a working-class sport. While this was not a problem up until the late 1960s, from that period on football's association with the working classes came to be perceived in an overwhelmingly negative light. This was partly as a result of the rise of hooliganism, but was also a product of wider social processes that led to an overall stigmatisation of cultural industries with working-class associations in the

1970s and 1980s. The massive socio-economic changes of that period, and the disintegration of consensus politics rooted in full employment led to the term 'working-class' often being stripped of any positive overtones in the 1980s, as it instead came to be associated with backwardness, conservatism, and irrelevance.

By the 1990s British football was again asserting its credibility as a national sport, drawing fans from all social classes. As, among other things, the new marketing of the English Premier League got under way after 1992, the game again began to attract a significant number of middle-class fans. The reception of this development among football journalists, fans and academics has been mixed. However, when set in historical context, it should not necessarily be seen as an unusual or unnatural circumstance.

Sources:

Fishwick, N., *English Football and Society, 1910–1950* (Manchester: Manchester University Press, 1989).

Mellor, G., 'The Social and Geographical Make-up of Football Crowds in the North-West of England, 1946–62: 'Super-Clubs', Local Loyalty and Regional Identities', *The Sports Historian*, 19: 2 (November 1999), 25–42.

Russell, D., *Football and the English: A Social History of Association Football in England, 1863–1995* (Preston: Carnegie Publishing, 1997).

Further Reading:

Giulianotti, R., *Football: A Sociology of the Global Game* (Cambridge: Polity, 1999).

Mason, T., *Association Football and English Society, 1863–1915* (Brighton: Harvester Press, 1980).

See also Amateurism

Gavin Mellor

Sociology of Football

The sociological study of football began in earnest in Britain in the early 1970s. Set against a backdrop of rising football hooli-ganism on the one hand, and increasing academic interest in popular culture and youth subcultures on the other, sociologists such as Ian Taylor began publishing work on the 'problems' of football, with particular emphasis on why young males were increasingly identifying football grounds as sites for violent exchanges. Taylor's work was largely Marxist in character and suggested that hooliganism resulted from the attempts of young working-class males to maintain a central role in a game that was becoming increasingly middle-class. Other work, not principally concerned with hooliganism, also began to appear during this period, with authors, such as Eric Dunning, exploring the history of football from a sociological perspective. Dunning, who worked at the University of Leicester, had been studying football since the late 1960s and advocated the use of the work of German sociologist Norbert Elias in the study of sport and society. The work of historical sociologists such as Dunning was complemented in the early 1970s by the publication of James Walvin's *The People's Game,* a social history of British football which, while less theoretical than many of its sociological counterparts, covered much the same ground.

As the issue of hooliganism came to dominate British, and especially English, football in the late 1970s and early 1980s, so the sociology of football turned almost exclusively to address that one issue. In the late 1970s, authors such as John Clarke and Stuart Hall followed the lead of Ian Taylor and produced further Marxist analyses of the hooligan problem, while Peter Marsh and his colleagues at Oxford University tackled the hooligan problem from a socio-biological perspective. However, it was Eric Dunning, along with Patrick Murphy, John Williams, Joe Maguire and others at the University of Leicester who came to dominate sociological debates around football hooliganism for much of the 1980s. The 'Leicester school', as that group of researchers came to be known, began work on the hooligan problem in 1979 with the support of the Economic and Social Research Council. By the time that their major findings were published in *The Roots of Football Hooliganism* in 1988, the Football Trust and the Department of the Environment had become the group's major sources of funding, enabling them to establish the Sir Norman Chester Football Research Centre at the University of Leicester: a body which remains dedicated to the sociological analysis of football in Britain and abroad.

As the work of the Leicester school continued to develop during the late 1980s and early 1990s, a growing number of sociologists and academics employing sociological theory began to study football as a serious academic pursuit. Authors like Steve Redhead, Richard Giulianotti, Bert Moorhouse and others approached football from various sociological traditions, all bringing their own distinctive analyses to the game. What united these authors in the late 1980s and early 1990s was their almost exclusive concern with football fans, rather than football *per se*. When they were not writing about football hooligans, most sociologists of football in this period were studying one football-fan subculture or another. Much of this work was conducted under the increasingly popular title of 'cultural studies' rather than sociology, thereby drawing heavily on postmodernism, poststructuralism and other contemporary theoretical concepts. Fan analysis remains a prominent strand among British sociological analyses of football today, with authors such as Anthony King, Adam Brown, and Gary Armstrong all publishing important works on football fans in the late 1990s.

In the later 1990s, the sociology of football has grown into a diverse subject area concerned with many more debates than those associated with fan cultures. In recent years a number of important sociological analyses have been published on football and politics; football player migration; players' employment and training conditions; football and social inequality; football and national identity; the globalisation of football; the relationship between football and the media; and the commercialisation and modernisation of football. Moreover, the first of a new breed of general sociological readers on football have been published, most notably by Richard Giulianotti and Anthony King, which set out the authors' vision of the current failings of the sociology of football. Giulianotti declares that sociological studies of football have hitherto suffered from a lack of empirical depth brought about by a culture of 'armchair theorising', while King criticises the lack of theoretical rigour in much football sociology and the discipline's failure to engage with mainstream sociological debates. Both of these problems are probably symptomatic of a new discipline that is still unsure of where its debates fit within wider academia. Hopefully they will both be resolved in the future as the sociology of football establishes itself with increasing confidence as an important academic exercise.

Sources:

Dunning, E. et al., *The Roots of Football Hooliganism: An Historical and Sociological Study* (London: Routledge, 1988).

Giulianotti, R., *Football: A Sociology of the Global Game* (Cambridge: Polity, 1999).

King, A., *The End of the Terraces: The Transformation of English Football in the 1990s* (London: Leicester University Press, 1998).

Redhead, S., *The Passion and the Fashion: Football Fandom in the New Europe* (Aldershot: Avebury, 1993).

Taylor, I., 'Football Mad: a Speculative Sociology of Football Hooliganism', in E. Dunning (ed.), *The Sociology of Sport: A Selection of Readings* (London: Frank Cass, 1971).

Further Reading:

Armstrong, G. and Giulianotti, R., *Entering the Field: New Perspectives on World Football* (Oxford: Berg, 1997).

Brown, A. (ed.), *Fanatics! Power, Identity and Fandom in Football* (London: Routledge, 1998).

Williams, J. and Wagg, S., *British Football and Social Change* (Leicester: Leicester University Press, 1991).

See also Anthropology of Football

Gavin Mellor

Sponsorship

Sponsorship is not an altruistic activity. It involves a commercial decision to provide funds in cash or kind to a sports organisation or player in return for securing publicity and product awareness. It enables the sponsor to become identified with a club or league without the risk of shareholding, and brings the benefits of increased sales and brand recognition as well as the opportunity to mix with the stars and supply corporate hospitality to major customers. Football has embraced sponsorship because it can help pay for enhanced facilities, better players and improved teams, all of which can bring success. In return for the money, the host league or club will be expected to advertise the product or service of the sponsors on their kit or around the ground, and perhaps utilise their name in the title of the competition, team or stadium, while players might be expected to attend corporate functions. At the elite level sponsorship of football has become a sophisticated marketing exercise involving both the commercial sponsor and the television broadcaster. The advent of colour television made sport a more attractive product and, despite the multi-million pound deals, a football match is still relatively inexpensive to produce compared to, say, costume drama. Clearly, the growth and ubiquity of football sponsorship suggests that many firms believe that such activity is to their benefit. Although substantial hard evidence is difficult to come by, in 1998 Bass reported that, during its sponsorship of football, sales of Carling lager had risen by 31 per cent, and in Scotland, the period of Bell's football sponsorship saw their brand awareness rise to 67 per cent, the highest for any brand of spirits in Britain.

At the competition level the beginning of the modern era of sponsorship was perhaps signalled by the introduction in 1970 of the Watney Cup, a knock out competition for Football League teams, and a similar venture by Drybrough in Scotland the following year. The last two decades have witnessed the wholesale re-branding of competitions to secure the sponsorship pound. All significant league or cup competitions – and many that are not – now carry the sponsor's name and logo. Here the alcohol trade has been to the fore, and indeed the FA Cup itself might well have been renamed the Fosters Cup, but commercial difficulties and an outcry against attaching an alcoholic label to this most famous of competitions caused the deal to fall through. Nevertheless, the anti-alcohol lobby cannot have been that strong because in 1993 Bass sponsored the inaugural Premier League competition via their Carling brand. Five years later the firm was pumping a million pounds a month into that league. Bass also sponsor the Worthington Cup and the Tennent's Scottish Cup.

At the club level sponsorship is now virtually obligatory. Few teams exist without some backing from a sponsor, be it Manchester United's £30 million over four years from Vodaphone, or a junior side having their shirts provided by the local supermarket. One of the first major deals was that of Arsenal in 1981, who secured £500,000 from JVC for having their initials on their shirts. This emblazonment required a change in Football League regulations that had prevented such on-field advertising, but which collapsed under the financial pressures facing clubs at the time. Others have opted for sponsored facilities, such as Bolton's Reebok Stadium. Perhaps two decades ago the sponsors relied on the clubs to provide the exposure that they were paying for, but now they also make available their

Thierry Henry displays the logo of Arsenal's sponsor

(© Stuart MacFarlane, Arsenal FC)

promotional and marketing expertise to the clubs. Strategic alliances are also developing which mutually facilitate the economic capabilities of the partners. Vodaphone may well use its technology to transmit Manchester United matches worldwide to paying customers, who, in turn, will form an expanded fan base and clientele for the club's merchandise.

Endorsement lies somewhere between sponsorship and advertising. It implies that a team or player recommends the use of a particular product, as with Carling becoming the 'official beer' of the England team in the 1998 World Cup. Sixty-four years earlier the FA Cup finalists promoted trousers, shoe-polish, and shredded wheat. In the 1970s Heineken used Scottish international Joe Jordan in its famous 'Heineken refreshes the parts other beers cannot reach' campaign. Walkers Crisps have used both ex-international Gary Lineker – 'Salt 'n' Lineker' – and current international Michael Owen – 'Cheese 'n' Owen' – though the latter has now been dropped from the crisp company's squad as his squeaky clean image based on youth, fitness, and clean-living was considered inappropriate to their new marketing campaign aimed at the public house customer. Owen may not mind: in 1999 he also had contracts with Umbro, Jaguar and Tissot. Whether the public really believe that sporting success can be associated with, and derived from, buying the advertised product is a moot point.

Sources:

Collins, T. and Vamplew, W., *Blood, Sweat and Beers: Sport and Alcohol* (forthcoming Oxford: Berg).

Szymanski, S. and Kuypers, T., *Winners and Losers: The Business Strategy of Football* (London: Viking, 1999).

Further Reading:

Hamil, S., Michie, J. and Oughton, C. (eds), *The Business of Football: A Game of Two Halves?* (Edinburgh: Mainstream, 1999).

Wray Vamplew

Success off the Pitch

Traditionally a professional reaching the end of his career would often use the proceeds from his benefit match to set himself up in a pub. John Charles, Jim Baxter and Martin Chivers are among the most noteworthy post-war players to have enjoyed a second career running licensed premises. What better place for their fame to live on than in a cosy bar, with the fans of their glory days as admirers and customers? Others, however, have made their mark outside the game – and often enjoyed substantial financial reward – in a variety of alternative ventures.

Blackburn Rovers' defender Dave Whelan was one of the victims of the infamous 'Wembley Jinx', breaking his leg in the 1960 FA Cup Final. He then ended his playing days with Crewe Alexandra in 1965, before setting up his own sports business that eventually expanded to a chain of 115 shops. The company was floated on the stock market in 1994, netting Whelan an estimated £13.5 million. The chain, JJB Sports, is prominent in the country's shopping districts, but few patrons are likely to be aware of its founder's playing career. Another ex-player to have seen his business venture spread to the nation's high streets is Frank McLintock, Scottish international defender and a member of the Arsenal double-winning side of 1971. In partnership with boxer Dave 'Boy' Green, McLintock set up the 'Cash Converter' chain of shops. Francis Lee, Manchester City's England winger of the 1960s and 1970s, kept up his sporting interests after his playing days were over by becoming a racehorse trainer, although the turf was always a sideline to his business interests (unlike former England striker Mick Channon, who has become a successful racehorse trainer). Lee's recycled paper business was profitable enough to enable him to head a consortium that took control of the Maine Road club in 1993. One of Lee's regular opponents on the field was Paul Madeley of Leeds United, who played over 500 times for the Elland Road club between

1963 and 1980. Madeley and his brothers shared £27 million when they sold their chain of 26 DIY shops in 1987. Paul then diversified into property consultancy. Lee's former team-mate Mike Summerbee, another England winger, set up his own made-to-measure shirt business which proved successful enough to attract such high-profile clients as Michael Caine, Sylvester Stallone and David Bowie.

If Summerbee's shirts brought him into contact with the entertainment world only peripherally, other ex-players have used their names and personalities to embrace it fully. The most obvious route open to ex-players wishing to extend their shelf-life is via television sports programmes: Ally McCoist is now a regular on the quiz show *A Question of Sport*, as was Emlyn Hughes before him. Ian St John and Jimmy Greaves' banter found an outlet in their own show, *The Saint and Greavesie*. Jimmy Hill waxed lyrical, if not always logical, for years on BBC's *Match of the Day*, long after his career as a Fulham inside-forward was forgotten. Trevor Brooking, Alan Hansen and Mark Lawrenson, among others, all extended their careers into the field of TV punditry on the same programme. The most successful in this field has proved to be Gary Lineker, who moved seamlessly into the show's top spot, taking over from Desmond Lynam after the latter's defection to ITV in 2000. It proved an inspired decision: a TV poll conducted to find the game's top presenter over Euro 2000 gave Lineker 60 per cent of the votes. Lynam came second with 18 per cent. At the turn of the millennium Lineker was also a regular team captain on the irreverent quiz show *They Think It's All Over*, as well as exhorting the game's younger fans to enjoy the delights of Walkers Crisps in a series of lucrative ads on the rival channel.

At the opposite end of the image spectrum from the fresh-faced, goody-goody Lineker is Vinny Jones, a member of the Wimbledon 'Crazy Gang' that won the FA Cup in 1988. The same year Jones hit the headlines for all the wrong reasons when, during a Wimbledon v Newcastle United game he was caught on camera getting to grips with Paul Gascoigne in what can best be described as the 'penalty area'. He was also reported as threatening to tear off Kenny Dalglish's ear and spit in the hole. In 1992 Jones was handed a record £20,000 fine by the FA, together with a suspended six-month ban, for his part in the release of the notorious 'video nasty' *Soccer's Hard Men*, which glorified foul and dangerous play. When he finally retired as a player, Jones's tough-guy image earned him a place in the 1998 gangster film *Lock, Stock and Two Smoking Barrels*, in which he played a fearsome character called Big Chris. Two years later he was back on the big screen, again playing to type, this time as Bullet Tooth Tony in *Snatch*. Jones has announced himself as being bound for Hollywood. If Jones's future career in films lasts long enough for his fans to forget his footballing past, then he will not be alone. Among today's stars who were once signed by professional clubs but failed to make the grade are singers Rod Stewart (Brentford) and Des O'Connor (Northampton Town), together with comedians Ronnie Corbett (Hearts), Stan Boardman (Liverpool) and Eddie Large (Manchester City). Charlie Williams, he of the 'Hello, me old flower' catchphrase, was one of Britain's few coloured players in the early post-war years, playing in Doncaster Rovers' defence for over a decade from 1949. Ever the dressing-room clown, he was encouraged by his team-mates to try his luck as a comedian on the northern working-men's club circuit, and proved so successful that he landed the job as presenter on the TV quiz show *The Golden Shot*. Another ex-player to have graced the small screen is ex-Glasgow Ranger Gordon Ramsay, one of the band of celebrity TV chefs to come to prominence in the 1990s. Named Chef of the Year for 2000, Ramsay became as well-known for his fiery temper, with customers and employees alike, as for his fine cuisine.

Following a less glamorous, but just as prestigious, course to fame was Albert Gudmundsson, who appeared for Arsenal in 1946 and 1947. After leaving Highbury to return to his native Iceland, Albert went on to become President of the Icelandic FA before joining the government and becoming Minister of Finance. Charles Buchan, the Sunderland, Arsenal and England inside-forward between 1911 and 1928, went on to become a celebrated journalist, reporting on golf and football for the *Daily News* and the *News Chronicle*. He was also one of the BBC's first radio commentators, and in 1951 was appointed editor of the newly launched magazine *Football Monthly*, which became *Charles Buchan's Football Monthly*. Although he died in 1960, the popular title continued to carry his name long after his death. Another ex-player with literary talent is former England manager Terry Venables, co-author of the 1971 novel *They Used To Play On Grass*, which foresaw the introduction of artificial pitches among other innovations. He also collaborated on the scripts for the TV drama series *Hazell*.

Sources:

Hazlewood, N., *In The Way! Goalkeepers: A Breed Apart?* (Edinburgh: Mainstream, 1998).

Matthews, P. and Buchanan, I., *The All-Time Greats of British and Irish Sport* (Enfield: Guinness, 1995).

Pringle, A. and Fissler, N., *Where Are They Now?* (London: Two Heads Publishing, 1996).

Further Reading:

Barrett, N., *The Daily Telegraph Football Chronicle* (London: Carlton, 1996).

Drewett, J. and Leith, A., *The Virgin Book of Football Records* (London: Virgin, 1996).

Tony Rennick

History Highlights 1960–1969

The 1960s will always be remembered as the decade in which the British game finally made an impact on the wider stages of European and world football, and shook off its insular image: one that had been summed up in the comment to journalist Brian Glanville by the Football League's Alan Hardaker that he didn't like getting involved with football on the Continent because of 'too many wogs and dagoes'. Neither was he impressed by the players'

trade union, the Professional Footballers' Association, in their attempts to have the maximum wage abolished and their members released from the contracts which bound them to their clubs for life. On Wednesday 18 January 1961 Hardaker, as League secretary, and PFA chairman Jimmy Hill, in the latest of a series of acrimonious meetings, spent five hours in discussion before the players' demands were finally met and a threatened strike the following Saturday was called off. The £20-a-week maximum was consigned to history and it appeared initially that the 'slavery' contract was to follow suit. However, at the Football League's June AGM the clubs voted against that part of the agreement and it was not until 1963 that the issue was finally resolved. In a test case instigated by the PFA Mr Justice Wilberforce declared that Newcastle United's refusal to let George Eastham join Arsenal in 1960 had amounted to a 'restraint of trade'. As a result, extensive reform of players' contracts finally took place in 1964. Jimmy Hill, who had become a national celebrity through the publicity generated by the affair, became manager of Coventry City in 1961, eventually entering the world of TV punditry.

If Hardaker appeared to lack vision with regard to what seem natural elements of the modern game – international club football and 'superstar' salaries for the top players – he can at least be given credit for another integral component, the Football League Cup (by the turn of the millennium known as the Worthington Cup), although this brainchild of his got off to a less than auspicious start. Dubbed 'Hardaker's Folly' when first launched in 1960, it was immediately snubbed by five of the top clubs of the time – Arsenal, Sheffield Wednesday, Tottenham Hotspur, West Bromwich Albion and Wolverhampton Wanderers – on the grounds that the fixture list was already congested and what the game needed was a smaller First Division rather than another knock-out competition. Nevertheless, the new Cup got under way on Monday 26 September 1960 when Bristol Rovers beat Fulham 2–1, and West Ham won a London derby 3–1 against Charlton. The trophy went that first season, 1960/61, to Aston Villa by a 3–2 margin after a two-legged final against Second Division Rotherham United, although the two games only managed to attract a total of 43,428 spectators. The following season, with many of the top clubs still not deigning to enter, Second Division Norwich City beat Rochdale of the Fourth 4–0 on aggregate. If the fledgling competition seemed destined to remain the province of the League's minnows, Hardaker had other ideas. From the 1966/67 season the competition was given a televised Wembley final and the winners granted automatic entry to the Inter-Cities Fairs Cup (the forerunner of the UEFA Cup), provided they were from the First Division. By 1969/70 every club in the League was entering, Liverpool and Everton being the last to submit to the lure of glory. Not that the big guns had it all their own way: the first Wembley final of 1967 saw top-flight West Brom go down 3–2 to Queen's Park Rangers of Division Three, and two years later the feat was repeated when another Third Division side, Swindon Town, humbled the mighty Arsenal 3–1.

On a broader stage, the first European Cup final to be staged in Britain was played on the evening of 18 May 1960 at Hampden Park, Glasgow. The Scottish national stadium held 127,000 fans, and millions more watched on television as Real Madrid won their fifth European Cup in a row, beating Eintracht Frankfurt 7–3 in what is still often described as the greatest match ever played. Many in the crowd would have witnessed Eintracht's demolition of Glasgow Rangers in the semi-final, by an aggregate score of 12–4. The *Daily Mail*'s Don Hardisty summed up the mood of the nation with his comment that he felt sorry for the fans having to return to English and Scottish League football the following season. British football seemed to have been left behind, but European success was not far away.

Rangers reached the final of the European Cup Winners' Cup in 1961, losing 4–1 on aggregate to Fiorentina in what was then a two-legged final, but in 1963 Tottenham Hotspur became the first British side to lift a European trophy.

Spurs, led by the inspirational Danny Blanchflower, demolished Atletico Madrid 5–1 in Rotterdam in the final of the European Cup Winners' Cup, two of the goals coming from diminutive left-winger Terry Dyson. Two years later London rivals West Ham United repeated the feat when they triumphed 2–0 over Munich 1860 in Wembley's first European final. In 1966 Hammers' captain Bobby Moore returned to Wembley to lift the ultimate prize, the World Cup, in England's historic extra-time 4–2 defeat of West Germany, thanks to Geoff Hurst's hat-trick. Further European success came close that year, with Liverpool losing the European Cup Winners' Cup final 2–1 to Borussia Dortmund. The following season Rangers reached the final of the same competition, only to lose 1–0 to another German side, Bayern Munich. Both these finals went to extra time.

The greatest European prize, the European Cup, finally came to Britain in the 1966/67 season when Celtic recovered from being a goal down to a sixth-minute penalty to beat the strongly-fancied Inter Milan 2–1 in Lisbon, the goals coming from Tommy Gemmell and Steve Chalmers. The following year finally saw the European Cup won by an English club when Manchester United beat Portuguese champions Benfica 4–1 at Wembley. Bobby Charlton's 52nd-minute strike had been cancelled out to take the match into injury time, but George Best, Brian Kidd and Charlton again scored to take the trophy to Old Trafford. This triumph was to result in a knighthood for manager Matt Busby. Further European success was achieved that season with Leeds United taking the Inter-Cities Fairs Cup with a 1–0 victory over Hungarian side Ferencvaros over a two-legged final. The following season Newcastle United lifted the same trophy, beating another Hungarian side, Ujpest Dozsa, 3–0 at home and 3–2 away, to complete an impressive decade for British clubs in Europe.

On the domestic front, history was made in England in the 1960/61 season when Spurs, managed by Bill Nicholson, became the first side in the twentieth century to achieve the coveted Football League and FA Cup double. Wolves had come tantalisingly close to what the experts had decided was a near-impossible feat the previous season, lifting the Cup with a 3–0 victory over Blackburn Rovers but losing 3–1 to Spurs in their penultimate League game and thereby, despite a 5–1 defeat of Chelsea at Stamford Bridge in their last match, but conceding the Championship to Burnley by a single point. Spurs, who finished third behind Wolves, began the following season with a record 11 straight league victories. By the turn of the year they had established such a lead that the bookmakers refused to take any further bets on their taking the title. They finally ended the campaign eight points ahead of second-placed Sheffield Wednesday, with Wolves a further point behind in third place. In the Cup final, they defeated Leicester City 2–0, with the young Gordon Banks in goal, though the game was marred by an early injury to the City right-back, Len Chalmers. Thanks to a 3–1 Wembley win over Burnley, Spurs retained the Cup the following year – a feat previously accomplished in the twentieth century only by Newcastle United in 1951 and 1952 – but lost the Championship to the unfancied Ipswich Town side managed by Alf Ramsey, the ex-Tottenham full-back. This was the first managerial success for the future knight who was to lead England to World Cup glory in 1966.

The most remarkable aspect of Scottish football was the re-emergence of Celtic as a major power in the second half of the decade. First championships for Dundee in 1962 and Kilmarnock in 1965 suggested that the relative openness marking the League in the previous decade might continue. However, under Jock Stein the championship success of 1966 began a run of nine consecutive titles. The club's European Cup success in 1967 capped a season which also saw it claim a League, Cup and League Cup treble, a domestic treble repeated in 1969.

Off the field the 1960s saw the emergence of what is now taken for granted as being an intrinsic part of the game – television coverage. During the 1950s the only regular live broadcast was the FA Cup final, with internationals and top club games occasionally being edited for the BBC's *Sports Special* programme, launched in 1955. But on 10 September 1960 ITV screened the First Division match between Blackpool and Bolton Wanderers. In 1964 the BBC launched *Match of the Day*, a 45-minute programme of edited highlights of a top League match. This was initially shown on the new minority channel, BBC2, but such was the demand that it was switched to BBC1, where it remained until very recently. The late 1960s also saw the introduction of closed-circuit TV coverage, to enable fans to watch their teams in away action without having to travel themselves. The first experiment was carried out on 7 October 1965 by Coventry City, who erected screens at Highfield Road for their Second Division visit to Cardiff City. Over 10,000 watched the game in Coventry – only a couple of thousand less than the actual gate. By 1967 the idea had really caught on and the fifth-round FA Cup derby between Everton and Liverpool was watched live at Goodison Park by 64,851, while 40,149 tuned in to the screens at Anfield. The power of television was capable of bringing the big events to the whole nation, as witnessed by the vast audiences for England's 1966 World Cup Final victory and the European Cup successes for Celtic in 1967 and Manchester United in 1968.

Another innovation of the 1960s was the introduction of substitutes. So many showpiece games, including several Wembley finals (see for example Spurs v Leicester City, above), had been affected by injuries to players that, commencing in the 1965/66 season, it became permissible for one player to be named as a possible substitute in FA Cup and Football League matches. The first such player to take the field was Charlton Athletic's Keith Peacock, in the match against Bolton Wanderers at Burnden Park on 21 August 1965. On the same day Barrow's Bobby Knox became the first substitute to score. Initially, substitutes were only allowed to replace genuinely injured players, but the rule was so open to abuse that it was relaxed the following season, allowing for the tactical switches that are so much a part of the modern game. The first substitute in a Scottish senior game was Archie Gemmill, who came on for St Mirren on 13 August 1966 in the League Cup tie against Clyde. In 1968 two other players got their names into the history books: Geoff Vowden of Birmingham City became the first 12th man to score a hat-trick, and Derek Clarke earned an FA Cup winner's medal after replacing John Kaye in West Bromwich Albion's Wembley victory over Everton.

Another kind of substitution had been forced on the game in 1963: in January of that year severe weather conditions had so decimated the fixture lists that for three successive weeks the pools companies had had to declare their coupons null and void, with only a handful of matches being played. If the fans couldn't have their football they still needed their flutter, so a panel of experts, comprising ex-players Ted Drake, Tom Finney, Tommy Lawton, George Young and former referee Arthur Ellis each received £100 on 26 January to forecast what the results would have been. One happy punter reaped a six-figure jackpot but the innovation was not universally acclaimed: 'Soccer Fans In Storm Over Phantom 12X' ran the *News of the World* headline. Nevertheless, the Pools Panel was here to stay.

The following year a much more serious story concerning payments of £100 hit the sports pages, when on 12 April 1964 the *People* ran an exposé concerning the Sheffield Wednesday players Peter Swan, Tony Kay and David Layne, who had each won that amount by backing their own side to lose against Ipswich Town in the First Division match played on 1 December 1962. All three players (by now Kay was with Everton) were banned for life and received prison sentences. Further investigations involving the *People* and the Football League revealed that on the same day as the Ipswich–Wednesday fixture, the matches between Lincoln City and Brentford in the Third Division, and York City and Oldham Athletic in the Fourth, had been similarly rigged. All three games resulted in home wins. Many more life bans followed for the players involved in one of the most discreditable episodes in

the game's history.

Despite this shameful chapter, however, the 'swinging sixties' evoke positive memories. After all, England won the World Cup, British clubs enjoyed regular success in European competitions, television coverage brought the game to millions and, with George Best being dubbed the 'fifth Beatle', football emerged as the new rock 'n' roll.

Sources:
Cottrell, J., *A Century of Great Soccer Drama* (London: Rupert Hart-Davis, 1970).
Kelly, S. F., *Back Page Football: A Century of Newspaper Coverage* (Harpenden: Aurora Publishing, 1995).
Nawrat, C. and Hutchings, S., *The Sunday Times Illustrated History of Football: The Post-War Years* (London: Chancellor Press, 1995).

Further Reading:
Butler, B., *The Official Illustrated History of the FA Cup* (London: Headline, 1996).
Hart, G. (ed)., *The Guinness Football Encyclopedia* (Enfield: Guinness, 1995).
Nawrat, C., Hutchings, S. and Struthers, G., *The Sunday Times Illustrated History of Twentieth Century Sport* (London: Hamlyn, 1996).

Tony Rennick

Tactics and Playing Formations

Football 'tactics' are those strategies employed by the members of one side to compete most effectively with their opponents. Tactics in football matches operate at five levels. First, at individual level, specific players seek to out-manoeuvre individual opponents. For example, full-backs may adopt the tactic of forcing wingers to run at the inside channel, onto their weaker foot. Second, during particular passages of play, pre-arranged tactical manoeuvres involving a few team-mates may be employed in defence or attack. For example, a zonal defence may deal with a group of attackers; or at a free-kick, the attacking players will make pre-arranged runs to open space for colleagues. Third, most importantly, tactics refers to the playing system or team formation that is generally employed by the team coach, as the underlying structure that organises players throughout the match. Fourth, particular tactics of movement and passing with the ball are employed. Examples here include individual dribbling, the long-ball game or triangular passing patterns. Fifth, tactics also include those practices that seek to control the tempo or flow of the game in both defence and attack. These may include holding on to the ball, hustling opponents, as well as more questionable practices, such as time-wasting, persistent fouling of opponents, or disputing the decisions of match officials.

The specific tactics selected by any one side should feature a careful integration of all five aspects. Key factors when deciding on tactics are the resources available to the team and its traditions. A balance must be struck between establishing a systematic and manageable pattern of play with the particular skills of individuals. For example, there is little point in playing with a zonal 'sweeper' in defence if the defenders lack anticipation and good technical skills. Similarly, in UK football there may be strong local hostility to a defensive playing formation if the club has an established pattern of play, such as the deliberately more spectacular styles of West Ham or Celtic. British football has embraced a great range of playing formations and specific playing styles, although it has been relatively less influential overseas throughout the post-war period. Historically, football has witnessed a general reduction in the emphasis on player individualism in favour of greater interplay with teammates, alongside a greater tactical concern with the defensive duties of players. The opportunity for managers and coaches to alter tactics as the game progressed was enhanced by the legalisation of tactical substitutions in 1966/67. Only one substitution was allowed initially, but the number was raised to two in 1986 and then to three in the 1990s.

At the foundation of association football, teams tended to contain eight forward players, with a goal-keeper, half-back, and three-quarter in support. This was reduced in the 1870s to seven players with two half-backs and a full-back. The favoured playing style centred on the dribbling skills of individuals. Scottish football is credited with the creation of the passing game in the late nineteenth century, which proved more competitively effective and aesthetically appealing to the development of individual and team skills. Playing formations were amended to provide the teams with greater depth, and thus more room for passing movements and effective defence against more concerted attacks. Until the 1920s, a particularly common playing style was the 2–3–5 formation, initiated by Preston North End, featuring two full-backs, three half-backs and five forwards. As goals in English football declined numerically, the offside laws were changed in 1925, although overseas commentators believed the English were simply not using sufficient guile to break defensive play. The major law change enabled a player to remain onside if, upon the ball being played forward to him, two or more opponents were nearer to their own goal-line (the previous rule had stipulated three). Herbert Chapman, the Arsenal manager, amended his playing formation accordingly, to create the WM formation. Five defenders lined up as a 'W' while five attackers lined up as an 'M'; crucially, the centre-half dropped into a defensive position. The formation relied heavily on the attacking, goal-scoring prowess of Arsenal's wingers, the ball-playing skills of the brilliant Scotsman Alex James, and an effective counter-attacking game. The new formation was embraced by most English clubs, but overseas sides tended to retain the attacking centre-half. British soccer was introduced to the tactical benefits of European innovation, first by the Austrian *wunderteam* in the 1930s, and following the war by the brilliant Hungary national team. The latter's 6–3 victory at Wembley was achieved tactically through having Hidekguti play as a withdrawn centre-forward, thus wrong-footing the WM defence. Overseas, further variations were introduced, such as the 4–2–4 system employed by Brazil, the Swiss Bolt system of Karl Rappan, and the *catenaccio* system of Helenio Herrera. Tactically, English football was moving towards more efficient play and 'scientific' thinking, thus curtailing some of the individual skills of players. Wolverhampton Wanderers pursued a 'long-ball' game with great effect in the 1950s, while coaching experts such as Charles Reep and then Charles Hughes drew upon statistical research to promote the quick delivery of the ball into attacking 'reacher areas'. Alf Ramsey's champions of 1966, playing to a 4–3–3 formation, solidified England's midfield but eradicated the creative winger's role. (This stood in some contrast to the attacking prowess of UK football's most effective club sides, especially Celtic.) Subsequently, a further forward slipped more regularly into midfield to provide a hustling, 4–4–2 system that proved highly effective for English club sides in the 1970s and 1980s. In Europe, AC Milan's immensely successful side during the late 1980s and early 1990s borrowed heavily from this model to establish a powerful 'pressing' game. However, the English national side struggled, especially with the inflexibility of 4–4–2, most recently at Euro 2000; by contrast, the semi-finals of the 1990 World Cup were reached through borrowing two continental features (a *libero* and play-making midfielder). Since the early 1990s, and following the influx of overseas players and coaches, UK clubs have employed a far more cosmopolitan range of playing formations; frequently, these appear in four-digit notation (such as 4–3–2–1). Perhaps the most significant innovation has involved the use of 'wing-backs' to bolster the midfield and add attacking options, such as through a 3–5–2 formation.

Sources:

Giulianotti, R., *Football: A Sociology of the Global Game* (Cambridge: Polity, 1999).

Joy, B., *Soccer Tactics* (London: Phoenix, 1957).

Further Reading:

Gray, A. with Drewett, J., *Flat Back Four: The Tactical Game* (London: Boxtree, 1998).

Richard Giulianotti

Talented Ball Players

It would be impossible to examine all the talented ball players who have featured in British football, but those highlighted here were particularly lauded for their passing and dribbling skills during different eras. Prior to 1914 the English game was notable for players with dribbling skills – that is, the ability to run while retaining possession of the ball. The star of the 1870s was Robert Sealy-Vidal of Wanderers, dubbed the 'prince of dribblers'. Under the influence of the many Scots who joined English sides, there was a growing emphasis on a passing style of play. Archie Hunter, a Scot who joined Aston Villa in the 1880s, was noted for his passing skills, and many Englishmen adopted this approach. The England centre-forward of the 1880s, Tinsley Lindley, was noted for his passing, as was his successor, G. O. Smith. Perhaps the real star of pre-1914 football, though, was the Welsh winger Billy Meredith, who represented both Manchester clubs. His ball skills and ability to beat defenders left many a crowd gasping with admiration.

When football resumed in 1919, spectators were entertained by forwards noted for their skill on the ball. Charles Buchan of Sunderland and Arsenal was famous for his intelligent passing and he was succeeded at Highbury by players such as David Jack, Alex James and Cliff Bastin. Jack and James could fool opponents with delightful body swerves, while Bastin was a speedy winger with a deadly shot. James and the brilliant Newcastle United forward Hughie Gallacher played for Scotland in the side that beat England 5–1 at Wembley in 1928. Another in the side dubbed the 'Wembley Wizards' was Alan Morton of Rangers, a winger blessed with great talent. Across Glasgow at Celtic Park was Patsy Gallacher, a brilliant dribbler who played internationally for Northern Ireland. Either side of the Second World War came three great inside-forwards. England's Raich Carter, whose ball skills enabled him to find space behind defences, was partnered by Wilf Mannion

Cliff Bastin
(Reproduced with the kind permission of Imperial
Tobacco Limited)

*George Best, Manchester United v Ipswich
Town, April 1971*
(Peter Robinson; © EMPICS Sports Photo Agency)

of Middlesbrough, noted for his incisive passing. Perhaps the finest of the era was Peter Doherty from Northern Ireland, a natural dribbler with speed off the mark and a deadly shot. For a time, Carter and Doherty formed an outstanding partnership at Derby County.

Another great player whose career spanned the war was Stanley Matthews, the Stoke City, Blackpool and England winger. Matthews was a fantastic dribbler with the ability to make pinpoint centres for waiting forwards. On the opposite flank for England was Preston's Tom Finney, who could destroy defences with speed and skill. They serviced forwards like Tommy Lawton, who allied a goal-scoring touch to great distribution, and Stan Mortensen. Succeeding Carter and Mannion were Johnny Haynes, whose trademark was the long, penetrating pass, and Manchester United's Bobby Charlton, scorer of 49 goals for England, maker of many more and winner in 1966 of a World Cup medal. Scotland continued to produce great ball players, including the Liverpool winger Billy Liddell, the exquisite passer Jim Baxter and the goal-poacher Denis Law, a team-mate of Charlton's at Old Trafford.

The 1960s and 1970s are remembered for some great ball-players, some of whom also acquired reputations for their behaviour off the field. George Best, a wonderful dribbler with superb balance, starred for Manchester United and Northern Ireland, but his career was blighted by personal problems. Others such as Alan Hudson, a superb passer, and Stan Bowles, a speedy and tricky winger, had brushes with authority. Hudson won only two caps, and other gifted players of the 1970s such as Charlie George, Rodney Marsh, Tony Currie and Peter Osgood did not receive the recognition their skills warranted. In this respect they were natural predecessors to England's most talented player of the 1980s – Glenn Hoddle of Tottenham Hotspur, whose ability to play long, accurate passes was not fully utilised at international level. Similarly, the Liverpool winger John Barnes was not able to fully deploy his gifts on the England stage.

The emphasis on speed and stamina in modern football has perhaps diminished the scope for the talented ball player, at least in Britain. England's last real star in this respect was that fine passer and dribbler Paul Gascoigne, a star of the 1990 World Cup, while Scotland's last great was perhaps Kenny Dalglish. However, the skills demonstrated by many leading continental players in Euro 2000 pointed to a welcome return in emphasis towards the ball player, and suggested that English and Scottish sides need to rediscover players who possess these arts.

Sources:

Lamming, D., *An England Football Internationalists' Who's Who 1872–1988* (Beverley: Hutton, 1990).

Lamming, D., *A Scottish Soccer Internationalists' Who's Who 1872–1986* (Beverley: Hutton, 1987).

Pawson, T., *The Goalscorers: From Bloomer to Keegan* (London: Cassell, 1978).

Further Reading:

Miller, D., *Stanley Matthews: The Authorised Biography* (London: Pavilion, 1989).

Woolnough, B., *Glenn Hoddle: The Man and the Manager* (London: Virgin, 1997).

John Coyle

Taylor Report

The Taylor Report was the ninth official report that dealt with issues of safety and control of spectators at football grounds. The inquiry, conducted by Lord Justice Taylor, was set up by the then Home Secretary, the Rt Hon Douglas Hurd, after the tragic events at Sheffield Wednesday's Hillsborough ground on 15 April 1989. The match was an FA Cup semi-final between Liverpool and Nottingham Forest, at which, as a result of overcrowding, 95 spectators were crushed to death. It was the worst disaster to hit modern British football since the Ibrox disaster in 1971 where 66 supporters died. The events at Hillsborough came only four years after the Bradford disaster, where an outbreak of fire led to 56 deaths. As a consequence of that tragedy Mr Justice Popplewell had produced two reports with a number of recommendations. Despite this and all the previous proposals from other reports a more serious disaster occurred. As Taylor commented: 'it seems astounding that 95 people could die from overcrowding before the very eyes of those controlling the event' (Taylor Report, 1990, paragraph 19).

There were two distinct questions to which the Taylor inquiry addressed itself. Firstly, the investigation of the events at Hillsborough and what short-term measures were required to prevent any repetition. Secondly, what action was required over the long term to improve, or on the worst analysis save, football as a spectator sport. Following on from the hooligan problems of the 1970s and 1980s, this was seen as perhaps the last opportunity for football to carve out a viable future. Taylor laid out the nature and extent of the problem:

Football is our national game. We gave it to the world. But its image in our country has been much tarnished. In my Interim Report I concentrated on overcrowding because it was the cause of the Hillsborough disaster. But wider and deeper inquiry shows that overcrowding is only one feature amongst a number causing danger or marring football as a spectator sport. The picture revealed is of a general malaise or blight over the game due to a number of factors. Principally these are: old grounds, poor facilities, hooliganism, excessive drinking and poor leadership. Crowd safety and crowd behaviour with which I am concerned are closely related to the quality of the accommodation and facilities offered and to the standards which are encouraged and enforced. (Taylor Report, 1990, paragraph 26)

Taylor led a root-and-branch analysis of the safety and control of spectators that went way beyond the disaster itself. He was in a rather peculiar position in that the Government had already introduced draft legislation as part of its proposals to develop some type of national membership scheme, and this then formed part of his remit. The Final Report made a total of 76 recommendations. These were wide-ranging and covered all aspects of stadium safety, crowd control and hooligan behaviour. It is the application of these recommendations that has changed the face of contemporary professional football at the highest levels.

The most obvious change has been the imposition of all-seated accommodation within grounds, and thus the abolition of standing terraces. This has not only changed the physical shape of grounds but has also had an impact on the economics of spectating. All-seated grounds have a smaller capacity than those with standing room, and this has led to a number of significant ground re-developments, such as that at Old Trafford, in order to regain some of the lost capacity. There have been complaints from some fans that the requirement for seating only has led to an impoverishment of the atmosphere within grounds, as those supporters wishing to sing are no longer able to gravitate towards one area.

Apart from the changes to grounds and the establishment of the Football Licensing Authority, a further area of change produced by the Taylor Report has been with respect to the policing of supporters. New legislation has been introduced that is specifically aimed at those attending football matches. The Football (Offences) Act 1991 has made it a criminal offence to throw missiles towards the pitch, take part in racist chanting, or go onto the playing area without lawful excuse. However, Taylor rejected the imposition of any national membership scheme based on the technology available at the time. Undoubtedly the Taylor Report has been the most influential document in the history of the modern game, and led to radical changes in not only the structure of grounds but also the experience of spectating.

Source:
The Taylor Report (London HMSO, 1990) (Cm 962).

Further Reading:
Greenfield, S. and Osborn, G., *Regulating Football* (London: Pluto Press, 2001).

Steve Greenfield and Guy Osborn

Technology

Technology has been applied in football to assist the players, officials and spectators. Players have gained from the use of improved training equipment, facilities, and knowledge on methods and diet. However, unlike in many sports, football players wear little protective gear, and so have not received the benefits of advances in safety technology enjoyed by racing drivers, jockeys, and other sportspersons. Since shin-guards were patented in 1874 by Sam Widdowson of Nottingham Forest, perhaps the greatest benefit to footballers has been afforded by changes to the ball itself. The valved ball that replaced the laced version in the 1950s made heading less dangerous, as did the plastic covering that prevented the leather soaking up water or becoming caked with mud. No doubt players also appreciated the emergence of screw-in studs and moulded rubber soles that ended the days of leather studs being nailed into boots. Whether the use of anaesthetic sprays is ultimately as good for the injured player as the 'magic sponge' is less obvious.

Referees and linesmen have been aided in deciding whether or not a goal has been scored by the use of goal nets, patented in 1890 by J. A. Brodie of Liverpool. Yet to date, despite the implementation of illuminated time-boards to inform spectators and giant television screens to entertain them, there has been an official reluctance to make electronic aids or light-sensitive equipment available to match officials. Video replays are confined to post-match disciplinary hearings rather than used as instant guides to decision-making.

Technology has offered significant benefits to those who choose to watch sport, either at home or at the stadium. Advances in cameras and their use have enabled the viewer to take advantage of the close-up and slow-motion replay, and have better than the best seats at the game. Even if a spectator is at the sporting venue, large video screens often ensure that the sports fan sees every detail of the action. Such spectators have gained from improved stadium architecture, with better roofing to combat the worst of the weather, better design to allow unobstructed viewing, and floodlights to enable sport to be watched at night or in gloomy weather.

Source:
Barrett, N., *The Daily Telegraph Football Chronicle* (London: Carlton, 1995).

See also Artificial Pitches, Floodlighting, Football Boots, Footballs

Wray Vamplew

Television

Once seen as a major threat to the future of football, television has transformed itself into the central driving force within the modern game, fundamental to its finances, marketing and public image. In turn, football has become central for both new and established television channels, and is the main explanation for the massive growth of channels like Rupert Murdoch's Sky.

Experimental coverage of the game began as early as September 1937, when a handful of London viewers were treated to footage of Arsenal playing Arsenal Reserves. The Cup final was televised in the next year and by the early 1950s had become a major televisual occasion, constructed as a 'national' event for all to enjoy. Despite this and the FA's willingness to allow coverage of internationals, the Football League was always reluctant to allow either highlights or live coverage of League fixtures to be shown, fearing a negative impact on live attendances. An attempt at live coverage in 1960 was abandoned after just one game following opposition from leading clubs, and it was not until 1964 that the BBC was allowed to show highlights of League games, with *Match of the Day* beginning its first edition with Arsenal's trip to Liverpool in August 1964. Since then, the history of the relationship between football and television has been one of constant tension. The non-commercially motivated administra-

tors at the FA and Football League were always suspicious of business developments within the game, an attitude central to the way they approached TV. Clauses like that preventing shirt sponsors from appearing on television during games (only revoked in 1983) affected the relationship between the game and what was to become its biggest source of income, and an increasingly important medium for the generation of supporters.

Widely recognised as the largest source of income top division clubs can generate, as well as the key to increasing revenues from other activities (sponsorship, advertising, non-active fan-bases), the rights to live and recorded football have been viciously fought over by television companies: when the League signed an exclusive deal with ITV in 1978 (in what became known as 'Snatch of the Day'), the BBC, recognising the importance of the decision, were furious and levelled accusations of bad faith. Rights to live coverage changed hands over the next decade, with the amount of money slowly increasing with each deal – although football would later claim that the BBC and ITV had operated a cartel to keep costs down. But, crucially, the growing revenue from exclusive live coverage created deep – maybe still unresolved – pressures within the game, particularly from the handful of top, rich clubs who felt they had the greatest TV appeal and so should receive a greater percentage of the money. Regular threats in the 1980s by the 'Big Five' (Manchester United, Liverpool, Arsenal, Tottenham Hotspur and Everton) to leave the League and form a Super League if they did not get a larger share, led to crucial changes to the financial balance of the game. As the clubs most often featured live (particularly on ITV in the late 1980s), fears of losing the Big Five always ensured compliance from the rest of football, increasing the revenue these clubs received from TV as well as indirectly increasing other revenues (such as sponsorship and advertising). TV and the revenue it could offer changed forever the economic balance of professional football (the big clubs kept 50 per cent of TV and sponsorship revenues from 1986, rising to 75 per cent in 1988).

The continual pressure from top clubs to retain a greater share of TV revenues eventually led to the creation of the FA Premier League in 1992: the new league was identical to the old Football League Division One, except that its clubs would keep all TV revenues, and it would be specifically designed for blanket coverage by Sky TV, with fixtures spread across the entire week, and new kick-off times. The scramble to secure Premier League rights testifies to the importance attached to owning exclusive rights for the top English division: Sky (in league with the BBC) and ITV between them offered nearly £600 million for five years' coverage, and there have been constant accusations that the Premier League, and Tottenham Hotspur in particular, unfairly favoured Sky in the bidding process. Sky won the rights with a bid worth £304 million over five years (renewed in 1997 for £670 million), and the effects on it have been astonishing, reflecting the enormous importance of football to a new channel's development. While Sky was expanding at the time of the 1992 Premier League deal (having successfully broadcast its first major event, the 1992 Cricket World Cup), it was still very much a minor player in the British TV market. Since then, the impetus given to the company by the Premier League rights (and later the Football League as well) has not just earned it hundreds of millions of pounds through six million new subscribers, but has given it the audience base and finances needed to buy the rights to other major sporting events in the country, coming to dominate the British sports rights market.

It would, however, be inaccurate to assume that the finance that has flowed into the game from television has been the primary, or most important, effect of the new coverage: Sky and the production values it pioneered has arguably contributed to a total transformation in the image of football, coinciding with the decline in violence, the Euro 96 experience and the fashionability of the game, to offer it a new marketing niche. Arguably, it is Sky and its production values (hype, multiple camera-angles, showing numerous games weekly and, for the first time, charging viewers to see fixtures) that has taken football to hundreds of thousands of people who never previously took an interest in it, and accelerated yet further the de-localisation of support for major clubs like Liverpool and, especially, Manchester United, that began in the 1960s. Gary Whannel also argues that TV has contributed to the creation of a star-system culture around the game, operating with highly personalised, hype-driven discourses that contribute to the individualisation of football culture, which in turn drives a significant proportion of its business. TV has thus been central to the re-alignment of football in the 1990s leisure market, and in some senses the fears expressed 30 years ago about the impact on the game may have come true.

The centrality of football as content is also evident in the strategies of new stations. Channel 5, launched in the UK in 1997, took an early decision to buy as much live football as possible, and its most popular programmes have been live European Cup ties; ITV2 has a similar focus on live football. TV has been perhaps the most important element of the football industry since the 1970s – the source of much of its finance and ability to project itself, as well as many of its discontents – and is likely to retain its major role in the future. It is universally accepted that offering pay-per-view subscriptions via new digital TV technology for live coverage will create massive new commercial opportunities for the biggest European clubs in the near future, as well as fundamentally redefining fandom. Other developments that offer similar opportunities include the creation of club Pay-TV stations, already started by Middlesbrough and Manchester United in 1999. The anticipated profits from such coverage explain the rush of TV companies seeking close relationships with clubs, with Granada buying 9.9 per cent of Liverpool in 1999, ntl signing a loan agreement with Newcastle, and Sky trying to buy Manchester United in 1998. Television has thus fundamentally reshaped the nature of football, threatens to reshape the nature of fandom (plus creating massive markets for English football abroad), and so represents the central variable within the modern industry.

At the time of going to press, ITV Digital has collapsed leaving many Football League clubs in financial crisis. In Scotland, wranglings over the distribution of TV revenue amongst the Scottish Premier League teams has forced a rift between the old firm (Glasgow Rangers and Glasgow Celtic) and the remaining 10 clubs in the league. What the future therefore holds and whether the days of lucrative TV contracts are over is an interesting subject for conjecture.

Sources:

Conn, D., *The Football Business: Fair Play in the 1990s?* (Edinburgh: Mainstream, 1997).
Fynn, A. and Guest, L., *Out of Time* (London: Simon & Schuster, 1994).
Szymanski, S. and Kuypers, T., *Winners and Losers: The Business Strategy of Football* (London: Viking Press, 1999).

Further Reading:

Whannel G., *Fields of Vision* (London: Routledge, 1992).
Haynes R., 'Pageant of Sound and Vision: Football's Relationship with Television', *International Journal of History of Sport*, 15 (1998), 211–26.

Rex Nash

Tobacco

Attitudes towards the smoking and advertising of tobacco by footballers have varied considerably, reflecting changes in medical knowledge and social attitudes. Cards picturing the top players of the day or the badges, emblems, or nicknames of clubs were included in cigarette packets to encourage sales by all the leading tobacco manufacturers from the 1900s. These cards were collected avidly, creating an early association between smoking and football.

Before the links made between smoking and cancer, respiratory, and other diseases were medically proved, there was still an appreciation that cigarettes could affect a player's wind unless moderation was exercised. Some footballers, from Billy Meredith onwards, demonstrated a serious commitment to their profession by proudly declaring that they maintained their fitness by neither smoking nor drinking alcohol. Others saw nothing wrong in indulging in such a popular and widespread habit: David Jack, the Bolton and Arsenal star of the inter-war period, was a chain-smoker. Consumption of tobacco, especially in cigarette form, grew rapidly in the inter-war period. Newspaper and magazine photographs of players at leisure often showed them smoking, but this was no different from the example set by film-stars and other personalities.

Famous footballers could supplement their incomes by advertising tobacco products. 'Dixie' Dean, the superstar Everton striker of the 1930s, promoted Carreras 'Clubs', 'the cigarettes with a kick in them'. Dean, pictured in the publicity with a lighted cigarette clamped firmly between his lips, was obviously chosen for his appeal to working-class men; 'Clubs' were a budget brand at five for two pence. Even that noted abstainer Stanley Matthews appeared in an advertisement for Craven 'A' cigarettes in 1954. This cleverly linked his 'smooth ball control and timing' with the smoothness of the cigarette, without ever suggesting that the ascetic Matthews himself smoked. However, there was some protest at the example this gave to young boys, suggesting that attitudes towards footballers' smoking were beginning to change.

Other top professionals prized smoking for its calming effect on the nerves. Newcastle United's prolific goal-scorer Jackie Milburn rushed off to the Wembley toilets for a relaxing cigarette before the 1951 FA Cup final, only to find four other players puffing away in there already. A half-time drag helped him steady himself and distract from the pain of a pulled stomach muscle during the 1955 final. Tom Finney, who kept himself very fit, admitted to smoking the occasional cigarette socially. By 1957 some football clubs had introduced rules to stop players smoking after 11 am on the day of a match, but this regulation was probably often flouted. In the 1960s players were still prepared to admit publicly that they smoked, even though the first Royal College of Physicians' Report on smoking had recommended restrictions on advertising and sales to children, and an increase in tax on cigarettes. Bobby Charlton, a ten-a-day man, and Jimmy Greaves, both claimed their stamina was unaffected by their moderate tobacco consumption.

Despite the new government restrictions, and the subsequent banning of tobacco advertisements on television in 1965, widespread tobacco sponsorship of sport in Britain began in the 1960s, as tobacco companies realised its marketing potential. However, although Rothmans sponsored an extremely influential football yearbook from 1970, as well as amateur leagues Isthmian and Hellenic for a period from 1973, football competitions did not receive lucrative tobacco sponsorship. This was because of perceptions that football had a younger audience than sports like snooker, cricket, or racing, which were the major beneficiaries. Voluntary agreements between tobacco companies and the government since 1977 have recognised that sports in which a substantial proportion of spectators are under 18 are not suitable for tobacco advertising. Thus, football was unaffected by the British government's implementation of the 1998 European Union directive completely banning all tobacco advertising and sponsorship by 2006.

In the 1990s the FA included information about the health risks associated with smoking in their education package for young players. Professional football clubs claimed to educate their squads about smoking, and preferred that players did not smoke because of its deleterious effects on fitness. How many modern footballers accept this advice is impossible to calculate. In a climate of growing concern about the increase in smoking among the young, public smoking by professionals has generally been greeted with disapproval. Paul Gascoigne's reported smoking habit of a packet a day, supposedly developed in Italy, was revealed during the England squad's preparation for the 1998 World Cup. Glenn Hoddle, the England manager, was criticised for refusing to force him to give it up, despite pressure in the tabloids and from anti-smoking campaigners. However, though spectators are forbidden to consume alcohol within sight of the pitch, they can and do smoke freely at football grounds.

Sources:
Charlton, B., *Forward For England* (London: Pelham, 1967).
Finney, T., *Finney on Football* (London: Nicholas Kaye, 1958).
Ford, T., *I Lead the Attack* (London: Stanley Paul, 1957).
Milburn, J., *Golden Goals* (London: Stanley Paul, 1957).
Randall, C., 'Carry on Smoking, Hoddle tells Gazza', *Daily Telegraph* (Wednesday, 13 May 1998).

Joyce Woolridge

Trainers

Britain initially exported methods of training, but the reverse is now true because of a belated realisation of the importance of the trainer's role. The figure of the trainer as physical instructor was separated from that of the manager responsible for the conduct of a football team, and was regarded for a long time as being of secondary importance. From the beginnings of professional football in England until the First World War, the trainer, very often a past footballer, had his role limited to rubbing the skin of players and accompanying them in an oxygenating walk before the match. Generally the flat-capped trainer would lead the players around the field, surveying tug-of-war and warming-up exercises, always following the specific instructions of the managers. A respected trainer of that period was J. Grierson, who looked after the physical conduct of Aston Villa players in all six of their league

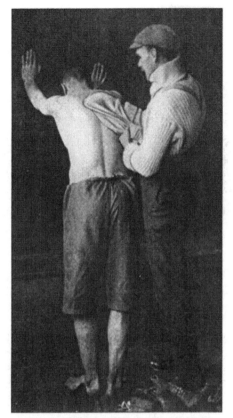

A rub down by the trainer, 1906
(National Football Museum)

championships between 1894 and 1910.

Until the1930s, Britain led international football in tactical and athletic conduct. The Scotsman Aitken shocked Italian football when, not being allowed to play for Juventus FC because he was British, he served as manager and taught the modern system of 'interval training', never adopted in Italy before. Jimmy Hogan too was an influential trainer, assisting Hugo Meisl, the manager of the national team of Austria, who challenged the English dominance in the game. Yet the career of Charlie Paynter at West Ham indicates the subsidiary position assigned to the trainer: he was assistant trainer from 1902, and trainer from 1912 to 1932, when he assumed the role of secretary-manager.

A revolution in training was pursued by Herbert Chapman, the famous manager of Arsenal, who expanded the role of the trainer. His assistant, Tom Whittaker, was a physiotherapist with modern medical equipment who was fully advanced in training techniques. But this remained an exception. After the Second World War, however, the figure of trainer assumed a more athleticist tone, even though they acquired popular fame as the first-aid men of the 'magic sponge' whose application would quickly revive injured players. Although the FA inaugurated courses for trainers, the participants were always recruited among former players and under the strict supervision of managers.

During his long career, the famous Liverpool manager Bob Paisley served initially as full-time trainer, with remarkable preparation of physiotherapy and training techniques, but once he became manager he absorbed these functions, giving no specialised space to the trainer, who basically remained a hybrid figure as fitness coach. On the other hand, Les Cocker, trainer for both Leeds and England under Don Revie, gained a reputation as a key element of Revie's assistance staff. Generally, however, the careers of trainers were mentioned in the historiography on the basis of not having missed any matches or staying with the same team for a long time, rather than as a reference point for the health and fitness of the players. Jack Wheeler, for example, is acclaimed for serving Notts County from 1957 to 1983, beating the previous record of long service of Williams as trainer of Sunderland from 1897 to 1929.

Presently, the teams of the leading countries of continental Europe require a state diploma or equivalent specialisation for their athletic supervisor, while this formal qualification is not obligatory for British teams. Nevertheless, the elite teams have improved the scientific basis of recruitment for their trainers, who must be acquainted with the modern techniques of physical training and able to carry out updated individual treatments. Moreover, the fact that teams in England and Scotland are increasingly filled with non-British players is assisting in bringing continental ideas on training to the British scene.

WEST BROMWICH ALBION OUT FOR A TRAINING-WALK.
Back Row: F. Shinton.   E. Bradley.   J. Stringer.   J. Pennington.   C. Simmons.   G. Young.
Front Row: W. Barber   J. Manners.   A. Haywood.
(Trainer).

West Bromwich Albion players out for a walk, 1906 (National Football Museum)

Sources:
Butler, B., *The Official History of Football League* (London: Queen Anne Press, 1990).
Golesworthy, M., *Encyclopedia of Football* (London: Robert Hale, 1975).
Nawrat, S. and Hutchings, G., *The Sunday Times Illustrated History of Twentieth Century Football* (London: Hamlyn, 1995).

Further Reading:
Young, P. M., *A History of British Football* (London: Arrow Books, 1975).

Gherardo Bonini

Transport

For over a century public transport, and particularly the railways, played a major part in the establishment of soccer as both spectator and participatory sport. But the ability of the railways to transport large numbers of spectators to major events, such as the FA Cup final or international matches, has overshadowed their key role in the fulfilment of a regular pattern of fixtures at local, regional and national level. Despite the granting of a Saturday afternoon half holiday to many industrial workers, and the gradual but inconsistent rise in disposable incomes between the formations of the FA in 1863 and the Football League in 1888 – by which time much of the country was served by an extensive rail network – soccer matches remained mainly the province of the players and their home supporters. Teams set up by factories, churches, and other organisations played on rented grounds, if recreation grounds were not made available by town councils, and the railways provided cheap travel to those fixtures in the local cup and league competitions which could not easily be reached on foot.

Many major football grounds were established near town centres, and most home supporters either walked or cycled to the match, or travelled a short distance by train or horse omnibus. By the first decade of the twentieth century electric tramways were providing an alternative and often more convenient means of access. The railways responded by providing extra stops and more local trains, and later, particularly in London, by the electrification of suburban lines, although travel by motorbus became more significant in country areas. Some towns and

Advertisement, London Underground, date? (London Underground Ltd)

cities could support two or more major teams, and any meeting between them was a 'local derby', with the majority of spectators living within easy reach of the ground – especially in the early days before supporting more distant teams became fashionable and practical in terms of both cost and time.

Tottenham Hotspur benefited from its proximity to White Hart Lane station, where 10,000 spectators could be easily handled by trains arriving every five minutes. Aston Villa was similarly served by the station at Witton, while Chelsea, at its formation in 1905, found a home at Stamford Bridge, close to Walham Green station (now Fulham Broadway). Two years later Queen's Park Rangers were provided with a new ground by the Great Western Railway's intelligent use of surplus land at Park Royal. Woolwich Arsenal's move to Highbury in 1913 enabled the London Underground station at Gillespie Road (renamed Arsenal in 1932) to deal with the crowds.

Although both rail fares and entrance to the ground were relatively cheap, only the more affluent or dedicated supporters would forfeit a Saturday morning's wages. So regular visits to away matches were rare at first, except in the industrial north, where journeys between important clubs (particularly in Lancashire) were generally short. The railways were quick to exploit this potential for leisure travel, advertising cheap excursion fares in the local press and by handbills and posters. But cheap fares did not guarantee a full train when any distance was involved or the match itself was not attractive enough. Yet the Hull and Barnsley Railway continued to make a profit from football excursions, and the Great Central Railway offset the constraints of its lines and running costs with special trains over circuitous routes at extremely low fares.

While the railways enabled wealthy amateur clubs, such as Queen's Park from Glasgow, to travel long distances to fulfil a single fixture, travel time and cost were major constraints for many professional clubs. Although the first clubs in the Football League were from the north and the Midlands, Sunderland was excluded largely because some clubs would have found the travel costs too great, while Blackpool was unable to visit Arsenal in 1899 because the club had insufficient money for the rail fares. Yet the railways did provide top teams with the means of both fulfilling their regular fixtures and going on tour at Christmas and Easter to raise both their profile and much-needed funds.

The first FA Cup final at The Oval in 1872 attracted only 2,000 spectators. But although Blackburn Olympic ended the domination of southern and public school teams in 1883, and only two southern clubs reached the final in the next 30 years, the fact that the venue remained in the London area, moving to Crystal Palace, near Sydenham, in 1894, did not inhibit crowd growth. Northern supporters saved for months through thrift clubs to pay for their trip and the necessary food and drink, in the hope that a local club might reach the final. As most long-distance excursions ran into the London termini rather than to the station nearest the ground, considerable traffic was generated on local lines. In 1901, when over 110,000 spectators watched the Cup final, about half were carried to Crystal Palace by the London, Brighton and South Coast, and the South Eastern and Chatham Railways, which both had stations there.

In 1923 the venue was moved to Wembley, where a stadium had been built for the British Empire Exhibition. The Cup final in that year between Bolton Wanderers and West Ham United saw 126,847 through the turnstiles, with about another 100,000 gaining access by other means. The railways brought some 270,000 hopefuls in 145 special services, as well as regular long-distance and local trains. New and enlarged stations had been provided for the Exhibition, and these helped to deal with the crowds of would-be spectators who left early, and caused wholesale revision of both surface and underground train services.

International matches were equally well patronised. The Scotland v England game at Hampden Park in 1931 generated 218 special trains from all parts of the country, and the railways carried a large proportion of the 130,000 spectators. There was now a greater incidence of away supporters, with 22,000 Scots, in 41 trains provided by the London Midland and Scottish Railway alone, making the journey to Wembley in 1936; whereas for a similar fixture at Crystal Palace in 1897 only 1,000 in total, including the team and its officials, had travelled south. Interestingly, while fans were moving happily around the country at this time, players sometimes found their movements constrained. The FA banned Plymouth Argyle from flying players to a

match in October 1932 on safety grounds, while some clubs banned players from using motor cycles following a number of accidents.

The special station provided by the London and North Eastern Railway at Wembley Stadium was used for all major sporting events, including the 1948 Olympic Games and the 1966 World Cup, but was closed three years later. Manchester United, itself a team of railway origin founded by the Carriage and Wagon Works at Newton Heath in 1878, benefited from the availability of the nearby Cricket Ground station on the Manchester South Junction and Altrincham line, when the club moved to Old Trafford for the 1909/10 season. The Cheshire Lines Committee planned to provide a special station for use on match days, as its Trafford Park station was some distance from the ground, but this did not happen until 1935. Some stations have alternated between opening only on match days and supporting a regular passenger service. Ashton Gate, opened in September 1906 to serve the Bristol City ground, was still used for football specials in the late 1980s, after serving the general public between 1926 and 1964. Ninian Park Halt, on the other hand, became a public station in September 1987, after 75 years of use by Cardiff City. The Hawthorns Halt was opened on Christmas Day 1931 for West Bromwich Albion home games, and closed in April 1968, but in recent years public stations close to the ground have been provided both on a re-opened railway and on the Midland Metro. After the Second World War special stations were opened at Boothferry Park (for Hull City), Easter Road Park Halt (for Hibernian), and a special platform was provided at Ibrox (for Glasgow Rangers), but these are now closed. Wadsley Bridge was retained for Sheffield Wednesday home games for 25 years after the withdrawal of regular passenger services.

Although some larger clubs had begun to establish sizeable car parks from the 1930s, and car travel to away games became ever more common, it was not until the 1960s that the combined effects of private car ownership, comfortable coach travel and television outside broadcasts really made their impact on the football special. Even in 1957 a fourth-round FA Cup tie at non-League Peterborough needed 20 trains to carry supporters. The 1960s also saw the acceleration of railway line and station closures in the wake of the Beeching Report, which affected minor and local fixtures most severely and moved their players and supporters permanently to road transport. Moreover, the rise of the football hooligan, coupled with the need to maximise rolling stock utilisation, turned the railways against the football excursion, or 'Footex', which had been part of the soccer scene for so many years.

Nevertheless new football ground stations were opened at Watford (1982) and Derby (1990), although this was done as much to segregate supporters as to provide easy access. The latter, in particular, was little used, and is no longer required, as Derby County left the Baseball Ground for Pride Park at the end of the 1996/97 season, while the railway line serving Watford Stadium is now closed. Manchester United now boasts the only football ground station in regular use, although services to public stations close to other major grounds are still augmented on match days.

But the growth of the 'armchair supporter', either in front of the television set or in relative comfort in a reduced-capacity stadium, has taken its toll on the travelling supporter. As private cars and luxury coaches are now the preferred option, new stadia at Bolton, Huddersfield, Middlesbrough and Sunderland have moved away from the town centre for ease of access and ample parking. Some supporters, however, still use railways for both short- and long-distance travel, the latter group typified by Manchester United supporters travelling from the London area. These normally travel on regular service trains, as football excursions run only to Cup finals or other fixtures of particular interest. Moreover, in the last 30 years both the horizons of the fans and the money at their disposal have markedly increased, and many now follow their teams by sea, rail, road, and air into Europe and beyond.

Sources:
Biddle, G. and Simmons, J. (eds), *The Oxford Companion to British Railway History* (Oxford: Oxford University Press, 1997).
Croughton, G., Kidner, R. W. and Young, A., *Private and Untimetabled Railway Stations, Halts and Stopping Places* (Trowbridge: Oakwood Press, 1982).
Huggins, M. J. and Tolson, J. M., 'The Railways and Sport in Victorian Britain', *The Journal of Transport History* (forthcoming)
Jordan, A. and E., *Away for the Day* (Kettering: Silver Link Publishing Ltd, 1991).

Further Reading:
Mason, T., *Association Football and English Society 1863–1915* (Brighton: Harvester Press, 1980).
Vamplew, W., *Pay Up and Play the Game* (Cambridge: Cambridge University Press, 1988).

John Tolson

Turf Management

Turf management is the process of producing and maintaining a natural grass playing surface for soccer. The management of grass soccer pitches will relate to the standard of construction and drainage, the climate, the intensity of use (one or several games each week), as well as the nature of use (junior or senior football, amateur or professional, etc.).

Of key influence will be the nature of the construction profile, ranging from perhaps a heavy clay pitch with little or no drainage (where one could expect very wet, maybe waterlogged conditions during wet winter weather), to very free-draining constructions formed by the laying of an intensive pipe drainage system over which is placed a complete carpet of porous aggregate, and then a suitable depth of purpose-prepared very sandy soil. The latter type of construction is invariably encountered in the best pitches used for professional soccer. Given appropriate maintenance, a well-constructed pitch with good drainage should support a much higher standard of playing surface, as well as being able to withstand significantly more games. It is possible to upgrade pitches by various drainage techniques.

The groundsman (or woman) is a significant factor in turf management. Good ground-staff will have an understanding of drainage and turf-grass science, as well as the practical skills to use that knowledge in the production of the playing surface. The availability of adequate resources (labour, machinery and materials) will also be crucial in achieving successful turf management. While each pitch or site will have its own specific requirements, there are a number of fundamental aspects which will be relevant to every site and pitch. These are summarised below.

The turf surface on a football pitch is invariably dominated by perennial ryegrass – a hard-wearing grass species which is also quick to germinate and establish. The latter characteristics are essential for successful renovation during the close season. There are some excellent cultivars (cultivated varieties) of perennial ryegrass with good wear tolerance, general appearance and resistance to turf-grass diseases.

A good sward of perennial ryegrass forms a suitable playing surface for soccer if cut at 20–30 mm. Various types of mowing equipment may be employed, such as gang mowers or perhaps rotary cutters, but for the best finish a large cylinder-type mower with a facility to box-off the clippings will be required. Mowing height during the close season (after renovation) should be raised some 10–15 mm until the start of the following playing season.

Appropriate fertilising will be essential for optimum grass performance. Analysis of the soil on the pitch will help determine the most appropriate fertiliser programme, which will probably involve applying suitable amounts of the main plant foods – nitrogen, phosphorus, and potash. More fertilising will be required on free-draining sandy pitches.

Irrigation is also likely to be an important requirement on free-draining pitches (many clubs spend money improving drainage but ignore the fact that a free-draining surface will tend to dry out quite quickly, and often badly, during long dry spells in the summer). The availability of an adequate irrigation system is fundamental in such circumstances. The results of the end-of-season renovation works can be disappointing in a dry summer unless adequate irrigation resources are available. Such irrigation resources range from a few hydrant points with a hose-pipe and sprinkler to a more sophisticated automatic pop-up irrigation system.

Mechanical treatments, such as scarifying (to remove any accumulations of dead material at the base of the turf), and particularly aeration (to relieve compaction, improve surface drainage, and generally create better conditions for improved root growth), are also fundamental management operations. They must, however, relate to growing and ground conditions.

Applications of sand or very sandy soils will be very important at appropriate times to sustain smooth and, hopefully, firm, free-draining playing surfaces. The quality of materials has to be carefully considered – sand applied to football pitches has to be very specific, neither too coarse nor too fine. Expert advice may be necessary for this very important and essential aspect of management.

Blemishes in the turf playing surface, such as weeds, worm casts (which in excess lead to muddy surfaces), pests and diseases, may need control with suitable approved pesticides. Other blemishes as a consequence of play, such as scars and divots, should receive attention by means of regular repair work.

The availability of adequate labour, suitable equipment, and appropriate materials cannot be over-stressed, but unfortunately at the lower levels and leagues of football, financial constraints are invariably a limiting factor in securing adequate resources.

In recent years, new challenges have arisen in turf management on football pitches. The renovation of old large stadia, or the construction of new large stadia, with stands that create large areas of shade and affect air movement have resulted in environmental problems for good turf performance. In such situations, those involved in turf management would be well advised to seek specialist consultancy assistance. Indeed, some environments are so unfriendly for natural grass surfaces that the future of grass playing surfaces in such circumstances must be questioned. The availability of much improved artificial grass surfaces which now seem to mimic the playing characteristics of good natural turf may well be the way forward at sites with very difficult grass-growing conditions.

Sources:

Evans, R. D. C., *Winter Games Pitches* (Bingley: The Sports Turf Research Institute, 1994).

Baker, S. W., *Sands for Sports Turf Construction and Maintenance* (Bingley: The Sports Turf Research Institute, 1990).

Further Reading:

Adams, W. A. and Gibbs, R. J., *Natural Turf for Sport and Amenity: Science and Practice* (Wallingford: C. A. B. International, 1994).

Lawson, D. M., *Fertilisers for Turf* (Bingley: The Sports Turf Research Institute, 1995).

Jeff Perris

UEFA

The formation of the Union des Associations Européennes de Football (UEFA) in Basle (Switzerland) on 15 June 1954 was a result of the initiative of a number of progressively minded European football administrators, most notably Dr Ottorino Barassi, the President of the Italian Football Association, and his counterparts in the French and Belgian Associations, Henri Delauney and José Crahay. Barassi in particular went to great lengths to win support for the idea of a union of European football associations, and during the first half of 1952 he courted the support of a number of prominent football associations. In May 1952 a meeting was called in Zurich for all those interested in the formation of a European confederation, and subsequent meetings in Paris in 1952 and Helsinki the following year brought this idea to the verge of fruition. Amendments to FIFA's statutes in 1953 cleared the way for the creation of continental football confederations, and in the following year UEFA was formally constituted.

While the rationale underpinning the confederation's inception was rooted in the idea of fostering unity and solidarity among Europe's football associations, world football politics were also crucial to the formation of UEFA. In terms of the organisation of national associations, Europe was particularly fragmented prior to the 1950s. There had always been small, insular groupings within Europe such as the separate British, Scandinavian, and former Eastern bloc associations. However, leading figures in European football began to recognise and voice concerns that they were being politically outmanoeuvred at FIFA Congresses by the Latin Americans, who had formed a confederation in 1916 and were thus in a position to vote on key issues in a collective manner. The establishment of UEFA served to co-ordinate European football politically, and provided it with a collective voice within the world governing body, and this in turn allowed Europe to remain at the vanguard of world football.

With Europe's central place in the governance of the international game secured, at least for the time being, UEFA turned its attention to formulating a series of club competitions for its member associations. In 1955, UEFA acted on the initiative of Gabriel Hanot, editor of the Paris sports newspaper *L'Equipe,* and decided to establish a European Champion Clubs' Cup, the first edition of which was played during the 1955/56 season. The Inter-Cities Fairs Cup, the forerunner to today's UEFA Cup, was inaugurated in the same season, and two years later the European Nations' Cup got under way. The expansion of opportunities for inter-European club competition continued in 1961 with the inception of the European Cup Winners' Cup (now defunct), and 12 years later the UEFA Super Cup, involving the winners of the Champions' Cup and the Cup Winners' Cup, was added to UEFA's portfolio of senior competitions. At the same time as it was enhancing opportunities for top-level competition, UEFA also undertook a programme of institutional restructuring and statutory change which allowed it successfully to manage the rapid growth and development of European football.

For much of the 1970s and 1980s UEFA experienced steady development and consolidation. The club competitions were progressing smoothly, apart from the Heysel disaster of 1985, and the number of affiliated members rose gradually. However, a series of political upheavals in the former Eastern bloc during the late 1980s were to have serious ramifications for UEFA. The fragmentation of the former Soviet Union and the collapse of communism throughout Eastern Europe led to the birth of 16 new nations and the rapid growth in the number of UEFA affiliates. As a result of these developments the European confederation sought to ensure that the enlargement of its constituency was reflected concomitantly within FIFA, and this heralded a period of intense conflict between the two bodies. This conflict took the form of an acrimonious power struggle between João Havelange, former head of FIFA, and Lennart Johansson, the Swede who had succeeded Ebbe Schwartz (1954–62), Gustav Weiderkehr (1962–72), Artemio Franchi (1973–83) and Jacques George (1984–90) as president of UEFA. It was widely anticipated that Johansson would replace Havelange as FIFA president, but during the world body's 1998 congress he was defeated by Sepp Blatter following a bitter electoral contest.

Despite UEFA's failure to reclaim the FIFA presidency, the period of Johansson's leadership has been one of innovation and expansion. For example, the Champions' League replaced the Champions' Cup as the premier European club competition in 1992 and, in a move to counter the threat of the formation of a breakaway European super league and satisfy the requirements of the top European club sides, UEFA expanded the Champions' League for the 1999/2000 season. Other initiatives included the launch of the Intertoto Cup in 1995, the expansion of the UEFA Cup in 1999 following the abandonment of the Cup Winners' Cup, and for the first time 16 teams participated in the European Nations' Cup in 1996. Away from its competitions, UEFA continues to respond to the many challenges which have confront-

ed European football during the 1990s, such as the *Bosman* ruling which drastically altered the regulations governing the transfer of players to clubs within the European Union, and the increasing influence of television and business interests in the game.

Sources:

Rothenbühler, U. R., *25 Years of UEFA* (Berne: UEFA Publications, 1979)

Sugden, J. and Tomlinson, A., *FIFA and the Contest for World Football: Who Rules the Peoples' Game* (Cambridge: Polity Press, 1998).

Sugden, J., Tomlinson, A. and Darby, P., 'FIFA Versus UEFA in the Struggle for the Control of World Football', in A. Brown (ed.), *Fanatics! Power, Identity and Fandom in Football* (New York and London: Routledge, 1998), pp. 11–31.

See also European Champions' Cup

Paul Darby

Veterans

When the 40-year-old Scottish goalkeeper Jim Leighton announced his retirement from international football in 1998, the sports page headlines took the 'Veteran Keeper Calls it a Day' line. Leighton is by no means unique among goalkeepers in playing beyond the two-score landmark at international level, however: Peter Shilton (England) and Pat Jennings (Northern Ireland) both gained their last caps at the age of 40.

Shilton made his debut for Leicester City in 1966 as a 16-year-old and went on to play for Stoke City, Nottingham Forest (with whom he won European Cup medals in 1979 and 1980, a League Championship medal in 1978 and a League Cup medal in 1979), Southampton, and Derby County before becoming player–manager of Plymouth Argyle in 1992. Other clubs to benefit from his vast experience were Wimbledon, Bolton Wanderers, Coventry City, West Ham United and Leyton Orient. During a

30-year career he earned a record 125 England caps between 1970 and 1990, and made a phenomenal 1,380 senior appearances, including a record 996 Football League games. In recognition of his long service to the game he was awarded the MBE in 1986 and the OBE in 1990.

Jennings began his long career with his home-town club, Newry Town, before moving to Watford in 1963. In June 1964 he signed for Tottenham Hotspur, where he spent the next 13 seasons, making a club record 472 League appearances, before moving down the road to join north London rivals Arsenal in 1977. While with Spurs he won medals in the FA Cup (1967), League Cup (1971 and 1973), and UEFA Cup (1972). He was also voted Footballer of the Year in 1973. As if to prove that he had not left his best years behind him at White Hart Lane, he lifted another FA Cup medal with the Gunners in 1979. On the international front, he earned a record 119 caps for Northern Ireland between 1964 and his retirement after the 1986 World Cup. In all, his senior appearances totalled 1,098. Like Shilton, he was honoured with the MBE and OBE, in 1976 and 1987 respectively.

All three of the above players were carrying on a long goalkeeping tradition. In 1873 Alexander Morton made his one and only appearance as England custodian against Scotland at the age of 40 (or 42: records were not kept so meticulously in those days). Not quite so old was England's most venerable twentieth-century debutant: Arsenal centre-half Leslie Compton was 38 when he won his two caps in 1950. Welsh outside-right Billy Meredith won the first of his 48 caps in 1895, and continued to serve his country until his final appearance in March 1920, when, at the age of 45, he helped Wales to their first ever victory over England. He soldiered on for another four years with Manchester City and ended his career with a losing FA Cup semi-final appearance at St Andrews in 1924 against the eventual winners, Newcastle United. By then he was approaching his 50th birthday. Newcastle went on to win the Cup that season, beating Aston Villa 2–0 in the second Wembley final. Appearing at right-back for the Magpies was Billy Hampson, a relative youngster at 41.

There must be something about the outside-right position. In 1957, in a European qualifier against Denmark, the legendary Stanley Matthews won the last of his 54 caps (he also played in 29 wartime internationals) at the age of 41. Known to generations of fans as the 'Wizard of Dribble', Matthews had joined Stoke City after leaving school in 1928 at the age of 14, making his League debut as a 17-year-old during the 1931/32 season. The following season Stoke won promotion to the First Division of the Football League and the young winger was in the England team. He left the Potteries club in 1947 and spent the next 14 years at Blackpool, with whom he made three FA Cup final appearances. Blackpool lost at Wembley in 1948 and 1951, but Stan finally won his cherished winner's medal in 1953 after an epic 4–3 win over Bolton Wanderers in what, despite Stan Mortensen's hat-trick, will always be known as the 'Matthews' Final'. In 1961 Matthews returned to Stoke and won another Second Division medal in 1963, an incredible 30 years after his first. He finally retired at the end of the 1964/65 season, his last League match being a First Division game against Fulham on 6 February 1965, five days after his 50th birthday. A crowd of almost 30,000 at the Victoria Ground saw the maestro set up the third goal in a 3–1 victory for the home side. It was his 886th senior appearance. He won the first ever Football Writers' Player of the Year award in 1948, and won it again in 1963. He also became the first European Footballer of the Year in 1956. His career was crowned in 1965 when he became the first professional footballer to be knighted.

Although Sir Stan holds the record as the oldest player to appear in the First Division, the Football League longevity record is held by New Brighton manager Neil McBain, who was forced to pick himself in a Third Division (North) match against Hartlepool United in 1947, at the age of 52.

If the modern game cannot boast any semi-centenarians, there are still examples of players in the top flight performing past the mid-point of their allotted three score years and ten. As the 1999/2000 season drew to a close, the Premiership could boast yet another 40-plus goalkeeper in ex-Welsh international Neville Southall of Bradford City, aged 41. Other veterans turning out for the Yorkshire club were Dean Saunders and Stuart McCall, both aged 35. Sunderland's early-season form had dipped after an injury to 37-year-old defender Steve Bould, while Bould's former club, Arsenal, continued to field such old hands as David Seaman, Nigel Winterburn and Lee Dixon, all 36. Everton had Mark Hughes, also 36, still chasing goals, with central defender Richard Gough, a year older, behind him. Other 35-year-olds included Alec Chamberlain, still keeping them out for Watford, and Robbie Earle, knocking them in for Wimbledon. In the Scottish Premier League, Jim Leighton was still around, helping Aberdeen in their fight against relegation.

All these players, however, would have been considered mere boys by Fred Rosner, who in 1995 was thought to be by far the oldest regular player in Britain. Aged 71, he was still appearing on the left wing for Downham FC, the amateur team he founded in 1948, in Division Four of the Hackney and Leyton League. Fred must also hold the record for being the oldest player to have been sent off, receiving his marching orders at the age of 68 from a lady referee.

Who said it was a young man's game?

Sources:

Kelly, S. F., *Back Page Football: A Century of Newspaper Coverage* (Harpenden: Aurora Publishing, 1995).

Lamming, D., *An English Football Internationalists' Who's Who* (Beverley: Houghton Press, 1990).

Matthews, P. and Buchanan, I., *All-Time Greats of British and Irish Sport* (Enfield: Guinness, 1995).

Pickering, D., *Cassell Soccer Companion* (London: Cassell, 1997).

Rollin, J., *Guinness Soccer Records, Facts and Champions* (Enfield: Guinness, 1988).

Further Reading:

Barrett, N., *Daily Telegraph Football Chronicle* (London: Carlton, 1995).

Freddi, C., *England Football Fact Book* (Enfield: Guinness, 1991).

Tony Rennick

Violence

Only a month into the 1999/2000 season, Premiership sendings-off had risen by 52 per cent compared to the previous season, mainly due to violent actions on the pitch. Media pundits castigated both referees and players; managers blamed their opponents and referees; and the match officials argued that players should learn to play within the rules. Gordon Taylor, Chief Executive of the Professional Footballers' Association, suggested that a sin-bin should be introduced to allow players to calm down and prevent indiscipline spiralling the game out of control. Yet violence in football is nothing new. The mayhem of folk football was often a time to settle old scores. Even when the game became codified, violence continued. In 1891 Blackburn Rovers players walked off during a match against local rivals Burnley after experiencing too many violent incidents, including a couple of fights. Sometimes, though much more rarely than incidents involving the opposition, violence occurs between players on the same side. In 1979 Derek Hales and his Charlton team-mate, Mike Flanagan, were sent off for fighting each other, and in 1995 Graham Le Saux and David Batty had a spat when playing in a demoralised Blackburn team.

Without doubt some players are thugs both on and off the field. Others – though not excluding the thugs – are enforcers: hard men whose task it is to intimidate the opposition. These men will go as far as the match officials will permit – and sometimes beyond if the end would justify the means. Yet probably most violence is not premeditated; rather, it is the product of a heat-of-the-moment adrenalin rush, when a key decision has gone against a team, when an opponent is perceived to have committed an offence, or as a response to barracking from the crowd.

Whoever the offender and whatever their motivation, on-field violence has to be punished. The question at issue is: by whom? Acts of violence, like other rule transgressions, are dealt with firstly by the referee officiating in the match, and, secondly, by the football authorities, either at local or regional association level, or, for Football League and Premier League players, by the FA and its equivalent in the other home nations. Frequent offenders can anticipate being suspended for a few matches and ultimately, at the lower echelons of the game, being banned for a season or even *sine die*. In the professional game fears of legal challenge have militated against such draconian sentencing. However, at the higher level leading clubs have been fined by the football authorities for the behaviour of their players. In 1990 both Arsenal and Manchester United had to pay £50,000 following a 21-man brawl, and five Arsenal players and their manager were fined. Arsenal were also deducted two points and Manchester one, a policy which many believe may be more effective than fines.

Much football violence is not only against the rules of sport, it also breaks the law of the land. Many players, and indeed most football fans, do not see violence on the field in the same light as an assault in the street. Partly this is because, historically, the sport has enjoyed immunity from prosecution where the rules of the game have sanctioned certain activities. Those playing football have, in effect, agreed to accept the risks of hard tackles, and the law has concurred, or at least turned a blind eye. Yet players do not consent to being punched or head-butted on the football field: these actions are illegitimate in sport and illegal in law. While most sports associations would prefer to handle these matters themselves, without the intervention of the courts, in Scotland at least, there has been less reluctance to act, as when Rangers player Duncan Ferguson was jailed for three months for head-butting a Raith Rovers opponent in 1994. Ferguson had been on probation for an off-field assault at the time. Earlier, in 1987, a clash between players in an 'Old Firm' derby in Glasgow led to legal action being taken against four of them, even though not all of them had been sent off by the referee. Two were eventually fined.

Although there is an economic argument against football violence, the available evidence suggests that the proportion of football injuries attributable to violent play is very small. Nevertheless, those individuals who are hospitalised or incapacitated by foul play certainly suffer economic disadvantage. Football is hazardous enough without adding to the risks by tolerating violent on-field behaviour. The main stance against sports violence is a moral one. Its proponents argue that the use of violence to secure an advantage is cheating: allowing the result to be determined by brutality rather than skill undermines the basic principles of fair play. Hopefully the 'fair play' campaigns instigated by FIFA and other ruling bodies may have an effect.

The media focus on violence in elite football, but there is no doubt that it is prevalent at all levels of the game. Many people are to blame for this. They include those coaches whose careers depend – or whose egos thrive – on the right result, and so instruct their players to take out opponents; selectors who continue to choose known enforcers in their teams; match officials who allow verbal and physical abuse to go on unchecked; and administrators who pay only lip service to the enforcement of codes of conduct. Ultimately, however, players must take responsibility for their own actions. Their challenge is to play football within the rules. Football violence, like most forms of violence, is generally learned behaviour and as such should be susceptible to modification. Physical hardness need not be removed from the game, but illegitimate violence should be eliminated. The club is the basic reference point for most players and it is here that an environment conducive to fair play can be engendered. If this does not occur then it is likely that a stricter interpretation of the law could lead to more players being charged with criminal assault; injured footballers, more aware of their legal rights than in the past, increasingly might sue not only their violent opponents, but also match officials and even selectors for failing in their duty of care.

Any discussion of player violence is of course bedevilled by problems of definition. One is whether verbal abuse, particularly racial, should be classed as player violence; another is the grey area between legitimate aggression and illegitimate assault as denoted by the rules of the game and the perceived motivation of the transgressor. The fans and manager of one side rarely share their opponents' views on violence committed by each other's players. Ultimately the match officials must decide, though there is a growing feeling that post-game videos should be utilised so that the violent player has nowhere to hide.

Source:
Williams, R., *Football Babylon* (London: Virgin, 1996).

See also Discipline and Punishment

Wray Vamplew

History Highlights 1970–1979

In British domestic football, the 1970s undoubtedly belonged to two teams. In Scotland, Celtic were the team of the decade, winning seven league championships and finishing runners-up on one occasion. In England, Liverpool, while not as dominant as Celtic, reigned supreme, winning the English League Championship four times, and finishing runners-up on two occasions. Both teams owed much of their success to those who managed them. Jock Stein guided Celtic for 13 years, prior to his sacking in 1978, and in that period won ten League Championships (including nine consecutive titles), eight Scottish Cups and six Scottish League Cups. Bill Shankly's reign between 1959 and 1974, brought Liverpool three League Championships and two FA Cups. For the remainder of the

1970s the club was led by Bob Paisley, who secured the club a further three League Championships during that decade. Other notable domestic teams of the 1970s include Arsenal, who in 1971 became the first team to win the League and FA Cup double since Tottenham ten years earlier; Leeds United, who under the leadership of Don Revie won the League Championship courtesy of a 29-game unbeaten run in 1973/74; and Nottingham Forest who won the League Championship and the League Cup in 1978, and the League Cup again the following year.

The strength of British club football in the 1970s was reflected in the number of European trophies that teams won in that decade. Between 1970 and 1979, British clubs won a total of 11 European competitions including three European Cups, three Cup Winners' Cups, and five Fairs/UEFA Cups. Liverpool alone accounted for four of these successes, winning the UEFA Cup in 1973 and 1976, the European Cup in 1977 and 1978, and the European Super Cup in 1977.

The success of British, and especially English, clubs in Europe in the 1970s afforded those clubs the unfortunate opportunity of exporting their growing supporter hooligan problems to the international stage. In the 1973/74 season, Tottenham Hotspur fans were involved in rioting in Rotterdam during and after the UEFA Cup final second leg against Feyenoord. The fighting led to 70 arrests and over 200 injuries. In 1975, Leeds United fans rioted as their club lost the European Cup final to Bayern Munich in Paris. This time, with disturbances involving English clubs in Europe becoming all too common, UEFA banned Leeds from all European competitions for four years.

The most unfortunate incident involving British football supporters in the 1970s was not an act of hooliganism, but rather the tragedy that befell Rangers and Celtic supporters at Ibrox stadium on 2 January 1971. A crush on a stairwell after the traditional New Year game between the two teams led to the death of 66 people and injuries to 200 others. This was the second major tragedy to hit the Ibrox stadium in the twentieth century, but despite the usual reports and calls for greater ground safety that followed the disaster, not enough was done to save the lives of the people who were to die at football matches in Britain in the 1980s.

The success of British club football in the 1970s was not reflected by the home nations' records at full international level. With the exception of their strong showing in the World Cup of 1970, England's record in international football during the 1970s was woeful. They failed to qualify for the World Cup in both 1974 and 1978, ending Alf Ramsey's successful reign as England manager on the first occasion and, albeit less directly, Don Revie's rather less successful tenure on the second. Scotland did qualify for the finals in 1974 and 1978, but having achieved what England could not, they failed to make it to the second round on both occasions. This was particularly unfortunate in 1974 as the Scots did not lose a game during the tournament, and achieved a creditable 0–0 draw with Brazil.

Returning to domestic football, at least two further events of note occurred during the 1970s. Firstly, Trevor Francis became the first player to be transferred between two British clubs for over £1 million, when he left Birmingham City for Nottingham Forest in 1979. Secondly, Laurie Cunningham became the first black footballer to represent England at any level when he was named in the under-21 squad in 1977. This was quickly followed by Viv Anderson's inclusion in the full squad in 1978. The emergence of players such as Cunningham and Anderson represented a significant step forward for black players in English football, but was unfortunately accompanied by a level of racism which continues to blight British football to this day.

Sources:

Nawrat, C. and Hutchings, S., *The Sunday Times Illustrated History of Football* (St Helens: The Book People Ltd, 1998).

Russell, D., *Football and the English: A Social History of Association Football in England, 1863–1995* (Preston: Carnegie Publishing, 1997).

Walvin, J., *The People's Game: The History of Football Revisited* (Edinburgh: Mainstream Publishing, 1994).

Gavin Mellor

Wages

Although relating only to a player's basic weekly remuneration, the 'wage' has often been used a catch-all term to refer to all aspects of a professional's earnings. Since the legalisation of professionalism in 1885, and even before this, pay has been one of football's most discussed and controversial issues. This can be explained, in part at least, by the secrecy associated with the subject. Like most businesses, football clubs have been loath to disclose to outsiders details of their financial dealings with employees.

In the late 1880s and early 1890s, levels and methods of payment varied considerably. Whether paid by the match, by the week or according to short-term arrangements embracing a series of games, few of the first football professionals, many of whom were part-time, seem to have collected more than £2 a week including bonuses. The Scot Nick Ross received £10 a month on signing for Everton in 1888, but he was probably the best paid footballer of his day. By the mid-1890s leading clubs like Aston Villa, Newcastle and Sunderland were paying their best players £3 or £4 per week, while the Liverpool players who won the First Division championship in the 1900/01 season were on £7, which with bonuses could reach £10 a week.

Introduced in time for the 1901/02 season, the maximum wage led to an overall levelling of pay. At many First Division clubs the maximum of £4 per week soon became standard, although it was often restricted to the first team. By 1910 the FA could report that 573 of an estimated total of 6,800, mostly Football League and southern professionals, were receiving the maximum.

In 1920 the wage structure was reformed. Wages were thereafter regulated according to a sliding scale, ranging from a maximum of £5 per week for 'new' players with annual rises of £1 weekly over four years, to a final ceiling of £9 per week. Two years later the maximum was reduced to £8 during the 37-week playing season and £6 in the remaining 15 weeks of the close season. The sliding scale was retained, but clubs could also increase the wages of those players picked for the first team and reduce those of players dropped through loss of form. This led many clubs to adopt a type of incentive scheme, in which the best players were guaranteed a weekly wage of just £6, with £2 extra providing they kept their first team place.

Pressure from the players' union led the wage limit to be pushed gradually upwards after the Second World War, from £10 in 1946 to £15 in 1951 and £20 in 1958, with a stipulated minimum introduced in 1947. But even the best footballers were earning comparatively less than they had between the wars. Whereas in 1939 the footballers' £8 was approximately double the average industrial wage, by 1960 the gap had narrowed to £5 with those figures standing at £20 and £15 respectively.

Even without a maximum wage, earnings tended to be no greater in Scotland. Celtic and Rangers were generally the only clubs who could afford to pay sums equivalent to the maximum in England, although Aberdeen did lead the pay scale in the late 1940s and early 1950s with £14 a week. Wage differentials, however, were much larger. Whereas the Celtic captain Billy McNeil was reputedly earning £15,000 per year in the 1970s, full-time players in the lower divisions could be retained for as little as £624 a year.

In England, the abolition of the maximum wage in 1961 had a profound effect on wage levels. Fulham's England captain Johnny Haynes saw his wages treble overnight when he became the first £100-per-week player, but for others the change was less immediate. A number of major clubs such as Liverpool and Manchester United attempted to enforce unofficial wage ceilings, the latter paying its players just £50 a week as late as 1965/66. More significant perhaps were the increasing dif-

ferentials between the star players and the rest of the profession. The average annual earnings of First Division footballers rose from £1,173 in 1960 to £2,680 by 1964, representing a 56 per cent increase, but in the Third and Fourth Divisions the figure was less than 30 per cent.

For the best players, the last two decades have brought unprecedented rewards. By the mid-1990s, salaries for a handful of players at the leading Premier League clubs had risen to £10,000 and even £15,000 a week. Recent contracts to secure the services of Roy Keane, David Beckham and Michael Owen in the twenty-first century are reputed to offer in excess of £50,000 per week. Earnings have been good but less impressive lower down the scale, with salaries and lifestyles equivalent to those of middle-class professionals rather than film and music stars.

Sources:

Crampsey, B., *The Scottish Footballer* (Edinburgh: William Blackwood, 1978).

Mason, T., *Association Football and English Society, 1863–1915* (Brighton: Harvester, 1980).

Russell, D., *Football and the English: A Social History of Association Football in England, 1863–1995* (Preston: Carnegie Press, 1997).

Vamplew, W., 'Playing for Pay: The Earnings of Professional Sportsmen in England 1870–1914', in R. Cashman and M. McKernan (eds), *Sport: Money, Morality and the Media* (Brisbane: New South Wales University Press, 1979), 104–30.

See also Professional Footballers' Association

Matt Taylor

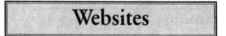

Websites

One of the more unexpected events of the 1990s was the remarkably rapid growth in usage of the Internet, and particularly the World Wide Web (usually abbreviated to WWW or just the Web). Initially developed in 1990 for the communication of scientific information between European physicists, the Web was quickly adopted by people and organisations from almost every aspect of society, including football.

In the simplest terms, the Web allows documents called pages stored on one computer to be distributed on request and viewed on any other computer connected to the Internet. Pages can contain text, multimedia elements such as graphics, photographs, sound and video, and even interactive computer programs. Perhaps most importantly, pages can also contain links to related information on other pages. A collection of pages on a particular subject, created and maintained by the same individual or organisation, is known as a website.

There are three main categories of website devoted to the topic of football. The first are those created by fans; second are the official websites run by clubs, players or administrative bodies; and finally there are sites run by organisations or businesses which are not directly involved in the sport, such as the media sites, created either by traditional media organisations such as newspapers and television broadcasters, or by more recent online media companies.

The fan sites were probably the first to come into existence, as much of the initial growth of the Web was due to personal pages created by people with access to the Internet, particularly those within academic or research institutions. Fan sites can be seen as the electronic equivalent of fanzines, allowing their creator to voice his or her opinion about the team, positive or negative. The main difference is that the website has a potential audience across the entire globe. Many fan sites also provide features such as message boards or chat rooms, which allow other fans of the club from around the world to discuss the team.

Occasionally these sites have been used to campaign actively on issues affecting the sport. For example, from 1995 to 1997 Brighton and Hove Albion supporters used the Web to protest about the decision to sell the club's ground (http://www.mistral.co.uk/timc/saveclub.htm).

Over the last few years, the majority of clubs have established official websites. As would be expected, official club and organisation websites are professionally run, and provide a wider range of features than the majority of fan sites. At their most basic, team websites offer an avenue of communication to the club's supporters similar to that provided by match programmes, but with added functionality such as video highlights of match footage. They are also increasingly being used to augment the commercial activities of the club, with most now offering online sales of team merchandise. These electronic commerce facilities extend the sales of the team shop to a worldwide audience, which is a huge potential source of revenue, particularly for teams with an international fan-base.

One indication of the perceived value of these sites is the fact that football club names have been targeted for 'cyber-squatting'. This practice involves registering a site name which is similar to that of a well-known company or brand, with the intention of later selling the rights to that name. For example, the official Manchester United site is at http://www.manutd.com, while the very similar http://www.manunited.com has been registered by a company which trades in domain names.

The explosion of football websites has also raised concern among some clubs that they might be missing out on a lucrative photography market. Images of footballers abound on the internet, but currently clubs receive nothing for such photographic rights. Although newspaper and picture agency photographers are licensed by the Premier League photography committee, there are no restrictions on fans taking their own pictures, because until now this has not been seen as a problem. However, with digital cameras becoming smaller and cheaper, it will become easier for unauthorised photographers to take good quality pictures from the stands and then distribute them over the net.

Interestingly, British football's administrative bodies were slower than the clubs to embrace Web technology as part of their operations, perhaps because there is less financial incentive to motivate such action. In late 1999, only two of the five national bodies had active websites (the Scottish Football Association at http://www.scottishfa.co.uk, and the Football Association of Ireland at http://www.fai.ie). The FA's site (http://www.the-FA.org) consisted only of a title page, the Welsh Football Association's site (http://www.faw.co.uk) failed to load and the UEFA website (http://www.uefa.org) did not list any site for the Irish Football Association. However, there has been drastic improvement in the past three years, particularly in the FA's site. The league bodies have been more active in establishing Web presences – the English Premier League (http://www.fa-premier.com), the Football League (http://www.football-league.co.uk/) and the Scottish Premier League (http://www.scot-prem.com) have all established official sites. These sites offer information about the organisation and affiliated bodies, and in some cases also provide electronic commerce facilities and access to travel details for international matches.

The League Managers Association website (http://www.leaguemanagers.co.uk/index.asp) provides press releases and contact information for the LMA, as well as providing details for all current managers, as well as CVs for managers who are currently not employed. Similarly, some player agents have used the Web to advertise the availability of their clients.

A recent trend has been the establishment of official sites devoted to individual players. As with team sites, these player sites are often used to promote and sell merchandise such as autographed memorabilia and autobiographies. Other common features include statistics and online diaries. Many of these player sites are run as subsections of more general sport-related sites, using the player's name as a means of attracting Internet users.

The football websites run by media outlets are for the most part an extension of traditional media organisations such as newspapers, magazines, television and radio stations. Much of the information on these sites is reproduced from these sources, with the main bonus to the user being the ability to access archived material such as results and match reports from earlier in the season. These sites are also often used to provide interactive competitions, such as fantasy football contests or online versions of the traditional 'spot the ball' game. As with more traditional media these sites are largely dependent on advertising to provide their revenue, often providing links to online suppliers of sporting equipment or memorabilia.

One use of the Web which has increased very rapidly and drawn large amounts of attention over the last few years is that of online gambling. Many of the sites are based in countries with liberal gambling laws, and accept wagers from international customers. While some focus on acting as online casinos, many accept bets on a wide range of sporting events, including British football. Over recent seasons there have been several incidents, such as bribery allegations and floodlight tampering, which have been traced back to overseas gambling on British games, and it is possible that increases in online gambling may lead to further such incidents in the future.

Websites are by nature more transient than other forms of media such as printed publications, while the Web itself is still in its infancy, and so many of the facts stated above will undoubtedly change over the next few years.

Peter Vamplew

Welsh Football

Throughout its history, football in Wales has struggled against the popularity of rugby union, financial constraints, divisions between north and south and perceptions that there was something un-Welsh about the sport. There is little that is actually distinct about Welsh football, and it is intimately linked to the game in England, but throughout its history its players, fans and administrators have all shared a pride in Wales.

Football emerged in Wales in the late nineteenth century and its early history owed much to the immigration of workers and industrialists from England, where the game was already established. It was in industrial north-east Wales in the 1870s that the sport first took hold. Small clubs and local competitions were established and by the late 1880s the region's more talented players were already moving into the English Football League. The most notable of such players was former miner Billy Meredith, widely regarded as the finest player in late-Victorian and Edwardian Britain.

In south Wales, small amateur teams existed in the late nineteenth century, but the sport was overshadowed by the more popular rugby union. Small semi-professional soccer clubs developed in the years immediately after the turn of the century, but it was not until just before the First World War that the senior game firmly established itself in the south. Professional clubs were formed in all the region's major urban centres and these teams soon graduated into the FA Cup and English Southern League. This growth continued into the inter-war period, with attendances swelling and the largest clubs joining the expanded Football League; there were six Welsh clubs in the League in the early 1920s. Cardiff City quickly became established as a leading First Division side, and won the FA Cup in 1927 amid wide acclaim across Wales. The mass unemployment of the inter-war depression brought such success to an end as gates plummeted. Consequently, many clubs went bankrupt, including Aberdare Athletic and Merthyr Town, both briefly members of the Football League.

Cardiff City's 1920s success was not repeated by any Welsh club in the post-war period. Cardiff and Swansea City both enjoyed brief flurries in the First Division and European competition but, for all Welsh clubs, the years after 1945 were characterised by financial problems and inconsistency. Newport County went bankrupt in 1989, leaving Cardiff, Swansea and Wrexham as the only Welsh teams in the Football League. All three remain firmly committed to competing in the English competition despite concern at this anomaly within the Football Association of Wales and UEFA. Worries about the future independence of Wales as a soc-

cer nation led to the formation of the League of Wales in 1992. However, consisting only of small semi-professional clubs, the League has failed to win credibility among many Welsh fans and, with only minimal financial rewards on offer, it seems unlikely that the leading Welsh clubs will ever join.

The national team enjoyed a period of success in the 1930s and qualified for the 1958 World Cup, but its dominant record has been one of failure. Wales has produced the occasional world-class player, such as John Charles and Ryan Giggs. However, when representing their country they have tended to be surrounded by a succession of journeymen. With the exception of the 1920s, domestic Welsh football has not been able to offer the wages or glory that English clubs could, and thus Wales' most talented players have plied their trade outside her borders. Similarly, Welsh professional clubs have employed strong contingents of English players. This has all contributed to a wide perception of football as 'not really a Welsh institution'.

Yet in north Wales the popularity of soccer continues to marginalise rugby. Wales is a divided nation, and the north has long since moved towards the economic and cultural rhythms of Merseyside, rather than those of the south of the principality. Football's popularity there owes much to such influences. It is also indicative of the fragility of any notion of a united Wales, and the domination of Welsh identity by the south.

Since the eve of the First World War, football across Wales has had more amateur players than rugby, and its senior clubs have enjoyed similar sized crowds. Yet its failure to enjoy any sustained success has left the game overshadowed by rugby union, whose repeated achievements have made the sport a central aspect of Welsh national identity. Thus, the popularity of football and its infusion with a national pride has not been enough on its own to represent the game as a Welsh sport. However, national identity is malleable and subject to reconstruction according to circumstance. Any sustained future success could easily transform the image of Welsh football.

Sources:

Corrigan, P., *A Hundred Years of Welsh Soccer* (Cardiff: Welsh Brewers, 1976).

Johnes, M., *That Other Game: A Social History of Soccer in South Wales, c. 1906–39*, Ph.D. thesis, University of Wales, Cardiff, 1998.

Johnes, M. 'Irredeemably English? Football in Wales', *Planet: The Welsh Internationalist*, 133 (February/March 1999), 72–8.

Morgan, K. O., *Rebirth of a Nation: Wales, 1880–1980* (Cardiff & Oxford: University of Wales Press & Oxford University Press, 1981).

Williams, G., *1905 and All That: Essays on Rugby Football, Sport and Welsh Society* (Llandysul: Gomer, 1991).

Further Reading:

Richards, H. and Stead, P. (eds), *In Association: The Character of Welsh Soccer* (Cardiff: University of Wales Press, 2000).

Smith, D. and Williams, G., *Fields of Praise: The Official History of the Welsh Rugby Union, 1881–1981* (Cardiff: University of Wales Press, 1980).

See also Welsh Football Association

Martin Johnes

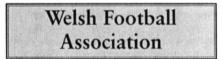

Welsh Football Association

The Football Association of Wales (FAW) is football's governing body in Wales. It was formed in 1876 by a solicitor, Llewelyn Kenrick, following an exchange of ideas in a London-based sporting paper. Its initial *raison d'être* was to select a team to accept Scotland's invitation to play an international match. That game went ahead in March 1876, thus making Wales the world's third oldest international team. Yet the FAW's history has been one of combating financial problems, the dominance of the English game, and the north–south rivalries within Wales. It is a national association that governs a football territory whose boundaries are neither clear nor self-sufficient. This is a reflection of Wales' tenuous position as a nation within the wider British state.

Inspired by the success of the FA Cup,

in 1877 the FAW ran the inaugural Welsh Cup competition. The trophy was intended to raise the standard of play and organisation of football in Wales, in the interests of which English border clubs were invited to participate. The prominent north–south divide within Wales meant that the association did not set up a national league. By the twentieth century Wales' senior clubs were competing in English league competitions, thus reducing the importance of the lower-standard and less glamorous Welsh Cup. The allocation of a place in the European Cup Winners' Cup from 1960 did boost interest in the competition, but it has remained secondary in the priorities of Wales' leading clubs.

The FAW is financially reliant on the proceeds of international matches. A lack of success on the pitch, Wales' unstable economy, and a recurring inability to pick its star players, have all meant that the Association has struggled to achieve financial security. In more recent years this has been compounded by a failure to take full advantage of the new commercial and television opportunities that the wider game has enjoyed. On occasions financial problems have led the FAW to stage Wales' home matches in English stadia, where capacities were larger than at domestic grounds.

The FAW's inability always to pick the best players for the national side is rooted in the Welsh game's subservience to English football. As a foreign association, the FAW had no powers to demand that players employed outside Wales be released for its international games. With Wales' best players traditionally employed by English clubs, its national team has been reliant on the willingness of clubs to release players. This has caused recurring tensions as the Football League and its clubs have tried to impose their authority over the national associations. Today, even with FIFA regulations demanding that players be released for competitive internationals, the increasingly mobile football labour market means that the FAW is far from unique in experiencing such problems.

Many of the FAW's members have also always been affiliated to the FA, thus creating an uncertainty over the association's responsibilities and powers. Its unwillingness and inability to assert its independence were illustrated when it followed the FA out of FIFA in 1919 and 1928, only to rejoin when its English counterparts did. Before the Second World War, like Wales as a whole, the FAW's ambitions for recognition were firmly within a British context. Its first international against opponents outside Britain was not until 1933, in a match against France. The development of the world game has brought the FAW onto a wider stage, but representing a small, stateless nation, it has failed to make much impact on or off the pitch.

The FAW's internal relationships were no easier, due to a history of tension between members from north and south. Before the Second World War it did not even have complete control over football in the whole nation. The South Wales and Monmouthshire FA (founded in 1893) essentially acted as an independent association for all purposes except the national team. Although the south was represented on the FAW, the north effectively retained control of its decision-making council until the 1970s. The location of home internationals was the most common source of tension until 1989, when it was decided to hold all home games in the National Stadium at rugby's Cardiff Arms Park. When in 1985 the FAW moved its headquarters from Wrexham in the north to the capital Cardiff, the balance of power shifted firmly to the south.

By the 1980s there was concern within the FAW that its very existence was under threat. The UK's four independent associations within a single state were a unique result of football's British origins. As pressure grew from non-European associations for a greater say in the running of football, Britain's special position became vulnerable. The case for Wales as a football nation was particularly weak in foreign eyes, given the absence of any national league. Thus the FAW founded the League of Wales in 1992 to try and ensure its very future. Over 100 years after the formation of its national association, Wales finally became a football nation with its own national League.

Yet, despite the entry to European competitions that the League offered, Welsh clubs playing in England were less than enthusiastic about its prospects, and a prolonged battle with the association ensued. This ended up in the High Court, and resulted in defeat for the FAW's attempt to coerce clubs to join the League of Wales. The League and the FAW emerged with their credibility and finances damaged, and Wales' best teams and players continue to play outside the immediate jurisdiction of their national association.

In recent years the FAW has struggled to establish its credibility with Welsh fans. Its choice of national manager, the weaknesses of its national League, and its unmeritocratic committee structure, have left the association vulnerable to public criticism. As football in the twenty-first century becomes increasingly dominated by commercial concerns and a handful of influential nations and clubs, the future looks no easier for the FAW at home or abroad.

Sources:

Corrigan, P., *A Hundred Years of Welsh Soccer* (Cardiff: Welsh Brewers, 1976).

Evans, A., *Football on the Edge: The Relationship Between Welsh Football Policy-Making and the British International Championship*, MA dissertation, De Montfort University, 1996.

Johnes, M., 'That Other Game: A Social History of Soccer in South Wales, c. 1906–39', Ph.D. thesis, University of Wales, Cardiff, 1998.

Further Reading:

Garland, I., *The History of the Welsh Cup, 1877–1993* (Wrexham: Bridge, 1993).

Lerry, G. G., *The Football Association of Wales: 75th Anniversary, 1876–1951* (Wrexham: FAW, 1952).

See also Welsh Football

Martin Johnes

Women and Football

In Britain today approximately two million girls play football in school and, in 1999, the English women's team was ranked eighth in the world, above Brazil. However, the journey towards this has been long and complex. The women's game has shifted between periods of great popularity, such as that which existed during and immediately after the First World War, and much bleaker times, typified by the years between the 1930s and 1950s.

Some of the earliest recordings of women's football can be traced back to the Highland region of Scotland during the eighteenth century, where the sport manifested itself as a form of folk football that

Drawing by A.S. Boyd of women's football, 1890s (National Football Museum)

Miss Nettie Honeyball, captain of the British Ladies' Football Club, in her football costume.
(From a photograph by Russell and Sons, Baker Street)

sporting phenomenon, but a novel aspect within a formative process extending women's access to sport.

During this period, the more progressive girls' schools, physical education colleges and universities began to develop forms of 'rationalised sport' for women. They advocated 'rough sports' for girls such as lacrosse, hockey and in more extreme instances football. However, these schools did not represent the dominant consensus on women's physical culture, which advocated clear distinctions between gender roles in sporting activity. In 1894 the *British Medical Journal* published an article condemning women who played football and stating that, 'We can in no way sanction the reckless exposure to violence, of organs which the common experience of women had led them in every way to protect.' Nevertheless, despite the dominant stance on sport for women and girls, ladies' football continued with quiet persistence up to the First World War, attracting little in the way of formal opposition, although much ridicule. The term 'ladies' football', with its connotation of a certain gentility and restraint, remained the preferred label for the game until the 1980s when, in a very different cultural climate, 'women's football' became the norm. Interestingly, however, some contemporary sides still retain 'Ladies' in their club name.

The First World War was to be a watershed in the lives of many women, suddenly thrown into roles that society had previously denied to them. Women were expected to enter male spheres in the workplace as part of the war effort, and for many this resulted in munitions work: by May 1918, there were over one million women working in this industry alone. This huge number of women and girls displaced from their home environments was the cause of major concern to the government and local authorities, who feared it would result in social problems. The response manifested itself in forms of social control, of which rational recreation was one element. Organisations such as the Young Women's Christian Association, Church Army, Girl's Friendly Society, National Union of Women Workers and

was also linked to local marriage customs. Single women would play married women, whilst prospective husbands watched and chose suitable brides from the singles side. The extent of this custom or its existence elsewhere is unknown. It was the latter end of the nineteenth century before formally organised matches were played. The first official match was played at Crouch End Athletic in north London on 23 March 1895, between teams of middle- and upper-class schoolgirls. It was organised by Nettie Honeyball, the Secretary of the British Ladies' Football Club, who promoted the game as a 'manly game that could be womanly as well'. The club president was Lady Florence Dixie, the youngest daughter of the Marquis of Queensbury, who acted as the first woman war correspondent during the Boer War. Florence Dixie was instrumental in organising the game in Scotland, setting up exhibition matches for charity. Honeyball and Dixie's work was not an isolated others organised 'girls' clubs' to entertain the munitions workers in their leisure time, and to act as counter-attractions to the public house. Sporting activities, including football, took their place in this process, using workers' sports facilities which had been made largely redundant by the mobilisation of male factory employees.

One of the first games to result from this took place on Christmas Day 1916 at Dragley Beck, near Ulverston, Lancashire, between Ulverston Munitions Girls and Ulverston Athletic, resulting in an 11–5 victory for the muntitionettes. The *Barrow Guardian* noted that, 'Owing to bad weather the girls did not turn out to full strength, but those who did played a very fine game.' Although the number of teams that emerged over the next two years is too extensive to list here, a random selection demonstrates the breadth of the sport across the country. In Wales, examples included teams representing Swansea National Shell Factory and Newport Shell Factory. In London, Hackney Marshes National Projectile Factory had 'girls' football, swimming and netball' on the sports list. In the north-west, Sutton Glassworks in St Helens had two teams representing the forging and shells shops and, in Cumbria, Vickers of Barrow and Barrow YMCA both had strong teams. In the north-east, Armstrong Whitworth and Co had a ladies' football team in 'nearly every branch' of their extensive works, according to an internal report – a significant statement considering that the company had 13 major works and these works incorporated 36 branches or 'shops' and 20,000 workers by November 1918. The teams were organised by the workers and encouraged by progressive middle-class welfare supervisors such as Miss E. B. Jayne, of the main munitions manufacturer Armstrong, Whitworth and Co, but were managed by male employees, who were either factory managers or fellow workers.

The government was supportive of the sport during the war as it helped reinforce the culture of the 'plucky heroine', and encouraged patriotism by raising money for ex-servicemen. Miss Jayne was sent a letter from the secretary of the Women's Work

Sub-Committee praising her work and expressing particular interest in the women's football teams. However, this support was to be for the duration of the war only. Football, like munitions work, was considered part of the war effort, and after the war moves were made to encourage women to return to pre-war gender roles.

Nevertheless, during the immediate post-war period, ladies' football continued to thrive due to the continuation of the 'plucky heroine' ideology and the degree of public support for the ladies' matches to be continued as fundraisers for the benefit of ex-servicemen and other war-time causes. The most enthusiastic members of many munitions factories' teams re-formed into local or regional teams: Sutton Glass Works reformed as St Helens Ladies' AFC, while others such as Dick, Kerr's in Preston and Heys Brewery, Bradford, continued with the support of their employers. The games could attract huge crowds, reaching an all-time high on Boxing Day 1920 when approximately 53,000 watched Dick, Kerr's play St Helens at Goodison Park. In 1921, when ladies' football reached its height in popularity, Dick, Kerr's Ladies alone were booked for two matches per week, every week, all over the British Isles; indeed, club historian Gail Newsham notes that they had to refuse 120 invitations from all over the country. In 1921 alone, Dick, Kerr's played 67 games for charity in front of 900,000 people, and for 25 of these matches alone, the gate receipts came to £22,525.

During the immediate post-war period, the game was used to serve the cause of international peace and reconciliation. On 29 April 1920 the first of many international matches took place at Preston North End's Deepdale ground, between Dick, Kerr's Ladies and an 11 drawn from the main nine French teams. This was part of a tour of four matches over a period of 12 days. Dick, Kerr's, made a reciprocal visit in October and November 1920. The tour was given popular endorsement as an extension of the women's roles during the war, with one of the objectives being the placing of wreathes on the graves of Lancashire football players killed in action. A wreath in Blackburn Rovers' colours was laid on the grave of Eddie Latherston, a Rovers inside-right killed in active service with the Royal Artillery at Passchendaele. The relationship between Dick, Kerr's (Preston Ladies) and the French lasted until the 1960s. During this period, international tours were also undertaken to Belgium and Holland, and the club also toured America in 1922, where they played men's soccer teams.

The early post-war years were characterised by industrial unrest, and it is in this context that ladies' football became temporarily associated with Labour politics, especially during the 1921 Miners' Lock-Out, and most notably in the area around Wigan in Lancashire and in the Ashington district in the north-east. Games were played to raise money for soup kitchens to feed the miners' children, and took on the name 'pea soup' football. These matches were organised by women from the local mining communities, encouraged by the labour movement and played on farmers' fields in front of crowds exceeding 5,000. 'Pea soup' football matches in the Wigan and Leigh area were played between untrained teams of miners' wives, daughters and other local women. The women had no kit or boots, and Jane Oakley, who played for Seven Stars' Ladies during the strike, recalls playing in her clogs. Eight 'pea soup' teams have been identified in the Wigan and Leigh district during the summer of 1921. In the north-east the game appears to be more organised and extensive, with the local media recording at least 15 teams in the district, of which Barrington Ladies was the strongest. Team managers placed advertisements in the local press to recruit players, and matches were reported in a far more objective manner. Although the coalfields of both the north-east and north-west were acutely affected by the General Strike in 1926, ladies' football was notably absent as a means of either fund-raising or entertainment. By 1926 the 'plucky heroine' ideology of the war had been forgotten, and the role of women's football in fund-raising had been significantly reduced. Most important of all, on 6 December 1921 ladies' football was banned from the grounds of FA member clubs, amid allegations of corruption with regard to gate receipts for charity matches. However, the FA's accompanying statement that 'the game of football is quite unsuitable for females and should not be encouraged' suggested deeper motives rooted in a dominant belief in the return to pre-war gender roles.

The ban marked the start of a decline in the game, and during the 1920s and 1930s ladies' football was reduced to a minor sub-culture. Educationalists, physicians and representatives of the FA opposed the game. Arsenal manager Leslie Knighton claimed that '[a]nyone acquainted with the nature of the injuries received by men could not help but think looking at girls playing – that should they get similar knocks and buffeting, their future duties as mothers would be seriously impaired'. The 1920s and 1930s saw much discussion of eugenics and racial quality, and women's roles as mothers were venerated, with any exhibitions of 'masculine' behaviour condemned as unnatural. The emphasis was on 'keep fit', as satirised in the George Formby film of the same name. Women joined the League of Health and Beauty, whose mission was to use callisthenic style exercises to develop fit yet 'feminine' women. In an age of increasing consumerism, the American idea of obtaining the ideal body was extremely popular among women and girls.

During this period, women's football was obliged to emphasise its femininity. Arthur Frankland, the manager of Dick, Kerr's Ladies, insisted that all his players wore smart dresses or skirts when going to matches. Women's football had no formal structure and consisted of *ad hoc* matches for charity arranged between different team managers. Part of this charity work involved attending numerous celebrity functions and dinner dances, where the players were expected to stick to the dress code of ball gowns and cocktail dresses. A 1937 press-cutting from one Preston player's scrap book stated that '[t]he football girls are going to make whoopee, casting aside shorts and jerseys, they are preparing to wear their daintiest frocks for a celebration dinner'. These attitudes continued to restrict women's football up to the 1940s. After the release of the Kinsey

Report in the 1950s the situation was complicated by a growth of public awareness regarding homosexuality. Women were sometimes jeered at during matches, with the result that many women players became victims of homophobia from both inside and outside the game. From the 1960s onwards, gay women have indeed become increasingly involved in women's football. A number of writers have argued that lesbians are attracted to football because the characteristics required to play are contrary to the dominant ideal of femininity. Whatever the motivation, it has not been uncommon for confrontations to arise between the heterosexual majority and the gay minority.

Perhaps because of the interest generated in the game in general by the 1966 World Cup finals, the women's game seems to have enjoyed a boost in popularity in the late 1960s, resulting in the foundation of the Women's Football Association in 1969. Bridges with the FA were gradually built, the ban on the use of FA grounds lifted, and finally, in 1983, the WFA affiliated to its old enemy on the same basis as a county association. A cup competition was founded as early as 1971, with Southampton the first winners, and international matches were put on an official footing in the following year. In the first match, Scotland defeated England 3–2. The English side reached the final of the first UEFA women's tournament in 1984, and won the first 'mini-World Cup' (a larger scale competition emerged in 1991) the next year.

Many were uncertain whether these promising signs represented anything beyond a fashionable ripple, but the 1990s saw growth continue to the point where the women's game appears to have sunk genuine roots. Within the United Kingdom, the number of women's teams increased from about 500 in 1993 to around 4,500 by 2000. In England, a national league of 24 clubs was founded in 1991, and by 2000 it had become the 34-strong AXA FA. Women's Premier League, astride a pyramid structure with clearly defined feeder leagues. The dominant clubs of the 1990s were Arsenal, Croydon, the Millwall Lionesses (at least earlier in

the decade) and the Doncaster Belles. The latter enjoyed a similar high public profile to that enjoyed by Dick, Kerr's earlier in the century, aided by Pete Davies' highly acclaimed story of one season, *I Lost my Heart to the Belles* (1996). By 2000, some 31 regional centres of excellence had been set up, offering 20-week courses for players in the 10–16 age group, as well as nine academies for older age-groups. In March 2000, the English FA rather surprised some commentators by arguing that the game was now strong enough to sustain a professional league by 2003; in anticipation, Fulham became the first professional women's team at the beginning of the 2000/01 season, taking on 16 players. While the initiative has been generally well received, concern has been expressed (and not least by those involved in the women's game) that the fan base may not be big enough to sustain such a development. While internationals and cup finals can attract crowds of several thousand, League matches usually attract only between 50 and 500. The nature and extent of media coverage, which has been generally thin and not always serious, will obviously be the crucial element in the success or otherwise of such initiatives.

One of the most important changes from the late 1990s has been the increasing sense that woman are beginning to have some real ownership of their game. It could be argued that women's football has never really belonged to them, with most teams traditionally being managed and coached by men. Similarly, from its inauguration in 1969, the Women's Football Association was run by David Marlowe and Arthur Hobbs. Marlowe continued to be involved up to 1993, when the organisation was taken under the auspices of the FA. However by 2000, although the FA Women's Committee was still chaired by a man, all other key posts were held by women, while the English and Scottish national teams were coached by Hope Powell and Vera Pauw respectively. By the same date, there were almost 6,500 women coaches active in the game. The increased involvement of women in key roles can only strengthen the game and enhance its chance of expansion.

Sources:

Melling, A., '"Plucky Lasses, Pea Soup and Politics": The Role of Ladies' Football during the 1922 Miners' Lock Out in Lancashire', *The International Journal of the History of Sport*, 17 (May 1999).

Newsham, G., *In a League of their Own!* (London: Scarlet, 1997).

Non League Club Directory (Guildford: Biddles, 2000).

Williamson, D., *Belles of the Ball* (Devon: R & D, 1991).

Williams, J. and Woodhouse, J., '"Can Play, Will Play": Women and Football in Britain', in Williams, J. and Wagg, S. (eds), *British Football and Social Change* (Leicester: Leicester University Press, 1991).

Further Reading:

Hargreaves, J., *Sporting Females: Critical Issues in the History and Sociology of Women's Sports* (London: Routledge, 1994).

Lopez, S., *Women on the Ball* (London: Scarlet, 1997).

Melling, A., 'Charging Amazons and Fair Invaders': The Dick, Kerr's Ladies' FC Soccer Tour of North America, 1922', *European Sports History Review*, 3 (2000).

Ali Melling

World Cup, The

While the idea of a World Championship for footballing nations was first mooted at the inaugural FIFA congress in Paris in 1904, it was not until the 1928 Congress held in Amsterdam that the concrete reality was put into place. The inaugural tournament was to be held in 1930, with the initial hosts being Uruguay. The trophy itself was to be named after FIFA president Jules Rimet who, with Henri Delauney, was credited with bringing the tournament to fruition. So began a tournament that in 70 years' time would become the most popular sporting contest in the world.

That the four British nations refused to compete until after the Second World War should have been of little surprise, given their general indifference to anything the international footballing community had to offer. Having withdrawn from FIFA in 1928, they gave a clear message as to what they thought of this new tournament by refusing to compete in the first tournament even though they were offered places as non-FIFA guests. Their arrogance was bolstered by the fact that domestic football was booming.

In the immediate post-war era the British nations deigned finally to join their international brethren, this being cemented by their return to FIFA in 1946. That is not to say that it was a comfortable transition. England's performances in the first four tournaments after the war (1950, 1954, 1958 and 1962) were notable for the fact that they were unable to qualify past the first round on each occasion. Their inadequacies were encapsulated by the 1–0 defeat to the amateurs from the USA in the 1950 tournament. Problems were caused by a distinct lack of organisation, borne from years of isolation, archaic methods in team selection, and by a domestic League that was in a post-war boom and therefore detracted from anything that could be achieved internationally.

Scotland, meanwhile, refused to compete in the 1950 tournament despite only having to finish second in the home internationals to qualify. Four years later Scotland decided to accept their fortunate passage into the finals, and were promptly humiliated, losing both games, the second of them 7–0 to Uruguay. They fared no better in the 1958 tournament, again going out in the first round. They also suffered from the same organisational problems that dogged England's progress, with the added disadvantage that their domestic football was suffering a recession of talent at the time.

The best British performances over the first four post-war tournaments were by Northern Ireland and Wales, who both reached the quarter-finals in 1958, with Wales only losing out to the eventual winners Brazil due to a lucky goal by Pele. The 1958 tournament is still the only tournament that all four British nations have qualified for. The 1962 tournament marked the end of one era and the beginning of another for England. The old-style methods practised by Walter Winterbottom (coach for the last four tournaments) were replaced by a new, more organised and invariably modern approach in the shape of Alf Ramsey. Gone were the old selectors and interference from on high: Ramsey was determined to do things his way.

Ironically, when England hosted the tournament in 1966, the organisation was exceptional. However, controversy followed the English team right up to their final dramatic triumph at Wembley Stadium on 30 July 1966. During the quarter-final against Argentina, when captain Antonio Rattin was sent off, comments about the Argentines by Alf Ramsey after the game merely added to the tension. There were also question marks surrounding Geoff Hurst's second goal against West Germany in the final: did it cross the line? Linesman Bakhramov certainly thought so, and that was all that mattered. England had finally won the tournament that they had previously treated with such disdain.

Mexico 1970 was significant in that widespread access to television around the world meant that this would be the first truly global World Cup. As holders, England were again expected to put up a stern challenge. However, a mixture of bad luck (injuries and illness), dubious tactics and the harsh climate were to be their undoing. Maybe it was the nature of their defeat in the quarter-finals against West Germany, losing after being up 2–0, but English international football began to suffer another slump after 1970, and they were not to reach another finals for 12 years.

Britain was represented, however, at the next series in 1974 and 1978 by the much-maligned Scots. On both occasions an early flight home was the inevitable outcome. This despite great shows of confidence before the event in 1978, where many Scots were predicting the ultimate triumph. However, a drugs scandal and poor performances meant that, even with a last gasp victory against finalists Holland, this was a tournament not to be remembered with pride.

By 1982 the odds on further British participation were greatly enhanced as the World Cup had grown, with 24 rather than 16 now competing. Thus England,

Northern Ireland and Scotland went to Spain. During the tournament it was again Northern Ireland who showed the greatest fight of all the home nations. While Scotland again went home in the first round and England's challenge withered and died after a promising beginning, it was the Northern Irish who, arguably, achieved the shock of the tournament by defeating hosts Spain after having a man sent off. This qualified them for the second-round groups, where their heartfelt challenge was not enough against classier opposition.

Again, the same three British nations qualified in 1986 and had little more positive affect than they had four years earlier, with Northern Ireland joining Scotland in first-round elimination. In fact, England nearly joined them, saved only by a tournament-saving hat-trick by Gary Lineker against Poland. However, they did qualify and reached the quarter-finals where they met a nation that had been their foes on the battlefield only four years earlier – Argentina. The match merely added to the antagonism between the countries as controversy again dominated. Argentina won the match 2–1, but only after star captain Diego Maradona had scored their first goal with what he called the 'hand of God'.

Drama would again feature high on the menu in the 1990 World Cup for England, both on and off the pitch. However, for Scotland, qualifying for their fifth series in succession, the requisite early exit again followed. There were a great many fears about England's hooligan element, and while there were occasional though much publicised clashes, the tournament went off relatively peacefully. After a very slow start the team were eventually able to return home to a hero's welcome. As England reached the semi-finals the tournament had caught hold back home and the match produced the biggest ever television audience for a sporting event on British TV – an estimated 30 million viewers. They lost the tie on penalties, however, to their old foes West Germany.

Although no British nation qualified for the 1994 series, France 98 promised to offer the biggest financial benefits yet, as it had again expanded, this time to 32 nations. England and Scotland both qualified. Scotland's fans added to their good reputation even though their team did not, with yet another early exit. Some England fans were at the sharp end of a great deal of scrutiny from both the law and the press. Again, some much-publicised skirmishes showed that hooliganism had certainly not disappeared. As far as the England team were concerned, this was the best-prepared team ever to go to a World Cup – apparently leaving aside the small matters of self-discipline and the practising of pentalty-taking, as again the lack of expertise in these departments let down the side against Argentina in the second round.

Sources:

Glanville, B., *The Story of the World Cup* (London: Faber & Faber, 1997).

Walvin, J., *The People's Game: The History of Football Revisited* (Edinburgh: Mainstream, 1994).

Further Reading:

Davies, P., *All Played Out* (London: Yellow Jersey Press, 1998).

See also FIFA

Roy Abbott

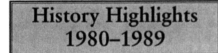

History Highlights 1980–1989

No matter what happened on the pitch, the 1980s will always be remembered for three tragedies that will be framed as a reference point for the decade. The first of these tragedies occurred at a Third Division match between Bradford City and Lincoln City, at Valley Parade on 11 May 1985. On that day 56 people died after a discarded cigarette turned a decrepit old stand into an all-engulfing blaze. Only 18 days later 39 people were killed during the European Cup final at the Heysel stadium in Brussels. The game was played at a stadium not suited for a match between such well-supported teams as Liverpool and Juventus. The clamour for tickets meant supporters of opposing teams were placed

at the same end of the ground without segregation. At a time when hooliganism was at its height, this proved to be a grievous error by the organisers. The tragedy occurred as Liverpool fans 'rushed' the opposition fans, who, while trying to get away, merely forced so much pressure onto their brethren that a fragile wall collapsed, crushing the victims. Finally, the worst of all these disasters in terms of loss of life occurred on 15 April 1989, during the FA Cup semi-final between Liverpool and Nottingham Forest at Hillsborough, home of Sheffield Wednesday. Ninety-six men, women and children lost their lives. Another fan died some years later when his life-support machine was turned off after he had failed to regain consciousness. A catalogue of errors meant that far too many fans were allowed into a small area of the Leppings Lane end of the ground. This led to a massive crush from which people were not able to escape owing to the police being reluctant to open gates in the fencing that would have saved many more lives.

That all these tragedies occurred in the 1980s seems no coincidence, as it was a decade that symbolised the decaying nature of football. Hooliganism was now becoming a part of football, with the threat of violence an occupational hazard for most football fans. Due to this, football was largely ostracised by the government and many sections of wider society. While a great deal of the violence that occurred in and around football may well have been exaggerated by a press always on the lookout for a good story, there is no doubt that there were some very real and extreme acts of hooliganism both at home and abroad.

After the Heysel tragedy all English clubs were banned from European competition. Although there was official culpability for the tragedy, most of the blame was placed at the feet of English hooligans. There was little protest at the ban, particularly from government, as it was felt that severe and decisive action needed to be taken. As the English national team was still allowed to compete internationally, hooliganism by English fans did continue in foreign climes. There were also hooligan outbreaks at home and several measures were put forward to try to stop this. The most controversial was the ID card scheme put forward under the Football Spectators Bill in 1988. This stated that fans would have to become members of their clubs so as to gain entry to matches. However, the tragedy at Hillsborough showed that this scheme would have become unworkable if put into practice, as it would merely have added to congestion before games.

Added to the hooligan problems were the state of facilities at British grounds and the lack of organisational and financial capabilities at the top level. The game was in serious trouble, with gates decreasing at a rapid rate while wages and transfer fees were rapidly increasing. What may have hidden the onset of an inevitable crisis was the success that English and Scottish clubs were having in European competition up to 1985, with Nottingham Forest in 1980, Liverpool in 1981 and 1984, and Aston Villa in 1982 all continuing the run of English European Cup success that had begun with Liverpool's victory in 1977. Once the ban had occurred domestic football had to face up to its general malaise.

New commercial possibilities had appeared during the decade: shirt sponsorship was permitted for the first time and regular live matches were broadcast on nation-wide television. As realisation grew that these new forms of revenue could prove to be very profitable, some of the bigger clubs threatened to break away from the League so as to receive a greater share of this income. On each occasion the threat was becalmed by promises of greater money-making autonomy. However, some semblance of sharing still occurred within these new deals. When television, the most profitable of these streams, moved into a new satellite age, these threats suddenly became a reality.

Off-the-field activity should not, however, overshadow achievements on it. Alongside their European success, Liverpool won seven titles between 1979/80 and 1989/90, managing the League and FA Cup double in 1986 and a hat-trick of Milk Cup victories between 1982 and 1984. Everton's two champi-

onships in 1985 and 1987 meant that football played a major role in maintaining local pride and identity at a time of political and social difficulties on Merseyside. Perhaps the most dramatic moment, though, was provided by Arsenal's 2–0 win at Liverpool in 1989, which saw the London club take the title from Liverpool on goal difference. Michael Thomas' crucial goal came one minute and 22 seconds into injury time in the final game of the season.

In Scotland, a realignment of footballing forces looked a real possibility earlier in the decade as a 'new firm' of Aberdeen and Dundee United emerged. Under Alex Ferguson, Aberdeen took the Scottish Premiership title in 1980, 1984 and 1985, won the Scottish Cup three times in succession from 1982 and again in 1986, and the European Cup Winners' Cup in 1983. Dundee United were less successful, but a championship in 1983, four Cup final appearances and a string of good performances in Europe – which included reaching the European Cup semifinal in 1984 – much enlivened the country's football scene. However, by the end of the decade, following a brief Celtic revival, Rangers were on the way to establishing the run of nine consecutive Premiership titles that stretched from 1989 to 1997. In a difficult period for domestic football in Northern Ireland, Linfield was very much the team of the decade, winning eight titles, including six in succession between 1982 and 1987. Under the management of Billy Bingham, the performance of the Northern Irish side in the 1982 World Cup finals was undoubtedly one of the international highlights of the period. A 1–0 defeat of Spain saw the team top its qualifying group, only for them to go out at the second group stage. At 17, Northern Ireland's Norman Whiteside, then of Manchester United, became the youngest ever player to appear in the World Cup.

Sources:

Conn, D., *The Football Business* (Edinburgh: Mainstream Publishing, 1998).

Scraton, P., *Hillsborough: The Truth* (Edinburgh: Mainstream Publishing, 1999).

Further Reading:
Szymanski, S. and Kuypers, T., *Winners and Losers: The Business Strategy of Football* (London: Viking, 1999).

Roy Abbott

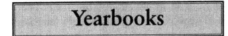

Yearbooks

The football yearbook or directory, a compendium of the previous season's records, players' career details, fixture lists and so on, has been a feature of the game almost from its beginning. Probably the first such title was *John Lilywhite's Football Annual*, which appeared in 1868 under the editorship of Charles Alcock, leading amateur footballer, FA secretary and journalist. Renamed *The Football Annual* in the following year, it ran until 1908. Other publishers swiftly entered the field and by the turn of the century it was possible to buy a range of publications serving the game at national, regional, or local level. Along with Alcock's title, perhaps the best known was the *Athletic News Football Annual*, founded in 1887 as an annual accompaniment to the popular weekly paper. It was incorporated into the *Sunday Chronicle Football Annual* in 1946, which in turn was absorbed by the *News of the World Football Annual* in 1965, under which guise it continues to operate. Other titles continued to appear, with the *Topical Times* (1927) and *News Chronicle* (1931) annuals proving successful in the inter-war period, and the *Playfair Football Annual* (1948) rapidly gaining a strong market position immediately after the Second World War. 1948 also saw the first appearance of the *FA Yearbook*, a source of record but also a publication consciously used by the FA to debate issues of the day.

Most yearbooks came in pocket-sized editions, and this format clearly imposed restrictions on the amount of data that could be carried. The genre thus really came of age in 1970 when the cigarette manufacturer Rothmans launched the first edition of a far more ambitious publication. Over 900 pages in length, *Rothmans Football Yearbook* provided (and contin-

ues to provide) comprehensive coverage of the contemporary English and Scottish game, as well as a substantial body of historical data and useful material on European and world football. Often nicknamed 'football's Wisden', it has become the leading yearbook. As a result of Rothmans' success and of football's resurgent position in the national culture, a steady stream of new titles of varying size and ambition appeared from the late 1980s. Although Scotland had a major yearbook as early as 1875 in the form of the *Scottish Football Association Annual*, Scottish provision improved considerably in this later period, while Wales, Northern Ireland and the Irish Republic gained their first really comprehensive titles in the form of the *Welsh Football Yearbook* (1991), the *Irish Football Yearbook* (1990) and the *Irish Football Handbook* (1991).

Yearbooks are generally commercial ventures and until the 1960s newspapers, both national and local, were at the forefront, using the annuals to raise brand awareness and as useful sources of external advertising revenue. From the 1970s, as demonstrated by Rothmans, a company which pioneered sponsorship deals within football, a wider range of companies have been attracted. The commercial imperative has generally meant that yearbooks have been safely factual and have eschewed controversy, although the Rothmans editorial team have made critical comments on the state of the game, particularly in the 1980s. For fans, the yearbook fulfils many practical functions, providing an easy source of quick reference and a final arbiter in quizzes and competitions. However, perhaps its greatest role is to provide hours of absorbing and joyous browsing which allows the reader to luxuriate in the obscure and to relive old glories and plan new ones. Such pleasures are central – perhaps even essential – to the maintenance of football fandom.

Sources:
Seddon, P., *A Football Compendium* (Boston Spa: The British Library, 1999).

Dave Russell

Yo-Yo Clubs

'Yo-yo clubs' is a slang term used to describe those clubs that have become synonymous with the travails of regular promotion and relegation between divisions. A great deal of this can depend on the organisation of the leagues at any particular time. For example, if the League has increased or decreased the number of promotion and relegation places, then 'yo-yo clubs' are likely to become more prevalent. So when the number of promoted and relegated clubs from the top three divisions was increased from two to three for the 1973/74 season, there was a natural increase in the number of 'yo-yo clubs'.

The late 1970s and early '80s were notable for three clubs that had a particular notoriety as 'yo-yo clubs': they were Leicester City, Wolverhampton Wanderers and Birmingham City, all of whom were relegated from the then First Division three times and promoted twice between 1976 and 1987. While these clubs may have been victims of league restructuring, the recent increase in the 'yo-yo clubs' phenomenon should be put down to financial issues. While the 'yo-yo' tendencies of the above-mentioned clubs may have had something to do with a disparity in finances, the differences in revenue between the top two divisions is far greater today.

With the inception of the Premier League, finances changed dramatically as the top division monopolised the revenue that was coming into the game. Now the Premier League organises all its own finances and has, in a sense, sealed itself off from the other leagues. While the traditional three up–three down was maintained, the benefits that Premier League clubs awarded themselves meant that newly-arrived teams in the top division were competing against others that had had the benefit of Premiership income. Clubs were now in a Catch-22 situation: should they overspend their budget in an attempt to get into the Premier League, or should they try to achieve promotion through frugal accounting and intuitive management? Both have been tried and the difficulties remain. The ultimate challenge for a club newly arrived in the top division it therefore to stay there.

The statistics back up the belief that the number of 'yo-yo clubs', rather than remaining an abnormality for particular clubs, will no doubt increase as the financial gaps become greater, with increased revenues pouring into the Premier League. The ultimate proof of the way clubs have begun to struggle when promoted occurred at the end of the 1997/98 season, when all three clubs that had been promoted the season before (Bolton Wanderers, Barnsley and Crystal Palace) were relegated again straight away. In fact there have only been three clubs that have been promoted to the Premier League and have stayed there, without having been relegated and then returning: Newcastle United, West Ham United and Derby County.

However, it isn't all about getting relegated, as many of the clubs who have gone down have the added advantage of the extra revenue the Premier League has provided during their stay. They should also have a squad that is well equipped to make a concerted challenge for a quick return. In fact, of the 19 clubs that were relegated from the Premier League, up to and including those relegated in the 1997/98 season, nine were able to regain their places in the Premiership. It seems that it will be these clubs who will lead a nomadic existence between the Premiership and the First Division. However, it would seem this existence could only go on for so long. Finances may well dictate that a club cannot go on paying out consistently high wages while they are only sporadically gaining the financial rewards. They will either, therefore, eventually establish a consistent level in the Premiership (Leicester City), or they will begin to flounder under the heavy financial burden (Crystal Palace).

At the lower league level there has constantly been a healthy exchange of clubs between the leagues. The 'yo-yo clubs' here tend to be more extreme, as the highs and lows of success are exacerbated by the number of divisions that can be travelled. The extreme examples of the ups and downs that can be reached are provided by two clubs that left the Fourth Division to reach the First Division, only to return to the Fourth a few years later: Northampton Town (left 1961, returned 1969) and Swansea City (left 1978, returned 1986). In fact these movements are so extreme that they might be termed 'bungee clubs'.

Source:

Szymanski, S. and Kuypers, T., *Winners & Losers: The Business Strategy of Football* (London: Viking, 1999).

Roy Abbott

Youth Groups

'Youth' football traditionally referred to participation in the game by those under the age of 21, and only incorporated male football. Today youth football is a term that would seem to represent football for all participants under 18. Almost always the term has referred to the game outside schools.

In 1926, the FA's Council decided to appoint a special committee to report on the desirability of assisting elementary schools in developing football among boys while at school. At the same time, the committee was to examine the possibility of providing for the continued interest of participants with junior clubs until they became 'eligible' to play in matches with higher-grade clubs. The committee called upon every county association to form a minor association or 'committee' to organise, affiliate and control Old Boys clubs of elementary and secondary schools consisting of players between the ages of 14 and 18. In addition, they were asked to affiliate and control other youth clubs comprising participants of the same age. The minor associations were to foster football in all its aspects, including co-operation with the English Schools FA, organising minor leagues, and the arrangement of inter-county games. The FA felt that minor competition should be self-supporting: they would reimburse county associations for any deficits incurred by

clubs, and a grant of £50 (later increased to £75) would be granted to county associations for administrative expenses, but, incredibly, the FA reserved the right to criticise the annual reports of minor associations.

It would be true to say that youth football outside schools in Britain began because once young players left school they were forced to work long hours and excluded from competitive frameworks. In July 1926 model rules for youth football were drawn up, but the next ten years saw little progress. In 1936, the FA encouraged its county associations to make stringent efforts to create youth leagues. Prior to the Second World War very few young players played professional football before their 21st birthday. Exceptions included Stanley Matthews, Cliff Bastin and Tommy Lawton.

Outside the FA's jurisdiction youth football took place under the auspices of groups and societies such as the Boys' Brigade. The first uniformed organisation for boys or girls, Sir William Alexander Smith founded the Boys' Brigade in 1883. In an attempt to instil 'drill and discipline' into young boys, sport, and in particular, football emerged as a mechanism for providing young people with a positive focus in their activities within society. Currently the Boys' Brigade in Britain runs five national competitions, one of which is five-a-side football. National finals usually take place in April or May. As well as the competition, standards of behaviour and a sense of fair play are expected to be exemplary. Many local leagues also take place, and in Scotland and Northern Ireland particularly leagues such as the Belfast Battalion Intermediate League continue to thrive. In this league teams must have an average age of 15 or under (a total team age of 165 or less). The Boys' Brigade has many famous alumni, introduced to football through the society, the most famous of whom is Sir Alex Ferguson.

Cub Scout and Scout Societies have also utilised sport as a focus for young people. Football has historically been one of the 'core' sports in its programme of developing well-rounded young people. Cub Scouts may obtain their 'Sportsman

Badge' through 'reasonable proficiency' and 'regular participation' in at least one sport. Scouts may obtain badges in 'Physical Recreation' where wider issues such as officiating, understanding of the rules and a wider knowledge of the sport is expected. Football is one of the most popular sports for those who are awarded this badge.

The first national competition for youth players began in the 1944/45 season. The FA County Youth Challenge Cup was for representative players of county associations under the age of 18. The tournament continues today, but with the best players snapped up by professional clubs long before they reach 18 the standard of play is not always particularly strong. The FA Council introduced the FA Youth Challenge Cup in 1952 for the youth teams of Football League clubs and other approved youth teams. In the first year, youth groups were permitted to enter teams. The Hereford Lads Club and Pinehurst Youth Centre from Swindon both lost heavily in the first round, but Huntley and Palmers of Reading reached the semi-finals. In its current format youth groups and clubs cannot now qualify for the tournament. The Manchester United youth team that included Colman, Edwards, Pegg and Whelan beat Nantwich 23–0 on their way to eventual success in the first final, emphasising the gulf in abilities between the youth teams of professional and non-league clubs. Gradually, the tournament became increasingly structured and is now highly reflective of the FA Cup.

Until very recently youth football meant boys' football. Women and girls had begun to play football regularly during the First World War, as they established teams whilst working in wartime munitions factories. However, the chauvinistic attitude of the FA during the early 1920s nullified the development of women's and girls' football, and it was not until 1969 that the Women's Football Association was formed. In 1978, Theresa Bennett, a 12-year-old girl, was banned by the FA from playing football in a local league with boys. This action prevented mixed football for young people for another decade. The case generated growing interest in girls' football and sensitised primary schools to the contradictions between their equal opportunity policies and the FA's banning order on mixed participation. In 1990 the FA lifted the ruling and girls under 11 could finally participate in mixed football. At the same time the English Schools Football Association (ESFA) was made responsible for the development of girls' football. The ESFA has recently introduced four competitions for schoolgirl teams, each with corporate sponsorship: at under-16s level the Vimto Trophy attracted 500 school teams in 1999, a fivefold increase since the competition started in 1997. Research for the FA shows that in 1993 there were 800 registered girls' footballers aged under 18. By 1996 this number had increased to 750 girls' teams, with 7,500 players, and by 2000 there were 23,000 registered girls' soccer players. The number of women players had increased from 10,400 to 18,200. This makes the sport of women's football the fastest-growing team sport in Britain, and with an ever-increasing number of participants aged under 18, policy-makers are having to respond with unprecedented speed to address the huge gap between the access girls and boys have to playing the game.

In 1998, 20 Female Centres of Excellence were approved under the FA's *Programme for Excellence and Talent Development Plan*, with all but one, Dorset, attached to league football clubs. Each Centre is funded to a minimum of £5,000 per annum by the FA, and given leave to apply for further funding via Sport England's access to National Lottery money. In January 2000, Reading FC set up a comprehensive football development programme for girls aged between eight and 16, to become the only club in the south of England outside London to operate a women's academy. Three Development Centres were opened to all aspiring girl football players in the catchment area. The development centres provided players to an elite squad, and it was also planned to extend the scheme to provide scholarships for girls aged 16 to 18 as they graduate from the Centre of Excellence.

Girls' football is now represented at international level in the under-16 and under-18 age groups, while a number of regional leagues such as that in the West Midlands have competitions for under-12 age-groups. Girls' football has also been included as one of nine sports in Sport England's 'Active Sport' programme, a five-year development programme that aims to build on current good practice within these sports, the programme's main aim being to help young people get more from their involvement in sport.

Sources:

Carvosso, J. W. 'Youth Football', in Fabian, A. H. and Green, G. (eds), *Association Football*, vol. 2 (London: Caxton, 1959) pp. 159–76.

Hargreaves, J., *Sporting Females: Critical Issues in the History and Sociology of Women's Sports* (London: Routledge, 1994)

McFarlan, D. M., 'First for Boys: The Story of the Boys' Brigade 1883–1983', published online at: www.boys-brigade.org.uk/bgrnd/ffb-cont.htm, retrieved on December 14 2000.

Williams, J. and Woodhouse, J., 'Can Play? Will Play? Women and Football in Britain', in Williams, J. and Wagg, S. (eds), *Getting into Europe: British Football and Social Change* (Leicester: Leicester University Press, 1991).

Further Reading:
On the Ball – the official women's football magazine.

Marc Keech

Youth Training

The purpose of any form of training is twofold. Firstly, to supply the trainer with a more skilled future workforce, and secondly, to provide the individual with skills and knowledge that can be utilised to enhance his or her future career prospects. The training of young professional footballers follows the structure of training in most industries, combining educational and vocational enhancement with job-specific development. Only recently, however, has the football industry embraced the need for young professionals to be encouraged to further their education. Given the small percentage of trainees who actually become professional players – historically, only about 25 per cent of apprentices remain in the game at 21, this is a vital aspect of their training period.

West Ham v Arsenal Under-17 match
(© Stuart MacFarlane, Arsenal FC)

Training of young professionals has been commonplace in football since clubs were formed. However, the first structured scheme for youth training came as late as 1960, when the FA inserted a new Rule (32), which described a new category of player – 'The Apprentice'. This allowed clubs to sign boys as professionals from the age of 15 (the limit had previously been 17) and stated that clubs should 'make provision for the player to continue his further education or to take up vocational training'. However, in reality this rarely happened. Under the guise of an apprenticeship young boys would do menial tasks around the club, such as painting, cleaning and groundwork, denying them purposeful career-related training.

Despite attempts to revamp the Apprenticeship Scheme during the 1960s and 1970s the inherent structure of the scheme remained the same. However, moves by the Professional Footballers Association (PFA) played a major part in advancing youth training provision. In 1971 Bob Kerry was appointed as the Association's first full-time Education Officer. He sought to offer young players an education which would provide them with opportunities in their careers beyond football. In 1978 the PFA and the Football League jointly launched the Footballers Further Education and Vocational Training Society (FFE and VTS) with the brief of ensuring that all the educational and vocational requirements of PFA members, both past and present, were being catered for.

A change of government in 1979 brought new objectives to youth training as a whole. In response to general skills shortages and rising youth unemployment a number of training schemes aimed at the 16 to 25 age group were initiated. In 1983 the Youth Training Scheme (YTS) replaced the Youth Opportunity Programme (YOP). YTS changed the perspective of previous schemes, with central government rather than individual firms funding training. Despite criticism of the scheme by many industrial unions, in June 1983 the PFA agreed to introduce YTS into professional football. The one-year scheme, becoming

two-year in 1985, was administered by the FFE and VTS, and brought compulsory continuing education to a football traineeship for the first time. Young professionals had to attend a local college to follow an educational course, mainly BTEC leisure and tourism based. They also received football training and guidance in all areas of the football industry.

With decreasing investment in training from central government, further change in the training of young professionals ensued. In April 1990 Training and Enterprise Councils were created from the 'privatisation' of training. Rather than receiving funding for training, clubs, through the FFE and VTS, now had to apply for financial support. YTS was also replaced by a new scheme, Youth Training (YT) in May 1990. The main difference between the schemes was the greater emphasis on attaining qualifications to a pre-determined level. Rather than just attending college, trainees now took examinations at National Vocational Qualification (NVQ) Level II, equivalent to four GCSEs.

YT in football continued through the 1990s. However, the advent of football academies in November 1997 brought a change in the structure of a young professional's training. The academies evolved from recommendations made by the FA's Chief Technical Officer, Howard Wilkinson, in his report, *A Charter for Quality*. Each academy employs a full-time Education and Welfare Officer who is charged with monitoring educational provision for the trainees. Rather than a two-year YT, at the age of 16 young professionals now embark on a three-year scholarship through their academy. As before, college courses are offered, with 'A' levels and GNVQs being the most common qualifications studied for. If a player so wishes clubs must continue his or her education for the full three years, even if it does not intend to retain him.

The progression of youth training in football, from being a side issue to becoming an important element in a young professional's development, has been a long process. However, clubs now realise that youngsters have to gain academic and vocational development alongside their football training in order to help provide for their futures.

Sources:
The Football Association, 'The Apprentice Player', *FA News XIII*, 11 (June 1960), 395.
Bradley, L., 'Youth Training Initiatives in English Professional Football: An Economic Analysis of the Training Schemes Implemented By Football Clubs For Boys Aged 16 To 18 In The Period 1960–1996', MA Dissertation, De Montfort University, 1997.

Further Reading:
Harding, J., *For the Good of the Game: The Official History of the Professional Footballers Association* (London: Robson, 1991).
Monk, D. and Russell, D., 'Training Apprentices: Tradition Versus modernity in the Football Industry', *Soccer and Society*, 1: 1 (2000), 62–79.

Lee Bradley

History Highlights 1990–1999

The 1990s will be seen as a decade of change, during which football moved away from its traditional centre and into a new, highly commercialised sector of the entertainment industry. The seeds for this change were sewn at the end of the 1980s, when the Taylor Report was published in response to the Hillsborough disaster. The technological revolution in satellite broadcasting also helped shape the way television would be perceived in future.

There was also a change of attitude towards football, most aptly symbolised by reactions to the 1990 World Cup finals in Italy. Throughout the tournament England was gripped with football fever, as the national team advanced to the semifinals. The event produced enthralling drama, encapsulated by the television audience figures for the fateful semi-final against West Germany. Thirty million people in England watched the match – the single biggest domestic television audience

for any sporting event. Even though England lost the match after a tense penalty shoot-out, it showed that football could still grip the nation like no other sport, and that it provided great television entertainment.

As the Taylor Report was instigated, with the modernised all-seater stadium increasingly becoming the norm, football began to gain a positive high profile. This was enhanced by the exposure provided by the new Premier League. With the aid of satellite company BSkyB and the FA, top division clubs colluded to rid themselves of commercial restrictions placed on them by the Football League. They withdrew and formed their own league so that they could take sole control of assets garnered from television and sponsorship deals. After the League had been formed, with 22 clubs, a huge contract with BSkyB, worth £304 million over five years, was signed. The inaugural Premier League season was begun in 1992. The financial success of the BSkyB deal became a catalyst for future financial deals within the game, as realisation dawned that football could be profitable. Throughout the decade clubs sought to float on the stock exchange, encouraged by the promise of ever-increasing wealth. This wealth was to come from all sorts of profitable ventures, such as corporate entertainment, sponsorship, merchandising and promises of even greater television inducements, such as the increased BSkyB deal signed in 1997, for £670 million over four years.

A decision by the European Court in 1995 also changed the nature of football in Britain. The *Bosman* ruling stated that there could be no restrictions in the number of players from European Union countries in other member states. It also stated that when a player had ended his contract with one club, that club could not demand a transfer fee from another club for that player. This decision, combined with the increased monies coming into the game, encouraged a sudden influx of foreign talent into the country, much of which was extremely high-profile. These players in turn added a visible glamour to the Premier League, thus increasing commercial interest. Before the *Bosman* ruling there was very little foreign talent in the country, due to a UEFA rule that meant players from other British nations were themselves deemed 'foreigners' when it came to club football. When the English were readmitted to UEFA competition in the 1990/91 season, clubs tended to look to players who were English due to these 'foreigner' restrictions.

Like domestic football, the European competitions were also becoming extremely lucrative, and the European Cup was constantly being restructured so as to become more profitable to the bigger clubs. These included a few high-profile English clubs who would soon benefit from the commercial patronage of the revamped European Champions League.

The nation also received a high international profile after hosting the 1996 European Championship finals. The newly modernised stadia that were now in place helped the event, as did an emphasis on the theme of 'Football's Coming Home'. The tournament was well organised and popular, and saw little of the hooliganism that many had feared. These fears were still very reasonable, as was shown only a year before the tournament, when rioting England fans forced the abandonment of a friendly match in Dublin against the Republic of Ireland. The success of Euro 96, as it was more popularly called, encouraged the FA to apply to host the 2006 World Cup, their campaign focusing on the attributes and profile which had been brought to the domestic game through its resurgence during the 1990s. Unfortunately, it was to fail. There were feelings of uncertainty, however, as to where this revolution was taking football as the new millennium approached.

In terms of playing success, Rangers dominated Scottish football, winning eight consecutive League titles from 1990 to 1997 and a ninth in 1999. Annual European campaigns were invariably disappointing, however. Most neutrals were pleased to see Dundee United at last win the Scottish Cup in 1994, after five Cup Final defeats in the previous 13 years. In 1992, Wales finally gained its own national league, the League of Wales, with Barry Town taking four consecutive titles between 1996 and 1999. In Northern Ireland, while Linfield's stranglehold was to some extent broken, with four other sides also managing to win League titles, the decade proved problematic. Uneconomically high wage bills following the introduction of promotion and relegation in the Irish League in 1994, and the problems of releasing ground improvement money because of continuing political uncertainties, pushed a number of clubs into or close to bankruptcy.

In England, Nationwide Division Two side Chesterfield's remarkable run to the FA Cup semi-finals in 1997 gave sustenance to all fans not associated with the big battalions. However, the decade was dominated by Manchester United, a club that became the biggest battalion over the 1990s. Winners of the Premiership six times between 1993 and 2000 and runners-up in the other two seasons, they also managed League and Cup doubles in 1994 and 1996, and a European Cup triumph in 1999 which gave them an unprecedented (for an English club) treble. The European final victory against Bayern Munich was extraordinarily dramatic. Losing 1–0 after 90 minutes, and with at least one eminent radio commentator claiming that the German side deserved its victory, substitutes Teddy Sheringham and Ole Gunnar Solskjaer scored the winning goals in injury time.

Sources:

Conn, D., *The Football Business: Fair Game in the 90s* (Edinburgh: Mainstream Publishing, 1998).

Dempsey, P. and Reilly, K., *Big Money, Beautiful Game: Saving Soccer From Itself* (London: Nicholas Brearley Publishing, 1998).

Further Reading:

Flynn, A. and Guest, L., *For Love or Money: Manchester United and England – The Business of Winning* (London: André Deutsch, 1999).

Roy Abbott

A Chronology of British Football Highlighting Important Landmarks and Events

1508
Alexander Barclay's poem *Eclogues* wrote that 'foote-ball' was the winter pastime of the 'sturdie plowman'

1846
Shrovetide matches between parishes of All Saints and St Peter's in Derby broken up by the military
first rules drawn up by Cambridge University

1855
Sheffield FC founded – the oldest football club still in existence

1856
Publication of the 'Sheffield Rules'

1862
Notts County FC founded
publication of J. C. Thring's *The Simplest Game,* containing a code for the game

1863
Stoke City FC founded
the Football Association founded

1865
Nottingham Forest FC founded

1866
Chester City FC founded

1867
Sheffield FC founded
Queen's Park FC founded – first Scottish club
Sheffield Wednesday FC founded

1868
First edition of *John Lillywhite's Football Annual*; renamed *The Football Annual* in 1908

1869
Goal kick introduced
Kilmarnock FC founded

1870
Stranraer FC founded
Charles Alcock appointed Secretary and Treasurer of the FA
eleven-a-side becomes standard

1871
First deaf football club founded in Glasgow
first time goalkeepers mentioned in laws of the game
Reading FC founded

1872
First FA Cup final – won by the Royal Engineers
first England v Scotland football international – all Scottish players from Queen's Park
corners introduced
Dumbarton FC founded

1873
Wrexham FC founded
Glasgow Rangers FC founded
Scottish Football Association founded at Dewar's Temperance Hotel, Glasgow
Glasgow Rangers FC founded
first Scottish Cup Competition – organised by the Scottish FA, won by Queen's Park
first Cap awarded for international recognition in football, by the Scottish FA for match against England

1874
Umpires mentioned in the laws of the game for the first time
Morton FC founded
Heart of Midlothian FC founded
Major Francis Marindin of the Royal Engineers made president of the FA; resigned in 1889
Shin-guards said to have been invented by Sam Widdowson
Aston Villa FC founded by Villa Cross Wesleyan Church
Christ's Church Sunday School FC founded, later to become Bolton Wanderers (1877)

1875
Hamilton Academicals FC founded
first publication of the 'Athletic News'
Hibernian FC founded by Canon Hannan
first edition of the *Scottish FA Annual*
Birmingham City FC founded
first FA Cup match replayed: Royal Engineers beat Old Etonians 2–0 following a 1–1 draw
cross-bar replaces tapes on the goalposts
Small Heath Alliance FC founded, later to

become Birmingham City FC
Blackburn Rovers FC founded

1876
First Scotland v Wales international, Glasgow,
Scotland win 4–0
Partick Thistle FC founded
St Mirren FC founded
Port Vale FC founded
Falkirk FC founded
Middlesbrough FC founded
Football Association of Wales founded

1877
Bolton Wanderers FC founded
first Scotland v Wales international played in
Wales (Wrexham), Scotland win 2–0
Wolverhampton Wanderers FC founded
Crewe Alexandra FC founded

1878
Grimsby Town FC founded as Grimsby Pelham
Lancashire FA founded
first match played under floodlights – Bramall
Lane, Sheffield
Arbroath FC founded
Everton FC founded
Bootle FC founded; wound up in 1893 after
one season in the Football League
Alloa Athletic FC founded
Clyde FC founded
first Welsh FA Cup final – Wrexham beat The
Ruabon Druids 1–0
The Lancashire and Yorkshire Railway
Company Carriage and Wagon Works, at
Newton Heath FC founded; later to
become Manchester United FC
referees use whistles for first time
Airdrieonians FC founded

1879
Doncaster Rovers FC founded
first England v Wales international at the
Kennington Oval; England win 2–1
Sunderland FC founded
West Bromwich Albion FC founded

1880
Ardwick Football Club founded, later to
become Manchester City FC
Fulham FC founded
Preston North End Cricket and Rugby Club
play their first football match; forerunner
of Preston North End FC
Irish Football Association founded

1881
Albion Rovers FC founded
East Stirlingshire FC founded
Cowdenbeath FC founded

Berwick Rangers FC founded
East Stirlingshire FC founded
Swindon Town FC founded
Leyton Orient FC founded
referee granted power to order a player off the
field

1882
Burnley FC founded
International Football Association Board created by the national associations of England,
Ireland, Scotland and Wales; exerted a
dominent role in making and amending
rules of the game
two handed throw-in introduced
Newcastle United FC founded
Albion Rovers FC founded
first football special published *Saturday Night*
in Birmingham; lasts until 1898
first Wales v Ireland match
first England v Ireland international match
Tottenham Hotspur FC founded

1883
Lincoln City FC founded
Heaton Norris Rovers founded; later to
become Stockport County FC
Bristol Rovers FC founded
Coventry City FC founded
Tranmere Rovers FC founded
Darlington FC founded

1884
Preston North End ejected from the FA Cup
for fielding 'professionals'
Stenhousemuir FC founded
St Johnstone FC founded
Rotherham United FC founded
Forfar Athletic FC founded
Derby County FC founded
first Scotland v Ireland international match;
Scotland win 5–0 in Belfast
Leicester Fosse FC founded; later to become
Leicester City FC

1885
Motherwell FC founded
Dunfermline Athletic FC founded
Southampton FC founded
Queen's Park Rangers FC founded
professionalism legalised by the FA
Millwall FC founded
Luton Town FC founded
Bury FC founded

1886
Plymouth Argyle FC founded
Linfield FC founded
Shrewsbury Town FC founded
FA surrenders its rights as chief law-maker to

the International Football Association
Board
Arsenal FC founded

1887
Scottish FA withdraws its members from the
English FA
Barnsley FC founded by St Peter's Church
first edition of *Athletic News Football Annual*
(previously *John Lillywhite's Football
Annual*)
Manchester City FC founded
Ipswich Town FC founded
Blackpool FC founded

1888
Glasgow Celtic FC founded
first Army Challenge Cup, won by the Second
Battalion of the Argyll and Sutherland
Highlanders
Football League founded by 12 clubs; first
match 8 September
Walsall FC founded as Walsall Town Swifts
British Army Football Association founded

1889
Leyland footballer James Tattershall indicted
for manslaughter of referee; later acquitted
on the grounds that the referee had a prior
medical condition
Wimbledon FC founded
Brentford FC founded; first English team to
win the Football League and FA Cup
double
Preston North End FC founded
Sheffield United Football Club founded

1890
Scottish League and Irish League founded
FA introduces rules for the protection of goal-
keepers

1891
Mansfield Town FC founded as Mansfield
Wesleyans
Retain and Transfer system introduced
Football League decrees that all clubs register
their colours during the close season
Watford FC founded
goal nets first used
penalty kick introduced at the wish of the Irish
FA
first *FA Handbook* published

1892
Liverpool FC founded
Division Two of the Football League introduced
first time goal nets used in FA Cup final

Celtic Park, Glasgow, opened
William McGregor elected President of the FA
(held the position until 1894)

1893
Accrington not re-elected to the Football
League
South Wales and Monmouth FA founded
first time professionalism legalised by the
Scottish FA
Bootle leaves the Football League
Rotherham elected to the Football League
Raith Rovers FC founded
Dundee FC founded
Newcastle United FC founded
first FA Amateur Cup competition
Gillingham FC founded
Referees Association founded
Raith Rovers FC founded

1894
Fred Wall appointed secretary of the FA
Oldham Athletic FC founded
Northwich Victoria resigned from the Football
League
Bristol City FC founded
Corinthians supplied all 11 players for the
England v Wales match at Wrexham
Southern League founded

1895
West Ham United FC founded as Thames
Ironworks, but folded in 1900
FA Cup stolen from a Birmingham shop
window

1896
Belfast Celtic FC founded
Accrington FC folded after five seasons in the
Football League
Oxford United FC founded
Rotherham not re-elected to the Football
League

1897
Second English team to win the Football
League and FA Cup double, Aston Villa FC
Northampton Town FC founded
Burton Wanderers not re-elected to the
Football League
Ibrox Stadium, Glasgow, opened

1898
Portsmouth FC founded
Torquay United FC founded
first time automatic promotion and relegation
between divisions of the Football League
introduced, previously settled by 'test
matches'
New Brighton Tower FC founded, lasted 3

seasons in the Football League
Player Union founded
first black professional footballer in Britain, Arthur 'Darkie' Wharton signs as a professional with Rotherham Town FC

1899
Cardiff City FC founded
Bournemouth FC founded as Boscombe
Darwen FC folded after eight years in the Football League

1900
Swansea City FC founded as Swansea Town
FA introduce maximum wage which took effect from the 1901/02 season
Brighton and Hove Albion FC founded

1901
First FA Cup final to be filmed
first non-League club to win the FA Cup: Tottenham Hotspur
New Brighton resigned from the Football League

1902
First £500 transfer: Alf Common from Sheffield United to Sunderland
military football leagues sanctioned
Ibrox disaster – 25 spectators killed and 163 seriously injured when terracing collapses
Newton Heath FC went into voluntary liquidation
South East Counties Amateur Championship inaugurated

1903
First Arthur Dunn Cup final – contested for by 'old boys' teams of the Public Schools
East Fife FC founded
Bradford City FC founded
Aberdeen FC founded
New Hampden Park opened

1904
Exeter City FC founded
Federation of International Football Associations (FIFA) founded
Scunthorpe United FC founded
Royal Navy Football Association founded
Leeds City FC founded, lasted until 1919
Carlisle United FC founded
Hull City FC founded

1905
FA makes it a legal requirement for the outer casing of a football to be made out of leather
FA impose a limit on transfer fee of £350, it

lasted only 3 months
first £1,000 transfer fee paid: Alf Common from Sunderland to Middlesbrough
Stamford Bridge football stadium opened, previously used as an athletics stadium
Chelsea FC founded
Mansfield Town FC founded
Charlton Athletic FC founded
Billy Meredith of Manchester City suspended following bribe to Aston Villa captain Alec Leake to throw match
Crystal Palace FC founded
Southend United FC founded
Norwich City FC founded

1906
Both major football trophies won by Liverpool teams – Liverpool FC the League, Everton FC the FA Cup
Southend United FC founded
Prevention of Corruption Act – makes bribes offered to footballers a punishable offence
first England v France amateur international

1907
Rochdale FC founded
Bradford Park Avenue FC founded
Glasgow Celtic become first Scottish club to win League and Cup double
first England v Ireland amateur international
Burton United not re-elected to the Football League
first time Wales win the Home International series
break-away Amateur Football Association founded, lasted until 1914
Football Players' and Trainers' Association Union founded

1908
Hartlepool United FC founded
first England match against foreign opposition – they defeated Austria 6–1 in Vienna
England win Gold Medal at the Olympic Games
Huddersfield Town FC founded

1909
Scottish Amateur Football Association founded
goalkeepers required to wear scarlet, blue or white shirts to distinguish them from other players – previously they had worn the same as their fellow players
riot at Hampden Park in Celtic v Rangers Scottish Cup final, match abandoned

1910
Ayr United FC founded
Dundee United FC founded
Manchester United move to new stadium at

Old Trafford
first penalty awarded in FA Cup final, scored
by Albert Shepherd of Newcastle in match
against Barnsley
West Auckland win First World ('Lipton') Cup
tournament
Irish, Scottish and Welsh FAs allowed to join
FIFA

1911
Halifax Town FC founded
first Welsh Junior Cup competition (for amateur clubs, equivalent to the FA Amateur
Cup)
first Scottish Amateur FA Cup, won by
Queen's Park
first time deadline for the transfer of Football
League players introduced
first FA Cup final replay at Old Trafford, won
by Bradford City
first known football film, *Harry the Footballer*
released

1912
Goalkeepers no longer allowed to handle the
ball outside the penalty area, previously
they could handle it anywhere within their
own half of the pitch
goalkeepers permitted to wear green as well as
scarlet, blue or white shirts
England win Gold Medal at the Olympic
Games
first £2,000 transfer: Danny O'Shea from West
Ham United to Blackburn Rovers
Gainsborough Trinity not re-elected to the
Football League
John Bentley appointed Chairman and
Secretary of the FA (held the position until
1916)

1913
Arsenal move from Woolwich to Highbury

1914
Footballers' Battalion formed
first FA Cup to be presented by a reigning
monarch, King George V
first time Ireland win the Home International
series
FA and the Amateur Football Association
reconcile their differences

1915
Football League programme suspended for
duration of the First World War – limited
regional programme was later introduced
Enoch West of Manchester United given life
ban for engineering result of Manchester
United v Liverpool result – 9 other players
suspended

1919
Leeds City expelled from second division for
making illegal payment to players – folded
soon after
Leeds United FC founded
Port Vale elected to the Football League
Queen of the South FC founded
Cambridge United FC founded
South Shields elected to the Football League,
later to transfer to Gateshead
Football League increased to 44 clubs
Glossop resigned from the Football League

1920
First £3,000 transfer: Joseph Lane from
Blackpool to Birmingham City
biggest ever crowd for women's match in
Britain: 53,000 spectators watch Dick,
Kerr's Ladies play St Helens Ladies at
Goodison Park on Boxing Day
Northern Irish Football Association founded
British Football Associations leave FIFA after
disagreement over playing against First
World War powers
Third Division of the Football League formed

1921
FA ban women's football
goalkeepers required to wear yellow shirts in
international matches
first Kentish Cup final, contested between the
armies of Britain, Belgium and France;
Third Division renamed Third Division
(South) and foundation of the Football
League's Third Division (North)

1922
First £5,000 transfer: Syd Puddefoot from
West Ham United to Falkirk
York City FC founded
maximum wage reduced from £9 per week to
£8

1923
First time the Corinthians entered FA Cup
competition
first FA Cup final at Wembley Stadium
Stalybridge Celtic resigned from the Football
League
Peterborough United FC founded
New Brighton re-elected to the Football
League
Third Division created in the Scottish League,
lasted only three seasons.

1924
British Football Associations rejoin FIFA
Hereford United FC founded
first international played at Wembley Stadium:
England v Scotland
became legal to score directly from a corner

1925
First inter-county championship competition
   organised by the Northern Counties
   Amateur Football Association
off-side rule amended reducing the number of
   defenders between the attacker and the
   opponent's goal-line from 3 to 2 leading to
   new tactics and more goals

1926
First BBC radio broadcast of the FA Cup final
Aldershot FC founded
film *Ball of Fortune* released starring Billy
   Meredith
first team to win the Football League title 3
   years running.: Huddersfield Town FC

1927
National Federation of Supporters' Clubs
   founded
last amateur to captain full England national
   team
Aberdare Athletic not re-elected to the
   Football League
first live radio broadcast, BBC Radio Arsenal v
   Sheffield United at Highbury
Cardiff City FC win FA Cup – first non-
   English team to win. Also First FA Cup
   final to be broadcast on radio

1928
The FA severs ties with FIFA over disagreement over 'Broken Time' payments to
   amateur players
Durham City FC withdrawn from the Football
   League, eventually collapsing altogether in
   1938
first £10,000 transfer: David Jack from Bolton
   Wanderers to Arsenal
first Spot-the-Ball competition in the *Athletic
   News*
Glasgow Rangers win the League and Cup
   double
W. R. 'Dixie' Dean sets new record of 60 goals
   in a season
Carlisle United elected to the Football League
Arsenal fined by FA over inducements to
   players
first time numbers worn on shirts in the
   Football League, by Arsenal and Chelsea in
   separate matches
Scotland beat England at Wembley for the first
   time. England 1 Scotland 5 'Wembley
   Wizards' enter Scottish folklore

1929
First time England lose all three Home
   Internationals; first Scotland match against
   foreign opposition: Norway
FA Cup final not broadcast due to dispute

between the BBC and the FA on fees
first England defeat by non-British team: Spain
   4 England 3 in Madrid

1930
Film *The Great Game* released
Thames elected to the Football League
Merthyr Town not re-elected to the Football
   League
FA ban floodlighting of football matches
   (reinstated 1950)
new record for lowest attendance at a League
   fixture: 469 spectators at the Thames v
   Luton match
first World Cup in football – Uruguay. Event
   boycotted by British Football Associations

1931
Glasgow Celtic goalkeeper James Thomson
   badly injured in match against Rangers
   dying several days later
Wigan Borough resigned from the Football
   League
Football League bans all broadcasts of its
   fixtures
Chester City elected to the Football League
Nelson not re-elected to the Football League
first time Scotland beaten by non-British
   opposition, 5–0 to Austria in Vienna
first team to win the FA Cup and the Second
   Division of the Football League in the same
   season: West Bromwich Albion

1932
Wigan Athletic FC founded

1933
First time numbers required to be worn on the
   back of shirts in the FA Cup final. Everton
   wore numbers 1–11, Manchester City
   12-22
first Wales match against foreign opposition:
   France
attempt to allow unemployed to attend League
   matches for half price by Sheffield United
   defeated

1934
Sudden death of highly successful Arsenal
   manager Herbert Chapman
first FA coaching course held
Fred Wall retired as Secretary of the FA with
   £10,000 'Golden Handshake'
Peterborough United FC founded
second World Cup Competition – Italy. British
   teams do not take part. Won by Italy
Stanley Rous appointed Secretary of the FA

1935
Managers banned from the touch line

first time the Football League imposes fines as
punishment
Arsenal win Football League for third year
running

1936
Charles Sutcliffe elected President of the FA
first time ten goals scored in a League match
by one player: Joe Payne of Luton Town
against Bristol Rovers
first BBC televised League match – highlights
of Arsenal v Everton match

1937
149,547 spectators watch Scotland v England
game at Hampden Park. Record crowd to
date for Home International
first professional player imported from
Argentina: Casco Rinaldi and Augustus
Corpa signed by Barrow of the Northern
League
first time FA Cup final televised (not live!).
Parts of the Sunderland v Preston North
End match
Colchester United FC founded

1938
England beat Rest of the World team in FA
75th anniversary match
first match televised live, Preston North End v
Huddersfield
first time the entire FA Cup final broadcast
live on television
first time the FA Cup final win on a penalty:
Preston North End victors
England players give Nazi salute before match
against Germany in Berlin
first time the Scottish Cup won by a Second
Division side. East Fife beat Kilmarnock
4–2
third World Cup – France. Won by Italy. No
British teams took part

1939
Film *The Arsenal Stadium Mystery* released
the FA halts all matches and suspends players'
contracts in aid of the War effort
numbers on shirts made compulsory by the
Football League

1940
Villa Park football ground reopened

1945
Stirling Albion FC founded
Matt Busby appointed manager of Manchester
United

1946
First FA National Coach – Walter
Winterbottom

FA and WFA re-unite with FIFA
Burnden Park disaster – 33 spectators killed,
400 injured when stand collapses at Bolton
v Stoke City game. Criticism in the press
that the game still went ahead
first edition of the *Sunday Chronicle Football
Annual*. Later absorbed by the *News of the
World Football Annual*
first Scottish League Cup competition final

1947
First £15,000 transfer: Billy Steel from
Morton to Derby County
Great Britain side beat Rest of Europe 6–1 at
Hampden Park
first £20,000 transfer: Tommy Lawton from
Chelsea to Notts County

1948
First edition of *The Playfair Football Annual*
first edition of the *FA Yearbook*
first Football Writers' Association Footballer of
the Year award: won by Stanley Matthews
of Blackpool

1949
First £25,000 transfer: Johnny Morris bought
by Derby County from Manchester United
record Football League attendance for a single
day when on 27 December, 1,272,155 fans
passed through the turnstiles
Stanley Rous knighted for services to football
former FA Secretary Fred Wall knighted for
services to football
first FA Amateur Cup final played at Wembley
Stadium
first time England team defeated on home soil
by Ireland: 2–0 at Goodison Park,
Liverpool
first BBC Radio *Sports Report*
Glasgow Rangers become first club to win
Scottish League, League Cup and FA Cup
in same season

1950
First £30,000 transfer: Trevor Ford from
Aston Villa to Sunderland
ban on use of floodlights for football lifted
(see 1930)
Football League extended from 88 to 92 clubs
Scotland beaten on home turf for first time by
a non-British team: Austria win 1–0 at
Hampden Park
first time England compete in the World Cup
competition. Finals held in Brazil. Won by
Uruguay. England do not get beyond the
group stage losing 1–0 to the USA in the
process. Scotland did not enter
first Charles *Buchan's Football Monthly*: ran
until 1973 when it became *Football*

Monthly Digest, then monthly one year later

1951
First foreign side to play England at Wembley Stadium – Argentina
Workington Town elected to the Football League
New Brighton FC folded after 28 years in the Football League
first Northern Ireland match against foreign opposition – France
white football introduced in the professional game for the first time. Inspired by the need to help vision of the ball when playing under floodlights
first Scottish player sent off in international match: Billy Steel in match against Northern Ireland

1952
First team to successfully defend the FA Cup title in the twentieth century: Newcastle United FC
first FA Youth Challenge Cup competition

1953
England draw 4–4 against a Rest of the World team at Wembley
first time England beaten on home soil by a continental side: 6–3 by Hungary at Wembley
'Stanley Matthews Cup Final'. Blackpool beat Bolton Wanderers 4–3, allowing Stanley Matthews to win a Cup Winners' medal, an honour that up until now had eluded him
film *Small Town Story* released starring Denis Compton

1954
UEFA founded
first appearance of 'Roy of the Rovers' in *Tiger*
fifth World Cup – Switzerland, won by West Germany
England lose to Hungary in Budapest, 7–1, their heaviest defeat to date

1955
First FA Cup floodlit match: Kidderminster v Brierley Hill
Duke of Edinburgh becomes President of the FA
first BBC television *Sports Special* broadcast
first floodlit England international match: England v Spain at Wembley
first Scottish Cup final televised live: Clyde v Celtic
comedian Tommy Trinder appointed Chairman of Fulham FC

first Scottish League game televised live: Clyde v Aberdeen
first European Cup competition commenced. No British teams entered. The final held in 1956.

1956
First League Game under floodlights: Portsmouth v Newcastle United
first ITV televised game: Bedford Town v Arsenal in the FA Cup third round
Bert Trautmann breaks his neck in FA Cup final playing for Manchester City
Stanley Matthews is named European Footballer of the Year in the inaugural competition

1957
First £65,000 transfer: John Charles from Leeds United to Juventus
first British team to enter the European Cup Competition – Manchester United
Entertainment Tax imposed on football in the First World War is withdrawn
Hughie Gallacher, former Scottish international committed suicide whilst awaiting a hearing on charges of cruelty against his daughter
Alan Hardaker appointed Secretary of the Football League
Stanley Matthews becomes the first footballer to be awarded the CBE
Sunderland Football Club fined £5,000 for irregular payments to players
Jimmy Hill elected Chairman of the Association Football Players' and Trainers' Union
Bishop Auckland win FA Amateur Cup for third successive year
first player to win Footballer of the Year for a second time: Tommy Finney of Preston North End

1958
The Association Football Players' and Trainers' Union renamed the Professional Footballers' Association (PFA)
first British football club to record a £100,000 operating profit: Manchester United
sixth World Cup, Sweden: won by Brazil. First time all 4 home-nations qualify for the final stages. England and Scotland knocked out in the first stage but Northern Ireland and Wales get through to the quarter-finals
Everton becomes the first League club to install underground heating of the pitch at Goodison Park
Football League reorganised Divisions 3 and 4 replace separate Division 3 North and Division 3 South

Munich air disaster: 8 Manchester United
players killed on their return flight from
European Cup match

first British £45,000 transfer: Albert Quixall
from Sheffield Wednesday to Manchester
United

Bobby Charlton makes his international debut
against Scotland at Hampden Park

1959

The Football League win judgement against
Littlewoods Pools copyrighting fixtures list

Walter Winterbottom appointed manager of
England football team

first player to be awarded his 100th cap for
England: Billy Wright of Wolverhampton
Wanderers

1960

Gateshead FC not re-elected to the Football
League after 41 years

introduction of the apprentice footballer category by the FA

League Cup Competition inaugurated

first League match to be televised live: ITV's
coverage of the Blackpool v Bolton
Wanderers game

first European Cup final to be played in
Britain: Hampden Park. Real Madrid beat
Eintracht 7–3

first time the FA recognises Sunday football

Peterborough United elected to the Football
League

first £50,000 transfer: Denis Law from
Huddersfield Town to Manchester City

1961

Sir Stanley Rous elected President of FIFA

new record £100,000 transfer fee: Denis Law
from Manchester City to Torino

Danny Blanchflower becomes the first footballer to be featured on BBC's *This is Your
Life*. Unfortunately for the BBC he declines
to appear

Tottenham Hotspur FC win the Football
League and FA Cup double

first £100 a week player in Britain: Johnny
Haynes of Fulham

Professional Footballers' Association issue
strike notice that would expire on 21
January 1961

abolition of the maximum wage by the FA

1962

Denis Law transferred from Torino to
Manchester United for £115,000

Accrington Stanley FC loses Football League
status

first video highlights of football match –
Anglia TV

TV documentary *The Saturday Men* broadcast.
A behind-the-scenes look at West
Bromwich Albion FC

seventh World Cup – Chile: won by Brazil.
England qualify but do not reach quarter
finals

1963

First British team to win a European title:
Tottenham Hotspur FC beat Atletico
Madrid 5–1 in the final of the European
Cup Winners' Cup in Rotterdam

first time the Pools Panel meet to predict
results of games postponed due to the
weather

George Best makes his debut for Manchester
United first team

Alf Ramsey appointed manager of the England
team

'Retain and Transfer System' modified by the
FA following the George Eastham case in
which the courts declared it 'a restraint of
trade'

1964

First *Match of the Day* programme broadcast
on BBC television: Liverpool v Arsenal

first 'official' British 'European Footballer of
the Year': Denis Law of Manchester United

Peter Swan, Tony Kaye and David 'Bronco'
Lane of Sheffield Wednesday jailed after
being found guilty of throwing match
against Ipswich Town

1965

First substitute in a Football League match:
Keith Peacock of Charlton Athletic in
match against Bolton Wanderers. The new
law permits substitutes for injured players

first closed circuit live TV broadcast of matches to fans: Coventry City of their match
against Cardiff City

Clydebank FC founded

first edition of the *News of the World Football
Annual*

West Ham United win the European Cup
Winners' Cup, beating Munich 1860 at
Wembley

Stanley Matthews retires from professional
football aged 50

first football player knighted for services to
football: Stanley Matthews of Stoke City
FC

first time winners of the League Cup given
automatic entry into European competition

first Scottish Football Writers' Association
Footballer of the Year award, won by Billy
McNeill of Glasgow Celtic

first executive boxes introduced at a Football
League ground – Old Trafford

1966

First £110,000 transfer between British clubs: Alan Ball from Blackpool to Everton

first official drug testing in football in Britain: World Cup final 1966

first Northern Ireland player to be sent off in an international match: Billy Ferguson in match against Wales

first British club to win the European Cup: Glasgow Celtic

Bobby Moore wins BBC Sports Personality of the Year award

eighth World Cup – England: England beat West Germany 4–2 in final. Northern Ireland, Scotland and Wales fail to qualify

1967

Alf Ramsey, England manager knighted

first time Football League fixtures generated by computer

League Cup final reduced to one match final played at Wembley. Previously, the final like all the rounds had been played on a home and away basis

Third Lanark FC folded after 79 seasons in the Scottish League

first British club to win the European Cup, then contest the World Club Championship: Celtic lost to Racing Club (Argentina) 0–1, 2–1, 1–0

1968

First England player to be sent off in an international match: Alan Mullery in England v Yugoslavia, Florence

first *Big Match* programme on ITV

first English club side to win the European Cup: Manchester United beat Benfica in final at Wembley Stadium

England beat a Rest of the World Team 2–1 at Wembley in FA centenary game

first British team to win the Inter Cities Fairs Cup: Leeds United

Department of Education and Science Report into Football (The Chester Report)

1969

First FA Trophy Competition

first match broadcast live in colour: Liverpool v West Ham

first Barassi Cup, played between the winners of the FA Amateur Cup and the Italian equivalent

Matt Busby retires as manager of Manchester United and is knighted for services to football

Women's FA founded

Wolves and England U23 international, Peter Knowles leaves the professional game to become a Jehovah's Witness

1970

Bradford Park Avenue FC not re-elected to the Football League

Manchester City win European Cup Winners' Cup beating Gornik Zabrze 2–1 in Vienna final

Cambridge United elected to the Football League

Derby County FC fined £10,000 for 'administrative irregularities'

ninth World Cup – Mexico. Only England of the home nations qualified for the final stages but were eliminated in quarter finals by West Germany

first £200,000 transfer: Martin Peters from West Ham United to Tottenham Hotspur FC

first time penalty shoot-out introduced into the professional game in Britain in the Watney Mann Trophy

first 'football song' to reach number one in charts: *Back Home* by the England World Cup squad

The Ford Sporting League (a fair play award) and the Watney Mann Invitation Trophy introduces the concept of commercial sponsorship of football competitions

1971

First British team to win the European Inter Cities Fairs Cup for the second time – Leeds United beat Juventus in the finals

Arsenal FC won the Football League and FA Cup double

Scottish Women's FA founded

disaster at Ibrox Stadium when 66 spectators killed and over 200 injured as they leave the ground

Chelsea win European Cup Winners' Cup beating Real Madrid 2–1 in Athens replay final

1972

Glasgow Rangers win European Cup Winners' Cup beating Dynamo Moscow 3–0 in Barcelona final

Dumbarton FC founded

Barrow not re-elected to the Football League; Hereford United elected to the Football League

release of *Blue is the Colour* song recording produced by Chelsea FC

inaugural UEFA Cup win by Tottenham Hotspur FC beating Wolverhampton Wanderers in the finals

1973

First English team to win the League Championship and a European title in the same season: Liverpool FC; also won the

UEFA Cup
Ted Croker appointed Secretary of the FA
first Welsh player to be sent off in an international match: Trevor Hockey in match against Poland
Rothmans begin sponsorship of amateur leagues
last FA Amateur Cup Competition
second division Sunderland beat strong favourites and first division leaders Leeds United 1–0 in FA Cup final

1974
First Professional Footballers' Association Young Player of the Year award won by Kevin Beattie of Ipswich Town
Meadowbank Thistle FC founded
Don Revie appointed manager of England
Bill Shankly steps down as manager of Liverpool FC
Alf Ramsey sacked as England manager
first League match played on a Sunday: Millwall v Fulham at the Den. This was due to industrial action preventing amenities being available to play a night match. Sunday Trading Laws prevented a charge being made for spectators
first Charity Shield Match at Wembley
first Professional Footballers' Association Player of the Year award won by Norman Hunter of Leeds United
FA formally abolished separate amateur and professional international teams
lowest recorded League attendance: 450 at the Rochdale v Cambridge Town match
first players to be sent off in a Charity Shield match – Billy Bremner of Leeds United and Kevin Keegan of Liverpool FC
Bobby Tambling, Crystal Palace and England international leaves the profession to become a Jehovah's Witness
tenth World Cup – West Germany. England, Northern Ireland and Wales all failed to qualify. Scotland had mixed fortunes beating the eventual winners Holland but failing to progress to the knockout stage
Meadowbank Thistle FC founded
new tax guidelines to remove the distinction between amateur and professional sportsman abandoned

1975
Safety of Sports Grounds Act

1976
First issue of *Roy of the Rovers* comic. Stories originally published in *Tiger*
Liverpool win the UEFA Cup beating FC Brugge in the finals
first female to referee match between two

men's teams: Joan Bazely
first use of shirt advertisements by non-League Kettering Town. Football League allows clubs to have sponsor's logos on shirts, provided they are not worn on televised games
second division Southampton FC beat Manchester United in FA Cup final
first time the yellow card introduced

1977
Don Revie resigns as England manager to take up position in United Arab Emirates
Ron Greenwood appointed England manager
Workington Town not re-elected to the Football League
Scottish fans invade Wembley pitch after their 2–1 win over England in the Home International Series
Liverpool win European Cup for first time
first British team to contest and win the European Super Cup, Liverpool FC beat Hamburg SV 1–1, 6–0
Wimbledon elected to the Football League
Bobby Moore retired from playing

1978
First all-seater football stadium in Britain – Pittodrie, home of Aberdeen FC
Southport not re-elected to the Football League
FA ban on overseas players lifted
eleventh World Cup – Argentina. England failed to qualify, Scotland knocked out at the group stage
first black footballer to play full international for England – Viv Anderson
Liverpool FC won European Cup for second time
The Football Experts Association founded by Ray Spiller
Wigan elected to the Football League
Theresa Bennett, a 12-year-old girl, was banned by the FA from playing football in a local league with boys
first official testing for drug abuse in British football

1979
Film *Yesterday's Hero* released
first time two players of the same side sent off for fighting each other: Derek Hales and Mike Flanagan of Charlton Athletic
Graham Kelly appointed Secretary of the Football League aged 33
restructuring of non-league football leads to the creation of Alliance Premier League, now the Football Conference
Nottingham Forest win European Cup for first time

first £1,000,000 transfer in Britain: Trevor Francis from Birmingham City to Nottingham Forest

first £1,500,000 transfer in Britain: David Mills from Middlesbrough to West Brom

The Football Experts becomes the Association of Football Statisticians. Their newsletter *The Football Experts* was published the same year

first League side to wear shirts bearing sponsor's name: Liverpool Football Club promote Hitachi electrical goods

1980

First time referees allowed to send players off for spitting

Peter Storey of Arsenal FC sent to prison for his part in a counterfeiting scheme

Nottingham Forest FC won European Cup for second time

film *Gregory's Girl* released

1981

First Football League ground with an artificial playing surface.: Loftus Road, home of Queen's Park Rangers

Arsenal sign shirt sponsorship deal worth £500,000 with JVC: first deal of such magnitude

probable first fanzine published: York City's fanzine *Terrace Talk*

Liverpool FC win European Cup for third time

1982

The League Cup becomes known as the Milk Cup sponsored by the Milk Marketing Board

twelfth World Cup – Spain. Both England and Northern Ireland finish top of their group but fail to progress beyond the second stage. Scotland defeated in the opening round

Bobby Robson appointed manager of England

1983

Aberdeen win the European Cup Winners' Cup beating Real Madrid in the final 2–1

TV Drama *Those Glory Glory Days* broadcast: starred Danny Blanchflower

the Youth Training Scheme introduced into professional football

first Football League club to be floated on the Stock Exchange: Tottenham Hotspur

first sponsorship of the Football League, sponsored by Japanese company Canon

live television broadcast of League matches introduced on a regular basis

1984

Liverpool FC win European Cup for the

fourth time

first FA National School of Football established at Lilleshall

first European Championships for women

1985

Chelsea FC attempt to erect electric perimeter fence around pitch to keep fans at bay but refused planning permission by the local authority

Heysel Stadium disaster, Brussel: 39 spectators killed, 400 injured in stampede during match, Liverpool v Juventus in the final of the European Cup, leads to European ban on English football clubs

first life-time ban imposed on fan from attending football matches

Millwall fans run amok at Luton drawing public attention to the growing problem

Valley Parade disaster, 56 supporters killed and over 200 injured

Exeter City FC professional Symon Burgher quits the game due to religious beliefs which prevent him working on Saturdays

UEFA ban British football clubs from European Club competition indefinitely

foundation of the Football Supporters' Association

first player to be sent off in an FA Cup final: Kevin Moran of Manchester United

1986

First Independent Football Supporters' Club: Chelsea

Liverpool FC win the Football League and FA Cup double

first England player sent off in World Cup match: Ray Wilkins in match against Morocco

Manchester United Football Museum opened

first issue of hugely popular and influential magazine *When Saturday Comes*

thirteenth World Cup – Mexico: England reach quarter finals before being defeated by Argentinian Diego Maradona's 'Hand of God'. Northern Ireland and Scotland fail to progress beyond the qualifying rounds. Wales failed to qualify for the finals

first PFA Football in the Community schemes set up

Bristol Rovers forced by mounting debts to sell their ground and move in with Bath City

1987

FA intervenes to prevent business tycoon Robert Maxwell taking control of Watford FC, because of his control, directly or indirectly, through his sons at Derby, Oxford and Reading

the League Cup becomes known as the

Littlewoods Cup sponsored by Littlewoods Pools

first World Congress on Science and Football, Liverpool: hosted by Liverpool Polytechnic

unsuccessful bid to merge Chelsea and Fulham football clubs

first automatic promotion and relegation between Football League and GM Vauxhall Conference. Lincoln city were the first to be relegated and Scarborough Town, the first to be promoted under this system

first time players tried in a court of law for offences committed on the field of play: Chris Woods, Graham Roberts, Terry Butcher and Frank McAvennie following an 'Old firm' game.

1988

Graham Kelly appointed Chief Executive of the FA

new record £2.8m transfer fee: Ian Rush from Juventus to Liverpool FC

1989

Football Spectators Act

Glasgow Rangers sign first Catholic player for many years: Maurice Johnston

Hillsborough disaster – 96 football supporters killed at Liverpool v Nottingham Forest FA Cup semi-final match. Leads to Justice Taylor being commissioned to look into safety at sports grounds

interim version of the Taylor Report published

drug testing in British football made compulsory as opposed to voluntary (see 1978)

Gay Footballers' Support Network established

first Christie's auction of football memorabilia

1990

Swindon Town promotion to second division overturned due to financial irregularities

FA lifted the ruling preventing girls under 11 participating in mixed football

Tony Adams of Arsenal and England sent to prison for reckless driving whilst drunk. He later went on to captain England

fourteenth World Cup – Italy. England progress to semi-finals where they are beaten on penalties by West Germany. Scotland, the only other home nation to qualify for the finals failed to progress beyond the preliminary rounds

first League match to be televised live on satellite television: Rangers v Celtic, BSky

UEFA ban on English clubs in European competitions lifted

first edition of the *Irish Football Yearbook*

first BBC Radio 5 606 programme broadcast

'Professional Foul' introduced into the FA rules

Paul Gascoigne wins BBC Sports Personality of the Year award

the League Cup becomes known as the Rumbelows Cup sponsored by high street electrical retail company Rumbelows

1991

Reduction in Pools Betting Duty of 2.4 per cent. Used to pass onto the Football Trust to improve safety at sports grounds

Finance Act 1991, Section 121 Reduction in pools betting levy to finance Football Trust and Foundation for Sports and Arts in association with Football Pools Companies

first FA Cup semi-final to be played at Wembley: Tottenham defeated Arsenal 3–1

first £5.5m transfer: David Platt Aston Villa to Bari

first £2.9m transfer between British clubs. Dean Saunders from Derby County to Liverpool FC

Manchester United win European Cup Winners' Cup beating Barcelona 2–1 in Rotterdam final

the Football League demands that artificial pitches be phased out

Manchester United floated on the Stock Exchange

Graham Taylor appointed manager of the England football team replacing Bobby Robson

Kenny Dalglish resigns as Liverpool FC manager, reason given as 'too much pressure'

Lord Justice Taylor's final report on the Hillsborough disaster published. A swingeing criticism of the state of modern football

Chelsea Football Club fined a record £105,000 by the FA for making irregular payments to players

FA's Blueprint for the Future of Football published leading to the Founding of the Premier League in 1992

first Professional Footballers' Association Full-time Education Officer appointed: Bob Kerry

first Gay football club: Stonewall FC

Women's FA founds National League, later renamed FA Women's Premier League

Football (Offences) Act passed

first edition of the *Welsh Football Yearbook*

Terry Fenwick of Tottenham Hotspur FC jailed on drink driving charges

1992

League of Wales founded by the Football Association of Wales

Charlton Athletic return to The Valley after a couple of seasons at Selhurst Park (Crystal Palace's home ground)

Nick Hornby's *Fever Pitch* published and becomes a top seller, later to be turned into a film

the first matches of the newly founded Premier League commence

Aldershot FC goes into voluntary liquidation

Liverpool FC sign largest shirt sponsorship to date. £4m from brewers Carlsberg

exclusive TV rights to broadcast Premier League matches won by BSkyB

1993

First issue of *Sweet FA* magazine published

first team to win the League Cup and FA Cup double: Arsenal

first issue of *Manchester United* magazine published

George Graham, manager of Arsenal, banned for a year following irregular payments

first manager to win League titles both in the Scottish and English Leagues, Alex Ferguson with Aberdeen and then Manchester United

Mickey Thomas of Wrexham FC and Wales sent to prison for passing forged bank notes to the club's YTS players

Terry Venables appointed manager of England football team replacing Graham Taylor

the League Cup becomes known as the Coca-Cola Cup

1994

Tottenham Hotspur FC fined £600,000 and banned from the FA Cup following 40 charges of financial irregularities

Arsenal won European Cup Winners' Cup beating Parma 1–0 in Copenhagen final

Paul Merson publicly acknowledges alcohol, drug and gambling addiction

fifteenth World Cup – USA, England, Scotland, N. Ireland and Wales all failed to qualify for the final stages. The competition was won by Brazil

Bobby Charlton knighted for services to football

Manchester United win League and FA Cup double

first *FourFourTwo* magazine published

first £5m transfer between British clubs: Chris Sutton from Norwich City to Blackburn Rovers

Scottish Football Museum established (Hampden Park)

1995

First *Total Football* magazine published

first £8.5m transfer between British clubs: Stan Collymore from Nottingham Forest to Liverpool FC

film *When Saturday Comes* released

Bosman ruling lifted the restriction on players from the European Union playing in other member states: this facilitated freedom of movement for out-of-contract players

Manchester United's Eric Cantona arrested after leaping into the crowd to attack a belligerent spectator during a match against Crystal Palace at Selhurst Park, Cantona is banned for 6 months

Duncan Ferguson sentenced to 3 months in prison for assaulting Raith Rovers full-back John McStay

University of Liverpool Football Research Unit opened

Ireland v England International in Dublin abandoned following fan violence

1996

First £15m transfer between British clubs: Alan Shearer from Blackburn Rovers to Newcastle United

Aston Villa win the League Cup for an unprecedented fifth time beating Leeds United 3–0 in the final at Wembley

first player to complete 1,000 matches in the Football League: Peter Shilton

Manchester United win League and FA Cup double for second time

first BBC *Match of the Day* magazine published

Terry Venables resigns as England manager

Glenn Hoddle appointed manager of England team

England hosts European Championships, Germany beat Czechoslovakia in final at Wembley

House of Commons motion called for a reduction in the 'excessive' use of yellow cards

1997

Football Academies introduced by professional clubs

first edition of *Insight*, the FA Coaches' Association journal published

Pride Park football stadium, Derby opened. Derby County Football Club moving from the Baseball Ground

first FA *Charter for Quality*

the FA Coaches Association established

1998

Newcastle United Director Douglas Hall and Freddie Shepherd resign after allegations that they described Newcastle women as 'dogs' and their supporters as gullible for buying overpriced replica shirts

sixteenth World Cup Competition – France. England progress to quarter-finals only to be beaten by Argentina after extra time. Scotland, the only other home country to reach the finals failed to progess beyond the first stage

Arsenal win the League and FA Cup double

Football Museum project at Preston awarded a Heritage Lottery grant of £7.5m

first women's inter-services tournament

Arsenal player guilty of breaking code of ethics following the injury to a player in match against Sheffield United

first time laws passed to use penalties to decide outcome of FA Cup Final if scores still level after extra-time

Chelsea win European Cup Winners' Cup beating Stuttgart 1–0 in Stockholm final

Chelsea win European Super Cup beating Real Madrid 1–0

Michael Owen wins BBC Sports Personality of the Year award

first female head coach of the England women's football team

1999

Glenn Hoddle forced to resign as England team manager following comments made to the press about his religious beliefs

Alex Ferguson knighted for services to football

Geoff Hurst knighted for services to football

Kevin Keegan appointed manager of England

Robbie Fowler of Liverpool FC fined £32,000 for 'pretending' to sniff cocaine when celebrating scoring a goal

the Football League becomes known as the Nationwide League sponsored by Nationwide Building Society

first Compliance Officer appointed by the FA: Graham Bean

Bradford City's Gordon Watson successfully claims in court against Kevin Gray for career-threatening injury from a tackle

Football (Offences and Disorder) Act

the League Cup becomes known as The Worthington Cup sponsored by brewing company Bass

FA closes its football academy at Lilleshall

Manchester United win an unprecedented Triple – Premier League title, FA Cup and European Cup championship within a 4-week period

2000

Sculpture of Manchester United and England soccer star David Beckham integrated into base of Buddha's effigy in Bangkok's Pariwas Temple

Kevin Keegan resigns as England manager following poor performances in Euro 2000

Football Disorder Act

first Deaf World Cup

first non-English manager appointed coach of England team: Swede Sven-Göran Eriksson

last match at Wembley Stadium before being demolished to make way for controversial new stadium

£18m transfer of Rio Ferdinand from West Ham United to Leeds United

2001

Manchester United pay record British transfer fee of £19m to PSV Eindhoven for Ruud Van Nistelroy. This was eclipsed by the same club in July when they paid Lazio £28m for Juan Veron

Liverpool won unprecedented treble of FA Cup, League Cup and EUEFA Cup

Leeds United's Jonathan Woodgate found guilty of affray and ordered to give 100 hours of community service.

Index

Lightning Source UK Ltd.
Milton Keynes UK
UKOW04n0612100114

224291UK00001B/33/P